# Investment Banking

## UNIVERSITY EDITION

# Investment Banking

## Valuation, LBOs, M&A, and IPOs

### THIRD EDITION

### UNIVERSITY EDITION

JOSHUA ROSENBAUM

JOSHUA PEARL

FOREWORD BY JOSEPH R. PERELLA
AFTERWORD BY JOSHUA HARRIS

www.investmentbankingbook.com

WILEY

Published by John Wiley & Sons, Inc., Hoboken, New Jersey.
Second Edition published by John Wiley & Sons, Inc. in 2013.
First Edition published by John Wiley & Sons, Inc. in 2009.
Published simultaneously in Canada.

For general information on our other products and services or for technical support, please contact our Customer Care Department within the United States at (800) 762-2974, outside the United States at (317) 572-3993 or fax (317) 572-4002.

Wiley publishes in a variety of print and electronic formats and by print-on-demand. Some material included with standard print versions of this book may not be included in e-books or in print-on-demand. If this book refers to media such as a CD or DVD that is not included in the version you purchased, you may download this material at booksupport.wiley.com. For more information about Wiley products, visit www.wiley.com.

*Library of Congress Cataloging-in-Publication Data is Available:*

ISBN 978-1-119-82337-7 (paperback)
ISBN 978-1-119-82343-8 (ePDF)
ISBN 978-1-119-82342-1 (ePub)

SKY10079839_071824

*In loving memory of Ronie Rosenbaum, an inspiration
for strength and selflessness.*

—J.R.

*To the memory of my grandfather, Joseph Pearl, a Holocaust
survivor, for his inspiration to persevere and succeed.*[*]

—J.P.

---

[*]A portion of the authors' royalties will be donated to The Blue Card Fund aiding destitute
Holocaust survivors—www.bluecardfund.org

# Contents

## PART TWO

## CHAPTER 9
### The IPO Process

# Instructor and Student Resources

## OVERVIEW

Written to reflect today's dynamic market conditions, *Investment Banking, University Edition* skillfully:

- Introduces students to the primary valuation methodologies currently used on Wall Street
- Uses a step-by-step how-to approach for each methodology and builds a chronological knowledge base
- Defines key terms, financial concepts, and processes throughout
- Provides a comprehensive overview of the fundamentals of LBOs and an organized M&A sale process
- Presents new coverage of M&A buy-side analytical tools—which includes both qualitative aspects, such as buyer motivations and strategies, along with technical financial and valuation assessment tools
- Includes a comprehensive merger consequences analysis, including accretion/(dilution) and balance sheet effects
- Outlines IPO valuation, including equity value, implied multiples, offering size, and pro forma credit statistics
- Contains challenging end-of-chapter questions to reinforce concepts covered

## INSTRUCTOR RESOURCES

An extensive support package, including print and online tools, helps instructors maximize their teaching effectiveness. It offers useful supplements for instructors with varying levels of experience and different instructional circumstances. These resources can be accessed at Wiley's Global Education website by searching the book title or by visiting www.wiley.com/go/ib3euniv.

Instructor resources include:

- **Test Bank.** Over 500 questions and answers available in Microsoft Word and as a computerized test bank. The computerized test bank is available through Respondus (Respondus.com) and is a powerful tool for creating and managing exams. It can be printed or published directly to ANGEL, Blackboard, Desire2Learn, eCollege, WebCT, and other eLearning systems. Questions are presented in multiple choice and true/false format.

- **Solutions Manual.** The solutions manual includes detailed solutions to end of chapter questions.

- **Case Studies with Video Commentary.** 14 University of Virginia, Darden School of Business case studies complete with companion video commentary by the authors. The video commentary presents an overview of the case material and key issues to address.

- **Image Gallery.** Each exhibit in the *University Edition* is available for instructors in PowerPoint format.

- **Valuation Models.** Five templates and five completed models, along with user guides for the valuation methodologies discussed in the book, including:

  - Comparable Companies
  - Precedent Transactions
  - DCF Analysis
  - LBO Analysis
  - Merger Consequences Analysis
  - IPO Valuation

## WORKBOOK

The *Investment Banking Workbook* is designed for use both as a companion to *Investment Banking, Third Edition*, as well as on a standalone basis. The *Workbook* provides a mix of multi-step problem set exercises, as well as multiple choice and essay questions—over 500 questions in total. It also provides a comprehensive answer key that aims to truly teach and explain as opposed to simply identify the correct answer. Therefore, the answers themselves are an effective learning tool. The completion of this comprehensive guide will help ensure the achievement of your professional and educational milestones.

JOSHUA ROSENBAUM is a Managing Director and Head of the Industrials & Diversified Services Group at RBC Capital Markets, where he also serves on the Management Committee for the U.S. Investment Bank. He originates, structures, and advises on M&A, corporate finance, and capital markets transactions. Previously, he worked at UBS Investment Bank and the International Finance Corporation, the direct investment division of the World Bank. He received his AB from Harvard and his MBA with Baker Scholar honors from Harvard Business School. He is also the co-author of *Investment Banking: Valuation, LBOs, M&A, and IPOs* and *The Little Book of Investing Like the Pros*.

JOSHUA PEARL is the Founder and Chief Investment Officer of Hickory Lane Capital Management, a long/short equity asset manager. He focuses on public equity investments and special situations utilizing a fundamentals-based approach. From 2011 to 2020, he served as a Managing Director and Partner at Brahman Capital. Previously, he structured high yield financings, leveraged buyouts, and restructurings as a Director at UBS Investment Bank. Prior to UBS, he was an investment banker at Moelis & Company and Deutsche Bank. He received his BS in Business from Indiana University's Kelley School of Business. He is also the co-author of *Investment Banking: Valuation, LBOs, M&A, and IPOs* and *The Little Book of Investing Like the Pros*.

## CONTACT THE AUTHORS

Please feel free to contact JOSHUA ROSENBAUM and JOSHUA PEARL with any questions, comments, or suggestions at josh@investmentbankingbook.com

JOSEPH GASPARRO is Head of Americas Capital Services Content at Credit Suisse. He advises on capital raising and operations for alternative asset managers. Previously, he executed M&A and capital markets transactions in the firm's Investment Banking Division. Prior to Credit Suisse, he worked at BofA Securities and UBS. He received his BA from Gettysburg College and his MBA from Rutgers Business School. He is a two-time recipient of the President's Volunteer Service Award, bestowed by the President of the United States. He is also an editor of *Investment Banking: Valuation, LBOs, M&A, and IPOs* and *The Little Book of Investing Like the Pros.*

RAYMOND AZIZI is a Portfolio Manager at Weiss Multi-Strategy Advisers where he manages a long/short equity portfolio. Previously, he was an investment professional at Lehman Brothers Merchant Banking where he focused on leveraged buyouts and growth capital investments. Prior to his private equity role, he worked in the Investment Banking Division at Lehman Brothers. He received his BS in Business from Rutgers University and his MBA from The Wharton School of the University of Pennsylvania. He is also an editor of *Investment Banking: Valuation, LBOs, M&A, and IPOs* and *The Little Book of Investing Like the Pros.*

# Foreword

Mark Twain, long known for his critical views of formal education, once wisely noted: "I never let my schooling interfere with my education."

Twain's one-liner strikes at the core of investment banking, where deals must be lived before proper knowledge and understanding can be obtained. Hard time must be spent doing deals, with complexities in valuation, terms, and negotiations unique to every situation. The truly great firms and dealmakers have become so by developing cultures of apprenticeship that transfer knowledge and creativity from one generation to the next. The task of teaching aspiring investment bankers and finance professionals has been further complicated by the all-consuming nature of the trade, as well as its constantly evolving art and science.

Therefore, for me personally, it's exciting to see Joshua Rosenbaum and Joshua Pearl take the lead in training a new generation of investment bankers. Their work in documenting valuation and deal process in an accessible manner is a particularly important contribution as many aspects of investment banking cannot be taught, even in the world's greatest universities and business schools. Rosenbaum and Pearl provide aspiring—and even the most seasoned—investment bankers with a unique real-world education inside Wall Street's less formal classroom, where deals come together at real-time speed.

The school of hard knocks and of learning-by-doing, which was Twain's classroom, demands strong discipline and sound acumen in the core fundamentals of valuation. It requires applying these techniques to improve the quality of deals for all parties, so that dealmakers can avoid critical and costly mistakes, as well as unnecessary risks. My own 50 years of Wall Street education has clearly demonstrated that valuation is at the core of investment banking. Any banker worth his salt must possess the ability to properly value a business in a structured and defensible manner. This logic and rationale must inspire clients and counterparties alike, while spurring strategic momentum and comprehension into the art of doing the deal.

Rosenbaum and Pearl succeed in providing a systematic approach to addressing a critical issue in any M&A, IPO, or investment situation—namely, how much is a business or transaction worth. They also put forth the framework for helping approach more nuanced questions such as how much to pay for the business and how to get the deal done. Due to the lack of a comprehensive written reference material on valuation, the fundamentals and subtlety of the trade are often passed on orally from banker-to-banker on a case-by-case basis. In codifying the art and science of investment banking, the authors convert this oral history into an accessible framework by bridging the theoretical to the practical with user-friendly, step-by-step approaches to performing primary valuation methodologies.

Many seasoned investment bankers commonly lament the absence of relevant and practical "how-to" materials for newcomers to the field. The reality is that most financial texts on valuation and M&A are written by academics. The few books written by practitioners tend to focus on dramatic war stories and hijinks, rather than the nuts-and-bolts of the techniques used to get deals done. Rosenbaum and Pearl fill this heretofore void for practicing and aspiring investment bankers and finance professionals. Their book is designed to prove sufficiently accessible to a wide audience, including those with a limited finance background.

It is true that we live in uncertain and volatile times—times that have destroyed or consumed more than a few of the most legendary Wall Street institutions. However, one thing will remain a constant in the long-term—the need for skilled finance professionals with strong technical expertise. Companies will always seek counsel from experienced and independent professionals to analyze, structure, negotiate, and close deals as they navigate the market and take advantage of value-creating opportunities. Rosenbaum and Pearl promulgate a return to the fundamentals of due diligence and the use of well-founded realistic assumptions governing growth, profitability, and approach to risk. Their work toward instilling the proper skill set and mindset in aspiring generations of Wall Street professionals will help establish a firm foundation for driving a brighter economic future.

JOSEPH R. PERELLA
Founding Partner, Perella Weinberg Partners

# Acknowledgments

We are deeply indebted to the numerous colleagues, peers, and industry-leading professionals who provided sage guidance, input, and hard work to help make this book possible.

We would like to highlight the contributions made by Joseph Gasparro toward the successful revision and production of the third edition of this book. His contributions were multi-dimensional and his unwavering enthusiasm, insights, and support were nothing short of exemplary. In general, Joe's work ethic, creativity, "can-do" attitude, and commitment to perfection are a true inspiration.

To the outstanding team at RBC Capital Markets, thank you for your insightful comments and support. Larry Grafstein, Deputy Chairman, is a true sage advisor who has seen it all in M&A and possesses unique wisdom and bedside manner. Andrew Schwartz, Managing Director in Leveraged Finance, helped ensure that the LBO content is timely and leading edge. Hank Johnson, Managing Director in M&A, provided helpful input on the sell-side process content as that part of the M&A market evolves and grows.

We'd like to thank the talented team of lawyers from Latham & Watkins. As the world's leading capital markets, M&A, and finance law firm, the Latham team provided us with vital insight and guidance on several chapters, including those on capital markets and IPOs, M&A, and LBOs. As Latham has long shared their collective wisdom on the law and the lore of Wall Street through their publications, they are well-practiced at delivering the kind of demystifying explanations that are valued by dealmakers. Recognized as trailblazers in the capital markets arena, especially for their work around IPOs, direct listings, and convertible notes, Marc Jaffe, Greg Rodgers, Benjamin Cohen, Arash Aminian Baghai, and Brittany Ruiz, were instrumental in ensuring the accuracy, timeliness, and relevancy of our capital markets content at the time of publication. Christopher Drewry, part of a team who see and close more deals than almost any group in the country, shared his seasoned and extensive perspective on M&A. Senet Bischoff similarly leveraged his market-leading expertise to contribute to our LBO chapters.

For the third edition, Robin Feiner's contributions to the IPO chapters were invaluable, reflecting her leading edge expertise and transaction experience. Robin is a corporate partner at Winston & Strawn LLP and a former business executive with over 20 years of experience in corporate finance and IPOs. Adam Fleisher, a partner at Cleary Gottlieb Steen & Hamilton LLP, made valuable contributions to the new chapters on both traditional IPOs and direct listings. With over 30 years of writing and teaching on IPOs, Professor Jay Ritter of the University of Florida, Warrington College of Business, helped us marry the theory and practice of going public. Lastly, we want to highlight the insights from Dan Hennessy and Nick Petruska of Hennessy

Capital on our new SPAC content—they are true leaders and innovators in the space and continue to create successful SPACs.

We also want to reiterate our thanks to those who were so instrumental in the success of the first and second editions of *Investment Banking*. Joseph Meisner's technical insights on M&A buy-side and sell-side analysis were priceless, as was his unique ability to marry the academic with the practical. Jeffrey Groves provided us with valuable contributions on the leveraged buyouts content. Jeff is a highly skilled and experienced leveraged finance professional with a soft client touch and his pulse on the market. Daniel Plaxe was also helpful in enriching our LBO content with his technical and precise approach. Vijay Kumra made a valuable contribution to our updated M&A content, providing practical and grounding insights to help preserve the accessibility of a highly complex and technical topic.

The book could never have come to fruition without the sage advice and enthusiasm of Steve Momper, Director of Darden Business Publishing at the University of Virginia. Steve believed in our book from the beginning and supported us throughout the entire process. Most importantly, he introduced us to our publisher, John Wiley & Sons, Inc. Special thanks to Ryan Drook, Milwood Hobbs, Jr., Eric Klar, James Paris, Michael Lanzarone, Joseph Bress, and Benjamin Hochberg for their insightful editorial contributions. As top-notch professionals in investment banking and private equity, their expertise and practical guidance proved invaluable. Many thanks to Steven Sherman, Eric Leicht, Greg Pryor, Mark Gordon, Jennifer Fonner Fitchen, and Ante Vucic for their exhaustive work in assisting with the legal nuances of our book. As partners at the nation's leading corporate law firms, their oversight helped ensure the accuracy and timeliness of the content.

We'd like to thank the outstanding team at Wiley, who have been our partners for over a decade on all of our books. Bill Falloon, our acquisition editor, brought us into the Wiley family and never wavered in his vision and support. He has provided strong leadership over the years and has become a true friend. Susan Cerra, Steven Kyritz, Samantha Enders, and Purvi Patel on the editorial and production side, worked diligently to ensure all the details were addressed and facilitated a smooth production process. Evan Burton, Doug Salvemini, Claire Brock, Sadhika Salariya, and Amanda Wainer were critical in the production and editorial process of our Wiley Efficient Learning (WEL) Investment Banking Course. Jean-Karl Martin, our marketing manager, helped us realize our vision through his creativity and foresight.

We also want to express immeasurable gratitude to our families and friends. Margo and Alex, and Masha, Jonathan, and Olivia, thank you so much for your support, patience, and sacrifice! You were always in our hearts and minds as we worked diligently to produce a book that would make us all proud.

This book could not have been completed without the efforts and reviews of the following individuals:

Jonathan Ackerman, *Moda Midstream*

Mark Adler, *Piper Jaffray*

Kenneth Ahern, *University of Southern California, Marshall School of Business*

Marc Auerbach, *LevFin Insights*

Raymond Azizi, *Weiss Multi-Strategy Advisers*

Arash Aminian Baghai, *Latham & Watkins LLP*

Carliss Baldwin, *Harvard Business School*

Kyle Barker, *APC Automotive Technologies*

Ronnie Barnes, *Cornerstone Research*

Joshua Becker, *Antares Capital*

Senet Bischoff, *Latham & Watkins LLP*

Christopher Blum, *BNP Paribas*

Bernard Bolduc, *Altrum*

Catherine Bolduc, *Altrum*

Louis-David Bourque, *Altrum*

Joseph Bress, *The Carlyle Group*

William Briganti, *Nasdaq*

Geoff Burt, *Latham & Watkins LLP*

Gabrielle Bustamante, *Nasdaq*

Stephen Catera, *Siris Capital Group*

Eric Coghlin, *Bank of America Merrill Lynch*

Benjamin Cohen, *Latham & Watkins LLP*

Thomas Cole, *Citigroup*

Lawrence A. Cook, CFA, CAIA, *Tippie College of Business - University of Iowa*

Ryan Corbett, *MP Materials, JHL Capital Group*

Lawrence Cort, *Jefferies Group*

Jason Cruise, *Latham & Watkins LLP*

Aswath Damodaran, *New York University, Stern School of Business*

Thomas Davidoff, *University of British Columbia*

Victor Delaglio, *Province Advisors*

Nicholas DeNovio, *Latham & Watkins LLP*

Jennifer Fonner DiNucci, *Cooley Godward Kronish LLP*

Michael Dirla, *Lightyear Capital*

Wojciech Domanski, *Coast2Coast Capital*

Diana Doyle, *Latham & Watkins LLP*

Christopher Drewry, *Latham & Watkins LLP*

Ryan Drook, *Deutsche Bank*

Chris Falk, *University of Florida, Warrington College of Business*

Ezra Faham, *Brahman Capital*

Robin Feiner, *Winston & Strawn LLP*

Bryan Fingeroot, *Raymond James*

Adam Fleisher, *Cleary Gottlieb Steen & Hamilton LLP*

Adam Friedman, *Seaport Global Holdings*

Heiko Freitag, *Anschutz Investment Company*

Mark Funk, *BBCA Compass*

Joseph Gasparro, *Credit Suisse*

Andrew Gladston, *MJM Capital Group*

Michael Goldberg, *RBC Capital Markets*

Peter D. Goodson, *University of California Berkeley, Haas School of Business*

Peter M. Goodson, *Eminence Capital*

Mark Gordon, *Wachtell, Lipton, Rosen & Katz*

Steven Gordon, *J. Goldman & Co.*

Larry Grafstein, *RBC Capital Markets*

Gary Gray, *Pennsylvania State University, Smeal School of Business*

Jailan Griffiths, *Nasdaq*

Michael Groner, *Millennium Partners*

Jeffrey Groves, *UBS Investment Bank*

David Haeberle, *Indiana University, Kelley School of Business*

Tim Hani, *Bloomberg*

John Haynor, *Solebury Capital*

Han He, *Oaktree Capital Management*

Dan Hennessy, *Hennessy Capital*

Milwood Hobbs, Jr., *Oaktree Capital Management*

Benjamin Hochberg, *Lee Equity Partners, LLC*

Alec Hufnagel, *Kelso & Company*

Jon Hugo, *BlackRock*

Cal Hunter, *Barnes & Noble*

Roger Ibbotson, *Yale School of Management, Zebra Capital Management*

Marc Jaffe, *Latham & Watkins LLP*

Cedric Jarrett, *Deutsche Bank*

Robert Jermain, *SearchOne Advisors*

Hank Johnson, *RBC Capital Markets*

John Joliet, *American Discovery Capital*

Mitchell Julis, *Canyon Partners*

Tamir Kaloti, *Deutsche Bank*

Michael Kamras, *Credit Suisse*

Kenneth Kim, *State University of New York at Buffalo, School of Management*

Eric Klar, *White & Case LLP*

Jennifer Klein, *Sequence Capital*

Kenneth Kloner, *UBS Investment Bank*

Philip Konnikov, *Three Keys Capital Advisors*

Kush Kothary, *BlackRock*

Vijay Kumra, *UBS Investment Bank*

Tracy Lacovelli, *Latham & Watkins LLP*

Alex Lajoux, *National Association of Corporate Directors*

Nathan Laliberte, *Brahman Capital*

Ian Lampl, *LoanStreet*

Michael Lanzarone, CFA, *Time Inc.*

Eu-Han Lee, *Baring Private Equity Asia*

Franky Lee, *Providence Equity Partners*

Eric Leicht, *White & Case LLP*

Shaya Lesches, *Young Jewish Professionals*

Marshall Levine, *GMT Capital*

Dan Levy, *Credit Suisse*

Jay Lurie, *International Finance Corporation (IFC)*

Christine Marron, *Nasdaq*

David Mayhew, *GE Ventures*

Coley McMenamin, *Bank of America Merrill Lynch*

Joseph Meisner, *RBC Capital Markets*

Jeff Mensch, *Deutsche Bank*

Brian Miller, *Altrum*

Steve Momper, *University of Virginia, Darden Business Publishing*

Kirk Murphy, *MKM Partners*

Joshua Neren, *Barron Point Advisors*

Peter Nieberg, *Altrum*

Paul Pai, *U.S. Bank*

James Paris, *Avant*

Dan Park, *Clutch*

Dom Petrosino, *Moelis & Company*

Nick Petruska, *Hennessy Capital*

Daniel Plaxe, *Pioneer Funding Group, LLC*

Gregory Pryor, *White & Case LLP*

Daniel Reichgott, *Federal Reserve Bank of New York*

Eric Ritter, *Needham & Company*

Jay R. Ritter, *University of Florida, Warrington College of Business*

Greg Rodgers, *Latham & Watkins LLP*

David Ross, *Credit Suisse*

Ashish Rughwani, *Dominus Capital*

Brittany Ruiz, *Latham & Watkins LLP*

David Sanford, *Hitchwood Capital*

Jeff Schachter, *Crawford Lake Capital*

Allan Schoenberg, *Nasdaq*

Arnold Schneider, *Georgia Tech College of Management*

Andrew Schwartz, *RBC Capital Markets*

Howard A. Scott, *Park Hill Group*

Mustafa Singaporewalla, *Amazon Web Services*

Steven Sherman, *Shearman & Sterling LLP*

Andrew Shogan, *CTSI Oncology Solutions*

Karen Snow, *Nasdaq*

Emma Squires, *Value Retail*

David Spalding, *Dean, Iowa State University College of Business*

Andrew Steinerman, *J.P. Morgan*

Diana Tas, *Nasdaq*

Suvir Thadani, *RBC Capital Markets*

Matthew Thomson, *RBC Capital Markets*

Robb Tretter, *Ropes & Gray LLP*

John Tripodoro, *Cahill Gordon & Reindel LLP*

Charles VanderLinden, *Sysco*

Ante Vucic, *Wachtell, Lipton, Rosen & Katz*

Siyu Wang, CFA, *TX Investment Consulting (China)*

Brian Weiss, *RBC Capital Markets*

Jeremy Weisstub, *Aryeh Capital Management*

Jack Whalen, *Kensico Capital*

Chris Wright, *Crescent Capital Group*

# Disclaimer

*Views Expressed* All views expressed herein are those of the Authors as of the date of publication and do not represent the views of their respective current or former employers, or any entity with which the Authors ever have been, are now, or will be affiliated. The information and views expressed herein are subject to change at any time without notice. The Authors and John Wiley & Sons, Inc. (the "Publisher") are not under any obligation to update or correct any information provided in this book.

*Informational Only; No Investment Advice* The information provided herein is for general informational purposes only and is not and should not be regarded as "investment advice", a "recommendation" of any kind (whether investment, financial, accounting, tax, or legal), or "marketing material" of any kind. This book does not provide recommendations or views as to whether a stock or investment approach is suited to the financial needs of a specific individual. Your needs, goals, and circumstances are unique and may require the individualized attention of a licensed financial advisor.

*References and Examples Illustrative Only* Any and all examples included herein are for illustrative purposes only, and do not constitute recommendations of any kind, and are not intended to be reflective of results you can expect to achieve. Any reference to any company in this book is not intended to refer to, nor should it be considered, an endorsement of any stock, brand, or product.

*Information Accuracy* Although the information provided herein is obtained or compiled from sources believed to be reliable, the Authors cannot and do not guarantee the accuracy, validity, timeliness, or completeness of any information or data made available to you for any particular purpose. Neither the Authors, nor the Publisher, will be liable or have any responsibility of any kind for any loss or damage that you incur in the event of errors, inaccuracies, or omissions.

*Risk* Investing involves risk including possible loss of principal. An investor should consider his or her own investment objectives and risks carefully before investing. There is no guarantee that investments will result in profits or that they will not result in losses. All investors need to fully understand the risks associated with any kind of investing he or she chooses to do. Economic factors, market conditions, and investment strategies will affect the performance of any portfolio and there are no assurances that it will match or outperform any particular benchmark.

*No Reliance* The Authors will not be liable, whether in contract, tort (including, but not limited to, negligence) or otherwise, in respect to any damage, expense or other loss you may suffer arising out of or in connection with any information or content provided herein or any reliance you may place upon such information, content, or views. Any investments you make are at your sole discretion and risk.

*Disclaimer of Warranty and Limitation of Liability* In no event will the Authors, the Publisher, their affiliates, or any such parties be liable to you for any direct, indirect, special, consequential, incidental, or any other damages of any kind.

# Introduction

In the constantly evolving world of finance, a solid technical foundation is an essential tool for success. Due to the fast-paced nature of this world, however, no one was able to take the time to properly codify the lifeblood of the corporate financier's work—namely, valuation and dealmaking. We originally responded to this need in 2009 by writing the first edition of the book we wish had existed when we were trying to break into Wall Street. *Investment Banking: Valuation, LBOs, M&A, and IPOs, Third Edition* is a highly accessible and authoritative book written by investment bankers that explains how to perform the valuation work at the core of the financial world. Our book fills a noticeable gap in contemporary finance literature, which tends to focus on theory rather than practical application.

As the world of finance adjusts to the new normal of the post–Great Recession era, it merits revisiting the pillars of our second edition for today's environment. While the fundamentals of valuation and critical due diligence for mergers & acquisitions (M&A), capital markets, LBOs, initial public offerings (IPOs), and other public investment opportunities remain intact, the environment is constantly evolving. This involves the use of more realistic assumptions governing approach to growth and risk, including expected financial performance, discount rates, multiples, leverage levels, and financing terms. While valuation has always involved a great deal of "art" in addition to time-tested "science", the artistry must adapt to changing market developments and conditions. *As a result, we have updated our widely adopted book accordingly, while adding two new chapters on IPOs.*

The genesis for the original book stemmed from our personal experiences as students seeking to break into Wall Street. As we both independently went through the rigorous process of interviewing for associate and analyst positions at investment banks, we realized that our classroom experience was a step removed from how valuation and financial analysis are performed in real-world situations. This was particularly evident during the technical portion of the interviews, which is often the differentiator for recruiters trying to select among hundreds of qualified candidates.

Faced with this reality, we searched in vain for a practical how-to guide on the primary valuation methodologies used on Wall Street. At a loss, we resorted to compiling bits and pieces from various sources and conversations with friends and contacts already working in investment banking, private equity, and hedge funds. Needless to say, we didn't feel as prepared as we would have liked. While we were fortunate enough to secure job offers, the process left a deep impression on us. In fact, we continued to refine the comprehensive preparatory materials we had created as students, which served as the foundation for this book. And even today, we continue to refine and augment this material for new developments.

Once on Wall Street, we both went through mandatory training consisting of crash courses on finance and accounting, which sought to teach us the skill set necessary to become effective investment bankers. Months into the job, however, even the limitations of this training were revealed. Actual client situations and deal complexities, combined with evolving market conditions, accounting guidelines, and technologies stretched our knowledge base and skills. In these situations, we were forced to consult with senior colleagues for guidance, but often the demands of the job left no one accessible in a timely manner. Given these realities, it is difficult to overstate how helpful a reliable handbook based on years of "best practices" and deal experience would have been.

Consequently, we created this book to provide a leg up to those individuals seeking or beginning careers on Wall Street—from students at undergraduate universities and graduate schools to "career changers" looking to break into finance. This book has also served as important reference material for existing finance professionals. Our experience has demonstrated that given the highly specialized nature of many finance jobs, there are noticeable gaps in skill sets that need to be addressed. Furthermore, many professionals seek to continuously brush up on their skills as well as broaden and refine their knowledge base. This book has also proven invaluable for trainers and trainees at Wall Street firms, both within the context of formal training programs and informal on-the-job training.

Many private equity firms and hedge funds use our book to help train their investment professionals and key portfolio company executives. Many of these professionals come from a consulting or operational background and do not have a finance pedigree. Furthermore, the vast majority of buy-side investment firms do not have in-house training programs and rely heavily upon on-the-job learning. Consequently, our book has served as a helpful reference guide for individuals joining, or seeking jobs at, these institutions.

This book also provides essential tools for professionals at corporations, including members of business development, M&A, finance, and treasury departments. These specialists are responsible for corporate finance, valuation, and transaction-related deliverables on a daily basis. They also work with investment bankers on various M&A transactions (including leveraged buyouts (LBOs) and related financings), as well as IPOs, restructurings, and other capital markets transactions. Similarly, this book is intended to provide greater context for the legions of attorneys, consultants, and accountants focused on M&A, corporate finance, and other transaction advisory services.

Given the increasing globalization of the financial world, this book is designed to be sufficiently universal for use outside of North America. Our work on cross-border transactions in markets such as Asia, Europe, Latin America, India, and the Middle East has revealed a tremendous appetite for skilled resources throughout the globe. Therefore, this book fulfills an important need as a valuable training material and reliable handbook for finance professionals in these markets.

## STRUCTURE OF THE BOOK

Our book focuses on the primary valuation methodologies currently used on Wall Street, namely comparable companies analysis, precedent transactions analysis, discounted cash flow analysis, and leveraged buyout analysis. These methodologies are used to determine valuation for public and private companies within the context of M&A transactions, LBOs, IPOs, restructurings, and investment decisions. They also form the cornerstone for valuing companies on a standalone basis, including an assessment of whether a given public company is overvalued or undervalued. As such, these fundamental skills are just as relevant for private equity and hedge fund analysis as for investment banking. Using a step-by-step, how-to approach for each methodology, we build a chronological knowledge base and define key terms, financial concepts, and processes throughout the book.

We also provide context for the various valuation methodologies through a comprehensive overview of the fundamentals of LBOs, M&A, and IPOs. For these core transaction types, we discuss process and analytics in detail, including walking through illustrative analyses as would be performed on live deals. This discussion also provides detailed information on key participants, financing sources and terms, strategies, milestones, and legal and marketing documentation.

This body of work builds on our combined experience on a multitude of transactions, as well as input received from numerous investment bankers, investment professionals at private equity firms and hedge funds, attorneys, corporate executives, peer authors, and university professors. By drawing upon our own transaction and classroom experience, as well as that of a broad network of professional and professorial sources, we bridge the gap between academia and industry as it relates to the practical application of finance theory. The resulting product is accessible to a wide audience—including those with a limited finance background—as well as sufficiently detailed and comprehensive to serve as a primary reference tool and training guide for finance professionals.

This book is organized into four primary parts, as summarized below.

### Part One: Valuation (Chapters 1–3)

Part One focuses on the three most commonly used methodologies that serve as the core of a comprehensive valuation toolset—comparable companies analysis (Chapter 1), precedent transactions analysis (Chapter 2), and discounted cash flow analysis (Chapter 3). Each of these chapters employs a user-friendly, how-to approach for performing the given valuation methodology while defining key terms, detailing various calculations, and explaining advanced financial concepts. At the end of each chapter, we use our step-by-step approach to determine a valuation range for an illustrative target company, ValueCo Corporation ("ValueCo"), in accordance with the given methodology. The Base Case set of financials for ValueCo that forms the basis for our valuation work throughout the book is provided in Exhibits I.I to I.III.

In addition, the full set of valuation models and output pages used in this book are accessible on our website: www.wiley.com/go/investmentbanking3e

**Chapter 1: Comparable Companies Analysis**    Chapter 1 provides an overview of comparable companies analysis ("comparable companies", "trading comps", or simply, "comps"), one of the primary methodologies used for valuing a given focus company, division, business, or collection of assets ("target"). Comps provides a market benchmark against which a banker can establish valuation for a private company or analyze the value of a public company at a given point in time. It has a broad range of applications, most notably for various M&A situations, IPOs, restructurings, and investment decisions.

The foundation for comps is built upon the premise that similar companies provide a highly relevant reference point for valuing a given target as they share key business and financial characteristics, performance drivers, and risks. Therefore, valuation parameters can be established for the target by determining its relative positioning among peer companies. The core of this analysis involves selecting a universe of comparable companies for the target. These peer companies are benchmarked against one another and the target based on various financial statistics and ratios. Trading multiples—which utilize a measure of value in the numerator and an operating metric in the denominator—are then calculated for the universe. These multiples provide a basis for extrapolating a valuation range for the target.

**Chapter 2: Precedent Transactions Analysis**    Chapter 2 focuses on precedent transactions analysis ("precedent transactions" or "precedents"), which, like comparable companies, employs a multiples-based approach to derive an implied valuation range for a target. Precedents is premised on multiples paid for comparable companies in prior transactions. It has a broad range of applications, most notably to help determine a potential sale price range for a company, or part thereof, in an M&A or restructuring transaction.

The selection of an appropriate universe of comparable acquisitions is the foundation for performing precedent transactions. The best comparable acquisitions typically involve companies similar to the target on a fundamental level. As a general rule, the most recent transactions (i.e., those that have occurred within the previous two to three years) are the most relevant as they likely took place under similar market conditions to the contemplated transaction. Potential buyers and sellers look closely at the multiples that have been paid for comparable acquisitions. As a result, bankers and investors are expected to know the transaction multiples for their sector focus areas.

**Chapter 3: Discounted Cash Flow Analysis**    Chapter 3 discusses discounted cash flow analysis ("DCF analysis" or the "DCF"), a fundamental valuation methodology broadly used by investment bankers, corporate officers, academics, investors, and other finance professionals. The DCF has a wide range of applications, including valuation for various M&A situations, IPOs, restructurings, and investment decisions. It is premised on the principle that a target's value can be derived from the present value of its projected *free cash flow* (FCF). A company's projected FCF is derived from a variety of assumptions and judgments about its expected future financial performance, including sales growth rates, profit margins, capital expenditures, and net working capital requirements.

The valuation implied for a target by a DCF is also known as its *intrinsic value*, as opposed to its *market value*, which is the value ascribed by the market at a given point in time. Therefore, a DCF serves as an important alternative to market-based valuation techniques such as comparable companies and precedent transactions, which can be distorted by a number of factors, including market aberrations (e.g., the tech bubble of the late 1990s and the Great Recession). As such, a DCF plays a valuable role as a check on the prevailing market valuation for a publicly traded company. A DCF is also critical when there are limited (or no) "pure play" peer companies or comparable acquisitions.

## Part Two: Leveraged Buyouts (Chapters 4 & 5)

Part Two focuses on leveraged buyouts, which comprise a large part of the capital markets and M&A landscape due to the proliferation of private investment vehicles (e.g., private equity firms, hedge funds, and family offices) and their considerable pools of capital, as well as structured credit vehicles. We begin with a discussion in Chapter 4 of the fundamentals of LBOs, including an overview of key participants, characteristics of a strong LBO candidate, economics of an LBO, exit strategies, and key financing sources and terms. Once this framework is established, we apply our step-by-step, how-to approach in Chapter 5 to construct a comprehensive LBO model and perform an LBO analysis for our illustrative target company, ValueCo. LBO analysis is a core tool used by bankers and private equity professionals alike to determine financing structure and valuation for leveraged buyouts.

**Chapter 4: Leveraged Buyouts**  Chapter 4 provides an overview of the fundamentals of leveraged buyouts. An LBO is the acquisition of a target using debt to finance a large portion of the purchase price. The remaining portion of the purchase price is funded with an equity investment by funds managed by a private equity firm, also referred to as a financial sponsor ("sponsor"). In this chapter, we provide an overview of the economics of LBOs and how they are used to generate returns for sponsors. We also dedicate a significant portion of Chapter 4 to a discussion of LBO financing sources, particularly the various debt instruments and their terms and conditions.

LBOs are used by sponsors to acquire a broad range of businesses, including both public and private companies, as well as their divisions and subsidiaries. Generally speaking, companies with stable and predictable cash flows as well as substantial asset bases represent attractive LBO candidates. However, sponsors tend to be flexible investors provided the expected returns on the investment meet required thresholds. In an LBO, the disproportionately high level of debt incurred by the target is supported by its projected FCF and asset base, which enables the sponsor to contribute a small equity investment relative to the purchase price. This, in turn, enables the sponsor to realize an acceptable return on its equity investment upon exit, typically through a sale or IPO of the target.

**Chapter 5: LBO Analysis**   Chapter 5 removes the mystery surrounding LBO analysis, the core analytical tool used to assess financing structure, investment returns, and valuation in leveraged buyout scenarios. These same techniques can also be used to assess refinancing opportunities and restructuring alternatives for corporate issuers. LBO analysis is more complex than those methodologies previously discussed as it requires specialized knowledge of financial modeling, leveraged finance markets, M&A, and accounting. At the center of LBO analysis is a financial model, which is constructed with the flexibility to analyze a given target under multiple financing structures and operating scenarios.

As with the methodologies discussed in Part One, LBO analysis is an essential component of a comprehensive valuation toolset. On the debt financing side, LBO analysis is used to help craft a viable financing structure for the target on the basis of its cash flow generation, debt repayment, credit statistics, and investment returns over the projection period. Sponsors work closely with financing providers (e.g., investment banks) to determine the preferred financing structure for a particular transaction. In an M&A advisory context, LBO analysis provides the basis for determining an implied valuation range for a given target in the eyes of sponsors.

## Part Three: Mergers & Acquisitions (Chapters 6 & 7)

Part Three provides a comprehensive foundation for M&A, including process, strategies, deal structure, and analytics. M&A is a catch-all phrase for the purchase, sale, spin-off, and combination of companies and their parts and subsidiaries. M&A facilitates a company's ability to continuously grow, evolve, and re-focus in accordance with ever-changing market conditions, industry trends, and shareholder demands. M&A advisory assignments are core to investment banking, traditionally representing a substantial portion of the firm's annual corporate finance revenues. In addition, most M&A transactions require financing on the part of the acquirer through the issuance of debt and/or equity.

In Chapter 6, we focus on sell-side M&A, including the key process points and stages for running an effective M&A sale process, the medium whereby companies are bought and sold in the marketplace. This discussion serves to provide greater context for the topics discussed earlier in the book as theoretical valuation methodologies and analytics are tested based on what a buyer can afford to pay . . . and ultimately decide to bid. We also describe how valuation analysis is used to frame the seller's price expectations, set guidelines for the range of acceptable bids, evaluate offers received, and, ultimately, guide negotiations of the final purchase price.

Chapter 7 focuses on buy-side M&A. It builds upon the fundamental valuation material discussed earlier in the book by performing detailed valuation and merger consequences analysis on ValueCo from an illustrative strategic buyer's perspective, BuyerCo. As the name suggests, merger consequences analysis centers on examining the pro forma effects of a given transaction on the acquirer.

**Chapter 6: Sell-Side M&A**   The sale of a company, division, business, or collection of assets is a major event for its owners (shareholders), management, employees, and other stakeholders. It is an intense, time-consuming process with high stakes, usually spanning several months. Consequently, the seller typically hires an investment bank ("sell-side advisor") and its team of trained professionals to ensure that key objectives are met—namely an optimal mix of value maximization, speed of execution, and certainty of completion, among other deal-specific considerations. Prospective buyers also often hire an investment bank ("buy-side advisor") to perform valuation work, interface with the seller, and conduct negotiations, among other critical tasks.

The sell-side advisor is responsible for identifying the seller's priorities from the onset and crafts a tailored sale process accordingly. From an analytical perspective, a sell-side assignment requires a comprehensive valuation of the target using those methodologies discussed in this book. Perhaps the most basic decision, however, relates to whether to run a broad or targeted auction, or pursue a negotiated sale. Generally, an auction requires more upfront organization, marketing, process points, and resources than a negotiated sale with a single party. Consequently, Chapter 6 focuses primarily on the auction process.

**Chapter 7: Buy-Side M&A**   Chapter 7 begins by discussing buyer M&A strategies and motivations, including deal rationale and synergies. We also discuss form of financing and deal structure, which are critical components for performing detailed buy-side M&A analysis. We then perform a comprehensive valuation and merger consequences analysis for ValueCo from the perspective of a strategic acquirer, BuyerCo. This analysis starts with an overview of the primary valuation methodologies for ValueCo discussed in Chapters 1–3 and 5—namely, comparable companies, precedent transactions, DCF, and LBO analysis. The results of these analyses are displayed on a graphic known as a "football field" for easy comparison and analysis.

The next level of detail in our buy-side M&A work involves analysis at various prices (AVP) and contribution analysis. AVP, also known as a valuation matrix, displays the implied multiples paid at a range of transaction values and offer prices (for public targets) at set intervals. Contribution analysis analyzes the financial "contributions" made by the acquirer and target to the pro forma entity prior to any transaction adjustments. We then conduct a detailed merger consequences analysis for ValueCo in order to fine-tune the ultimate purchase price, deal structure, and financing mix. This analysis examines the pro forma impact of the transaction on the acquirer. The impact on earnings is known as accretion/(dilution) analysis, while the impact on credit statistics is known as balance sheet effects.

## Part Four: Initial Public Offerings (Chapters 8 & 9)

Part Four dives into the intricacies of initial public offerings. We kick off the discussion in Chapter 8 with an overview of the decision to go public, characteristics of strong IPO candidates, key participants, and key terms, as well as the nuances around running a dual-track process. We also address market developments around special purpose acquisition companies (SPACs) and direct listings. Once the IPO basics are addressed, we turn our focus to the stages of an IPO process, including critical analysis related to structure and valuation. Throughout, investment banks advise on all aspects of the IPO, culminating in the ultimate launch decision.

**Chapter 8: Initial Public Offerings**   Chapter 8 provides an overview of the fundamentals of initial public offerings. An IPO represents the first time a company sells its stock to public investors. It is a transformational event for a company, its owners, and employees. The company and the way it operates will never be the same again. Once a company "goes public", its shares will trade daily on the open market where buyers and sellers determine its prevailing equity value in real time. Detailed business and financial information will be made public and subject to analysis. Management will conduct quarterly earnings calls and field questions from sell-side research analysts. They will also speak regularly with existing and potential new investors.

While IPO candidates vary broadly in terms of sector, size, and financial profile, they need to feature performance and growth attributes that public investors would find compelling. Is the company and its addressable market large enough to warrant attention? Is it a market leader? How exciting is the growth opportunity? Is the cycle entry point attractive? How capable is the management team? Market conditions must also be conducive. The number of IPO offerings over a given time period is strongly correlated to the performance of the overall stock market. The better the market, the more plentiful the IPO pipeline.

**Chapter 9: The IPO Process**   As with an M&A sell-side, the IPO process is intense and time-consuming with high stakes for the company and its stakeholders. The typical process spans several months, although IPO-readiness activities and preparation may begin years in advance. Once the IPO decision has been made, the company chooses its team of investment banks, lawyers, accountants, and other key advisors. As with any other organized process, teamwork and cultural fit help ensure efficiency, quality, and success. Therefore, it is critical to get the right team in place upfront.

The IPO process consists of multiple stages and discrete milestones within each of these stages. There are numerous variations within this structure that allow the bookrunners to customize, as appropriate, for a given situation. In the event the company has long-standing banking relationships and current public audited financials (e.g., a public bond issuer), the prep stage can move quickly. On the other end of the spectrum, some companies may spend months or even years preparing their organization for an IPO. This extends to putting in place the right management and internal support, as well as getting the financials "IPO-ready". Proper company positioning is one of the foremost responsibilities for the deal team, most notably the bankers. This extends to IPO structure and valuation. Getting it right requires extensive thought, analysis, and market insight. Hence, the importance of choosing bankers that have a deep understanding of the company, sector, and equity market sentiment.

## VALUECO SUMMARY FINANCIAL INFORMATION

Exhibits I.I through I.III display the historical and projected financial information for ValueCo. These financials—as well as the various valuation multiples, financing terms, and other financial statistics discussed throughout the book—are purely illustrative and designed to represent normalized economic and market conditions.

**EXHIBIT I.I**    ValueCo Summary Historical Operating Data

*($ in millions)*

**ValueCo Summary Historical Operating Data**

| | Fiscal Year Ending December 31, | | | LTM |
|---|---|---|---|---|
| | **2016** | **2017** | **2018** | **9/30/2019** |
| **Sales** | **$2,600.0** | **$2,900.0** | **$3,200.0** | **$3,385.0** |
| *% growth* | *NA* | *11.5%* | *10.3%* | *NA* |
| Cost of Goods Sold | 1,612.0 | 1,769.0 | 1,920.0 | 2,030.0 |
| **Gross Profit** | **$988.0** | **$1,131.0** | **$1,280.0** | **$1,355.0** |
| *% margin* | *38.0%* | *39.0%* | *40.0%* | *40.0%* |
| Selling, General & Administrative | 496.6 | 551.0 | 608.0 | 655.0 |
| **EBITDA** | **$491.4** | **$580.0** | **$672.0** | **$700.0** |
| *% margin* | *18.9%* | *20.0%* | *21.0%* | *20.7%* |
| Depreciation & Amortization | 155.0 | 165.0 | 193.0 | 200.0 |
| **EBIT** | **$336.4** | **$415.0** | **$479.0** | **$500.0** |
| *% margin* | *12.9%* | *14.3%* | *15.0%* | *14.8%* |
| Capital Expenditures | 114.4 | 116.0 | 144.0 | 152.3 |
| *% sales* | *4.4%* | *4.0%* | *4.5%* | *4.5%* |

Note: For modeling purposes (e.g., DCF analysis and LBO analysis), D&A is broken out separately from COGS & SG&A as its own line item.

**EXHIBIT I.II**    ValueCo Summary Projected Operating Data

*($ in millions)*

**ValueCo Summary Projected Operating Data**

| | Fiscal Year Ending December 31, | | | | | |
|---|---|---|---|---|---|---|
| | **2019E** | **2020E** | **2021E** | **2022E** | **2023E** | **2024E** |
| **Sales** | **$3,450.0** | **$3,708.8** | **$3,931.3** | **$4,127.8** | **$4,293.0** | **$4,421.7** |
| *% growth* | *7.8%* | *7.5%* | *6.0%* | *5.0%* | *4.0%* | *3.0%* |
| Cost of Goods Sold | 2,070.0 | 2,225.3 | 2,358.8 | 2,476.7 | 2,575.8 | 2,653.0 |
| **Gross Profit** | **$1,380.0** | **$1,483.5** | **$1,572.5** | **$1,651.1** | **$1,717.2** | **$1,768.7** |
| *% margin* | *40.0%* | *40.0%* | *40.0%* | *40.0%* | *40.0%* | *40.0%* |
| Selling, General & Administrative | 655.0 | 704.1 | 746.4 | 783.7 | 815.0 | 839.5 |
| **EBITDA** | **$725.0** | **$779.4** | **$826.1** | **$867.4** | **$902.1** | **$929.2** |
| *% margin* | *21.0%* | *21.0%* | *21.0%* | *21.0%* | *21.0%* | *21.0%* |
| Depreciation & Amortization | 207.0 | 222.5 | 235.9 | 247.7 | 257.6 | 265.3 |
| **EBIT** | **$518.0** | **$556.9** | **$590.3** | **$619.8** | **$644.6** | **$663.9** |
| *% margin* | *15.0%* | *15.0%* | *15.0%* | *15.0%* | *15.0%* | *15.0%* |
| Capital Expenditures | 155.3 | 166.9 | 176.9 | 185.8 | 193.2 | 199.0 |
| *% sales* | *4.5%* | *4.5%* | *4.5%* | *4.5%* | *4.5%* | *4.5%* |

**EXHIBIT I.III** ValueCo Summary Historical Balance Sheet Data

*($ in millions)*

| ValueCo Summary Historical Balance Sheet Data | | | | | |
|---|---|---|---|---|---|
| | Fiscal Year Ended December 31, | | | As of | FYE |
| | 2016 | 2017 | 2018 | 9/30/2019 | 2019E |
| Cash and Cash Equivalents | $627.1 | $392.8 | $219.8 | $183.1 | $250.0 |
| Accounts Receivable | 317.0 | 365.5 | 417.4 | 441.5 | 450.0 |
| Inventories | 441.6 | 496.8 | 556.5 | 588.4 | 600.0 |
| Prepaid and Other Current Assets | 117.0 | 142.1 | 162.3 | 171.7 | 175.0 |
| **Total Current Assets** | **$1,502.7** | **$1,397.1** | **$1,356.0** | **$1,384.8** | **$1,475.0** |
| | | | | | |
| Property, Plant and Equipment, net | 2,571.1 | 2,565.6 | 2,564.6 | 2,501.3 | 2,500.0 |
| Goodwill | 1,000.0 | 1,000.0 | 1,000.0 | 1,000.0 | 1,000.0 |
| Intangible Assets | 1,018.3 | 974.8 | 926.8 | 891.8 | 875.0 |
| Other Assets | 150.0 | 150.0 | 150.0 | 150.0 | 150.0 |
| **Total Assets** | **$6,242.1** | **$6,087.5** | **$5,997.4** | **$5,927.8** | **$6,000.0** |
| | | | | | |
| Accounts Payable | 189.9 | 189.0 | 199.4 | 210.8 | 215.0 |
| Accrued Liabilities | 221.0 | 237.8 | 255.1 | 269.8 | 275.0 |
| Other Current Liabilities | 75.4 | 84.1 | 92.8 | 98.1 | 100.0 |
| **Total Current Liabilities** | **$486.3** | **$510.9** | **$547.2** | **$578.8** | **$590.0** |
| | | | | | |
| Total Debt | 2,500.0 | 2,150.0 | 1,800.0 | 1,500.0 | 1,500.0 |
| Other Long-Term Liabilities | 410.0 | 410.0 | 410.0 | 410.0 | 410.0 |
| **Total Liabilities** | **$3,396.3** | **$3,070.9** | **$2,757.2** | **$2,488.8** | **$2,500.0** |
| Noncontrolling Interest | - | - | - | - | - |
| Shareholders' Equity | 2,845.8 | 3,016.6 | 3,240.2 | 3,439.1 | 3,500.0 |
| **Total Liabilities and Equity** | **$6,242.1** | **$6,087.5** | **$5,997.4** | **$5,927.8** | **$6,000.0** |
| | | | | | |
| *Balance Check* | *0.000* | *0.000* | *0.000* | *0.000* | *0.000* |

# CHAPTER 1

# Comparable Companies Analysis

**C**omparable companies analysis ("comparable companies", "trading comps", or simply "comps") is one of the primary methodologies used for valuing a given focus company, division, business, or collection of assets ("target"). It provides a market benchmark against which a banker can establish valuation for a private company or analyze the value of a public company at a given point in time. Comps has a broad range of applications, most notably for various mergers & acquisitions (M&A) situations, initial public offerings (IPOs), restructurings, and investment decisions.

The foundation for comps is built upon the premise that similar companies provide a highly relevant reference point for valuing a given target due to the fact that they share key business and financial characteristics, performance drivers, and risks. Therefore, the banker can establish valuation parameters for the target by determining its relative positioning among peer companies. The core of this analysis involves selecting a universe of comparable companies for the target ("comparables universe"). These peer companies are benchmarked against one another and the target based on various financial statistics and ratios. Trading multiples are then calculated for the universe, which serve as the basis for extrapolating a valuation range for the target. This valuation range is calculated by applying the selected multiples to the target's relevant financial statistics.

While valuation metrics may vary by sector, this chapter focuses on the most widely used trading multiples. These multiples—such as enterprise value-to-earnings before interest, taxes, depreciation, and amortization (EV/EBITDA) and price-to-earnings (P/E)—utilize a measure of value in the numerator and a financial statistic in the denominator. While P/E is the most broadly recognized in circles outside Wall Street, multiples based on enterprise value are widely used by bankers because they are independent of capital structure and other factors unrelated to business operations (e.g., differences in tax regimes and certain accounting policies).

Comps is designed to reflect "current" valuation based on prevailing market conditions and sentiment. As such, it is often more relevant than *intrinsic valuation* techniques, such as the DCF (see Chapter 3). At the same time, market trading levels may be subject to periods of irrational investor sentiment that skew valuation either too high or too low. Furthermore, no two companies are exactly the same, so assigning a valuation based on the trading characteristics of similar companies may fail to accurately capture a given company's true value.

As a result, comps should be used in conjunction with the other valuation methodologies discussed in this book. A material disconnect between the derived valuation ranges from the various methodologies might be an indication that key assumptions or calculations need to be revisited. Or, it may indicate that you have discovered true valuation arbitrage in the market. Therefore, when performing comps and other valuation methodologies, it is imperative to diligently footnote key sources and assumptions both for review and defense of conclusions.

This chapter provides a highly practical, step-by-step approach to performing comps consistent with how this valuation methodology is performed in real world applications (see Exhibit 1.1). Once this framework is established, we walk through an illustrative comparable companies analysis using our target company, ValueCo (see Introduction for reference).

**EXHIBIT 1.1** Comparable Companies Analysis Steps

Step I.    Select the Universe of Comparable Companies
Step II.   Locate the Necessary Financial Information
Step III.  Spread Key Statistics, Ratios, and Trading Multiples
Step IV.   Benchmark the Comparable Companies
Step V.    Determine Valuation

## SUMMARY OF COMPARABLE COMPANIES ANALYSIS STEPS

- Step I. Select the Universe of Comparable Companies. The selection of a universe of comparable companies for the target is the foundation of comps. While this exercise can be fairly simple and intuitive for companies in certain sectors, it can prove challenging for others whose peers are not readily apparent. To identify companies with similar business and financial characteristics, it is first necessary to gain a sound understanding of the target.

  As a starting point, the banker typically consults with peers or senior colleagues to see if a relevant set of comparable companies already exists internally. If beginning from scratch, the banker casts a broad net to review as many potential comparable companies as possible. This broader group is eventually narrowed, and then typically further refined to a subset of "closest comparables". A survey of the target's public competitors is generally a good place to start this exercise.

- Step II. Locate the Necessary Financial Information. Once the initial comparables universe is determined, the banker locates the financial information necessary to analyze the selected comparable companies and calculate ("spread[1]") key financial statistics, ratios, and trading multiples (see Step III). The primary data for calculating these metrics is compiled from various sources, including a company's SEC filings,[2] consensus research estimates, equity research reports, and press releases.

---

[1]The notion of "spreading" refers to performing calculations in a spreadsheet program such as Microsoft Excel.
[2]The Securities and Exchange Commission (SEC) is a federal agency created by the Securities Exchange Act of 1934 that regulates the U.S. securities industry. SEC filings can be located online at www.sec.gov.

- **Step III. Spread Key Statistics, Ratios, and Trading Multiples.** The banker is now prepared to spread key statistics, ratios, and trading multiples for the comparables universe. This involves calculating market valuation measures such as enterprise value and equity value, as well as key income statement items, such as EBITDA and net income. A variety of ratios and other metrics measuring profitability, growth, returns, and credit strength are also calculated at this stage. Selected financial statistics are then used to calculate trading multiples for the comparables.

  As part of this process, the banker needs to employ various financial concepts and techniques, including the calculation of *last twelve months* (LTM)[3] financial statistics, *calendarization* of company financials, and adjustments for *non-recurring items*. These calculations are imperative for measuring the comparables accurately on both an absolute and relative basis (see Step IV).

- **Step IV. Benchmark the Comparable Companies.** The next level of analysis requires an in-depth examination of the comparable companies in order to determine the target's relative ranking and closest comparables. This requires laying out the calculated financial statistics and ratios for the comparable companies (as calculated in Step III) alongside those of the target in spreadsheet form for easy comparison (see Exhibits 1.53 and 1.54). This exercise is known as "benchmarking".

  Benchmarking serves to determine the relative strength of the comparable companies versus one another and the target. The similarities and discrepancies in size, growth rates, margins, and leverage, for example, among the comparables and the target are closely examined. This analysis provides the basis for establishing the target's relative ranking as well as determining those companies most appropriate for framing its valuation. The trading multiples are also laid out in a spreadsheet form for benchmarking purposes (see Exhibits 1.2 and 1.55). At this point, it may become apparent that certain outliers need to be eliminated or that the comparables should be further tiered (e.g., on the basis of size, sub-sector, or ranging from closest to peripheral).

- **Step V. Determine Valuation.** The trading multiples of the comparable companies serve as the basis for deriving a valuation range for the target. The banker typically begins by using the means and medians for the relevant trading multiples (e.g., EV/EBITDA) as the basis for extrapolating an initial range. The high and low multiples for the comparables universe provide further guidance in terms of a potential ceiling or floor. The key to arriving at the tightest, most appropriate range, however, is to rely upon the multiples of the closest comparables as guideposts. Consequently, only a few carefully selected companies typically serve as the ultimate basis for valuation, with the broader group serving as additional reference points. As this process involves as much "art" as "science", industry veterans are typically consulted for guidance on the final decision. The chosen range is then applied to the target's relevant financial statistics to produce an implied valuation range.

---

[3]The sum of the prior four quarters of a company's financial performance, also known as Trailing Twelve Months (TTM).

**EXHIBIT 1.2** Comparable Companies Analysis—Trading Multiples Output Page

## ValueCo Corporation
### Comparable Companies Analysis
($ in millions, except per share data)

| Company | Ticker | Current Share Price | % of 52-wk. High | Equity Value | Enterprise Value | EV/ LTM Sales | EV/ 2019E Sales | EV/ 2020E Sales | EV/ LTM EBITDA | EV/ 2019E EBITDA | EV/ 2020E EBITDA | EV/ LTM EBIT | EV/ 2019E EBIT | EV/ 2020E EBIT | LTM EBITDA Margin | Total Debt / EBITDA | Price/ LTM EPS | Price/ 2019E EPS | Price/ 2020E EPS | LT EPS Growth |
|---|---|---|---|---|---|---|---|---|---|---|---|---|---|---|---|---|---|---|---|---|
| **Tier I: Specialty Chemicals** | | | | | | | | | | | | | | | | | | | | |
| BuyerCo | BUY | $70.00 | 91% | $9,800 | $11,600 | 1.8x | 1.7x | 1.6x | 8.0x | 7.8x | 7.3x | 9.1x | 8.8x | 8.2x | 22% | 1.5x | 11.5x | 11.1x | 10.3x | 7% |
| Sherman Co. | SHR | 40.00 | 76% | 5,600 | 8,101 | 1.4x | 1.4x | 1.3x | 7.7x | 7.7x | 7.2x | 10.8x | 10.7x | 10.1x | 18% | 3.0x | 11.0x | 10.6x | 9.7x | 9% |
| Pearl Corp. | PRL | 68.50 | 95% | 5,172 | 5,856 | 1.4x | 1.4x | 1.3x | 7.0x | 7.0x | 6.5x | 9.4x | 9.4x | 8.7x | 20% | 1.8x | 13.1x | 12.2x | 11.1x | 11% |
| Gasparro Corp. | JDG | 50.00 | 80% | 5,000 | 6,750 | 1.4x | 1.4x | 1.3x | 7.5x | 7.1x | 6.6x | 9.3x | 8.8x | 8.2x | 19% | 2.1x | 10.7x | 9.8x | 9.1x | 12% |
| Kumra Inc. | KUM | 52.50 | 88% | 4,852 | 5,345 | 1.7x | 1.7x | 1.5x | 8.0x | 7.9x | 7.4x | 10.6x | 10.4x | 9.7x | 21% | 1.3x | 15.8x | 13.6x | 11.8x | 10% |
| **Mean** | | | | | | 1.5x | 1.5x | 1.4x | 7.7x | 7.5x | 7.0x | 9.8x | 9.6x | 9.0x | 20% | 1.9x | 12.4x | 11.5x | 10.4x | 10% |
| **Median** | | | | | | 1.4x | 1.4x | 1.3x | 7.7x | 7.7x | 7.2x | 9.4x | 9.4x | 8.7x | 20% | 1.8x | 11.5x | 11.1x | 10.3x | 10% |
| **Tier II: Commodity / Diversified Chemicals** | | | | | | | | | | | | | | | | | | | | |
| Falloon Group | FLN | $31.00 | 87% | $7,480 | $11,254 | 1.0x | 1.0x | 0.9x | 6.9x | 7.0x | 6.7x | 10.8x | 11.0x | 10.5x | 14% | 2.5x | 13.3x | 12.4x | 10.8x | 5% |
| Goodson Corp. | GDS | 64.00 | 83% | 4,160 | 5,660 | 1.2x | 1.2x | 1.1x | 7.4x | 7.5x | 7.2x | 10.8x | 11.0x | 10.4x | 16% | 2.9x | 16.1x | 15.4x | 13.5x | 9% |
| Pryor Industries | PRI | 79.00 | 88% | 3,926 | 4,166 | 1.1x | 1.2x | 1.1x | 7.3x | 7.4x | 7.1x | 9.9x | 10.1x | 9.6x | 15% | 1.1x | 14.3x | 13.9x | 12.7x | 10% |
| Lanzarone Global | LNZ | 32.25 | 95% | 3,230 | 3,823 | 1.0x | 1.0x | 1.0x | 6.6x | 6.7x | 6.4x | 8.9x | 9.0x | 8.6x | 16% | 1.3x | 11.5x | 10.7x | 9.7x | 8% |
| McMenamin & Co. | MCM | 33.50 | 80% | 3,193 | 3,193 | 1.0x | 0.9x | 0.8x | 9.0x | 8.4x | 7.5x | 14.2x | 13.1x | 11.8x | 11% | 1.2x | 22.2x | 19.3x | 16.8x | 12% |
| **Mean** | | | | | | 1.1x | 1.1x | 1.0x | 7.4x | 7.4x | 7.0x | 10.9x | 10.8x | 10.2x | 14% | 1.8x | 15.5x | 14.3x | 12.7x | 9% |
| **Median** | | | | | | 1.0x | 1.0x | 1.0x | 7.3x | 7.4x | 7.1x | 10.8x | 11.0x | 10.4x | 15% | 1.3x | 14.3x | 13.9x | 12.7x | 9% |
| **Tier III: Small-Cap Chemicals** | | | | | | | | | | | | | | | | | | | | |
| S. Momper & Co. | MOMP | $28.00 | 95% | $2,240 | $2,921 | 1.4x | 1.4x | 1.2x | 7.7x | 7.4x | 6.7x | 9.9x | 9.5x | 8.6x | 18% | 2.6x | 14.2x | 14.4x | 13.4x | 5% |
| Adler Worldwide | ADL | 10.50 | 80% | 1,217 | 1,463 | 0.9x | 1.0x | 0.9x | 6.0x | 6.1x | 5.8x | 8.0x | 8.1x | 7.7x | 16% | 1.6x | 11.3x | 12.2x | 11.3x | 7% |
| Schachter & Sons | STM | 4.50 | 89% | 1,125 | 1,674 | 1.0x | 0.9x | 0.8x | 7.0x | 6.5x | 5.7x | 9.8x | 9.1x | 7.9x | 14% | 2.5x | 12.2x | 11.3x | 10.0x | 11% |
| Girshin Holdings | MGP | 50.00 | 67% | 1,035 | 1,298 | 0.8x | 0.8x | 0.7x | 7.3x | 6.8x | 6.1x | 11.5x | 10.7x | 9.7x | 11% | 1.8x | 16.5x | 15.6x | 14.2x | 8% |
| Crespin International | MCR | 27.00 | 80% | 872 | 1,222 | 0.8x | 0.8x | 0.7x | 6.4x | 6.0x | 5.4x | 9.2x | 8.6x | 7.7x | 13% | 2.1x | 11.8x | 11.6x | 10.5x | 6% |
| **Mean** | | | | | | 1.0x | 1.0x | 0.9x | 6.9x | 6.6x | 5.9x | 9.7x | 9.2x | 8.3x | 14% | 2.1x | 13.2x | 13.0x | 11.9x | 7% |
| **Median** | | | | | | 0.9x | 0.9x | 0.8x | 7.0x | 6.5x | 5.8x | 9.8x | 9.1x | 7.9x | 14% | 2.1x | 12.2x | 12.2x | 11.3x | 7% |
| **Overall** | | | | | | | | | | | | | | | | | | | | |
| **Mean** | | | | | | 1.2x | 1.2x | 1.1x | 7.3x | 7.2x | 6.6x | 10.1x | 9.9x | 9.2x | 16% | 2.0x | 13.7x | 12.9x | 11.7x | 9% |
| **Median** | | | | | | 1.1x | 1.2x | 1.1x | 7.3x | 7.1x | 6.7x | 9.9x | 9.5x | 8.7x | 16% | 1.8x | 13.1x | 12.2x | 11.1x | 9% |
| **High** | | | | | | 1.8x | 1.7x | 1.6x | 9.0x | 8.4x | 7.5x | 14.2x | 13.1x | 11.8x | 22% | 3.0x | 22.2x | 19.3x | 16.8x | 12% |
| **Low** | | | | | | 0.8x | 0.8x | 0.7x | 6.0x | 6.0x | 5.4x | 8.0x | 8.1x | 7.7x | 11% | 1.1x | 10.7x | 9.8x | 9.1x | 5% |

Source: Company filings, Bloomberg, Consensus Estimates
Note: Last twelve months data based on September 30, 2019. Estimated annual financial data based on a calendar year.

## STEP I. SELECT THE UNIVERSE OF COMPARABLE COMPANIES

The selection of the right universe of comparable companies is the foundation for performing trading comps. To find companies with similar business and financial characteristics, you must first truly understand the target. At its base, the methodology for determining comparable companies is relatively intuitive. Companies in the same sector (or, preferably, "sub-sector") with similar size tend to serve as good comparables. While this can be a fairly simple exercise for certain companies, it may prove challenging for others with no readily apparent peers.

For a target with no clear, publicly traded comparables, the banker seeks companies outside the target's core sector that share business and financial characteristics on some fundamental level. For example, a medium-sized manufacturer of residential windows may have limited or no truly direct publicly traded peers in terms of products, namely companies that produce windows. If the universe is expanded to include companies that manufacture building products, serve homebuilders, or have exposure to the housing cycle, however, the probability of locating companies with similar business drivers is increased. In this case, the list of potential comparables could be expanded to include manufacturers of related building products such as decking, roofing, siding, doors, and cabinets.

### Study the Target

The process of learning the in-depth "story" of the target should be exhaustive. Toward this end, the banker is encouraged to read and study as much company- and sector-specific material as possible. *The actual selection of comparable companies should only begin once this research is completed.*

For targets that are public registrants,[4] annual (10-K) and quarterly (10-Q) SEC filings, consensus research estimates, equity and fixed income research reports, press releases, earnings call transcripts, investor presentations,[5] and corporate websites provide key business and financial information. Private companies present a greater challenge as the banker is forced to rely upon sources such as corporate websites, sector research reports, news runs, and trade journals for basic company data. Public competitors' SEC filings, research reports, and investor presentations may also serve as helpful sources of information on private companies. In an organized M&A sale process[6] for a private company, however, the banker is provided with detailed business and financial information on the target (see Chapter 6).

---

[4]Public or publicly traded companies refer to those listed on a public stock exchange where their shares can be traded. Public filers ("public registrants"), however, may include privately held companies that are issuers of public debt securities and, therefore, subject to SEC disclosure requirements.

[5]Presentations at investment conferences or regular performance reports, typically posted on a company's corporate website. Investor presentations may also be released for significant M&A events or as part of Regulation FD requirements. They are typically posted on the company's corporate website under "Investor Relations" and filed in an 8-K (current report).

[6]A process through which a target is marketed to prospective buyers, typically run by an investment banking firm (see Chapter 6).

## Identify Key Characteristics of the Target for Comparison Purposes

A simple framework for studying the target and selecting comparable companies is shown in Exhibit 1.3. This framework, while by no means exhaustive, is designed to determine commonality with other companies by profiling and comparing key business and financial characteristics.

**EXHIBIT 1.3**    Business and Financial Profile Framework

| Business Profile | Financial Profile |
| --- | --- |
| ■ Sector | ■ Size |
| ■ Products and Services | ■ Profitability |
| ■ Customers and End Markets | ■ Growth Profile |
| ■ Distribution Channels | ■ Return on Investment |
| ■ Geography | ■ Credit Profile |

### Business Profile

Companies that share core business characteristics tend to serve as good comparables. These core traits include sector, products and services, customers and end markets, distribution channels, and geography.

Sector

Sector refers to the industry or markets in which a company operates (e.g., consumer products, financials, healthcare, industrials, and technology). A company's sector can be further divided into sub-sectors, which facilitates the identification of the target's closest comparables. Within the industrials sector, for example, there are numerous sub-sectors, such as aerospace and defense, automotive, building products, chemicals, and paper and packaging. Even these sub-sectors can be further segmented—for example, chemicals can be divided into specialty and commodity chemicals. For companies with distinct business divisions, the segmenting of comparable companies by sub-sector may be critical for valuation.

A company's sector conveys a great deal about its key drivers, risks, and opportunities. For example, a cyclical sector such as oil & gas will have dramatically different earnings volatility from consumer staples. On the other hand, cyclical or highly fragmented sectors may present growth opportunities that are unavailable to companies in more stable or consolidated sectors. The proper identification and classification of the target's sector and sub-sector is an essential step toward locating comparable companies.

Products and Services

A company's products and services are at the core of its business model. Accordingly, companies that produce similar products or provide similar services typically serve as good comparables. Products are commodities or value-added goods that a company creates, produces, or refines. Examples of products include auto supplies, lumber, oil, machinery, prescription drugs, and steel. Services are acts or functions performed by one entity for the benefit of another. Examples of common services include banking, consulting, installation, lodging, facilities maintenance, and transportation. Many companies provide both products and services to their customers, while others offer one or the other. Similarly, some companies offer a diversified product and/or service mix, while others are more focused.

Within a given sector or sub-sector, comparable companies may be tiered according to their products and services. For example, within the chemicals sector, specialty chemicals producers tend to consistently trade at a premium to commodity chemicals producers. Hence, they are often grouped together in a tighter comparables category within the broader chemicals universe.

## Customers and End Markets

*Customers*  A company's customers refer to the purchasers of its products and services. Companies with a similar customer base tend to share similar opportunities and risks. For example, companies supplying automobile manufacturers abide by certain manufacturing and distribution requirements, and are subject to the automobile purchasing cycles and trends.

The quantity and diversity of a company's customers are also important. Some companies serve a broad customer base while others may target a specialized or niche market. While it is generally positive to have low customer concentration from a risk management perspective, it is also beneficial to have a stable customer core to provide visibility and comfort regarding future revenues.

*End Markets*  A company's end markets refer to the broad underlying markets into which it sells its products and services. For example, a plastics manufacturer may sell into several end markets, including automotive, construction, consumer products, medical devices, and packaging. End markets need to be distinguished from customers. For example, a company may sell into the housing end market, but to retailers or suppliers as opposed to homebuilders.

A company's performance is generally tied to economic and other factors that affect its end markets. A company that sells products into the housing end market is susceptible to macroeconomic factors that affect the overall housing cycle, such as interest rates and unemployment levels. Therefore, companies that sell products and services into the same end markets generally share a similar performance outlook, which is important for determining appropriate comparable companies.

## Distribution Channels

Distribution channels are the avenues through which a company sells its products and services to the end user. As such, they are a key driver of operating strategy, performance, and, ultimately, value. Companies that sell primarily to the wholesale channel, for example, often have significantly different organizational and cost structures from those selling directly to retailers or end users. Selling to a superstore or value retailer requires a physical infrastructure, salesforce, and logistics that may be unnecessary for serving the professional or wholesale channels.

Some companies sell at several levels of the distribution chain, such as wholesale, retail, online, and direct-to-customer. A flooring manufacturer, for example, may distribute its products through selected wholesale distributors and retailers, as well as directly to homebuilders and end users.

Geography

Companies that are based in (and sell to) different regions of the world often differ substantially in terms of fundamental business drivers and characteristics. These may include growth rates, macroeconomic environment, competitive dynamics, path(s)-to-market, organizational and cost structure, and potential opportunities and risks. Such differences—which result from local demographics, regulatory regimes, consumer buying patterns and preferences, and cultural norms—can vary greatly from country to country and, particularly, from continent to continent. Consequently, there are often valuation disparities for similar companies in different global regions or jurisdictions.[7] For comps, bankers tend to group U.S.-based (or focused) companies in a separate category from European- or Asian-based companies even if their basic business models are the same.

For example, a banker seeking comparable companies for a U.S. retailer would focus primarily on U.S. companies with relevant foreign companies providing peripheral guidance. This geographic grouping is slightly less applicable for truly global industries such as oil and aluminum, for example, where domicile is less indicative than global commodity prices and supply/demand dynamics. Even in these instances, however, valuation disparities by geography are often evident.

### Financial Profile

Key financial characteristics must also be examined both as a means of understanding the target and identifying the best comparable companies.

Size

Size is typically measured in terms of market valuation (e.g., equity value and enterprise value), as well as key financial statistics (e.g., sales, gross profit, EBITDA, EBIT, and net income). Companies of similar size in a given sector are more likely to have similar multiples than companies with significant size discrepancies. This reflects the fact that companies of similar size are also likely to be analogous in other respects (e.g., economies of scale, purchasing power, pricing leverage, customers, growth prospects, and the trading liquidity of their shares in the stock market).

Consequently, differences in size often map to differences in valuation. Hence, the comparables are often tiered based on size categories. For example, companies with under $5 billion in equity value (or enterprise value, sales) may be placed in one group and those with greater than $5 billion in a separate group. This tiering, of course, assumes a sufficient number of comparables to justify organizing the universe into sub-groups.

---

[7]Other factors, such as the local capital markets conditions, including volume, liquidity, transparency, shareholder base, and investor perceptions, as well as political risk, also contribute to these disparities.

## Profitability

A company's profitability measures its ability to convert sales into profit. Profitability ratios ("margins") employ a measure of profit in the numerator, such as gross profit, EBITDA, EBIT, or net income, and sales in the denominator.[8] As a general rule, for companies in the same sector, higher profit margins translate into higher valuations, all else being equal. Consequently, determining a company's relative profitability versus peers is a core component of the benchmarking analysis (see Step IV).

## Growth Profile

A company's growth profile, as determined by its historical and estimated future financial performance, is a critical driver of valuation. Equity investors reward high growth companies with higher trading multiples than slower growing peers. They also discern whether the growth is primarily organic or acquisition-driven, with the former generally viewed as preferable. In assessing a company's growth profile, historical and estimated future growth rates for various financial statistics (e.g., sales, EBITDA, and earnings per share (EPS)) are examined at selected intervals. For mature public companies, EPS growth rates are typically more meaningful. For early stage or emerging companies with little or no earnings, however, sales or EBITDA growth trends may be more relevant.

## Return on Investment

Return on investment (ROI) measures a company's ability to provide earnings (or returns) to its capital providers. ROI ratios employ a measure of profitability (e.g., EBIT, NOPAT,[9] or net income) in the numerator and a measure of capital (e.g., invested capital, shareholders' equity, or total assets) in the denominator. The most commonly used ROI metrics are return on invested capital (ROIC), return on equity (ROE), and return on assets (ROA). Dividend yield, which measures the dividend payment that a company's shareholders receive for each share owned, is another type of return metric.

## Credit Profile

A company's credit profile refers to its creditworthiness as a borrower. It is typically measured by metrics relating to a company's overall debt level ("leverage") as well as its ability to make interest payments ("coverage"), and reflects key company and sector-specific benefits and risks. Moody's Investors Service (Moody's), Standard & Poor's (S&P), and Fitch Ratings (Fitch) are the three primary independent credit rating agencies that provide formal assessments of a company's credit profile.

---

[8]Depending on the sector, profitability may be measured on a per unit basis (e.g., per ton or pound).
[9]Net operating profit after taxes, also known as tax-effected EBIT or earnings before interest after taxes (EBIAT).

## Screen for Comparable Companies

Once the target's basic business and financial characteristics are researched and understood, the banker uses multiple resources to screen for potential comparable companies. At the initial stage, the focus is on identifying companies with a similar business profile. While basic financial information (e.g., sales, enterprise value, or equity value) should be assessed early on, more detailed financial benchmarking is performed in Step IV.

Investment banks generally have established lists of comparable companies by sector containing relevant multiples and other financial data, which are updated on a quarterly basis and for appropriate company-specific actions. Often, however, the banker needs to start from scratch. In these cases, an examination of the target's public competitors is usually the best place to begin. Competitors generally share key business and financial characteristics and are susceptible to similar opportunities and risks. Public companies typically discuss their primary competitors in their 10-Ks, annual proxy statement (DEF14A),[10] and, potentially, in investor presentations. Furthermore, equity research reports, especially those known as *initiating coverage*,[11] often explicitly list the research analyst's views on the target's comparables and/or primary competitors. For private targets, public competitors' 10-Ks, proxy statements, investor presentations, research reports, and broader industry reports are often helpful sources.

An additional source for locating comparables is the proxy statement for a relatively recent M&A transaction in the sector ("merger proxy"),[12] as it contains excerpts from a *fairness opinion*. As the name connotes, a fairness opinion opines on the "fairness" of the purchase price and deal terms offered by the acquirer from a financial perspective (see Chapter 6). The fairness opinion is supported by a detailed overview of the methodologies used to perform a valuation of the target, typically including comparable companies, precedent transactions, DCF analysis, and LBO analysis, if applicable.[13] The trading comps excerpt from the fairness opinion generally provides a list of the comparable companies used to value the M&A target as well as the selected range of multiples used in the valuation analysis.

---

[10]A company's annual proxy statement typically provides a suggested peer group of companies that is used for benchmarking purposes.

[11]An initiating coverage equity research report refers to the first report published by an equity research analyst beginning coverage on a particular company. This report often provides a comprehensive business description, sector analysis, and commentary.

[12]A solicitation of shareholder votes in a business combination is initially filed under SEC Form PREM14A (preliminary merger proxy statement) and then DEFM14A (definitive merger proxy statement).

[13]Not all companies are LBO candidates. See Chapter 4 for an overview of the characteristics of strong LBO candidates.

The banker may also screen for companies that operate in the target's sector using SIC, NAICS, or other industry codes.[14] This type of screen is typically used either to establish a broad initial universe of comparables or to ensure that no potential companies have been overlooked. Sector reports published by the credit rating agencies (e.g., Moody's, S&P, and Fitch) may also provide helpful lists of peer companies.

In addition to the aforementioned, senior bankers and industry experts are perhaps the most valuable resources. Given their sector knowledge and familiarity with the target, a brief conversation is usually sufficient to provide a strong starting point. Toward the end of the process—once the legwork to craft and refine a robust list of comparables has been completed—a senior banker should be called upon to provide the finishing touches.

At this stage of the process, there may be sufficient information to eliminate certain companies from the group or tier the selected companies by size, business focus, or geography, for example.

## STEP II. LOCATE THE NECESSARY FINANCIAL INFORMATION

This section provides an overview of the relevant sources for locating the necessary financial information to calculate key financial statistics, ratios, and multiples for the selected comparable companies (see Step III). The most common sources for public company financial data are SEC filings (such as 10-Ks, 10-Qs, and 8-Ks), as well as earnings announcements, investor presentations, equity research reports, consensus estimates, and press releases. A summary list of where to locate key financial data is provided in Exhibit 1.4.

In trading comps, valuation is driven on the basis of both historical performance (e.g., LTM financial data) and expected future performance (e.g., consensus estimates for future calendar years). Depending on the sector and point in the cycle, however, financial projections tend to be more meaningful. Estimates for forward-year financial performance are typically sourced from consensus estimates[15] as well as individual company equity research reports. In the context of an M&A or debt capital raising transaction, by contrast, more emphasis is placed on LTM financial performance. LTM financial information is calculated on the basis of data obtained from a company's public filings (see Exhibits 1.24 and 1.25).

---

[14]Standard Industrial Classification (SIC) is a system established by the U.S. government for classifying the major business operations of a company with a numeric code. Some bankers use the newer North American Industry Classification System (NAICS) codes in lieu of SIC codes. The SEC, however, still uses SIC codes.

[15]Bloomberg Estimates, Refinitiv IBES (Institutional Brokers Estimate System), S&P Capital IQ Estimates, and Thomson First Call provide consensus analyst estimates for thousands of publicly traded companies.

## SEC Filings: 10-K, 10-Q, 8-K, and Proxy Statement

As a general rule, the banker uses SEC filings to source historical financial information for comparable companies. This financial information is used to determine historical sales, gross profit, EBITDA, EBIT, and net income (and EPS) on both an annual and LTM basis. SEC filings are also the primary source for other key financial items such as balance sheet data, capital expenditures ("capex"), basic shares outstanding, stock options/warrants data, and information on non-recurring items. SEC filings can be obtained through numerous mediums, including a company's corporate website (typically through an "Investor Relations" link) as well as EDGAR[16] and other financial information services.

**10-K (Annual Report)**   The 10-K is an annual report filed with the SEC by a public registrant that provides a comprehensive overview of the company and its prior year performance.[17] It is required to contain an exhaustive list of disclosure items including, but not limited to, a detailed business description, management's discussion & analysis (MD&A),[18] audited financial statements[19] and supplementary data, outstanding debt detail, basic shares outstanding, and stock options/warrants data. It also contains an abundance of other pertinent information about the company and its sector, such as business segment detail, customers, end markets, competition, insight into material opportunities (and challenges and risks), significant recent events, and acquisitions.

**10-Q (Quarterly Report)**   The 10-Q is a quarterly report filed with the SEC by a public registrant that provides an overview of the most recent quarter and year-to-date (YTD) period.[20] It is less comprehensive than the 10-K, but provides financial statements as well as MD&A relating to the company's financial performance for the most recent quarter and YTD period versus the prior year periods.[21] The 10-Q also provides the most recent share count information and may also contain the most recent stock options/warrants data. For detailed financial information on a company's final quarter of the fiscal year, the banker refers to the 8-K containing the fourth quarter earnings press release that usually precedes the filing of the 10-K.

---

[16]The Electronic Data Gathering, Analysis, and Retrieval (EDGAR) system performs automated collection, validation, indexing, acceptance, and forwarding of submissions by companies and others who are required to file forms with the SEC.

[17]The deadline for the filing of the 10-K ranges from 60 to 90 days after the end of a company's fiscal year depending on the size of its public float.

[18]A section in a company's 10-K and 10-Q that provides a discussion and analysis of the prior reporting period's financial performance. It also contains forward-looking information about the possible future effects of known and unknown events, market conditions, and trends.

[19]The financial statements in a 10-K are audited and certified by a Certified Public Accountant (CPA) to meet the requirements of the SEC.

[20]The deadline for the filing of the 10-Q ranges from 40 to 45 days after the end of a company's fiscal quarter depending on the size of its public float. The 10-K, instead of the 10-Q, is filed after the end of a company's fiscal fourth quarter.

[21]The financial statements in a company's 10-Q are reviewed by a CPA, but not audited.

**8-K (Current Report)**   The 8-K, or current report, is filed by a public registrant to report the occurrence of *material* corporate events or changes ("triggering event") that are of importance to shareholders or security holders.[22] For the purposes of preparing trading comps, key triggering events include, but are not limited to, earnings announcements, entry into a definitive purchase/sale agreement,[23] completion of an acquisition or disposition of assets, capital markets transactions, investor days,[24] and Regulation FD disclosure requirements.[25] The corresponding 8-Ks for these events often contain important information necessary to calculate a company's updated financial statistics, ratios, and trading multiples that may not be reflected in the most recent 10-K or 10-Q (see "Adjustments for Recent Events").

**Proxy Statement**   A proxy statement is a document that a public company sends to its shareholders prior to a shareholder meeting containing material information regarding matters on which the shareholders are expected to vote. It is also filed with the SEC on Schedule 14A. For the purposes of spreading trading comps, the annual proxy statement provides a basic shares outstanding count that may be more recent than that contained in the latest 10-K or 10-Q. As previously discussed, the annual proxy statement also typically contains a suggested peer group for benchmarking purposes.

## Equity Research

**Research Reports**   Equity research reports provide individual analyst estimates of future company performance, which may be used to calculate forward-looking multiples. They generally include estimates of sales, EBITDA and/or EBIT, and EPS for future quarters and the future two- or three-year period (on an annual basis). More comprehensive reports provide additional estimated financial information from the research analyst's model, including key items from the income statement, balance sheet, and cash flow statement. These reports may also provide segmented financial projections, such as sales and EBIT at the business division level.

Equity research reports often provide commentary on non-recurring items and recent M&A and capital markets transactions, which are helpful for determining *pro forma* adjustments and normalizing financial data. They may also provide helpful sector and market information, as well as explicitly list the research analyst's view on the company's comparables universe. Initiating coverage research reports tend to be more comprehensive than normal interim reports. As a result, it is beneficial to mine these reports for financial, market, and competitive insights.

---

[22] Depending on the particular triggering event, the 8-K is typically filed within four business days after occurrence.

[23] The legal contract between a buyer and seller detailing the terms and conditions of an M&A transaction. See Chapter 6 for additional information.

[24] From time to time, companies hold investor days to tell their in-depth story directly to current and prospective shareholders. These are typically large public events spanning several hours and can include product demos and facility tours (if held on site). They are led by the senior management team, often including division heads and business development executives.

[25] Regulation FD (Fair Disclosure) provides that when a public filer discloses material nonpublic information to certain persons, as defined by the SEC, it must make public disclosure of that information typically through the filing of an 8-K.

Research reports can be located through various subscription financial information services. If you're currently working at an investment bank, you should have access to the bank's research reports through the internal portal. Also, if you're an individual investor reading this book, you should have access to research through your brokerage account(s) as most brokerage houses provide customers with access to in-house or affiliate research.

**Consensus Estimates**     Consensus research estimates for selected financial statistics are widely used by bankers as the basis for calculating forward-looking trading multiples in trading comps. The primary sources for consensus estimates are Bloomberg Estimates, Refinitiv IBES, S&P Capital IQ Estimates, and Thomson First Call, among other financial information services. Investment banks typically choose one source or the other so as to maintain consistency throughout the analysis.[26]

## Press Releases and News Runs

A company issues a press release when it has something important to report to the public. Standard press releases include earnings announcements, declaration of dividends, and management changes, as well as M&A and capital markets transactions. Earnings announcements, which are accompanied by the filing of an 8-K, are typically issued prior to the filing of a 10-K or 10-Q. Therefore, the banker relies upon the financial data provided in the earnings announcement to update trading comps in a timely manner. A company may also release an investor presentation to accompany its quarterly earnings call, which may be helpful in readily identifying key financial data and obtaining additional color and commentary. In the event that certain financial information is not provided in the earnings press release, the banker must wait until the filing of the 10-K or 10-Q for complete information. A company's press releases and recent news articles are available on its corporate website.

## Financial Information Services

As discussed throughout this section, financial information services are a key source for obtaining SEC filings, research reports, consensus estimates, and press releases, among other items. They are also a primary source for current and historical company share price information, which is essential for calculating equity value and determining a company's current share price as a percentage of its 52-week high. Corporate credit ratings information can be gleaned form various financial information services. If practical, however, we suggest sourcing credit ratings directly from the official Moody's, S&P, and Fitch websites and attributing such information to its original sources.[27]

---

[26]Once a given consensus estimates source is selected, it is important to screen individual estimates for obsolescent data and outliers. For example, if a company has recently made a transformative acquisition, some analysts may have revised their estimates accordingly, while others may have not. Bloomberg and other sources allow the banker to view individual estimates (and the date when they were posted), which allows for the identification and removal of inconsistent estimates as appropriate.

[27]Access to these websites requires a subscription.

## Summary of Financial Data Primary Sources

Exhibit 1.4 provides a summary of the primary sources used to obtain the necessary financial information to perform trading comps.

**EXHIBIT 1.4**  Summary of Financial Data Primary Sources

| Information Item | Source |
|---|---|
| **Income Statement Data** | |
| Sales | |
| Gross Profit | |
| EBITDA[a] | Most recent 10-K, 10-Q, 8-K, Press Release |
| EBIT | |
| Net Income / EPS | |
| Research Estimates | Bloomberg Estimates, Refinitiv IBES, S&P Capital IQ Estimates, Thomson First Call, individual equity research reports |
| **Balance Sheet Data** | |
| Cash Balance | |
| Debt Balance | Most recent 10-K, 10-Q, 8-K, Press Release |
| Shareholders' Equity | |
| **Cash Flow Statement Data** | |
| Depreciation & Amortization | Most recent 10-K, 10-Q, 8-K, Press Release |
| Capital Expenditures | |
| **Share Data** | |
| Basic Shares Outstanding | 10-K, 10-Q, or Proxy Statement, whichever is most recent |
| Options and Warrants Data | 10-K or 10-Q, whichever is more recent |
| **Market Data** | |
| Share Price Data | Financial information service |
| Credit Ratings | Rating agencies' websites |

[a] As a non-GAAP (generally accepted accounting principles) financial measure, EBITDA is not reported on a public filer's income statement. It may, however, be disclosed as supplemental information in the company's public filings.

## STEP III. SPREAD KEY STATISTICS, RATIOS, AND TRADING MULTIPLES

Once the necessary financial information for each of the comparables has been located, it is entered into an input page (see Exhibit 1.5).[28] This sample input page is designed to assist the banker in calculating the key financial statistics, ratios, and multiples for the comparables universe.[29] The input page data, in turn, feeds into output sheets that are used to benchmark the comparables (see Exhibits 1.53, 1.54, and 1.55).

In the pages that follow, we discuss the financial data displayed on the sample input sheet, as well as the calculations behind them. We also describe the mechanics for calculating LTM financial statistics, calendarizing company financials, and adjusting for non-recurring items and recent events.

### Calculation of Key Financial Statistics and Ratios

In this section, we outline the calculation of key financial statistics, ratios, and other metrics in accordance with the financial profile framework introduced in Step I.

- Size (Market Valuation: equity value and enterprise value; and Key Financial Data: sales, gross profit, EBITDA, EBIT, and net income)

- Profitability (gross profit, EBITDA, EBIT, and net income margins)

- Growth Profile (historical and estimated growth rates)

- Return on Investment (ROIC, ROE, ROA, and dividend yield)

- Credit Profile (leverage ratios, coverage ratios, and credit ratings)

---

[28]For modeling/data entry purposes, manual inputs are typically formatted in blue font and yellow shading, while formula cells (calculations) are in black font (electronic versions of our models are available on our website, www.wiley.com/go/investmentbanking3e).
[29]This template should be adjusted as appropriate in accordance with the specific company/ sector (see Exhibit 1.33).

# EXHIBIT 1.5 Sample Comparable Company Input Page

## Company A (Nasdaq:AAA)
### Input Page
*($ in millions, except per share data)*

### General Information

| | |
|---|---|
| Company Name | Company A |
| Ticker | AAA |
| Stock Exchange | Nasdaq |
| Fiscal Year Ending | Dec-31 |
| Moody's Corporate Rating | NA |
| S&P Corporate Rating | NA |
| Predicted Beta | 1.00 |
| Marginal Tax Rate | 25.0% |

### Selected Market Data

| | | |
|---|---|---|
| Current Price | 1/1/2000 | - |
| % of 52-week High | | NA |
| 52-week High Price | 1/1/2000 | - |
| 52-week Low Price | 1/1/2000 | - |
| Dividend Per Share (MRQ) | 1/1/2000 | - |
| Fully Diluted Shares Outstanding | | - |
| **Equity Value** | | - |
| Plus: Total Debt | | - |
| Plus: Preferred Stock | | - |
| Plus: Noncontrolling Interest | | - |
| Less: Cash and Cash Equivalents | | - |
| **Enterprise Value** | | - |

### Trading Multiples

| | LTM 9/30/2019 | NFY 2019E | NFY+1 2020E | NFY+2 2021E |
|---|---|---|---|---|
| EV/Sales | NA | NA | NA | NA |
| Metric | - | - | - | - |
| EV/EBITDA | NA | NA | NA | NA |
| Metric | - | - | - | - |
| EV/EBIT | NA | NA | NA | NA |
| Metric | - | - | - | - |
| P/E | NA | NA | NA | NA |
| Metric | - | - | - | - |
| FCF Yield | NA | NA | NA | NA |
| Metric | - | | | |

### LTM Return on Investment Ratios

| | |
|---|---|
| Return on Invested Capital | - |
| Return on Equity | - |
| Return on Assets | - |
| Implied Annual Dividend Per Share | NA |

### LTM Credit Statistics

| | |
|---|---|
| Debt/Total Capitalization | - |
| Total Debt/EBITDA | NA |
| Net Debt/EBITDA | NA |
| (EBITDA-capex)/Interest Expense | NA |
| EBIT/Interest Expense | NA |

### Growth Rates

| Historical | Sales | EBITDA | FCF | EPS |
|---|---|---|---|---|
| 1-year | - | - | - | - |
| 2-year CAGR | - | - | - | - |
| **Estimated** | | | | |
| 1-year | - | - | - | - |
| 2-year CAGR | - | - | - | - |
| Long-term | | | | NA |

### Reported Income Statement

| | Fiscal Year Ending December 31, | | | Prior Stub | Current Stub | LTM |
|---|---|---|---|---|---|---|
| | 2016A | 2017A | 2018A | 9/30/2018 | 9/30/2019 | 9/30/2019 |
| Sales | - | - | - | - | - | NA |
| COGS (incl. D&A) | - | - | - | - | - | NA |
| **Gross Profit** | - | - | - | - | - | NA |
| SG&A | - | - | - | - | - | NA |
| Other Expense / (Income) | - | - | - | - | - | NA |
| **EBIT** | - | - | - | - | - | NA |
| Interest Expense | - | - | - | - | - | NA |
| **Pre-tax Income** | - | - | - | - | - | NA |
| Income Taxes | - | - | - | - | - | NA |
| Noncontrolling Interest | - | - | - | - | - | NA |
| Preferred Dividends | - | - | - | - | - | NA |
| **Net Income** | - | - | - | - | - | NA |
| *Effective Tax Rate* | *NA* | *NA* | *NA* | *NA* | *NA* | *NA* |
| Weighted Avg. Diluted Shares | - | - | - | - | - | |
| **Diluted EPS** | NA | NA | NA | NA | NA | NA |

### Adjusted Income Statement

| | | | | | | |
|---|---|---|---|---|---|---|
| Reported Gross Profit | - | - | - | - | - | NA |
| Non-recurring Items in COGS | - | - | - | - | - | NA |
| **Adj. Gross Profit** | - | - | - | - | - | NA |
| *% margin* | *-* | *-* | *-* | *-* | *-* | *NA* |
| Reported EBIT | - | - | - | - | - | NA |
| Non-recurring Items in COGS | - | - | - | - | - | NA |
| Other Non-recurring Items | - | - | - | - | - | NA |
| **Adjusted EBIT** | - | - | - | - | - | NA |
| *% margin* | *-* | *-* | *-* | *-* | *-* | *NA* |
| Depreciation & Amortization | - | - | - | - | - | NA |
| **Adjusted EBITDA** | - | - | - | - | - | NA |
| *% margin* | *-* | *-* | *-* | *-* | *-* | *NA* |
| Reported Net Income | - | - | - | - | - | NA |
| Non-recurring Items in COGS | - | - | - | - | - | NA |
| Other Non-recurring Items | - | - | - | - | - | NA |
| Non-operating Non-rec. Items | - | - | - | - | - | NA |
| Tax Adjustment | - | - | - | - | - | NA |
| **Adjusted Net Income** | - | - | - | - | - | NA |
| *% margin* | *-* | *-* | *-* | *-* | *-* | *NA* |
| **Adjusted Diluted EPS** | - | - | - | - | - | NA |

### Cash Flow Statement Data

| | | | | | | |
|---|---|---|---|---|---|---|
| Cash From Operations | - | - | - | - | - | NA |
| Capital Expenditures | - | - | - | - | - | NA |
| *% sales* | *NA* | *NA* | *NA* | *NA* | *NA* | *NA* |
| **Free Cash Flow** | - | - | - | - | - | NA |
| *% margin* | *NA* | *NA* | *NA* | *NA* | *NA* | *NA* |
| **FCF / Share** | - | - | - | - | - | NA |
| Depreciation & Amortization | - | - | - | - | - | NA |
| *% sales* | *NA* | *NA* | *NA* | *NA* | *NA* | *NA* |

### Notes

(1) [to come]
(2) [to come]
(3) [to come]
(4) [to come]

### Business Description

[to come]

### Balance Sheet Data

| | 2018A | 9/30/2019 |
|---|---|---|
| Cash and Cash Equivalents | - | - |
| Accounts Receivable | - | - |
| Inventories | - | - |
| Prepaids and Other Current Assets | - | - |
| **Total Current Assets** | - | - |
| Property, Plant and Equipment, net | - | - |
| Goodwill and Intangible Assets | - | - |
| Other Assets | - | - |
| **Total Assets** | - | - |
| Accounts Payable | - | - |
| Accrued Liabilities | - | - |
| Other Current Liabilities | - | - |
| **Total Current Liabilities** | - | - |
| Total Debt | - | - |
| Other Long-Term Liabilities | - | - |
| **Total Liabilities** | - | - |
| Noncontrolling Interest | - | - |
| Preferred Stock | - | - |
| Shareholders' Equity | - | - |
| **Total Liabilities and Equity** | - | - |
| *Balance Check* | *0.000* | *0.000* |

### Calculation of Fully Diluted Shares Outstanding

| | |
|---|---|
| Basic Shares Outstanding | - |
| Plus: Shares from In-the-Money Options | - |
| Less: Shares Repurchased | - |
| **Net New Shares from Options** | - |
| Plus: Shares from Convertible Securities | - |
| **Fully Diluted Shares Outstanding** | - |

### Options/Warrants

| Tranche | Number of Shares | Exercise Price | In-the-Money Shares | Proceeds |
|---|---|---|---|---|
| Tranche 1 | - | - | - | - |
| Tranche 2 | - | - | - | - |
| Tranche 3 | - | - | - | - |
| Tranche 4 | - | - | - | - |
| Tranche 5 | - | - | - | - |
| **Total** | - | | - | - |

### Convertible Securities

| | Amount | Conversion Price | Conversion Ratio | New Shares |
|---|---|---|---|---|
| Issue 1 | - | - | - | - |
| Issue 2 | - | - | - | - |
| Issue 3 | - | - | - | - |
| Issue 4 | - | - | - | - |
| Issue 5 | - | - | - | - |
| **Total** | - | | | - |

## Size: Market Valuation

**Equity Value**   Equity value ("market capitalization") is the value represented by a given company's basic shares outstanding plus "in-the-money" stock options,[30] warrants,[31] and convertible securities—collectively, "fully diluted shares outstanding". It is calculated by multiplying a company's current share price[32] by its fully diluted shares outstanding (see Exhibit 1.6).

**EXHIBIT 1.6**   Calculation of Equity Value

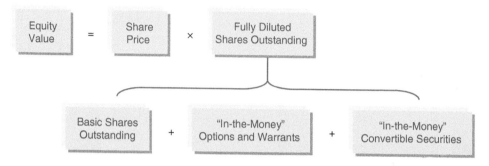

While equity value provides perspective on relative size, it does not lend insight on share price performance. The company's current share price as a percentage of its 52-week high is much more informative in this respect. This is a widely used metric that provides perspective on valuation and gauges current market sentiment and outlook for both the individual company and its broader sector. If a given company's percentage is significantly out of line with that of its peers, it is generally an indicator of company-specific (as opposed to sector-specific) issues. For example, a company may have missed its earnings guidance or underperformed versus its peers over the recent quarter(s). It may also be a sign of more entrenched issues involving management, operations, or specific markets.

---

[30]Stock options are granted to employees as a form of non-cash compensation. They provide the right to buy (call) shares of the company's common stock at a set price ("exercise" or "strike" price) during a given time period. Employee stock options are subject to vesting periods that restrict the number of shares available for exercise according to a set schedule. They become eligible to be converted into shares of common stock once their vesting period expires ("exercisable"). An option is considered "in-the-money" when the underlying company's share price surpasses the option's exercise price.

[31]A warrant is a security typically issued in conjunction with a debt instrument that entitles the purchaser of that instrument to buy shares of the issuer's common stock at a set price during a given time period. In this context, warrants serve to entice investor interest (usually as a detachable equity "sweetener") in riskier classes of securities such as non-investment-grade bonds and mezzanine debt, by providing an increase to the security's overall return.

[32]For trading comps, the banker typically uses the company's share price as of the prior day's close as the basis for calculating equity value and trading multiples.

*Calculation of Fully Diluted Shares Outstanding*   A company's fully diluted shares are calculated by adding the number of shares represented by its in-the-money options, warrants, and convertible securities to its basic shares outstanding.[33] A company's most recent basic shares outstanding count is typically sourced from the first page of its 10-K or 10-Q (whichever is most recent). In some cases, however, the latest proxy statement may contain more updated data and, therefore, should be used in lieu of the 10-K or 10-Q. The most recent stock options/warrants information is obtained from a company's latest 10-K or, in some cases, the 10-Q.

The incremental shares represented by a company's in-the-money options and warrants are calculated in accordance with the treasury stock method (TSM). Those shares implied by a company's in-the-money convertible and equity-linked securities are calculated in accordance with the if-converted method or net share settlement (NSS), as appropriate.

*Options and Warrants—The Treasury Stock Method*   The TSM assumes that all tranches of in-the-money options and warrants are exercised at their weighted average strike price with the resulting option proceeds used to repurchase outstanding shares of stock at the company's current share price. In-the-money options and warrants are those that have an exercise price lower than the current market price of the underlying company's stock. As the strike price is lower than the current market price, the number of shares repurchased is less than the additional shares outstanding from exercised options. This results in a net issuance of shares, which is dilutive.

In Exhibit 1.7, we provide an example of how to calculate fully diluted shares outstanding using the TSM.

**EXHIBIT 1.7**   Calculation of Fully Diluted Shares Using the Treasury Stock Method

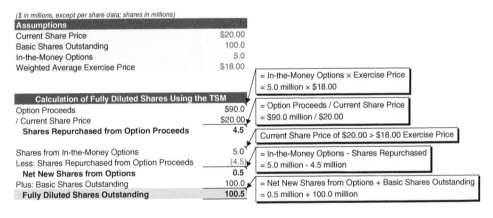

($ in millions, except per share data; shares in millions)

| Assumptions | |
|---|---|
| Current Share Price | $20.00 |
| Basic Shares Outstanding | 100.0 |
| In-the-Money Options | 5.0 |
| Weighted Average Exercise Price | $18.00 |

= In-the-Money Options × Exercise Price
= 5.0 million × $18.00

| Calculation of Fully Diluted Shares Using the TSM | |
|---|---|
| Option Proceeds | $90.0 |
| / Current Share Price | $20.00 |
| **Shares Repurchased from Option Proceeds** | **4.5** |

= Option Proceeds / Current Share Price
= $90.0 million / $20.00

Current Share Price of $20.00 > $18.00 Exercise Price

| Shares from In-the-Money Options | 5.0 |
|---|---|
| Less: Shares Repurchased from Option Proceeds | (4.5) |
| **Net New Shares from Options** | **0.5** |
| Plus: Basic Shares Outstanding | 100.0 |
| **Fully Diluted Shares Outstanding** | **100.5** |

= In-the-Money Options - Shares Repurchased
= 5.0 million - 4.5 million

= Net New Shares from Options + Basic Shares Outstanding
= 0.5 million + 100.0 million

[33]Investment banks and finance professionals may differ as to whether they use "outstanding" or "exercisable" in-the-money options and warrants in the calculation of fully diluted shares outstanding when performing trading comps. For conservatism (i.e., assuming the most dilutive scenario), many firms employ all outstanding in-the-money options and warrants as opposed to just exercisable as they represent future claims against the company.

As shown in Exhibit 1.7, the 5 million options are in-the-money as the exercise price of $18.00 is lower than the current share price of $20.00. This means that the holders of the options have the right to buy the company's shares at $18.00 and sell them at $20.00, thereby realizing the $2.00 differential. Under the TSM, it is assumed that the $18.00 of potential proceeds received by the company is used to repurchase shares that are currently trading at $20.00. Therefore, the number of shares repurchased is 90% ($18.00 / $20.00) of the options, or 4.5 million shares in total (90% × 5 million). To calculate net new shares, the 4.5 million shares repurchased are subtracted from the 5 million options, resulting in 0.5 million. These new shares are added to the company's basic shares outstanding to derive fully diluted shares of 100.5 million.

*Convertible and Equity-Linked Securities*   Outstanding convertible and equity-linked securities also need to be factored into the calculation of fully diluted shares outstanding. Convertible and equity-linked securities bridge the gap between traditional debt and equity, featuring characteristics of both. They include a broad range of instruments, such as traditional cash-pay convertible bonds, convertible hybrids, perpetual convertible preferred, and mandatory convertibles.[34]

This section focuses on the traditional cash-pay convertible bond as it is the most "plain-vanilla" and commonly issued structure. A cash-pay convertible bond ("convert") represents a straight debt instrument and an embedded equity call option that provides for the convert to be exchanged into a defined number of shares of the issuer's common stock under certain circumstances. The value of the embedded call option allows the issuer to pay a lower coupon than a straight debt instrument of the same credit. The strike price of the call option ("conversion price") is typically set at a premium to the company's underlying share price at the time the offering of the converts is priced.

The conversion feature can have different settlement mechanics. The simplest, "physical settlement", requires the issuer to settle conversions entirely in shares (together with cash in lieu of any fractional share). On the other end of the spectrum is "flexible settlement" (sometimes called "Instrument X"), which allows the issuer to settle conversion by delivering any combination of cash and shares, at its election. Finally, "net share settlement" requires the issuer to settle the conversion value in cash up to the principal amount being converted, with any excess of the conversion value of over the principal amount settled in shares.

For the purposes of performing trading comps, to calculate fully diluted shares outstanding, it is standard practice to first determine whether the company's outstanding converts are in-the-money, meaning that the current share price is above the conversion price. The number of diluted shares underlying cash-pay converts is often calculated using either the if-converted method or the treasury stock method, as applicable. Out-of-the-money converts, by contrast, remain treated as debt. Proper treatment of converts requires a careful reading of the relevant footnotes in the company's 10-K or prospectus for the security.

---

[34]While the overall volume of issuance for convertible and equity-linked securities is less than that for straight debt instruments, they are relatively common in certain sectors, such as healthcare and technology.

*If-Converted Method* In accordance with the if-converted method, the impact of physically settled converts on the number of diluted shares is calculated by adding an amount equal to the outstanding principal amount of the convert divided by the conversion price.[35] The convert is then treated as equity and included in the calculation of the company's fully diluted shares outstanding and equity value. The equity value represented by the convert is calculated by multiplying the number of dilutive shares underlying the convert by the company's current share price. The convert is then excluded from the calculation of the company's total debt.

As shown in Exhibit 1.8, as the company's current share price of $20.00 is greater than the conversion price of $15.00, we determine that the $150 million convert is in-the-money. Therefore the convert's outstanding principal amount is simply divided by the conversion price to calculate new shares of 10 million ($150 million / $15.00). The number of underlying shares is then added to the company's basic shares outstanding of 100 million and net new shares from in-the-money options of 0.5 million to calculate fully diluted shares outstanding of 110.5 million.

The assumed conversion of in-the-money converts also requires an upward adjustment to the company's net income to account for the forgone interest expense payments associated with the coupon on the convert. This amount must be tax-effected before being added back to net income. Therefore, while the if-converted method can be EPS dilutive due to the additional number of shares, net income is actually higher on a pro forma basis.

**EXHIBIT 1.8**   Calculation of Fully Diluted Shares Using the If-Converted Method

*($ in millions, except per share data; shares in millions)*

| Assumptions | |
|---|---|
| **Company** | |
| Current Share Price | $20.00 |
| Basic Shares Outstanding | 100.0 |
| | |
| **Convertible** | |
| Amount Outstanding | $150.0 |
| Conversion Price | $15.00 |

| If-Converted | | |
|---|---|---|
| Amount Outstanding | $150.0 | = Amount Outstanding / Conversion Price |
| / Conversion Price | $15.00 | = $150.0 million / $15.00 |
| **Incremental Shares** | **10.0** | Calculated in Exhibit 1.7 |
| Plus: Net New Shares from Options | 0.5 | = New Shares from Conversion |
| Plus: Basic Shares Outstanding | 100.0 | + Net New Shares from Options |
| **Fully Diluted Shares Outstanding** | **110.5** | + Basic Shares Outstanding |
| | | = 10.0 million + 0.5 million + 100.0 million |

---

[35]For GAAP reporting purposes (e.g., for EPS and fully diluted shares outstanding), the if-converted method requires issuers to measure the dilutive impact of the security through a two-test process. First, the issuer needs to test the security as if it were debt on its balance sheet, with the stated interest expense reflected in net income and the underlying shares omitted from the share count. Second, the issuer needs to test the security as if it were converted into equity at the beginning of the reporting period (or, if later, the date when the security was issued), which involves excluding the after-tax interest expense of the convert from net income and including the full underlying shares in the share count (or on a weighted average basis, if the convert was issued in the middle of the reporting period). Upon completion of the two tests, the issuer is required to use the more dilutive of the two methodologies.

*Net Share Settlement* Net share settlement and flexible settlement are common features in convertible bonds and often used by more mature, larger capitalized issuers.[36] These settlement methods serve to limit the dilutive effects of conversion and can in some cases afford the issuer TSM accounting treatment. For example, in net share settlement, only the value represented by the excess of the current share price over the conversion price is assumed to be settled with the issuance of additional shares, which results in less share issuance.[37]

As shown in Exhibit 1.9, the if-converted method results in incremental dilutive shares of 10 million, while NSS results in incremental dilutive shares of only 2.5 million. The NSS calculation is conducted by first multiplying the number of shares underlying the convert of 10 million by the company's current share price of $20.00 to determine the implied conversion value of $200 million. The $50 million spread between the conversion value and par ($200 million – $150 million) is then divided by the current share price to determine the number of incremental dilutive shares of 2.5 million ($50 million / $20.00).[38] The $150 million principal amount of the convert remains treated as debt due to the fact that the issuer typically must settle this amount in cash at maturity.

**EXHIBIT 1.9**    Incremental Shares from If-Converted versus Net Share Settlement

*($ in millions, except per share data; shares in millions)*

| If-Converted | | Net Share Settlement | |
|---|---|---|---|
| Amount Outstanding | $150.0 | Amount Outstanding | $150.0 |
| / Conversion Price | $15.00 | / Conversion Price | $15.00 |
| **Incremental Shares** | **10.0** | **Incremental Shares** | **10.0** |
| | | × Current Share Price | $20.00 |
| | | **Total Conversion Value** | **$200.0** |
| | | Less: Par Value of Amount Outstanding | (150.0) |
| | | **Excess Over Par Value** | **$50.0** |
| | | / Current Share Price | $20.00 |
| **Incremental Shares – If-Converted** | **10.0** | **Incremental Shares – NSS** | **2.5** |

= Excess Over Par Value / Current Share Price
= $50.0 million / $20.00

= Total Conversion Value - Par Value of Amt. Out.
= $200.0 million - $150.0 million

= Incremental Shares × Current Share Price
= 10.0 million × $20.00

= Amount Outstanding / Conversion Price
= $150.0 million / $15.00

---

[36]Effective for fiscal years beginning after December 15, 2008, the Financial Accounting Standards Board (FASB) put into effect guidelines for accounting for converts whose conversion can be settled in cash. These changes effectively bifurcate such converts into their debt and equity components, resulting in higher reported GAAP interest expense due to the higher imputed cost of debt. However, the guidelines do not change the calculation of shares outstanding in accordance with the TSM. Moreover, in July 2019, FASB proposed to eliminate this bifurcated accounting. Therefore, one should consult with a capital markets specialist for accounting guidance on in-the-money converts with NSS features.

[37]The NSS feature may also be structured so that the issuer can elect to settle the excess conversion value in cash.

[38]As the company's share price increases, the amount of incremental shares issued also increases as the spread between conversion and par value widens.

**Enterprise Value**   Enterprise value ("total enterprise value" or "firm value") is the sum of all ownership interests in a company and claims on its assets from both debt and equity holders. As the graphic in Exhibit 1.10 depicts, it is defined as equity value + total debt + preferred stock + noncontrolling interest[39] – cash and cash equivalents. The equity value component is calculated on a fully diluted basis.

**EXHIBIT 1.10**   Calculation of Enterprise Value

Theoretically, enterprise value is considered independent of capital structure, meaning that changes in a company's capital structure do not affect its enterprise value. For example, if a company raises additional debt that is held on the balance sheet as cash, its enterprise value remains constant as the new debt is offset by the increase in cash (i.e., net debt remains the same, see Scenario I in Exhibit 1.11). Similarly, if a company issues equity and uses the proceeds to repay debt, the incremental equity value is offset by the decrease in debt on a dollar-for-dollar basis (see Scenario II in Exhibit 1.11).[40] Therefore, these transactions are enterprise value neutral.

In both Scenario I and II, enterprise value remains constant despite a change in the company's capital structure. Hence, similar companies would be expected to have consistent enterprise value multiples despite differences in capital structure. One notable exception concerns highly leveraged companies, which may trade at a discount relative to their peers due to the perceived higher risk of financial distress[41] and potential constraints to growth.

---

[39]Formerly known as "minority interest", noncontrolling interest is a significant, but non-majority, interest (less than 50%) in a company's voting stock by another company or an investor. Effective for fiscal years beginning after December 15, 2008, FAS 160 changed the accounting and reporting for minority interest, which is now called noncontrolling interest and can be found in the shareholders' equity section of a company's balance sheet. On the income statement, the noncontrolling interest holder's share of income is subtracted from net income.
[40]These illustrative scenarios ignore financing fees associated with the debt and equity issuance as well as potential breakage costs associated with the repayment of debt (see Chapter 4).
[41]Circumstances whereby a company is unable or struggles to meet its credit obligations, typically resulting in business disruption, insolvency, or bankruptcy. As the perceived risk of financial distress increases, equity value generally decreases accordingly.

**EXHIBIT 1.11**   Effects of Capital Structure Changes on Enterprise Value

*($ in millions)*

| | Scenario I: Issuance of Debt | | | |
|---|---|---|---|---|
| | Actual 2018 | Adjustments + | Adjustments - | Pro forma 2018 |
| Equity Value | $750 | | | $750 |
| Plus: Total Debt | 250 | 100 | | 350 |
| Plus: Preferred Stock | 35 | | | 35 |
| Plus: Noncontrolling Interest | 15 | | | 15 |
| Less: Cash and Cash Equivalents | (50) | | (100) | (150) |
| **Enterprise Value** | **$1,000** | | | **$1,000** |

| | Scenario II: Issuance of Equity to Repay Debt | | | |
|---|---|---|---|---|
| | Actual 2018 | Adjustments + | Adjustments - | Pro forma 2018 |
| Equity Value | $750 | 100 | | $850 |
| Plus: Total Debt | 250 | | (100) | 150 |
| Plus: Preferred Stock | 35 | | | 35 |
| Plus: Noncontrolling Interest | 15 | | | 15 |
| Less: Cash and Cash Equivalents | (50) | | | (50) |
| **Enterprise Value** | **$1,000** | | | **$1,000** |

## Size: Key Financial Data

- Sales (or revenue) is the first line item, or "top line", on an income statement. Sales represents the total dollar amount realized by a company through the sale of its products and services during a given time period. Sales levels and trends are a key factor in determining a company's relative positioning among its peers. All else being equal, companies with greater sales volumes tend to benefit from scale, market share, purchasing power, and lower risk profile, and are often rewarded by the market with a premium valuation relative to smaller peers.

- Gross Profit, defined as sales less cost of goods sold (COGS),[42] is the profit earned by a company after subtracting costs directly related to the production of its products and services. As such, it is a key indicator of operational efficiency and pricing power, and is usually expressed as a percentage of sales for analytical purposes (gross profit margin, see Exhibit 1.12). For example, if a company sells a product for $100, and that product costs $60 in materials, manufacturing, and direct labor to produce, then the gross profit on that product is $40 and the gross profit margin is 40%.

- EBITDA (earnings before interest, taxes, depreciation and amortization) is an important measure of profitability. As EBITDA is a non-GAAP financial measure and typically not reported by public filers within their 10-Ks and 10-Qs, it is generally calculated by taking EBIT (or operating income/profit as often reported on the income statement) and adding back the depreciation and amortization

---

[42]COGS, as reported on the income statement, may include or exclude D&A depending on the filing company. If D&A is excluded, it is reported as a separate line item on the income statement.

(D&A) as sourced from the cash flow statement.[43] EBITDA is a widely used proxy for operating cash flow as it reflects the company's total cash operating costs for producing its products and services. In addition, EBITDA serves as a fair "apples-to-apples" means of comparison among companies in the same sector because it is free from differences resulting from capital structure (i.e., interest expense) and tax regime (i.e., tax expense).

- EBIT (<u>e</u>arnings <u>b</u>efore <u>i</u>nterest and <u>t</u>axes) is often the same as reported operating income, operating profit, or income from operations[44] on the income statement found in a company's SEC filings. Like EBITDA, EBIT is independent of tax regime and serves as a useful metric for comparing companies with different capital structures. It is, however, less indicative as a measure of operating cash flow than EBITDA because it includes non-cash D&A expense. Furthermore, D&A reflects discrepancies among different companies in capital spending and/or depreciation policy as well as acquisition histories (amortization).

- Net income ("earnings" or the "bottom line") is the residual profit after all of a company's expenses have been netted out. Net income can also be viewed as the earnings available to equity holders once all of the company's obligations have been satisfied (e.g., to suppliers, vendors, service providers, employees, utilities, lessors, lenders, state and local treasuries). Wall Street tends to view net income on a per share basis (i.e., earnings per share or EPS).

## Profitability

- Gross profit margin ("gross margin") measures the percentage of sales remaining after subtracting COGS (see Exhibit 1.12). It is driven by a company's direct cost per unit, such as materials, manufacturing, and direct labor involved in production. These costs are typically largely variable, as opposed to corporate overhead, which is more fixed in nature.[45] Companies ideally seek to increase their gross margin through a combination of improved sourcing/procurement of raw materials and enhanced pricing power, as well as by improving the efficiency of manufacturing facilities and processes.

---

[43]In the event a company reports D&A as a separate line item on the income statement (i.e., broken out separately from COGS and SG&A), EBITDA can be calculated as sales less COGS less SG&A.

[44]EBIT may differ from operating income/profit due to the inclusion of income generated outside the scope of a company's ordinary course business operations ("other income").

[45]*Variable* costs change depending on the volume of goods produced and include items such as materials, direct labor, transportation, and utilities. *Fixed* costs remain more or less constant regardless of volume and include items such as lease expense, advertising and marketing, insurance, corporate overhead, and administrative salaries. These costs are usually captured in the SG&A (or equivalent) line item on the income statement.

**EXHIBIT 1.12**   Gross Profit Margin

$$\text{Gross Profit Margin} = \frac{\text{Gross Profit (Sales - COGS)}}{\text{Sales}}$$

- EBITDA and EBIT margin are accepted standards for measuring a company's operating profitability (see Exhibit 1.13). Accordingly, they are used to frame relative performance both among peer companies and across sectors.

**EXHIBIT 1.13**   EBITDA and EBIT Margin

$$\text{EBITDA Margin} = \frac{\text{EBITDA}}{\text{Sales}} \qquad \text{EBIT Margin} = \frac{\text{EBIT}}{\text{Sales}}$$

- Net income margin measures a company's overall profitability as opposed to its operating profitability (see Exhibit 1.14). It is net of interest expense and, therefore, affected by capital structure. As a result, companies with similar operating margins may have substantially different net income margins due to differences in leverage. Furthermore, as net income is impacted by taxes, companies with similar operating margins may have varying net income margins due to different tax rates.

**EXHIBIT 1.14**   Net Income Margin

$$\text{Net Income Margin} = \frac{\text{Net Income}}{\text{Sales}}$$

### Growth Profile

A company's growth profile is a critical value driver. In assessing a company's growth profile, the banker typically looks at historical and estimated future growth rates as well as compound annual growth rates (CAGRs) for selected financial statistics (see Exhibit 1.15).

**EXHIBIT 1.15**   Historical and Estimated Diluted EPS Growth Rates

| | Fiscal Year Ending December 31, | | | | | | |
|---|---|---|---|---|---|---|---|
| | 2016A | 2017A | 2018A | CAGR ('16 - '18) | 2019E | 2020E | CAGR ('18 - '20) |
| Diluted Earnings Per Share | $1.00 | $1.20 | $1.40 | 18.3%▲ | $1.60 | $1.80 | 13.4% |
| *% growth* | | 20.0% | 16.7% | | 14.3% | 12.5% | |
| *Long-term growth rate* | | | | | | | 12.5%▲ |

= (Ending Value / Beginning Value) ^ (1 / Ending Year - Beginning Year) - 1
= ($1.40 / $1.00) ^ (1 / (2018 - 2016)) - 1

*Source: Consensus Estimates*

Historical annual EPS data is typically sourced directly from a company's 10-K or a financial information service that sources SEC filings. As with the calculation of any financial statistic, historical EPS must be adjusted for non-recurring items to be meaningful. The data that serves as the basis for a company's projected 1-year, 2-year, and long-term[46] EPS growth rates is generally obtained from consensus estimates.

### Return on Investment

- Return on invested capital (ROIC) measures the return generated by all capital provided to a company. As such, ROIC utilizes a pre-interest earnings statistic in the numerator, such as EBIT or tax-effected EBIT (also known as NOPAT or EBIAT) and a metric that captures both debt and equity in the denominator (see Exhibit 1.16). The denominator is typically calculated on an average basis (e.g., average of the balances as of the prior annual and most recent periods).

**EXHIBIT 1.16**  Return on Invested Capital

$$ROIC = \frac{EBIT}{Average\ Net\ Debt\ +\ Equity}$$

- Return on equity (ROE) measures the return generated on the equity provided to a company by its shareholders. As a result, ROE incorporates an earnings metric net of interest expense, such as net income, in the numerator and average shareholders' equity in the denominator (see Exhibit 1.17). ROE is an important indicator of performance as companies are intently focused on shareholder returns.

**EXHIBIT 1.17**  Return on Equity

$$ROE = \frac{Net\ Income}{Average\ Shareholders'\ Equity}$$

- Return on assets (ROA) measures the return generated by a company's asset base, thereby providing a barometer of the asset efficiency of a business. ROA typically utilizes net income in the numerator and average total assets in the denominator (see Exhibit 1.18).

**EXHIBIT 1.18**  Return on Assets

$$ROA = \frac{Net\ Income}{Average\ Total\ Assets}$$

---

[46]Represents a three-to-five-year estimate of annual EPS growth, as reported by equity research analysts.

- Dividend yield is a measure of returns to shareholders, but from a different perspective than earnings-based ratios. Dividend yield measures the annual dividends per share paid by a company to its shareholders (which can be distributed either in cash or additional shares), expressed as a percentage of its share price. Dividends are typically paid on a quarterly basis and therefore must be annualized to calculate the implied dividend yield (see Exhibit 1.19).[47] For example, if a company pays a quarterly dividend of $0.05 per share ($0.20 per share on an annualized basis) and its shares are currently trading at $10.00, the dividend yield is 2% (($0.05 × 4 payments) / $10.00).

**EXHIBIT 1.19**   Implied Dividend Yield

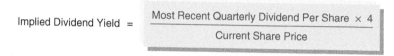

$$\text{Implied Dividend Yield} = \frac{\text{Most Recent Quarterly Dividend Per Share} \times 4}{\text{Current Share Price}}$$

### Credit Profile

Leverage   Leverage refers to a company's debt level. It is typically measured as a multiple of EBITDA (e.g., debt-to-EBITDA) or as a percentage of total capitalization (e.g., debt-to-total capitalization). Both debt and equity investors closely track a company's leverage as it reveals a great deal about financial policy, risk profile, and capacity for growth. As a general rule, the higher a company's leverage, the higher its risk of financial distress due to the burden associated with greater interest expense and principal repayments.

- Debt-to-EBITDA depicts the ratio of a company's debt to its EBITDA, with a higher multiple connoting higher leverage (see Exhibit 1.20). It is generally calculated on the basis of LTM financial statistics. There are several variations of this ratio, including total debt-to-EBITDA, senior secured debt-to-EBITDA, net debt-to-EBITDA, and total debt-to-(EBITDA less capex). As EBITDA is typically used as a rough proxy for operating cash flow, this ratio can be viewed as a measure of how many years of a company's cash flows are needed to repay its debt.

**EXHIBIT 1.20**   Leverage Ratio

$$\text{Leverage} = \frac{\text{Debt}}{\text{EBITDA}}$$

---

[47]Not all companies choose to pay dividends to their shareholders.

■ **Debt-to-total capitalization** measures a company's debt as a percentage of its total capitalization (debt + preferred stock + noncontrolling interest + equity) (see Exhibit 1.21). This ratio can be calculated on the basis of book or market values depending on the situation. As with debt-to-EBITDA, a higher debt-to-total capitalization ratio connotes higher debt levels and risk of financial distress.

**EXHIBIT 1.21**  Capitalization Ratio

$$\text{Debt-to-Total Capitalization} = \frac{\text{Debt}}{\text{Debt} + \text{Preferred Stock} + \text{Noncontrolling Interest} + \text{Equity}}$$

**Coverage**   Coverage is a broad term that refers to a company's ability to meet ("cover") its interest expense obligations. Coverage ratios are generally comprised of a financial statistic representing operating cash flow (e.g., LTM EBITDA) in the numerator and LTM interest expense in the denominator. There are several variations of the coverage ratio, including EBITDA-to-interest expense, (EBITDA less capex)-to-interest expense, and EBIT-to-interest expense (see Exhibit 1.22). Intuitively, the higher the coverage ratio, the better positioned the company is to meet its debt obligations and, therefore, the stronger its credit profile.

**EXHIBIT 1.22**   Interest Coverage Ratio

$$\text{Interest Coverage Ratio} = \frac{\text{EBITDA, (EBITDA} - \text{Capex), or EBIT}}{\text{Interest Expense}}$$

**Credit Ratings**   A credit rating is an assessment[48] by an independent rating agency of a company's ability and willingness to make full and timely payments of amounts due on its debt obligations. Credit ratings are typically required for companies seeking to raise debt financing in the capital markets as only a limited class of investors will participate in a corporate debt offering without an assigned credit rating on the new issue.[49]

The three primary credit rating agencies are Moody's, S&P, and Fitch. Nearly every public debt issuer receives a rating from Moody's, S&P, and/or Fitch. Moody's uses an alphanumeric scale, while S&P and Fitch both use an alphabetic system combined with pluses (+) and minuses (−) to rate the creditworthiness of an issuer. The ratings scales of the primary rating agencies are shown in Exhibit 1.23.

---

[48]Ratings agencies provide opinions, but do not conduct audits.
[49]Ratings are assessed on the issuer (corporate credit ratings) as well as on the individual debt instruments (facility ratings).

**EXHIBIT 1.23**   Ratings Scales of the Primary Rating Agencies

| | Moody's | S&P | Fitch | Definition |
|---|---|---|---|---|
| **Investment Grade** | Aaa | AAA | AAA | Highest Quality |
| | Aa1 | AA+ | AA+ | Very High Quality |
| | Aa2 | AA | AA | |
| | Aa3 | AA– | AA– | |
| | A1 | A+ | A+ | High Quality |
| | A2 | A | A | |
| | A3 | A– | A– | |
| | Baa1 | BBB+ | BBB+ | Medium Grade |
| | Baa2 | BBB | BBB | |
| | Baa3 | BBB– | BBB– | |
| **Non-Investment Grade** | Ba1 | BB+ | BB+ | Speculative |
| | Ba2 | BB | BB | |
| | Ba3 | BB– | BB– | |
| | B1 | B+ | B+ | Highly Speculative |
| | B2 | B | B | |
| | B3 | B– | B– | |
| | Caa1 | CCC+ | CCC+ | Substantial Risk |
| | Caa2 | CCC | CCC | |
| | Caa3 | CCC– | CCC– | |
| | Ca | CC | CC | Extremely Speculative / Default |
| | C | C | C | |
| | – | D | D | |

## Supplemental Financial Concepts and Calculations

**Calculation of LTM Financial Data**   U.S. public filers are required to report their financial performance on a quarterly basis, including a full year report filed at the end of the fiscal year. Therefore, in order to measure financial performance for the most recent annual or LTM period, the company's financial results for the previous four quarters are summed. This financial information is sourced from the company's most recent 10-K and 10-Q, as appropriate. As previously discussed, however, prior to the filing of the 10-Q or 10-K, companies typically issue a detailed earnings press release in an 8-K with the necessary financial data to help calculate LTM performance. Therefore, it may be appropriate to use a company's earnings announcement to update trading comps on a timely basis.

As the formula in Exhibit 1.24 illustrates, LTM financials are typically calculated by taking the full prior fiscal year's financial data, adding the YTD financial data for the current year period ("current stub"), and then subtracting the YTD financial data from the prior year ("prior stub").

**EXHIBIT 1.24**   Calculation of LTM Financial Data

$$\text{LTM} = \boxed{\begin{array}{c}\text{Prior}\\ \text{Fiscal Year}\end{array}} + \boxed{\begin{array}{c}\text{Current}\\ \text{Stub}\end{array}} - \boxed{\begin{array}{c}\text{Prior}\\ \text{Stub}\end{array}}$$

In the event that the most recent quarter is the fourth quarter of a company's fiscal year, then no LTM calculations are necessary as the full prior fiscal year (as reported) serves as the LTM period. Exhibit 1.25 shows an illustrative calculation for a given company's LTM sales for the period ending 9/30/2019.

**EXHIBIT 1.25**   Calculation of LTM 9/30/2019 Sales

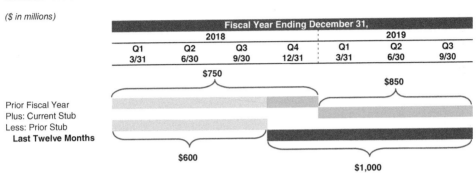

**Calendarization of Financial Data**   The majority of U.S. public filers report their financial performance in accordance with a fiscal year (FY) ending December 31, which corresponds to the calendar year (CY) end. Some companies, however, report on a different schedule (e.g., a fiscal year ending April 30). Any variation in fiscal year ends among comparable companies must be addressed for benchmarking purposes. Otherwise, the trading multiples will be based on financial data for different periods and, therefore, not truly "comparable".

To account for variations in fiscal year ends among comparable companies, each company's financials are adjusted to conform to a calendar year end in order to produce a "clean" basis for comparison, a process known as "calendarization". This is a relatively straightforward algebraic exercise, as illustrated by the formula in Exhibit 1.26, used to calendarize a company's fiscal year sales projection to produce a calendar year sales projection.[50]

**EXHIBIT 1.26**   Calendarization of Financial Data

$$\text{Next Calendar (CY) Sales} = \frac{(\text{Month \#}) \times (\text{FYA Sales})}{12} + \frac{(12 - \text{Month \#}) \times (\text{NFY Sales})}{12}$$

Note: "Month #" refers to the month in which the company's fiscal year ends (e.g., the Month # for a company with a fiscal year ending April 30 would be 4). FYA = Fiscal Year Actual and NFY = Next Fiscal Year.

Exhibit 1.27 provides an illustrative calculation for the calendarization of a company's calendar year 2019 estimated (E) sales, assuming a fiscal year ending April 30.

---

[50] If available, quarterly estimates should be used as the basis for calendarizing financial projections.

**EXHIBIT 1.27**   Calendarization of Sales

*($ in millions)*

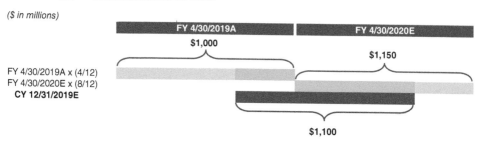

**Adjustments for Non-Recurring Items**   To assess a company's financial performance on a "normalized" basis, it is standard practice to adjust reported financial data for non-recurring items, a process known as "scrubbing" or "sanitizing" the financials. Failure to do so may lead to the calculation of misleading ratios and multiples, which, in turn, may produce a distorted view of valuation. These adjustments involve the add-back or elimination of one-time charges and gains, respectively, to create a more indicative view of ongoing company performance. Typical charges include those incurred for restructuring events (e.g., store/plant closings and headcount reduction), losses on asset sales, changes in accounting principles, inventory write-offs, goodwill impairment, extinguishment of debt, and losses from litigation settlements, among others. Typical benefits include gains from asset sales, favorable litigation settlements, and tax adjustments, among others.

Non-recurring items are often described in the MD&A section and financial footnotes in a company's public filings (e.g., 10-K and 10-Q) and earnings announcements. These items are often explicitly depicted as "non-recurring", "extraordinary", "unusual", or "one-time". Therefore, the banker is encouraged to comb electronic versions of the company's public filings and earnings announcements using word searches for these adjectives. Often, non-recurring charges or benefits are explicitly broken out as separate line items on a company's reported income statement and/or cash flow statement. Research reports can be helpful in identifying these items, while also providing color commentary on the reason they occurred.

In many cases, however, the banker must exercise discretion as to whether a given charge or benefit is non-recurring or part of normal business operations. This determination is sometimes relatively subjective, further compounded by the fact that certain events may be considered non-recurring for one company, but customary for another. For example, a generic pharmaceutical company may find itself in court frequently due to lawsuits filed by major drug manufacturers related to patent challenges. In this case, expenses associated with a lawsuit should not necessarily be treated as non-recurring because these legal expenses are a normal part of ongoing operations. While financial information services provide a breakdown of recommended adjustments that can be helpful in identifying potential non-recurring items, ultimately professional judgment needs to be exercised.

When adjusting for non-recurring items, it is important to distinguish between pre-tax and after-tax amounts. For a pre-tax restructuring charge, for example, the full amount is simply added back to calculate adjusted EBIT and EBITDA. To calculate adjusted net income, however, the pre-tax restructuring charge needs to be tax-effected[51] before being added back. Conversely, for after-tax amounts, the disclosed amount is simply added back to net income, but must be "grossed up" at the company's tax rate (t) (i.e., divided by $(1 - t)$) before being added back to EBIT and EBITDA.

Exhibit 1.28 provides an illustrative income statement for the fiscal year 2018 as it might appear in a 10-K. Let's assume the corresponding notes to the financials mention that the company recorded one-time charges related to an inventory write-down ($5 million pre-tax) and restructuring expenses from downsizing the salesforce ($10 million pre-tax). Provided we gain comfort that these charges are truly non-recurring, we would need to normalize the company's earnings statistics accordingly for these items in order to arrive at adjusted EBIT, EBITDA, and diluted EPS.

**EXHIBIT 1.28**  Reported Income Statement

| ($ in millions, except per share data) **Income Statement** | Reported 2018 |
|---|---|
| Sales | $1,000.0 |
| Cost of Goods Sold | 625.0 |
| **Gross Profit** | **$375.0** |
| Selling, General & Administrative | 230.0 |
| Restructuring Charges | 10.0 |
| **Operating Income (EBIT)** | **$135.0** |
| Interest Expense | 35.0 |
| **Pre-tax Income** | **$100.0** |
| Income Taxes | 25.0 |
| **Net Income** | **$75.0** |
| | |
| Weighted Average Diluted Shares | 30.0 |
| Diluted Earnings Per Share | $2.50 |

As shown in Exhibit 1.29, to calculate adjusted EBIT and EBITDA, we add back the full pre-tax charges of $5 million and $10 million ($15 million in total). This provides adjusted EBIT of $150 million and adjusted EBITDA of $200 million. To calculate adjusted net income and diluted EPS, however, the tax expense on the incremental $15 million pre-tax earnings must be subtracted. Assuming a 25% marginal tax rate, we calculate tax expense of $3.8 million and additional net income of $11.3 million ($15 million – $3.8 million). The $11.3 million is added to reported net income, resulting in adjusted net income of $86.3 million. We then divide the $86.3 million by weighted average fully diluted shares outstanding of 30 million to calculate adjusted diluted EPS of $2.88.

---

[51]In the event the SEC filing's footnotes do not provide detail on the after-tax amounts of such adjustments, the banker typically uses the marginal tax rate. The marginal tax rate for U.S. corporations is the rate at which a company is required to pay federal, state, and local taxes. The Tax Cuts and Jobs Act of 2017 lowered the U.S. federal corporate tax rate from 35% to 21%. State and local taxes typically add another 2% to 5% or more (depending on the state). Most public companies disclose their federal, state, and local tax rates in their 10-Ks in the notes to their financial statements. We have assumed a federal corporate tax rate of 21% and marginal tax rate of 25% for all analyses in this book.

**EXHIBIT 1.29**  Adjusted Income Statement

*($ in millions, except per share data)*

| Income Statement | Reported 2018 | Adjustments + | Adjustments − | Adjusted 2018 | |
|---|---|---|---|---|---|
| **Sales** | $1,000.0 | | | $1,000.0 | |
| Cost of Goods Sold | 625.0 | | (5.0) | 620.0 | Inventory write-down |
| **Gross Profit** | $375.0 | | | $380.0 | |
| Selling, General & Administrative | 230.0 | | | 230.0 | |
| Restructuring Charges | 10.0 | | (10.0) | - | Restructuring charge related to severance from downsizing the salesforce |
| **Operating Income (EBIT)** | $135.0 | | | $150.0 | |
| Interest Expense | 35.0 | | | 35.0 | |
| **Pre-tax Income** | $100.0 | | | $115.0 | |
| Income Taxes | 25.0 | 3.8 | | 28.8 | = (Inventory write-down + Restructuring charge) x Marginal Tax Rate |
| **Net Income** | $75.0 | | | $86.3 | = ($5 million + $10 million) x 25% |
| Operating Income (EBIT) | $135.0 | 15.0 | | $150.0 | |
| Depreciation & Amortization | 50.0 | | | 50.0 | D&A is sourced from the company's cash flow statement although it is sometimes broken out on the income statement |
| **EBITDA** | $185.0 | | | $200.0 | |
| Weighted Avg. Diluted Shares | 30.0 | | | 30.0 | |
| Diluted EPS | $2.50 | | | $2.88 | |

$15 million add-back of total non-recurring items

## Adjustments for Recent Events

In normalizing a company's financials, adjustments also need to be made for recent events, such as M&A transactions, financing activities, conversion of convertible securities, stock splits, or share repurchases in between reporting periods. Therefore, prior to performing trading comps, the banker checks company SEC filings (e.g., 8-Ks, registration statements/prospectuses[52]) and press releases since the most recent reporting period to determine whether the company has announced such activities.

For a recently announced M&A transaction, for example, the company's financial statements must be adjusted accordingly. The balance sheet is adjusted for the effects of the transaction by adding the purchase price financing (including any refinanced or assumed debt), while the LTM income statement is adjusted for the target's incremental sales and earnings. Equity research analysts typically update their estimates for a company's future financial performance promptly following the announcement of an M&A transaction. Therefore, the banker can use updated consensus estimates in combination with the pro forma balance sheet to calculate forward-looking multiples.[53]

---

[52]A registration statement/prospectus is a filing prepared by an issuer upon the registration/issuance of public securities, including debt and equity. The primary SEC forms for registration statements are S-1, S-3, and S-4; prospectuses are filed pursuant to Rule 424. When a company seeks to register securities with the SEC, it must file a registration statement. Within the registration statement is a preliminary prospectus. Once the registration statement is deemed effective, the company files the final prospectus as a 424 (includes final pricing and other key terms).

[53]As previously discussed, however, the banker needs to confirm beforehand that the estimates have been updated for the announced deal prior to usage. Furthermore, certain analysts may only update NFY estimates on an "as contributed" basis for the incremental earnings from the transaction for the remainder of the fiscal year (as opposed to adding a pro forma full year of earnings).

## Calculation of Key Trading Multiples

Once the key financial statistics are spread, the banker proceeds to calculate the relevant trading multiples for the comparables universe. While various sectors may employ specialized or sector-specific valuation multiples (see Exhibit 1.33), the most generic and widely used multiples employ a measure of market valuation in the numerator (e.g., enterprise value, equity value) and a universal measure of financial performance in the denominator (e.g., EBITDA, net income). For enterprise value multiples, the denominator employs a financial statistic that flows to both debt and equity holders, such as sales, EBITDA, and EBIT. For equity value (or share price) multiples, the denominator must be a financial statistic that flows only to equity holders, such as net income (or diluted EPS). Among these multiples, EV/EBITDA and P/E are the most common.

The following sections provide an overview of the more commonly used equity value and enterprise value multiples.

### Equity Value Multiples

**Price-to-Earnings Ratio / Equity Value-to-Net Income Multiple**  The P/E ratio, calculated as current share price divided by diluted EPS (or equity value divided by net income), is the most widely recognized trading multiple. Assuming a constant share count, the P/E ratio is equivalent to equity value-to-net income. These ratios can also be viewed as a measure of how much investors are willing to pay for a dollar of a company's current or future earnings. P/E ratios are typically based on forward one- or two-year EPS (and, to a lesser extent, LTM EPS) as investors are focused on future growth. Companies with higher P/Es than their peers tend to have higher earnings growth expectations.

The P/E ratio is particularly relevant for mature companies that have a demonstrated ability to consistently grow earnings. However, while the P/E ratio is broadly used and accepted, it has certain limitations. For example, it is not relevant for companies with little or no earnings as the denominator in these instances is *de minimis*, zero, or even negative. In addition, as previously discussed, net income (and EPS) is net of interest expense and, therefore, dependent on capital structure. As a result, two otherwise similar companies in terms of size and operating margins can have substantially different net income margins (and consequently P/E ratios) due to differences in leverage. Similarly, accounting discrepancies, such as for depreciation or taxes, can also produce meaningful disparities in P/E ratios among comparable companies.

The two formulas for calculating the P/E ratio (both equivalent, assuming a constant share count) are shown in Exhibit 1.30.

**EXHIBIT 1.30**   Equity Value Multiples

$$\frac{\text{Share Price}}{\text{Diluted EPS}} \qquad \frac{\text{Equity Value}}{\text{Net Income}}$$

### Enterprise Value Multiples

Given that enterprise value represents the interests of both debt and equity holders, it is used as a multiple of unlevered financial statistics such as sales, EBITDA, and EBIT. The most generic and widely used enterprise value multiples are EV/EBITDA, EV/EBIT, and EV/sales (see Exhibits 1.31 and 1.32). As with P/E ratios, enterprise value multiples tend to focus on forward estimates in addition to LTM statistics for framing valuation.

**Enterprise Value-to-EBITDA and Enterprise Value-to-EBIT Multiples**   EV/EBITDA serves as a valuation standard for most sectors. It is independent of capital structure and taxes, as well as any distortions that may arise from differences in D&A among different companies. For example, one company may have spent heavily on new machinery and equipment in recent years, resulting in increased D&A for the current and future years, while another company may have deferred its capital spending until a future period. In the interim, this situation would produce disparities in EBIT margins between the two companies that would not be reflected in EBITDA margins.

For the reasons outlined above, as well as potential discrepancies due to acquisition-related amortization, EV/EBIT is less commonly used than EV/EBITDA. However, EV/EBIT may be helpful in situations where D&A is unavailable (e.g., when valuing divisions of public companies) or for companies with high capex.

**EXHIBIT 1.31**   Enterprise Value-to-EBITDA and Enterprise Value-to-EBIT

**Enterprise Value-to-Sales Multiple**   EV/sales is also analyzed, although it is typically less relevant than the other multiples discussed. Sales may provide an indication of size, but it does not necessarily translate into profitability or cash flow generation, both of which are key value drivers. Consequently, EV/sales is used largely as a sanity check on the earnings-based multiples discussed above.

In certain sectors, however, as well as for companies with little or no earnings, EV/sales may be relied upon as a meaningful reference point for valuation. For example, EV/sales may be used to value an early stage technology company that is aggressively growing sales, but has yet to achieve profitability.

**EXHIBIT 1.32**   Enterprise Value-to-Sales

## Sector-Specific Multiples

Many sectors employ specific valuation multiples in addition to, or instead of, the traditional metrics previously discussed. These multiples use an indicator of market valuation in the numerator and a key sector-specific financial, operating, or production/capacity statistic in the denominator. Selected examples are shown in Exhibit 1.33.

**EXHIBIT 1.33**   Selected Sector-Specific Valuation Multiples

| Valuation Multiple | Sector |
|---|---|
| **Enterprise Value /** | |
| Broadcast Cash Flow (BCF) | ▪ Media<br>▪ Telecommunications |
| Earnings Before Interest Taxes, Depreciation, Amortization, and Rent Expense (EBITDAR) | ▪ Casinos<br>▪ Restaurants<br>▪ Retail |
| Earnings Before Interest Taxes, Depreciation, Depletion, Amortization, and Exploration Expense (EBITDAX) | ▪ Natural Resources<br>▪ Oil & Gas |
| Population (POP) | ▪ Metals & Mining<br>▪ Natural Resources<br>▪ Oil & Gas<br>▪ Paper and Forest Products |
| Reserves | ▪ Metals & Mining<br>▪ Natural Resources<br>▪ Oil & Gas |
| Square Footage | ▪ Real Estate<br>▪ Retail |
| Subscriber | ▪ Media<br>▪ Telecommunications |
| **Equity Value (Price) /** | |
| Book Value (per share) | ▪ Financial Institutions<br>▪ Homebuilders |
| Cash Available for Distribution (per share) | ▪ Real Estate |
| Discretionary Cash Flow (per share) | ▪ Natural Resources |
| Funds from Operations (FFO) (per share) | ▪ Real Estate |
| Net Asset Value (NAV) (per share) | ▪ Financial Institutions<br>▪ Mining<br>▪ Real Estate |

## STEP IV. BENCHMARK THE COMPARABLE COMPANIES

Once the initial universe of comparable companies is selected and key financial statistics, ratios, and trading multiples are spread, the banker is set to perform benchmarking analysis. Benchmarking centers on analyzing and comparing each of the comparable companies with one another and the target. The ultimate objective is to determine the target's relative ranking so as to frame valuation accordingly. While the entire universe provides a useful perspective, the banker typically hones in on a selected group of closest comparables as the basis for establishing the target's implied valuation range. The closest comparables are generally those most similar to the target in terms of business and financial profile.

We have broken down the benchmarking exercise into a two-stage process. First, we benchmark the key financial statistics and ratios for the target and its comparables in order to establish relative positioning, with a focus on identifying the closest or "best" comparables and noting potential outliers. Second, we analyze and compare the trading multiples for the peer group, placing particular emphasis on the best comparables.

### Benchmark the Financial Statistics and Ratios

The first stage of the benchmarking analysis involves a comparison of the target and comparables universe on the basis of key financial performance metrics. These metrics, as captured in the financial profile framework outlined in Steps I and III, include measures of size, profitability, growth, returns, and credit strength. They are core value drivers and typically translate directly into relative valuation. The results of the benchmarking exercise are displayed on spreadsheet output pages that present the data for each company in an easy-to-compare format (see Exhibits 1.53 and 1.54). These pages also display the mean, median, maximum (high), and minimum (low) for the universe's selected financial statistics and ratios.

A thoughtful benchmarking analysis goes beyond a quantitative comparison of the comparables' financial metrics. In order to truly assess the target's relative strength, the banker needs to have a strong understanding of each comparable company's story. For example, what are the reasons for high or low growth rates and profit margins? Is the company a market leader or laggard, gaining or losing market share? Has the company been successful in delivering upon announced strategic initiatives or meeting earnings guidance? Has the company announced any recent M&A transactions or significant ownership/management changes? The ability to interpret these issues, in combination with the above-mentioned financial analysis, is critical to assessing the performance of the comparable companies and determining the target's relative position.

### Benchmark the Trading Multiples

The trading multiples for the comparables universe are also displayed on a spreadsheet output page for easy comparison and analysis (see Exhibit 1.55). This enables the banker to view the full range of multiples and assess relative valuation for each of the comparable companies. As with the financial statistics and ratios, the means, medians, highs, and lows for the range of multiples are calculated and displayed, providing a preliminary reference point for establishing the target's valuation range.

Once the trading multiples have been analyzed, the banker conducts a further refining of the comparables universe. Depending on the resulting output, it may become apparent that certain outliers need to be excluded from the analysis or that the comparables should be further tiered (e.g., on the basis of size, sub-sector, or ranging from closest to peripheral). The trading multiples for the best comparables are also noted as they are typically assigned greater emphasis for framing valuation.

## STEP V. DETERMINE VALUATION

The trading multiples for comparable companies serve as the basis for deriving an appropriate valuation range for the target. The banker typically begins by using the means and medians of the most relevant multiple for the sector (e.g., EV/EBITDA or P/E) to extrapolate a defensible range of multiples. The high and low multiples of the comparables universe provide further guidance. The multiples of the best comparables, however, are typically relied upon as guideposts for selecting the tightest, most appropriate range.

Consequently, as few as two or three carefully selected comparables often serve as the ultimate basis for valuation, with the broader group providing reference points. Hence, the selected multiple range is typically tighter than that implied by simply taking the high and low multiples for the universe. As part of this exercise, the banker must also determine which period financial data is most relevant for calculating the trading multiples. Depending on the sector, point in the business cycle, and comfort with consensus estimates, the comparable companies may be trading on the basis of LTM, one or two-year forward financials.

As shown in the illustrative example in Exhibit 1.34, the target has three closest comparables that trade in the range of approximately 6.5x to 7.5x 2019E EBITDA, versus a high/low range of 5.5x to 8.5x, a mean of 7.0x and a median of 6.8x.

**EXHIBIT 1.34**    Selected Enterprise Value-to-EBITDA Multiple Range

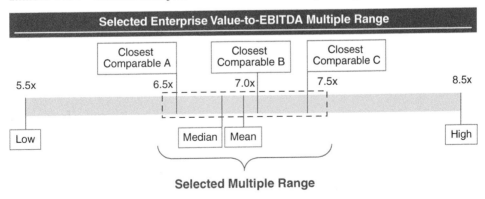

The selected multiple range is then applied to the target's appropriate financial statistics to derive an implied valuation range.

## Valuation Implied by EV/EBITDA

Exhibit 1.35 demonstrates how a given EV/EBITDA multiple range translates into an implied range for enterprise value, equity value, and share price. For these calculations, we assume net debt[54] of $500 million and fully diluted shares outstanding of 100 million.[55]

**EXHIBIT 1.35**  Valuation Implied by EV/EBITDA

*($ in millions, except per share data)*

| EBITDA | Financial Metric | Multiple Range | | Implied Enterprise Value | | Less: Net Debt | Implied Equity Value | | Fully Diluted Shares | Implied Share Price | |
|---|---|---|---|---|---|---|---|---|---|---|---|
| LTM | $200 | 7.0x | – 8.0x | $1,400 | – $1,600 | (500) | $900 | – $1,100 | 100 | $9.00 | – $11.00 |
| 2019E | 215 | 6.5x | – 7.5x | 1,398 | – 1,613 | (500) | 898 | – 1,113 | 100 | $8.98 | – $11.13 |
| 2020E | 230 | 6.0x | – 7.0x | 1,380 | – 1,610 | (500) | 880 | – 1,110 | 100 | $8.80 | – $11.10 |

At a 6.5x to 7.5x multiple range for 2019E EBITDA, the endpoints are multiplied by the target's 2019E EBITDA of $215 million to produce an implied enterprise value range of $1,398 million to $1,613 million.

To calculate implied equity value, we subtract net debt of $500 million from enterprise value, which results in a range of $898 million to $1,113 million. For public companies, the implied equity value is then divided by fully diluted shares outstanding to yield implied share price. Dividing the endpoints of the equity value range by fully diluted shares outstanding of 100 million provides an implied share price range of $8.98 to $11.13. The same methodology can then be performed using the selected multiple range for EV/LTM EBITDA and EV/2020E EBITDA.

## Valuation Implied by P/E

Exhibits 1.36 and 1.37 demonstrate how the P/E ratio translates into implied share price and enterprise value ranges. As with the example in Exhibit 1.35, we assume net debt of $500 million and a static fully diluted shares outstanding count of 100 million.

**Implied Share Price**  For a public company, the banker typically begins with net income and builds up to implied equity value. The implied equity value is then divided by fully diluted shares outstanding to calculate implied share price. A P/E multiple range of 12.0x to 15.0x 2019E net income, for example, yields an implied equity value of $900 million to $1,125 million when multiplied by the target's 2019E net income of $75 million. Dividing this range by fully diluted shares outstanding of 100 million produces an implied share price range of $9.00 to $11.25.

---

[54]"Net debt" is often defined to include all obligations senior to common equity.

[55]For illustrative purposes, we assume that the number of fully diluted shares outstanding remains constant for each of the equity values presented. As discussed in Chapter 3: Discounted Cash Flow Analysis, however, assuming the existence of stock options, the number of fully diluted shares outstanding as determined by the TSM is dependent on share price, which in turn is dependent on equity value and shares outstanding (see Exhibit 3.31). Therefore, the target's fully diluted shares outstanding and implied share price vary in accordance with its amount of stock options and their weighted average exercise price.

**EXHIBIT 1.36**   Valuation Implied by P/E – Share Price

*($ in millions, except per share data)*

| Net Income | Financial Metric | Multiple Range | | Implied Equity Value | | Fully Diluted Shares | Implied Share Price | |
|---|---|---|---|---|---|---|---|---|
| LTM | $70 | 13.0x | – | 16.0x | $910 – $1,120 | 100 | $9.10 – $11.20 |
| 2019E | 75 | 12.0x | – | 15.0x | 900 – 1,125 | 100 | $9.00 – $11.25 |
| 2020E | 80 | 11.0x | – | 14.0x | 880 – 1,120 | 100 | $8.80 – $11.20 |

**Implied Enterprise Value**   To calculate an implied enterprise value range using the assumptions above, the same P/E multiple range of 12.0x to 15.0x is multiplied by 2019E net income of $75 million to produce an implied equity value range of $900 million to $1,125 million. Net debt of $500 million is added to the low and high endpoints of the implied equity value range to calculate an implied enterprise value range of $1,400 million to $1,625 million.

**EXHIBIT 1.37**   Valuation Implied by P/E – Enterprise Value

*($ in millions)*

| Net Income | Financial Metric | Multiple Range | | Implied Equity Value | | Plus: Net Debt | Implied Enterprise Value | |
|---|---|---|---|---|---|---|---|---|
| LTM | $70 | 13.0x | – | 16.0x | $910 – $1,120 | 500 | $1,410 – $1,620 |
| 2019E | 75 | 12.0x | – | 15.0x | 900 – 1,125 | 500 | 1,400 – 1,625 |
| 2020E | 80 | 11.0x | – | 14.0x | 880 – 1,120 | 500 | 1,380 – 1,620 |

As a final consideration, it is necessary to analyze the extrapolated valuation range for the target and test the key assumptions and conclusions. The banker should also compare the valuation derived from comparable companies to other methodologies, such as precedent transactions, DCF analysis, and LBO analysis (if applicable). Significant discrepancies may signal incorrect assumptions, misjudgment, or even mathematical error, thereby prompting the banker to reexamine the inputs and assumptions used in each technique. Common errors in trading comps typically involve the inclusion or overemphasis of inappropriate comparable companies, incorrect calculations (e.g., fully diluted equity value, enterprise value, LTM financial data, or calendarization), as well as the failure to accurately scrub the financials for non-recurring items and recent events.

## KEY PROS AND CONS

### Pros

- *Market-based* – information used to derive valuation for the target is based on actual public market data, thereby reflecting the market's growth and risk expectations, as well as overall sentiment

- *Relativity* – easily measurable and comparable versus other companies

- *Quick and convenient* – valuation can be determined on the basis of a few easy-to-calculate inputs

- *Current* – valuation is based on prevailing market data, which can be updated on a daily (or intraday) basis

### Cons

- *Market-based* – valuation that is completely market-based can be skewed during periods of irrational exuberance or bearishness

- *Absence of relevant comparables* – "pure play" comparables may be difficult to identify or even nonexistent, especially if the target operates in a niche sector, in which case the valuation implied by trading comps may be less meaningful

- *Potential disconnect from cash flow* – valuation based on prevailing market conditions or expectations may have significant disconnect from the valuation implied by a company's projected cash flow generation (e.g., DCF analysis)

- *Company-specific issues* – valuation of the target is based on the valuation of other companies, which may fail to capture target-specific strengths, weaknesses, opportunities, and risks

## ILLUSTRATIVE COMPARABLE COMPANIES ANALYSIS FOR VALUECO

The following section provides a detailed, step-by-step example of how comps is used to establish a valuation range for our illustrative target company, ValueCo. For the purposes of Chapters 1 through 6, we assume that ValueCo is a private company and that the financial statistics and valuation multiples throughout the book represent normalized economic and market conditions.

### Step I. Select the Universe of Comparable Companies

**Study the Target**   Our first task was to learn ValueCo's "story" in as much detail as possible so as to provide a frame of reference for locating comparable companies. As ValueCo is a private company, for the purposes of this exercise we assumed that it is being sold through an organized M&A sale process (see Chapter 6). Therefore, we were provided with substantive information on the company, its sector, products, customers, competitors, distribution channels, and end markets, as well as historical financial performance and projections. We sourced this information from the confidential information memorandum/presentation (CIM/CIP, see Exhibit 6.5), management presentation (see Exhibit 6.6), and data room, such as those provided by Datasite (formerly Merrill Corporation, see Exhibit 6.7).[56]

**Identify Key Characteristics of the Target for Comparison Purposes**   This exercise involved examining ValueCo's key business and financial characteristics in accordance with the framework outlined in Exhibit 1.3, which provided us with a systematic approach for identifying companies that shared key similarities with ValueCo.

**Screen for Comparable Companies**   Our search for comparable companies began by examining ValueCo's public competitors, which we initially identified from the CIM as well as selected industry reports. We then searched through equity research reports on these public competitors for the analysts' views on comparable companies, which provided us with additional companies to evaluate. We also reviewed the proxy statements for recent M&A transactions involving companies in ValueCo's sector, and found ideas for additional comparable companies from the enclosed fairness opinion excerpts. To ensure that no potential comparables were missed, we screened companies using SIC/NAICS codes corresponding to ValueCo's sector.

These sources provided us with enough information to create a solid initial list of comparable companies (see Exhibit 1.38). We also compiled summary financial information using data downloaded from a financial information service in order to provide a basic understanding of their financial profiles.

---

[56]See Chapter 6 for an overview of the key documents and sources of information in an organized sale process.

**EXHIBIT 1.38**  List of Comparable Companies

*($ in millions)*

## List of Comparable Companies

| Company | Ticker | Business Description | Equity Value | Enterprise Value | LTM Sales | LTM EBITDA |
|---|---|---|---|---|---|---|
| BuyerCo | BUY | Produces chemicals and advanced materials including acetyl, acetate, vinyl emulsion, and engineered polymers | $9,800 | $11,600 | $6,560 | $1,443 |
| Falloon Group | FLN | Manufactures differentiated and commodity chemical products including those in adhesives, aerospace, automotive, and consumer products | 7,480 | 11,254 | 11,835 | 1,636 |
| Sherman Co. | SHR | Produces chemicals and plastics including coatings, adhesives, specialty polymers, inks, and intermediates, performance polymers | 5,600 | 8,101 | 5,895 | 1,047 |
| Pearl Corp. | PRL | Supplies specialty chemical, construction, and container products for the food, consumer products, petroleum refinery, and construction industries | 5,172 | 5,804 | 4,284 | 839 |
| Gasparro Corp. | JDG | Develops various chemical products for use in crop protection, pharmaceuticals, and electronics applications | 5,000 | 6,750 | 4,725 | 900 |
| Kumra Inc. | KUM | Manufactures brominated flame retardants, refinery catalysts, and fine chemistry products | 4,852 | 5,345 | 3,187 | 665 |
| Goodson Corp. | GDS | Manufactures and markets basic chemicals, vinyls, polymers, and fabricated products | 4,160 | 5,660 | 4,769 | 763 |
| Pryor Industries | PRI | Develops and manufactures specialty chemicals for various end users including aerospace, plastics, coatings, and mining industries | 3,926 | 4,166 | 3,682 | 569 |
| Lanzarone Global | LNZ | Manufactures plastics and other chemicals including urethane polymers, flame retardants, seed treatment, and petroleum additives | 3,230 | 3,823 | 3,712 | 578 |
| McMenamin & Co. | MCM | Manufactures thermoplastic compounds, specialty resins, specialty polymer formulations, engineered films, and additive systems | 3,193 | 3,193 | 3,223 | 355 |
| Momper & Co. | MOMP | Manufactures chlorine, caustic soda, sodium hydrosulfite, hydrochloric acid, bleach products, and potassium hydroxide | 2,240 | 2,921 | 2,077 | 378 |
| Adler Worldwide | ADL | Produces titanium dioxide pigments for paints, plastics, inks, and cosmetics | 1,217 | 1,463 | 1,550 | 245 |
| Schachter & Sons | STM | Manufactures and markets chemical and plastic products including electrochemicals, methanol, and aromatic chemicals | 1,125 | 1,674 | 1,703 | 238 |
| Girshin Holdings | MGP | Manufactures carbon compounds and wood treatments | 1,035 | 1,298 | 1,606 | 177 |
| Crespin International | MCR | Produces engineered polymers and styrenic block copolymers used in adhesives, coatings, consumer, and personal care products | 872 | 1,222 | 1,443 | 190 |

## Step II. Locate the Necessary Financial Information

In Step II, we set out to locate the financial information necessary to spread the key financial statistics and ratios for each of the companies that we identified as being comparable to ValueCo. For Gasparro Corp. ("Gasparro"), one of ValueCo's closest comparables, for example, this information was obtained from its most recent SEC filings, consensus estimates, and equity research. Additional financial information was sourced from financial information services.

**10-K and 10-Q**   We used Gasparro's most recent 10-K and 10-Q for the periods ending December 31, 2018, and September 30, 2019, respectively, as the primary sources for historical financial information. Specifically, these filings provided us with the prior year annual as well as current and prior year YTD financial statistics necessary to calculate LTM data. They also served as sources for the most recent basic shares outstanding count, options/warrants data, and balance sheet and cash flow statement information. The MD&A and notes to the financials were key for identifying non-recurring items (see Exhibit 1.47).

**Earnings Announcement and Earnings Call Transcript**   We read through the most recent earnings announcement and earnings call transcript to gain further insight on Gasparro's financial performance and outlook.

**8-K/Press Releases**   We confirmed via a search of Gasparro's corporate website that there were no intra-quarter press releases, 8-Ks, or other SEC filings disclosing new M&A, capital markets, or other activities since the filing of its most recent 10-Q that would affect the relevant financial statistics.

**Consensus Estimates and Equity Research**   Consensus estimates formed the basis for the 2019E and 2020E income statement inputs, namely sales, EBITDA, EBIT, and EPS. We also read individual equity research reports for further color on factors driving Gasparro's growth expectations as well as insights on non-recurring items.

**Financial Information Service**   We used a financial information service to source Gasparro's closing share price on December 20, 2019 (the day we performed the analysis), as well as its 52-week high and low share price data.

**Moody's and S&P Websites**   We obtained the Moody's and S&P credit ratings for Gasparro from the respective credit rating agencies' websites.

## Step III. Spread Key Statistics, Ratios, and Trading Multiples

After locating the necessary financial information for the selected comparable companies, we created input sheets for each company, as shown in Exhibit 1.39 for Gasparro. These input sheets link to the output pages used for benchmarking the comparables universe (see Exhibits 1.53, 1.54, and 1.55).

Below, we walk through each section of the input sheet in Exhibit 1.39.

# EXHIBIT 1.39   Comparable Companies Analysis—Trading Multiples Output Page

## Gasparro Corp. (Nasdaq:JDG)
### Input Page
*($ in millions, except per share data)*

### General Information

| | |
|---|---|
| Company Name | Gasparro Corp. |
| Ticker | JDG |
| Stock Exchange | Nasdaq |
| Fiscal Year Ending | Dec-31 |
| Moody's Corporate Rating | Ba2 |
| S&P Corporate Rating | BB |
| Predicted Beta | 1.30 |
| Marginal Tax Rate | 25.0% |

### Selected Market Data

| | | |
|---|---|---|
| Current Price | 12/20/2019 | $50.00 |
| % of 52-week High | | 80.0% |
| 52-week High Price | 7/19/2019 | 62.50 |
| 52-week Low Price | 4/5/2019 | 46.00 |
| Dividend Per Share (MRQ) | | 0.25 |
| Fully Diluted Shares Outstanding | | 100.0 |
| **Equity Value** | | **$5,000.0** |
| Plus: Total Debt | | 1,850.0 |
| Plus: Preferred Stock | | - |
| Plus: Noncontrolling Interest | | - |
| Less: Cash and Cash Equivalents | | (100.0) |
| **Enterprise Value** | | **$6,750.0** |

### Trading Multiples

| | LTM 9/30/2019 | NFY 2019E | NFY+1 2020E | NFY+2 2021E |
|---|---|---|---|---|
| **EV/Sales** | 1.4x | 1.4x | 1.3x | 1.2x |
| Metric | $4,725.0 | $5,000.0 | $5,350.0 | $5,825.0 |
| **EV/EBITDA** | 7.5x | 7.1x | 6.6x | 6.3x |
| Metric | $900.0 | $950.0 | $1,025.0 | $1,075.0 |
| **EV/EBIT** | 9.3x | 8.8x | 8.2x | 7.8x |
| Metric | $725.0 | $765.0 | $825.0 | $865.0 |
| **P/E** | 10.7x | 9.8x | 9.1x | 8.7x |
| Metric | $4.69 | $5.10 | $5.50 | $5.75 |
| **FCF Yield** | 6.3% | 7.5% | 8.3% | 9.1% |
| Metric | $3.15 | $3.75 | $4.15 | $4.55 |

### LTM Return on Investment Ratios

| | |
|---|---|
| Return on Invested Capital | 21.1% |
| Return on Equity | 28.2% |
| Return on Assets | 9.5% |
| Implied Annual Dividend Per Share | 2.0% |

### LTM Credit Statistics

| | |
|---|---|
| Debt / Total Capitalization | 51.7% |
| Total Debt / EBITDA | 2.1x |
| Net Debt / EBITDA | 1.9x |
| EBITDA / Interest Expense | 9.0x |
| (EBITDA-capex) / Interest Expense | 7.0x |
| EBIT / Interest Expense | 7.3x |

### Growth Rates

| | Sales | EBITDA | FCF | EPS |
|---|---|---|---|---|
| **Historical** | | | | |
| 1-year | 8.4% | 5.1% | 13.2% | 6.4% |
| 2-year CAGR | 9.5% | 8.2% | 14.2% | 11.6% |
| **Estimated** | | | | |
| 1-year | 11.1% | 15.2% | 25.0% | 24.1% |
| 2-year CAGR | 9.0% | 11.5% | 17.6% | 15.7% |
| Long-term | | | | 12.0% |

### Business Description

Develops various chemical products for use in crop protection, pharmaceuticals, and electronics applications

### Balance Sheet Data

| | 2018A | 9/30/2019 |
|---|---|---|
| Cash and Cash Equivalents | $75.0 | $100.0 |
| Accounts Receivable | 625.0 | 650.0 |
| Inventories | 730.0 | 750.0 |
| Prepaids and Other Current Assets | 225.0 | 250.0 |
| **Total Current Assets** | **$1,655.0** | **$1,750.0** |
| Property, Plant and Equipment, net | 1,970.0 | 2,000.0 |
| Goodwill and Intangible Assets | 775.0 | 800.0 |
| Other Assets | 425.0 | 450.0 |
| **Total Assets** | **$4,825.0** | **$5,000.0** |
| Accounts Payable | 275.0 | 300.0 |
| Accrued Liabilities | 450.0 | 475.0 |
| Other Current Liabilities | 125.0 | 150.0 |
| **Total Current Liabilities** | **$850.0** | **$925.0** |
| Total Debt | 1,875.0 | 1,850.0 |
| Other Long-Term Liabilities | 500.0 | 500.0 |
| **Total Liabilities** | **$3,225.0** | **$3,275.0** |
| Noncontrolling Interest | - | - |
| Preferred Stock | - | - |
| Shareholders' Equity | 1,600.0 | 1,725.0 |
| **Total Liabilities and Equity** | **$4,825.0** | **$5,000.0** |
| Balance Check | 0.000 | 0.000 |

### Calculation of Fully Diluted Shares Outstanding

| | |
|---|---|
| Basic Shares Outstanding | 98.500 |
| Plus: Shares from In-the-Money Options | 2.750 |
| Less: Shares Repurchased | (1.250) |
| Net New Shares from Options | 1.500 |
| Plus: Shares from Convertible Securities | - |
| Fully Diluted Shares Outstanding | 100.000 |

### Options/Warrants

| Tranche | Number of Shares | Exercise Price | In-the-Money Shares | Proceeds |
|---|---|---|---|---|
| Tranche 1 | 1.250 | $10.00 | 1.250 | $12.5 |
| Tranche 2 | 1.000 | 30.00 | 1.000 | 30.0 |
| Tranche 3 | 0.500 | 40.00 | 0.500 | 20.0 |
| Tranche 4 | 0.250 | 60.00 | | |
| Tranche 5 | | | | |
| **Total** | **3.000** | | **2.750** | **$62.5** |

### Convertible Securities

| | Amount | Conversion Price | Conversion Ratio | New Shares |
|---|---|---|---|---|
| Issue 1 | | | | |
| Issue 2 | | | | |
| Issue 3 | | | | |
| Issue 4 | | | | |
| Issue 5 | | | | |
| **Total** | | | | |

### Reported Income Statement

| | Fiscal Year Ending December 31 | | | Prior Stub 9/30/2018 | Current Stub 9/30/2019 | LTM 9/30/2019 |
|---|---|---|---|---|---|---|
| | 2016A | 2017A | 2018A | | | |
| Sales | $3,750.0 | $4,150.0 | $4,500.0 | $3,375.0 | $3,600.0 | $4,725.0 |
| COGS (incl. D&A) | 2,450.0 | 2,700.0 | 2,925.0 | 2,200.0 | 2,350.0 | 3,075.0 |
| **Gross Profit** | **$1,300.0** | **$1,450.0** | **$1,575.0** | **$1,175.0** | **$1,250.0** | **$1,650.0** |
| SG&A | 750.0 | 830.0 | 900.0 | 675.0 | 720.0 | 945.0 |
| Other Expense / (Income) | - | - | - | - | - | - |
| **EBIT** | **$550.0** | **$620.0** | **$675.0** | **$500.0** | **$530.0** | **$705.0** |
| Interest Expense | 110.0 | 105.0 | 102.0 | 75.0 | 73.0 | 100.0 |
| **Pre-tax Income** | **$440.0** | **$515.0** | **$573.0** | **$425.0** | **$457.0** | **$605.0** |
| Income Taxes | 110.0 | 128.8 | 143.3 | 106.3 | 114.3 | 151.3 |
| Noncontrolling Interest | - | - | - | - | - | - |
| Preferred Dividends | - | - | - | - | - | - |
| **Net Income** | **$330.0** | **$386.3** | **$429.8** | **$318.8** | **$342.8** | **$453.8** |
| *Effective Tax Rate* | *25.0%* | *25.0%* | *25.0%* | *25.0%* | *25.0%* | *25.0%* |
| Weighted Avg. Diluted Shares | 100.0 | 100.0 | 100.0 | 100.0 | 100.0 | 100.0 |
| **Diluted EPS** | **$3.30** | **$3.86** | **$4.30** | **$3.19** | **$3.43** | **$4.54** |

### Adjusted Income Statement

| | 2016A | 2017A | 2018A | 9/30/2018 | 9/30/2019 | 9/30/2019 |
|---|---|---|---|---|---|---|
| Reported Gross Profit | $1,300.0 | $1,450.0 | $1,575.0 | $1,175.0 | $1,250.0 | $1,650.0 |
| Non-recurring Items in COGS | - | - | - | - | - | 30.0 (1) |
| **Adj. Gross Profit** | **$1,300.0** | **$1,450.0** | **$1,575.0** | **$1,175.0** | **$1,260.0** | **$1,680.0** |
| *% margin* | *34.7%* | *34.9%* | *35.0%* | *34.8%* | *35.6%* | *35.6%* |
| Reported EBIT | $550.0 | $620.0 | $675.0 | $500.0 | $530.0 | $705.0 |
| Non-recurring Items in COGS | - | - | (25.0) | - | 30.0 | 30.0 |
| Other Non-recurring Items | - | - | - | - | 15.0 | (10.0) (2), (3) |
| **Adjusted EBIT** | **$550.0** | **$620.0** | **$650.0** | **$500.0** | **$575.0** | **$725.0** |
| *% margin* | *14.7%* | *14.9%* | *14.4%* | *14.8%* | *16.0%* | *15.3%* |
| Depreciation & Amortization | 155.0 | 165.0 | 175.0 | 125.0 | 125.0 | 175.0 |
| **Adjusted EBITDA** | **$705.0** | **$785.0** | **$825.0** | **$625.0** | **$700.0** | **$900.0** |
| *% margin* | *18.8%* | *18.9%* | *18.3%* | *18.5%* | *19.4%* | *19.0%* |
| Reported Net Income | $330.0 | $386.3 | $429.8 | $318.8 | $342.8 | $453.8 |
| Non-recurring Items in COGS | - | - | (25.0) | - | 30.0 | 30.0 |
| Other Non-recurring Items | - | - | - | - | 15.0 | (10.0) |
| Non-operating Non-rec. Items | - | - | 6.3 | - | (11.3) | (5.0) |
| Tax Adjustment | - | - | (25.0) | - | - | - |
| **Adjusted Net Income** | **$330.0** | **$386.3** | **$411.0** | **$318.8** | **$376.5** | **$468.8** |
| *% margin* | *8.8%* | *9.3%* | *9.1%* | *9.4%* | *10.5%* | *9.9%* |
| Adjusted Diluted EPS | $3.30 | $3.86 | $4.11 | $3.19 | $3.77 | $4.69 |

### Cash Flow Statement Data

| | 2016A | 2017A | 2018A | 9/30/2018 | 9/30/2019 | 9/30/2019 |
|---|---|---|---|---|---|---|
| Cash From Operations | 400.0 | 450.0 | 500.0 | 360.0 | 380.0 | 520.0 |
| Capital Expenditures | 170.0 | 185.0 | 200.0 | 150.0 | 155.0 | 205.0 |
| *% sales* | *4.5%* | *4.5%* | *4.4%* | *4.4%* | *4.3%* | *4.3%* |
| **Free Cash Flow** | **$230.0** | **$265.0** | **$300.0** | **$210.0** | **$225.0** | **$315.0** |
| *% margin* | *6.1%* | *6.4%* | *6.7%* | *6.2%* | *6.3%* | *6.7%* |
| FCF / Share | $2.30 | $2.65 | $3.00 | $2.10 | $2.25 | $3.15 |
| Depreciation & Amortization | 155.0 | 165.0 | 175.0 | 125.0 | 125.0 | 175.0 |
| *% sales* | *4.1%* | *4.0%* | *3.9%* | *3.7%* | *3.5%* | *3.7%* |

### Notes

(1) In Q2 2019, Gasparro Corp. recorded a $30 million pre-tax inventory valuation change related to product obsolescence (see Q2 2019 10-Q MD&A, page 14).

(2) In Q4 2018, Gasparro Corp. realized a $25 million pre-tax gain on the sale of a non-core business (see 2018 10-K MD&A, page 45).

(3) In Q3 2019, Gasparro Corp. recognized $15 million of pre-tax restructuring costs in connection with the closure of a manufacturing facility (see Q3 2019 10-Q MD&A, page 15).

**General Information**   In the "General Information" section of the input page, we entered various basic company data (see Exhibit 1.40). Gasparro Corp., ticker symbol JDG, is a U.S.-based company that is listed on Nasdaq. Gasparro reports its financial results based on a fiscal year ending December 31 and has corporate credit ratings of Ba2 and BB as rated by Moody's and S&P, respectively. Gasparro's predicted levered beta is 1.3, as sourced from Barra (see Chapter 3). We also determined a 25% marginal tax rate from Gasparro's tax rate disclosures in its 10-K.

**EXHIBIT 1.40**   General Information Section

| General Information | |
| --- | --- |
| Company Name | Gasparro Corp. |
| Ticker | JDG |
| Stock Exchange | Nasdaq |
| Fiscal Year Ending | Dec-31 |
| Moody's Corporate Rating | Ba2 |
| S&P Corporate Rating | BB |
| Predicted Beta | 1.30 |
| Marginal Tax Rate | 25.0% |

**Selected Market Data**   Under "Selected Market Data", we entered Gasparro's share price information as well as the most recent quarterly (MRQ) dividend paid of $0.25 per share (as sourced from the latest 10-Q, see Exhibit 1.41). Gasparro's share price was $50.00 as of market close on December 20, 2019, representing 80% of its 52-week high. As the trading multiples benchmarking output page shows (see Exhibit 1.55), this percentage is consistent with that of most of the comparables, which indicates that the market expects Gasparro to perform roughly in line with its peers.

This section also calculates equity value and enterprise value once the appropriate basic shares outstanding count, options/warrants data, and most recent balance sheet data are entered (see Exhibits 1.42, 1.43, 1.44, and 1.45).

**EXHIBIT 1.41**   Selected Market Data Section

*($ in millions, except per share data)*

| Selected Market Data | | | |
| --- | --- | --- | --- |
| Current Price | 12/20/2019 | $50.00 | = Closing Share Price on December 20, 2019 |
| % of 52-week High | | 80.0% | |
| 52-week High Price | 7/19/2019 | 62.50 | = Closing Share Price / 52-week High Price |
| 52-week Low Price | 4/5/2019 | 40.00 | |
| Dividend Per Share (MRQ) | | 0.25 | |
| | | | |
| Fully Diluted Shares Outstanding | | - | |
| **Equity Value** | | - | |
| | | | |
| Plus: Total Debt | | - | |
| Plus: Preferred Stock | | - | |
| Plus: Noncontrolling Interest | | - | |
| Less: Cash and Cash Equivalents | | - | |
| **Enterprise Value** | | - | |

**Calculation of Fully Diluted Shares Outstanding**   Gasparro's most recent basic shares outstanding count is 98.5 million, as sourced from the first page of its latest 10-Q. We searched recent press releases and SEC filings to ensure that no stock splits, follow-on offerings, or major share buybacks, for example, took place following the most recent 10-Q filing. We also confirmed that Gasparro does not have convertible securities outstanding. However, Gasparro has several tranches of options, which must be reflected in the calculation of fully diluted shares in accordance with the TSM.

As shown in Exhibit 1.42 under the "Options/Warrants" heading, Gasparro has four tranches of options, each consisting of a specified number of shares and corresponding weighted average exercise price. The first tranche, for example, represents a group of options collectively owning the right to buy 1.25 million shares at a weighted average exercise price of $10.00. This tranche is deemed in-the-money given that Gasparro's current share price of $50.00 is above the weighted average strike price. The exercise of this tranche generates proceeds of $12.5 million (1.25 million × $10.00), which are assumed to repurchase Gasparro shares at the current share price of $50.00.

**EXHIBIT 1.42**   Calculation of Fully Diluted Shares Outstanding Section

*($ in millions, except per share data)*

**Calculation of Fully Diluted Shares Outstanding**

| | |
|---|---|
| Basic Shares Outstanding | 98.500 |
| Plus: Shares from In-the-Money Options | 2.750 |
| Less: Shares Repurchased | (1.250) |
| **Net New Shares from Options** | **1.500** |
| Plus: Shares from Convertible Securities | - |
| **Fully Diluted Shares Outstanding** | **100.000** |

= Total In-the-Money Shares

= Total Option Proceeds / Current Share Price
= $62.5 million / $50.00

**Options/Warrants**

| Tranche | Number of Shares | Exercise Price | In-the-Money Shares | Proceeds |
|---|---|---|---|---|
| Tranche 1 | 1.250 | $10.00 | 1.250 | $12.5 |
| Tranche 2 | 1.000 | 30.00 | 1.000 | 30.0 |
| Tranche 3 | 0.500 | 40.00 | 0.500 | 20.0 |
| Tranche 4 | 0.250 | 60.00 | - | - |
| Tranche 5 | - | - | - | - |
| **Total** | **3.000** | **-** | **2.750** | **$62.5** |

= IF(Weighted Average Strike Price < Current Share Price, display Number of Shares, otherwise display 0)
= IF($10.00 < $50.00, 1.250, 0)

= IF(In-the-Money Shares > 0, then In-the-Money Shares x Weighted Average Strike Price, otherwise display 0)
= IF(1.250 > 0, 1.250 x $10.00, 0)

**Convertible Securities**

| | Amount | Conversion Price | Conversion Ratio | New Shares |
|---|---|---|---|---|
| Issue 1 | - | - | - | - |
| Issue 2 | - | - | - | - |
| Issue 3 | - | - | - | - |
| Issue 4 | - | - | - | - |
| Issue 5 | - | - | - | - |
| **Total** | **-** | **-** | **-** | **-** |

We utilized this same approach for the other tranches of options. The fourth tranche, however, has a weighted average exercise price of $60.00 (above the current share price of $50.00) and was therefore identified as out-of-the-money. Consequently, these options were excluded from the calculation of fully diluted shares outstanding.

In aggregate, the 2.75 million shares from the in-the-money options generate proceeds of $62.5 million. At Gasparro's current share price of $50.00, these proceeds are used to repurchase 1.25 million shares ($62.5 million/$50.00). The repurchased shares are then subtracted from the 2.75 million total in-the-money shares to provide net new shares of 1.5 million, as shown under the net new shares from options line item in Exhibit 1.42. These incremental shares are added to Gasparro's basic shares to calculate fully diluted shares outstanding of 100 million.

Equity Value    The 100 million fully diluted shares outstanding output feeds into the "Selected Market Data" section, where it is multiplied by Gasparro's current share price of $50.00 to produce an equity value of $5,000 million (see Exhibit 1.43). This calculated equity value forms the basis for calculating enterprise value.

**EXHIBIT 1.43**    Equity Value

*($ in millions, except per share data)*

| Selected Market Data | | |
| --- | --- | --- |
| Current Price | 12/20/2019 | $50.00 |
| % of 52-week High | | 80.0% |
| 52-week High Price | 7/19/2012 | 62.50 |
| 52-week Low Price | 4/5/2012 | 40.00 |
| Dividend Per Share (MRQ) | | 0.25 |
| | | |
| Fully Diluted Shares Outstanding | | 100.000 |
| **Equity Value** | | **$5,000.0** |
| | | |
| Plus: Total Debt | | - |
| Plus: Preferred Stock | | - |
| Plus: Noncontrolling Interest | | - |
| Less: Cash and Cash Equivalents | | - |
| **Enterprise Value** | | - |

= Current Share Price × Fully Diluted Shares Outstanding
= $50.00 × 100 million

**Balance Sheet Data**   In the "Balance Sheet Data" section, we entered Gasparro's balance sheet data for the prior fiscal year ending 12/31/2018 and the most recent quarter ending 9/30/2019, as sourced directly from its 10-Q (see Exhibit 1.44).

**EXHIBIT 1.44**   Balance Sheet Data Section

*($ in millions)*

| Balance Sheet Data | | |
| --- | --- | --- |
| | **2018A** | **9/30/2019** |
| Cash and Cash Equivalents | $75.0 | $100.0 |
| Accounts Receivable | 625.0 | 650.0 |
| Inventories | 730.0 | 750.0 |
| Prepaids and Other Current Assets | 225.0 | 250.0 |
| **Total Current Assets** | **$1,655.0** | **$1,750.0** |
| | | |
| Property, Plant and Equipment, net | 1,970.0 | 2,000.0 |
| Goodwill and Intangible Assets | 775.0 | 800.0 |
| Other Assets | 425.0 | 450.0 |
| **Total Assets** | **$4,825.0** | **$5,000.0** |
| | | |
| Accounts Payable | 275.0 | 300.0 |
| Accrued Liabilities | 450.0 | 475.0 |
| Other Current Liabilities | 125.0 | 150.0 |
| **Total Current Liabilities** | **$850.0** | **$925.0** |
| | | |
| Total Debt | 1,875.0 | 1,850.0 |
| Other Long-Term Liabilities | 500.0 | 500.0 |
| **Total Liabilities** | **$3,225.0** | **$3,275.0** |
| | | |
| Noncontrolling Interest | - | - |
| Preferred Stock | - | - |
| Shareholders' Equity | 1,600.0 | 1,725.0 |
| **Total Liabilities and Equity** | **$4,825.0** | **$5,000.0** |
| | | |
| *Balance Check* | *0.000* | *0.000* |

Enterprise Value   We used selected balance sheet data, specifically total debt and cash, together with the previously calculated equity value to determine Gasparro's enterprise value. As shown in Exhibit 1.45, Gasparro had $1,850 million of total debt outstanding and cash and cash equivalents of $100 million as of 9/30/2019. The net debt balance of $1,750 million was added to equity value of $5,000 million to produce an enterprise value of $6,750 million.

**EXHIBIT 1.45**   Enterprise Value

*($ in millions, except per share data)*

| Selected Market Data | | |
|---|---|---|
| Current Price | 12/20/2019 | $50.00 |
| *% of 52-week High* | | *80.0%* |
| 52-week High Price | 7/19/2019 | 62.50 |
| 52-week Low Price | 4/5/2019 | 40.00 |
| Dividend Per Share (MRQ) | | 0.25 |
| | | |
| Fully Diluted Shares Outstanding | | 100.000 |
| **Equity Value** | | **$5,000.0** |
| | | |
| Plus: Total Debt | | 1,850.0 |
| Plus: Preferred Stock | | - |
| Plus: Noncontrolling Interest | | - |
| Less: Cash and Cash Equivalents | | (100.0) |
| **Enterprise Value** | | **$6,750.0** |

= Equity Value + Total Debt - Cash
= $5,000 million + $1,850 million - $100 million

**Reported Income Statement**   In the "Reported Income Statement" section, we entered the historical income statement items directly from Gasparro's most recent 10-K and 10-Q. The LTM column automatically calculates Gasparro's LTM financial data on the basis of the prior annual year, and the prior and current year stub inputs (see Exhibit 1.46).

**EXHIBIT 1.46**   Reported Income Statement Section

*($ in millions, except per share data)*

| Reported Income Statement | | | | | | |
|---|---|---|---|---|---|---|
| | Fiscal Year Ending December 31, | | | Prior Stub 9/30/2018 | Current Stub 9/30/2019 | LTM 9/30/2019 |
| | 2016A | 2017A | 2018A | | | |
| Sales | $3,750.0 | $4,150.0 | $4,500.0 | $3,375.0 | $3,600.0 | $4,725.0 |
| COGS (incl. D&A) | 2,450.0 | 2,700.0 | 2,925.0 | 2,200.0 | 2,350.0 | 3,075.0 |
| **Gross Profit** | **$1,300.0** | **$1,450.0** | **$1,575.0** | **$1,175.0** | **$1,250.0** | **$1,650.0** |
| SG&A | 750.0 | 830.0 | 900.0 | 675.0 | 720.0 | 945.0 |
| Other Expense / (Income) | - | - | - | - | - | - |
| **EBIT** | **$550.0** | **$620.0** | **$675.0** | **$500.0** | **$530.0** | **$705.0** |
| Interest Expense | 110.0 | 105.0 | 102.0 | 75.0 | 73.0 | 100.0 |
| **Pre-tax Income** | **$440.0** | **$515.0** | **$573.0** | **$425.0** | **$457.0** | **$605.0** |
| Income Taxes | 110.0 | 128.8 | 143.3 | 106.3 | 114.3 | 151.3 |
| Noncontrolling Interest | - | - | - | - | - | - |
| Preferred Dividends | - | - | - | - | - | - |
| **Net Income** | **$330.0** | **$386.3** | **$429.8** | **$318.8** | **$342.8** | **$453.8** |
| *Effective Tax Rate* | *25.0%* | *25.0%* | *25.0%* | *25.0%* | *25.0%* | *25.0%* |
| | | | | | | |
| Weighted Avg. Diluted Shares | 100.0 | 100.0 | 100.0 | 100.0 | 100.0 | 100.0 |
| **Diluted EPS** | **$3.30** | **$3.86** | **$4.30** | **$3.19** | **$3.43** | **$4.54** |

= Prior Fiscal Year + Current Stub - Prior Stub
= $4,500 million + $3,600 million - $3,375 million

**Adjusted Income Statement**    After entering the reported income statement, we made adjustments in the "Adjusted Income Statement" section, as appropriate, for those items we determined to be non-recurring (see Exhibit 1.47), namely:

- $25 million pre-tax gain on the sale of a non-core business in Q4 2018

- $30 million pre-tax inventory valuation charge in Q2 2019 related to product obsolescence

- $15 million pre-tax restructuring charge in Q3 2019 related to severance costs

As the adjustments for non-recurring items relied on judgment, we carefully footnoted our assumptions and sources.

**EXHIBIT 1.47**    Adjusted Income Statement Section

Inventory valuation charge ("write-off")

Gain on sale of non-core business ("asset sale")

Restructuring charge

*($ in millions, except per share data)*

**Adjusted Income Statement**

| | Fiscal Year Ending December 31, | | | Prior Stub | Current Stub | LTM |
|---|---|---|---|---|---|---|
| | **2016A** | **2017A** | **2018A** | **9/30/2018** | **9/30/2019** | **9/30/2019** |
| Reported Gross Profit | $1,300.0 | $1,450.0 | $1,575.0 | $1,175.0 | $1,250.0 | $1,650.0 |
| Non-recurring Items in COGS | - | - | - | - | 30.0 | 30.0 (1) |
| **Adj. Gross Profit** | **$1,300.0** | **$1,450.0** | **$1,575.0** | **$1,175.0** | **$1,280.0** | **$1,680.0** |
| % margin | 34.7% | 34.9% | 35.0% | 34.8% | 35.6% | 35.6% |
| | | | | | | |
| Reported EBIT | $550.0 | $620.0 | $675.0 | $500.0 | $530.0 | $705.0 |
| Non-recurring Items in COGS | - | - | - | - | 30.0 | 30.0 |
| Other Non-recurring Items | - | - | (25.0) | - | 15.0 | (10.0) (2), (3) |
| **Adjusted EBIT** | **$550.0** | **$620.0** | **$650.0** | **$500.0** | **$575.0** | **$725.0** |
| % margin | 14.7% | 14.9% | 14.4% | 14.8% | 16.0% | 15.3% |
| | | | | | | |
| Depreciation & Amortization | 155.0 | 165.0 | 175.0 | 125.0 | 125.0 | 175.0 |
| **Adjusted EBITDA** | **$705.0** | **$785.0** | **$825.0** | **$625.0** | **$700.0** | **$900.0** |
| % margin | 18.8% | 18.9% | 18.3% | 18.5% | 19.4% | 19.0% |
| | | | | | | |
| Reported Net Income | $330.0 | $386.3 | $429.8 | $318.8 | $342.8 | $453.8 |
| Non-recurring Items in COGS | - | - | - | - | 30.0 | 30.0 |
| Other Non-recurring Items | - | - | (25.0) | - | 15.0 | (10.0) |
| Non-operating Non-rec. Items | - | - | - | - | - | - |
| Tax Adjustment | - | - | 6.3 | - | (11.3) | (5.0) |
| **Adjusted Net Income** | **$330.0** | **$386.3** | **$411.0** | **$318.8** | **$376.5** | **$468.8** |
| % margin | 8.8% | 9.3% | 9.1% | 9.4% | 10.5% | 9.9% |
| | | | | | | |
| Adjusted Diluted EPS | $3.30 | $3.86 | $4.11 | $3.19 | $3.77 | $4.69 |

**Notes**

(1) In Q2 2019, Gasparro Corp. recorded a $30 million pre-tax inventory valuation charge related to product obsolescence (see Q2 2019 10-Q MD&A, page 14).

(2) In Q4 2018, Gasparro Corp. realized a $25 million pre-tax gain on the sale of a non-core business (see 2018 10-K MD&A, page 45).

(3) In Q3 2019, Gasparro Corp. recognized $15 million of pre-tax restructuring costs in connection with the closure of a manufacturing facility (see Q3 2019 10-Q MD&A, page 15).

= Negative adjustment for pre-tax gain on asset sale × Marginal tax rate
= - ($25) million × 25%

= Add-back for pre-tax inventory and restructuring charges × Marginal tax rate
= - ($30 million + $15 million) × 25%

As shown in Exhibit 1.47, we entered the $30 million non-recurring product obsolescence charge as an add-back in the non-recurring items in COGS line item under the "Current Stub 9/30/2019" column heading. We also added back the $15 million restructuring charge in the other non-recurring items line under the "Current Stub 9/30/2019" column. The $25 million gain on asset sale, on the other hand, was backed out of reported earnings (entered as a negative value) under the "2018A" column. These calculations resulted in adjusted LTM EBIT and EBITDA of $725 million and $900 million, respectively.

To calculate LTM adjusted net income after adding back the full non-recurring charges of $30 million and $15 million, respectively, and subtracting the full $25 million gain on sale amount, we made tax adjustments in the tax adjustment line item. These adjustments were calculated by multiplying each full amount by Gasparro's marginal tax rate of 25%. This resulted in adjusted net income and diluted EPS of $468.8 million and $4.69, respectively. The adjusted financial statistics then served as the basis for calculating the various LTM profitability ratios, credit statistics, and trading multiples used in the benchmarking analysis (see Exhibits 1.53, 1.54, and 1.55).

**Cash Flow Statement Data**   Gasparro's historical *cash from operations,* D&A, and capex were entered directly into the input page as they appeared in the cash flow statement from its 10-K and 10-Q with adjustments made as necessary for non-recurring items (see Exhibit 1.48). We also calculated free cash flow (FCF) by subtracting capex from cash from operations for each reporting period. This enabled us to calculate a FCF-to-sales margin of 6.7% and FCF per share of $3.15 for LTM 9/30/2019.

**EXHIBIT 1.48**   Cash Flow Statement Data Section

*($ in millions, except per share data)*

| Cash Flow Statement Data | | | | | | |
|---|---|---|---|---|---|---|
| | Fiscal Year Ending December 31, | | | Prior Stub 9/30/2018 | Current Stub 9/30/2019 | LTM 9/30/2019 |
| | 2016A | 2017A | 2018A | | | |
| Cash From Operations | 400.0 | 450.0 | 500.0 | 360.0 | 380.0 | 520.0 |
| Capital Expenditures | 170.0 | 185.0 | 200.0 | 150.0 | 155.0 | 205.0 |
| % sales | 4.5% | 4.5% | 4.4% | 4.4% | 4.3% | 4.3% |
| **Free Cash Flow** | **$230.0** | **$265.0** | **$300.0** | **$210.0** | **$225.0** | **$315.0** |
| % margin | 6.1% | 6.4% | 6.7% | 6.2% | 6.3% | 6.7% |
| **FCF / Share** | **$2.30** | **$2.65** | **$3.00** | **$2.10** | **$2.25** | **$3.15** |
| | | | | | | |
| Depreciation & Amortization | 155.0 | 165.0 | 175.0 | 125.0 | 125.0 | 175.0 |
| % sales | 4.1% | 4.0% | 3.9% | 3.7% | 3.5% | 3.7% |

### LTM Return on Investment Ratios

**Return on Invested Capital**   For ROIC, we calculated 21.1% (see Exhibit 1.49) by dividing Gasparro's LTM 9/30/2019 adjusted EBIT of $725 million (as calculated in Exhibit 1.47) by the sum of its average net debt and shareholders' equity balances for the periods ending 12/31/2018 and 9/30/2019 ($725 million / (($1,875 million − $75 million + $1,600 million) + ($1,850 million − $100 million + $1,725 million) / 2)).

**Return on Equity**   For ROE, we calculated 28.2% by dividing Gasparro's LTM 9/30/2019 adjusted net income of $468.8 million (as calculated in Exhibit 1.47) by its average shareholders' equity balance for the periods ending 12/31/2018 and 9/30/2019 (($1,600 million + $1,725 million) / 2).

**Return on Assets**   For ROA, we calculated 9.5% by dividing Gasparro's LTM 9/30/2019 adjusted net income of $468.8 million by its average total assets for the periods ending 12/31/2018 and 9/30/2019 (($4,825 million + $5,000 million) / 2).

**Dividend Yield**   To calculate dividend yield, we annualized Gasparro's dividend payment of $0.25 per share for the most recent quarter (see Exhibit 1.41), which implied an annual dividend payment of $1.00 per share. We checked recent press releases to ensure there were no changes in dividend policy after the filing of the 10-Q. The implied annualized dividend payment of $1.00 per share was then divided by Gasparro's current share price of $50.00 to calculate an implied annual dividend yield of 2%.

**EXHIBIT 1.49**   LTM Return on Investment Ratios Section

| LTM Return on Investment Ratios | |
|---|---|
| Return on Invested Capital | 21.1% |
| Return on Equity | 28.2% |
| Return on Assets | 9.5% |
| Implied Annual Dividend Per Share | 2.0% |

= LTM Adjusted EBIT / Average (Total Debt$_{2018}$ - Cash$_{2018}$ + Shareholders' Equity$_{2018}$, Total Debt$_{9/30/2019}$ - Cash$_{9/30/2019}$ + Shareholders' Equity$_{9/30/2019}$)
= $725 million / (($1,875 million - $75 million + $1,600 million) + ($1,850 million - $100 million + $1,725 million) / 2)

= LTM Adjusted Net Income / Average (Shareholders' Equity$_{2018}$, Shareholders' Equity$_{9/30/2019}$)
= $468.8 million / ($1,600 million + $1,725 million) / 2

= LTM Adjusted Net Income / Average (Total Assets$_{2018}$, Total Assets$_{9/30/2019}$)
= $468.8 million / ($4,825 million + $5,000 million) / 2

= (Quarterly Dividend × 4) / Current Share Price
= ($0.25 × 4) / $50.00

## LTM Credit Statistics

**Debt-to-Total Capitalization**   For debt-to-total capitalization, we divided Gasparro's total debt of $1,850 million as of 9/30/2019 by the sum of its total debt and shareholders' equity for the same period ($1,850 million + $1,725 million). This provided a debt-to-total capitalization ratio of 51.7% (see Exhibit 1.50).

**Total Debt-to-EBITDA**   For total debt-to-EBITDA, we divided Gasparro's total debt of $1,850 million by its LTM 9/30/2019 adjusted EBITDA of $900 million. This provided a total leverage multiple of 2.1x (1.9x on a net debt basis).

**EBITDA-to-Interest Expense**   For EBITDA-to-interest expense, we divided Gasparro's LTM 9/30/2019 adjusted EBITDA of $900 million by its interest expense of $100 million for the same period. This provided a ratio of 9.0x. We also calculated the company's (EBITDA – capex)-to-interest expense and EBIT-to-interest expense ratios at 7.0x and 7.3x, respectively.

**EXHIBIT 1.50**   LTM Credit Statistics Section

| LTM Credit Statistics | |
| --- | --- |
| Debt / Total Capitalization | 51.7% |
| Total Debt / EBITDA | 2.1x |
| Net Debt / EBITDA | 1.9x |
| EBITDA / Interest Expense | 9.0x |
| (EBITDA-capex) / Interest Expense | 7.0x |
| EBIT / Interest Expense | 7.3x |

= Total Debt$_{9/30/2019}$ / (Total Debt$_{9/30/2019}$ + Shareholders' Equity$_{9/30/2019}$)
= $1,850 million / ($1,850 million + $1,725 million)

= Total Debt$_{9/30/2019}$ / LTM Adjusted EBITDA
= $1,850 million / $900 million

= (Total Debt$_{9/30/2019}$ - Cash$_{9/30/2019}$) / LTM Adjusted EBITDA
= ($1,850 million - $100 million) / $900 million

= LTM Adjusted EBITDA / LTM Interest Expense
= $900 million / $100 million

## Trading Multiples

In the "Trading Multiples" section, we entered consensus estimates for Gasparro's 2019E, 2020E, and 2021E sales, EBITDA, EBIT, and EPS (see Exhibit 1.51). These estimates, along with the calculated enterprise and equity values, were used to calculate forward trading multiples. Gasparro's LTM adjusted financial data is also linked to this section and used to calculate trailing trading multiples.

**Enterprise Value Multiples**   For enterprise value-to-LTM EBITDA, we divided Gasparro's enterprise value of $6,750 million by its LTM 9/30/2019 adjusted EBITDA of $900 million, providing a multiple of 7.5x. For EV/2019E EBITDA, we divided the same enterprise value of $6,750 million by Gasparro's 2019E EBITDA of $950 million to calculate a multiple of 7.1x. This same methodology was used for EV/2020E EBITDA and EV/2021E EBITDA, as well as for the trailing and forward sales and EBIT enterprise value multiples.

**Price-to-Earnings Ratio**   The approach for calculating P/E mirrors that for EV/EBITDA. We divided Gasparro's current share price of $50.00 by its LTM, 2019E, 2020E, and 2021E EPS of $4.69, $5.10, $5.50, and $5.75, respectively. These calculations provided P/E ratios of 10.7x, 9.8x, 9.1x, and 8.7x respectively.

**Free Cash Flow Yield**   Free cash flow (FCF) generation is an important metric for determining valuation. FCF is an indicator of a company's ability to return capital to shareholders or repay debt, which accrues to equity holders. Therefore, many investors focus on FCF yield, calculated as (cash from operations – capex) / market capitalization or FCF per share / share price. Gasparro's FCF yield for LTM, 2019E, 2020E, and 2021E is 6.3%, 7.5%, 8.3%, and 9.1%, respectively.

**EXHIBIT 1.51**  Trading Multiples Section

*($ in millions, except per share data)*

**Trading Multiples**

|  | LTM 9/30/2019 | NFY 2019E | NFY+1 2020E | NFY+2 2021E |
|---|---|---|---|---|
| EV/Sales | 1.4x | 1.4x | 1.3x | 1.2x |
| Metric | $4,725.0 | $5,000.0 | $5,350.0 | $5,625.0 |
| EV/ EBITDA | 7.5x | 7.1x | 6.6x | 6.3x |
| Metric | $900.0 | $950.0 | $1,025.0 | $1,075.0 |
| EV/EBIT | 9.3x | 8.8x | 8.2x | 7.8x |
| Metric | $725.0 | $765.0 | $825.0 | $865.0 |
| P/E | 10.7x | 9.8x | 9.1x | 8.7x |
| Metric | $4.69 | $5.10 | $5.50 | $5.75 |
| *FCF Yield* | 6.3% | 7.5% | 8.3% | 9.1% |
| Metric | $3.15 | $3.75 | $4.15 | $4.55 |

= Enterprise Value / LTM Sales
= $6,750 million / $4,750 million

= Enterprise Value / 2019E EBITDA
= $6,750 million / $950 million

= Current Share Price / 2020 EPS
= $50.00 / $5.50

= 2021E FCF per Share / Current Share Price
= $4.55 / $50.00

## Growth Rates

In the "Growth Rates" section, we calculated Gasparro's historical and estimated growth rates for sales, EBITDA, and EPS for various periods. For historical data, we used the adjusted income statement financials from Exhibit 1.47. As shown in Exhibit 1.52, Gasparro's EPS grew 6.4% over the past year (1-year historical growth) and at an 11.6% CAGR over the past two years (2-year historical compounded growth).

For the forward growth rates, we used consensus estimates from the "Trading Multiples" section. On a forward year basis, Gasparro's expected EPS growth rate for 2018A to 2019E is 24.1%, with an expected 2018A to 2020E CAGR of 15.7%. We sourced Gasparro's long-term EPS growth rate of 12%, which is based on equity research analysts' estimates, from consensus estimates.

**EXHIBIT 1.52**  Growth Rates Section

**Growth Rates**

|  | Sales | EBITDA | FCF | EPS |
|---|---|---|---|---|
| **Historical** | | | | |
| 1-year | 8.4% | 5.1% | 13.2% | 6.4% |
| 2-year CAGR | 9.5% | 8.2% | 14.2% | 11.6% |
| **Estimated** | | | | |
| 1-year | 11.1% | 15.2% | 25.0% | 24.1% |
| 2-year CAGR | 9.0% | 11.5% | 17.6% | 15.7% |
| Long-term | | | | 12.0% |

= 2019E Sales / 2018A Sales - 1
= $5,000 million / $4,500 million - 1

= (2020E EBITDA / 2018A Adjusted EBITDA) ^ (1 / (2020E - 2018A)) - 1
= ($1,025 million / $825 million) ^ (1/2) - 1

## Step IV. Benchmark the Comparable Companies

After completing Steps I through III, we were prepared to perform the benchmarking analysis for ValueCo.

The first two benchmarking output pages focused on the comparables' financial characteristics, enabling us to determine ValueCo's relative position among its peers for key value drivers (see Exhibits 1.53 and 1.54). This benchmarking analysis, in combination with a review of key business characteristics (outlined in Exhibit 1.3), also enabled us to identify ValueCo's closest comparables—in this case, BuyerCo, Gasparro Corp., and Sherman Co. These closest comparables were instrumental in helping to frame the ultimate valuation range.

Similarly, the benchmarking analysis allowed us to identify outliers, such as McMenamin & Co. and Adler Worldwide among others, which were determined to be less relevant due to their profitability and size, respectively. In this case, we did not eliminate the outliers altogether. Rather, we elected to group the comparable companies into three tiers based on subsector and size—Specialty Chemicals, Commodity/Diversified Chemicals, and Small-Cap Chemicals. The companies in the "Specialty Chemicals" group are more similar to ValueCo in terms of key business and financial characteristics and therefore more relevant. The companies in the "Commodity/Diversified Chemicals" and "Small-Cap Chemicals" groups, however, provided further perspective as part of a more thorough analysis.

We used the output page in Exhibit 1.55 to analyze and compare the trading multiples for ValueCo's comparables. As previously discussed, financial performance typically translates directly into valuation (i.e., the top performers tend to receive a premium valuation to their peers, with laggards trading at a discount). Therefore, we focused on the multiples for ValueCo's closest comparables as the basis for framing valuation.

Exhibit 1.55(a) presents a comparable companies output page in a format preferred by certain equity research analysts and equity investors, namely those focused primarily on FCF generation for their valuation and investment decisions.

**EXHIBIT 1.53**  ValueCo Corporation: Benchmarking Analysis – Financial Statistics and Ratios, Page 1

## ValueCo Corporation
### Benchmarking Analysis – Financial Statistics and Ratios, Page 1
($ in millions, except per share data)

| Company | Ticker | Market Valuation: Equity Value | Enterprise Value | LTM Financial Statistics: Sales | Gross Profit | EBITDA | EBIT | Net Income | LTM Profitability Margins: Gross Profit (%) | EBITDA (%) | EBIT (%) | Net Income (%) | Growth Rates Sales Hist. 1-year | Sales Est. 1-year | EBITDA Hist. 1-year | EBITDA Est. 1-year | EPS Hist. 1-year | EPS Est. 1-year | EPS Est. LT |
|---|---|---|---|---|---|---|---|---|---|---|---|---|---|---|---|---|---|---|---|
| ValueCo Corporation | NA | - | - | $3,385 | $1,155 | $700 | $500 | $300 | 34% | 21% | 15% | 9% | 10% | 9% | 15% | 9% | NA | NA | NA |
| **Tier I: Specialty Chemicals** | | | | | | | | | | | | | | | | | | | |
| BuyerCo | BUY | $9,800 | $11,600 | $6,560 | $2,329 | $1,443 | $1,279 | $853 | 36% | 22% | 20% | 13% | 14% | 8% | 22% | 8% | 27% | 9% | 7% |
| Sherman Co. | SHR | 5,600 | 8,101 | 5,895 | 1,945 | 1,047 | 752 | 507 | 33% | 18% | 13% | 9% | 10% | 7% | 10% | 7% | 11% | 11% | 9% |
| Pearl Corp. | PRL | 5,172 | 5,804 | 4,284 | 1,585 | 839 | 625 | 393 | 37% | 20% | 15% | 9% | 10% | 7% | 10% | 7% | 10% | 15% | 11% |
| Gasparro Corp. | JDG | 5,000 | 6,750 | 4,725 | 1,680 | 900 | 725 | 469 | 36% | 19% | 15% | 10% | 8% | 11% | 5% | 15% | 6% | 24% | 12% |
| Kumra Inc. | KUM | 4,852 | 5,345 | 3,187 | 922 | 665 | 506 | 306 | 29% | 21% | 16% | 10% | 10% | 8% | 10% | 8% | 11% | 20% | 10% |
| **Mean** | | | | | | | | | **34%** | **20%** | **16%** | **10%** | **10%** | **8%** | **11%** | **9%** | **13%** | **16%** | **10%** |
| **Median** | | | | | | | | | **36%** | **20%** | **15%** | **10%** | **10%** | **8%** | **10%** | **8%** | **11%** | **15%** | **10%** |
| **Tier II: Commodity / Diversified Chemicals** | | | | | | | | | | | | | | | | | | | |
| Falloon Group | FLN | $7,480 | $11,254 | $11,835 | $3,373 | $1,636 | $1,044 | $563 | 29% | 14% | 9% | 5% | 5% | 4% | 5% | 4% | 5% | 18% | 5% |
| Goodson Corp. | GDS | 4,160 | 5,660 | 4,769 | 1,431 | 763 | 525 | 258 | 30% | 16% | 11% | 5% | 10% | 5% | 10% | 5% | 17% | 16% | 9% |
| Pryor Industries | PRI | 3,926 | 4,166 | 3,682 | 1,178 | 569 | 421 | 275 | 32% | 15% | 11% | 7% | 5% | 5% | 5% | 5% | 2% | 11% | 10% |
| Lanzarone Global | LNZ | 3,230 | 3,823 | 3,712 | 854 | 578 | 430 | 282 | 23% | 16% | 12% | 8% | 5% | 5% | 4% | 5% | 4% | 16% | 8% |
| McMenamin & Co. | MCM | 3,193 | 3,193 | 3,223 | 903 | 355 | 226 | 144 | 28% | 11% | 7% | 4% | 5% | 15% | 5% | 15% | 7% | 20% | 12% |
| **Mean** | | | | | | | | | **28%** | **14%** | **10%** | **6%** | **6%** | **7%** | **6%** | **7%** | **7%** | **16%** | **9%** |
| **Median** | | | | | | | | | **29%** | **15%** | **11%** | **5%** | **5%** | **5%** | **5%** | **5%** | **5%** | **16%** | **9%** |
| **Tier III: Small-Cap Chemicals** | | | | | | | | | | | | | | | | | | | |
| Momper & Co. | MOMP | $2,240 | $2,921 | $2,077 | $457 | $378 | $295 | $158 | 22% | 18% | 14% | 8% | 5% | 11% | 5% | 11% | 7% | 8% | 5% |
| Adler Worldwide | ADL | 1,217 | 1,463 | 1,550 | 387 | 245 | 183 | 108 | 25% | 16% | 12% | 7% | 5% | 5% | 5% | 5% | 7% | 8% | 7% |
| Schachter & Sons | STM | 1,125 | 1,674 | 1,703 | 426 | 238 | 170 | 92 | 25% | 14% | 10% | 5% | 11% | 15% | 11% | 15% | 16% | 19% | 11% |
| Girshin Holdings | MGP | 1,035 | 1,298 | 1,606 | 273 | 177 | 112 | 63 | 17% | 11% | 7% | 4% | 5% | 15% | 5% | 15% | 11% | 15% | 8% |
| Crespin International | MCR | 872 | 1,222 | 1,443 | 390 | 190 | 133 | 74 | 27% | 13% | 9% | 5% | 5% | 15% | 4% | 14% | 5% | 10% | 6% |
| **Mean** | | | | | | | | | **23%** | **14%** | **10%** | **6%** | **6%** | **12%** | **6%** | **12%** | **9%** | **12%** | **7%** |
| **Median** | | | | | | | | | **25%** | **14%** | **10%** | **5%** | **5%** | **15%** | **5%** | **14%** | **7%** | **10%** | **7%** |
| **Overall** | | | | | | | | | | | | | | | | | | | |
| **Mean** | | | | | | | | | **29%** | **16%** | **12%** | **7%** | **8%** | **9%** | **8%** | **9%** | **10%** | **15%** | **9%** |
| **Median** | | | | | | | | | **29%** | **16%** | **12%** | **7%** | **5%** | **8%** | **5%** | **8%** | **7%** | **15%** | **9%** |
| **High** | | | | | | | | | **37%** | **22%** | **20%** | **13%** | **14%** | **15%** | **22%** | **15%** | **27%** | **24%** | **12%** |
| **Low** | | | | | | | | | **17%** | **11%** | **7%** | **4%** | **5%** | **4%** | **4%** | **4%** | **2%** | **8%** | **5%** |

Source: Company filings, Bloomberg, Consensus Estimates
Note: Last twelve months data based on September 30, 2019. Estimated annual financial data based on a calendar year.

## ValueCo Corporation

**Benchmarking Analysis – Financial Statistics and Ratios, Page 2**
*($ in millions, except per share data)*

| Company | Ticker | General | | Return on Investment | | | | LTM Leverage Ratios | | | LTM Coverage Ratios | | | Credit Ratings | |
|---|---|---|---|---|---|---|---|---|---|---|---|---|---|---|---|
| | | FYE | Predicted Beta | ROIC (%) | ROE (%) | ROA (%) | Implied Div. Yield (%) | Debt/Tot. Cap. (%) | Debt/EBITDA (x) | Net Debt/EBITDA (x) | EBITDA/Int. Exp. (x) | EBITDA - Cpx/Int. (x) | EBIT/Int. Exp. (x) | Moody's | S&P |
| ValueCo Corporation | NA | Dec-31 | NA | 10% | 9% | 5% | NA | 30% | 2.1x | 1.9x | 7.0x | 5.5x | 5.0x | NA | NA |
| **Tier I: Specialty Chemicals** | | | | | | | | | | | | | | | |
| BuyerCo | BUY | Dec-31 | 1.35 | 30% | 35% | 11% | 0% | 47% | 1.5x | 1.2x | 10.1x | 8.8x | 9.0x | Baa3 | BBB- |
| Sherman Co. | SHR | Dec-31 | 1.46 | 16% | 22% | 7% | 2% | 57% | 3.0x | 2.4x | 13.8x | 10.7x | 9.9x | Ba1 | BB+ |
| Pearl Corp. | PRL | Dec-31 | 1.28 | 20% | 17% | 9% | 0% | 37% | 1.8x | 0.8x | 8.4x | 7.1x | 6.2x | Ba1 | BB+ |
| Gasparro Corp. | JDG | Dec-31 | 1.30 | 21% | 28% | 10% | 2% | 52% | 2.1x | 1.9x | 9.0x | 7.0x | 7.3x | Ba2 | BB |
| Kumra Inc. | KUM | Dec-31 | 1.50 | 17% | 12% | 7% | 2% | 25% | 1.3x | 0.6x | 11.0x | 8.7x | 8.4x | Ba1 | BB+ |
| **Mean** | | | 1.38 | 21% | 23% | 9% | 1% | 44% | 1.9x | 1.4x | 10.5x | 8.4x | 8.2x | | |
| **Median** | | | 1.35 | 20% | 22% | 9% | 2% | 47% | 1.8x | 1.2x | 10.1x | 8.7x | 8.4x | | |
| **Tier II: Commodity / Diversified Chemicals** | | | | | | | | | | | | | | | |
| Falloon Group | FLN | Dec-31 | 1.39 | 16% | 17% | 5% | 3% | 55% | 2.5x | 2.2x | 5.7x | 3.8x | 3.6x | Ba3 | BB |
| Goodson Corp. | GDS | Dec-31 | 1.53 | 15% | 13% | 5% | 1% | 52% | 2.9x | 2.0x | 4.2x | 3.0x | 2.9x | Ba2 | BB- |
| Pryor Industries | PRI | Dec-31 | 1.26 | 14% | 10% | 6% | 1% | 19% | 1.1x | 0.4x | 11.1x | 8.9x | 8.2x | Ba2 | BB |
| Lanzarone Global | LNZ | Dec-31 | 1.28 | 17% | 14% | 7% | 0% | 27% | 1.3x | 1.0x | 10.7x | 7.9x | 7.9x | Ba3 | BB- |
| McMenamin & Co. | MCM | Dec-31 | 1.34 | 12% | 8% | 5% | 1% | 18% | 1.2x | 0.0x | 10.6x | 8.2x | 6.7x | Ba2 | BB- |
| **Mean** | | | 1.36 | 15% | 12% | 6% | 1% | 34% | 1.8x | 1.1x | 8.5x | 6.4x | 5.9x | | |
| **Median** | | | 1.34 | 15% | 13% | 5% | 1% | 27% | 1.3x | 1.0x | 10.6x | 7.9x | 6.7x | | |
| **Tier III: Small-Cap Chemicals** | | | | | | | | | | | | | | | |
| Momper & Co. | MOMP | Dec-31 | 1.50 | 19% | 17% | 7% | 4% | 50% | 2.6x | 1.8x | 4.5x | 3.7x | 3.5x | Ba1 | BB |
| Adler Worldwide | ADL | Dec-31 | 1.46 | 12% | 8% | 4% | 4% | 22% | 1.6x | 1.0x | 6.2x | 5.0x | 4.7x | Ba2 | BB |
| Schachter & Sons | STM | Dec-31 | 1.40 | 12% | 10% | 4% | 1% | 38% | 2.5x | 2.3x | 5.0x | 3.2x | 3.6x | Ba3 | BB- |
| Girshin Holdings | MGP | Dec-31 | 1.55 | 13% | 11% | 5% | 3% | 34% | 1.8x | 1.4x | 6.3x | 4.7x | 4.0x | Ba3 | BB- |
| Crespin International | MCR | Dec-31 | 1.70 | 10% | 8% | 5% | 0% | 28% | 2.1x | 1.8x | 5.7x | 4.4x | 3.9x | Ba3 | B+ |
| **Mean** | | | 1.52 | 13% | 11% | 5% | 2% | 35% | 2.1x | 1.7x | 5.5x | 4.2x | 3.9x | | |
| **Median** | | | 1.50 | 12% | 10% | 5% | 3% | 34% | 2.1x | 1.8x | 5.7x | 4.4x | 3.9x | | |
| **Overall** | | | | | | | | | | | | | | | |
| **Mean** | | | 1.42 | 16% | 15% | 7% | 1% | 37% | 2.0x | 1.4x | 8.2x | 6.3x | 6.0x | | |
| **Median** | | | 1.40 | 16% | 13% | 6% | 1% | 37% | 1.8x | 1.4x | 8.4x | 7.0x | 6.2x | | |
| **High** | | | 1.70 | 30% | 35% | 11% | 4% | 57% | 3.0x | 2.4x | 13.8x | 10.7x | 9.9x | | |
| **Low** | | | 1.26 | 10% | 8% | 4% | 0% | 18% | 1.1x | 0.0x | 4.2x | 3.0x | 2.9x | | |

*Source: Company filings; Bloomberg, Consensus Estimates*
Note: Last twelve months data based on September 30, 2019. Estimated annual financial data based on a calendar year.

**EXHIBIT 1.55** ValueCo Corporation: Comparable Companies Analysis—Trading Multiples Output Page

## ValueCo Corporation
### Comparable Companies Analysis
($ in millions, except per share data)

| Company | Ticker | Current Share Price | % of 52-wk. High | Equity Value | Enterprise Value | Enterprise Value / LTM Sales | 2019E Sales | 2020E Sales | LTM EBITDA | 2019E EBITDA | 2020E EBITDA | LTM EBIT | 2019E EBIT | 2020E EBIT | LTM EBITDA Margin | Total Debt / EBITDA | Price / LTM EPS | 2019E EPS | 2020E EPS | LT EPS Growth |
|---|---|---|---|---|---|---|---|---|---|---|---|---|---|---|---|---|---|---|---|---|
| **Tier I: Specialty Chemicals** | | | | | | | | | | | | | | | | | | | | |
| BuyerCo | BUY | $70.00 | 91% | $9,800 | $11,600 | 1.8x | 1.7x | 1.6x | 8.0x | 7.8x | 7.3x | 9.1x | 8.8x | 8.2x | 22% | 1.5x | 11.5x | 11.1x | 10.3x | 7% |
| Sherman Co. | SHR | 40.00 | 76% | 5,600 | 8,101 | 1.4x | 1.4x | 1.3x | 7.7x | 7.7x | 7.2x | 10.8x | 10.7x | 10.1x | 18% | 3.0x | 11.0x | 10.6x | 9.7x | 9% |
| Pearl Corp. | PRL | 68.50 | 95% | 5,172 | 5,856 | 1.4x | 1.4x | 1.3x | 7.0x | 7.0x | 6.5x | 9.4x | 9.4x | 8.7x | 20% | 1.8x | 13.1x | 12.2x | 11.1x | 11% |
| Gasparro Corp. | JDG | 50.00 | 80% | 5,000 | 6,750 | 1.4x | 1.4x | 1.3x | 7.5x | 7.1x | 6.6x | 9.3x | 8.8x | 8.2x | 19% | 2.1x | 10.7x | 9.8x | 9.1x | 12% |
| Kumra Inc. | KUM | 52.50 | 88% | 4,852 | 5,345 | 1.7x | 1.7x | 1.5x | 8.0x | 7.9x | 7.4x | 10.6x | 10.4x | 9.7x | 21% | 1.3x | 15.8x | 13.6x | 11.8x | 10% |
| **Mean** | | | | | | 1.5x | 1.5x | 1.4x | 7.7x | 7.5x | 7.0x | 9.8x | 9.6x | 9.0x | 20% | 1.9x | 12.4x | 11.5x | 10.4x | 10% |
| **Median** | | | | | | 1.4x | 1.4x | 1.3x | 7.7x | 7.7x | 7.2x | 9.4x | 9.4x | 8.7x | 20% | 1.8x | 11.5x | 11.1x | 10.3x | 10% |
| **Tier II: Commodity / Diversified Chemicals** | | | | | | | | | | | | | | | | | | | | |
| Falloon Group | FLN | $31.00 | 87% | $7,480 | $11,254 | 1.0x | 1.0x | 0.9x | 6.9x | 7.0x | 6.7x | 10.8x | 11.0x | 10.5x | 14% | 2.5x | 13.3x | 12.4x | 10.8x | 5% |
| Goodson Corp. | GDS | 64.00 | 83% | 4,160 | 5,660 | 1.2x | 1.2x | 1.1x | 7.4x | 7.5x | 7.2x | 10.8x | 11.0x | 10.4x | 16% | 2.9x | 16.1x | 15.4x | 13.5x | 9% |
| Pryor Industries | PRI | 79.00 | 88% | 3,926 | 4,166 | 1.1x | 1.2x | 1.1x | 7.3x | 7.4x | 7.1x | 9.9x | 10.1x | 9.6x | 15% | 1.1x | 14.3x | 13.9x | 12.7x | 10% |
| Lanzarone Global | LNZ | 32.25 | 95% | 3,230 | 3,823 | 1.0x | 1.0x | 1.0x | 6.6x | 6.7x | 6.4x | 8.9x | 9.0x | 8.6x | 16% | 1.3x | 11.5x | 10.7x | 9.7x | 8% |
| McMenamin & Co. | MCM | 33.50 | 80% | 3,193 | 3,193 | 1.0x | 0.9x | 0.8x | 9.0x | 8.4x | 7.5x | 14.2x | 13.1x | 11.8x | 11% | 1.2x | 22.2x | 19.3x | 16.8x | 12% |
| **Mean** | | | | | | 1.1x | 1.1x | 1.0x | 7.4x | 7.4x | 7.0x | 10.9x | 10.8x | 10.2x | 14% | 1.8x | 15.5x | 14.3x | 12.7x | 9% |
| **Median** | | | | | | 1.0x | 1.0x | 1.0x | 7.3x | 7.4x | 7.1x | 10.8x | 11.0x | 10.4x | 15% | 1.3x | 14.3x | 13.9x | 12.7x | 9% |
| **Tier III: Small-Cap Chemicals** | | | | | | | | | | | | | | | | | | | | |
| S. Momper & Co. | MOMP | $28.00 | 95% | $2,240 | $2,921 | 1.4x | 1.4x | 1.2x | 7.7x | 7.4x | 6.7x | 9.9x | 9.5x | 8.6x | 18% | 2.6x | 14.2x | 14.4x | 13.4x | 5% |
| Adler Worldwide | ADL | 10.50 | 80% | 1,217 | 1,463 | 0.9x | 1.0x | 0.9x | 6.0x | 6.1x | 5.8x | 8.0x | 8.1x | 7.7x | 16% | 1.6x | 11.3x | 12.2x | 11.3x | 7% |
| Schachter & Sons | STM | 4.50 | 89% | 1,125 | 1,674 | 1.0x | 0.9x | 0.8x | 7.0x | 6.5x | 5.7x | 9.8x | 9.1x | 7.9x | 14% | 2.5x | 12.2x | 11.3x | 10.0x | 11% |
| Girshin Holdings | MGP | 50.00 | 67% | 1,035 | 1,298 | 0.8x | 0.8x | 0.7x | 7.3x | 6.8x | 6.1x | 11.5x | 10.7x | 9.7x | 11% | 1.8x | 16.5x | 15.6x | 14.2x | 8% |
| Crespin International | MCR | 27.00 | 80% | 872 | 1,222 | 0.8x | 0.8x | 0.7x | 6.4x | 6.0x | 5.4x | 9.2x | 8.6x | 7.7x | 13% | 2.1x | 11.8x | 11.6x | 10.5x | 6% |
| **Mean** | | | | | | 1.0x | 1.0x | 0.9x | 6.9x | 6.6x | 5.9x | 9.7x | 9.2x | 8.3x | 14% | 2.1x | 13.2x | 13.0x | 11.9x | 7% |
| **Median** | | | | | | 0.9x | 0.9x | 0.8x | 7.0x | 6.5x | 5.8x | 9.8x | 9.1x | 7.9x | 14% | 2.1x | 12.2x | 12.2x | 11.3x | 7% |
| **Overall** | | | | | | | | | | | | | | | | | | | | |
| **Mean** | | | | | | 1.2x | 1.2x | 1.1x | 7.3x | 7.2x | 6.6x | 10.1x | 9.9x | 9.2x | 16% | 2.0x | 13.7x | 12.9x | 11.7x | 9% |
| **Median** | | | | | | 1.1x | 1.2x | 1.1x | 7.3x | 7.1x | 6.7x | 9.9x | 9.5x | 8.7x | 16% | 1.8x | 13.1x | 12.2x | 11.1x | 9% |
| **High** | | | | | | 1.8x | 1.7x | 1.6x | 9.0x | 8.4x | 7.5x | 14.2x | 13.1x | 11.8x | 22% | 3.0x | 22.2x | 19.3x | 16.8x | 12% |
| **Low** | | | | | | 0.8x | 0.8x | 0.7x | 6.0x | 6.0x | 5.4x | 8.0x | 8.1x | 7.7x | 11% | 1.1x | 10.7x | 9.8x | 9.1x | 5% |

Source: Company filings, Bloomberg, Consensus Estimates
Note: Last twelve months data based on September 30, 2019. Estimated annual financial data based on a calendar year.

# ValueCo Corporation
## Comparable Companies Analysis
*($ in millions, except per share data)*

| Company | Ticker | Current Share Price | % of 52-wk. High | Equity Value | Enterprise Value | EV / EBITDA | | 2019E EBITDA Margin | LTM Debt / EBITDA | LTM Int Exp / EBITDA | P / E | | LT EPS Growth | Div Yield | FCF Yield | |
|---|---|---|---|---|---|---|---|---|---|---|---|---|---|---|---|---|
| | | | | | | 2019E | 2020E | | | | 2019E | 2020E | | | 2019E | 2020E |
| **Tier I: Specialty Chemicals** | | | | | | | | | | | | | | | | |
| BuyerCo | BUY | $70.00 | 91% | $9,800 | $11,600 | 7.8x | 7.3x | 22% | 1.5x | 10.1x | 11.1x | 10.3x | 7% | 0.0% | 8.6% | 8.9% |
| Sherman Co. | SHR | $40.00 | 76% | 5,600 | 8,101 | 7.7x | 7.2x | 18% | 3.0x | 13.8x | 10.6x | 9.7x | 9% | 1.8% | 10.4% | 11.5% |
| Pearl Corp. | PRL | $68.50 | 95% | 5,172 | 5,804 | 6.9x | 6.5x | 20% | 1.8x | 8.4x | 12.2x | 11.1x | 11% | 0.0% | 9.4% | 10.4% |
| Gasparro Corp. | JDG | $50.00 | 80% | 5,000 | 6,750 | 7.1x | 6.6x | 19% | 2.1x | 9.0x | 9.8x | 9.1x | 12% | 2.0% | 7.5% | 8.3% |
| Kumra Inc. | KUM | $52.50 | 88% | 4,852 | 5,345 | 7.9x | 7.4x | 21% | 1.3x | 11.0x | 13.6x | 11.8x | 10% | 1.5% | 7.1% | 7.8% |
| **Mean** | | | | | | 7.5x | 7.0x | 20% | 1.9x | 10.5x | 11.5x | 10.4x | 10% | 1.1% | 8.6% | 9.4% |
| **Median** | | | | | | 7.7x | 7.2x | 20% | 1.8x | 10.1x | 11.1x | 10.3x | 10% | 1.5% | 8.6% | 8.9% |
| **Tier II: Commodity / Diversified Chemicals** | | | | | | | | | | | | | | | | |
| Falloon Group | FLN | $31.00 | 87% | $7,480 | $11,254 | 7.0x | 6.7x | 14% | 2.5x | 5.7x | 12.4x | 10.8x | 5% | 2.6% | 8.4% | 9.2% |
| Goodson Corp. | GDS | $64.00 | 83% | 4,160 | 5,660 | 7.5x | 7.2x | 16% | 2.9x | 4.2x | 15.4x | 13.5x | 9% | 1.0% | 6.8% | 7.4% |
| Pryor Industries | PRI | $79.00 | 88% | 3,926 | 4,166 | 7.4x | 7.1x | 15% | 1.1x | 11.1x | 13.9x | 12.7x | 10% | 0.8% | 8.1% | 8.8% |
| Lanzarone Global | LNZ | $32.25 | 95% | 3,230 | 3,823 | 6.7x | 6.4x | 16% | 1.3x | 10.7x | 10.7x | 9.7x | 8% | 0.0% | 8.9% | 9.7% |
| McMenamin & Co. | MCM | $33.50 | 80% | 3,193 | 3,193 | 8.4x | 7.5x | 11% | 1.2x | 10.6x | 19.3x | 16.8x | 12% | 1.2% | 6.2% | 6.8% |
| **Mean** | | | | | | 7.4x | 7.0x | 14% | 1.8x | 8.5x | 14.3x | 12.7x | 9% | 1.1% | 7.7% | 8.4% |
| **Median** | | | | | | 7.4x | 7.1x | 15% | 1.3x | 10.1x | 13.9x | 12.7x | 9% | 1.0% | 8.1% | 8.8% |
| **Tier III: Small-Cap Chemicals** | | | | | | | | | | | | | | | | |
| Momper & Co. | MOMP | $28.00 | 95% | $2,240 | $2,921 | 7.4x | 6.7x | 18% | 2.6x | 4.5x | 14.4x | 13.4x | 5% | 3.7% | 8.0% | 8.7% |
| Adler Worldwide | ADL | $10.50 | 80% | 1,217 | 1,463 | 6.1x | 5.8x | 16% | 1.6x | 6.2x | 12.2x | 11.3x | 7% | 4.0% | 9.6% | 10.5% |
| Schachter & Sons | STM | $4.50 | 89% | 1,125 | 1,674 | 6.5x | 5.7x | 14% | 2.5x | 5.0x | 11.3x | 10.0x | 11% | 0.8% | 6.7% | 7.3% |
| Girshin Holdings | MGP | $50.00 | 67% | 1,035 | 1,298 | 6.8x | 6.1x | 11% | 1.8x | 6.3x | 15.6x | 14.2x | 8% | 2.8% | 8.1% | 8.9% |
| Crespin International | MCR | $27.00 | 80% | 872 | 1,222 | 6.0x | 5.4x | 13% | 2.1x | 5.7x | 11.6x | 10.5x | 6% | 0.0% | 10.4% | 11.3% |
| **Mean** | | | | | | 6.6x | 5.9x | 14% | 2.1x | 5.5x | 13.0x | 11.9x | 7% | 2.2% | 8.6% | 9.3% |
| **Median** | | | | | | 6.5x | 5.8x | 14% | 2.1x | 5.7x | 12.2x | 11.3x | 7% | 2.8% | 8.1% | 8.9% |
| **Overall** | | | | | | | | | | | | | | | | |
| **Mean** | | | | | | 7.2x | 6.6x | 16% | 2.0x | 8.2x | 12.9x | 11.7x | 9% | 1.5% | 8.3% | 9.0% |
| **Median** | | | | | | 7.1x | 6.7x | 16% | 1.8x | 8.4x | 12.2x | 11.1x | 9% | 1.2% | 8.1% | 8.9% |
| High | | | | | | 8.4x | 7.5x | 22% | 3.0x | 13.8x | 19.3x | 16.8x | 12% | 4.0% | 10.4% | 11.5% |
| Low | | | | | | 6.0x | 5.4x | 11% | 1.1x | 4.2x | 9.8x | 9.1x | 5% | 0.0% | 6.2% | 6.8% |

*Source: Company filings, Bloomberg, Consensus Estimates*

## Step V. Determine Valuation

The means and medians for the Specialty Chemicals comparables universe helped establish an initial valuation range for ValueCo, with the highs and lows providing further perspective. We also looked to the Commodity/Diversified Chemicals and Small-Cap Chemicals comparables for peripheral guidance. To fine-tune the range, however, we focused on those comparables deemed closest to ValueCo in terms of business and financial profile—namely, BuyerCo, Gasparro Corp., and Sherman Co., as well as Goodson Corp. and Momper & Co. to a lesser extent.

Companies in ValueCo's sector tend to trade on the basis of forward EV/EBITDA multiples. Therefore, we framed our valuation of ValueCo on the basis of the forward EV/EBITDA multiples for its closest comparables, selecting ranges of 6.75x to 7.75x 2019E EBITDA, and 6.5x to 7.5x 2020E EBITDA. We also looked at the implied valuation based on a range of 7.0x to 8.0x LTM EBITDA.

**EXHIBIT 1.56**    ValueCo Corporation: Implied Valuation Range – Enterprise Value

**ValueCo Corporation**
**Implied Valuation Range**
*($ in millions, last twelve months ending 9/30/2019)*

| EBITDA | Metric | Multiple Range | | | Implied Enterprise Value | | |
|--------|--------|------|---|------|---------|---|---------|
| LTM | $700.0 | 7.00x | – | 8.00x | $4,900.0 | – | $5,600.0 |
| 2019E | 725.0 | 6.75x | – | 7.75x | 4,893.8 | – | 5,618.8 |
| 2020E | 779.4 | 6.50x | – | 7.50x | 5,065.9 | – | 5,845.3 |

The chosen multiple ranges in Exhibit 1.56 translated into an implied enterprise value range of approximately $4,900 million to $5,850 million. This implied valuation range is typically displayed in a format such as that shown in Exhibit 1.57 (known as a "football field") for eventual comparison against other valuation methodologies, which we discuss in the following chapters.

**EXHIBIT 1.57**    ValueCo Football Field Displaying Comparable Companies

*($ in millions)*

**Comparable Companies**

7.0x – 8.0x LTM EBITDA

6.75x – 7.75x 2019E EBITDA

6.5x – 7.5x 2020E EBITDA

$4,500    $4,750    $5,000    $5,250    $5,500    $5,750    $6,000

**CHAPTER 1 QUESTIONS**

1) Which of the following is the correct order of steps to complete comparable companies analysis?

   I. Locate the necessary financial information
   II. Select the universe of comparable companies
   III. Spread key statistics, ratios, and trading multiples
   IV. Determine valuation
   V. Benchmark the comparable companies

   A. II, I, III, V, IV
   B. I, II, III, IV, V
   C. II, I, III, IV, V
   D. III, I, IV, V, II

2) Which of the following are key business characteristics to examine when screening for comparable companies?

   I. Sector
   II. Return on investment
   III. End markets
   IV. Distribution channels
   V. Return on assets

   A. I and III
   B. II and IV
   C. I, III, and IV
   D. I, II, III, IV, and V

3) Which of the following are key financial characteristics to examine when screening for comparable companies?

   I. Customers
   II. Profitability
   III. Growth profile
   IV. Credit profile
   V. End markets

   A. II and III
   B. II, III, and IV
   C. I, II, and IV
   D. II, III, and V

4) Which of the following is NOT a source for locating financial information for comparable companies?

   A. 10-K
   B. 13-D
   C. Investor Presentations
   D. Equity Research

5) Which of the following is the correct calculation for fully diluted shares outstanding when used in trading comps?

   A. "Out-of-the money" options and warrants + "in-the-money" convertible securities
   B. Basic shares outstanding + "in-the-money" options and warrants + "in-the-money" convertible securities
   C. "In-the-money" options and warrants + "in-the-money" convertible securities
   D. Basic shares outstanding + "out-of-the money" options and warrants

6) Which methodology is used to determine additional shares from "in-the-money" options and warrants when determining fully diluted shares?

   A. Treasury Stock Method
   B. "If-Converted" Method
   C. Net Share Settlement Method
   D. "In-the-Money" Method

7) Calculate fully diluted shares using the information below

*($ in millions, except per share data; shares in millions)*

| Assumptions | |
|---|---|
| Current Share Price | $25.00 |
| Basic Shares Outstanding | 200.0 |
| Exercisable Options | 20.0 |
| Weighted Average Exercise Price | $10.00 |

   A. 150.4 million
   B. 200.5 million
   C. 212.0 million
   D. 220.0 million

8) What is the most conservative (most dilutive scenario) way to treat options and warrants when calculating fully diluted shares outstanding?

    A. Use all outstanding "in-the-money" options and warrants
    B. Use all exercisable "in-the-money" options and warrants
    C. Ignore all "in-the-money" options and warrants
    D. Ignore all outstanding "in-the-money" options and warrants

9) What is the formula for calculating enterprise value?

    A. Equity value + total debt
    B. Equity value + total debt + preferred stock + noncontrolling interest – cash
    C. Equity value + total debt – preferred stock – noncontrolling interest – cash
    D. Equity value + total debt + preferred stock + noncontrolling interest + cash

10) All else being constant, how does enterprise value change if a company raises equity and uses the entire amount to repay debt?

    A. Stays constant
    B. Increases
    C. Decreases
    D. Not enough information to answer the question

11) Show the necessary adjustments and pro forma amounts if a company issues $200.0 million of equity and uses the proceeds to repay debt (excluding fees and expenses).

*($ in millions)*

| **Capital Structure** | | | | |
|---|---|---|---|---|
| | **Actual 2018** | **Adjustments +** | **-** | **Pro forma 2018** |
| Equity Value | $1,200.0 | | | |
| Plus: Total Debt | 750.0 | | | |
| Plus: Preferred Stock | 100.0 | | | |
| Plus: Minority Interest | 50.0 | | | |
| Less: Cash and Cash Equivalents | (100.0) | | | |
| **Enterprise Value** | **$2,000.0** | | | |

12) When calculating an interest coverage ratio, which of the following is NOT used in the numerator?

    A. Net income
    B. EBIT
    C. EBITDA
    D. (EBITDA – capex)

13) Calculate adjusted net income, EBITDA, and EPS, respectively, assuming $50 million of D&A, and adjusting for the $10.0 million restructuring charge as well as an inventory write-down of $5 million

*($ in millions, except per share data)*

| Income Statement | |
| --- | --- |
| | Reported 2018 |
| **Sales** | **$1,000.0** |
| Cost of Goods Sold | 625.0 |
| **Gross Profit** | **$375.0** |
| Selling, General & Administrative | 230.0 |
| Restructuring Charges | 10.0 |
| **Operating Income (EBIT)** | **$135.0** |
| Interest Expense | 35.0 |
| **Pre-tax Income** | **$100.0** |
| Income Taxes @ 25% | 25.0 |
| **Net Income** | **$75.0** |
| | |
| Weighted Average Diluted Shares | 30.0 |
| Diluted Earnings Per Share | $2.50 |

A. $75.0 million, $185.0 million, $2.88
B. $86.3 million, $200.0 million, $2.88
C. $88.8 million, $200.0 million, $2.50
D. $88.8 million, $100.0 million, $2.50

14) The P/E ratio is equivalent to

A. Equity value/net income
B. Enterprise value/net income
C. Enterprise value/EBITDA
D. Share price/free cash flow

15) Which of the following is not an appropriate valuation multiple?

A. Enterprise value/EBITDA
B. Enterprise value/EBIT
C. Enterprise value/net income
D. Enterprise value/sales

# CHAPTER 2

# Precedent Transactions Analysis

**P**recedent transactions analysis ("precedent transactions" or "precedents"), like comps, employs a multiples-based approach to derive an implied valuation range for a given company, division, business, or collection of assets ("target"). It is premised on multiples paid for comparable companies in prior M&A transactions. Precedent transactions has a broad range of applications, most notably to help determine a potential sale price range for a company, or part thereof, in an M&A, capital markets, or restructuring transaction.

The selection of an appropriate universe of comparable acquisitions is the foundation for performing precedent transactions. This process incorporates a similar approach to that for determining a universe of comparable companies. The best comparable acquisitions typically involve companies similar to the target on a fundamental level (i.e., sharing key business and financial characteristics such as those outlined in Chapter 1, see Exhibit 1.3).

As with trading comps, it is often challenging to obtain a robust universe of truly comparable acquisitions. This exercise may demand some creativity and perseverance on the part of the banker. For example, it is not uncommon to consider transactions involving companies in different, but related, sectors that may share similar end markets, distribution channels, or financial profiles. As a general rule, the most recent transactions (i.e., those that have occurred within the previous two to three years) are the most relevant as they likely took place under similar market conditions to the contemplated transaction. In some cases, however, older transactions may be appropriate to evaluate if they occurred during a similar point in the target's business cycle or macroeconomic environment.

Under normal market conditions, precedents tend to provide a higher multiple range than trading comps for two principal reasons. First, buyers generally pay a "control premium" when purchasing another company. In return for this premium, the acquirer receives the right to control decisions regarding the target's business and its underlying cash flows. Second, strategic buyers often have the opportunity to realize synergies, which supports the ability to pay higher purchase prices. Synergies refer to the expected cost savings, growth opportunities, and other financial benefits that occur as a result of the combination of two businesses.

Potential acquirers look closely at the multiples that have been paid for comparable acquisitions. As a result, bankers and investment professionals are expected to know the transaction multiples for their sector focus areas. As in Chapter 1, this chapter employs a step-by-step approach to performing precedent transactions, as shown in Exhibit 2.1, followed by an illustrative analysis for ValueCo.

**EXHIBIT 2.1**   Precedent Transactions Analysis Steps

Step I.    Select the Universe of Comparable Acquisitions
Step II.   Locate the Necessary Deal-Related and Financial Information
Step III.  Spread Key Statistics, Ratios, and Transaction Multiples
Step IV.   Benchmark the Comparable Acquisitions
Step V.    Determine Valuation

## SUMMARY OF PRECEDENT TRANSACTIONS ANALYSIS STEPS

- Step I. Select the Universe of Comparable Acquisitions. The identification of a universe of comparable acquisitions is the first step in performing precedents. This exercise, like determining a universe of comparable companies for trading comps, can often be challenging and requires a strong understanding of the target and its sector. As a starting point, the banker typically consults with peers or senior colleagues to see if a relevant set of comparable acquisitions already exists internally. In the event the banker is starting from scratch, we suggest searching through M&A databases, examining the M&A history of the target and its comparable companies, and reviewing merger proxies of comparable companies for lists of selected comparable acquisitions disclosed in the fairness opinions. Equity and fixed income research reports for the target (if public), its comparable companies, and overall sector may also provide lists of comparable acquisitions, including relevant financial data (for reference purposes only).

  As part of this process, the banker seeks to learn as much as possible regarding the specific circumstances and deal dynamics for each transaction. This is particularly important for refining the universe and, ultimately, honing in on the "best" comparable acquisitions.

- Step II. Locate the Necessary Deal-Related and Financial Information. This section focuses on the sourcing of deal-related and financial information for M&A transactions involving both public and private companies. Locating information on comparable acquisitions is invariably easier for transactions involving public companies (including private companies with publicly registered debt securities) due to SEC disclosure requirements. For competitive reasons, however, public acquirers sometimes safeguard these details and only disclose information that is required by law or regulation. For M&A transactions involving private companies, it is often difficult—and sometimes impossible—to obtain complete (or any) financial information necessary to determine their transaction multiples.

- Step III. Spread Key Statistics, Ratios, and Transaction Multiples. Once the relevant deal-related and financial information has been located, the banker is prepared to spread each selected transaction. This involves entering the key transaction data relating to purchase price, form of consideration, and target financial statistics into an input page, where the relevant multiples for each transaction are calculated. The key multiples used for precedent transactions mirror those used for comparable companies (e.g., enterprise value-to-EBITDA and equity value-to-net income). As with comparable companies, certain sectors may also rely on other metrics to derive valuation (see Chapter 1, Exhibit 1.33). The notable difference is that multiples for precedent transactions often reflect a premium paid by the acquirer for control and potential synergies. In addition, multiples for precedent transactions are typically calculated on the basis of actual LTM financial statistics (available at the time of deal announcement).

▪ **Step IV. Benchmark the Comparable Acquisitions.** As with trading comps, the next level of analysis involves an in-depth study of the selected comparable acquisitions so as to identify those most relevant for valuing the target. As part of this benchmarking analysis, the banker examines key financial statistics and ratios for the acquired companies, with an eye toward those most comparable to the target. Output pages, such as those shown in Exhibits 1.53 and 1.54 in Chapter 1, facilitate this analysis. Other relevant deal circumstances and dynamics are also examined.

The transaction multiples for each selected acquisition are linked to an output sheet where they can be easily benchmarked against one another and the broader universe (see Exhibit 2.2). Each precedent transaction is closely examined as part of the final refining of the universe, with the best comparable transactions identified and obvious outliers eliminated. Ultimately, an experienced sector banker is consulted to help determine the final universe.

▪ **Step V. Determine Valuation.** In precedent transactions, the multiples of the selected comparable acquisitions universe are used to derive an implied valuation range for the target. The banker typically uses the mean and median multiples from the universe as a guide to establish a preliminary valuation range for the target, with the high and low ends also serving as reference points. These calculations often serve as the precursor for a deeper level of analysis whereby the banker uses the multiples from the most relevant transactions to anchor the ultimate valuation range. Often, the banker focuses on as few as two or three of the most similar transactions. Once the chosen multiples range is finalized, the endpoints are multiplied by the target's appropriate LTM financial statistics to produce an implied valuation range. As with trading comps, the target's implied valuation range is then given a sanity check and compared to the output from other valuation methodologies.

**EXHIBIT 2.2** Precedent Transactions Analysis Output Page

## ValueCo Corporation
### Precedent Transactions Analysis
($ in millions)

| Date Announced | Acquirer | Target | Transaction Type | Purchase Consideration | Equity Value | Enterprise Value | Enterprise Value / LTM Sales | Enterprise Value / LTM EBITDA | LTM EBIT | LTM EBITDA Margin | Equity Value / LTM Net Income | Premiums Paid / Days Prior to Unaffected 1 | 7 | 30 |
|---|---|---|---|---|---|---|---|---|---|---|---|---|---|---|
| 11/4/2019 | Pearl Corp. | Rosenbaum Industries | Public / Public | Cash | $2,500 | $3,825 | 1.6x | 8.5x | 11.2x | 19% | 13.7x | 35% | 33% | 37% |
| 7/22/2019 | Goodson Corp. | Schneider & Co. | Public / Public | Cash / Stock | 5,049 | 6,174 | 1.4x | 8.1x | 10.3x | 18% | 12.7x | 29% | 32% | 31% |
| 6/24/2019 | Domanski Capital | Ackerman Industries | Sponsor / Public | Cash | 8,845 | 9,995 | 1.7x | 8.0x | 10.2x | 21% | 13.1x | 35% | 37% | 39% |
| 4/15/2019 | The Hochberg Group | Whalen Inc. | Sponsor / Private | Cash | 1,250 | 1,350 | 1.9x | 7.5x | 9.6x | 26% | 12.6x | NA | NA | NA |
| 8/8/2018 | Cole Manufacturing | Gordon Inc. | Public / Public | Stock | 2,620 | 3,045 | 1.5x | 9.0x | 12.2x | 17% | 16.8x | 47% | 44% | 49% |
| 7/9/2018 | Eu-Han Capital | Rughwani International | Sponsor / Public | Cash | 3,390 | 4,340 | 1.6x | 7.8x | 9.4x | 21% | 11.4x | 38% | 40% | 43% |
| 3/20/2018 | Lanzarone Global | Falk & Sons | Public / Private | Cash | 8,750 | 10,350 | 1.7x | 8.4x | 10.5x | 21% | 13.3x | NA | NA | NA |
| 11/9/2017 | Meisner Global Management | Kamras Brands | Sponsor / Private | Cash | 1,765 | 2,115 | 1.5x | 7.9x | 9.3x | 19% | 11.4x | NA | NA | NA |
| 6/22/2017 | Pryor, Inc. | ParkCo | Public / Private | Cash | 6,450 | 8,700 | 1.1x | 7.0x | 7.9x | 16% | 9.8x | NA | NA | NA |
| 4/17/2017 | Leicht & Co. | Bress Products | Public / Public | Stock | 12,431 | 12,681 | 1.5x | 8.2x | 12.1x | 19% | 16.3x | 29% | 36% | 34% |
| | | | | | | | | | | | | | | |
| Mean | | | | | | | 1.6x | 8.0x | 10.3x | 19% | 13.1x | 36% | 37% | 39% |
| Median | | | | | | | 1.6x | 8.0x | 10.3x | 19% | 12.9x | 35% | 36% | 38% |
| | | | | | | | | | | | | | | |
| High | | | | | | | 1.9x | 9.0x | 12.2x | 26% | 16.8x | 47% | 44% | 49% |
| Low | | | | | | | 1.1x | 7.0x | 7.9x | 16% | 9.8x | 29% | 32% | 31% |

Source: Company filings

## STEP I. SELECT THE UNIVERSE OF COMPARABLE ACQUISITIONS

The identification of a universe of comparable acquisitions is the first step in performing precedents. This exercise, like determining a universe of comparable companies for trading comps, can often be challenging and requires a strong understanding of the target and its sector. Investment banks generally have internal M&A transaction databases containing relevant multiples and other financial data for focus sectors, which are updated as appropriate for newly announced deals. Often, however, the banker needs to start from scratch.

When practical, the banker consults with peers or senior colleagues with first-hand knowledge of relevant transactions. Senior bankers can be helpful in establishing the basic landscape by identifying the key transactions in a given sector. Toward the end of the screening process, an experienced banker's guidance is beneficial for the final refining of the universe.

### Screen for Comparable Acquisitions

The initial goal when screening for comparable acquisitions is to locate as many potential transactions as possible for a relevant, recent time period and then further refine the universe. Below are several suggestions for creating an initial list.

- Search M&A databases using a financial information service, which allows for the screening of M&A transactions through multiple search criteria, including industry, transaction size, form of consideration, time period, and geography, among others

- Examine the target's M&A history and determine the multiples it has paid and received for the purchase and sale, respectively, of its businesses

- Revisit the target's universe of comparable companies (as determined in Chapter 1) and examine the M&A history of each comparable company

- Search merger proxies for comparable acquisitions, as they typically contain excerpts from fairness opinion(s) that cite a list of selected transactions analyzed by the financial advisor(s)

- Review equity and fixed income research reports for the target (if public), its comparable companies, and sector as they may provide lists of comparable acquisitions, including relevant financial data (for reference purposes only)

### Examine Other Considerations

Once an initial set of comparable acquisitions is selected, it is important to gain a better understanding of the specific circumstances and context for each transaction. Although these factors generally do not change the list of comparable acquisitions to be examined, understanding the "story" behind each transaction helps to better interpret the multiple paid, as well as its relevance to the target being valued. This next level of analysis involves examining factors such as market conditions and deal dynamics.

**Market Conditions**    Market conditions refer to the business and economic environment, as well as the prevailing state of the capital markets, at the time of a given transaction. They must be viewed within the context of specific sectors and cycles (e.g., housing, steel, and technology). These conditions directly affect availability and cost of acquisition financing and, therefore, influence the price an acquirer is willing, or able, to pay. They also affect buyer confidence with respect to the target's growth prospects, as well as its own ability to undertake a transaction.

For example, at the height of the technology bubble in the late 1990s and early 2000s, many technology and telecommunications companies were acquired at unprecedented multiples. Equity financing was prevalent during this period as companies used their stock, which was valued at record levels, as acquisition currency. Boardroom confidence was also high—growth prospects appeared unlimited—which lent support to contemplated M&A activity. After the bubble burst and market conditions adjusted, M&A activity slowed dramatically, and companies changed hands for fractions of the valuations seen just a couple of years earlier. The multiples paid for companies during this period quickly became irrelevant for assessing value in the following era.

Similarly, during the low-rate debt financing environment of the mid-2000s, acquirers (financial sponsors, in particular) were able to support higher than historical purchase prices due to the market's willingness to supply abundant and inexpensive debt with favorable terms. In the ensuing credit crunch that began during the second half of 2007, however, debt financing became scarce and expensive, thereby dramatically changing value perceptions. Over the subsequent couple of years, the entire M&A landscape changed, with the LBO market grinding to a halt and overall deal volume and valuations falling dramatically.

**Deal Dynamics**    Deal dynamics refer to the specific circumstances surrounding a given transaction. For example:

- Was the acquirer a strategic buyer or a financial sponsor?
- What were the buyer's and seller's motivations for the transaction?
- Was the target sold through an *auction process* or *negotiated sale*? Was the nature of the deal *friendly* or *hostile*?
- What was the purchase consideration (i.e., mix of cash and stock)?

This information often provides valuable insight into factors that may have impacted the price paid by the acquirer.

**Strategic Buyer vs. Financial Sponsor**   Traditionally, strategic buyers have been able to pay higher purchase prices than financial sponsors due to their ability to realize synergies from the transaction, among other factors, including lower cost of capital and return thresholds. During periods of robust credit markets, such as the mid-2000s and mid-2010s, however, sponsors were able to place higher leverage on targets and, therefore, compete more effectively with strategic buyers on purchase price. In the credit crunch of 2008/2009, the advantage shifted back to strategic buyers as only the strongest and most creditworthy companies were able to source acquisition financing.

**Motivations**   Buyer and seller motivations may also play an important role in interpreting purchase price. For example, a strategic buyer may "stretch" to pay a higher price for an asset if there are substantial synergies to be realized and/or the asset is critical to its strategic plan ("scarcity value"). Similarly, a financial sponsor may be more aggressive on price if synergies can be realized by combining the target with an existing portfolio company. Or, if the target fits particularly well with the sponsor's investment priorities in terms of sector or situation (e.g., carve-outs, operational turnarounds, or family-owned). From the seller's perspective, motivations may also influence purchase price. A corporation in need of cash that is selling a non-core business, for example, may prioritize speed of execution, certainty of completion, and other structural considerations, which may result in a lower valuation than a pure value maximization strategy.

**Sale Process and Nature of the Deal**   The type of sale process and nature of the deal should also be examined. For example, auctions, whereby the target is shopped to multiple prospective buyers, are designed to maximize competitive dynamics with the goal of producing the best offer at the highest possible price. Hostile situations, whereby the target actively seeks alternatives to a proposed takeover by a particular buyer, may also produce higher purchase prices. A *merger of equals* (MOE) transaction, on the other hand, is premised on partnership with the target, thereby forgoing a typical takeover premium as both sides collectively participate in the upside (e.g., growth and synergies) over time.

**Purchase Consideration**   The use of stock as a meaningful portion of the purchase consideration tends to result in a lower valuation (measured by multiples and premiums paid) than for an all-cash transaction. This is largely due to the fact that the receipt of stock means that target shareholders retain an equity interest in the combined entity and the ability to share in the upside (driven by growth and realizing synergies). Target shareholders also maintain the opportunity to obtain a control premium at a later date through a future sale of the company. As a result, target shareholders may require less upfront compensation than for an all-cash transaction in which they are unable to participate in value creation opportunities that result from combining the two companies.

## STEP II. LOCATE THE NECESSARY DEAL-RELATED AND FINANCIAL INFORMATION

This section focuses on the sourcing of key deal-related and financial information for M&A transactions involving both public and private targets. Locating information on comparable acquisitions is invariably easier for transactions involving public targets (including private companies with publicly registered debt securities) due to SEC disclosure requirements.

For M&A transactions involving private targets, the availability of sufficient information typically depends on whether public securities were used as the acquisition financing. In many cases, it is often challenging and sometimes impossible to obtain complete (or any) financial information necessary to determine the transaction multiples in such deals. For competitive reasons, even public acquirers may safeguard these details and only disclose information that is required by law or regulation. Nonetheless, the resourceful banker conducts searches for information on private transactions via news runs and various databases. In some cases, these searches yield enough data to determine purchase price and key target financial statistics; in other cases, there simply may not be enough relevant information available.

Below, we grouped the primary sources for locating the necessary deal-related and financial information for spreading comparable acquisitions into separate categories for public and private targets.

### Public Targets

**Proxy Statement**   In a one-step merger transaction,[1] the target obtains approval from its shareholders through a vote at a shareholder meeting. Prior to the vote, the target provides appropriate disclosure to the shareholders via a proxy statement. The proxy statement contains a summary of the background and terms of the transaction, a description of the financial analysis underlying the fairness opinion(s) of the financial advisor(s), a copy of the definitive purchase/sale agreement ("definitive agreement"), and summary and pro forma financial data (if applicable, depending on the form of consideration). As such, it is a primary source for locating key information used to spread a precedent transaction. The proxy statement is filed with the SEC under the codes PREM14 (preliminary) and DEFM14A (definitive).

In the event that a public acquirer is issuing new shares equal to or greater than 20% of its pre-deal shares outstanding to fund the purchase consideration,[2] it will also need to file a proxy statement for its shareholders to vote on the proposed transaction. In addition, a registration statement to register the offer and sale of shares must be filed with the SEC if no exemption from the registration requirements is available.[3]

---

[1]An M&A transaction for public targets where shareholders approve the deal at a formal shareholder meeting pursuant to relevant state law. See Chapter 6 for additional information.
[2]The requirement for a shareholder vote in this situation arises from the listing rules of the Nasdaq Stock Market and the New York Stock Exchange. If the amount of shares being issued is less than 20% of pre-deal levels, or if the merger consideration consists entirely of cash or debt, the acquirer's shareholders are typically not entitled to vote on the transaction.
[3]When both the acquirer and target are required to prepare proxy and/or registration statements, they typically combine the statements in a joint disclosure document.

**Schedule TO/Schedule 14D-9**   In a tender offer, the acquirer offers to buy shares directly from the target's shareholders.[4] As part of this process, the acquirer mails an Offer to Purchase to the target's shareholders and files a Schedule TO. In response to the tender offer, the target files a Schedule 14D-9 within ten business days of commencement. The Schedule 14D-9 contains a recommendation from the target's board of directors to the target's shareholders on how to respond to the tender offer, typically including a fairness opinion. The Schedule TO and the Schedule 14D-9 include the same type of information with respect to the terms of the transaction as set forth in a proxy statement.

**Registration Statement/Prospectus (S-4, 424B)**   When a public acquirer issues shares as part of the purchase consideration for a public target, the acquirer is typically required to file a registration statement/prospectus in order for those shares to be freely tradeable by the target's shareholders. Similarly, if the acquirer is issuing public debt securities (or debt securities intended to be registered)[5] to fund the purchase, it must also file a registration statement/prospectus. The registration statement/prospectus contains the terms of the issuance, material terms of the transaction, and purchase price detail. It may also contain acquirer and target financial information, including on a pro forma basis to reflect the consummation of the transaction (if applicable, depending on the materiality of the transaction).[6]

**Schedule 13E-3**   Depending on the nature of the transaction, a "going private"[7] deal may require enhanced disclosure. For example, in an LBO of a public company where an "affiliate" (such as a senior company executive or significant shareholder) is part of the buyout group, the SEC requires broader disclosure of information used in the decision-making process on a Schedule 13E-3. Disclosure items on Schedule 13E-3 include materials such as presentations to the target's board of directors by its financial advisor(s) in support of the actual fairness opinion(s).

---

[4]A tender offer is an offer to purchase shares for cash. An acquirer can also effect an exchange offer, pursuant to which the target's shares are exchanged for shares of the acquirer.

[5]Debt securities are typically sold to qualified institutional buyers (QIBs) through a private placement under Rule 144A of the Securities Act of 1933 initially, and then registered with the SEC within one year after issuance so that they can be traded on an open exchange. This is done to expedite the sale of the debt securities as SEC registration, which involves review of the registration statement by the SEC, can take several weeks or months. Once the SEC review of the documentation is complete, the issuer conducts an exchange offer pursuant to which investors exchange the unregistered bonds for registered bonds.

[6]A joint proxy/registration statement typically incorporates the acquirer's and target's applicable 10-K and 10-Q by reference as the source for financial information.

[7]A company "goes private" when it engages in certain transactions that have the effect of delisting its shares from a public stock exchange. In addition, depending on the circumstances, a publicly held company may no longer be required to file reports with the SEC when it reduces the number of its shareholders to fewer than 300.

**8-K**  In addition to the SEC filings mentioned above, key deal information can be obtained from the 8-K that is filed upon announcement of the transaction. Generally, a public target is required to file an 8-K within four business days of the transaction announcement. In the event a public company is selling a subsidiary or division that is significant in size, the parent company typically files an 8-K upon announcement of the transaction. Public acquirers are also required to file an 8-K upon announcement of material transactions.[8] A private acquirer does not need to file an 8-K as it is not subject to the SEC's disclosure requirements. When filed in the context of an M&A transaction, the 8-K contains a brief description of the transaction, as well as the corresponding press release and definitive agreement as exhibits.

The press release filed upon announcement typically contains a summary of the deal terms, transaction rationale, and a description of the target and acquirer. In the event there are substantial changes to the terms of the transaction following the original announcement, the banker uses the 8-K for the final announced deal (and enclosed press release) as the basis for calculating the deal's transaction multiples. This is a relatively common occurrence in competitive situations where two or more parties enter into a bidding war for a target.

**10-K and 10-Q**  The target's 10-K and 10-Q are the primary sources for locating the information necessary to calculate its relevant LTM financial statistics, including adjustments for non-recurring items and significant recent events. The most recent 10-K and 10-Q for the period ending prior to the announcement date typically serve as the source for the necessary information to calculate the target's LTM financial statistics and balance sheet data. In some cases, the banker may use a filing after announcement if the financial information is deemed more relevant. The 10-K and 10-Q are also relied upon to provide information on the target's shares outstanding and options/warrants.[9]

**Equity and Fixed Income Research**  Equity and fixed income research reports often provide helpful deal insight, including information on pro forma adjustments and expected synergies. Furthermore, research reports typically provide color on deal dynamics and other circumstances.

---

[8]Generally, an acquisition is required to be reported in an 8-K if the assets, income, or value of the target comprise 10% or greater of the acquirer's. Furthermore, for larger transactions where assets, income, or value of the target comprise 20% or greater of the acquirer's, the acquirer must file an 8-K containing historical financial information on the target and pro forma financial information within 75 days of the completion of the acquisition.

[9]The proxy statement may contain more recent share count information than the 10-K or 10-Q.

## Private Targets

A private target (i.e., a non-public filer) is not required to publicly file documentation in an M&A transaction as long as it is not subject to SEC disclosure requirements. Therefore, the sourcing of relevant information on private targets depends on the type of acquirer and/or acquisition financing.

When a public acquirer buys a private target (or a division/subsidiary of a public company), it may be required to file certain disclosure documents. For example, in the event the acquirer is using public securities as part of the purchase consideration for a private target, it is required to file a registration statement/prospectus. Furthermore, if the acquirer is issuing shares in excess of 20% of its pre-deal shares, a proxy statement is filed with the SEC and mailed to its shareholders so they can evaluate the proposed transaction and vote. As previously discussed, regardless of the type of financing, the acquirer files an 8-K upon announcement and completion of material transactions.

For LBOs of private targets, the availability of necessary information depends on whether public debt securities (typically high yield bonds) are issued as part of the financing. In this case, the S-4 contains the relevant data on purchase price and target financials to spread the precedent transaction.

Private acquirer/private target transactions (including LBOs) involving nonpublic financing are the most difficult transactions for which to obtain information because there are no SEC disclosure requirements. In these situations, the banker must rely on less formal sources for deal information, such as press releases and news articles. These news pieces can be found by searching a company's corporate website as well as through information services such as Bloomberg, Factiva, and Thomson Reuters. The banker should also search relevant sector-specific trade journals for potential disclosures. Any information provided on these all-private transactions, however, relies on discretionary disclosure by the parties involved. As a result, in many cases it is impossible to obtain even basic deal information that can be relied upon, thus precluding these transactions from being used in precedents.

## Summary of Primary SEC Filings in M&A Transactions

Exhibit 2.3 provides a list of key SEC filings that can be used to source relevant deal-related data and target financial information for performing precedent transactions. If applicable, the definitive proxy statement or tender offer document should serve as the primary source for deal-related data.

**EXHIBIT 2.3**   Primary SEC Filings in M&A Transaction—U.S. Issuers

| SEC Filings | Description |
|---|---|
| **Proxy Statements and Other Disclosure Documents** | |
| PREM14A/DEFM14A | Preliminary/definitive proxy statement relating to an M&A transaction |
| PREM14C/DEFM14C[a] | Preliminary/definitive information statement relating to an M&A transaction |
| Schedule 13E-3 | Filed to report going private transactions initiated by certain issuers or their affiliates |
| **Tender Offer Documents** | |
| Schedule TO | Filed by an acquirer upon commencement of a tender offer |
| Schedule 14D-9 | Recommendation from the target's board of directors on how shareholders should respond to a tender offer |
| **Registration Statement/Prospectus** | |
| S-4 | Registration statement for securities issued in connection with a business combination or exchange offer. May include proxy statement of acquirer and/or public target |
| 424B | Prospectus |
| **Current and Periodic Reports** | |
| 8-K | When filed in the context of an M&A transaction, used to disclose a material acquisition or sale of the company or a division/subsidiary |
| 10-K and 10-Q | Target company's applicable annual and quarterly reports |

[a]In certain circumstances, an *information statement* is sent to shareholders instead of a proxy statement. This occurs if one or more shareholders comprise a majority and can approve the transaction via a written consent, in which case a shareholder vote is not required. An information statement generally contains the same information as a proxy statement.

Exhibit 2.4 provides an overview of the sources for transaction information in public and private company transactions.

**EXHIBIT 2.4**   Transaction Information by Target Type

| Information Item | Target Type | |
| --- | --- | --- |
| | Public | Private |
| Announcement Date | ▪ 8-K / Press Release | ▪ Acquirer 8-K / Press Release ▪ News Run |
| Key Deal Terms[a] | ▪ 8-K / Press Release ▪ Proxy ▪ Schedule TO ▪ 14D-9 ▪ Registration Statement / Prospectus (S-4, 424B) ▪ 13E-3 | ▪ Acquirer 8-K / Press Release ▪ Acquirer Proxy ▪ Registration Statement / Prospectus (S-4, 424B) ▪ M&A Database ▪ News Run ▪ Trade Publications |
| Target Description and Financial Data | ▪ Target 10-K / 10-Q ▪ 8-K ▪ Proxy ▪ Registration Statement / Prospectus (S-4, 424B) ▪ 13E-3 | ▪ Acquirer 8-K ▪ Acquirer Proxy ▪ Registration Statement / Prospectus (S-4, 424B) ▪ M&A Database ▪ News Run ▪ Trade Publications |
| Target Historical Share Price Data | ▪ Financial Information Service | NA |

[a]Should be updated for amendments to the definitive agreement or a new definitive agreement for a new buyer.

## STEP III. SPREAD KEY STATISTICS, RATIOS, AND TRANSACTION MULTIPLES

Once the relevant deal-related and financial information has been located, the banker is prepared to spread each selected transaction. This involves entering the key transaction data relating to purchase price, form of consideration, and target financial statistics into an input page, such as that shown in Exhibit 2.5, where the relevant multiples for each transaction are calculated. An input sheet is created for each comparable acquisition, which, in turn, feeds into summary output sheets used for the benchmarking analysis. In the pages that follow, we explain the financial data on the input page and the calculations behind them.

### Calculation of Key Financial Statistics and Ratios

The process for spreading the key financial statistics and ratios for precedent transactions is similar to that outlined in Chapter 1 for comparable companies (see Exhibits 1.53 and 1.54). Our focus for this section, therefore, is on certain nuances for calculating equity value and enterprise value in precedent transactions, including under different purchase consideration scenarios. We also discuss the analysis of premiums paid and synergies.

**Equity Value**   Equity value ("equity purchase price" or "offer value") for public targets in precedent transactions is calculated in a similar manner as that for comparable companies. However, it is based on the announced offer price per share as opposed to the closing share price on a given day. To calculate equity value for public M&A targets, the offer price per share is multiplied by the target's fully diluted shares outstanding at the given offer price. For example, if the acquirer offers the target's shareholders $20.00 per share and the target has 50 million fully diluted shares outstanding (based on the treasury stock method at that price), the equity purchase price would be $1,000 million ($20.00 × 50 million). In those cases where the acquirer purchases less than 100% of the target's outstanding shares, equity value must be grossed up to calculate the implied equity value for the entire company.

In calculating fully diluted shares for precedent transactions, all outstanding in-the-money options and warrants are converted at their weighted average strike prices regardless of whether they are exercisable or not.[10] As with the calculation of fully diluted shares outstanding for comparable companies, out-of-the money options and warrants are not assumed to be converted. For convertible and equity-linked securities, the banker must determine whether they are in-the-money and perform conversion in accordance with the terms and *change of control* provisions as detailed in the registration statement/prospectus.

For M&A transactions in which the target is private, equity value is simply enterprise value less any assumed/refinanced net debt.

---

[10]Assumes that all unvested options and warrants vest upon a change of control (which typically reflects actual circumstances) and that no better detail exists for strike prices than that mentioned in the 10-K or 10-Q.

**EXHIBIT 2.5** Precedent Transactions Input Page Template

## Acquisition of Target by Acquirer
### Input Page
*($ in millions, except per share data)*

### General Information

| Target | Target |
|---|---|
| Ticker | TRGT |
| Fiscal Year End | Dec-31 |
| Marginal Tax Rate | |

| Acquirer | Acquirer |
|---|---|
| Ticker | ACQR |
| Fiscal Year End | Dec-31 |

| | |
|---|---|
| Date Announced | 1/0/2000 |
| Date Effective | 1/0/2000 |
| Transaction Type | NA |
| Purchase Consideration | NA |

### Calculation of Equity and Enterprise Value

| Offer Price per Share | |
|---|---|
| Cash Offer Price per Share | - |
| Stock Offer Price per Share | - |
| Exchange Ratio | - |
| Acquirer Share Price | - |
| **Offer Price per Share** | **-** |

| | |
|---|---|
| Fully Diluted Shares Outstanding | - |
| **Implied Equity Value** | **-** |

| Implied Enterprise Value | |
|---|---|
| Plus: Total Debt | - |
| Plus: Preferred Stock | - |
| Plus: Noncontrolling Interest | - |
| Less: Cash and Cash Equivalents | - |
| **Implied Enterprise Value** | **-** |

### LTM Transaction Multiples

| EV/Sales | NA |
|---|---|
| Metric | NA |
| EV/EBITDA | NA |
| Metric | NA |
| EV/EBIT | NA |
| Metric | NA |
| P/E | NA |
| Metric | - |

### Premiums Paid

| Transaction Announcement | Premium |
|---|---|
| 1 Day Prior | NA |
| **Unaffected Share Price** | |
| 1 Day Prior | NA |
| 7 Days Prior | NA |
| 30 Days Prior | NA |

### Source Documents

| | Period | Date Filed |
|---|---|---|
| Target 10-K | 1/0/2000 | 1/0/2000 |
| Target 10-Q | 1/0/2000 | 1/0/2000 |
| Target 8-K | | 1/0/2000 |
| Target DEFM14A | | 1/0/2000 |
| Acquirer 424B | | 1/0/2000 |
| Acquirer 8-K | | 1/0/2000 |

### Reported Income Statement

| | FYE | Prior Stub | Current Stub | LTM |
|---|---|---|---|---|
| | 1/0/2000 | 1/0/2000 | 1/0/2000 | 1/0/2000 |
| Sales | - | - | - | - |
| COGS | - | - | - | - |
| **Gross Profit** | - | - | - | - |
| SG&A | - | - | - | - |
| Other (Income)/Expense | - | - | - | - |
| **EBIT** | - | - | - | - |
| Interest Expense | - | - | - | - |
| **Pre-tax Income** | - | - | - | - |
| Income Taxes | - | - | - | - |
| Noncontrolling Interest | - | - | - | - |
| Preferred Dividends | - | - | - | - |
| **Net Income** | *NA* | *NA* | *NA* | *NA* |
| | | | | |
| Weighted Avg. Diluted Shares | | | | |
| Diluted EPS | NA | NA | NA | NA |

| Effective Tax Rate | *NA* | *NA* | *NA* | *NA* |
|---|---|---|---|---|

### Adjusted Income Statement

| Reported Gross Profit | - | - | - | - |
|---|---|---|---|---|
| Non-recurring Items in COGS | - | - | - | - |
| **Adjusted Gross Profit** | *NA* | *NA* | *NA* | *NA* |
| *% margin* | | | | |
| Reported EBIT | - | - | - | - |
| Non-recurring Items in COGS | - | - | - | - |
| Other Non-recurring Items | - | - | - | - |
| **Adjusted EBIT** | *NA* | *NA* | *NA* | *NA* |
| *% margin* | | | | |
| Depreciation & Amortization | - | - | - | - |
| **Adjusted EBITDA** | *NA* | *NA* | *NA* | *NA* |
| *% margin* | | | | |
| Reported Net Income | - | - | - | - |
| Non-recurring Items in COGS | - | - | - | - |
| Other Non-recurring Items | - | - | - | - |
| Non-operating Non-rec. Items | - | - | - | - |
| Tax Adjustment | - | - | - | - |
| **Adjusted Net Income** | *NA* | *NA* | *NA* | *NA* |
| *% margin* | | | | |
| Adjusted Diluted EPS | *NA* | *NA* | *NA* | *NA* |

### Cash Flow Statement Data

| Depreciation & Amortization | NA | NA | NA | NA |
|---|---|---|---|---|
| *% sales* | | | | |
| Capital Expenditures | NA | NA | NA | NA |
| *% sales* | | | | |

### Notes

(1) [to come]
(2) [to come]
(3) [to come]
(4) [to come]
(5) [to come]

### Target Description

[to come]

### Acquirer Description

[to come]

### Comments

[to come]

### Calculation of Fully Diluted Shares Outstanding

| Basic Shares Outstanding | |
|---|---|
| Plus: Shares from In-the-Money Options | |
| Less: Shares Repurchased from Option Proceeds | |
| **Net New Shares from Options** | - |
| Plus: Shares from Convertible Securities | - |
| **Fully Diluted Shares Outstanding** | - |

### Options/Warrants

| Tranche | Number of Shares | Exercise Price | In-the-Money Shares | Proceeds |
|---|---|---|---|---|
| Tranche 1 | - | - | - | - |
| Tranche 2 | - | - | - | - |
| Tranche 3 | - | - | - | - |
| Tranche 4 | - | - | - | - |
| Tranche 5 | - | - | - | - |
| **Total** | - | | - | - |

### Convertible Securities

| | Amount | Conversion Price | Conversion Ratio | New Shares |
|---|---|---|---|---|
| Issue 1 | - | - | - | - |
| Issue 2 | - | - | - | - |
| Issue 3 | - | - | - | - |
| Issue 4 | - | - | - | - |
| Issue 5 | - | - | - | - |
| **Total** | | | | - |

**Purchase Consideration**   Purchase consideration refers to the mix of cash, stock, and/or other securities that the acquirer offers to the target's shareholders. In some cases, the form of consideration can affect the target shareholders' perception of the value embedded in the offer. For example, some shareholders may prefer cash over stock as payment due to its guaranteed value. On the other hand, some shareholders may prefer stock compensation in order to participate in the upside potential of the combined companies. Tax consequences and other issues may also play a decisive role in guiding shareholder preferences.

The three primary types of consideration for a target's equity are all-cash, stock-for-stock, and cash/stock mix.

**All-Cash Transaction**   As the term implies, in an all-cash transaction, the acquirer makes an offer to purchase all or a portion of the target's shares outstanding for cash (see Exhibit 2.6). This makes for a simple equity value calculation by multiplying the cash offer price per share by the number of fully diluted shares outstanding. Cash represents the cleanest form of currency and certainty of value for all shareholders. However, it also typically triggers a taxable event as opposed to the exchange or receipt of shares of stock, which, if structured properly, is not taxable until the shares are eventually sold.

**EXHIBIT 2.6**   Press Release Excerpt for All-Cash Transaction

> CLEVELAND, Ohio – June 10, 2019 – AcquirerCo and TargetCo today announced the two companies have entered into a definitive agreement for AcquirerCo to acquire the equity of TargetCo, a publicly held company, in an all-cash transaction at a price of approximately $1 billion, or $20.00 per share. The acquisition is subject to TargetCo shareholder and regulatory approvals and other customary closing conditions, and is expected to close in the fourth quarter of 2019.

**Stock-for-Stock Transaction**   In a stock-for-stock transaction, the calculation of equity value is based on either a *fixed exchange ratio* or a *floating exchange ratio* ("fixed price"). The exchange ratio is calculated as offer price per share divided by the acquirer's share price. A fixed exchange ratio, which is more common than a fixed price structure, is a ratio of how many shares of the acquirer's stock are exchanged for each share of the target's stock. In a floating exchange ratio, the number of acquirer shares exchanged for target shares fluctuates so as to ensure a fixed value for the target's shareholders.

*Fixed Exchange Ratio*   A fixed exchange ratio defines the number of shares of the acquirer's stock to be exchanged for each share of the target's stock. As per Exhibit 2.7, if AcquirerCo agrees to exchange one half share of its stock for every one share of TargetCo stock, the exchange ratio is 0.5.

**EXHIBIT 2.7** Press Release Excerpt for Fixed Exchange Ratio Structure

CLEVELAND, Ohio – June 10, 2019 – AcquirerCo has announced a definitive agreement to acquire TargetCo in an all-stock transaction valued at $1 billion. Under the terms of the agreement, which has been approved by both boards of directors, TargetCo stockholders will receive, at a fixed exchange ratio, 0.50 shares of AcquirerCo common stock for every share of TargetCo common stock. Based on AcquirerCo's stock price on June 7, 2019 of $40.00, this represents a price of $20.00 per share of TargetCo common stock.

For precedent transactions, offer price per share is calculated by multiplying the exchange ratio by the share price of the acquirer, typically one day prior to announcement (see Exhibit 2.8).

**EXHIBIT 2.8** Calculation of Offer Price per Share & Equity Value in a Fixed Exchange Ratio Structure

$$\text{Offer Price per Share} = \left( \text{Exchange Ratio} \times \text{Acquirer's Share Price} \right)$$

$$\text{Equity Value} = \left( \text{Exchange Ratio} \times \text{Acquirer's Share Price} \right) \times \text{Target's Fully Diluted Shares Outstanding}$$

In a fixed exchange ratio structure, the offer price per share (value to target) moves in line with the underlying share price of the acquirer. The amount of the acquirer's shares received, however, is constant (see Exhibit 2.9). For example, assuming TargetCo has 50 million fully diluted shares outstanding, it will receive 25 million shares of AcquirerCo stock. The shares received by the target and the respective ownership percentages for the acquirer and target remain fixed regardless of share price movement between execution of the definitive agreement ("signing") and transaction close (assuming no structural protections for either the acquirer or target, such as a *collar*).[11]

Following a deal's announcement, the market immediately starts to assimilate the publicly disclosed information. In response, the target's and acquirer's share prices begin to trade in line with the market's perception of the transaction.[12] Therefore, the target assumes the risk of a decline in the acquirer's share price, but preserves the potential to share in the upside, both immediately and over time. The fixed exchange ratio is more commonly used than the floating exchange ratio as it "links" both parties' share prices, thereby enabling them to share the risk (or opportunity) from movements post-announcement.

---

[11]In a fixed exchange ratio deal, a collar can be used to guarantee a certain range of prices to the target's shareholders. For example, a target may agree to a $20.00 offer price per share based on an exchange ratio of 1:2, with a collar guaranteeing that the shareholders will receive no less than $18.00 and no more than $22.00, regardless of how the acquirer's shares trade between signing and closing.

[12]Factors considered by the market when evaluating a proposed transaction include strategic merit, economics of the deal, synergies, and likelihood of closing.

**EXHIBIT 2.9**    Fixed Exchange Ratio – Value to Target and Shares Received

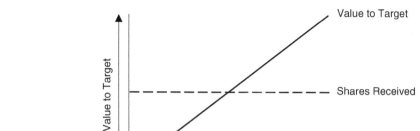

*Floating Exchange Ratio*    A floating exchange ratio represents the set dollar amount per share that the acquirer has agreed to pay for each share of the target's stock in the form of shares of the acquirer's stock. As per Exhibit 2.10, TargetCo shareholders will receive $20.00 worth of AcquirerCo shares for each share of TargetCo stock they own.

**EXHIBIT 2.10**    Press Release Excerpt for Floating Exchange Ratio Structure

CLEVELAND, Ohio – June 10, 2019 – AcquirerCo and TargetCo today announced the execution of a definitive agreement pursuant to which AcquirerCo will acquire TargetCo in an all stock transaction. Pursuant to the agreement, TargetCo stockholders will receive $20.00 of AcquirerCo common stock for each share of TargetCo common stock they hold. The number of AcquirerCo shares to be issued to TargetCo stockholders will be calculated based on the average closing price of AcquirerCo common stock for the 30 trading days immediately preceding the third trading day before the closing of the transaction.

In a floating exchange ratio structure, as opposed to a fixed exchange ratio, the dollar offer price per share (value to target) is set, and the number of shares exchanged fluctuates in accordance with the movement of the acquirer's share price (see Exhibit 2.11).

The number of shares to be exchanged is typically based on an average of the acquirer's share price for a specified time period prior to transaction close. This structure presents target shareholders with greater certainty in terms of value received as the acquirer assumes the full risk of a decline in its share price (assuming no structural protections for the acquirer). In general, a floating exchange ratio is used when the acquirer is significantly larger than the target. A larger acquirer can absorb potential downside from the acquisition of a much smaller target while providing certainty to the seller.

**EXHIBIT 2.11** Floating Exchange Ratio – Value to Target and Shares Received

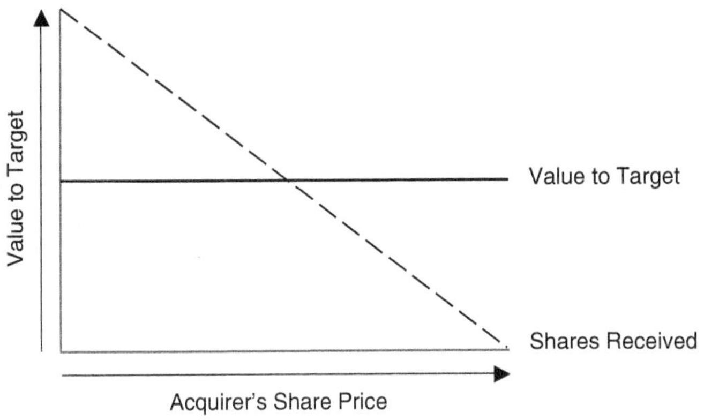

**Cash and Stock Transaction** In a cash and stock transaction, the acquirer offers a combination of cash and stock as purchase consideration (see Exhibit 2.12).

**EXHIBIT 2.12** Press Release Excerpt for Cash and Stock Transaction

> CLEVELAND, Ohio – June 10, 2019 – AcquirerCo and TargetCo announced today that they signed a definitive agreement whereby AcquirerCo will acquire TargetCo for a purchase price of approximately $1 billion in a mix of cash and AcquirerCo stock. Under the terms of the agreement, which was unanimously approved by the boards of directors of both companies, TargetCo stockholders will receive $10.00 in cash and 0.25 shares of AcquirerCo common stock for each outstanding TargetCo share. Based on AcquirerCo's closing price of $40.00 on June 7, 2019, AcquirerCo will issue an aggregate of approximately 12.5 million shares of its common stock and pay an aggregate of approximately $500 million in cash in the transaction.

The cash portion of the offer represents a fixed value per share for target shareholders. The stock portion of the offer can be set according to either a fixed or floating exchange ratio. The calculation of offer price per share and equity value in a cash and stock transaction (assuming a fixed exchange ratio) is shown in Exhibit 2.13.

**EXHIBIT 2.13** Calculation of Offer Price per Share and Equity Value in a Cash and Stock Transaction

Offer Price per Share = Cash Offer per Share + (Exchange Ratio × Acquirer's Share Price)

Equity Value = (Cash Offer per Share + (Exchange Ratio × Acquirer's Share Price)) × Target's Fully Diluted Shares Outstanding

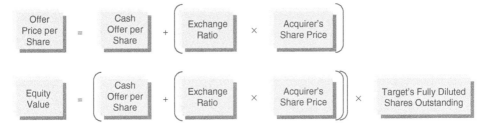

**Enterprise Value**  Enterprise value is often referred to as "transaction value" in an M&A context. It is the total value offered by the acquirer for the target's equity interests, as well as the assumption or refinancing of the target's net debt. It is calculated for precedent transactions in the same manner as for comparable companies, comprising the sum of equity, net debt, preferred stock, and noncontrolling interest. Exhibit 2.14 illustrates the calculation of enterprise value, with equity value calculated as offer price per share (the sum of the target's "unaffected" share price and premium paid, see "Premiums Paid") multiplied by the target's fully diluted shares outstanding.

**EXHIBIT 2.14**    Calculation of Enterprise Value

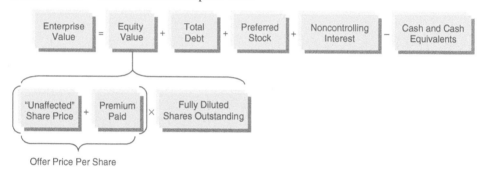

**Calculation of Key Transaction Multiples**

The key transaction multiples used in precedents mirror those used for trading comps. Equity value, as represented by the offer price for the target's equity, is used as a multiple of net income (or offer price per share as a multiple of diluted EPS) and enterprise value (or transaction value) is used as a multiple of EBITDA, EBIT, and, to a lesser extent, sales. In precedent transactions, these multiples are typically higher than those in trading comps due to the premium paid for control and/or synergies.

Multiples for precedent transactions are typically calculated on the basis of actual LTM financial statistics available at the time of announcement. The full projections that an acquirer uses to frame its purchase price decision are generally not public and subject to a confidentiality agreement.[13] Therefore, while equity research may offer insights into future performance for a public target, identifying the actual projections that an acquirer used when making its acquisition decision is typically not feasible. Furthermore, buyers are often hesitant to give sellers full credit for projected financial performance as they assume the risk for realization.

As previously discussed, whenever possible, the banker sources the information necessary to calculate the target's LTM financials directly from SEC filings and other public primary sources. As with trading comps, the LTM financial data needs to be adjusted for non-recurring items and recent events in order to calculate clean multiples that reflect the target's normalized performance.

---

[13]Legal contract between a buyer and seller that governs the sharing of confidential company information (see Chapter 6). In the event the banker performing precedents is privy to non-public information regarding one of the selected comparable acquisitions, the banker must refrain from using that information in order to maintain client confidentiality.

## Equity Value Multiples

**Offer Price per Share-to-LTM EPS / Equity Value-to-LTM Net Income**  The most broadly used equity value multiple is the P/E ratio, namely offer price per share divided by LTM diluted earnings per share (or equity value divided by LTM net income, see Exhibit 2.15).

**EXHIBIT 2.15**  Equity Value Multiples

## Enterprise Value Multiples

**Enterprise Value-to-LTM EBITDA, EBIT, and Sales**  As in trading comps, enterprise value is used in the numerator when calculating multiples for financial statistics that apply to both debt and equity holders. The most common enterprise value multiples are shown in Exhibit 2.16, with EV/LTM EBITDA being the most prevalent. As discussed in Chapter 1, however, certain sectors may rely on additional or other metrics to drive valuation (see Exhibit 1.33).

**EXHIBIT 2.16**  Enterprise Value Multiples

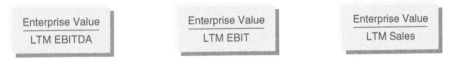

**Premiums Paid**  The *premium paid* refers to the incremental dollar amount per share that the acquirer offers relative to the target's unaffected share price, expressed as a percentage. As such, it is only relevant for public target companies. In calculating the premium paid relative to a given date, it is important to use the target's unaffected share price so as to isolate the true effect of the purchase offer.

The closing share price on the day prior to the official transaction announcement typically serves as a good proxy for the unaffected share price. However, to isolate for the effects of market gyrations and potential share price "creep" due to rumors or information leakage regarding the deal, the banker examines the offer price per share relative to the target's share price at multiple time intervals prior to transaction announcement (e.g., one trading day, seven calendar days, and 30 calendar days or more).[14]

---

[14]60, 90, 180, or an average of a set number of calendar days prior, as well as the 52-week high and low, may also be reviewed.

In the event the seller has publicly announced its intention to pursue "strategic alternatives" or there is a major leak prior to announcement, the target's share price may increase in anticipation of a potential takeover. In this case, the target's share price on the day(s) prior to the official transaction announcement is not truly unaffected. Instead, look at premiums paid relative to the target's share price at various intervals prior to such an announcement or leak in addition to the actual transaction announcement.

The formula for calculating the percentage premium paid, as well as an illustrative example, is shown in Exhibit 2.17. In this example, we calculate a 35% premium assuming that the target's shareholders are being offered $67.50 per share for a stock that was trading at an unaffected share price of $50.00.

**EXHIBIT 2.17**    Calculation of Premium Paid

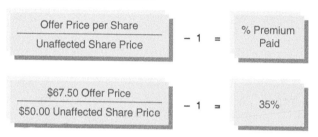

**Synergies**    Synergies refer to the expected cost savings, growth opportunities, and other financial benefits that occur as a result of the combination of two businesses. Consequently, the assessment of synergies is most relevant for transactions where a strategic buyer is purchasing a target in a related business.

Synergies represent tangible value to the acquirer in the form of future cash flow and earnings above and beyond what can be achieved by the target on a stand-alone basis. Therefore, the size and degree of likelihood for realizing potential synergies play an important role for the acquirer in framing the purchase price for a particular target. Theoretically, higher synergies translate into a higher potential price that the acquirer can pay. In analyzing a given comparable acquisition, the amount of announced synergies provides important perspective on the purchase price and multiple paid.

Upon announcement of a material acquisition, public acquirers often provide guidance on the nature and amount of expected synergies. This information is typically communicated via the press release announcing the transaction (see illustrative press release excerpt in Exhibit 2.18) and potentially an investor presentation.

**EXHIBIT 2.18**   Press Release Excerpt Discussing Synergies in a Strategic Acquisition

CLEVELAND, Ohio – June 10, 2019 – AcquirerCo and TargetCo announced today that they have signed a definitive agreement to merge the two companies…The proposed transaction is expected to provide substantial benefits for shareholders of the combined company and significant value creation through identified highly achievable synergies of $25 million in the first year after closing, and $50 million annually beginning in 2021. As facilities and operations are consolidated, a substantial portion of cost synergies and capital expenditure savings are expected to come from increased scale. Additional savings are expected to result from combining staff functions and the elimination of a significant amount of SG&A expenses that would be duplicative in the combined company.

Equity research reports also may provide helpful commentary on the value of expected synergies, including the likelihood of realization. Depending on the situation, investors afford varying degrees of credit for announced synergies, as reflected in the acquirer's post-announcement share price. In precedent transactions, it is helpful to note the announced expected synergies for each transaction where such information is available. However, the transaction multiples are typically shown on the basis of the target's reported LTM financial information (i.e., without adjusting for synergies). To better understand the multiple paid, it is common practice to also calculate adjusted multiples that reflect expected synergies. This typically involves adding the full effect of expected annual run-rate cost savings synergies (excluding costs to achieve) to an earnings metric in the denominator (e.g., EBITDA and EPS).

Exhibit 2.19 shows the calculation of an EV/LTM EBITDA transaction multiple before and after the consideration of expected synergies, assuming a purchase price of $1,200 million, LTM EBITDA of $150 million, and synergies of $25 million.

**EXHIBIT 2.19**   Synergies-Adjusted Multiple

$$\frac{\text{Enterprise Value}}{\text{LTM EBITDA}} = \frac{\$1,200 \text{ million}}{\$150 \text{ million}} = 8.0x$$

$$\frac{\text{Enterprise Value}}{\text{LTM EBITDA + Synergies}} = \frac{\$1,200 \text{ million}}{\$150 \text{ million} + \$25 \text{ million}} = 6.9x$$

## STEP IV. BENCHMARK THE COMPARABLE ACQUISITIONS

As with trading comps, the next level of analysis involves an in-depth study of the selected comparable acquisitions so as to determine those most relevant for valuing the target. The business profile is reexamined and key financial statistics and ratios for each of the acquired companies are benchmarked, with an eye toward identifying those most comparable to the target. Output sheets, such as those shown in Exhibits 1.53 and 1.54 in Chapter 1, facilitate this analysis.

The transaction multiples and deal information for each selected acquisition are also linked to an output sheet where they can be easily benchmarked against one another and the broader universe (see Exhibit 2.35). Each comparable acquisition is closely examined as part of the final refining of the universe, with the best comparable transactions identified and obvious outliers eliminated. As would be expected, a recently consummated deal involving a direct competitor with a similar financial profile is typically more relevant than, for example, an older transaction from a different point in the business or credit cycle, or for a marginal player in the sector. A thoughtful analysis weighs other considerations such as market conditions and deal dynamics in conjunction with the target's business and financial profile.

## STEP V. DETERMINE VALUATION

In precedent transactions, the multiples of the selected comparable acquisitions universe are used to derive an implied valuation range for the target. While standards vary by sector, the key multiples driving valuation in precedent transactions tend to be enterprise value-to-LTM EBITDA and equity value-to-net income (or offer price per share-to-LTM diluted EPS, if public). Therefore, the banker typically uses the means and medians of these multiples from the universe to establish a preliminary valuation range for the target, with the highs and lows also serving as reference points.

As noted earlier, valuation requires a significant amount of art in addition to science. Therefore, while the mean and median multiples provide meaningful valuation guideposts, often the banker focuses on as few as two or three of the best transactions (as identified in Step IV) to establish valuation. For example, if the banker calculates a mean 7.5x EV/LTM EBITDA multiple for the comparable acquisitions universe, but the most relevant transactions were consummated in the 8.0x to 8.5x area, a 7.5x to 8.5x range might be more appropriate. This would place greater emphasis on the best transactions. The chosen multiple range would then be applied to the target's LTM financial statistics to derive an implied valuation range for the target, using the methodology described in Chapter 1 (see Exhibits 1.35, 1.36, and 1.37).

As with other valuation methodologies, once a valuation range for the target has been established, it is necessary to analyze the output and test conclusions. A common red flag for precedent transactions is when the implied valuation range is lower than the range derived using comparable companies. In this instance, revisit the assumptions underlying the selection of both the universes of comparable acquisitions and comparable companies, as well as the calculations behind the multiples. However, it is important to note that this may not always represent a flawed analysis. If a particular sector is "in play" or benefiting from a cyclical high, for example, the implied valuation range from comparable companies might be higher than that from precedent transactions. The results should be examined in isolation, using best judgment as well as guidance from senior colleagues to determine whether the results make sense.

## KEY PROS AND CONS

### Pros

- *Market-based* – analysis is based on actual acquisition multiples and premiums paid for similar companies

- *Current* – recent transactions tend to reflect prevailing M&A, capital markets, and general economic conditions

- *Relativity* – multiples approach provides straightforward reference points across sectors and time periods

- *Simplicity* – key multiples for a few selected transactions can anchor valuation

- *Objectivity* – precedent-based and avoids making assumptions about a company's future performance

### Cons

- *Market-based* – multiples may be skewed depending on capital markets and/or economic environment at the time of the transaction

- *Time lag* – precedent transactions, by definition, have occurred in the past and, therefore, may not be truly reflective of prevailing market conditions (e.g., the LBO boom in the mid-2000s versus the 2008/2009 credit crunch)

- *Existence of comparable acquisitions* – in some cases it may be difficult to find a robust universe of precedent transactions

- *Availability of information* – information may be insufficient to determine transaction multiples for many comparable acquisitions

- *Acquirer's basis for valuation* – multiple paid by the buyer may be based on expectations governing the target's future financial performance (which is typically not publicly disclosed) rather than on reported LTM financial information

## ILLUSTRATIVE PRECEDENT TRANSACTION ANALYSIS FOR VALUECO

The following section provides a detailed, step-by-step example of how precedent transactions analysis is applied to establish a valuation range for our illustrative target company, ValueCo.

### Step I. Select the Universe of Comparable Acquisitions

**Screen for Comparable Acquisitions**  Our screen for comparable acquisitions began by searching M&A databases for past transactions involving companies similar to ValueCo in terms of sector and size. We focused on transactions that occurred over the past three years with enterprise value between approximately $1 billion and $15 billion. At the same time, we examined the acquisition history of ValueCo's comparable companies (as determined in Chapter 1) for relevant transactions.

The comparable companies' public filings (including merger proxies) were helpful for identifying and analyzing past acquisitions and sales of relevant businesses. Research reports for individual companies as well as sector reports also provided valuable information. In total, these resources produced a sizable list of potential precedent transactions. Upon further scrutiny, we eliminated several transactions where the target's size or business model differed significantly from that of ValueCo.

**Examine Other Considerations**  For each of the selected transactions, we examined the specific deal circumstances, including market conditions and deal dynamics. For example, we discerned whether the acquisition took place during a cyclical high or low in the target's sector as well as the prevailing capital markets conditions. We also determined whether the acquirer was a strategic buyer or a financial sponsor and noted whether the target was sold through an auction process or a negotiated/ friendly transaction, and if it was contested. The form of consideration (i.e., cash versus stock) was also analyzed. While these deal considerations did not change the list of comparable acquisitions, the context helped us better interpret and compare the acquisition multiples and premiums paid.

By the end of Step I, we established a solid initial list of comparable acquisitions to be further analyzed. Exhibit 2.20 displays basic data about the selected transactions and target companies for easy comparison.

## Step II. Locate the Necessary Deal-Related and Financial Information

In Step II, we set out to locate the relevant deal-related and financial information necessary to spread each comparable acquisition. To illustrate this task, we highlighted Pearl Corp.'s ("Pearl") acquisition of Rosenbaum Industries ("Rosenbaum"), the most recent transaction on our list.[15] As this transaction involved a public acquirer and a public target, the necessary information was readily accessible via the relevant SEC filings.

**EXHIBIT 2.20**    Initial List of Comparable Acquisitions

*($ in millions)*

| Initial List of Comparable Acquisitions | | | | | | | | |
|---|---|---|---|---|---|---|---|---|
| Date Announced | Acquirer | Target | Transaction Type | Target Business Description | Equity Value | Enterprise Value | LTM Sales | LTM EBITDA |
| 11/4/2019 | Pearl Corp. | Rosenbaum Industries | Public / Public | Engages in the manufacture and sale of chemicals, plastics, and fibers | $2,500 | $3,825 | $2,385 | $450 |
| 7/22/2019 | Goodson Corp. | Schneider & Co. | Public / Public | US-based company engaged in providing water treatment and process chemicals | 5,049 | 6,174 | 4,359 | 764 |
| 6/24/2019 | Domanski Capital | Ackerman Industries | Sponsor / Public | Specialty chemical company that supplies technologies and produces additives, ingredients, resins, and compounds | 8,845 | 9,995 | 5,941 | 1,248 |
| 4/15/2019 | The Hochberg Group | Whalen Inc. | Sponsor / Private | World's largest producer of alkylamines and derivatives | 1,250 | 1,350 | 700 | 180 |
| 8/8/2018 | Cole Manufacturing | Gordon Inc. | Public / Public | Provider of cleaning, sanitizing, food safety, and infection prevention products and services | 2,620 | 3,045 | 1,989 | 340 |
| 7/9/2018 | Eu-Han Capital | Rughwani International | Sponsor / Public | Supplies products for the manufacturing, construction, automotive, chemical processing, and other industries worldwide | 3,390 | 4,340 | 2,722 | 558 |
| 3/20/2018 | Lanzarone Global | Falk & Sons | Public / Private | Manufactures specialty chemicals and functional ingredients for personal care, pharmaceutical, oral care, and institutional cleaning applications | 8,750 | 10,350 | 5,933 | 1,235 |
| 11/9/2017 | Meisner Global Management | Kamras Brands | Sponsor / Private | Manufactures and markets basic chemicals, vinyls, polymers, and fabricated building products | 1,765 | 2,115 | 1,416 | 269 |
| 6/22/2017 | Pryor, Inc. | ParkCo | Public / Private | Offers a broad range of chemicals and solutions used in consumer products applications | 6,450 | 8,700 | 7,950 | 1,240 |
| 4/17/2017 | Leicht & Co. | Bress Products | Public / Public | Engages in the development, production, and sale of food ingredients, enzymes, and bio-based solutions | 12,431 | 12,681 | 8,250 | 1,550 |

**8-K/Press Release**    Our search for relevant deal information began by locating the 8-K filed upon announcement of the transaction. The 8-K contained the press release announcing the transaction as well as a copy of the definitive agreement as an exhibit. The press release provided an overview of the basic terms of the deal, including the offer price per share, enterprise value, and purchase consideration, as well as a description of both the acquirer and target and a brief description of the transaction rationale (see Exhibit 2.21). The definitive agreement contained the detailed terms and conditions of the transaction.

---

[15]Pearl is also a comparable company to ValueCo (see Chapter 1, Exhibits 1.53, 1.54, and 1.55).

We also checked to see whether the original transaction changed for any new announced terms. As previously discussed, this is a relatively common occurrence in competitive situations where two or more parties enter into a bidding war for a given target.

**EXHIBIT 2.21**   Press Release Excerpt from Announcement of Pearl/Rosenbaum Deal

CLEVELAND, Ohio – November 4, 2019 – PEARL CORP. (Nasdaq: PRL), a producer of specialty chemical products, announced today that it has entered into a definitive agreement to acquire ROSENBAUM INDUSTRIES (Nasdaq: JNR), a manufacturer of plastics and fibers, for an aggregate consideration of approximately $3.825 billion, including the payment of $20.00 per outstanding share in cash and the assumption of $1.325 billion in net debt. The strategic business combination of Pearl and Rosenbaum will create a leading provider of "best-in-class" chemical products in North America. When completed, Pearl anticipates the combined companies will benefit from a broader product offering, complementary distribution channels, and efficiencies from streamlining its facilities.

**Proxy Statement (DEFM14A)**   As Rosenbaum is a public company, its board of directors sought approval for the transaction from Rosenbaum's shareholders via a proxy statement. The proxy statement contained Rosenbaum's most recent basic share count, a detailed background of the merger, discussion of the premium paid, and an excerpt from the fairness opinion, among other items. The background described key events leading up to the transaction announcement and provided us with helpful insight into other deal considerations useful for interpreting purchase price, including buyer/seller dynamics (see excerpt in Exhibit 2.22).

**EXHIBIT 2.22**   Excerpt from Rosenbaum's Proxy Statement

On June 3, 2019, Rosenbaum's CEO was informed of a financial sponsor's interest in a potential takeover and request for additional information in order to make a formal bid. This unsolicited interest prompted Rosenbaum's board of directors to form a special committee and engage an investment bank and legal counsel to explore strategic alternatives. Upon being contacted by Rosenbaum's advisor, the sponsor submitted a written indication of interest containing a preliminary valuation range of $15.00 to $17.00 per share and outlining a proposed due diligence process. Subsequently, certain media outlets reported that a sale of Rosenbaum was imminent, prompting the company to publicly announce its decision to explore strategic alternatives on August 15, 2019.

One week later, Pearl sent Rosenbaum a preliminary written indication of interest with a price range of $17.00 to $18.00. In addition, Rosenbaum's advisor contacted an additional 5 strategic buyers and 10 financial sponsors, although these parties did not ultimately participate in the formal process. Both the bidding financial sponsor and Pearl were then invited to attend a management presentation and perform due diligence, after which the financial sponsor and Pearl presented formal letters with bids of $18.00 and $20.00 per share in cash, respectively. Pearl's offer, as the highest cash offer, was accepted.

This background highlights the competitive dynamics involved in the process, which helped explain why the multiple paid for Rosenbaum is above the mean of the selected comparable acquisitions (see Exhibit 2.35).

**Rosenbaum's 10-K and 10-Q**　Rosenbaum's 10-K and 10-Q for the period prior to the transaction announcement provided us with the financial data necessary to calculate its LTM financial statistics as well as equity value and enterprise value (based on the offer price per share). We also read through the MD&A and notes to the financials for further insight into Rosenbaum's financial performance as well as for information on potential non-recurring items and recent events. *These public filings provided us with the remaining information necessary to calculate the transaction multiples.*

**Research Reports**　We read through equity research reports for Pearl and Rosenbaum following the transaction announcement for further color on the circumstances of the deal, including Pearl's strategic rationale and expected synergies.

**Investor Presentation**　In addition, Pearl posted an investor presentation to its corporate website under an "Investor Relations" link, which confirmed the financial information and multiples calculated in Exhibit 2.23.

**Financial Information Service**　We used a financial information service to source key historical share price information for Rosenbaum. These data points included the share price on the day prior to the actual transaction announcement, the unaffected share price (i.e., on the day prior to Rosenbaum's announcement of the exploration of strategic alternatives), and the share price at various intervals prior to the unaffected share price. This share price information served as the basis for the premiums paid calculations in Exhibit 2.33.

## Step III. Spread Key Statistics, Ratios, and Transaction Multiples

After locating the necessary deal-related and financial information for the selected comparable acquisitions, we created input pages for each transaction, as shown in Exhibit 2.23 for the Pearl/Rosenbaum transaction.

# EXHIBIT 2.23 Input Page for the Acquisition of Rosenbaum by Pearl

## Acquisition of Rosenbaum Industries by Pearl Corp.
### Input Page
*($ in millions, except per share data)*

### General Information

| Target | Rosenbaum Industries |
|---|---|
| Ticker | JNR |
| Fiscal Year End | Dec-31 |
| Marginal Tax Rate | 25.0% |

| Acquirer | Pearl Corp. |
|---|---|
| Ticker | PRL |
| Fiscal Year End | Dec-31 |

| | |
|---|---|
| Date Announced | 11/4/2019 |
| Date Effective | Pending |
| Transaction Type | Public / Public |
| Purchase Consideration | Cash |

### Calculation of Equity and Enterprise Value

**Offer Price per Share**

| | |
|---|---|
| Cash Offer Price per Share | $20.00 |
| Stock Offer Price per Share | - |
| Exchange Ratio | - |
| Pearl Corp. Share Price | - |
| **Offer Price per Share** | **$20.00** |

| | |
|---|---|
| Fully Diluted Shares Outstanding | 125.000 |
| **Implied Equity Value** | **$2,500.0** |

**Implied Enterprise Value**

| | |
|---|---|
| Plus: Total Debt | 1,375.0 |
| Plus: Preferred Stock | - |
| Plus: Noncontrolling Interest | - |
| Less: Cash and Cash Equivalents | (50.0) |
| **Implied Enterprise Value** | **$3,825.0** |

### LTM Transaction Multiples

| | |
|---|---|
| **EV/Sales** | |
| Metric | 1.6x |
| Metric | $2,385.0 |
| **EV/EBITDA** | |
| Metric | 8.5x |
| Metric | $450.0 |
| **EV/EBIT** | |
| Metric | 11.2x |
| Metric | $343.0 |
| **P/E** | |
| Metric | 13.7x |
| Metric | $1.46 |

### Premiums Paid

| Transaction Announcement | | Premium |
|---|---|---|
| 1 Day Prior | $17.39 | 15.0% |
| **Unaffected Share Price** | | (2) |
| 1 Day Prior | $14.81 | 35.0% |
| 7 Days Prior | 15.04 | 33.0% |
| 30 Days Prior | 14.60 | 37.0% |

### Source Documents

| | Period | Date Filed |
|---|---|---|
| Rosenbaum Industries 10-K | 12/31/2018 | 2/14/2019 |
| Rosenbaum Industries 10-Q | 9/30/2019 | 10/30/2019 |
| Rosenbaum Industries 8-K | | 11/4/2019 |
| Rosenbaum Industries DEFM14A | | 12/15/2019 |

### Reported Income Statement

| | FYE 12/31/2011 | Prior Stub 9/30/2018 | Current Stub 9/30/2019 | LTM 9/30/2019 |
|---|---|---|---|---|
| Sales | $2,250.0 | $1,687.5 | $1,822.5 | $2,385.0 |
| COGS | 1,500.0 | 1,125.0 | 1,215.0 | 1,590.0 |
| Gross Profit | $750.0 | $562.5 | $607.5 | $795.0 |
| SG&A | 450.0 | 337.5 | 364.5 | 477.0 |
| Other (Income)/Expense | - | - | - | - |
| EBIT | $300.0 | $225.0 | $243.0 | $318.0 |
| Interest Expense | 100.0 | 75.0 | 75.0 | 100.0 |
| Pre-tax Income | $200.0 | $150.0 | $168.0 | $218.0 |
| Income Taxes | 50.0 | 37.5 | 42.0 | 54.5 |
| Noncontrolling Interest | - | - | - | - |
| Preferred Dividends | - | - | - | - |
| Net Income | $150.0 | $112.5 | $126.0 | $163.5 |
| Effective Tax Rate | 25.0% | 25.0% | 25.0% | 26.0% |
| | | | | |
| Weighted Avg. Diluted Shares | 125.0 | 125.0 | 125.0 | 125.0 |
| Diluted EPS | $1.20 | $0.90 | $1.01 | $1.31 |

### Adjusted Income Statement

| | FYE 12/31/2011 | Prior Stub 9/30/2018 | Current Stub 9/30/2019 | LTM 9/30/2019 |
|---|---|---|---|---|
| Reported Gross Profit | $750.0 | $562.5 | $607.5 | $795.0 |
| Non-recurring Items in COGS | - | - | - | - |
| Adjusted Gross Profit | $750.0 | $562.5 | $607.5 | $795.0 |
| % margin | 33.3% | 33.3% | 33.3% | 33.3% |
| | | | | |
| Reported EBIT | $300.0 | $225.0 | $243.0 | $318.0 |
| Non-recurring Items in COGS | - | - | - | - |
| Other Non-recurring Items | 25.0 | - | - | 25.0 (1) |
| Adjusted EBIT | $325.0 | $225.0 | $243.0 | $343.0 |
| % margin | 14.4% | 13.3% | 13.3% | 14.4% |
| | | | | |
| Depreciation & Amortization | 100.0 | 75.0 | 82.0 | 107.0 |
| Adjusted EBITDA | $425.0 | $300.0 | $325.0 | $450.0 |
| % margin | 18.9% | 17.8% | 17.8% | 18.9% |
| | | | | |
| Reported Net Income | $150.0 | $112.5 | $126.0 | $163.5 |
| Non-recurring Items in COGS | - | - | - | - |
| Other Non-recurring Items | 25.0 | - | - | 25.0 |
| Non-operating Non-rec. Items | - | - | - | - |
| Tax Adjustment | (6.3) | - | - | (6.3) |
| Adjusted Net Income | $168.8 | $112.5 | $126.0 | $182.3 |
| % margin | 7.5% | 6.7% | 6.9% | 7.6% |
| Adjusted Diluted EPS | $1.35 | $0.90 | $1.01 | $1.46 |

### Cash Flow Statement Data

| | FYE 12/31/2011 | Prior Stub 9/30/2018 | Current Stub 9/30/2019 | LTM 9/30/2019 |
|---|---|---|---|---|
| Depreciation & Amortization | 100.0 | 75.0 | 82.0 | 107.0 |
| % sales | 4.4% | 4.4% | 4.5% | 4.5% |
| Capital Expenditures | 105.0 | 75.0 | 85.0 | 115.0 |
| % sales | 4.7% | 4.4% | 4.7% | 4.8% |

### Notes

(1) In Q4 2018, Rosenbaum Industries recorded a $25 million pre-tax payment in regards to a litigation settlement (see 2018 10-K MD&A, page 50).

(2) On August 15, 2019, Rosenbaum Industries announced the formation of a special committee to explore strategic alternatives.

### Target Description
Engages in the manufacture and sale of chemicals, plastics, and fibers

### Acquirer Description
Manufactures and markets performance materials and specialty chemicals

### Comments
The combined company will benefit from a broader product offering, complementary distribution channels, and efficiencies from streamlining facilities. The transaction also extends the acquirer's reach into emerging markets. Annual cost saving synergies of approximately $100 million expected by the end of 2014.

### Calculation of Fully Diluted Shares Outstanding

| | |
|---|---|
| Basic Shares Outstanding | 123.000 |
| Plus: Shares from In-the-Money Options | 3.750 |
| Less: Shares Repurchased from Option Proceeds | (1.750) |
| Net New Shares from Options | 2.000 |
| Plus: Shares from Convertible Securities | - |
| Fully Diluted Shares Outstanding | 125.000 |

**Options/Warrants**

| Tranche | Number of Shares | Exercise Price | In-the-Money Shares | Proceeds |
|---|---|---|---|---|
| Tranche 1 | 1.500 | $6.00 | 1.500 | $7.5 |
| Tranche 2 | 1.250 | 10.00 | 1.250 | 12.5 |
| Tranche 3 | 1.000 | 15.00 | 1.000 | 15.0 |
| Tranche 4 | - | - | - | - |
| Tranche 5 | - | - | - | - |
| Total | 3.750 | | 3.750 | $35.0 |

**Convertible Securities**

| Issue | Amount | Conversion Price | Conversion Ratio | New Shares |
|---|---|---|---|---|
| Issue 1 | - | - | - | - |
| Issue 2 | - | - | - | - |
| Issue 3 | - | - | - | - |
| Issue 4 | - | - | - | - |
| Issue 5 | - | - | - | - |
| Total | | | | |

Below, we walk through each section of the input sheet in Exhibit 2.23.

**General Information**   In the "General Information" section, we entered basic company and transaction information, such as the target's and acquirer's names and fiscal year ends, as well as the transaction announcement and closing dates, transaction type, and purchase consideration. As shown in Exhibit 2.24, Rosenbaum Industries (Nasdaq:JNR) was acquired by Pearl Corp. (Nasdaq:PRL) in an all-cash transaction. Both companies have a fiscal year ending December 31. The transaction was announced on November 4, 2019.

**EXHIBIT 2.24**   General Information Section

| General Information | |
| --- | --- |
| **Target** | **Rosenbaum Industries** |
| Ticker | JNR |
| Fiscal Year End | Dec-31 |
| Marginal Tax Rate | 25.0% |
| | |
| **Acquirer** | **Pearl Corp.** |
| Ticker | PRL |
| Fiscal Year End | Dec-31 |
| | |
| Date Announced | 11/4/2019 |
| Date Effective | Pending |
| Transaction Type | Public/Public |
| Purchase Consideration | Cash |

**Calculation of Equity and Enterprise Value**   Under "Calculation of Equity and Enterprise Value", we first entered Pearl's offer price per share of $20.00 in cash to Rosenbaum's shareholders, as disclosed in the 8-K and accompanying press release announcing the transaction (see Exhibit 2.25).

**EXHIBIT 2.25**   Calculation of Equity and Enterprise Value Section

*($ in millions, except per share data)*

| Calculation of Equity and Enterprise Value | |
| --- | --- |
| **Offer Price per Share** | |
| Cash Offer Price per Share | $20.00 |
| Stock Offer Price per Share | - |
| Exchange Ratio | - |
| Pearl Corp. Share Price | - |
| **Offer Price per Share** | **$20.00** ◢ |
| | |
| Fully Diluted Shares Outstanding | - |
| **Implied Equity Value** | - |
| | |
| **Implied Enterprise Value** | |
| Plus: Total Debt | - |
| Plus: Preferred Stock | - |
| Plus: Noncontrolling Interest | - |
| Less: Cash and Cash Equivalents | - |
| **Implied Enterprise Value** | - |

> = Cash Offer Price per Share + Stock Offer Price per Share
> = $20.00 + $0.00

**Calculation of Fully Diluted Shares Outstanding**    As sourced from the most recent proxy statement, Rosenbaum had basic shares outstanding of 123 million. Rosenbaum also had three "tranches" of options, as detailed in its most recent 10-K (see "Options/ Warrants" heading in Exhibit 2.26). At the $20.00 offer price, the three tranches of options are all in-the-money. In calculating fully diluted shares outstanding for precedent transactions, all outstanding in-the-money options and warrants are converted at their weighted average strike prices regardless of whether they are exercisable or not. These three tranches represent 3.75 million shares, which generate total proceeds of $35 million at their respective exercise prices. In accordance with the TSM, these proceeds are assumed to repurchase 1.75 million shares at the $20.00 offer price ($35 million/$20.00), thereby providing net new shares of 2 million. These incremental shares are added to Rosenbaum's basic shares to calculate fully diluted shares outstanding of 125 million.

**EXHIBIT 2.26**    Calculation of Fully Diluted Shares Outstanding Section

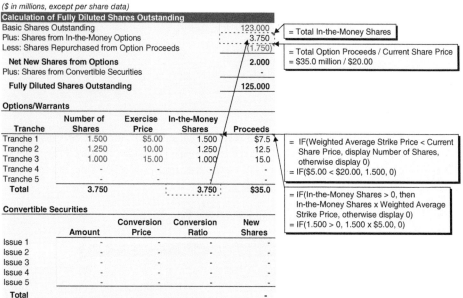

**Equity Value**    The 125 million fully diluted shares outstanding feeds into the "Calculation of Equity and Enterprise Value" section. It is then multiplied by the $20.00 offer price per share to produce an equity value of $2,500 million (see Exhibit 2.27).

**EXHIBIT 2.27** Equity Value

*($ in millions, except per share data)*

| Calculation of Equity and Enterprise Value | | |
|---|---|---|
| **Offer Price per Share** | | |
| Cash Offer Price per Share | | $20.00 |
| Stock Offer Price per Share | | - |
| Exchange Ratio | - | |
| Pearl Corp. Share Price | - | |
| **Offer Price per Share** | | **$20.00** |
| | | |
| Fully Diluted Shares Outstanding | | 125.000 |
| **Implied Equity Value** | | **$2,500.0** |

= Offer Price per Price × Fully Diluted Shares Outstanding
= $20.00 × 125 million

**Enterprise Value**   Rosenbaum's enterprise value was determined by adding net debt to the calculated equity value. We calculated net debt of $1,325 million by subtracting cash and cash equivalents of $50 million from total debt of $1,375 million, as sourced from Rosenbaum's 10-Q for the period ending September 30, 2019. The $1,325 million was then added to the calculated equity value of $2,500 million to derive an enterprise value of $3,825 million (see Exhibit 2.28).

**EXHIBIT 2.28** Enterprise Value

*($ in millions, except per share data)*

| Calculation of Equity and Enterprise Value | | |
|---|---|---|
| **Offer Price per Share** | | |
| Cash Offer Price per Share | | $20.00 |
| Stock Offer Price per Share | | - |
| Exchange Ratio | - | |
| Pearl Corp. Share Price | - | |
| **Offer Price per Share** | | **$20.00** |
| | | |
| Fully Diluted Shares Outstanding | | 125.000 |
| **Implied Equity Value** | | **$2,500.0** |
| | | |
| **Implied Enterprise Value** | | |
| Plus: Total Debt | | 1,375.0 |
| Plus: Preferred Stock | | - |
| Plus: Noncontrolling Interest | | - |
| Less: Cash and Cash Equivalents | | (50.0) |
| **Implied Enterprise Value** | | **$3,825.0** |

= Equity Value + Total Debt - Cash
= $2,500 million + $1,375 million - $50 million

**Reported Income Statement**   Next, we entered Rosenbaum's income statement information for the prior full year 2018 and YTD 2018 and 2019 periods directly from its most recent 10-K and 10-Q, respectively (see Exhibit 2.29). We also made adjustments for non-recurring items, as appropriate (see Exhibit 2.30).

**EXHIBIT 2.29** Rosenbaum's Reported Income Statement Section

*($ in millions, except per share data)*

**Reported Income Statement**

| | FYE 12/31/2018 | Prior Stub 9/30/2018 | Current Stub 9/30/2019 | LTM 9/30/2019 |
|---|---|---|---|---|
| Sales | $2,250.0 | $1,687.5 | $1,822.5 | $2,385.0 |
| COGS | 1,500.0 | 1,125.0 | 1,215.0 | 1,590.0 |
| **Gross Profit** | **$750.0** | **$562.5** | **$607.5** | **$795.0** |
| SG&A | 450.0 | 337.5 | 364.5 | 477.0 |
| Other (Income)/Expense | - | - | - | - |
| **EBIT** | **$300.0** | **$225.0** | **$243.0** | **$318.0** |
| Interest Expense | 100.0 | 75.0 | 75.0 | 100.0 |
| **Pre-tax Income** | **$200.0** | **$150.0** | **$168.0** | **$218.0** |
| Income Taxes | 50.0 | 37.5 | 42.0 | 54.5 |
| Noncontrolling Interest | - | - | - | - |
| Preferred Dividends | - | - | - | - |
| **Net Income** | **$150.0** | **$112.5** | **$126.0** | **$163.5** |
| *Effective Tax Rate* | *25.0%* | *25.0%* | *25.0%* | *25.0%* |
| | | | | |
| Weighted Avg. Diluted Shares | 125.0 | 125.0 | 125.0 | 125.0 |
| Diluted EPS | $1.20 | $0.90 | $1.01 | $1.31 |

**EXHIBIT 2.30** Rosenbaum's Adjusted Income Statement Section

*($ in millions, except per share data)*

Litigation Settlement

**Adjusted Income Statement**

| | FYE 12/31/2018 | Prior Stub 9/30/2018 | Current Stub 9/30/2019 | LTM 9/30/2019 |
|---|---|---|---|---|
| Reported Gross Profit | $750.0 | $562.5 | $607.5 | $795.0 |
| Non-recurring Items in COGS | - | - | - | - |
| **Adjusted Gross Profit** | **$750.0** | **$562.5** | **$607.5** | **$795.0** |
| *% margin* | *33.3%* | *33.3%* | *33.3%* | *33.3%* |
| | | | | |
| Reported EBIT | $300.0 | $225.0 | $243.0 | $318.0 |
| Non-recurring Items in COGS | - | - | - | - |
| Other Non-recurring Items | 25.0 | - | - | 25.0 |
| **Adjusted EBIT** | **$325.0** | **$225.0** | **$243.0** | **$343.0** |
| *% margin* | *14.4%* | *13.3%* | *13.3%* | *14.4%* |
| | | | | |
| Depreciation & Amortization | 100.0 | 75.0 | 82.0 | 107.0 |
| **Adjusted EBITDA** | **$425.0** | **$300.0** | **$325.0** | **$450.0** |
| *% margin* | *18.9%* | *17.8%* | *17.8%* | *18.9%* |
| | | | | |
| Reported Net Income | $150.0 | $112.5 | $126.0 | $163.5 |
| Non-recurring Items in COGS | - | - | - | - |
| Other Non-recurring Items | 25.0 | - | - | 25.0 |
| Non-operating Non-rec. Items | - | - | - | - |
| Tax Adjustment | (6.3) | - | - | (6.3) |
| **Adjusted Net Income** | **$168.8** | **$112.5** | **$126.0** | **$182.3** |
| *% margin* | *7.5%* | *6.7%* | *6.9%* | *7.6%* |
| | | | | |
| Adjusted Diluted EPS | $1.35 | $0.90 | $1.01 | $1.46 |

**Notes**

(1) In Q4 2018, Rosenbaum Industries recorded a $25 million pre-tax payment in regards to a litigation settlement (see 2018 10-K MD&A, page 50).

= Negative Adjustment for Pre-tax Gain on Litigation Settlement × Marginal Tax Rate
= - ($25 million × 25%)

**Adjusted Income Statement** A review of Rosenbaum's financial statements and MD&A revealed that it made a $25 million pre-tax payment regarding a litigation settlement in Q4 2018, which we construed as non-recurring. Therefore, we added this charge back to Rosenbaum's reported financials, resulting in adjusted EBITDA, EBIT, and EPS of $450 million, $343 million and $1.46, respectively, on an LTM basis. These adjusted financials served as the basis for calculating Rosenbaum's transaction multiples in Exhibit 2.32.

**Cash Flow Statement Data** Rosenbaum's D&A and capex information was sourced directly from its cash flow statement, as it appeared in the 10-K and 10-Q (see Exhibit 2.31).

**EXHIBIT 2.31** Cash Flow Statement Data Section

*($ in millions)*

| Cash Flow Statement Data | | | | |
|---|---|---|---|---|
| | FYE 12/31/2018 | Prior Stub 9/30/2018 | Current Stub 9/30/2019 | LTM 9/30/2019 |
| Depreciation & Amortization | 100.0 | 75.0 | 82.0 | 107.0 |
| % sales | 4.4% | 4.4% | 4.5% | 4.5% |
| Capital Expenditures | 105.0 | 75.0 | 85.0 | 115.0 |
| % sales | 4.7% | 4.4% | 4.7% | 4.8% |

**LTM Transaction Multiples** For the calculation of Rosenbaum's transaction multiples, we applied enterprise value and offer price per share to the corresponding adjusted LTM financial data (see Exhibit 2.32). These multiples were then linked to the precedent transactions output sheet (see Exhibit 2.35) where the multiples for the entire universe are displayed.

**EXHIBIT 2.32** LTM Transaction Multiples Section

*($ in millions, except per share data)*

| LTM Transaction Multiples | |
|---|---|
| EV/Sales | 1.6x |
| Metric | $2,385.0 |
| EV/EBITDA | 8.5x |
| Metric | $450.0 |
| EV/EBIT | 11.2x |
| Metric | $343.0 |
| P/E | 13.7x |
| Metric | $1.46 |

= Enterprise Value / LTM 9/30/2019 EBITDA
= $3,825 million / $450 million

Adjusted for $100 million of expected synergies, the LTM EV/EBITDA multiple would be approximately 7.0x ($3,825 million / $550 million).

**Enterprise Value-to-LTM EBITDA**   For EV/LTM EBITDA, we divided Rosenbaum's enterprise value of $3,825 million by its LTM 9/30/2019 adjusted EBITDA of $450 million to provide a multiple of 8.5x. We used the same approach to calculate the LTM EV/sales and EV/EBIT multiples.

**Offer Price per Share-to-LTM Diluted Earnings per Share**   For P/E, we divided the offer price per share of $20.00 by Rosenbaum's LTM diluted EPS of $1.46 to provide a multiple of 13.7x.

**Premiums Paid**   The premiums paid analysis for precedent transactions does not apply when valuing private companies such as ValueCo. However, as Rosenbaum was a public company, we performed this analysis for illustrative purposes (see Exhibit 2.33).

**EXHIBIT 2.33**   Premiums Paid Section

| Premiums Paid | | |
|---|---|---|
| **Transaction Announcement** | | **Premium** |
| 1 Day Prior | $17.39 | *15.0%* |
| **Unaffected Share Price** | | (2) |
| 1 Day Prior | $14.81 | *35.0%* |
| 7 Days Prior | 15.04 | *33.0%* |
| 30 Days Prior | 14.60 | *37.0%* |

= Offer Price per Price / Share Price One Day Prior to Announcement - 1
= $20.00 / $17.39 - 1

| Notes |
|---|
| (2) On August 15, 2019, Rosenbaum Industries announced the formation of a special committee to explore strategic alternatives. |

The $20.00 offer price per share served as the basis for performing the premiums paid analysis, representing a 15% premium to Rosenbaum's share price of $17.39 on the day prior to transaction announcement. However, as shown in Exhibit 2.34, Rosenbaum's share price was directly affected by the announcement that it was exploring strategic alternatives on August 15, 2019 (even though the actual deal wasn't announced until November 4, 2019). Therefore, we also analyzed the unaffected premiums paid on the basis of Rosenbaum's closing share prices of $14.81, $15.04, and $14.60, for the one-, seven-, and 30-calendar-day periods prior to August 15, 2019. This provided us with premiums paid of 35%, 33%, and 37%, respectively, which are more in line with traditional public M&A premiums.

**EXHIBIT 2.34** Rosenbaum's Annotated Price/Volume Graph

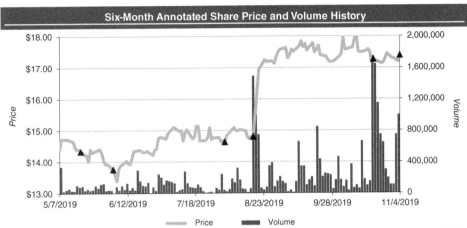

| Δ Date | Event |
|---|---|
| 5/15/2019 | Rosenbaum Industries reports earnings results for the first quarter ended March 31, 2019 |
| 6/3/2019 | Rosenbaum's CEO receives unsolicited bid by a financial sponsor |
| 7/31/2019 | Media reports that a sale of Rosenbaum Industries is likely |
| 8/15/2019 | Rosenbaum reports earnings results for the second quarter ended June 30, 2019 |
| **8/15/2019** | **Rosenbaum's Board of Directors forms a Special Committee to explore strategic alternatives** |
| 10/18/2019 | Media reports that Rosenbaum is close to signing a deal |
| 11/4/2019 | Rosenbaum reports earnings results for the third quarter ended September 30, 2019 |
| 11/4/2019 | Pearl Corp. enters into a Definitive Agreement to acquire Rosenbaum |

## Step IV. Benchmark the Comparable Acquisitions

In Step IV, we linked the key financial statistics and ratios for the target companies (calculated in Step III) to output sheets used for benchmarking purposes (see Chapter 1, Exhibits 1.53 and 1.54, for general templates). The benchmarking sheets helped us determine those targets most comparable to ValueCo from a financial perspective, namely Rosenbaum Industries, Schneider & Co., and Rughwani International. At the same time, our analysis in Step I provided us with sufficient information to confirm that these companies were highly comparable to ValueCo from a business perspective.

The relevant transaction multiples and deal information for each of the individual comparable acquisitions were also linked to an output sheet. As shown in Exhibit 2.35, ValueCo's sector experienced robust M&A activity during the 2017 to 2019 period, which provided us with sufficient relevant data points for our analysis. Consideration of the market conditions and other deal dynamics for each of these transactions further supported our selection of Pearl Corp./Rosenbaum Industries, Goodson Corp./Schneider & Co., and Eu-Han Capital/Rughwani International as the best comparable acquisitions. These multiples formed the primary basis for our selection of the appropriate multiple range for ValueCo.

**EXHIBIT 2.35** Precedent Transactions Analysis Output Page

## ValueCo Corporation
### Precedent Transactions Analysis
($ in millions)

| Date Announced | Acquirer | Target | Transaction Type | Purchase Consideration | Equity Value | Enterprise Value | Enterprise Value / | | | LTM EBITDA Margin | Equity Value / LTM Net Income | Premiums Paid Days Prior to Unaffected | | |
|---|---|---|---|---|---|---|---|---|---|---|---|---|---|---|
| | | | | | | | LTM Sales | LTM EBITDA | LTM EBIT | | | 1 | 7 | 30 |
| 11/4/2019 | Pearl Corp. | Rosenbaum Industries | Public / Public | Cash | $2,500 | $3,825 | 1.6x | 8.5x | 11.2x | 19% | 13.7x | 35% | 33% | 37% |
| 7/22/2019 | Goodson Corp. | Schneider & Co. | Public / Public | Cash / Stock | 5,049 | 6,174 | 1.4x | 8.1x | 10.3x | 18% | 12.7x | 29% | 32% | 31% |
| 6/24/2019 | Domanski Capital | Ackerman Industries | Sponsor / Public | Cash | 8,845 | 9,995 | 1.7x | 8.0x | 10.2x | 21% | 13.1x | 35% | 37% | 39% |
| 4/15/2019 | The Hochberg Group | Whalen Inc. | Sponsor / Private | Cash | 1,250 | 1,350 | 1.9x | 7.5x | 9.6x | 26% | 12.6x | NA | NA | NA |
| 8/8/2018 | Cole Manufacturing | Gordon Inc. | Public / Public | Stock | 2,620 | 3,045 | 1.5x | 9.0x | 12.2x | 17% | 16.8x | 47% | 44% | 49% |
| 7/9/2018 | Eu-Han Capital | Rughwani International | Sponsor / Public | Cash | 3,390 | 4,340 | 1.6x | 7.8x | 9.4x | 21% | 11.4x | 38% | 40% | 43% |
| 3/20/2018 | Lanzarone Global | Falk & Sons | Public / Private | Cash | 8,750 | 10,350 | 1.7x | 8.4x | 10.5x | 21% | 13.3x | NA | NA | NA |
| 11/9/2017 | Meisner Global Management | Kamras Brands | Sponsor / Private | Cash | 1,765 | 2,115 | 1.5x | 7.9x | 9.3x | 19% | 11.4x | NA | NA | NA |
| 6/22/2017 | Pryor, Inc. | FeinerCo | Public / Private | Cash | 6,450 | 8,700 | 1.1x | 7.0x | 7.9x | 16% | 9.8x | NA | NA | NA |
| 4/17/2017 | Leicht & Co. | Bress Products | Public / Public | Stock | 12,431 | 12,681 | 1.5x | 8.2x | 12.1x | 19% | 16.3x | 29% | 36% | 34% |
| **Mean** | | | | | | | 1.6x | 8.0x | 10.3x | 19% | 13.1x | 36% | 37% | 39% |
| **Median** | | | | | | | 1.6x | 8.0x | 10.3x | 19% | 12.9x | 35% | 36% | 38% |
| **High** | | | | | | | 1.9x | 9.0x | 12.2x | 26% | 16.8x | 47% | 44% | 49% |
| **Low** | | | | | | | 1.1x | 7.0x | 7.9x | 16% | 9.8x | 29% | 32% | 31% |

Source: Company filings

## Step V. Determine Valuation

In ValueCo's sector, companies are typically valued on the basis of EV/EBITDA multiples. Therefore, we employed an LTM EV/EBITDA multiple approach in valuing ValueCo using precedent transactions. We placed particular emphasis on those transactions deemed most comparable, namely the acquisitions of Rosenbaum Industries, Schneider & Co., and Rughwani International to frame the range (as discussed in Step IV).

This approach led us to establish a multiple range of 7.5x to 8.5x LTM EBITDA. We then multiplied the endpoints of this range by ValueCo's LTM 9/30/2019 EBITDA of $700 million to calculate an implied enterprise value range of approximately $5,250 million to $5,950 million (see Exhibit 2.36).

**EXHIBIT 2.36**   ValueCo's Implied Valuation Range

| ValueCo Corporation | | | | |
|---|---|---|---|---|
| **Implied Valuation Range** | | | | |
| *($ in millions, LTM 9/30/2019)* | | | | |
| **EBITDA** | **Metric** | **Multiple Range** | | **Implied Enterprise Value** |
| LTM | $700 | 7.50x – 8.50x | | $5,250 – $5,950 |

As a final step, we analyzed the valuation range derived from precedent transactions versus that derived from comparable companies. As shown in the football field in Exhibit 2.37, this range is at a slight premium to comparable companies, which is attributable to premiums paid in M&A transactions.

**EXHIBIT 2.37**   ValueCo Football Field Displaying Comps & Precedents

*($ in millions)*

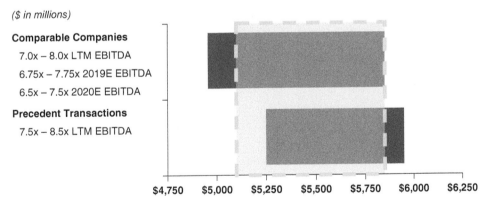

**Comparable Companies**

7.0x – 8.0x LTM EBITDA

6.75x – 7.75x 2019E EBITDA

6.5x – 7.5x 2020E EBITDA

**Precedent Transactions**

7.5x – 8.5x LTM EBITDA

$4,750   $5,000   $5,250   $5,500   $5,750   $6,000   $6,250

1) Which of the following is NOT a traditional source when creating an initial list of comparable acquisitions?

   A. M&A databases
   B. Target's M&A history
   C. Credit reports
   D. Fairness opinions for recent transactions in the target's sector

2) Which question(s) would a banker typically ask to better understand the context of an M&A deal?

   I. Was the acquirer a strategic buyer or financial sponsor?
   II. Was the nature of the deal friendly or hostile?
   III. Was the target sold through an auction process or negotiated sale?
   IV. What were the buyer's and seller's motivations for the transaction?

   A. I and IV
   B. II and III
   C. III and IV
   D. I, II, III, and IV

3) In addition to a high purchase price, what other factors are important to the seller in assessing the value of a proposed bid?

   I. Speed of execution
   II. Date of management presentation
   III. Certainty of completion
   IV. Regulatory approvals needed

   A. II and III
   B. II and IV
   C. I, II, and IV
   D. I, III, and IV

4) Which of following is NOT contained in a merger proxy?

   A. Terms of transaction
   B. Description of the financial analysis underlying the fairness opinion
   C. Definitive purchase/sale agreement
   D. Target's customer list

5) A target has _____ days to respond to a tender offer and file a _____

    A. 10; 10-Q
    B. 10; Schedule 14D-9
    C. 15; 10-Q
    D. 15; Schedule TO

6) Which exchange ratio is most common in a stock-for-stock transaction?

    A. Linear
    B. Floating
    C. Fixed
    D. Non-Floating

7) What is the exchange ratio if an acquirer agrees to exchange 0.5 shares of its stock for every 2 shares of the target's stock?

    A. 0.25
    B. 0.45
    C. 2.0
    D. 4.0

8) Assuming no structural protections for the acquirer, in which structure does the acquirer assume the full risk of a decline in its share price?

    A. Fixed
    B. Floating
    C. Both
    D. Neither

9) Calculate the implied premium paid, assuming the target has an unaffected share price of $50.00 and the offer price is $67.50 per share

    A. 20%
    B. 25%
    C. 30%
    D. 35%

10) Why is "time lag" a potential weakness when using precedent transactions?

    A. If the target company in an M&A transaction had a fiscal year ending April 30, it is difficult to include them in the group
    B. Precedent transactions, by definition, took place in the past and it is possible that they do not reflect prevailing market conditions
    C. It is complex to spread precedent transactions
    D. Certain precedent transactions were completed in a shorter time period than other deals

11) What are the primary types of synergies?

    I. Revenue
    II. Transaction
    III. Cost
    IV. Time

    A. I and II
    B. I and III
    C. III and IV
    D. I, II, and III

12) Assuming a stock-for-stock transaction, determine the exchange ratio

*($ in millions, except per share data; shares in millions)*

| Assumptions | |
|---|---|
| Office Price Per Share | $15.00 |
| Acquirer Share Price | $30.00 |
| Unaffected Target Share Price | $12.50 |
| Target Basic Shares Outstanding | 250.0 |
| Outstanding Options | 10.0 |
| Exercise Price | $10.00 |
| Target LTM Revenue | $4,500.0 |
| Target LTM EBITDA | 650.0 |
| Target Net Debt | 1,000.0 |

    A. 0.50
    B. 0.75
    C. 1.1
    D. 2.0

13) What is the premium paid for the target?

    A. 15.0%
    B. 17.0%
    C. 20.0%
    D. 25.0%

14) Calculate the target's offer value and enterprise value

    A. $3,800 million and $4,800 million
    B. $4,250 million and $5,250 million
    C. $4,750 million and $5,150 million
    D. $5,250 million and $6,250 million

15) Calculate the target's LTM enterprise value-to-EBITDA

    A. 9.0x
    B. 8.4x
    C. 6.4x
    D. 7.4x

# Discounted Cash Flow Analysis

**D**iscounted cash flow analysis ("DCF analysis" or the "DCF") is a fundamental valuation methodology broadly used by investment bankers, corporate officers, university professors, investors, and other finance professionals. It is premised on the principle that the value of a company, division, business, or collection of assets ("target") can be derived from the present value of its projected *free cash flow* (FCF). A company's projected FCF is derived from a variety of assumptions and judgments about expected financial performance, including sales growth rates, profit margins, capital expenditures, and *net working capital* (NWC) requirements. The DCF has a wide range of applications, including valuation for various M&A situations, IPOs, restructurings, and investment decisions.

The valuation implied for a target by a DCF is also known as its *intrinsic value*, as opposed to its market value, which is the value ascribed by the market at a given point in time. As a result, when performing a comprehensive valuation, a DCF serves as an important alternative to market-based valuation techniques such as comparable companies and precedent transactions, which can be distorted by a number of factors, including market aberrations (e.g., the post-subprime credit crunch). As such, a DCF plays an important role as a check on the prevailing market valuation for a publicly traded company. A DCF is also valuable when there are limited (or no) pure play, peer companies or comparable acquisitions.

In a DCF, a company's FCF is typically projected for a period of five years. The projection period, however, may be longer depending on the company's sector, stage of development, and the underlying predictability of its financial performance. Given the inherent difficulties in accurately projecting a company's financial performance over an extended period of time (and through various business and economic cycles), a *terminal value* is used to capture the remaining value of the target beyond the projection period (i.e., its "going concern" value).

The projected FCF and terminal value are discounted to the present at the target's *weighted average cost of capital* (WACC), which is a discount rate commensurate with its business and financial risks. The present value of the FCF and terminal value are summed to determine an enterprise value, which serves as the basis for the DCF valuation. The WACC and terminal value assumptions typically have a substantial impact on the output, with even slight variations producing meaningful differences in valuation. As a result, a DCF output is viewed in terms of a valuation range based on a range of key input assumptions, rather than as a single value. The impact of these assumptions on valuation is tested using *sensitivity analysis*.

The assumptions driving a DCF are both its primary strength and weakness versus market-based valuation techniques. On the positive side, the use of defensible assumptions regarding financial projections, WACC, and terminal value helps shield the target's valuation from market distortions that occur periodically. A DCF also provides the flexibility to analyze the target's valuation under different scenarios by changing the underlying inputs and examining the resulting impact. On the negative side, a DCF is only as strong as its assumptions. Hence, assumptions that fail to adequately capture the realistic set of opportunities and risks facing the target will also fail to produce a meaningful valuation.

This chapter walks through a step-by-step construction of a DCF, or its science (see Exhibit 3.1). At the same time, it provides the tools to master the art of the DCF, namely the ability to craft a logical set of assumptions based on an in-depth analysis of the target and its key performance drivers. Once this framework is established, we perform an illustrative DCF analysis for our target company, ValueCo.

**EXHIBIT 3.1**    Discounted Cash Flow Analysis Steps

| |
|---|
| Step I.    Study the Target and Determine Key Performance Drivers |
| Step II.   Project Free Cash Flow |
| Step III.  Calculate Weighted Average Cost of Capital |
| Step IV.  Determine Terminal Value |
| Step V.   Calculate Present Value and Determine Valuation |

## Summary of Discounted Cash Flow Analysis Steps

- **Step I. Study the Target and Determine Key Performance Drivers.** The first step in performing a DCF, as with any valuation exercise, is to study and learn as much as possible about the target and its sector. Shortcuts in this critical area of due diligence may lead to misguided assumptions and valuation distortions later on. This exercise involves determining the key drivers of financial performance (in particular sales growth, profitability, and FCF generation), which enables the banker to craft (or support) a defensible set of projections for the target. Step I is invariably easier when valuing a public company as opposed to a private company due to the availability of information from sources such as SEC filings (e.g., 10-Ks, 10-Qs, and 8-Ks), equity research reports, earnings call transcripts, and investor presentations.

  For private, non-filing companies, the banker often relies upon company management to provide materials containing basic business and financial information. In an organized M&A sale process, this information is typically provided in the form of a CIM (see Chapter 6). In the absence of this information, alternative sources (e.g., company websites, trade journals, and news articles, as well as SEC filings and research reports for public competitors, customers, and suppliers) must be used to learn basic company information and form the basis for developing the assumptions to drive financial projections.

■ **Step II. Project Free Cash Flow.** The projection of the target's *unlevered* FCF forms the core of a DCF. Unlevered FCF, which we simply refer to as FCF in this chapter, is the cash generated by a company after paying all cash operating expenses and taxes, as well as the funding of capex and working capital, but prior to the payment of any interest expense.[1] The target's projected FCF is driven by assumptions underlying its future financial performance, including sales growth rates, profit margins, capex, and working capital requirements. Historical performance, combined with third-party and/or management guidance, helps in developing these assumptions. The use of realistic FCF projections is critical as it has the greatest effect on valuation in a DCF.

In a DCF, the target's FCF is typically projected for a period of five years, but this period may vary depending on the target's sector, stage of development, and the predictability of its FCF. However, five years is typically sufficient for spanning at least one business/economic cycle and allowing for the successful realization of in-process or planned initiatives. The goal is to project FCF to a point in the future when the target's financial performance is deemed to have reached a "steady state" that can serve as the basis for a terminal value calculation (see Step IV).

■ **Step III. Calculate Weighted Average Cost of Capital.** In a DCF, WACC is the rate used to discount the target's projected FCF and terminal value to the present. It is designed to fairly reflect the target's business and financial risks. As its name connotes, WACC represents the "weighted average" of the required return on the invested capital (customarily debt and equity) in a given company. It is also commonly referred to as a company's *discount rate* or *cost of capital*. As debt and equity components generally have significantly different risk profiles and tax ramifications, WACC is dependent on capital structure.

■ **Step IV. Determine Terminal Value.** The DCF approach to valuation is based on determining the present value of future FCF produced by the target. Given the challenges of projecting the target's FCF indefinitely, a terminal value is used to quantify the remaining value of the target after the projection period. The terminal value typically accounts for a substantial portion of the target's value in a DCF. Therefore, it is important that the target's financial data in the final year of the projection period ("terminal year") represents a steady state or normalized level of financial performance, as opposed to a cyclical high or low.

There are two widely accepted methods used to calculate a company's terminal value—the exit multiple method (EMM) and the perpetuity growth method (PGM). The EMM calculates the remaining value of the target after the projection period on the basis of a multiple of the target's terminal year EBITDA (or EBIT). The PGM calculates terminal value by treating the target's terminal year FCF as a perpetuity growing at an assumed rate.

---

[1]See Chapter 4: Leveraged Buyouts and Chapter 5: LBO Analysis for a discussion of *levered* free cash flow or cash available for debt repayment.

▪ Step V. Calculate Present Value and Determine Valuation. The target's projected FCF and terminal value are discounted to the present and summed to calculate its enterprise value. Implied equity value and share price (if relevant) can then be derived from the calculated enterprise value. The present value calculation is performed by multiplying the FCF for each year in the projection period, as well as the terminal value, by its respective *discount factor*. The discount factor represents the present value of one dollar received at a given future date assuming a given discount rate.[2]

As a DCF incorporates numerous assumptions about key performance drivers, WACC, and terminal value, it is used to produce a valuation range rather than a single value. The exercise of driving a valuation range by varying key inputs is called sensitivity analysis. Core DCF valuation drivers such as WACC, exit multiple or perpetuity growth rate, sales growth rates, and margins are the most commonly sensitized inputs. Once determined, the valuation range implied by the DCF should be compared to those derived from other methodologies such as comparable companies, precedent transactions, and LBO analysis (if applicable) as a sanity check.

Once the step-by-step approach summarized above is complete, the final DCF output page should look similar to the one shown in Exhibit 3.2.

---

[2]For example, assuming a 10% discount rate and a one-year time horizon, the discount factor is 0.91 (1/(1+10%)^1), which implies that one dollar received one year in the future would be worth $0.91 today.

**EXHIBIT 3.2** DCF Analysis Output Page

# ValueCo Corporation
## Discounted Cash Flow Analysis
*($ in millions, fiscal year ending December 31)*

Operating Scenario: 1 / Y — Operating Scenario: Base

| Mid-Year Convention | Historical Period 2016 | 2017 | 2018 | CAGR ('16 - '18) | 2019 | Projection Period 2020 | 2021 | 2022 | 2023 | 2024 | CAGR ('19 - '24) |
|---|---|---|---|---|---|---|---|---|---|---|---|
| Sales | $2,600.0 | $2,900.0 | $3,200.0 | 10.9% | $3,450.0 | $3,708.8 | $3,931.3 | $4,127.8 | $4,293.0 | $4,421.7 | 5.1% |
| % growth | NA | 11.5% | 10.3% | | 7.8% | 7.5% | 6.0% | 5.0% | 4.0% | 3.0% | |
| EBITDA | $491.4 | $580.0 | $672.0 | 16.9% | $725.0 | $779.4 | $826.1 | $867.4 | $902.1 | $929.2 | 5.1% |
| % margin | 18.9% | 20.0% | 21.0% | | 21.0% | 21.0% | 21.0% | 21.0% | 21.0% | 21.0% | |
| Depreciation & Amortization | 155.0 | 165.0 | 193.0 | | 207.0 | 222.5 | 235.9 | 247.7 | 257.6 | 265.3 | |
| EBIT | $336.4 | $415.0 | $479.0 | 19.3% | $518.0 | $556.9 | $590.3 | $619.8 | $644.6 | $663.9 | 5.1% |
| % margin | 12.9% | 14.3% | 15.0% | | 15.0% | 15.0% | 15.0% | 15.0% | 15.0% | 15.0% | |
| Taxes | 84.1 | 103.8 | 119.8 | | 129.5 | 139.2 | 147.6 | 154.9 | 161.1 | 166.0 | |
| EBIAT | $252.3 | $311.3 | $359.3 | 19.3% | $388.5 | $417.6 | $442.7 | $464.8 | $483.4 | $497.9 | 5.1% |
| Plus: Depreciation & Amortization | 155.0 | 165.0 | 193.0 | | 207.0 | 222.5 | 235.9 | 247.7 | 257.6 | 265.3 | |
| Less: Capital Expenditures | (114.4) | (116.0) | (144.0) | | (155.3) | (166.9) | (176.9) | (185.8) | (193.2) | (199.0) | |
| Less: Inc./(Dec.) in Net Working Capital | | | | | | (47.6) | (41.0) | (36.2) | (30.4) | (23.7) | |
| Unlevered Free Cash Flow | | | | | | $425.6 | $460.7 | $490.6 | $517.4 | $540.5 | |
| WACC | 11.0% | | | | | | | | | | |
| Discount Period | | | | | | 0.5 | 1.5 | 2.5 | 3.5 | 4.5 | |
| Discount Factor | | | | | | 0.95 | 0.86 | 0.77 | 0.69 | 0.63 | |
| Present Value of Free Cash Flow | | | | | | $404.0 | $393.9 | $377.9 | $359.1 | $338.0 | |

### Enterprise Value

| Cumulative Present Value of FCF | $1,872.9 |
|---|---|
| **Terminal Value** | |
| Terminal Year EBITDA (2024E) | $929.2 |
| Exit Multiple | 7.5x |
| Terminal Value | $6,969.0 |
| Discount Factor | 0.59 |
| Present Value of Terminal Value | $4,135.8 |
| % of Enterprise Value | 68.8% |
| **Enterprise Value** | **$6,008.7** |

### Implied Equity Value and Share Price

| Enterprise Value | $6,008.7 |
|---|---|
| Less: Total Debt | (1,500.0) |
| Less: Preferred Stock | - |
| Less: Noncontrolling Interest | - |
| Plus: Cash and Cash Equivalents | 250.0 |
| **Implied Equity Value** | **$4,758.7** |
| Fully Diluted Shares Outstanding | 80.0 |
| **Implied Share Price** | **$59.48** |

### Implied Perpetuity Growth Rate

| Terminal Year Free Cash Flow (2024E) | $540.5 |
|---|---|
| WACC | 11.0% |
| Terminal Value | $6,969.0 |
| **Implied Perpetuity Growth Rate** | **2.6%** |

### Implied EV/EBITDA

| Enterprise Value | $6,008.7 |
|---|---|
| LTM 9/30/2019 EBITDA | 700.0 |
| **Implied EV/EBITDA** | **8.6x** |

**Enterprise Value**

| WACC | Exit Multiple 6.5x | 7.0x | 7.5x | 8.0x | 8.5x |
|---|---|---|---|---|---|
| 10.0% | 5,665 | 5,953 | 6,242 | 6,530 | 6,819 |
| 10.5% | 5,560 | 5,842 | 6,124 | 6,406 | 6,688 |
| 11.0% | 5,457 | 5,733 | 6,009 | 6,284 | 6,560 |
| 11.5% | 5,357 | 5,627 | 5,897 | 6,166 | 6,436 |
| 12.0% | 5,260 | 5,524 | 5,787 | 6,051 | 6,315 |

**Implied Perpetuity Growth Rate**

| WACC | Exit Multiple 6.5x | 7.0x | 7.5x | 8.0x | 8.5x |
|---|---|---|---|---|---|
| 10.0% | 0.6% | 1.2% | 1.7% | 2.2% | 2.6% |
| 10.5% | 1.0% | 1.6% | 2.2% | 2.7% | 3.1% |
| 11.0% | 1.4% | 2.1% | 2.6% | 3.1% | 3.5% |
| 11.5% | 1.9% | 2.5% | 3.1% | 3.5% | 4.0% |
| 12.0% | 2.3% | 2.9% | 3.5% | 4.0% | 4.4% |

## STEP I. STUDY THE TARGET AND DETERMINE KEY PERFORMANCE DRIVERS

### Study the Target

The first step in performing a DCF, as with any valuation exercise, is to study and learn as much as possible about the target and its sector. A thorough understanding of the target's business model, financial profile, value proposition for customers, end markets, competitors, and key risks is essential for developing a framework for valuation. The banker needs to be able to craft (or support) a realistic set of financial projections, as well as WACC and terminal value assumptions, for the target. Performing this task is invariably easier when valuing a public company as opposed to a private company due to the availability of information.

For a public company,[3] a careful reading of its recent SEC filings (e.g., 10-Ks, 10-Qs, and 8-Ks), earnings call transcripts, and investor presentations provides a solid introduction to its business and financial characteristics. To determine key performance drivers, the MD&A sections of the most recent 10-K and 10-Q are an important source of information as they provide a synopsis of the company's financial and operational performance during the prior reporting periods, as well as management's outlook for the company. Equity research reports add additional color and perspective while typically providing financial performance estimates for the future two- or three-year period.

For private, non-filing companies or smaller divisions of public companies (for which segmented information is not provided), company management is often relied upon to provide materials containing basic business and financial information. In an organized M&A sale process, this information is typically provided in the form of a CIM. In the absence of this information, alternative sources must be used, such as company websites, trade journals, and news articles, as well as SEC filings and research reports for public competitors, customers, and suppliers. For those private companies that were once public filers, or operated as a subsidiary of a public filer, it can be informative to read through old filings or research reports.

### Determine Key Performance Drivers

The next level of analysis involves determining the key drivers of a company's performance (particularly sales growth, profitability, and FCF generation) with the goal of crafting (or supporting) a defensible set of FCF projections. These drivers can be both internal (such as opening new facilities/stores, developing new products, securing new customer contracts, and improving operational and/or working capital efficiency) as well as external (such as acquisitions, end market trends, consumer buying patterns, macroeconomic factors, or even legislative/regulatory changes).

---

[3]Including those companies that have outstanding registered debt securities, but do not have publicly traded stock.

A given company's growth profile can vary significantly from that of its peers within the sector with certain business models and management teams more focused on, or capable of, expansion. Profitability may also vary for companies within a given sector depending on a multitude of factors, including management, brand, customer base, operational focus, product mix, sales/marketing strategy, scale, and technology. Similarly, in terms of FCF generation, there are often meaningful differences among peers in terms of capex (e.g., expansion projects or owned versus leased machinery) and working capital efficiency, for example.

## STEP II. PROJECT FREE CASH FLOW

After studying the target and determining key performance drivers, the stage is set to project FCF. As previously discussed, FCF is the cash generated by a company after paying all cash operating expenses and associated taxes, as well as the funding of capex and working capital, but prior to the payment of any interest expense (see Exhibit 3.3). FCF is independent of capital structure as it represents the cash available to all capital providers (both debt and equity holders).

**EXHIBIT 3.3**  Free Cash Flow Calculation

| |
| --- |
| Earnings Before Interest and Taxes |
| Less: Taxes (at the Marginal Tax Rate) |
| **Earnings Before Interest After Taxes** |
| Plus: Depreciation & Amortization |
| Less: Capital Expenditures |
| Less: Increase/(Decrease) in Net Working Capital |
| **Free Cash Flow** |

### Considerations for Projecting Free Cash Flow

**Historical Performance**  Historical performance provides valuable insight for developing defensible assumptions to project FCF. Past growth rates, profit margins, and other ratios are usually a reliable indicator of future performance, especially for mature companies in non-cyclical sectors. While it is informative to review historical data from as long a time horizon as possible, typically the prior three-year period (if available) serves as a good proxy for projecting future financial performance.

Therefore, as the output in Exhibit 3.2 demonstrates, the DCF customarily begins by laying out the target's historical financial data for the prior three-year period. This historical financial data is sourced from the target's financial statements with adjustments made for non-recurring items and recent events, as appropriate, to provide a normalized basis for projecting financial performance.

**Projection Period Length**   Typically, the banker projects the target's FCF for a period of five years depending on its sector, stage of development, and the predictability of its financial performance. As discussed in Step IV, it is critical to project FCF to a point in the future where the target's financial performance reaches a steady state or normalized level. For mature companies in established industries, five years is often sufficient for allowing a company to reach its steady state. A five-year projection period typically spans at least one business cycle and allows sufficient time for the successful realization of in-process or planned initiatives.

In situations where the target is in the early stages of rapid growth, however, it may be more appropriate to build a longer-term projection model (e.g., ten years or more) to allow the target to reach a steady state level of cash flow. A longer projection period may also be relevant for businesses in sectors with long-term, contracted revenue streams such as natural resources, satellite communications, or utilities.

**Alternative Cases**   Whether advising on the buy-side or sell-side of an organized M&A sale process, the company typically provides five years of financial projections for the target, which is usually labeled "Management Case". At the same time, you must develop a sufficient degree of comfort to support and defend these assumptions. This typically requires adjustments to management's projections that incorporate assumptions deemed more probable, known as the "Base Case", while also crafting upside and downside cases.

The development of alternative cases requires a sound understanding of company-specific performance drivers as well as sector trends. The various assumptions that drive these cases are entered into assumptions pages (see Chapter 5, Exhibits 5.52 and 5.53), which feed into the DCF output page (see Exhibit 3.2). A "switch" or "toggle" function in the model allows you to move between cases without having to re-input the financial data by entering a number or letter (that corresponds to a particular set of assumptions) into a single cell.

**Projecting Financial Performance without Management Guidance**   In some instances, a DCF is performed without the benefit of receiving an initial set of projections. For publicly traded companies, consensus research estimates for financial statistics such as sales, EBITDA, and EBIT (which are generally provided for a future two- or three-year period) are typically used to form the basis for developing a set of projections. Individual equity research reports may provide additional financial detail, including (in some instances) a full scale two-year (or more) projection model. For private companies, a robust DCF often depends on receiving financial projections from company management. In practice, however, this is not always possible. Therefore, the banker must develop the skill set necessary to reasonably forecast financial performance in the absence of management projections. In these instances, the banker typically relies upon historical financial performance, sector trends, and consensus estimates for public comparable companies to drive defensible projections. The remainder of this section provides a detailed discussion of the major components of FCF, as well as practical approaches for projecting FCF *without the benefit of readily available projections or management guidance.*

### Projection of Sales, EBITDA, and EBIT

**Sales Projections** For public companies, the banker often sources top line projections for the first two or three years of the projection period from consensus estimates. Similarly, for private companies, consensus estimates for peer companies can be used as a proxy for expected sales growth rates, provided the trend line is consistent with historical performance and sector outlook.

As equity research normally does not provide estimates beyond a future two- or three-year period, the banker must derive growth rates in the outer years from alternative sources. Without the benefit of management guidance, this typically involves more art than science. Often, industry reports and consulting studies provide estimates on longer-term sector trends and growth rates. In the absence of reliable guidance, the banker typically steps down the growth rates incrementally in the outer years of the projection period to arrive at a reasonable long-term growth rate by the terminal year (e.g., 2% to 4%).

For a highly cyclical business such as a steel or lumber company, however, sales levels need to track the movements of the underlying commodity cycle. Consequently, sales trends are typically more volatile and may incorporate dramatic peak-to-trough swings depending on the company's point in the cycle at the start of the projection period. Regardless of where in the cycle the projection period begins, it is crucial that the terminal year financial performance represents a normalized level as opposed to a cyclical high or low. Otherwise, the company's terminal value, which usually comprises a substantial portion of the overall value in a DCF, will be skewed toward an unrepresentative level. Therefore, in a DCF for a cyclical company, top line projections might peak (or trough) in the early years of the projection period and then decline (or increase) precipitously before returning to a normalized level by the terminal year.

Once the top line projections are established, it is essential to give them a sanity check versus the target's historical growth rates as well as peer estimates and sector/market outlook. Even when sourcing information from consensus estimates, each year's growth assumptions need to be justifiable, whether on the basis of market share gains/declines, end market trends, product mix changes, demand shifts, pricing increases, or acquisitions, for example. Furthermore, the banker must ensure that sales projections are consistent with other related assumptions in the DCF, such as those for capex and working capital. For example, higher top line growth typically requires the support of higher levels of capex and working capital.

**COGS and SG&A Projections**    For public companies, the banker typically relies upon historical COGS[4] (gross margin) and SG&A levels (as a percentage of sales) and/or sources estimates from research to drive the initial years of the projection period, if available. For the outer years of the projection period, it is common to hold gross margin and SG&A as a percentage of sales constant, although the banker may assume a slight improvement (or decline) if justified by company trends or outlook for the sector/market. Similarly, for private companies, the banker usually relies upon historical trends to drive gross profit and SG&A projections, typically holding margins constant at the prior historical year levels. At the same time, the banker may also examine research estimates for peer companies to help craft/support the assumptions and provide insight on trends.

In some cases, the DCF may be constructed on the basis of EBITDA and EBIT projections alone, thereby excluding line item detail for COGS and SG&A. This approach generally requires that NWC be driven as a percentage of sales as COGS detail for driving inventory and accounts payable is unavailable (see Exhibits 3.9, 3.10, and 3.11). However, the inclusion of COGS and SG&A detail provides greater flexibility to drive multiple operating scenarios on the basis of gross margins and/ or SG&A efficiency.

**EBITDA and EBIT Projections**    For public companies, EBITDA and EBIT projections for the future two- or three-year period are typically sourced from (or benchmarked against) consensus estimates, if available.[5] These projections inherently capture both gross profit performance and SG&A expenses. A common approach for projecting EBITDA and EBIT for the outer years is to hold their margins constant at the level represented by the last year provided by consensus estimates (assuming the last year of estimates is representative of a steady state level). As previously discussed, however, increasing (or decreasing) levels of profitability may be modeled throughout the projection period, perhaps due to product mix changes, cyclicality, operating leverage,[6] or pricing power/pressure.

For private companies, the banker looks at historical trends as well as consensus estimates for peer companies for insight on projected margins. In the absence of sufficient information to justify improving or declining margins, the banker may simply hold margins constant at the prior historical year level to establish a baseline set of projections.

---

[4]For companies with COGS that can be driven on a unit volume/cost basis, COGS is typically projected on the basis of expected volumes sold and cost per unit. Assumptions governing expected volumes and cost per unit can be derived from historical levels, production capacity, and/or sector trends.

[5]If the model is built on the basis of COGS and SG&A detail, the banker must ensure that the EBITDA and EBIT consensus estimates dovetail with those assumptions. This exercise may require some triangulation among the different inputs to ensure consistency.

[6]The extent to which sales growth results in growth at the operating income level; it is a function of a company's mix of fixed and variable costs.

## Projection of Free Cash Flow

In a DCF analysis, EBIT typically serves as the springboard for calculating FCF (see Exhibit 3.4). To bridge from EBIT to FCF, several additional items need to be determined, including the marginal tax rate, D&A, capex, and changes in net working capital.

**EXHIBIT 3.4**   EBIT to FCF

| EBIT |
| --- |
| Less: Taxes (at the Marginal Tax Rate) |
| **EBIAT** |
| Plus: Depreciation & Amortization |
| Less: Capital Expenditures |
| Less: Increase/(Decrease) in NWC |
| **FCF** |

**Tax Projections**   The first step in calculating FCF from EBIT is to net out estimated taxes. The result is tax-effected EBIT, also known as EBIAT or NOPAT. This calculation involves multiplying EBIT by $(1 - t)$, where "t" is the target's marginal tax rate. A marginal tax rate of 25% is generally assumed for modeling purposes, but the company's actual tax rate (effective tax rate) in previous years can also serve as a reference point.[7]

**Depreciation & Amortization Projections**   Depreciation is a non-cash expense that approximates the reduction of the book value of a company's long-term fixed assets or property, plant, and equipment (PP&E) over an estimated *useful life*. As an expense, it reduces reported earnings. Amortization, like depreciation, is a non-cash expense that reduces the value of a company's *definite life* intangible assets and also reduces reported earnings.[8]

Some companies report D&A together as a separate line item on their income statement, but these expenses are more commonly included in COGS (especially for manufacturers of goods) and, to a lesser extent, SG&A. Regardless, D&A is explicitly disclosed in the cash flow statement as well as the notes to a company's financial statements. As D&A is a non-cash expense, it is added back to EBIAT in the calculation of FCF (see Exhibit 3.4). Hence, while D&A decreases a company's reported earnings, it does not decrease its FCF.

---

[7]It is important to understand that a company's effective tax rate, or the rate that it actually pays in taxes, often differs from the marginal tax rate due to the use of tax credits, nondeductible expenses (such as government fines), deferred tax asset valuation allowances, and other company-specific tax policies.

[8]D&A for GAAP purposes typically differs from that for federal income taxes. For example, federal government tax rules generally permit a company to depreciate assets on a more accelerated basis than GAAP. These differences create deferred liabilities. Due to the complexity of calculating tax D&A, GAAP D&A is typically used as a proxy for tax D&A.

Depreciation   Depreciation expenses are typically scheduled over several years corresponding to the useful life of each of the company's respective asset classes. The *straight-line depreciation* method assumes a uniform depreciation expense over the estimated useful life of an asset. For example, an asset purchased for $100 million that is determined to have a ten-year useful life would be assumed to have an annual depreciation expense of $10 million per year for ten years. Most other depreciation methods fall under the category of *accelerated depreciation*, which assumes that an asset loses most of its value in the early years of its life (i.e., the asset is depreciated on an accelerated schedule, allowing for greater deductions earlier on).

For DCF modeling purposes, depreciation is often projected as a percentage of sales or capex based on historical levels as it is directly related to a company's capital spending, which, in turn, tends to support top line growth. An alternative approach is to build a detailed PP&E schedule[9] based on the company's existing depreciable net PP&E base and incremental capex projections. This approach involves assuming an average remaining life for current depreciable net PP&E as well as a depreciation period for new capex. While more technically sound than the "quick-and-dirty" method of projecting depreciation as a percentage of sales or capex, building a PP&E schedule generally does not yield a substantially different result.

For a DCF constructed on the basis of EBITDA and EBIT projections, depreciation (and amortization) can simply be calculated as the difference between the two. In this scenario, however, the banker must ensure that the implied D&A is consistent with historical levels as well as capex projections.[10] Regardless of which approach is used, the banker often makes a simplifying assumption that depreciation and capex are in line by the final year of the projection period so as to ensure that the company's PP&E base remains steady in perpetuity. Otherwise, the company's valuation would be influenced by an expanding or diminishing PP&E base, which would not be representative of a steady state business.

Amortization   Amortization differs from depreciation in that it reduces the value of definite life intangible assets as opposed to tangible assets. Definite life intangible assets include contractual rights such as non-compete clauses, copyrights, licenses, patents, trademarks, or other intellectual property, as well as information technology and customer lists, among others. These intangible assets are amortized according to a determined or useful life.[11]

---

[9]A schedule for determining a company's PP&E for each year in the projection period on the basis of annual capex (additions) and depreciation (subtractions). PP&E for a particular year in the projection period is the sum of the prior year's PP&E plus the projection year's capex less the projection year's depreciation.

[10]When using consensus estimates for EBITDA and EBIT, the difference between the two may imply a level of D&A that is not defensible. This situation is particularly common when there are a different number of research analysts reporting values for EBITDA than for EBIT.

[11]Indefinite life intangible assets, most notably goodwill (value paid in excess over the book value of an asset), are not amortized. Rather, goodwill is held on the balance sheet and tested annually for impairment.

Like depreciation, amortization can be projected as a percentage of sales or by building a detailed schedule based upon a company's existing intangible assets. However, amortization is often combined with depreciation as a single line item within a company's financial statements. Therefore, it is more common to simply model amortization with depreciation as part of one line-item (D&A).

Assuming depreciation and amortization are combined as one line item, D&A is projected in accordance with one of the approaches described under the "Depreciation" heading (e.g., as a percentage of sales or capex, through a detailed schedule, or as the difference between EBITDA and EBIT).

**Capital Expenditures Projections**   Capital expenditures are the funds that a company uses to purchase, improve, expand, or replace physical assets such as buildings, equipment, facilities, machinery, and other assets. Capex is an expenditure as opposed to an expense. It is capitalized on the balance sheet once the expenditure is made and then expensed over its useful life as depreciation through the company's income statement. As opposed to depreciation, capital expenditures represent actual cash outflows and, consequently, must be subtracted from EBIAT in the calculation of FCF (in the year in which the purchase is made).

Historical capex is disclosed directly on a company's cash flow statement under the investing activities section and also discussed in the MD&A section of a public company's 10-K and 10-Q. Historical levels generally serve as a reliable proxy for projecting future capex. However, capex projections may deviate from historical levels in accordance with the company's strategy, sector, or phase of operations. For example, a company in expansion mode might have elevated capex levels for some portion of the projection period, while one in harvest or cash conservation mode might limit its capex.

For public companies, future planned capex is often discussed in the MD&A of its 10-K. Research reports may also provide capex estimates for the future two- or three-year period. In the absence of specific guidance, capex is generally driven as a percentage of sales in line with historical levels due to the fact that top line growth typically needs to be supported by growth in the company's asset base.

**Change in Net Working Capital Projections**   Net working capital is typically defined as non-cash current assets ("current assets") less non-interest-bearing current liabilities ("current liabilities"). It serves as a measure of how much cash a company needs to fund its operations on an ongoing basis. All of the necessary components to determine a company's NWC can be found on its balance sheet. Exhibit 3.5 displays the main current assets and current liabilities line items.

**EXHIBIT 3.5**   Current Assets and Current Liabilities Components

| Current Assets | Current Liabilities |
|---|---|
| ▪ Accounts Receivable (A/R) | ▪ Accounts Payable (A/P) |
| ▪ Inventory | ▪ Accrued Liabilities |
| ▪ Prepaid Expenses and Other Current Assets | ▪ Other Current Liabilities |

The formula for calculating NWC is shown in Exhibit 3.6.

**EXHIBIT 3.6**   Calculation of Net Working Capital

$$
\text{NWC} = \frac{(\text{Accounts Receivable} + \text{Inventory} + \text{Prepaid Expenses and Other Current Assets})}{\textit{less}}
$$
$$
(\text{Accounts Payable} + \text{Accrued Liabilities} + \text{Other Current Liabilities})
$$

The change in NWC from year to year is important for calculating FCF as it represents an annual source or use of cash for the company. An increase in NWC over a given period (i.e., when current assets increase by more than current liabilities) is a use of cash. This is typical for a growing company, which tends to increase its spending on inventory to support sales growth. Similarly, A/R tends to increase in line with sales growth, which represents a use of cash as it is incremental cash that has not yet been collected. Conversely, an increase in A/P represents a source of cash as it is money that has been retained by the company as opposed to paid out.

As an increase in NWC is a use of cash, it is subtracted from EBIAT in the calculation of FCF. If the net change in NWC is negative (source of cash), then that value is added back to EBIAT. The calculation of a year-over-year (YoY) change in NWC is shown in Exhibit 3.7.

**EXHIBIT 3.7**   Calculation of a YoY Change in NWC

$$
\Delta \text{NWC} = \text{NWC}_n - \text{NWC}_{(n-1)}
$$

where:       n = the most recent year
        (n − 1) = the prior year

A "quick-and-dirty" shortcut for projecting YoY changes in NWC involves projecting NWC as a percentage of sales at a designated historical level and then calculating the YoY changes accordingly. This approach is typically used when a company's detailed balance sheet and COGS information is unavailable and working capital ratios cannot be determined. A more granular and recommended approach (where possible) is to project the individual components of both current assets and current liabilities for each year in the projection period. NWC and YoY changes are then calculated accordingly.

A company's current assets and current liabilities components are typically projected on the basis of historical ratios from the prior year level or a three-year average. In some cases, the company's trend line, management guidance, or sector trends may suggest improving or declining working capital efficiency ratios, thereby impacting FCF projections. In the absence of such guidance, constant working capital ratios in line with historical levels are typically assumed throughout the projection period.[12]

---

[12]For the purposes of the DCF, working capital ratios are generally measured on an annual basis.

Current Assets

*Accounts Receivable*   Accounts receivable refers to amounts owed to a company for its products and services sold on credit. A/R is customarily projected on the basis of days sales outstanding (DSO), as shown in Exhibit 3.8.

**EXHIBIT 3.8**   Calculation of DSO

$$DSO = \frac{A/R}{Sales} \times 365$$

DSO provides a gauge of how well a company is managing the collection of its A/R by measuring the number of days it takes to collect payment after the sale of a product or service. For example, a DSO of 45 implies that the company, on average, receives payment 45 days after an initial sale is made. The lower a company's DSO, the faster it receives cash from credit sales.

An increase in A/R represents a use of cash. Hence, companies strive to minimize their DSO so as to speed up their collection of cash. Increases in a company's DSO can be the result of numerous factors, including customer leverage or renegotiation of terms, worsening customer credit, poor collection systems, or change in product mix, for example. This increase in the cash cycle decreases short-term liquidity as the company has less cash on hand to fund short-term business operations and meet current debt obligations.

*Inventory*   Inventory refers to the value of a company's raw materials, work in progress, and finished goods. It is customarily projected on the basis of days inventory held (DIH), as shown in Exhibit 3.9.

**EXHIBIT 3.9**   Calculation of DIH

$$DIH = \frac{Inventory}{COGS} \times 365$$

DIH measures the number of days it takes a company to sell its inventory. For example, a DIH of 90 implies that, on average, it takes 90 days for the company to turn its inventory (or approximately four "inventory turns" per year, as discussed in more detail below). An increase in inventory represents a use of cash. Therefore, companies strive to minimize DIH and turn their inventory as quickly as possible so as to minimize the amount of cash it ties up. Additionally, idle inventory is susceptible to damage, theft, or obsolescence due to newer products or technologies.

An alternative approach for measuring a company's efficiency at selling its inventory is the inventory turns ratio. As depicted in Exhibit 3.10, inventory turns measures the number of times a company turns over its inventory in a given year. As with DIH, inventory turns is used together with COGS to project future inventory levels.

**EXHIBIT 3.10**    Calculation of Inventory Turns

$$\text{Inventory Turns} = \boxed{\text{COGS / Inventory}}$$

*Prepaid Expenses and Other Current Assets*    Prepaid expenses are payments made by a company before a product has been delivered or a service has been performed. For example, insurance premiums are typically paid upfront although they cover a longer-term period (e.g., six months or a year). Prepaid expenses and other current assets are typically projected as a percentage of sales in line with historical levels. As with A/R and inventory, an increase in prepaid expenses and other current assets represents a use of cash.

Current Liabilities

*Accounts Payable*    Accounts payable refers to amounts owed by a company for products and services already purchased. A/P is customarily projected on the basis of days payable outstanding (DPO), as shown in Exhibit 3.11.

**EXHIBIT 3.11**    Calculation of DPO

$$DPO = \boxed{\frac{\text{A/P}}{\text{COGS}} \times 365}$$

DPO measures the number of days it takes for a company to make payment on its outstanding purchases of goods and services. For example, a DPO of 45 implies that the company takes 45 days on average to pay its suppliers. The higher a company's DPO, the more time it has available to use its cash on hand for various business purposes before paying outstanding bills.

An increase in A/P represents a source of cash. Therefore, as opposed to DSO, companies aspire to maximize or "push out" (within reason) their DPO so as to increase short-term liquidity.

*Accrued Liabilities and Other Current Liabilities*    Accrued liabilities are expenses such as salaries, rent, interest, and taxes that have been incurred by a company but not yet paid. As with prepaid expenses and other current assets, accrued liabilities and other current liabilities are typically projected as a percentage of sales in line with historical levels. As with A/P, an increase in accrued liabilities and other current liabilities represents a source of cash.

**Free Cash Flow Projections**    Once all of the above items have been projected, annual FCF for the projection period is relatively easy to calculate in accordance with the formula first introduced in Exhibit 3.3. The projection period FCF, however, represents only a portion of the target's value. The remainder is captured in the terminal value, which is discussed in Step IV.

## STEP III. CALCULATE WEIGHTED AVERAGE COST OF CAPITAL

WACC is a broadly accepted standard for use as the discount rate to calculate the present value of a company's projected FCF and terminal value. It represents the weighted average of the required return on the invested capital (customarily debt and equity) in a given company. As debt and equity components have different risk profiles and tax ramifications, WACC is dependent on a company's "target" capital structure.

WACC can also be thought of as an opportunity cost of capital or what an investor would expect to earn in an alternative investment with a similar risk profile. Companies with diverse business segments may have different costs of capital for their various businesses. In these instances, it may be advisable to conduct a DCF using a "sum of the parts" approach in which a separate DCF analysis is performed for each distinct business segment, each with its own WACC. The values for each business segment are then summed to arrive at an implied enterprise valuation for the entire company.

The formula for the calculation of WACC is shown in Exhibit 3.12.

**EXHIBIT 3.12**   Calculation of WACC

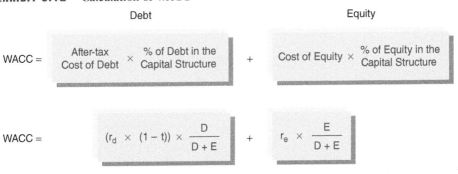

where:  $r_d$ = cost of debt
$\phantom{where:}$ $r_e$ = cost of equity
$\phantom{where:}$ t  = marginal tax rate
$\phantom{where:}$ D = market value of debt
$\phantom{where:}$ E = market value of equity

A company's capital structure or total capitalization is comprised of two main components, debt and equity (as represented by D + E). The rates—$r_d$ (return on debt) and $r_e$ (return on equity)—represent the company's market cost of debt and equity, respectively. As its name connotes, the ensuing weighted average cost of capital is simply a weighted average of the company's cost of debt (tax-effected) and cost of equity based on an assumed or "target" capital structure.

Below we demonstrate a step-by-step process for calculating WACC, as outlined in Exhibit 3.13.

**EXHIBIT 3.13** Steps for Calculating WACC

> Step III(a): Determine Target Capital Structure
> Step III(b): Estimate Cost of Debt ($r_d$)
> Step III(c): Estimate Cost of Equity ($r_e$)
> Step IV(d): Calculate WACC

## Step III(a): Determine Target Capital Structure

WACC is predicated on choosing a target capital structure for the company that is consistent with its long-term strategy. This target capital structure is represented by the debt-to-total capitalization (D/(D + E)) and equity-to-total capitalization (E/(D + E)) ratios (see Exhibit 3.12). In the absence of explicit company guidance on target capital structure, the banker examines the company's current and historical debt-to-total capitalization ratios as well as the capitalization of its peers. Public comparable companies provide a meaningful benchmark for target capital structure as it is assumed that their management teams are seeking to maximize shareholder value.

In the finance community, the approach used to determine a company's target capital structure may differ from firm to firm. For public companies, existing capital structure is generally used as the target capital structure as long as it is comfortably within the range of the comparables. If it is at the extremes of, or outside, the range, then the mean or median for the comparables may serve as a better representation of the target capital structure. For private companies, the mean or median for the comparables is typically used. Once the target capital structure is chosen, it is assumed to be held constant throughout the projection period.

The graph in Exhibit 3.14 shows the impact of capital structure on a company's WACC. When there is no debt in the capital structure, WACC is equal to the cost of equity. As the proportion of debt in the capital structure increases, WACC gradually decreases due to the tax deductibility of interest expense. WACC continues to decrease up to the point where the *optimal capital structure*[13] is reached. Once this threshold is surpassed, the cost of potential financial distress (i.e., the negative effects of an over-leveraged capital structure, including the increased probability of insolvency) begins to override the tax advantages of debt. As a result, both debt and equity investors demand a higher yield for their increased risk, thereby driving WACC upward beyond the optimal capital structure threshold.

---

[13]The financing mix that minimizes WACC, thereby maximizing a company's theoretical value.

**EXHIBIT 3.14** Optimal Capital Structure

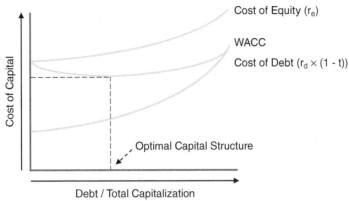

## Step III(b): Estimate Cost of Debt ($r_d$)

A company's cost of debt reflects its credit profile at the target capital structure, which is based on a multitude of factors including size, sector, outlook, cyclicality, credit ratings, credit statistics, cash flow generation, financial policy, and acquisition strategy, among others. Assuming the company is currently at its target capital structure, cost of debt is generally derived from the blended yield on its outstanding debt instruments, which may include a mix of public and private debt. In the event the company is not currently at its target capital structure, the cost of debt must be derived from peer companies.

For publicly traded bonds, cost of debt is determined on the basis of the *current yield*[14] on all outstanding issues. For private debt, such as revolving credit facilities and term loans,[15] the banker typically consults with an in-house debt capital markets (DCM) specialist to ascertain the current yield. Market-based approaches such as these are generally preferred as the current yield on a company's outstanding debt serves as the best indicator of its expected cost of debt and reflects the risk of default.

In the absence of current market data (e.g., for companies with debt that is not actively traded), an alternative approach is to calculate the company's weighted average cost of debt on the basis of the at-issuance coupons of its current debt maturities. This approach, however, is not always accurate as it is backward-looking and may not reflect the company's cost of raising debt capital under prevailing market conditions. A preferred, albeit more time-consuming, approach in these instances is to approximate a company's cost of debt based on its current (or implied) credit ratings at the target capital structure and the cost of debt for comparable credits. This invariably requires guidance from an in-house leveraged finance or debt capital markets professional.

---

[14]Technically, a bond's current yield is calculated as the annual coupon on the par value of the bond divided by the current price of the bond. However, callable bond yields are typically quoted at the yield-to-worst call (YTW). A callable bond has a call schedule (defined in the bond's indenture) that lists several call dates and their corresponding call prices. The YTW is the lowest calculated yield when comparing all of the possible yield-to-calls from a bond's call schedule given the initial offer price or current trading price of the bond.

[15]See Chapter 4 for additional information on term loans and other debt instruments.

Once determined, the cost of debt is tax-effected at the company's marginal tax rate as interest payments are tax deductible.

## Step III(c): Estimate Cost of Equity ($r_e$)

Cost of equity is the required annual rate of return that a company's equity investors expect to receive (including dividends). Unlike the cost of debt, which can be deduced from the yield on a company's outstanding maturities, a company's cost of equity is not readily observable in the market. To calculate the expected return on a company's equity, a formula known as the capital asset pricing model (CAPM) is employed.

**Capital Asset Pricing Model**    CAPM is based on the premise that equity investors need to be compensated for their assumption of systematic risk in the form of a risk premium, or the amount of market return in excess of a stated risk-free rate. Systematic risk is the risk related to the overall market, which is also known as non-diversifiable risk. A company's level of systematic risk depends on the covariance of its share price with movements in the overall market, as measured by its *beta* ($\beta$) (discussed later in this section).

By contrast, unsystematic or "specific" risk is company- or sector-specific and can be avoided through diversification. Hence, equity investors are not compensated for it (in the form of a premium). As a general rule, the smaller the company and the more specified its product offering, the higher its unsystematic risk.

The formula for the calculation of CAPM is shown in Exhibit 3.15.

**EXHIBIT 3.15**    Calculation of CAPM

Cost of Equity ($r_e$) =    Risk-free Rate + Levered Beta × Market Risk Premium

Cost of Equity ($r_e$) =    $r_f$ + $\beta_L$ × ($r_m$ − $r_f$)

where:     $r_f$ = risk-free rate
$\beta_L$ = levered beta
$r_m$ = expected return on the market
$r_m - r_f$ = market risk premium

**Risk-Free Rate** ($r_f$)  The risk-free rate is the expected rate of return obtained by investing in a "riskless" security. U.S. government securities such as T-bills, T-notes, and T-bonds[16] are accepted by the market as "risk-free" because they are backed by the full faith of the U.S. federal government. Interpolated yields[17] for government securities can be located on Bloomberg[18] as well as the U.S. Department of Treasury website,[19] among others. The actual risk-free rate used in CAPM varies with the prevailing yields for the chosen security.

Investment banks may differ on accepted proxies for the appropriate risk-free rate. In theory, the longest-dated risk-free debt instrument would be ideal so as to match the expected life of the company (assuming a going-concern). In practice, however, many use the 10-year U.S. Treasury note given the depth and liquidity of its markets and accessibility of information. Due to the moratorium on the issuance of 30-year Treasury bonds and shortage of securities with 30-year maturities, Duff & Phelps uses an interpolated yield for a 20-year bond as the basis for the risk-free rate.[20]

**Market Risk Premium** ($r_m - r_f$ or mrp)  The market risk premium is the spread of the expected market return[21] over the risk-free rate. Finance professionals, as well as academics, often differ over which historical time period is most relevant for observing the market risk premium. Some believe that more recent periods, such as the last ten years or the post–World War II era are more appropriate, while others prefer to examine the pre–Great Depression era to the present.

Duff & Phelps tracks data on the equity risk premium dating back to 1926. Depending on which time period is referenced, the premium of the market return over the risk-free rate ($r_m - r_f$) may vary substantially. Duff & Phelps calculates a market risk premium of nearly 7%.[22]

---

[16]T-bills are non-interest-bearing securities issued with maturities of 3 months, 6 months, and 12 months at a discount to face value. T-notes and bonds, by contrast, have a stated coupon and pay semiannual interest. T-notes are issued with maturities of between one and ten years, while T-bonds are issued with maturities of more than ten years.

[17]Yields on nominal Treasury securities at "constant maturity" are interpolated by the U.S. Treasury from the daily yield curve for non-inflation-indexed Treasury securities. This curve, which relates the yield on a security to its time-to-maturity, is based on the closing market bid yields on actively traded Treasury securities in the over-the-counter market.

[18]Bloomberg function: ICUR{# years}<GO>. For example, the interpolated yield for a 10-year Treasury note can be obtained from Bloomberg by typing "ICUR10", then pressing <GO>. Bloomberg also provides a U.S. Treasury Interpolated Benchmark Monitor, which displays yields for 1-month to 30-year Treasuries (USTI<GO>).

[19]www.treasury.gov/resource-center/data-chart-center/Pages/index.aspx and located under "Daily Treasury Yield Curve Rates".

[20]In early 2020, the U.S. Treasury stated they will begin issuing 20-year bonds in the first half of the year. In the interim, while there are currently no 20-year Treasury bonds issued by the U.S. Treasury, as long as there are bonds being traded with at least 20 years to maturity, there will be a proxy for the yield on 20-year Treasury bonds.

[21]The S&P 500 is typically used as the proxy for the return on the market.

[22]Expected risk premium for equities is based on the difference of historical arithmetic mean returns for the 1926 through 2019 period. Arithmetic annual returns are independent of one another. Geometric annual returns are dependent on the prior year's returns.

Many investment banks have a firm-wide policy governing market risk premium in order to ensure consistency in valuation work across various projects and departments. The equity risk premium employed on Wall Street typically ranges from approximately 5% to 8%. Consequently, it is important to consult with senior colleagues and firm-specific practices for guidance on the appropriate market risk premium to use in the CAPM formula.

**Beta (β)**   Beta is a measure of the covariance between the rate of return on a company's stock and the overall market return (systematic risk), with the S&P 500 traditionally used as a proxy for the market. As the S&P 500 has a beta of 1.0, a stock with a beta of 1.0 should have an expected return equal to that of the market. A stock with a beta of less than 1.0 has lower systematic risk than the market, and a stock with a beta greater than 1.0 has higher systematic risk. Mathematically, this is captured in the CAPM, with a higher beta stock exhibiting a higher cost of equity, and vice versa for lower beta stocks.

A public company's historical beta may be sourced from financial information resources such as Bloomberg,[23] FactSet, or Thomson Reuters. Recent historical equity returns (i.e., over the previous two to five years), however, may not be a reliable indicator of future returns. Therefore, many bankers prefer to use a predicted beta (e.g., provided by MSCI Barra[24]) whenever possible as it is meant to be forward-looking.

The exercise of calculating WACC for a private company involves deriving beta from a group of publicly traded peer companies that may or may not have similar capital structures to one another or the target. To neutralize the effects of different capital structures (i.e., remove the influence of leverage), the banker must *unlever* the beta for each company in the peer group to achieve the *asset beta* ("unlevered beta").

The formula for unlevering beta is shown in Exhibit 3.16.

**EXHIBIT 3.16**   Unlevering Beta

$$\beta_U = \frac{\beta_L}{\left(1 + \frac{D}{E} \times (1 - t)\right)}$$

where:   $\beta_U$ = unlevered beta
$\beta_L$ = levered beta
D/E = debt-to-equity[26] ratio
t = marginal tax rate

---

[23]Bloomberg function: Ticker symbol <Equity> BETA <GO>.
[24]MSCI Barra is a leading provider of investment decision support tools and supplies predicted betas for most public companies among other products and services. MSCI Barra uses a proprietary multifactor risk model, known as the Multiple-Horizon U.S. Equity Model™, which relies on market information, fundamental data, regressions, historical daily returns, and other risk analyses to predict beta. MSCI Barra betas can be obtained from Alacra, among other financial information services.

After calculating the unlevered beta for each company, the average unlevered beta for the peer group is determined.[25] This average unlevered beta is then *relevered* using the company's <u>target</u> capital structure and marginal tax rate. The formula for relevering beta is shown in Exhibit 3.17.

**EXHIBIT 3.17**   Relevering Beta

$$\beta_L = \beta_U \times \left(1 + \frac{D}{E} \times (1 - t)\right)$$

where:  D/E = <u>target</u> debt-to-equity ratio

The resulting levered beta serves as the beta for calculating the private company's cost of equity using the CAPM. Similarly, for a public company that is not currently at its target capital structure, its asset beta must be calculated and then relevered at the target D/E.

Size Premium (SP)   The concept of a size premium is based on empirical evidence suggesting that smaller-sized companies are riskier and, therefore, should have a higher cost of equity. This phenomenon, which to some degree contradicts the CAPM, relies on the notion that smaller companies' risk is not entirely captured in their betas given limited trading volumes of their stock, making covariance calculations inexact. Therefore, a comprehensive WACC analysis typically involves adding a size premium to the CAPM formula for smaller companies to account for the perceived higher risk and, therefore, expected higher return (see Exhibit 3.18). Duff & Phelps provides size premia for companies based on their market capitalization, tiered in deciles.

**EXHIBIT 3.18**   CAPM Formula Adjusted for Size Premium

$$r_e = r_f + \beta_L \times (r_m - r_f) + SP$$

where:  SP = size premium

---

[25]Average unlevered beta may be calculated on a market-cap-weighted basis.

## Step III(d): Calculate WACC

Once all of the above steps are completed, the various components are entered into the formula in Exhibit 3.19 to calculate the company's WACC. Given the numerous assumptions involved in determining a company's WACC and its sizable impact on valuation, its key inputs are typically sensitized to produce a WACC range (see Exhibit 3.49). This range is then used in conjunction with other sensitized inputs, such as exit multiple, to produce a valuation range for the target.

**EXHIBIT 3.19**   WACC Formula

$$WACC = \left( r_d \times (1 - t) \right) \times \frac{D}{D+E} \quad + \quad r_e \times \frac{E}{D+E}$$

## STEP IV. DETERMINE TERMINAL VALUE

The DCF approach to valuation is based on determining the present value of all future FCF produced by a company. As it is infeasible to project a company's FCF indefinitely, the banker uses a terminal value to capture the value of the company beyond the projection period. As its name suggests, terminal value is typically calculated on the basis of the company's FCF (or a proxy such as EBITDA) in the final year of the projection period.

The terminal value typically accounts for a substantial portion of a company's value in a DCF, sometimes as much as three-quarters or more. Therefore, it is important that the company's terminal year financial data represent a steady state level of financial performance, as opposed to a cyclical high or low. Similarly, the underlying assumptions for calculating the terminal value must be carefully examined and sensitized.

There are two widely accepted methods used to calculate a company's terminal value—the *exit multiple method* and the *perpetuity growth method*. Depending on the situation and company being valued, the banker may use one or both methods, with each serving as a check on the other.

### Exit Multiple Method

The EMM calculates the remaining value of a company's FCF produced after the projection period on the basis of a multiple of its terminal year EBITDA (or EBIT). This multiple is typically based on the current LTM trading multiples for comparable companies. As current multiples may be affected by sector or economic cycles, it is important to use both a normalized trading multiple and EBITDA. The use of a peak or trough multiple and/or an un-normalized EBITDA level can produce a skewed result. This is especially important for companies in cyclical industries.

As the exit multiple is a critical driver of terminal value, and hence overall value in a DCF, the banker subjects it to sensitivity analysis. For example, if the selected exit multiple range based on comparable companies is 7.0x to 8.0x, a common approach would be to create a valuation output table premised on exit multiples of 6.5x, 7.0x, 7.5x, 8.0x, and 8.5x (see Exhibit 3.32). The formula for calculating terminal value using the EMM is shown in Exhibit 3.20.

**EXHIBIT 3.20**    Exit Multiple Method

$$\text{Terminal Value} = \text{EBITDA}_n \times \text{Exit Multiple}$$

where: n = terminal year of the projection period

### Perpetuity Growth Method

The PGM calculates terminal value by treating a company's terminal year FCF as a perpetuity growing at an assumed rate. As the formula in Exhibit 3.21 indicates, this method relies on the WACC calculation performed in Step III and requires the banker to make an assumption regarding the company's long-term, sustainable growth rate ("perpetuity growth rate"). The perpetuity growth rate is typically chosen on the basis of the company's expected long-term industry growth rate, which generally tends to be within a range of 2% to 4% (i.e., nominal GDP growth). As with the exit multiple, the perpetuity growth rate is also sensitized to produce a valuation range.

**EXHIBIT 3.21**    Perpetuity Growth Method

$$\text{Terminal Value} = \frac{\text{FCF}_n \times (1 + g)}{(r - g)}$$

where:  FCF = unlevered free cash flow
        n = terminal year of the projection period
        g = perpetuity growth rate
        r = WACC

The PGM is often used in conjunction with the EMM, with each serving as a sanity check on the other. For example, if the implied perpetuity growth rate as derived from the EMM is too high or low (see Exhibits 3.22(a) and 3.22(b)), it could be an indicator that the exit multiple assumptions are unrealistic.

**EXHIBIT 3.22(a)**    Implied Perpetuity Growth Rate (End-of-Year Discounting)

$$\text{Implied Perpetuity Growth Rate} = \frac{((\text{Terminal Value}^{(a)} \times \text{WACC}) - \text{FCF}_{\text{Terminal Year}})}{(\text{Terminal Value}^{(a)} + \text{FCF}_{\text{Terminal Year}})}$$

**EXHIBIT 3.22(b)**    Implied Perpetuity Growth Rate (Mid-Year Discounting, see Exhibit 3.26)

$$\text{Implied Perpetuity Growth Rate} = \frac{((\text{Terminal Value}^{(a)} \times \text{WACC}) - \text{FCF}_{\text{Terminal Year}} \times (1 + \text{WACC})^{0.5})}{(\text{Terminal Value}^{(a)} + \text{FCF}_{\text{Terminal Year}} \times (1 + \text{WACC})^{0.5})}$$

[a]Terminal Value calculated using the EMM.

Similarly, if the implied exit multiple from the PGM (see Exhibits 3.23(a) and 3.23(b)) is not in line with normalized trading multiples for the target or its peers, the perpetuity growth rate should be revisited.

**EXHIBIT 3.23(a)**    Implied Exit Multiple (End-of-Year Discounting)

$$\text{Implied Exit Multiple} = \frac{\text{Terminal Value}^{(a)}}{\text{EBITDA}_{\text{Terminal Year}}}$$

**EXHIBIT 3.23(b)**    Implied Exit Multiple (Mid-Year Discounting, see Exhibit 3.26))

$$\text{Implied Exit Multiple} = \frac{\text{Terminal Value}^{(a)} \times (1 + \text{WACC})^{0.5}}{\text{EBITDA}_{\text{Terminal Year}}}$$

[a]Terminal Value calculated using the PGM.

## STEP V. CALCULATE PRESENT VALUE AND DETERMINE VALUATION

### Calculate Present Value

Calculating present value centers on the notion that a dollar today is worth more than a dollar tomorrow, a concept known as the *time value of money*. This is due to the fact that a dollar earns money through investments (capital appreciation) and/or interest (e.g., in a money market account). In a DCF, a company's projected FCF and terminal value are discounted to the present at the company's WACC in accordance with the time value of money.

The present value calculation is performed by multiplying the FCF for each year in the projection period and the terminal value by its respective discount factor. The discount factor is the fractional value representing the present value of one dollar received at a future date given an assumed discount rate. For example, assuming a 10% discount rate, the discount factor for one dollar received at the end of one year is 0.91 (see Exhibit 3.24).

**EXHIBIT 3.24**    Discount Factor

$$\text{Discount Factor} = \frac{1}{(1 + \text{WACC})^n}$$

$$0.91 = \frac{\$1.00}{(1 + 10\%)^1}$$

where:  n = year in the projection period

The discount factor is applied to a given future financial statistic to determine its present value. For example, given a 10% WACC, FCF of $100 million at the end of the first year of a company's projection period (Year 1) would be worth $91 million today (see Exhibit 3.25).

**EXHIBIT 3.25**    Present Value Calculation Using a Year-End Discount Factor

$$\text{PV of FCF}_n = \text{FCF}_n \times \text{Discount Factor}_n$$

$$\$91 \text{ million} = \$100 \text{ million} \times 0.91$$

where:  n = year in the projection period

**Mid-Year Convention**   To account for the fact that annual FCF is usually received throughout the year rather than at year-end, it is typically discounted in accordance with a *mid-year convention*. Mid-year convention assumes that a company's FCF is received evenly throughout the year, thereby approximating a steady (and more realistic) FCF generation.[26]

The use of mid-year convention results in a slightly higher valuation than year-end discounting due to the fact that FCF is received sooner. As Exhibit 3.26 depicts, if one dollar is received evenly over the course of the first year of the projection period rather than at year-end, the discount factor is calculated to be 0.95 (assuming a 10% discount rate). Hence, $100 million received throughout Year 1 would be worth $95 million today in accordance with a mid-year convention, as opposed to $91 million using the year-end approach in Exhibit 3.25.

**EXHIBIT 3.26**   Discount Factor Using a Mid-Year Convention

$$\text{Discount Factor} = \frac{1}{(1 + \text{WACC})^{(n - 0.5)}}$$

$$0.95 = \frac{\$1.00}{(1 + 10\%)^{0.5}}$$

where:   n = year in the projection period
0.5 = is subtracted from n in accordance with a mid-year convention

**Terminal Value Considerations**   When employing mid-year convention for the projection period, mid-year discounting is also applied for the terminal value under the PGM, as the banker is discounting perpetual future FCF assumed to be received throughout the year. The EMM, however, which is typically based on the LTM trading multiples of comparable companies for a calendar-year-end EBITDA (or EBIT), uses year-end discounting.

---

[26]May not be appropriate for highly seasonal businesses.

## Determine Valuation

**Calculate Enterprise Value**  A company's projected FCF and terminal value are each discounted to the present and summed to provide an enterprise value. Exhibit 3.27 depicts the DCF calculation of enterprise value for a company with a five-year projection period, incorporating a mid-year convention and the EMM.

**EXHIBIT 3.27**  Enterprise Value Using Mid-Year Discounting

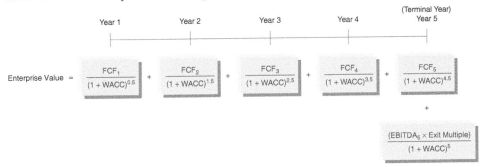

**Derive Implied Equity Value**  To derive implied equity value, the company's net debt, preferred stock, and noncontrolling interest are subtracted from the calculated enterprise value (see Exhibit 3.28).

**EXHIBIT 3.28**  Equity Value

**Derive Implied Share Price**  For publicly traded companies, implied equity value is divided by the company's fully diluted shares outstanding to calculate an implied share price (see Exhibit 3.29).

**EXHIBIT 3.29**  Share Price

The existence of in-the-money options and warrants, however, creates a *circular reference* in the basic formula shown in Exhibit 3.29 between the company's fully diluted shares outstanding count and implied share price. In other words, equity value per share is dependent on the number of fully diluted shares outstanding, which, in turn, is dependent on the implied share price. This is remedied in the model by activating the *iteration* function in Microsoft Excel (see Exhibit 3.30).

**EXHIBIT 3.30**   Iteration Function in Microsoft Excel

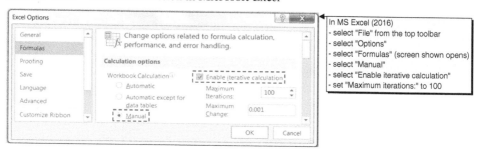

Once the iteration function is activated, the model is able to iterate between the cell determining the company's implied share price (see shaded area "A" in Exhibit 3.31) and those cells determining whether each option tranche is in-the-money (see shaded area "B" in Exhibit 3.31). At an assumed enterprise value of $6,000 million, implied equity value of $4,500 million, 80 million basic shares outstanding, and the options data shown in Exhibit 3.31, we calculate an implied share price of $55.00.

**EXHIBIT 3.31**   Calculation of Implied Share Price

*($ in millions, except per share data)*

| Calculation of Implied Share Price | |
| --- | --- |
| Enterprise Value | $6,000.0 |
| Less: Total Debt | (1,650.0) |
| Less: Preferred Securities | - |
| Less: Noncontrolling Interest | (100.0) |
| Plus: Cash and Cash Equivalents | 250.0 |
| **Implied Equity Value** | **$4,500.0** |

**Options/Warrants**

| Tranche | Number of Shares | Exercise Price | In-the-Money Shares | Proceeds | |
| --- | --- | --- | --- | --- | --- |
| Options 1 | 2.250 | $25.00 | 2.250 | 56.3 | In-the-money options are dependent on implied share price... |
| Options 2 | 1.000 | 30.00 | 1.000 | 30.0 | = IF (Exercise Price < Implied Share Price, then display Number of Shares, otherwise display 0) |
| Options 3 | 0.750 | 45.00 | 0.750 | 33.8 | = IF ($25.00 < $55.00, 2.25, 0) |
| Options 4 | 0.500 | 57.50 | - | - | |
| Options 5 | 0.250 | 75.00 | - | - | = Exercise Price × In-the-Money Shares |
| **Total** | **4.750** | | **4.000** | **$120.0** | = $45.00 × 0.750 |
| Basic Shares Outstanding | | | | 80.000 | = - Total Option Proceeds / Implied Share Price |
| Plus: Shares from In-the-Money Options | | | | 4.000 | = ($120) million / $55.00 |
| Less: Repurchased Shares | | | | (2.182) | Shares repurchased is dependent on implied share price... |
| **Net New Shares from Options** | | | | 1.818 | |
| Plus: Securities Convertible from Shares | | | | - | |
| **Fully Outstanding Shares Diluted** | | | | 81.818 | = Implied Equity Value / Fully Diluted Shares |
| | | | | | = $4.5 billion / 81.818 |
| **Implied Share Price** | | | | **$55.00** | Implied share price is dependent on in-the-money options... |

## Perform Sensitivity Analysis

The DCF incorporates numerous assumptions, each of which can have a sizable impact on valuation. As a result, the DCF output is viewed in terms of a valuation range based on a series of key input assumptions, rather than as a single value. The exercise of deriving a valuation range by varying key inputs is called sensitivity analysis.

Sensitivity analysis is a testament to the notion that valuation is as much an art as a science. Key valuation drivers such as WACC, exit multiple, and perpetuity growth rate are the most commonly sensitized inputs in a DCF. Additional sensitivity analysis is also commonly performed on key financial performance drivers, such as sales growth rates and profit margins (e.g., EBITDA or EBIT). The valuation output produced by sensitivity analysis is typically displayed in a data table, such as that shown in Exhibit 3.32.

The center shaded portion of the sensitivity table in Exhibit 3.32 displays an enterprise value range of $5,627 million to $6,406 million assuming a WACC range of 10.5% to 11.5% and an exit multiple range of 7x to 8x. As the exit multiple increases, enterprise value increases accordingly; conversely, as the discount rate increases, enterprise value decreases.

**EXHIBIT 3.32**   Sensitivity Analysis

Linked to the model output for enterprise value (cell containing $6,009 value in DCF model)

**Enterprise Value**

| | | Exit Multiple | | | |
|---|---|---|---|---|---|
| | **6.5x** | **7.0x** | **7.5x** | **8.0x** | **8.5x** |
| **10.0%** | 5,665 | 5,953 | 6,242 | 6,530 | 6,819 |
| **10.5%** | 5,560 | 5,842 | 6,124 | 6,406 | 6,688 |
| **11.0%** | 5,457 | 5,733 | **$6,009** | 6,284 | 6,560 |
| **11.5%** | 5,357 | 5,627 | 5,897 | 6,166 | 6,436 |
| **12.0%** | 5,260 | 5,524 | 5,787 | 6,051 | 6,315 |

WACC

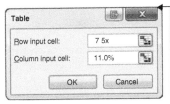

| Table | | |
|---|---|---|
| Row input cell: | 7 5x | |
| Column input cell: | 11.0% | |
| OK | Cancel | |

The sensitivity analysis above can be performed in MS Excel (2016) using the following process:
- create an output table similar to the format above
- input the WACC and exit multiple ranges
- link the top left corner (shaded orange for presentation purposes) to the model output for enterprise value (cell containing $6,009 value in DCF model)
- highlight entire data table
- select Data from top bar, What-if Analysis drop down, and Data Table from the menu: the input box to the left will appear
- link the "Row input cell:" to the cell containing the exit multiple driver of 7.5x in the DCF model
- link the "Column input cell:" to the cell containing the WACC driver of 11.0% in the DCF model
- click the "OK" button and the data table will populate

As with comparable companies and precedent transactions, once a DCF valuation range is determined, it should be compared to the valuation ranges derived from other methodologies. If the output produces notably different results, it is advisable to revisit the assumptions and fine-tune, if necessary. Common missteps that can skew the DCF valuation include the use of unrealistic financial projections (which generally has the largest impact),[27] WACC, or terminal value assumptions. A substantial difference in the valuation implied by the DCF versus other methodologies, however, does not necessarily mean the analysis is flawed. Multiples-based valuation methodologies may fail to account for company-specific factors that may imply a higher or lower valuation.

## KEY PROS AND CONS

### Pros

- *Cash flow-based* – reflects value of projected FCF, which represents a more fundamental approach to valuation than using multiples-based methodologies

- *Market independent* – more insulated from market aberrations such as bubbles and distressed periods

- *Self-sufficient* – does not rely entirely upon truly comparable companies or transactions, which may or may not exist, to frame valuation; a DCF is particularly important when there are limited or no "pure play" public comparables to the company being valued

- *Flexibility* – allows the banker to run multiple financial performance scenarios, including improving or declining growth rates, margins, capex requirements, and working capital efficiency

### Cons

- *Dependence on financial projections* – accurate forecasting of financial performance is challenging, especially as the projection period lengthens

- *Sensitivity to assumptions* – relatively small changes in key assumptions, such as growth rates, margins, WACC, or exit multiple, can produce meaningfully different valuation ranges

- *Terminal value* – the present value of the terminal value can represent as much as three-quarters or more of the DCF valuation, which decreases the relevance of the projection period's annual FCF

- *Assumes constant capital structure* – basic DCF does not provide flexibility to change the company's capital structure over the projection period

---

[27]This is a common pitfall in the event that management projections (Management Case) are used without independently analyzing and testing the underlying assumptions.

## ILLUSTRATIVE DISCOUNTED CASH FLOW ANALYSIS FOR VALUECO

The following section provides a detailed, step-by-step construction of a DCF analysis and illustrates how it is used to establish a valuation range for our target company, ValueCo. As discussed in the Introduction, ValueCo is a private company for which we are provided detailed historical financial information. However, for our illustrative DCF analysis, we assume that no management projections were provided in order to cultivate the ability to develop financial projections with limited information. We do, however, assume that we were provided with basic information on ValueCo's business and operations.

### Step I. Study the Target and Determine Key Performance Drivers

As a first step, we reviewed the basic company information provided on ValueCo. This foundation, in turn, allowed us to study ValueCo's sector in greater detail, including the identification of key competitors (and comparable companies), customers, and suppliers. Various trade journals and industry studies, as well as SEC filings and research reports of public comparables, were particularly important in this respect.

From a financial perspective, ValueCo's historical financials provided a basis for developing our initial assumptions regarding future performance and projecting FCF. Consensus estimates for public comparables were invaluable in guiding us toward supportable growth rates and margin trends for ValueCo's Base Case projections.

### Step II. Project Free Cash Flow

#### Historical Financial Performance

We began the projection of ValueCo's FCF by laying out its income statement through EBIT for the historical three-year and LTM periods (see Exhibit 3.33). We also entered ValueCo's historical capex and working capital data. The historical period provided important perspective for developing defensible Base Case projection period financials.

As shown in Exhibit 3.33, ValueCo's historical period includes financial data for 2016 to 2018 as well as for LTM 9/30/2019. The company's sales and EBITDA grew at a 10.9% and 16.9% CAGR, respectively, over the 2016 to 2018 period. In addition, ValueCo's EBITDA margin was in the approximately 19% to 21% range over this period, and average capex as a percentage of sales was 4.3%.

The historical working capital levels and ratios are also shown in Exhibit 3.33. ValueCo's average DSO, DIH, and DPO for the 2016 to 2018 period were 46.0, 102.8, and 40.0 days, respectively. For the LTM period, ValueCo's EBITDA margin was 20.7% and capex as a percentage of sales was 4.5%.

**EXHIBIT 3.33**  ValueCo Summary Historical Operating and Working Capital Data

*($ in millions, fiscal year ending December 31)*

| ValueCo Summary Historical Operating and Balance Sheet Data | | | | | |
|---|---|---|---|---|---|
| | Historical Period | | | CAGR | LTM |
| | **2016** | **2017** | **2018** | **('16 - '18)** | **9/30/2019** |
| **Operating Data** | | | | | |
| **Sales** | $2,600.0 | $2,900.0 | $3,200.0 | 10.9% | $3,385.0 |
| % growth | NA | 11.5% | 10.3% | | NA |
| Cost of Goods Sold | 1,612.0 | 1,769.0 | 1,920.0 | | 2,035.0 |
| % sales | 62.0% | 61.0% | 60.0% | | 60.1% |
| **Gross Profit** | $988.0 | $1,131.0 | $1,280.0 | 13.8% | $1,350.0 |
| % margin | 38.0% | 39.0% | 40.0% | | 39.9% |
| Selling, General & Administrative | 496.6 | 551.0 | 608.0 | | 650.0 |
| % sales | 19.1% | 19.0% | 19.0% | | 19.2% |
| **EBITDA** | $491.4 | $580.0 | $672.0 | 16.9% | $700.0 |
| % margin | 18.9% | 20.0% | 21.0% | | 20.7% |
| Depreciation | 116.0 | 121.5 | 145.0 | | 150.0 |
| % sales | 4.5% | 4.2% | 4.5% | | 4.4% |
| Amortization | 39.0 | 43.5 | 48.0 | | 50.0 |
| % sales | 1.5% | 1.5% | 1.5% | | 1.5% |
| **EBIT** | $336.4 | $415.0 | $479.0 | 19.3% | $500.0 |
| % margin | 12.9% | 14.3% | 15.0% | | 14.8% |
| | | | | **3-year Average** | |
| Capex | 114.4 | 116.0 | 144.0 | | 152.3 |
| % sales | 4.4% | 4.0% | 4.5% | 4.3% | 4.5% |
| **Balance Sheet Data** | | | | | |
| ***Current Assets*** | | | | | |
| Accounts Receivable | 317.0 | 365.5 | 417.4 | | |
| DSO | 44.5 | 46.0 | 47.6 | 46.0 | |
| Inventory | 441.6 | 496.8 | 556.5 | | |
| DIH | 100.0 | 102.5 | 105.8 | 102.8 | |
| Prepaid Expenses and Other | 117.0 | 142.1 | 162.3 | | |
| % sales | 4.5% | 4.9% | 5.1% | 4.8% | |
| ***Current Liabilities*** | | | | | |
| Accounts Payable | 189.9 | 189.0 | 199.4 | | |
| DPO | 43.0 | 39.0 | 37.9 | 40.0 | |
| Accrued Liabilities | 221.0 | 237.8 | 255.1 | | |
| % sales | 8.5% | 8.2% | 8.0% | 8.2% | |
| Other Current Liabilities | 75.4 | 84.1 | 92.8 | | |
| % sales | 2.9% | 2.9% | 2.9% | 2.9% | |

## Projection of Sales, EBITDA, and EBIT

**Sales Projections**    We projected ValueCo's top line growth for the first three years of the projection period on the basis of consensus research estimates for public comparable companies. Using the average projected sales growth rate for ValueCo's closest peers, we arrived at 2020E, 2021E, and 2022E YoY growth rates of 7.5%, 6%, and 5%, respectively, which are consistent with a maturing business coming off cyclical tailwinds.[28] These growth rate assumptions (as well as the assumptions for all of our model inputs) formed the basis for the Base Case financial projections and were entered into an assumptions page that drives the DCF model (see Chapter 5, Exhibits 5.52 and 5.53).

As the projections indicate, Wall Street expects ValueCo's peers (and, by inference, we expect ValueCo) to continue to experience steady albeit declining growth through 2022E. Beyond 2022E, in the absence of additional company-specific information or guidance, we decreased ValueCo's growth to a sustainable long-term rate of 3% for the remainder of the projection period.

**EXHIBIT 3.34**    ValueCo Historical and Projected Sales

*($ in millions, fiscal year ending December 31)*

| | Historical Period | | | CAGR | | Projection Period | | | | | CAGR |
|---|---|---|---|---|---|---|---|---|---|---|---|
| | 2016 | 2017 | 2018 | ('16 - '18) | 2019 | 2020 | 2021 | 2022 | 2023 | 2024 | ('19 - '24) |
| **Sales** | $2,600.0 | $2,900.0 | $3,200.0 | 10.9% | $3,450.0 | $3,708.8 | $3,931.3 | $4,127.8 | $4,293.0 | $4,421.7 | 5.1% |
| *% growth* | *NA* | *11.5%* | *10.3%* | | *7.8%* | *7.5%* | *6.0%* | *5.0%* | *4.0%* | *3.0%* | |

**COGS and SG&A Projections**    As shown in Exhibit 3.35, we held COGS and SG&A constant at the prior historical year levels of 60% and 19% of sales, respectively. Accordingly, ValueCo's gross profit margin remains at 40% throughout the projection period.

**EXHIBIT 3.35**    ValueCo Historical and Projected COGS and SG&A

*($ in millions, fiscal year ending December 31)*

| | Historical Period | | | CAGR | | Projection Period | | | | | CAGR |
|---|---|---|---|---|---|---|---|---|---|---|---|
| | 2016 | 2017 | 2018 | ('16 - '18) | 2019 | 2020 | 2021 | 2022 | 2023 | 2024 | ('19 - '24) |
| **Sales** | $2,600.0 | $2,900.0 | $3,200.0 | 10.9% | $3,450.0 | $3,708.8 | $3,931.3 | $4,127.8 | $4,293.0 | $4,421.7 | 5.1% |
| *% growth* | *NA* | *11.5%* | *10.3%* | | *7.8%* | *7.5%* | *6.0%* | *5.0%* | *4.0%* | *3.0%* | |
| COGS | 1,612.0 | 1,769.0 | 1,920.0 | | | 2,070.0 | 2,225.3 | 2,358.8 | 2,476.7 | 2,575.8 | 2,653.0 |
| *% sales* | *62.0%* | *61.0%* | *60.0%* | | | *60.0%* | *60.0%* | *60.0%* | *60.0%* | *60.0%* | *60.0%* |
| **Gross Profit** | $988.0 | $1,131.0 | $1,280.0 | 13.8% | $1,380.0 | $1,483.5 | $1,572.5 | $1,651.1 | $1,717.2 | $1,768.7 | 5.1% |
| *% margin* | *38.0%* | *39.0%* | *40.0%* | | *40.0%* | *40.0%* | *40.0%* | *40.0%* | *40.0%* | *40.0%* | |
| SG&A | 496.6 | 551.0 | 608.0 | | | 655.0 | 704.1 | 746.4 | 783.7 | 815.0 | 839.5 |
| *% sales* | *19.1%* | *19.0%* | *19.0%* | | | *19.0%* | *19.0%* | *19.0%* | *19.0%* | *19.0%* | *19.0%* |

**EBITDA Projections**    In the absence of guidance or management projections for EBITDA, we simply held ValueCo's margins constant throughout the projection period at prior historical year levels. These constant margins fall out naturally due to the fact that we froze COGS and SG&A as a percentage of sales at 2017 levels. As shown in Exhibit 3.36, ValueCo's EBITDA margins remain constant at 21% throughout the projection period. We also examined the consensus estimates for ValueCo's peer

---

[28]We also displayed ValueCo's full year 2019E financial data, for which we have reasonable comfort given its proximity at the end of Q3'19. For the purposes of the DCF valuation, we used 2020E as the first full year of projections. An alternative approach is to include the "stub" period FCF (i.e., for Q4'19E) in the projection period and adjust the discounting for a quarter year.

group, which provided comfort that the assumption of constant EBITDA margins was justifiable.

**EXHIBIT 3.36**　ValueCo Historical and Projected EBITDA

*($ in millions, fiscal year ending December 31)*

| | Historical Period | | | CAGR | | Projection Period | | | | | CAGR |
|---|---|---|---|---|---|---|---|---|---|---|---|
| | 2016 | 2017 | 2018 | ('16 - '18) | 2019 | 2020 | 2021 | 2022 | 2023 | 2024 | ('19 - '24) |
| Sales | $2,600.0 | $2,900.0 | $3,200.0 | 10.9% | $3,450.0 | $3,708.8 | $3,931.3 | $4,127.8 | $4,293.0 | $4,421.7 | 5.1% |
| % growth | NA | 11.5% | 10.3% | | 7.8% | 7.5% | 6.0% | 5.0% | 4.0% | 3.0% | |
| COGS | 1,612.0 | 1,769.0 | 1,920.0 | | 2,070.0 | 2,225.3 | 2,358.8 | 2,476.7 | 2,575.8 | 2,653.0 | |
| % sales | 62.0% | 61.0% | 60.0% | | 60.0% | 60.0% | 60.0% | 60.0% | 60.0% | 60.0% | |
| Gross Profit | $988.0 | $1,131.0 | $1,280.0 | 13.8% | $1,380.0 | $1,483.5 | $1,572.5 | $1,651.1 | $1,717.2 | $1,768.7 | 5.1% |
| % margin | 38.0% | 39.0% | 40.0% | | 40.0% | 40.0% | 40.0% | 40.0% | 40.0% | 40.0% | |
| SG&A | 496.6 | 551.0 | 608.0 | | 655.0 | 704.1 | 746.4 | 783.7 | 815.0 | 839.5 | |
| % sales | 19.1% | 19.0% | 19.0% | | 19.0% | 19.0% | 19.0% | 19.0% | 19.0% | 19.0% | |
| EBITDA | $491.4 | $580.0 | $672.0 | 16.9% | $725.0 | $779.4 | $826.1 | $867.4 | $902.1 | $929.2 | 5.1% |
| % margin | 18.9% | 20.0% | 21.0% | | 21.0% | 21.0% | 21.0% | 21.0% | 21.0% | 21.0% | |

**EBIT Projections**　To drive EBIT projections, we held D&A as a percentage of sales constant at the 2018 level of 6%. We gained comfort that these D&A levels were appropriate as they were consistent with historical data as well as our capex projections (see Exhibit 3.39). EBIT was then calculated in each year of the projection period by subtracting D&A from EBITDA (see Exhibit 3.37). As previously discussed, an alternative approach is to construct the DCF on the basis of EBITDA and EBIT projections, with D&A simply calculated by subtracting EBIT from EBITDA.

**EXHIBIT 3.37**　ValueCo Historical and Projected EBIT

*($ in millions, fiscal year ending December 31)*

| | Historical Period | | | CAGR | | Projection Period | | | | | CAGR |
|---|---|---|---|---|---|---|---|---|---|---|---|
| | 2016 | 2017 | 2018 | ('16 - '18) | 2019 | 2020 | 2021 | 2022 | 2023 | 2024 | ('19 - '24) |
| Sales | $2,600.0 | $2,900.0 | $3,200.0 | 10.9% | $3,450.0 | $3,708.8 | $3,931.3 | $4,127.8 | $4,293.0 | $4,421.7 | 5.1% |
| % growth | NA | 11.5% | 10.3% | | 7.8% | 7.5% | 6.0% | 5.0% | 4.0% | 3.0% | |
| COGS | 1,612.0 | 1,769.0 | 1,920.0 | | 2,070.0 | 2,225.3 | 2,358.8 | 2,476.7 | 2,575.8 | 2,653.0 | |
| % sales | 62.0% | 61.0% | 60.0% | | 60.0% | 60.0% | 60.0% | 60.0% | 60.0% | 60.0% | |
| Gross Profit | $988.0 | $1,131.0 | $1,280.0 | 13.8% | $1,380.0 | $1,483.5 | $1,572.5 | $1,651.1 | $1,717.2 | $1,768.7 | 5.1% |
| % margin | 38.0% | 39.0% | 40.0% | | 40.0% | 40.0% | 40.0% | 40.0% | 40.0% | 40.0% | |
| SG&A | 496.6 | 551.0 | 608.0 | | 655.0 | 704.1 | 746.4 | 783.7 | 815.0 | 839.5 | |
| % sales | 19.1% | 19.0% | 19.0% | | 19.0% | 19.0% | 19.0% | 19.0% | 19.0% | 19.0% | |
| EBITDA | $491.4 | $580.0 | $672.0 | 16.9% | $725.0 | $779.4 | $826.1 | $867.4 | $902.1 | $929.2 | 5.1% |
| % margin | 18.9% | 20.0% | 21.0% | | 21.0% | 21.0% | 21.0% | 21.0% | 21.0% | 21.0% | |
| D&A | 155.0 | 165.0 | 193.0 | | 207.0 | 222.5 | 235.9 | 247.7 | 257.6 | 265.3 | |
| % of sales | 6.0% | 5.7% | 6.0% | | 6.0% | 6.0% | 6.0% | 6.0% | 6.0% | 6.0% | |
| EBIT | $336.4 | $415.0 | $479.0 | 19.3% | $518.0 | $556.9 | $590.3 | $619.8 | $644.6 | $663.9 | 5.1% |
| % margin | 12.9% | 14.3% | 15.0% | | 15.0% | 15.0% | 15.0% | 15.0% | 15.0% | 15.0% | |

## Projection of Free Cash Flow

**Tax Projections** We calculated tax expense for each year at ValueCo's marginal tax rate of 25%. This tax rate was applied on an annual basis to EBIT to arrive at EBIAT (see Exhibit 3.38).

**EXHIBIT 3.38** ValueCo Projected Taxes

*($ in millions, fiscal year ending December 31)*

| | Historical Period | | | CAGR | | Projection Period | | | | | CAGR |
| --- | --- | --- | --- | --- | --- | --- | --- | --- | --- | --- | --- |
| | 2016 | 2017 | 2018 | ('16 - '18) | 2019 | 2020 | 2021 | 2022 | 2023 | 2024 | ('19 - '24) |
| EBIT | $336.4 | $415.0 | $479.0 | 19.3% | $518.0 | $556.9 | $590.3 | $619.8 | $644.6 | $663.9 | 5.1% |
| *% margin* | *12.9%* | *14.3%* | *15.0%* | | *15.0%* | *15.0%* | *15.0%* | *15.0%* | *15.0%* | *15.0%* | |
| Taxes @ 25% | | | | | | 139.2 | 147.6 | 154.9 | 161.1 | 166.0 | |
| EBIAT | | | | | | $417.6 | $442.7 | $464.8 | $483.4 | $497.9 | 5.1% |

**Capex Projections** We projected ValueCo's capex as a percentage of sales in line with historical levels. As shown in Exhibit 3.39, this approach led us to hold capex constant throughout the projection period at 4.5% of sales. Based on this assumption, capex increases from $166.9 million in 2020E to $199 million in 2024E.

**EXHIBIT 3.39** ValueCo Historical and Projected Capex

*($ in millions, fiscal year ending December 31)*

| | Historical Period | | | CAGR | | Projection Period | | | | | CAGR |
| --- | --- | --- | --- | --- | --- | --- | --- | --- | --- | --- | --- |
| | 2016 | 2017 | 2018 | ('16 - '18) | 2019 | 2020 | 2021 | 2022 | 2023 | 2024 | ('19 - '24) |
| Sales | $2,600.0 | $2,900.0 | $3,200.0 | 10.9% | $3,450.0 | $3,708.8 | $3,931.3 | $4,127.8 | $4,293.0 | $4,421.7 | 5.1% |
| *% growth* | *NA* | *11.5%* | *10.3%* | | *7.8%* | *7.5%* | *6.0%* | *5.0%* | *4.0%* | *3.0%* | |
| Capex | 114.4 | 116.0 | 144.0 | | 155.3 | 166.9 | 176.9 | 185.8 | 193.2 | 199.0 | |
| *% sales* | *4.4%* | *4.0%* | *4.5%* | | *4.5%* | *4.5%* | *4.5%* | *4.5%* | *4.5%* | *4.5%* | |

**Change in Net Working Capital Projections** As with ValueCo's other financial performance metrics, historical working capital levels normally serve as reliable indicators of future performance. The direct prior year's ratios are typically the most indicative provided they are consistent with historical levels. This was the case for ValueCo's 2018 working capital ratios, which we held constant throughout the projection period (see Exhibit 3.40).

For A/R, inventory, and A/P, respectively, these ratios are DSO of 47.6, DIH of 105.8, and DPO of 37.9. For prepaid expenses and other current assets, accrued liabilities, and other current liabilities, the percentage of sales levels are 5.1%, 8.0%, and 2.9%, respectively. For ValueCo's Base Case financial projections, we conservatively did not assume any improvements in working capital efficiency.

As depicted in the callouts in Exhibit 3.40, using ValueCo's 2018 ratios, we projected 2019E NWC to be $635 million. To determine the 2020E YoY change in NWC, we then subtracted this value from ValueCo's 2020E NWC of $682.6 million. The $47.6 million difference is a use of cash and is, therefore, subtracted from EBIAT, resulting in a reduction of ValueCo's 2020E FCF. Hence, it is shown in Exhibit 3.41 as a negative value.

**EXHIBIT 3.40**  ValueCo Historical and Projected Net Working Capital

## ValueCo Corporation
## Working Capital Projections
*($ in millions, fiscal year ending December 31)*

| | Historical Period | | | | Projection Period | | | | |
|---|---|---|---|---|---|---|---|---|---|
| | 2016 | 2017 | 2018 | 2019 | 2020 | 2021 | 2022 | 2023 | 2024 |
| Sales | $2,600.0 | $2,900.0 | $3,200.0 | $3,450.0 | $3,708.8 | $3,931.3 | $4,127.8 | $4,293.0 | $4,421.7 |
| Cost of Goods Sold | 1,612.0 | 1,769.0 | 1,920.0 | 2,070.0 | 2,225.3 | 2,358.8 | 2,476.7 | 2,575.8 | 2,653.0 |
| **Current Assets** | | | | | | | | | |
| Accounts Receivable | 317.0 | 365.5 | 417.4 | 450.0 | 483.8 | 512.8 | 538.4 | 560.0 | 576.7 |
| Inventories | 441.6 | 496.8 | 556.5 | 600.0 | 645.0 | 683.7 | 717.9 | 746.6 | 769.0 |
| Prepaid Expenses and Other | 117.0 | 142.1 | 162.3 | 175.0 | 188.1 | 199.4 | 209.4 | 217.8 | 224.3 |
| **Total Current Assets** | **$875.6** | **$1,004.4** | **$1,136.2** | **$1,225.0** | **$1,316.9** | **$1,395.9** | **$1,465.7** | **$1,524.3** | **$1,570.0** |
| **Current Liabilities** | | | | | | | | | |
| Accounts Payable | 189.9 | 189.0 | 199.4 | 215.0 | 231.1 | 245.0 | 257.2 | 267.5 | 275.6 |
| Accrued Liabilities | 221.0 | 237.8 | 255.1 | 275.0 | 295.6 | 313.4 | 329.0 | 342.2 | 352.5 |
| Other Current Liabilities | 75.4 | 84.1 | 92.8 | 100.0 | 107.5 | 114.0 | 119.6 | 124.4 | 128.2 |
| **Total Current Liabilities** | **$486.3** | **$510.9** | **$547.2** | **$590.0** | **$634.3** | **$672.3** | **$705.9** | **$734.2** | **$756.2** |
| **Net Working Capital** | **$389.4** | **$493.5** | **$589.0** | **$635.0** | **$682.6** | **$723.6** | **$759.8** | **$790.2** | **$813.9** |
| *% sales* | *15.0%* | *17.0%* | *18.4%* | *18.4%* | *18.4%* | *18.4%* | *18.4%* | *18.4%* | *18.4%* |
| **(Increase)/Decrease in NWC** | | ($104.1) | ($95.5) | ($46.0) | ($47.6) | ($41.0) | ($36.2) | ($30.4) | ($23.7) |
| **Assumptions** | | | | | | | | | |
| **Current Assets** | | | | | | | | | |
| Days Sales Outstanding | 44.5 | 46.0 | 47.6 | 47.6 | 47.6 | 47.6 | 47.6 | 47.6 | 47.6 |
| Days Inventory Held | 100.0 | 102.5 | 105.8 | 105.8 | 105.8 | 105.8 | 105.8 | 105.8 | 105.8 |
| Prepaids and Other CA (% of sales) | 4.5% | 4.9% | 5.1% | 5.1% | 5.1% | 5.1% | 5.1% | 5.1% | 5.1% |
| **Current Liabilities** | | | | | | | | | |
| Days Payable Outstanding | 43.0 | 39.0 | 37.9 | 37.9 | 37.9 | 37.9 | 37.9 | 37.9 | 37.9 |
| Accrued Liabilities (% of sales) | 8.5% | 8.2% | 8.0% | 8.0% | 8.0% | 8.0% | 8.0% | 8.0% | 8.0% |
| Other Current Liabilities (% of sales) | 2.9% | 2.9% | 2.9% | 2.9% | 2.9% | 2.9% | 2.9% | 2.9% | 2.9% |

Annotations:

$= (\text{Sales}_{2020E} / 365) \times \text{DSO} = (\$3,708.8 \text{ million} / 365) \times 47.6$

$= (\text{COGS}_{2020E} / 365) \times \text{DIH} = (\$2,225.3 \text{ million} / 365) \times 105.8$

$= \text{Sales}_{2020E} \times \% \text{ of Sales} = \$3,708.8 \text{ million} \times 5.1\%$

$= (\text{COGS}_{2020E} / 365) \times \text{DPO} = (\$2,225.3 \text{ million} / 365) \times 37.9$

$= \text{Sales}_{2020E} \times \% \text{ of Sales} = \$3,708.8 \text{ million} \times 8\%$

$= \text{Sales}_{2020E} \times \% \text{ of Sales} = \$3,708.8 \text{ million} \times 2.9\%$

$= \text{Total CA}_{2020E} - \text{Total CL}_{2020E} = \$1,316.9 \text{ million} - \$634.3 \text{ million}$

$= \text{NWC}_{2019E} - \text{NWC}_{2020E} = \$635 \text{ million} - \$682.6 \text{ million}$

$= (\text{A/R}_{2018} / \text{Sales}_{2018}) \times 365 = (\$417.4 \text{ million} / \$3,200 \text{ million}) \times 365$

$= (\text{Inventories}_{2018} / \text{COGS}_{2018}) \times 365 = (\$556.5 \text{ million} / \$1,920 \text{ million}) \times 365$

$= \text{Prepaids and Other Current Assets}_{2018} / \text{Sales}_{2018} = \$162.3 \text{ million} / \$3,200 \text{ million}$

$= (\text{A/P}_{2018} / \text{COGS}_{2018}) \times 365 = (\$199.4 \text{ million} / \$1,920 \text{ million}) \times 365$

$= \text{Accrued Liabilities}_{2018} / \text{Sales}_{2018} = \$255.1 \text{ million} / \$3,200 \text{ million}$

$= \text{Other Current Liabilities}_{2018} / \text{Sales}_{2018} = \$92.8 \text{ million} / \$3,200 \text{ million}$

**EXHIBIT 3.41**  ValueCo's Projected Changes in Net Working Capital

*($ in millions, fiscal year ending December 31)*

| | 2019 | Projection Period | | | | |
| --- | --- | --- | --- | --- | --- | --- |
| | | 2020 | 2021 | 2022 | 2023 | 2024 |
| Total Current Assets | $1,225.0 | $1,316.9 | $1,395.9 | $1,465.7 | $1,524.3 | $1,570.0 |
| Less: Total Current Liabilities | 590.0 | 634.3 | 672.3 | 705.9 | 734.2 | 756.2 |
| **Net Working Capital** | $635.0 | $682.6 | $723.6 | $759.8 | $790.2 | $813.9 |
| **(Increase)/Decrease in NWC** | | ($47.6) | ($41.0) | ($36.2) | ($30.4) | ($23.7) |

= Total Current Assets$_{2019E}$ - Total Current Liabilities$_{2019E}$
= $1,225 million - $590 million

= Net Working Capital$_{2019E}$ - Net Working Capital$_{2020E}$
= $635 million - $682.6 million

The methodology for determining ValueCo's 2019E NWC was then applied in each year of the projection period. Each annual change in NWC was added to the corresponding annual EBIAT (with increases in NWC expressed as negative values) to calculate annual FCF.

A potential shortcut to the detailed approach outlined in Exhibits 3.40 and 3.41 is to bypass projecting individual working capital components and simply project NWC as a percentage of sales in line with historical levels. For example, we could have used ValueCo's 2018 NWC percentage of sales ratio of 18.4% to project its NWC for each year of the projection period. We would then have simply calculated YoY changes in ValueCo's NWC and made the corresponding subtractions from EBIAT.

**Free Cash Flow Projections**  Having determined all of the above line items, we calculated ValueCo's annual projected FCF, which increases from $425.6 million in 2020E to $540.5 million in 2024E (see Exhibit 3.42).

**EXHIBIT 3.42**  ValueCo Projected FCF

*($ in millions, fiscal year ending December 31)*

| | Historical Period | | | CAGR | | Projection Period | | | | | CAGR |
| --- | --- | --- | --- | --- | --- | --- | --- | --- | --- | --- | --- |
| | 2016 | 2017 | 2018 | ('16 - '18) | 2019 | 2020 | 2021 | 2022 | 2023 | 2024 | ('19 - '24) |
| **Sales** | $2,600.0 | $2,900.0 | $3,200.0 | 10.9% | $3,450.0 | $3,708.8 | $3,931.3 | $4,127.8 | $4,293.0 | $4,421.7 | 5.1% |
| *% growth* | *NA* | *11.5%* | *10.3%* | | *7.8%* | *7.5%* | *6.0%* | *5.0%* | *4.0%* | *3.0%* | |
| COGS | 1,612.0 | 1,769.0 | 1,920.0 | | 2,070.0 | 2,225.3 | 2,358.8 | 2,476.7 | 2,575.8 | 2,653.0 | |
| *% sales* | *62.0%* | *61.0%* | *60.0%* | | *60.0%* | *60.0%* | *60.0%* | *60.0%* | *60.0%* | *60.0%* | |
| **Gross Profit** | $988.0 | $1,131.0 | $1,280.0 | 13.8% | $1,380.0 | $1,483.5 | $1,572.5 | $1,651.1 | $1,717.2 | $1,768.7 | 5.1% |
| *% margin* | *38.0%* | *39.0%* | *40.0%* | | *40.0%* | *40.0%* | *40.0%* | *40.0%* | *40.0%* | *40.0%* | |
| SG&A | 496.6 | 551.0 | 608.0 | | 655.0 | 704.1 | 746.4 | 783.7 | 815.0 | 839.5 | |
| *% sales* | *19.1%* | *19.0%* | *19.0%* | | *19.0%* | *19.0%* | *19.0%* | *19.0%* | *19.0%* | *19.0%* | |
| **EBITDA** | $491.4 | $580.0 | $672.0 | 16.9% | $725.0 | $779.4 | $826.1 | $867.4 | $902.1 | $929.2 | 5.1% |
| *% margin* | *18.9%* | *20.0%* | *21.0%* | | *21.0%* | *21.0%* | *21.0%* | *21.0%* | *21.0%* | *21.0%* | |
| D&A | 155.0 | 165.0 | 193.0 | | 207.0 | 222.5 | 235.9 | 247.7 | 257.6 | 265.3 | |
| *% of sales* | *6.0%* | *5.7%* | *6.0%* | | *6.0%* | *6.0%* | *6.0%* | *6.0%* | *6.0%* | *6.0%* | |
| **EBIT** | $336.4 | $415.0 | $479.0 | 19.3% | $518.0 | $556.9 | $590.3 | $619.8 | $644.6 | $663.9 | 5.1% |
| *% margin* | *12.9%* | *14.3%* | *15.0%* | | *15.0%* | *15.0%* | *15.0%* | *15.0%* | *15.0%* | *15.0%* | |
| Taxes | | | | | | 139.2 | 147.6 | 154.9 | 161.1 | 166.0 | |
| **EBIAT** | | | | | | $417.6 | $442.7 | $464.8 | $483.4 | $497.9 | 5.1% |
| Plus: D&A | | | | | | 222.5 | 235.9 | 247.7 | 257.6 | 265.3 | |
| Less: Capex | | | | | | (166.9) | (176.9) | (185.8) | (193.2) | (199.0) | |
| Less: Inc./(Dec.) in NWC | | | | | | (47.6) | (41.0) | (36.2) | (30.4) | (23.7) | |
| **Unlevered Free Cash Flow** | | | | | | $425.6 | $460.7 | $490.6 | $517.4 | $540.5 | |

## Step III. Calculate Weighted Average Cost of Capital

Below, we demonstrate the step-by-step calculation of ValueCo's WACC, which we determined to be 11%.

**Step III(a): Determine Target Capital Structure**  Our first step was to determine ValueCo's target capital structure. For private companies, the target capital structure is generally extrapolated from peers. As ValueCo's peers have an average (mean) D/E of 42.9%—or debt-to-total capitalization (D/(D+E)) of 30%—we used this as our target capital structure (see Exhibit 3.45).

**Step III(b): Estimate Cost of Debt**  We estimated ValueCo's long-term cost of debt based on the current yields on its existing term loan and senior notes (see Exhibit 3.43).[29] The term loan, which for illustrative purposes we assumed is trading at par, is priced at a spread of 350 basis points (bps)[30] to LIBOR[31] (L+350 bps). Based on LIBOR of 185 bps, we estimated ValueCo's term loan has a cost of debt of 5.35%. The senior notes are also assumed to be trading at par and have a coupon of 8%. Based on the rough average cost of debt across ValueCo's capital structure, we estimated ValueCo's cost of debt at roughly 6.5% (or approximately 4.9% on an after-tax basis).

**EXHIBIT 3.43**  ValueCo Capitalization

($ in millions)

| | Amount | % of Total Capitalization | Term | Coupon |
|---|---|---|---|---|
| Cash and Cash Equivalents | $250.0 | | | |
| Revolving Credit Facility | - | - % | 6 years | L+325 bps |
| Term Loan | 1,000.0 | 20.0% | 7 years | L+350 bps |
| **Senior Secured** | **$1,000.0** | **20.0%** | | |
| Senior Notes | 500.0 | 10.0% | 8 years | 8.000% |
| **Total Debt** | **$1,500.0** | **30.0%** | | |
| Shareholders' Equity | 3,500.0 | 70.0% | | |
| **Total Capitalization** | **$5,000.0** | **100.0%** | | |
| Net Debt | $1,250.0 | | | |
| Debt / Equity | 42.9% | | | |
| Debt / Total Capitalization | 30.0% | | | |

[29]Alternatively, ValueCo's cost of debt could be extrapolated from that of its peers. We took comfort with using the current yield on ValueCo's existing debt instruments because its current capital structure is in line with peers.

[30]A basis point is a unit of measure equal to 1/100th of 1% (100 bps = 1%).

[31]The London Interbank Offered Rate (LIBOR) is the rate of interest at which banks can borrow funds from other banks, in marketable size, in the London interbank market.

**Step III(c): Estimate Cost of Equity**   We calculated ValueCo's cost of equity in accordance with the CAPM formula shown in Exhibit 3.44.

**EXHIBIT 3.44**   CAPM Formula

$$r_e = r_f + \beta_L \times (r_m - r_f) + SP$$

**Determine Risk-free Rate and Market Risk Premium**   We assumed a risk-free rate ($r_f$) of 2.5% based on the interpolated yield of the 20-year Treasury bond. For the market risk premium ($r_m - r_r$), we used the arithmetic mean of approximately 7% (for the 1926–2019 period) in accordance with Duff & Phelps.

**Determine the Average Unlevered Beta of ValueCo's Comparable Companies**   As ValueCo is a private company, we extrapolated beta from its closest comparables (see Chapter 1). We began by sourcing predicted levered betas for each of ValueCo's closest comparables.[32] We then entered the market values for each comparable company's debt[33] and equity, and calculated the D/E ratios accordingly. This information, in conjunction with the marginal tax rate assumptions, enabled us to unlever the individual betas and calculate an average unlevered beta for the peer group (see Exhibit 3.45).

**EXHIBIT 3.45**   Average Unlevered Beta

|  |  |  |  |  |  | = Predicted Levered Beta / (1 + (Debt/Equity) × (1 - t))<br>= 1.46 / (1 + (56.3%) × (1 - 25%)) |
|---|---|---|---|---|---|---|

*($ in millions)*

| Company | Predicted Levered Beta | Market Value of Debt | Market Value of Equity | Debt/ Equity | Marginal Tax Rate | Unlevered Beta |
|---|---|---|---|---|---|---|
| BuyerCo | 1.35 | $2,200.0 | $9,800.0 | 22.4% | 25% | 1.16 |
| Sherman Co. | 1.46 | 3,150.0 | 5,600.0 | 56.3% | 25% | 1.03 |
| Gasparro Corp. | 1.30 | 1,850.0 | 5,000.0 | 37.0% | 25% | 1.02 |
| Goodson Corp | 1.53 | 2,250.0 | 4,160.0 | 54.1% | 25% | 1.09 |
| S. Momper & Co. | 1.50 | 1,000.0 | 2,240.0 | 44.6% | 25% | 1.12 |
| **Mean** | **1.43** |  |  | **42.9%** |  | **1.08** |
| **Median** | **1.46** |  |  | **44.6%** |  | **1.09** |

Comparable Companies Unlevered Beta

For example, based on Sherman Co.'s predicted levered beta of 1.46, D/E of 56.3%, and a marginal tax rate of 25%, we calculated an unlevered beta of 1.03. We performed this calculation for each of the selected comparable companies and then calculated an average unlevered beta of 1.08 for the group.

---

[32]An alternative approach is to use historical betas (e.g., from Bloomberg), or both historical and predicted betas, and then show a range of outputs.

[33]For simplicity, we assumed that the market value of debt was equal to the book value.

Relever Average Unlevered Beta at ValueCo's Capital Structure  We then relevered the average unlevered beta of 1.08 at ValueCo's previously determined target capital structure of 42.9% D/E, using its marginal tax rate of 25%. This provided a levered beta of 1.29 (see Exhibit 3.46).

**EXHIBIT 3.46**  ValueCo Relevered Beta

| = Average Unlevered Beta × (1 + (Target Debt/Equity) × (1 - Target Marginal Tax Rate) |
| = 1.08 × (1 + (42.9%) × (1 - 25%)) |

**ValueCo Relevered Beta**

| | Mean Unlevered Beta | Target Debt/ Equity | Target Marginal Tax Rate | Relevered Beta |
|---|---|---|---|---|
| Relevered Beta | 1.08 | 42.9% | 25% | 1.43 |

| = Debt-to-Total Capitalization / Equity-to-Total Capitalization |
| = 30% / 70% |

Calculate Cost of Equity  Using the CAPM, we calculated a cost of equity for ValueCo of 13.6% (see Exhibit 3.47), which is higher than the expected return on the market (calculated as 9.5% based on a risk-free rate of 2.5% and a market risk premium of 7%). This relatively high cost of equity was driven by the relevered beta of 1.43, versus 1.0 for the market as a whole, as well as a size premium of approximately 1.1%.[34]

**EXHIBIT 3.47**  ValueCo Cost of Equity

| **Cost of Equity** | |
|---|---|
| Risk-free Rate | 2.5% |
| Market Risk Premium | 7.0% |
| Levered Beta | 1.43 |
| Size Premium | 1.1% |
| **Cost of Equity** | **13.6%** |

| = Risk-free Rate + (Levered Beta × Market Risk Premium) + Size Premium |
| = 2.5% + (1.43 × 7.0%) + 1.10% |

---

[34] Duff & Phelps estimates a size premium of approximately 0.85% for the #4 Market Capitalization Decile and 1.28% for the #5 Decile. We used a blended average for our analysis.

**Step III(d): Calculate WACC** Having calculated all of the critical WACC components, they were entered into the formula in Exhibit 3.12, resulting in a WACC of 11%. Exhibit 3.48 displays each of the assumptions and calculations for determining ValueCo's WACC.

As previously discussed, the DCF is highly sensitive to WACC, which itself is dependent on numerous assumptions governing target capital structure, cost of debt, and cost of equity. Therefore, a sensitivity analysis is typically performed on key WACC inputs to produce a WACC range. In Exhibit 3.49, we sensitized target capital structure and pre-tax cost of debt to produce a WACC range of approximately 10.5% to 11.5% for ValueCo.

**EXHIBIT 3.48** ValueCo WACC Calculation

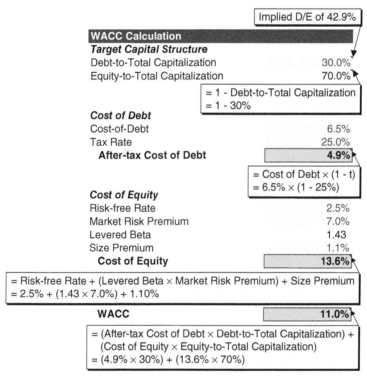

**EXHIBIT 3.49**  ValueCo Weighted Average Cost of Capital Analysis

## ValueCo Corporation
## Weighted Average Cost of Capital Analysis
*($ in millions)*

### WACC Calculation

**Target Capital Structure**

| | |
|---|---|
| Debt-to-Total Capitalization | 30.0% |
| Equity-to-Total Capitalization | 70.0% |

**Cost of Debt**

| | |
|---|---|
| Cost-of-Debt | 6.5% |
| Tax Rate | 25.0% |
| After-tax Cost of Debt | 4.9% |

**Cost of Equity**

| | |
|---|---|
| Risk-free Rate (1) | 2.5% |
| Market Risk Premium (2) | 7.0% |
| Levered Beta | 1.43 |
| Size Premium (3) | 1.1% |
| Cost of Equity | 13.6% |

| | |
|---|---|
| WACC | 11.0% |

### Comparable Companies Unlevered Beta

| Company | Predicted Levered Beta | Market Value of Debt | Market Value of Equity | Debt/ Equity | Marginal Tax Rate | Unlevered Beta |
|---|---|---|---|---|---|---|
| BuyerCo | 1.35 | $2,200.0 | $9,800.0 | 22.4% | 25% | 1.16 |
| Sherman Co. | 1.46 | 3,150.0 | 5,600.0 | 56.3% | 25% | 1.03 |
| Gasparro Corp. | 1.30 | 1,850.0 | 5,000.0 | 37.0% | 25% | 1.02 |
| Goodson Corp | 1.53 | 2,250.0 | 4,160.0 | 54.1% | 25% | 1.09 |
| S. Momper & Co. | 1.50 | 1,000.0 | 2,240.0 | 44.6% | 25% | 1.12 |
| Mean | 1.43 | | | 42.9% | | 1.08 |
| Median | 1.46 | | | 44.6% | | 1.09 |

### ValueCo Relevered Beta

| | Mean Unlevered Beta | Target Debt/ Equity | Target Marginal Tax Rate | Relevered Beta |
|---|---|---|---|---|
| Relevered Beta | 1.08 | 42.9% | 25% | 1.43 |

### WACC Sensitivity Analysis

| | | Pre-tax Cost of Debt | | | |
|---|---|---|---|---|---|
| | 5.50% | 6.00% | 6.50% | 7.00% | 7.50% |
| Debt-to-Total Capitalization — 10.0% | 12.7% | 12.7% | 12.7% | 12.8% | 12.8% |
| 20.0% | 11.7% | 11.8% | 11.9% | 11.9% | 12.0% |
| 30.0% | 10.8% | 10.9% | 11.0% | 11.1% | 11.2% |
| 40.0% | 9.8% | 10.0% | 10.1% | 10.3% | 10.4% |
| 50.0% | 8.9% | 9.1% | 9.2% | 9.4% | 9.6% |

(1) Interpolated yield on 20-year U.S. Treasury, sourced from Treasury.gov.
(2) Obtained from *Duff & Phelps SBBI Valuation Yearbook*.
(3) Blend of Duff & Phelps Market Capitalization Deciles 4 and 5.

## Step IV. Determine Terminal Value

**Exit Multiple Method**   We used the LTM EV/EBITDA trading multiples for ValueCo's closest public comparable companies as the basis for calculating terminal value in accordance with the EMM. These companies tend to trade in a range of 7.0x to 8.0x LTM EBITDA. Multiplying ValueCo's terminal year EBITDA of $929.2 million by the 7.5x midpoint of this range provided a terminal value of $6,969 million (see Exhibit 3.50).

**EXHIBIT 3.50**   Exit Multiple Method

*($ in millions)*

| Calculation of Terminal Value using EMM | |
| --- | --- |
| Terminal Year EBITDA (2024E) | $2.929 |
| Exit Multiple | 7.5x |
| **Terminal Value** | **$6,969.0** |

$= \text{EBITDA}_{\text{Terminal Year}} \times \text{Exit Multiple}$
$= \$929.2 \text{ million} \times 7.5\text{x}$

We then solved for the perpetuity growth rate implied by the exit multiple of 7.5x EBITDA. Given the terminal year FCF of $540.5 million and 11% midpoint of the selected WACC range, and adjusting for the use of a mid-year convention for the PGM terminal value, we calculated an implied perpetuity growth rate of 2.6% (see Exhibit 3.51).

**EXHIBIT 3.51**   Implied Perpetuity Growth Rate

*($ in millions)*

| Implied Perpetuity Growth Rate | |
| --- | --- |
| Terminal Year Free Cash Flow (2024E) | $540.5 |
| Discount Rate | 11.0% |
| Terminal Value | $6,969.0 |
| **Implied Perpetuity Growth Rate** | **2.6%** |

$= ((\text{EMM Terminal Value} \times \text{WACC}) - \text{FCF}_{\text{Terminal Year}} \times (1 + \text{WACC})^{0.5}) /$
$\quad (\text{EMM Terminal Value} + \text{FCF}_{\text{Terminal Year}} \times (1 + \text{WACC})^{0.5})$
$= ((\$6,969 \text{ million}) \times 11\%) - \$540.5 \text{ million} \times (1 + 11\%)^{0.5}) /$
$\quad (\$6,969 \text{ million} + \$540.5 \text{ million} \times (1 + 11\%)^{0.5})$

**Perpetuity Growth Method**    We selected a perpetuity growth rate range of 2% to 4% to calculate ValueCo's terminal value using the PGM. Using a perpetuity growth rate midpoint of 3%, WACC midpoint of 11%, and terminal year FCF of $540.5 million, we calculated a terminal value of $6,959.6 million for ValueCo (see Exhibit 3.52).

**EXHIBIT 3.52**    Perpetuity Growth Rate

*($ in millions)*

| Calculation of Terminal Value using PGM | |
| --- | --- |
| Terminal Year Free Cash Flow (2024E) | $540.5 |
| WACC | 11.0% |
| Perpetuity Growth Rate | 3.0% |
| **Terminal Value** | **$6,959.6** |

= FCF$_{\text{Terminal Year}}$ × (1 + Perpetuity Growth Rate) / (WACC - Perpetuity Growth Rate)
= $540.5 million × (1 + 3%) / (11% - 3%)

The terminal value of $6,959.6 million calculated using the PGM implied a 7.9x exit multiple, adjusting for year-end discounting using the EMM (see Exhibit 3.53). This is consistent with our assumptions using the EMM approach in Exhibit 3.50.

**EXHIBIT 3.53**    Implied Exit Multiple

*($ in millions)*

| Implied Exit Multiple | |
| --- | --- |
| Terminal Value | $6,959.6 |
| Terminal Year EBITDA (2024E) | 929.2 |
| WACC | 11.0% |
| | |
| **Implied Exit Multiple** | **7.9x** |

= PGM Terminal Value × (1 + WACC)$^{0.5}$ / EBITDA$_{\text{Terminal Year}}$
= $6,959.6 million × (1 + 11%)$^{0.5}$ / and $929.2 million

## Step V. Calculate Present Value and Determine Valuation

### Calculate Present Value

ValueCo's projected annual FCF and terminal value were discounted to the present using the selected WACC midpoint of 11% (see Exhibit 3.54). We used a mid-year convention to discount projected FCF. For the terminal value calculation using the EMM, however, we used year-end discounting.

**EXHIBIT 3.54**  Present Value Calculation

*($ in millions)*

**Present Value Calculation**

$$= 1 / ((1 + WACC)^{(n - .05)})$$
$$= 1 / ((1 + 11\%)^{(4.5)})$$
Note: Mid-Year Convention applied

| | | Projection Period | | | | |
|---|---|---|---|---|---|---|
| | | **2020** | **2021** | **2022** | **2023** | **2024** |
| **Unlevered Free Cash Flow** | | $425.6 | $460.7 | $490.6 | $517.4 | $540.5 |
| WACC | 11.0% | | | | | |
| Discount Period | | 0.5 | 1.5 | 2.5 | 3.5 | 4.5 |
| Discount Factor | | 0.95 | 0.86 | 0.77 | 0.69 | 0.63 |
| **Present Value of Free Cash Flow** | | $404.0 | $393.9 | $377.9 | $359.1 | $338.0 |

$$= \text{Unlevered FCF}_{2020E} \times \text{Discount Factor}$$
$$= \$404.0 \text{ million} \times 0.95$$

$$= \text{Exit Year EBITDA} \times \text{Exit Multiple}$$
$$= \$929.2 \text{ million} \times 7.5x$$

**Terminal Value**

| | |
|---|---|
| Terminal Year EBITDA (2024E) | $929.2 |
| Exit Multiple | 7.5x |
| **Terminal Value** | $6,969.0 |
| Discount Factor | 0.59 |
| **Present Value of Terminal Value** | $4,135.8 |

$$= 1 / ((1 + WACC)^{n})$$
$$= 1 / ((1 + 11\%)^{5})$$
Note: Mid-Year Convention not applied for Exit Multiple Method

## Determine Valuation

**Calculate Enterprise Value** The results of the present value calculations for the projected FCF and terminal value were summed to produce an enterprise value of $6,008.7 million for ValueCo (see Exhibit 3.55). The enterprise value is comprised of $1,872.9 million from the present value of the projected FCF and $4,135.8 million from the present value of the terminal value. This implies that ValueCo's terminal value represents 68.8% of the enterprise value.

**EXHIBIT 3.55**  Enterprise Value

($ in millions)

| Enterprise Value | | |
|---|---|---|
| **Present Value of Free Cash Flow** | **$1,872.9** | = SUM (FCF$_{2020E\text{-}2024E}$, discounted at 11%)<br>= SUM ($404 million : $338 million) |
| **Terminal Value** | | |
| Terminal Year EBITDA (2024E) | $929.2 | |
| Exit Multiple | 7.5x | |
| **Terminal Value** | **$6,969.0** | = Terminal Value × Discount Factor |
| Discount Factor | 0.59 | = $6,969 million × 0.59 |
| **Present Value of Terminal Value** | **$4,135.8** | = PV of Terminal Value / Enterprise Value |
| % of Enterprise Value | 68.8% | = $4,135.8 million / $6,008.7 million |
| **Enterprise Value** | **$6,008.7** | = PV of FCF$_{2020\text{-}2024}$ + PV of Terminal Value<br>= $1,872.9 million + $4,135.8 million |

**Derive Equity Value** We then calculated an implied equity value of $4,758.7 million for ValueCo by subtracting its net debt of $1,250 million ($1,500 million of debt – $250 million of cash) from enterprise value of $6,008.7 million (Exhibit 3.56). If ValueCo were a publicly traded company, we would then have divided the implied equity value by its fully diluted shares outstanding to determine an implied share price (see Exhibits 3.2 and 3.31).

**EXHIBIT 3.56**  Equity Value

($ in millions)

| Implied Equity Value and Share Price | |
|---|---|
| Enterprise Value | $6,008.7 |
| Less: Total Debt | (1,500.0) |
| Less: Preferred Stock | - |
| Less: Noncontrolling Interest | - |
| Plus: Cash and Cash Equivalents | 250.0 |
| **Implied Equity Value** | **$4,758.7** |

= Enterprise Value - Total Debt + Cash and Cash Equivalents
= $6,008.7 million - $1,500 million + $250 million

**DCF Output Page** Exhibit 3.57 displays a typical DCF output page for ValueCo using the EMM.

**EXHIBIT 3.57** ValueCo DCF Analysis Output Page

## ValueCo Corporation
### Discounted Cash Flow Analysis

*($ in millions, fiscal year ending December 31)* — Operating Scenario : Base

| Operating Scenario | 1 | | | | | | | | | | | |
|---|---|---|---|---|---|---|---|---|---|---|---|---|
| **Mid-Year Convention** | Y | Historical Period | | | CAGR | | Projection Period | | | | | CAGR |
| | | 2016 | 2017 | 2018 | ('16 - '18) | 2019 | 2020 | 2021 | 2022 | 2023 | 2024 | ('19 - '24) |
| **Sales** | | $2,600.0 | $2,900.0 | $3,200.0 | *10.9%* | $3,450.0 | $3,708.8 | $3,931.3 | $4,127.8 | $4,293.0 | $4,421.7 | *5.1%* |
| *% growth* | | *NA* | *11.5%* | *10.3%* | | *7.8%* | *7.5%* | *6.0%* | *5.0%* | *4.0%* | *3.0%* | |
| Cost of Goods Sold | | 1,612.0 | 1,769.0 | 1,920.0 | | 2,070.0 | 2,225.3 | 2,358.8 | 2,476.7 | 2,575.8 | 2,653.0 | |
| **Gross Profit** | | $988.0 | $1,131.0 | $1,280.0 | *13.8%* | $1,380.0 | $1,483.5 | $1,572.5 | $1,651.1 | $1,717.2 | $1,768.7 | *5.1%* |
| *% margin* | | *38.0%* | *39.0%* | *40.0%* | | *40.0%* | *40.0%* | *40.0%* | *40.0%* | *40.0%* | *40.0%* | |
| Selling, General & Administrative | | 496.6 | 551.0 | 608.0 | | 655.0 | 704.1 | 746.4 | 783.7 | 815.0 | 839.5 | |
| **EBITDA** | | $491.4 | $580.0 | $672.0 | *16.9%* | $725.0 | $779.4 | $826.1 | $867.4 | $902.1 | $929.2 | *5.1%* |
| *% margin* | | *18.9%* | *20.0%* | *21.0%* | | *21.0%* | *21.0%* | *21.0%* | *21.0%* | *21.0%* | *21.0%* | |
| Depreciation & Amortization | | 155.0 | 165.0 | 193.0 | | 207.0 | 222.5 | 235.9 | 247.7 | 257.6 | 265.3 | |
| **EBIT** | | $336.4 | $415.0 | $479.0 | *19.3%* | $518.0 | $556.9 | $590.3 | $619.8 | $644.6 | $663.9 | *5.1%* |
| *% margin* | | *12.9%* | *14.3%* | *15.0%* | | *15.0%* | *15.0%* | *15.0%* | *15.0%* | *15.0%* | *15.0%* | |
| Taxes | | 84.1 | 103.8 | 119.8 | | 129.5 | 139.2 | 147.6 | 154.9 | 161.1 | 166.0 | |
| **EBIAT** | | $252.3 | $311.3 | $359.3 | *19.3%* | $388.5 | $417.6 | $442.7 | $464.8 | $483.4 | $497.9 | *5.1%* |
| Plus: Depreciation & Amortization | | 155.0 | 165.0 | 193.0 | | 207.0 | 222.5 | 235.9 | 247.7 | 257.6 | 265.3 | |
| Less: Capital Expenditures | | (114.4) | (116.0) | (144.0) | | (155.3) | (166.9) | (176.9) | (185.8) | (193.2) | (199.0) | |
| Less: Inc./(Dec.) in Net Working Capital | | | | | | | (47.6) | (41.0) | (36.2) | (30.4) | (23.7) | |
| **Unlevered Free Cash Flow** | | | | | | | $425.6 | $460.7 | $490.6 | $517.4 | $540.5 | |
| WACC | | 11.0% | | | | | | | | | | |
| Discount Period | | | | | | | 0.5 | 1.5 | 2.5 | 3.5 | 4.5 | |
| Discount Factor | | | | | | | 0.95 | 0.86 | 0.77 | 0.69 | 0.63 | |
| **Present Value of Free Cash Flow** | | | | | | | $404.0 | $393.9 | $377.9 | $359.1 | $338.0 | |

| Enterprise Value | |
|---|---|
| **Cumulative Present Value of FCF** | $1,872.9 |
| **Terminal Value** | |
| Terminal Year EBITDA (2024E) | $929.2 |
| Exit Multiple | 7.5x |
| **Terminal Value** | $6,969.0 |
| Discount Factor | 0.59 |
| **Present Value of Terminal Value** | $4,135.8 |
| *% of Enterprise Value* | *68.8%* |
| **Enterprise Value** | $6,008.7 |

| Implied Equity Value and Share Price | |
|---|---|
| Enterprise Value | $6,008.7 |
| Less: Total Debt | (1,500.0) |
| Less: Preferred Stock | - |
| Less: Noncontrolling Interest | - |
| Plus: Cash and Cash Equivalents | 250.0 |
| **Implied Equity Value** | $4,758.7 |

| Implied Perpetuity Growth Rate | |
|---|---|
| Terminal Year Free Cash Flow (2024E) | $540.5 |
| WACC | 11.0% |
| Terminal Value | $6,969.0 |
| **Implied Perpetuity Growth Rate** | 2.6% |

| Implied EV/EBITDA | |
|---|---|
| Enterprise Value | $6,008.7 |
| LTM 9/30/2019 EBITDA | 700.0 |
| **Implied EV/EBITDA** | 8.6x |

**Enterprise Value**

| WACC \ Exit Multiple | 6.5x | 7.0x | 7.5x | 8.0x | 8.5x |
|---|---|---|---|---|---|
| **10.0%** | 5,665 | 5,953 | 6,242 | 6,530 | 6,819 |
| **10.5%** | 5,560 | 5,842 | 6,124 | 6,406 | 6,688 |
| **11.0%** | 5,457 | 5,733 | $6,009 | 6,284 | 6,560 |
| **11.5%** | 5,357 | 5,627 | 5,897 | 6,166 | 6,436 |
| **12.0%** | 5,260 | 5,524 | 5,787 | 6,051 | 6,315 |

**Implied Perpetuity Growth Rate**

| WACC \ Exit Multiple | 6.5x | 7.0x | 7.5x | 8.0x | 8.5x |
|---|---|---|---|---|---|
| **10.0%** | 0.6% | 1.2% | 1.7% | 2.2% | 2.6% |
| **10.5%** | 1.0% | 1.6% | 2.2% | 2.7% | 3.1% |
| **11.0%** | 1.4% | 2.1% | 2.6% | 3.1% | 3.5% |
| **11.5%** | 1.9% | 2.5% | 3.1% | 3.5% | 4.0% |
| **12.0%** | 2.3% | 2.9% | 3.5% | 4.0% | 4.4% |

**EXHIBIT 3.58** ValueCo Sensitivity Analysis

## ValueCo Corporation
## Sensitivity Analysis
*($ in millions, fiscal year ending December 31)*

### Enterprise Value

| | | | Exit Multiple | | |
|---|---|---|---|---|---|
| | **6.5x** | **7.0x** | **7.5x** | **8.0x** | **8.5x** |
| **10.0%** | 5,665 | 5,953 | 6,242 | 6,530 | 6,819 |
| **10.5%** | 5,560 | 5,842 | 6,124 | 6,406 | 6,688 |
| **11.0%** | 5,457 | 5,733 | **$6,009** | 6,284 | 6,560 |
| **11.5%** | 5,357 | 5,627 | 5,897 | 6,166 | 6,436 |
| **12.0%** | 5,260 | 5,524 | 5,787 | 6,051 | 6,315 |

WACC

### Implied Equity Value

| | | | Exit Multiple | | |
|---|---|---|---|---|---|
| | **6.5x** | **7.0x** | **7.5x** | **8.0x** | **8.5x** |
| **10.0%** | 4,415 | 4,703 | 4,992 | 5,280 | 5,569 |
| **10.5%** | 4,310 | 4,592 | 4,874 | 5,156 | 5,438 |
| **11.0%** | 4,207 | 4,483 | **$4,759** | 5,034 | 5,310 |
| **11.5%** | 4,107 | 4,377 | 4,647 | 4,916 | 5,186 |
| **12.0%** | 4,010 | 4,274 | 4,537 | 4,801 | 5,065 |

WACC

### Implied Perpetuity Growth Rate

| | | | Exit Multiple | | |
|---|---|---|---|---|---|
| | **6.5x** | **7.0x** | **7.5x** | **8.0x** | **8.5x** |
| **10.0%** | 0.6% | 1.2% | 1.7% | 2.2% | 2.6% |
| **10.5%** | 1.0% | 1.6% | 2.2% | 2.7% | 3.1% |
| **11.0%** | 1.4% | 2.1% | **2.6%** | 3.1% | 3.5% |
| **11.5%** | 1.9% | 2.5% | 3.1% | 3.5% | 4.0% |
| **12.0%** | 2.3% | 2.9% | 3.5% | 4.0% | 4.4% |

WACC

### Implied Enterprise Value / LTM EBITDA

| | | | Exit Multiple | | |
|---|---|---|---|---|---|
| | **6.5x** | **7.0x** | **7.5x** | **8.0x** | **8.5x** |
| **10.0%** | 8.1x | 8.5x | 8.9x | 9.3x | 9.7x |
| **10.5%** | 7.9x | 8.3x | 8.7x | 9.2x | 9.6x |
| **11.0%** | 7.8x | 8.2x | **8.6x** | 9.0x | 9.4x |
| **11.5%** | 7.7x | 8.0x | 8.4x | 8.8x | 9.2x |
| **12.0%** | 7.5x | 7.9x | 8.3x | 8.6x | 9.0x |

WACC

### PV of Terminal Value % of Enterprise Value

| | | | Exit Multiple | | |
|---|---|---|---|---|---|
| | **6.5x** | **7.0x** | **7.5x** | **8.0x** | **8.5x** |
| **10.0%** | 66.2% | 67.8% | 69.3% | 70.7% | 71.9% |
| **10.5%** | 65.9% | 67.6% | 69.1% | 70.4% | 71.7% |
| **11.0%** | 65.7% | 67.3% | **68.8%** | 70.2% | 71.4% |
| **11.5%** | 65.4% | 67.1% | 68.6% | 70.0% | 71.2% |
| **12.0%** | 65.2% | 66.8% | 68.3% | 69.7% | 71.0% |

WACC

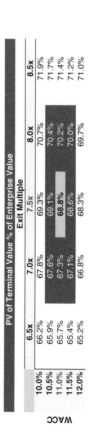

## Perform Sensitivity Analysis

We then performed a series of sensitivity analyses on WACC and exit multiple for several key outputs, including enterprise value, equity value, implied perpetuity growth rate, implied EV/LTM EBITDA, and PV of terminal value as a percentage of enterprise value (see Exhibit 3.58).

We also sensitized key financial assumptions, such as sales growth rates and EBIT margins, to analyze the effects on enterprise value. This sensitivity analysis provided helpful perspective on our assumptions and enabled us to study the potential value creation or erosion resulting from outperformance or underperformance versus the Base Case financial projections. For example, as shown in Exhibit 3.59, an increase in ValueCo's annual sales growth rates and EBIT margins by 50 bps each results in an increase of approximately $187 million in enterprise value from $6,009 million to $6,196 million.

**EXHIBIT 3.59**   Sensitivity Analysis on Sales Growth Rates and EBIT Margins

| | | Enterprise Value | | | | |
| | | Annual Sales Growth Inc. / (Dec.) | | | | |
| | | (1.0%) | (0.5%) | 0.0% | 0.5% | 1.0% |
| Annual EBIT Margin Inc. / (Dec.) | (1.0%) | 5,646 | 5,767 | 5,890 | 6,016 | 6,143 |
| | (0.5%) | 5,704 | 5,826 | 5,949 | 6,076 | 6,204 |
| | 0.0% | 5,761 | 5,884 | $6,009 | 6,136 | 6,265 |
| | 0.5% | 5,819 | 5,942 | 6,068 | 6,196 | 6,326 |
| | 1.0% | 5,877 | 6,001 | 6,127 | 6,256 | 6,387 |

After completing the sensitivity analysis, we proceeded to determine ValueCo's ultimate DCF valuation range. To derive this range, we focused on the shaded portion of the exit multiple / WACC data table (see top left corner of Exhibit 3.58). Based on an exit multiple range of 7.0x to 8.0x and a WACC range of 10.5% to 11.5%, we calculated an enterprise value range of approximately $5,627 million to $6,406 million for ValueCo.

We then added this range to our "football field" and compared it to the derived valuation ranges from our comparable companies analysis and precedent transactions analysis performed in Chapters 1 and 2 (see Exhibit 3.60).

**EXHIBIT 3.60**   ValueCo Football Field Displaying Comps, Precedents, and DCF Analysis

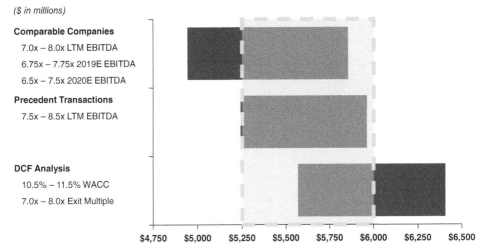

($ in millions)

**Comparable Companies**
  7.0x – 8.0x LTM EBITDA
  6.75x – 7.75x 2019E EBITDA
  6.5x – 7.5x 2020E EBITDA

**Precedent Transactions**
  7.5x – 8.5x LTM EBITDA

**DCF Analysis**
  10.5% – 11.5% WACC
  7.0x – 8.0x Exit Multiple

$4,750    $5,000    $5,250    $5,500    $5,750    $6,000    $6,250    $6,500

## CHAPTER 3 QUESTIONS

1) Which of the following is a current asset?

    A. Goodwill
    B. Property, plant, and equipment
    C. Accrued expenses
    D. Prepaid expenses

2) Calculate FCF using the information below

*($ in millions)*

| Assumptions | |
|---|---|
| EBIT | $300.0 |
| Depreciation & Amortization | 50.0 |
| Capital Expenditures | 25.0 |
| Inc./(Dec.) in Net Working Capital | 10.0 |
| Tax Rate | 25.0% |

    A. $151.0 million
    B. $189.0 million
    C. $240.0 million
    D. $389.0 million

3) How long is the typical DCF projection period?

    A. 1 year
    B. 3 years
    C. 5 years
    D. 30 years

4) Capex and depreciation share all of the following characteristics EXCEPT

    A. Used in the calculation of FCF
    B. Represent actual cash outflows
    C. Found on the cash flow statement
    D. Included in the calculation of PP&E

5) Calculate the (increase) / decrease in net working capital from 2018 to 2019 based on the following assumptions

*($ in millions)*

| Assumptions | | |
| --- | --- | --- |
| | **2018** | **2019** |
| Accounts Receivable | $325.0 | $350.0 |
| Inventories | 200.0 | 210.0 |
| Prepaid Expenses and Other | 35.0 | 45.0 |
| Accounts Payable | 300.0 | 315.0 |
| Accrued Liabilities | 150.0 | 160.0 |
| Other Current Liabilities | 60.0 | 65.0 |

A. $10.0 million
B. ($10.0 million)
C. $15.0 million
D. ($15.0 million)

6) An increase in inventory is

A. A use of cash
B. A source of cash
C. No change in cash
D. A decrease in PP&E

7) An increase in accounts payable is

A. A use of cash
B. A source of cash
C. No change in cash
D. An increase in PP&E

8) Calculate DSO assuming a company has $3.5 billion in revenue and $300 million in accounts receivable

A. 29 days
B. 30 days
C. 31 days
D. 43 days

9) Which of the following is the most appropriate market risk premium to use in the calculation of cost of equity?

A. 0%–1%
B. 2%–3%
C. 5%–8%
D. 10%+

10) Which of the following sectors should have the lowest beta?

    A. Social media
    B. Utility
    C. Homebuilder
    D. Chemicals

11) Which methodology is used to capture the value of a company beyond its projection period?

    A. Long-term value
    B. Long-term adjusted value
    C. Terminal value
    D. Projected value

12) How does using a mid-year convention affect valuation in a DCF?

    A. Higher value than year-end discounting
    B. Lower value than year-end discounting
    C. Same value as year-end discounting
    D. Not applicable

13) Using a mid-year convention and the assumptions below, calculate enterprise value

($ in millions)

| Assumptions | | | |
|---|---|---|---|
| FCF 2020E | $100.0 | Terminal Multiple | 7.5x |
| FCF 2021E | 110.0 | WACC | 10.0% |
| FCF 2022E | 120.0 | | |
| FCF 2023E | 125.0 | | |
| FCF 2024E | 130.0 | | |
| EBITDA 2024E | 250.0 | | |

    A. $1,710 million
    B. $1,725 million
    C. $1,624 million
    D. $1,986 million

14) Why might perpetuity growth method be used instead of exit growth method?

    A. Absence of relevant comparables to determine an exit multiple
    B. Difficult to determine a long-term growth rate
    C. Current economic environment is volatile
    D. Target company is private

15) Why may a banker choose to add a size premium to the CAPM formula?

    A. Empirical evidence suggesting that smaller companies are riskier and, therefore, should have a higher cost of equity

    B. Empirical evidence suggesting that larger companies are riskier and, therefore, should have a higher cost of equity

    C. To compensate for the market risk premium, which can vary

    D. To compensate for the risk-free rate, which can vary

# TWO

# Leveraged Buyouts

# Leveraged Buyouts

**A** leveraged buyout (LBO) is the acquisition of a company, division, business, or collection of assets ("target") using debt to finance a large portion of the purchase price. The remaining portion of the purchase price is typically funded with an equity contribution by a financial sponsor ("sponsor") or equivalent. LBOs are used by sponsors to acquire control of a broad range of businesses, including both public and private companies, as well as their divisions and subsidiaries. The sponsor's ultimate goal is to realize an acceptable return on its equity investment upon exit, typically through a sale or IPO of the target. Sponsors tend to seek a 15% to 20% annualized return and an investment exit within five years. PE funds range in size from tens of millions to tens of billions of dollars, and some sponsors manage numerous funds.

In a traditional LBO, debt typically comprises 60% to 70% of the financing structure with equity comprising the remaining 30% to 40% (see Exhibit 4.12). The relatively high level of debt incurred by the target is supported by its projected free cash flow[1] and asset base, which enables the sponsor to contribute a small equity investment relative to the purchase price. The ability to leverage the relatively small equity investment is important for sponsors to drive acceptable returns. The use of leverage provides the additional benefit of tax savings realized due to the tax deductibility of interest expense.

Companies with stable and predictable cash flow, as well as substantial assets, generally represent attractive LBO candidates due to their ability to support larger quantities of debt. Free cash flow is needed to service periodic interest payments and reduce the principal amount of debt over the life of the investment. In addition, a large tangible asset base increases the amount of *secured debt* available to the borrower (the least expensive source of debt financing) by providing greater comfort to lenders regarding the likelihood of principal recovery in the event of a bankruptcy. When credit markets are particularly robust, however, debt investors are increasingly willing to focus more on cash flow generation and less on the size and quality of the target's asset base.

During the time from which the sponsor acquires the target until its exit ("investment horizon"), lenders generally expect cash flow to be allocated toward interest payments and principal repayment. At the same time, the sponsor aims to improve the financial performance of the target and grow the existing business (including through future "bolt-on" acquisitions). Both debt repayment and cash flow growth serve to increase equity value and enhance potential returns. An appropriate LBO financing structure

---

[1]The "free cash flow" term ("levered free cash flow" or "cash available for debt repayment") used in LBO analysis differs from the "unlevered free cash flow" term used in DCF analysis as it includes the effects of leverage.

must balance the target's ability to service and repay debt with its need to use cash flow to manage and grow the business, including through acquisitions. In addition, sponsors will seek financing structures that permit them to achieve their desired returns, including through dividends and debt prepayment upon sale of the company.

A successful LBO relies upon the sponsor's ability to obtain the requisite financing needed to acquire the target. Investment banks traditionally play a critical role in this respect, primarily as arrangers/underwriters of the debt used to fund the purchase price.[2] Additionally, depending on the size and nature of the deal, credit funds may provide all or a portion of the debt. The investment banks and other debt providers compete to provide a financing commitment for the sponsor's preferred financing structure in the form of legally binding letters ("financing" or "commitment" letters). The commitment letters promise funding for the debt portion of the purchase price on pre-agreed terms in exchange for various fees and are subject to specific conditions, including the sponsor's contribution of an agreed minimum level of cash equity.[3]

The debt used in an LBO is raised through the issuance of various types of loans, securities, and other instruments that are classified based on their *security* status as well as their *seniority* in the capital structure. The condition of the prevailing debt capital markets plays a key role in determining leverage levels, as well as the cost of financing and key terms. The equity portion of the financing structure is usually sourced from a pool of capital ("fund") managed by the sponsor.

Due to the proliferation of private investment vehicles (e.g., private equity firms, family offices, hedge funds, and pension funds) and their considerable pools of capital, LBOs have become an increasingly large part of the bank lending, capital markets, and M&A landscape. Bankers who advise on LBO financings are tasked with helping to craft a financing structure that enables both the sponsor and debt investors to meet their respective investment objectives and return thresholds, while providing the target with sufficient financial flexibility and cushion needed to operate and grow the business. Investment banks also provide M&A advisory services to sponsors on LBO transactions. Post-LBO, investment banks have a multitude of opportunities to provide additional services, most notably for future acquisitions, carve-out dispositions, and refinancing opportunities, as well as traditional exit events, such as a sale of the target or an IPO.

This chapter provides an overview of the fundamentals of leveraged buyouts as depicted in the eight main categories shown in Exhibit 4.1.

**EXHIBIT 4.1**   LBO Fundamentals

- Key Participants
- Characteristics of a Strong LBO Candidate
- Economics of LBOs
- Primary Exit / Monetization Strategies
- LBO Financing: Structure
- LBO Financing: Primary Sources
- LBO Financing: Selected Key Terms
- LBO Financing: Determining Financing Structure

---

[2]The term "investment bank" is used broadly to refer to financial intermediaries that perform corporate finance and M&A advisory services, as well as capital markets underwriting activities.
[3]These letters are typically highly negotiated among the sponsor, the banks providing the financing, and their respective legal counsels before they are agreed upon.

## KEY PARTICIPANTS

This section provides an overview of the key participants in an LBO (see Exhibit 4.2).

**EXHIBIT 4.2**   Key Participants

- Financial Sponsors
- Investment Banks
- Bank and Institutional Lenders
- Bond Investors
- Private Credit Funds
- Target Management

### Financial Sponsors

The term "financial sponsor" refers to traditional private equity (PE) firms, family offices, merchant banking divisions of investment banks, hedge funds, venture capital funds, infrastructure funds, pension funds, and special purpose acquisition companies (SPACs), among other investment vehicles. PE firms, hedge funds, and venture capital funds raise the vast majority of their investment capital from third-party investors, which include public and corporate pension funds, insurance companies, endowments and foundations, sovereign wealth funds, and wealthy families/individuals. Sponsor partners and investment professionals also typically invest their own money into the fund(s) or in specific investment opportunities.

Capital raised from third-party investors and the sponsor partners and investment professionals is organized into funds that are usually structured as limited partnerships. Limited partnerships are typically established as a finite-life investment vehicle with a specific total capital commitment, in which the general partner (GP, i.e., the sponsor) manages the fund on a day-to-day basis and the limited partners (LPs) serve as passive financial investors.[4] LPs subscribe to fund a specific portion of the total fund's capital ("capital commitment"). These funds are considered "blind pools" in that the LPs subscribe to their capital commitment without specific knowledge of the investments that the sponsor plans to make.[5] However, sponsors are often limited in the amount of the fund's capital that can be invested in any particular business, typically no more than 10% to 20%.

Sponsors vary greatly in terms of fund size, focus, and investment strategy. The size of a sponsor's fund(s), which can range from tens of millions to tens of billions of dollars (based on its ability and willingness to raise capital), helps dictate its investment parameters. Some sponsors specialize in, or have particular funds focused on, specific sectors (such as industrials, technology, consumer products, or media, for example),

---

[4]To compensate the GP for management of the fund, LPs typically pay 1% to 2% per annum on committed funds as a management fee. In addition, once the LPs have received the return of their entire equity investment, plus an agreed minimum investment profit, the sponsor typically receives a 20% "carry" on every dollar of investment profit (known as "carried interest").

[5]LPs generally retain the capital they have committed to invest in a given fund until it is called by the GP in connection with a specific investment.

while others focus on specific situations (such as distressed companies/turnarounds, roll-ups, or corporate divestitures). Many PE firms are simply generalists that look at a broad spectrum of opportunities across multiple industries and investment strategies. They are staffed with investment professionals who fit their strategy, many of whom are former investment bankers or management consultants. They also typically employ (or engage the services of) operational professionals and industry experts, such as former CEOs and other company executives, who consult and advise the sponsor on specific transactions and the management of acquired companies.

In evaluating an investment opportunity, the sponsor performs detailed due diligence on the target, often through an organized M&A sale process (see Chapter 6). Due diligence is the process of learning as much as possible about all aspects of the target (e.g., business, industry, management, financial, accounting, tax, legal, regulatory, and environmental) to discover, confirm, or discredit information critical to the sponsor's investment thesis. Detailed information on the target is typically stored in an online data room, such as those provided by Datasite (see Exhibit 6.7). Sponsors use due diligence findings to develop a financial model and support purchase price assumptions (including a preferred financing structure), often hiring accountants, consultants, and industry and other functional experts to assist in the process. Sponsors typically engage operating experts, many of whom are former senior industry executives, to assist in the due diligence process and potentially join the management team or board of directors of the acquired companies.

## Investment Banks

Investment banks play a key role in LBOs, both as a provider and arranger of financing and as an M&A advisor to both sponsors and targets. Sponsors rely heavily on investment banks to help develop and market an optimal financing structure. They may also engage investment banks as buy-side M&A advisors in return for sourcing deals and/or for their expertise, relationships, and in-house resources. On the sell-side, sponsors typically engage bankers as M&A advisors (and potentially as *stapled financing* providers[6]) to market their portfolio companies to prospective buyers through an organized sale process.

Investment banks perform thorough due diligence on LBO targets (usually alongside their sponsor clients) and go through an extensive internal credit process in order to validate the target's business plan and underwrite a debt financing for the acquisition. They must gain comfort with the target's ability to service a highly leveraged capital structure and their ability to market the debt financing to the appropriate investors. Investment banks work closely with their sponsor clients to determine an appropriate financing structure for a particular transaction.[7] This tends to be an iterative process where the sponsor seeks the most issuer-friendly terms (including interest rates, maturity dates, prepayment premiums, and flexibility) while the banks push for terms that give them sufficient comfort that they can syndicate the debt, even if market conditions soften. Once the sponsor chooses the preferred financing structure for an LBO, the investment bank's deal team presents it to the bank's internal committee(s) for final approval.

---

[6]The investment bank running an auction process (or sometimes a "partner" bank) may offer a pre-packaged financing structure, typically for prospective financial buyers, in support of the target being sold. This is commonly referred to as stapled financing ("staple"), as discussed in Chapter 6.
[7]Alternatively, the banks may be asked to commit to a financing structure already developed by the sponsor.

Following credit (and potentially other) committee approval, the investment banks are able to provide a financing commitment to support the sponsor's bid. The financing commitment includes: a *commitment letter* for the secured revolver and term loans, and, if applicable, a bridge facility (to be provided by the lender in lieu of a bond financing if a planned bond offering is not successful); an *engagement letter*, in which the sponsor engages the investment banks to underwrite any bonds intended to be included in the planned financing on behalf of the issuer; and a *fee letter*, which sets forth the various fees to be paid to the investment banks in connection with the financing. Traditionally, in an LBO, the sponsor is required to provide certainty of financing to the seller and provides copies of the signed commitment letters to the seller at the time the acquisition agreement is signed.

The financing commitment offers funding for the debt portion of the transaction under proposed terms and conditions (including worst case maximum interest rates ("caps") and "flex"[8]) in exchange for various fees[9] and roles.[10] The commitment letters are typically subject to specific conditions, including the sponsor's contribution of an acceptable level of cash equity and a minimum level of EBITDA for the target. This is also known as an *underwritten* financing, which traditionally has been required for LBOs due to the need to provide certainty of closing to the seller (including financing). Commitment letters also typically provide for a marketing period during which the investment banks seek to syndicate their commitments to investors prior to the sponsor closing the transaction.

The secured debt component of the financing provided by investment banks is typically comprised of a revolving credit facility (a.k.a. "revolver"), which is typically held by the underwriting investment banks, and a term loan that is typically sold (or "syndicated") to a syndicate of institutional investors. The unsecured debt component of the financing, if any, provided by investment banks is often comprised of an offering of *high yield bonds*, which the investment banks attempt to sell to investors without being forced to hold any on their balance sheets after closing of the acquisition (similar to the institutional term loans).

However, in lieu of committing to purchase the high yield bonds, due to certain securities law and regulatory impediments, the investment banks instead commit to provide a bridge loan (in an equal amount) to the sponsor and the target. This provides

---

[8]"Flex" allows the underwriter to modify the terms of the debt during syndication to make it more attractive to potential debt investors, often including changes to covenants, increases to the interest rate "caps", changes to prepayment premiums, and allocations between classes of debt securities (e.g., shifting amounts between secured vs. unsecured tranches, or changes to the entities incurring certain tranches between operating company level ("OpCo") vs. holding company level ("HoldCo")).

[9]The fees associated with the commitment compensate the banks for their underwriting role and the risk associated with the pledge to fund the transaction in the event that a syndication to outside investors is not achievable.

[10]Investment banks compete for certain roles and associated titles in the debt syndicate. The lead investment bank responsible for marketing the loans, including the preparation of marketing materials and running the syndication, carries the title of "Lead Arranger". Other underwriters of the bank debt are "Joint Lead Arrangers" or "Joint Bookrunners". For high yield bonds, the lead bank is afforded the title of "Left Lead Bookrunner" with the other banks in the offering allotted "Joint Bookrunner" and "Co-Manager" titles. Roles and titles impact the amount of fees that an investment bank earns as well as the influence that the investment bank has over the underwriting and selling process. The Lead Arranger and the Left Lead Bookrunner are colloquially referred to as "left lead" and their names are positioned to the left of the other banks' names in marketing materials for the debt.

assurance that sufficient funding will be available to finance and close the acquisition even if the banks cannot sell the entire bond offering to investors. Typically, the bridge loans will only be funded if the bond offering is not successful (whether due to a deterioration in the capital markets or bond investors' unwillingness to purchase the bonds on the proposed terms) at the time the acquisition is consummated. Since the banks bear market risk on the bonds and bridge loans during the period from signing to closing, and have to reserve capital for those loans, they require the sponsors to pay for a bridge financing commitment even if the bond offering was successful and the bridge did not need to be funded.

## Bank and Institutional Lenders

Bank and institutional lenders are often the capital providers for the secured debt in an LBO financing structure. Although there is often overlap between them, traditional bank lenders provide capital for revolvers and amortizing term loans, while institutional lenders provide capital for longer tenored, limited amortization term loans. Bank lenders typically consist of commercial banks, savings and loan institutions, finance companies, and the investment banks serving as arrangers. The institutional lender base is largely comprised of hedge funds, pension funds, mutual funds, insurance companies, and structured vehicles such as collateralized loan obligation funds (CLOs).[11]

Like investment banks, lenders perform due diligence and undergo an internal credit process before participating in an LBO financing, although their diligence tends to be far more limited and focused on business and financial items. This involves analyzing the target's business and credit profile (with a focus on projected cash flow generation and credit statistics) to gain comfort that they will receive full future interest payments and principal repayment at maturity. Lenders also look to mitigate downside risk through covenants and collateral coverage. Prior experience with a given company, sector, or financial sponsor is also factored into the decision to participate. To a great extent, however, lenders rely on the due diligence performed (and materials prepared) by the investment banks acting as lead arrangers.

As part of their due diligence process, prospective lenders attend a group meeting known as a "lender meeting", which is organized by the lead arranger.[12] In a lender meeting, the target's senior management team gives a detailed slideshow presentation about the company and its investment/credit merits, followed by an overview of the debt offering by the lead arranger and a Q&A session. At the lender meeting, prospective lenders receive a hard copy of the presentation, as well as a confidential information memorandum/presentation (CIM/CIP or "bank book") prepared by management and the lead arrangers.[13] As lenders go through their internal credit processes and make their final investment decisions, they conduct follow-up diligence that often involves requesting additional information and analysis from the company.

---

[11]CLOs are asset-backed securities ("securitized") backed by interests in pools of loans.

[12]For particularly large or complex transactions, the target's management may present to certain lenders on a one-on-one basis.

[13]The bank book is a comprehensive document that contains a detailed description of the transaction, investment highlights, company, and sector, as well as preliminary term sheets and historical financials. A private supplement with financial projections is provided to non-public investors, i.e., those that intend to invest solely in the company's loans, but do not intend to invest in the company's equity or debt securities (such as high yield bonds). Both the bank meeting presentation and bank book are typically available to lenders through an online medium.

It is also common practice for the lead arranger bank to host small group meetings with some of the larger, more active institutional investors in advance to get early feedback on the term loan package that is eventually launched at the lender meeting.

## Bond Investors

The purchasers of the high yield bonds issued as part of the LBO financing structure are generally institutional investors, such as high yield mutual funds, hedge funds, pension funds, insurance companies, and collateralized debt obligations (CDOs).

As part of their investment assessment and decision-making process, bond investors often attend one-on-one meetings, known as "roadshow presentations", during which senior executives present the investment merits of the company and the proposed transaction. A roadshow is typically a three to five-day process (depending on the size and scope of the transaction), where bankers from the left lead bookrunner (and generally an individual from the sponsor) accompany the target's management on meetings with potential investors. These meetings may also be conducted as breakfasts or luncheons with groups of investors. The typical U.S. roadshow includes stops in the larger financial centers such as New York, Boston, Los Angeles, and San Francisco, as well as smaller cities throughout the country.[14],[15]

Prior to the roadshow meeting, bond investors receive a preliminary offering memorandum (OM), which is a legal document containing much of the target's business, industry, and financial information found in the bank book. The preliminary OM, however, must satisfy a higher degree of legal scrutiny and disclosure (including risk factors[16] and summaries of key affiliate contracts). Unlike loans, bonds are securities, and their sale is subject to regulation under the Securities Act of 1933 and the Securities Exchange Act of 1934.[17] As a result, the OM generally includes the same disclosures (and is subject to the same scrutiny) that are included in a prospectus filed in connection with an IPO. The preliminary OM contains very detailed information on the bonds, including a description of notes (DON) that includes all the terms of the high yield notes other than specific pricing information (e.g., the interest rate, redemption premium, and exact maturity and interest payment dates).[18] Once the roadshow concludes and the bonds have been priced, the final pricing terms are inserted into the document, which is then distributed to bond investors as the final OM.

---

[14]For example, roadshow schedules often include stops in Philadelphia, Baltimore, Minneapolis, Milwaukee, Chicago, and Houston, as well as various cities throughout New Jersey and Connecticut, in accordance with where the underwriters believe there will be investor interest.

[15]European roadshows include primary stops in London, Paris, and Frankfurt, as well as secondary stops typically in Milan, Edinburgh, Zurich, and Amsterdam.

[16]A discussion of the most significant factors that make the offering speculative or risky.

[17]Laws that set forth requirements for the issuance or sale of securities, including registration and periodic disclosures of financial status, among others.

[18] The preliminary OM contains a prominent notice on its cover, in red-colored font, explaining how it is preliminary and subject to change. As a result, it is also commonly referred to as the "red herring" or the "red". The DON contains a detailed, and often verbatim, description summary of the material provisions of the indenture that will govern the high yield notes, including definitions, terms, and covenants.

## Private Credit Funds

Private credit vehicles provide direct loans to finance LBOs in the form of secured debt, most notably first and second lien term loans. As opposed to investment banks, private credit funds hold onto the loans as investments without syndicating them broadly. Traditionally reserved primarily for smaller-size borrowers, they moved up-market in the mid-to-late 2010s in the pursuit of higher yields in a low interest rate environment. Today, they comprise a sizable portion of the leveraged finance market, often providing tailored solutions that are attractive to borrowers. They are particularly active in the second lien term loan market (see later in the chapter) where the tranches tend to be smaller in size and more tailored versus bonds.

Private credit funds tend to source their capital from large institutional investors, including pension funds, insurance companies, and alternative asset managers, with stable capital available to hold illiquid securities. The terms of the financing they provide are negotiated directly with sponsors. This stands in contrast to syndicated loans or offerings of high yield bonds, which are first underwritten by investment banks and then marketed to a broad group of debt investors. For borrowers, the certainty and simplicity of structuring a tailored financing with a direct lender, without the need to spend time on a roadshow, disclose their financials broadly, or subject themselves to the risk of changes to desired terms due to "flex", can be attractive. On the other hand, the terms of the financing, most notably price and covenants, may be more punitive than in a well-received fully marketed deal. Borrowers may also have concerns about concentrating their debt in the hands of one holder, as that can afford the direct lender "hold-up value" when they have the sole ability to permit (or deny) covenant amendments.

## Target Management

Management plays a crucial role in the marketing of the target to potential buyers (see Chapter 6) and lenders alike, working closely with the bankers on the preparation of marketing materials and financial information. Management also serves as the primary face of the company and must articulate the investment and credit merits of the transaction to these constituents. Consequently, in an LBO, a strong management team can create tangible value by driving favorable financing terms and pricing, as well as providing sponsors with comfort to stretch on valuation.

From a structuring perspective, management typically holds a meaningful equity interest in the post-LBO company through "rolling" its existing equity or investing in the business alongside the sponsor at closing, or success-based equity compensation. Several layers of management typically also have the opportunity to participate (on a post-closing basis) in a stock-based compensation package, generally tied to an agreed-upon set of financial targets for the company. This structure provides management with meaningful economic incentives to improve the company's performance as they share in the value created. As a result, the interests of management and sponsor are aligned in pursuing superior performance. The broad-based equity incentive program outlined above is often a key differentiating factor versus a public company ownership structure.

**Management Buyout**    An LBO originated and led by a target's existing management team is referred to as a management buyout (MBO). Often, an MBO is effected with the help of an equity partner, such as a financial sponsor, who provides capital support and access to debt financing through established investment banking relationships. The basic premise behind an MBO is that the management team believes it can create more value running the company on its own than under current ownership. The MBO structure also serves to eliminate the conflict between management and the board of directors/shareholders as owner-managers are able to run the company as they see fit.

Public company management may be motivated by the belief that the market is undervaluing the company, SEC and Sarbanes-Oxley (SOX)[19] compliance is too burdensome and costly (especially for smaller companies), and/or the company could operate more efficiently as a private entity. LBO candidates with sizable management ownership are generally strong MBO candidates. Another common MBO scenario involves a buyout by the management of a division or subsidiary of a larger corporation who believe they can run the business more effectively when separated from the parent company.

## CHARACTERISTICS OF A STRONG LBO CANDIDATE

Financial sponsors as a group are highly flexible investors that seek attractive investment opportunities across a broad range of sectors, geographies, and situations. While there are few steadfast rules, certain common traits emerge among traditional LBO candidates, as outlined in Exhibit 4.3.

**EXHIBIT 4.3**    Characteristics of a Strong LBO Candidate

- Strong Cash Flow Generation
- Leading and Defensible Market Positions
- Growth Opportunities
- Efficiency Enhancement Opportunities
- Low Capex Requirements
- Strong Asset Base
- Proven Management Team

During due diligence, the sponsor studies and evaluates an LBO candidate's key strengths and risks. Often, LBO candidates are identified among non-core or underperforming divisions of larger companies, neglected or troubled companies with turnaround potential, sponsor-owned businesses that have been held for an extended period, or companies in fragmented markets as platforms for a roll-up strategy.[20] In other instances, the target is simply a solidly performing company with a compelling business model, defensible competitive position, and strong growth opportunities. For a publicly traded LBO candidate, a sponsor may perceive the target as undervalued by the market or recognize opportunities for growth and efficiency not being exploited by current management. Regardless of the situation, the target only represents an attractive LBO opportunity if it can be purchased with a price and financing structure that provides sufficient returns with a viable exit strategy.

---

[19]The Sarbanes-Oxley Act of 2002 enacted substantial changes to the securities laws that govern public companies and their officers and directors in regards to corporate governance and financial reporting. Most notably, Section 404 of SOX requires public registrants to establish and maintain "Internal Controls and Procedures", which can consume significant internal resources, time, commitment, and expense.

[20]A roll-up strategy involves consolidating multiple companies in a fragmented market or sector to create an entity with increased size, scale, and efficiency.

## Strong Cash Flow Generation

The ability to generate strong, predictable cash flow is critical for LBO candidates given the highly leveraged capital structure. Debt investors require a business model that demonstrates the ability to support periodic interest payments and debt principal repayment over the life of the loans. Business characteristics that support the predictability of robust cash flow increase a company's attractiveness as an LBO candidate. For example, many strong LBO candidates operate a mature or niche business with stable customer demand and end markets. They often feature a strong brand name, established customer base, and/or long-term sales contracts, all of which serve to increase the predictability of cash flow. Prospective financial sponsors and financing providers seek to confirm a given LBO candidate's cash flow generation potential during due diligence to gain comfort with the target management's projections. Cash flow projections are usually stress-tested (sensitized) based on historical volatility and potential future business and economic conditions to ensure the ability to support the LBO financing structure under challenging circumstances.

## Leading and Defensible Market Positions

Leading and defensible market positions generally reflect entrenched customer relationships, brand name recognition, superior products and services, a favorable cost structure, and scale advantages, among other attributes. These qualities create barriers to entry and increase the stability and predictability of a company's cash flow. Accordingly, the sponsor spends a great deal of time during due diligence seeking assurance that the target's market positions are secure (and can potentially be expanded). Depending on the sponsor's familiarity with the sector, consultants may be hired to perform independent studies analyzing market share and barriers to entry.

## Growth Opportunities

Sponsors seek companies with growth potential, both organically and through potential future bolt-on acquisitions. Profitable top line growth at above-market rates helps drive outsized returns, generating greater cash available for debt repayment while also increasing EBITDA and equity value. Growth also enhances the speed and optionality for exit opportunities. For example, a strong growth profile is particularly important if the target is designated for an eventual IPO exit.

Companies with robust growth profiles have a greater likelihood of driving EBITDA "multiple expansion"[21] during the sponsor's investment horizon, which further enhances returns. Moreover, as discussed in Chapter 1, larger companies tend to benefit from their scale, market share, purchasing power, and lower risk profile, and are often rewarded with a premium valuation relative to smaller peers, all else being equal. In some cases, the sponsor opts not to maximize the amount of debt financing at purchase. This provides greater flexibility to pursue a growth strategy that may require future incremental debt to make acquisitions or build new facilities, for example.

---

[21]Selling the target for a higher multiple of EBITDA upon exit (i.e., purchasing the target for 8.0x EBITDA and selling it for 9.0x EBITDA).

## Efficiency Enhancement Opportunities

While an ideal LBO candidate should have a strong fundamental business model, sponsors seek opportunities to improve operational efficiencies and generate cost savings. Traditional cost-saving measures include lowering corporate overhead, streamlining operations, introducing *lean manufacturing* and *Six Sigma* processes,[22] reducing headcount, rationalizing the supply chain, and implementing new management information systems. The sponsor may also seek to source new (or negotiate better) terms with existing suppliers and customers. These initiatives are a primary focus for the consultants and industry experts hired by the sponsor to assist with due diligence and assess the opportunity represented by establishing "best practices" at the target. Their successful implementation often represents substantial value creation that accrues to equity value at a multiple of each dollar saved upon exit.

At the same time, sponsors must be careful not to jeopardize existing sales or attractive growth opportunities by starving the business of necessary capital. Extensive cuts in marketing, capex, or research & development, for example, may hurt customer retention, new product development, or other growth initiatives. Such moves could put the company at risk of deteriorating sales and profitability or loss of market position.

## Low Capex Requirements

All else being equal, low capex requirements enhance a company's cash flow generation capabilities. As a result, the best LBO candidates tend to have limited capital investment needs. However, a company with substantial capex requirements may still represent an attractive investment opportunity if they are consistent with a strong growth profile, high profit margins, and the business strategy is validated during due diligence.

During due diligence, the sponsor and its advisors focus on differentiating those expenditures deemed necessary to continue operating the business ("maintenance capex") from those that are discretionary ("growth capex"). Maintenance capex is capital required to sustain existing assets (typically PP&E) at their current output levels. Growth capex is used to purchase new assets, thereby expanding the existing asset base. In the event that economic conditions or operating performance decline, growth capex can potentially be reduced or eliminated.

---

[22]Lean manufacturing is a production practice and philosophy dedicated to eliminating waste, while Six Sigma is focused on improving output quality by identifying and eliminating defects and variability.

## Strong Asset Base

A strong asset base pledged as collateral against a loan benefits lenders by increasing the likelihood of principal recovery in the event of bankruptcy (and liquidation). This, in turn, increases their willingness to provide debt to the target. Strength is defined as size of the asset base (e.g., tangible assets as a percentage of total assets) as well as its quality. Accounts receivable and inventory are considered high quality assets given their liquidity. As opposed to long-term assets such as PP&E, they can be converted into cash easily and quickly.

The target's asset base is particularly important in the leveraged loan market, where the value of the assets helps dictate the amount of secured debt available (see "LBO Financing" sections for additional information). A strong asset base also tends to signify high barriers to entry because of the substantial capital investment required, which serves to deter new entrants in the target's markets. At the same time, a company with little or no assets can still be an attractive LBO candidate provided it generates sufficient cash flow.

## Proven Management Team

A proven management team serves to increase the attractiveness (and value) of an LBO candidate. Talented management is critical in an LBO scenario given the need to operate under a highly leveraged capital structure with ambitious performance targets. Prior experience operating under such conditions, as well as success in integrating acquisitions or implementing restructuring initiatives, is highly regarded by sponsors.

For LBO candidates with strong management, the sponsor usually seeks to keep the existing team in place post-acquisition. It is customary for management to retain, invest, or be granted a meaningful equity stake so as to align their incentives under the new ownership structure with that of the sponsor. Alternatively, in those instances where the target's management is weak, sponsors seek to add value by making key changes to the existing team or installing a new team altogether to run the company. In either circumstance, a strong management team is crucial for driving company performance going forward and helping the sponsor meet its investment objectives.

## ECONOMICS OF LBOs

### Returns Analysis—Internal Rate of Return

Internal rate of return (IRR) is the primary metric by which sponsors gauge the attractiveness of a potential LBO, as well as the performance of their existing investments. IRR measures the total return on a sponsor's equity investment, including any additional equity contributions made, or dividends received, during the investment horizon. The IRR approach factors in the time value of money—for a given amount of cash proceeds at exit, a shorter exit timeline produces a higher IRR for the sponsor. In contrast, if the investment proceeds take longer to realize, the IRR will decrease.

IRR is defined as the discount rate that must be applied to the sponsor's cash equity outflows and inflows during the investment horizon in order to produce a net present value (NPV) of zero. Although the IRR calculation can be performed with a financial calculator or by using the IRR function in Microsoft Excel, it is important to understand the supporting math. Exhibit 4.4 displays the equation for calculating IRR, assuming a five-year investment horizon.

**EXHIBIT 4.4** IRR Timeline

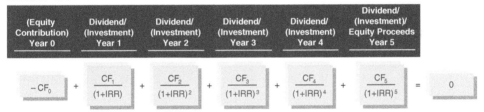

| (Equity Contribution) Year 0 | Dividend/ (Investment) Year 1 | Dividend/ (Investment) Year 2 | Dividend/ (Investment) Year 3 | Dividend/ (Investment) Year 4 | Dividend/ (Investment)/ Equity Proceeds Year 5 |
|---|---|---|---|---|---|

$$-CF_0 + \frac{CF_1}{(1+IRR)} + \frac{CF_2}{(1+IRR)^2} + \frac{CF_3}{(1+IRR)^3} + \frac{CF_4}{(1+IRR)^4} + \frac{CF_5}{(1+IRR)^5} = 0$$

While multiple factors affect a sponsor's ultimate decision to pursue a potential acquisition, comfort with meeting acceptable IRR thresholds is critical. Sponsors target superior returns for their fund's LPs, with a 15% to 20% threshold over a five-year investment horizon serving as a widely held "rule of thumb". This threshold, however, may increase or decrease depending on market conditions, the perceived risk of an investment, and other factors specific to the situation. The target return and holding period can vary depending on a variety of factors, including the type of fund, sector focus, and underlying investor base. The primary IRR drivers include the target's projected financial performance,[23] purchase price, and financing structure (particularly the size of the equity contribution), as well as the exit multiple and year. As would be expected, a sponsor seeks to minimize the price paid and equity contribution while gaining a strong degree of confidence in the target's future financial performance and the ability to exit at a higher valuation.

In Exhibit 4.5, we assume that a sponsor contributes $500 million of equity (cash outflow) at the end of Year 0 as part of the LBO financing structure and receives equity proceeds upon sale of $1,250 million (cash inflow) at the end of Year 5. This scenario produces an IRR of approximately 20%, as demonstrated by the NPV of zero.

---

[23]Based on the sponsor's model (see Chapter 5).

**EXHIBIT 4.5**   IRR Timeline Example

*($ in millions)*

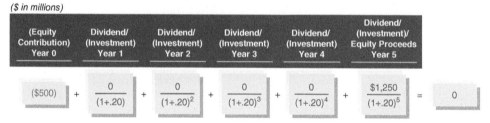

## Returns Analysis—Cash Return

In addition to IRR, sponsors also examine returns on the basis of a multiple of their cash investment ("cash return"). For example, assuming a sponsor contributes $500 million of equity and receives equity proceeds of $1,250 million at the end of the investment horizon, the cash return is 2.5x (assuming no additional equity investments or dividends during the period). While the cash return approach does not factor in the time value of money (versus IRR), it is an increasingly prevalent metric for PE funds. Cash returns are also referred to by the acronyms MOIC (multiple on invested capital) and CoC (cash on cash) return.

## How LBOs Generate Returns

LBOs generate returns through a combination of debt repayment and growth in enterprise value. Exhibit 4.6 depicts how each of these scenarios independently increases equity value, assuming a sponsor purchases a company for $1 billion, using $700 million of debt financing (70% of the purchase price) and an equity contribution of $300 million (30% of the purchase price). In each scenario, the returns are equivalent on both an IRR and cash return basis.

**Scenario I**   In Scenario I, we assume that the target generates cumulative free cash flow of $500 million, which is used to repay the principal amount of debt during the investment horizon. Although it does not change the enterprise value, debt repayment increases equity value on a dollar-for-dollar basis. Assuming the sponsor sells the target for $1 billion at exit, the value of the sponsor's equity investment increases from $300 million at purchase to $800 million even though there is no growth in the company's enterprise value. This scenario produces an IRR of 21.7% (assuming a five-year investment horizon) with a cash return of 2.7x.

**Scenario II** In Scenario II, we assume that the target does not repay any debt during the investment horizon. Rather, all cash generated by the target (after the payment of interest expense) is reinvested into the business, and the sponsor realizes 50% growth in enterprise value by selling the target for $1.5 billion after five years. This enterprise value growth can be achieved through EBITDA growth (e.g., organic growth, acquisitions, or streamlining operations) and/or achieving EBITDA multiple expansion.

As the debt represents a fixed claim on the business, the incremental $500 million of enterprise value accrues entirely to equity value. As in Scenario I, the value of the sponsor's equity investment increases from $300 million to $800 million, but this time without any debt repayment. Consequently, Scenario II produces an IRR and cash return equivalent to those in Scenario I (i.e., 21.7% and 2.7x, respectively).

**EXHIBIT 4.6** How LBOs Generate Returns

($ in millions)

**Scenaro I: Debt Repayment**

| Debt Repayment with No Enterprise Value Growth | |
|---|---|
| **Assumptions** | |
| Purchase Price | $1,000 |
| Equity Contribution | 300 |
| Debt Repayment | 500 |
| Sale Price (Year 5) | $1,000 |

| Equity Value Calculation and Returns | |
|---|---|
| Equity Contribution | $300 |
| *Increases to Equity Value:* | |
| Increase in Enterprise Value | - |
| Decrease in Debt from Repayment | 500 |
| **Equity Value At Exit** | **$800** |

| IRR | 21.7% |
|---|---|
| Cash Return | 2.7x |

**Scenario II: Enterprise Value Growth**

| Enterprise Value Growth with No Debt Repayment | |
|---|---|
| **Assumptions** | |
| Purchase Price | $1,000 |
| Equity Contribution | 300 |
| Debt Repayment | - |
| Sale Price (Year 5) | $1,500 |

| Equity Value Calculation and Returns | |
|---|---|
| Equity Contribution | $300 |
| *Increases to Equity Value:* | |
| Increase in Enterprise Value | 500 |
| Decrease in Debt from Repayment | - |
| **Equity Value At Exit** | **$800** |

| IRR | 21.7% |
|---|---|
| Cash Return | 2.7x |

## How Leverage Is Used to Enhance Returns

The concept of using leverage to enhance returns is fundamental to understanding LBOs. Assuming a fixed enterprise value at exit, using a higher percentage of debt in the financing structure (and a correspondingly smaller equity contribution) generates higher returns. Exhibit 4.7 illustrates this principle by analyzing the comparative returns of an LBO financed with 30% debt versus an LBO financed with 70% debt. A higher level of debt provides the additional benefit of greater tax savings realized due to the tax deductibility of a higher amount of interest expense.

While increased leverage may be used to generate enhanced returns, there are certain clear trade-offs. As discussed in Chapter 3, higher leverage increases the company's risk profile (and probability of financial distress), limiting financial flexibility and making the company more susceptible to business or economic downturns.

**EXHIBIT 4.7**    How Leverage Is Used to Enhance Returns

*($ in millions)*

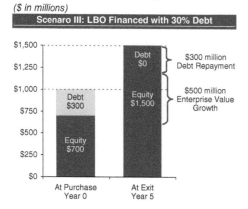
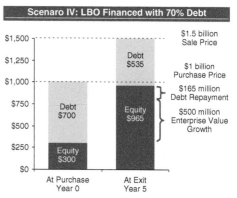

| 70% Equity Contribution / 30% Debt | |
|---|---|
| **Assumptions** | |
| Purchase Price | $1,000 |
| Equity Contribution | 700 |
| Cost of Debt | 8% |
| Cumulative FCF (after debt service) | 300 |
| Sale Price (Year 5) | $1,500 |

| **Equity Value and Returns** | |
|---|---|
| Equity Contribution | $700 |
| *Increases to Equity Value:* | |
| Increase in Enterprise Value | 500 |
| Decrease in Debt from Repayment | 300 |
| **Equity Value At Exit** | **$1,500** |

| | |
|---|---|
| IRR | 16.5% |
| Cash Return | 2.1x |

| 30% Equity Contribution / 70% Debt | |
|---|---|
| **Assumptions** | |
| Purchase Price | $1,000 |
| Equity Contribution | 300 |
| Cost of Debt[a] | 8% |
| Cumulative FCF (after debt service)[b] | 165 |
| Sale Price (Year 5) | $1,500 |

| **Equity Value and Returns** | |
|---|---|
| Equity Contribution | $300 |
| *Increases to Equity Value:* | |
| Increase in Enterprise Value | 500 |
| Decrease in Debt from Repayment | 165 |
| **Equity Value At Exit** | **$965** |

| | |
|---|---|
| IRR | 26.3% |
| Cash Return | 3.2x |

[a] In practice, the higher leverage in Scenario IV would require a higher blended cost of debt by investors versus Scenario III. For simplicity, we assume a constant cost of debt in this example.

[b] Reduced FCF in Scenario IV versus Scenario III reflects the incremental interest expense associated with the additional $400 million of debt, which results in less cash available for debt repayment.

**Scenario III**   In Scenario III, we assume a sponsor purchases the target for $1 billion using $300 million of debt (30% of the purchase price) and $700 million of equity (70% of the purchase price). After five years, the target is sold for $1.5 billion, thereby resulting in a $500 million increase in enterprise value ($1.5 billion sale price – $1 billion purchase price).

During the five-year investment horizon, we assume that the target generates annual free cash flow after the payment of interest expense of $60 million ($300 million on a cumulative basis), which is used for debt repayment. As shown in the timeline in Exhibit 4.8, the target completely repays the $300 million of debt by the end of Year 5.

By the end of the five-year investment horizon, the sponsor's original $700 million equity contribution is worth $1.5 billion as there is no debt remaining in the capital structure. This scenario generates an IRR of 16.5% and a cash return of approximately 2.1x after five years.

**EXHIBIT 4.8**   Scenario III Debt Repayment Timeline

= Beginning Debt Balance$_{Year\ 1}$ - Free Cash Flow$_{Year\ 1}$
= $300 million - $60 million

*($ in millions)*

**Scenario III - 70% Equity / 30% Debt**

| | Year 0 | Year 1 | Year 2 | Year 3 | Year 4 | Year 5 |
|---|---|---|---|---|---|---|
| **Equity Contribution** | ($700.0) | | | | | |
| Total Debt, beginning balance | | $300.0 | $240.0 | $180.0 | $120.0 | $60.0 |
| Free Cash Flow[a] | | $60.0 | $60.0 | $60.0 | $60.0 | $60.0 |
| **Total Debt, ending balance** | $300.0 | $240.0 | $180.0 | $120.0 | $60.0 | - |

| | |
|---|---|
| Sale Price | $1,500.0 |
| Less: Total Debt | (300.0) |
| Plus: Cumulative Free Cash Flow | 300.0 |
| **Equity Value at Exit** | **$1,500.0** |
| **IRR** | 16.5% |
| **Cash Return** | 2.1x |

[a] Annual free cash flow is after interest expense on the $300 million of debt. Also known as levered free cash flow or cash available for debt repayment (see Chapter 5).

**Scenario IV**   In Scenario IV, we assume that a sponsor buys the same target for $1 billion, but uses $700 million of debt (70% of the purchase price) and $300 million of equity (30% of the purchase price). As in Scenario III, we assume the target is sold for $1.5 billion at the end of Year 5. However, annual free cash flow is reduced due to the incremental interest expense on the $400 million of additional debt.

As shown in Exhibit 4.9, under Scenario IV, the additional $400 million of debt ($700 million – $300 million) creates incremental interest expense of $32 million ($24 million after-tax) in Year 1. The after-tax incremental interest expense of $24 million is calculated as the $400 million difference multiplied by an 8% assumed cost of debt and then tax-effected at a 25% assumed marginal tax rate. For each year of the projection period, we calculate incremental interest expense as the difference between total debt (beginning balance) in Scenario III versus Scenario IV multiplied by 8% (6% after tax).

By the end of Year 5, the sponsor's original $300 million equity contribution is worth $964.7 million ($1.5 billion sale price – $535.3 million of debt remaining in the capital structure). This scenario generates an IRR of 26.3% and a cash return of approximately 3.2x after five years.

**EXHIBIT 4.9**   Scenario IV Debt Repayment Timeline

> = Total Debt, beginning balance$_{Year\ 5}$ - Free Cash Flow, ending$_{Year\ 5}$
> = $565.0 million - $29.7 million

> = (Scenario IV Total Debt, beginning balance$_{Year\ 1}$ -
>   Scenario III Total Debt, beginning balance$_{Year\ 1}$) × Cost of Debt
> = ($700 million - $300 million) × 8%

*($ in millions)*

**Scenario IV - 30% Equity / 70% Debt**

|                                        | Year 0    | Year 1  | Year 2  | Year 3  | Year 4  | Year 5  |
|----------------------------------------|-----------|---------|---------|---------|---------|---------|
| **Equity Contribution**                | ($300.0)  |         |         |         |         |         |
|                                        |           |         |         |         |         |         |
| Total Debt, beginning balance          |           | $700.0  | $664.0  | $629.4  | $596.4  | $565.0  |
| Free Cash Flow, beginning[a]          |           | 60.0    | 60.0    | 60.0    | 60.0    | 60.0    |
| Incremental Interest Expense[b]       |           | 32.0    | 33.9    | 36.0    | 38.1    | 40.4    |
| Interest Tax Savings                   |           | (8.0)   | (8.5)   | (9.0)   | (9.5)   | (10.1)  |
| **Free Cash Flow, ending**             |           | $36.0   | $34.6   | $33.0   | $31.4   | $29.7   |
|                                        |           |         |         |         |         |         |
| **Total Debt, ending balance**         | $700.0    | $664.0  | $629.4  | $596.4  | $565.0  | $535.3  |

> = - Incremental Interest Expense$_{Year\ 2}$ × Marginal Tax Rate
> = ($33.9) million × 25%

| Sale Price                     | $1,500.0 |
|--------------------------------|----------|
| Less: Total Debt               | (700.0)  |
| Plus: Cumulative Free Cash Flow | 164.7   |
| **Equity Value at Exit**       | **$964.7** |

| IRR         | 26.3% |
|-------------|-------|

| Cash Return | 3.2x  |
|-------------|-------|

[a] Post-debt service on the $300 million of debt in Scenario III.

[b] Employs a beginning year as opposed to an average debt balance approach to calculating interest expense (see Chapter 5).

# PRIMARY EXIT/MONETIZATION STRATEGIES

Most sponsors aim to exit or monetize their investments within a five-year holding period in order to provide timely returns to their fund's LPs. These returns are typically realized via a sale to another company (commonly referred to as a "strategic sale"), a sale to another sponsor, or an IPO. Sponsors may also extract a return prior to exit through dividends, or even a dividend recapitalization, which is a dividend funded by the issuance of additional debt.

In addition, when the opportunity arises (e.g., during the 2008/2009 financial crisis), financial sponsors may opportunistically purchase the debt of their portfolio companies at a substantial discount to par.[24] These debt purchases may be made either directly by the issuer or by the sponsor. If purchased by the issuer, these debt purchases can allow incremental debt reduction since the amount of the principal reduction exceeds the amount of cash used to fund it. If purchased by the sponsor, they can realize an attractive return on their capital as markets normalize and the debt increases in price. This also enables them to gain leverage over other creditors in a future restructuring.

The ultimate decision regarding when to monetize an investment, however, depends on the performance of the target as well as prevailing market conditions. In some cases, such as when the target has performed particularly well or market conditions are favorable, the exit or monetization may occur within a year or two. Alternatively, the sponsor may be forced to hold an investment longer than desired as dictated by company performance or the market.

By the end of the investment horizon, ideally the sponsor has increased the target's EBITDA (e.g., through organic growth, acquisitions, and/or increased profitability) and reduced its debt, thereby substantially increasing the target's equity value. The sponsor also seeks to achieve multiple expansion upon exit. There are several strategies aimed at achieving a higher exit multiple, including an increase in the target's size and scale, meaningful operational improvements, a repositioning of the business toward more highly valued industry segments, an acceleration of the target's organic growth rate and/or profitability, and the accurate timing of a cyclical sector or economic upturn. Below, we discuss the primary LBO exit/monetization strategies for financial sponsors.

## Sale of Business

Traditionally, sponsors have sought to sell portfolio companies to strategic buyers, which typically represent the most attractive potential bidders due to their ability to realize synergies from the target and, therefore, pay a higher price. Strategic buyers may also benefit from a lower cost of capital and return thresholds. The proliferation of private equity funds, however, has made exits via a sale to another sponsor increasingly commonplace. Moreover, during robust debt financing markets, sponsors may be able to use high leverage levels and generous debt terms to support purchase prices competitive with (or even in excess of) those offered by strategic buyers.

---

[24]As permitted by the charter and mandate of the specific fund. Furthermore, such repurchases must be made in accordance with the specific debt instrument's credit agreement or indenture.

## Initial Public Offering

In an IPO exit, the sponsor sells a portion of its shares in the target to the public. As opposed to an outright majority sale for control, an IPO affords the sponsor only a partial monetization of its investment. Post-IPO, the sponsor typically retains the largest single equity stake in the target, with the understanding that a full exit will come through future follow-on equity offerings (see Chapter 8) or an eventual sale of the company. At the same time, the IPO provides the sponsor with a liquid market for its remaining equity investment while also preserving the opportunity to share in any future upside potential. Furthermore, depending on equity capital market conditions, an IPO may offer a compelling valuation premium to an outright sale.

## Dividends / Dividend Recapitalization

While not a true "exit strategy", a dividend provides the sponsor with a viable option for monetizing a portion of its investment prior to exit. At the same time, the sponsor retains its entire ownership interest in the target without any dilution resulting from the sale of equity to third parties. In a dividend recapitalization ("dividend recap"), instead of funding a dividend through cash flow generated by the target or proceeds from the sale of non-core assets, the target raises proceeds through the issuance of additional debt, and then uses those proceeds to pay shareholders a dividend. The incremental indebtedness may be issued in the form of an "add-on" to the target's existing credit facilities and/or bonds, a new security at the HoldCo level,[25] or as part of a complete refinancing of the existing capital structure. A dividend recap provides the sponsor with the added benefit of accelerating its return on investment while preserving the ability to share in any future upside potential and pursue a sale or IPO at a future date. Depending on the size and number of dividends, the sponsor may be able to recoup all of (or more than) its initial equity investment prior to any sale of the target or IPO.

## Below Par Debt Repurchase

Many PE funds have the flexibility to purchase the loans and high yield securities of their portfolio companies in the pursuit of acceptable risk-adjusted returns, either directly or through the issuer. As sponsors typically serve on the board of directors of their portfolio companies, they are well-positioned to evaluate the future prospects of the business, including its ability to service and eventually repay its indebtedness. Similarly, companies may opportunistically repurchase their own debt at discounts to par value, which can increase equity value and thus benefit the sponsors and PE funds.

This strategy is particularly attractive when the debt can be bought at distressed levels, which was relatively commonplace during the credit crisis of 2008 and 2009. In these instances, targets and sponsors found opportunities to purchase debt instruments at significant discounts to par value. In certain cases, the credit crisis created dramatic pricing changes in the trading value of debt that were uncorrelated to changes in the underlying performance of the borrower. Additionally, in those instances where the borrowers were negatively impacted by underlying economic conditions, as market conditions improved and the financial performance of these companies rebounded, the debt instruments increased in price commensurately. This debt repurchase strategy provides sponsors and portfolio companies with an additional tool for generating returns for PE funds, while still preserving future monetization opportunities via a refinancing, dividend, sale, or IPO.

---

[25]Debt incurrence and restricted payments covenants in the target's existing OpCo debt often substantially limit both incremental debt and the ability to pay a dividend to shareholders (see Exhibits 4.24 and 4.25). Therefore, dividend recaps frequently involve issuing new debt at the HoldCo, which is not subject to the existing OpCo covenants.

## LBO FINANCING: STRUCTURE

In a traditional LBO, debt typically comprises 60% to 70% of the financing structure, with the remainder of the purchase price funded by an equity contribution from a sponsor (or group of sponsors) and rolled/contributed equity from management. Given the inherently high leverage associated with an LBO, the various debt components of the capital structure are usually deemed non-investment grade, or rated 'Ba1' and below by Moody's Investor Service and 'BB+' and below by Standard and Poor's (see Chapter 1, Exhibit 1.23 for a ratings scale). The debt portion of the LBO financing structure may include a broad array of loans, bonds, or other debt or preferred equity instruments with varying terms and conditions that appeal to different classes of investors.

We have grouped the primary types of LBO financing sources into the categories shown in Exhibit 4.10, corresponding to their relative ranking in the capital structure. As a general rule, the higher a given debt instrument ranks in the capital structure hierarchy, the lower its risk and, consequently, the lower its cost of capital to the borrower/issuer. However, cost of capital tends to be inversely related to the flexibility permitted by the applicable debt instrument. For example, secured debt usually represents the least expensive form of LBO financing. At the same time, it is secured by various forms of collateral and governed by covenants that establish restrictions on how much incremental debt the borrower can incur, the parameters of future investments, and limitations on future dividends (see Exhibit 4.24).

**EXHIBIT 4.10**   General Ranking of Financing Sources in an LBO Capital Structure

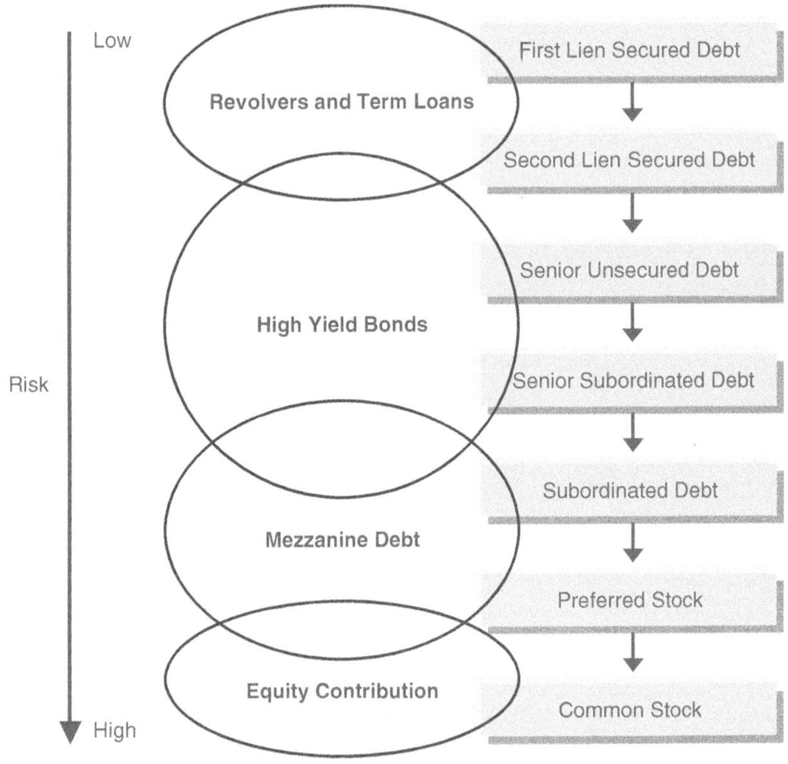

During the 2009 to 2018 period, the average LBO varied substantially in terms of leverage levels, purchase multiple, percentage of capital sourced from each class of debt, and equity contribution. As shown in Exhibit 4.11, average LBO leverage levels increased dramatically following the Great Recession, rising from 4.0x in 2009 to nearly 6.0x by 2018. At the same time, the average purchase price multiple increased from sub-8.0x in 2009 to over 10.5x by 2018.

After stabilizing from 2011 to 2013 following the depths of the recession, the LBO market accelerated in the ensuing years. The number of closed deals increased from 95 in 2013 to 157 in 2018 (see Exhibit 4.13) while transaction volume grew to $275 billion (see Exhibit 4.14). At the same time, average leverage grew from 5.3x to 5.8x, the average LBO purchase price increased from 8.8x to 10.6x, and the average equity contribution moved from 35% to 40% (see Exhibit 4.12).

**EXHIBIT 4.11** Average LBO Purchase Price Breakdown 2009 – 2018

Source: Standard & Poor's Leveraged Commentary & Data Group
Senior debt includes loans, 2nd lien debt, senior secured notes, and senior unsecured notes. Subordinated debt includes senior and junior subordinated debt. Equity includes HoldCo debt/seller notes, preferred stock, common stock, and rolled equity. Other is cash and any other unclassified sources.

**EXHIBIT 4.12** Average Sources of LBO Proceeds 2009 – 2018

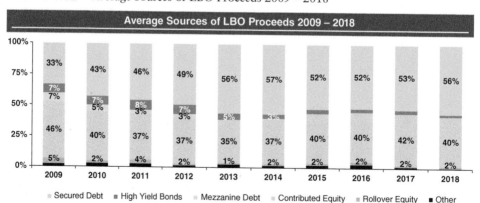

Source: Standard & Poor's Leveraged Commentary & Data Group
Note: Contributed equity includes HoldCo debt/seller notes, preferred stock, and common stock.

**EXHIBIT 4.13**   Number of Closed Deals 2009 – 2018

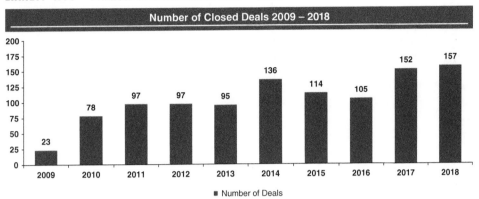

Source: Standard & Poor's Leveraged Commentary & Data Group
Note: U.S. deals.

**EXHIBIT 4.14**   LBO Transaction Volume 2009 – 2018

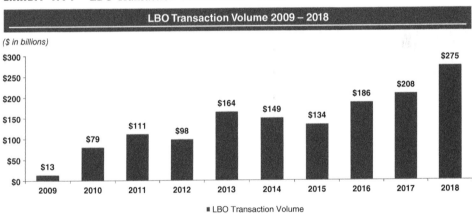

Source: Standard & Poor's Leveraged Commentary & Data Group
Note: U.S. volumes.

## LBO FINANCING: PRIMARY SOURCES

### Secured Debt

**EXHIBIT 4.15**    Secured Debt

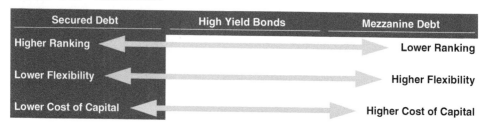

Secured debt, also known as *bank debt*, is an integral part of LBO financing, typically representing the largest part of the capital structure (as shown in Exhibit 4.12). It is generally comprised of a revolving credit facility (which may be borrowed, repaid, and reborrowed as needed during the term) and one or more term loan tranches (which may not be reborrowed once repaid). The revolving credit facility may take the form of a traditional "cash flow" revolver[26] or an asset-based lending (ABL) facility.[27]

Most secured debt is issued in the form of a loan (as opposed to a security), and is therefore not subject to SEC regulations and disclosure requirements imposed by law.[28] However, it has restrictive covenants that require the borrower to comply with certain provisions, reporting requirements, and financial tests throughout the life of the facility (see Exhibit 4.24).

Secured debt typically bears interest (payable on a quarterly basis) at a given benchmark rate, usually LIBOR[29] or the Base Rate,[30] plus an applicable margin ("spread") based on the creditworthiness of the borrower (or quality of the asset base in the case of ABL facilities). This type of debt is often referred to as floating rate due to the fact that the borrowing cost varies in accordance with changes to the underlying benchmark rate. In addition, the spread for revolver or ABL facilities may be adjusted downward (or upward) in accordance with a performance-based grid based on the borrower's leverage ratio or credit ratings.

---

[26]Lenders under a "cash flow" revolver focus on the ability of the borrower to cover debt service by generating cash flow. Cash flow revolvers are typically equally and ratably secured with the term loan.

[27]Lenders under an "ABL revolver" focus on the liquidation value of the assets comprising the facility's borrowing base, typically accounts receivable and inventory (see Exhibit 4.16). ABL facilities are generally viewed as the "safest" loan as the lenders have a first lien on assets that can be quickly liquidated, and they generally limit borrowings to a percentage of the liquidation value of that collateral. ABL revolvers typically have a 1st lien on those assets, with the term loan possessing a 2nd lien on property, plant, equipment and stock of subsidiaries (and vice versa).

[28]Loans are not subject to the Securities Act of 1933 or the Securities Exchange Act of 1934. Privately offered securities, such as bonds issued in "144A for life" offerings, are only subject to limited provisions of the '33 Act and the '34 Act. Public offerings of securities and publicly traded companies are subject to various registration and disclosure requirements, including periodic public reporting of financial and other information.

[29]In 2021, LIBOR is expected to transition to SOFR (secured overnight financing rate), which is published by the Federal Reserve Bank of New York.

[30]Base Rate is most often defined as a rate equal to the higher of the prime rate or the Federal Funds rate plus 1/2 of 1%.

**Revolving Credit Facility**    A traditional cash flow revolving credit facility ("revolver") is a line of credit extended by a bank or group of banks that permits the borrower to draw varying amounts up to a specified aggregate limit for a specified period of time. It is unique in that amounts borrowed can be freely repaid and reborrowed an unlimited number of times during the term of the facility, subject to agreed-upon conditions set forth in a credit agreement[31] (see Exhibit 4.24). The majority of companies utilize a revolver or equivalent lending arrangement to provide ongoing liquidity for seasonal working capital needs, capital expenditures, letters of credit (LC),[32] and other general corporate purposes. A revolver may also be used to fund a portion of the purchase price in an LBO, although it is usually undrawn at close.

Revolvers are typically held by the lead arranger investment banks. To compensate lenders for making this credit line available to the borrower (which may or may not be drawn upon and offers a less attractive return when unfunded), they are paid a commitment or underwriting fee upon entering into the facility based on the aggregate committed amount, and a nominal annual commitment fee on the undrawn portion of the facility.[33]

The revolver is generally the least expensive form of capital in the LBO financing structure, typically priced at, or slightly below, the interest rate applicable to the term loan. In return for the revolver's low cost, the borrower must sacrifice some flexibility. For example, lenders generally require a first priority security interest ("lien") on certain assets[34] of the borrower[35] (in the case of a cash flow revolver, shared with the term loan facilities) and compliance with various covenants. The first lien provides lenders greater comfort by granting their debt claims a higher priority in the event of bankruptcy relative to obligations owed to second priority secured debt and to unsecured creditors (see "Security"). The historical market standard for LBO revolvers has been a term ("tenor") of five to six years (and certainly prior to the term loan facilities), with no scheduled reduction to the committed amount of such facilities prior to maturity.

---

[31]The legal contract between the borrower and its lenders that governs loans. It contains key definitions, terms, representations and warranties, covenants, events of default, and other protective provisions.

[32]An LC is a document issued to a specified beneficiary that guarantees payment by an "issuing" lender under the credit agreement. For example, a supplier may require an LC from a borrower prior to shipping inventory to ensure that it will get paid by the issuing lender if the borrower fails to make required payments. LCs reduce revolver availability.

[33]The fee is assessed on an ongoing basis and accrues daily, typically at an annualized rate up to 50 basis points (bps) depending on the creditworthiness of the borrower. For example, an undrawn $100 million revolver would typically have an annual commitment fee of 50 bps or $500,000 ($100 million × 0.50%). Assuming the average daily revolver usage (including the outstanding LC amounts) is $25 million, the annual commitment fee would be $375,000 (($100 million – $25 million) × 0.50%). For any drawn portion of the revolver, the borrower pays interest on that dollar amount at LIBOR or the Base Rate plus a spread. To the extent the revolver's availability is reduced by outstanding LCs, the borrower pays a fee on the dollar amount of undrawn outstanding LCs at the full spread, but does not pay LIBOR or the Base Rate. Banks may also be paid an *up-front fee* upon the initial closing of the revolver and term loan(s) to incentivize participation.

[34]For example, in the tangible and intangible assets of the borrower, including capital stock of subsidiaries.

[35]As well as its domestic subsidiaries (in most cases).

**Asset-Based Lending Facility**    An ABL facility is a type of revolving credit facility that is available to current asset-intensive companies. ABL facilities are secured by a first priority lien on all current assets (typically accounts receivable and inventory) and may include a second priority lien on all other assets (typically PP&E). They are more commonly used by companies with sizable accounts receivable and inventory, and variable working capital needs that operate in seasonal or asset-intensive businesses. For example, ABL facilities are often used by retailers, selected commodity producers and distributors (e.g., chemicals, building products, and metals), manufacturers, and rental equipment businesses.

ABL facilities are subject to a borrowing base formula that limits availability based on "eligible" accounts receivable, inventory, and, in certain circumstances, fixed assets, real estate, or other specified assets of the borrower, all of which are pledged as collateral. The maximum amount available for borrowing under an ABL facility is capped by the size of the borrowing base at a given point in time or the committed amount of the facility, whichever is less. While the *borrowing base* formula varies depending on the individual borrower, a common example is shown in Exhibit 4.16.

**EXHIBIT 4.16**    ABL Borrowing Base Formula

ABL Borrowing Base   =   85% × Eligible Accounts Receivable + 60%[a] × Eligible Inventory

[a] Based on 85% of appraised net orderly liquidation value (expected net proceeds if inventory is liquidated) as determined by a third party firm.

ABL facilities provide lenders with certain additional protections not found in traditional cash flow revolvers, such as periodic collateral reporting requirements and appraisals. In addition, the assets securing ABLs (such as accounts receivable and inventory) are intended to be easier to monetize and turn into cash in the event of bankruptcy. As such, the interest rate spread on an ABL facility is lower than that of a cash flow revolver for the same credit. Given their reliance upon a borrowing base as collateral, ABL facilities traditionally have only one "springing" financial maintenance covenant.[36] Traditional loans, by contrast, often have multiple financial maintenance covenants restricting the borrower. The typical tenor of an ABL revolver is five years.

## Term Loan Facilities

A term loan ("leveraged loan", when non-investment grade) is a loan with a specified maturity that requires principal repayment ("amortization") according to a defined schedule, typically on a quarterly basis. Like a revolver, a traditional term loan for an LBO financing is structured as a first lien debt obligation[37] and requires the borrower to maintain a certain credit profile through compliance with covenants contained in the credit agreement. Unlike a revolver, however, a term loan is fully funded on the date of closing and once principal is repaid, it cannot be reborrowed. Term loans are classified by an identifying letter such as "A", "B", "C", etc. in accordance with their lender base, amortization schedule, maturity date, and other terms.

---

[36]The traditional springing financial covenant is a fixed charge coverage ratio of 1.0x and is tested only if "excess availability" falls below a certain level (usually 10% to 15% of the ABL facility). Excess availability is equal to the lesser of the ABL facility or the borrowing base less, in each case, outstanding amounts under the facility.

[37]Often *pari passu* (or on an equal basis) with the revolver, which entitles term loan lenders to an equal right of repayment upon bankruptcy of the borrower.

**Amortizing Term Loans**   "A" term loans ("Term Loan A" or "TLA") are commonly referred to as "amortizing term loans" because they typically require substantial principal repayment throughout the life of the loan.[38] Term loans with significant, annual required amortization are perceived by lenders as less risky than those with *de minimis* required principal repayments during the life of the loan due to their shorter average life. TLAs also often contain financial maintenance covenants that require quarterly compliance with specified financial ratios. Consequently, TLAs are often the lowest priced term loans in the capital structure. TLAs are syndicated to commercial banks and finance companies together with the revolver and are often referred to as "pro rata" tranches because lenders typically commit to equal ("ratable") percentages of the revolver and TLA during syndication. TLAs in LBO financing structures typically have a term that ends simultaneously ("co-terminus") with the revolver.

**Institutional Term Loans**   "B" term loans ("Term Loan B" or "TLB"), which are commonly referred to as "institutional term loans", are the lifeblood of LBO financings. They are typically larger in size than TLAs and sold to institutional investors (often the same investors who buy high yield bonds) rather than banks. This institutional investor class prefers non-amortizing loans with longer maturities and higher coupons. As a result, TLBs generally amortize at a nominal rate (e.g., 1% per annum) with a bullet payment at maturity.[39] TLBs are typically structured to have a longer term than the revolver and any TLA, as TLA and revolver lenders prefer to have their debt mature before the TLB. Hence, a tenor for TLBs of up to seven (or sometimes seven and one-half years) is market standard for LBOs. As discussed in more detail later in this chapter, TLBs are typically "covenant-lite", which means that they do not have financial maintenance covenants.

**Second Lien Term Loans**   Second lien term loans have been mainstays of the LBO market during the credit boom of the mid-2000s and at various points during the decade following the Great Recession. A second lien term loan is a floating rate loan that is secured by a second priority security interest in the assets of the borrower. It ranks junior to the first priority security interest in the assets of the borrower benefiting a revolver, TLA, and TLB. In the event of bankruptcy (and liquidation), second lien lenders are entitled to repayment from the proceeds of collateral sales <u>after</u> such proceeds have first been applied to the claims of first lien lenders, but <u>prior to</u> any application to unsecured claims, such as unsecured debt and trade creditors.[40] Unlike first lien term loans, second lien term loans generally do not amortize. Second lien term loans are typically structured to have a longer tenor than the first lien term loans as first lien lenders prefer to have a debt maturity inside that of the second lien term loan.

---

[38] An amortization repayment schedule for a TLA issued at the end of 2019 with a six-year maturity might be structured as follows: 2020: 10%, 2021: 10%, 2022: 15%, 2023: 15%, 2024: 25%, 2025: 25%. Another example might be: 2020: 0%, 2021: 0%, 2022: 5%, 2023: 5%, 2024: 10%, 2025: 80%. The amortization schedule is typically set on a quarterly basis.

[39] A large repayment of principal at maturity that is standard among institutional term loans. A typical mandatory amortization schedule for a TLB issued at the end of 2019 with a seven-year maturity would be as follows: 2020: 1%, 2021: 1%, 2022: 1%, 2023: 1%, 2024: 1%, 2025: 1%, 2026: 94%. Like TLAs, the amortization schedule for B term loans is typically set on a quarterly basis. The sizable 2026 principal repayment is referred to as a bullet.

[40] Exact terms and rights between first and second lien lenders are set forth in a negotiated *intercreditor agreement*.

For borrowers, second lien term loans offer an alternative to more traditional junior debt instruments, such as high yield bonds and mezzanine debt. As compared to traditional high yield bonds, second lien term loans provide borrowers with superior prepayment optionality, a floating interest rate, and no ongoing public disclosure requirements. They can also be issued in a smaller size than high yield bonds, which usually have a minimum issuance amount of $250+ million due to investors' desire for trading liquidity. Depending on the borrower and market conditions, second lien term loans may also provide a lower cost-of-capital. As with TLBs, they are increasingly structured as covenant-lite. For investors, which typically include hedge funds and CDOs, second lien term loans offer less risk (due to their secured status) than traditional unsecured high yield bonds while paying a higher coupon than first lien debt.

## High Yield Bonds

**EXHIBIT 4.17**  High Yield Bonds

| Secured Debt | High Yield Bonds | Mezzanine Debt |
| --- | --- | --- |
| Higher Ranking | | Lower Ranking |
| Lower Flexibility | | Higher Flexibility |
| Lower Cost of Capital | | Higher Cost of Capital |

High yield bonds are non–investment grade debt securities that obligate the issuer to make semiannual interest payments and repay the entire principal amount at a stated maturity date, usually seven to ten years after issuance. As opposed to term loans, high yield bonds are non-amortizing with the entire principal amount due as a bullet payment at maturity. Due to their junior, typically unsecured position in the capital structure,[41] fixed interest rate, longer maturities, absence of maintenance covenants, and less restrictive *incurrence* covenants as set forth in an indenture (see Exhibit 4.25),[42] high yield bonds feature a higher coupon than secured debt to compensate investors for the greater risk.

High yield bonds typically pay interest at a *fixed rate*, which is priced at issuance on the basis of a spread to a benchmark Treasury. As its name suggests, a fixed rate means that the interest rate is constant over the entire maturity. While high yield bonds may be structured with a floating rate coupon, this is not common.

Traditionally, high yield bonds have been a mainstay in LBO financings. Used in conjunction with secured term loans, high yield bonds enable sponsors to substantially

---

[41]High yield bonds can also be structured with a security interest.

[42]The indenture is the contract entered into by an issuer and corporate trustee (who acts on behalf of the bondholders) that defines the rights and obligations of the issuer and its creditors with respect to a bond issue. Similar to a credit agreement for a loan, an indenture sets forth the covenants and other terms of a bond issue.

increase leverage levels beyond those available in the leveraged loan market alone. This incremental debt permits sponsors to offer a higher purchase price and/or reduce the equity contribution. Furthermore, high yield bonds afford issuers greater flexibility than secured debt due to their less restrictive incurrence covenants, longer maturities, and lack of mandatory amortization. One offsetting factor, however, is that high yield bonds have non-call features (see Exhibit 4.23) that can negatively impact a sponsor's exit strategy due to onerous prepayment penalties.

Typically, high yield bonds are initially sold to qualified institutional buyers (QIBs)[43] through a private placement under Rule 144A of the Securities Act of 1933. The initial sale through a private placement helps expedite the process because SEC registration, which involves review of the registration statement by the SEC, can take several weeks or months. After closing, the issuer will be required to provide periodic reports to holders and prospective bond purchasers.[44]

During robust credit markets, companies may be able to issue bonds with atypical "issuer-friendly" provisions, such as a payment-in-kind (PIK) toggle. The PIK toggle allows an issuer to choose from time to time whether to make a particular interest payment "in-kind" (i.e., in the form of additional notes) or in cash. This optionality provides the issuer with the ability to preserve cash in times of challenging business or economic conditions, especially during the early years of the investment period when leverage is highest. If the issuer elects to pay PIK interest in lieu of cash, the coupon for that interest period typically increases by 75 bps.

As loans and high yield bonds are the primary debt instruments used in an LBO financing, a comparison of the key terms is shown in Exhibit 4.19.

**Bridge Loans**   A bridge loan facility ("bridge") is interim, committed financing provided to the borrower to "bridge" to the issuance of permanent capital, most often high yield bonds (the "take-out" securities). In an LBO, investment banks typically commit to provide funding for the secured debt and a bridge loan facility. The bridge usually takes the form of an unsecured term loan, which is only funded if the take-out securities cannot be issued and sold by the closing of the LBO.

Bridge loans are particularly important for LBO financings due to the sponsor's need to provide certainty of funding to the seller. The bridge financing gives comfort that the purchase consideration will be funded even in the event that market conditions for the take-out securities deteriorate between signing and closing of the transaction (subject to any conditions precedent to closing enumerated in the definitive agreement

---

[43]As part of Rule 144A, the SEC created another category of financially sophisticated investors known as qualified institutional buyers, or QIBs. Rule 144A provides a safe harbor exemption from SEC registration requirements for the resale of restricted securities to QIBs. QIBs generally are institutions or other entities that, in aggregate, own and invest (on a discretionary basis) at least $100 million in securities.

[44]In some instances, high yield bonds are offered with "registration rights", and the issuer is required to register them post-closing so that they can be traded on an open market. In that case, once the SEC review of the documentation is complete, the issuer conducts an exchange offer pursuant to which investors exchange the unregistered bonds for registered securities. Post-registration, the issuer is subject to the SEC's public disclosure requirements (e.g., the filing of 10-Ks, 10-Qs, 8-Ks, etc). However, while "144A for life" bonds have a marginally smaller market of purchasers, and thus should have slightly less liquidity than freely tradeable registered high yield bonds, as of 2020 "144A for life" bonds represented a substantial majority of new issuances of high yield bonds.

(see Chapter 6, Exhibit 6.9) or the commitment letter). If funded, the bridge loan can be replaced with the take-out securities at a future date, markets permitting.

In practice, however, the bridge loan is rarely intended to be funded, serving only as a financing of last resort. From the sponsor's perspective, the bridge loan is a potentially costly funding alternative due to the additional fees required to be paid to the arrangers.[45] The interest rate on a bridge loan also typically increases periodically the longer it is outstanding until it hits agreed-upon caps (maximum interest rate). The investment banks providing the bridge loan also hope that the bridge remains unfunded as it ties up capital and increases exposure to the borrower's credit. To mitigate the risk of funding a bridge, the lead arrangers often seek to syndicate all or a portion of the bridge loan commitment to institutional investors prior to the marketing of the high yield bonds.

### Mezzanine Debt

**EXHIBIT 4.18**   Mezzanine Debt

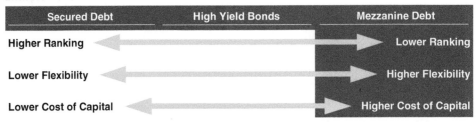

As its name suggests, mezzanine debt refers to a layer of capital that lies between traditional syndicated term loans / high yield bonds and equity. Mezzanine debt is a highly negotiated instrument between the issuer and investors that is tailored to meet the financing needs of the specific transaction and required investor returns. As such, mezzanine debt allows great flexibility in structuring terms conducive to issuer and investor alike.

For sponsors, mezzanine debt provides incremental capital at a cost below that of equity, which enables them to attain higher leverage levels and purchase price when alternative capital sources are inaccessible, or when funding that amount with equity would reduce their anticipated IRR. For example, mezzanine debt may serve to substitute for, or supplement, high yield financing when markets are unfavorable or even inaccessible (e.g., for smaller companies whose size needs are below high yield bond market minimum thresholds). In the United States, it is particularly prevalent in middle market transactions.[46]

---

[45]Investment banks are typically paid a commitment fee for arranging the bridge loan facility on the closing of the acquisition, regardless of whether the bridge is funded. In the event the bridge is funded, the banks and lenders receive an additional *funding fee*. Furthermore, if the bridge remains outstanding after one year, the borrower also pays a *conversion fee* (which is the same % as the fee the banks were supposed to receive under the engagement letter in connection with the planned bond offering).

[46]In Europe, mezzanine debt is used to finance large as well as middle market transactions. It is typically structured as a floating rate loan (with a combination of cash and PIK interest) that benefits from a second or third lien on the same collateral benefiting the loan (of the

Typical mezzanine debt investors include dedicated mezzanine funds, insurance companies, business development companies (BDCs), and hedge funds. For the investor, mezzanine debt typically offers a higher rate of return than traditional high yield bonds and can be structured to offer equity upside potential in the form of purchased equity or detachable warrants that are exchangeable into common stock of the issuer. The interest rate on mezzanine debt typically includes a combination of cash and non-cash PIK payments. Depending on available financing alternatives and market conditions, mezzanine investors typically target a "blended" return (including cash and non-cash components) in the low-to-mid teens (or higher) depending on market conditions. Maturities and terms for mezzanine debt may vary substantially, but tend to be similar to those for high yield bonds.[47]

### Equity Contribution

The remaining portion of LBO funding comes in the form of an equity contribution by the financial sponsor and rolled/contributed equity by the target's management, typically provided in the form of common equity. The equity contribution percentage typically ranges from approximately 30% to 40% of the LBO financing structure, although this may vary depending on debt market conditions, the type of company, and the purchase multiple paid.[48] For large LBOs, several sponsors may team up to create a consortium of buyers, thereby reducing the amount of each individual sponsor's equity contribution (known as a "club deal").

The equity contribution provides a cushion for lenders and bondholders in the event that the company's enterprise value deteriorates. For example, if a sponsor contributes 30% equity to a given deal, lenders gain comfort that the value of the business would have to decline by more than 30% from the purchase price before their principal is jeopardized. Sponsors may also choose to "over-equitize" certain LBOs, such as when they plan to issue incremental debt at a future date to fund acquisitions or fund growth initiatives for the company.

Rollover/contributed equity by existing company management and/or key shareholders varies according to the situation, but often ranges from approximately 2% to 5% (or more) of the overall equity portion. Management equity rollover/contribution is usually encouraged by the sponsor in order to align incentives.

---

same capital structure). U.S. mezzanine debt, on the other hand, is often structured with a fixed rate coupon and is unsecured and often times contractually subordinated (see Exhibit 4.21), as well as not benefiting from any security.

[47]However, if an LBO financing structure has both high yield bonds and mezzanine debt, the mezzanine debt will typically mature outside the high yield bonds, thereby reducing the risk to the more senior security.

[48]As previously discussed, the commitment papers for the debt financing are typically predicated on a minimum equity contribution by the sponsor.

**EXHIBIT 4.19**  Comparison of Secured Debt and High Yield Bonds

| | Secured Debt | High Yield Bonds |
|---|---|---|
| Seniority | ■ Most senior debt in capital structure | ■ Effectively subordinated to bank debt (by virtue of being unsecured)<br>■ Occasionally contractually subordinated to bank debt (in the case of "subordinated" or "senior subordinated" notes)<br>■ Rarely "structurally subordinated" to bank debt (by virtue of being incurred at a parent company without subsidiary guarantees from the secured debt's borrower and guarantors) |
| Prepayability | ■ Prepayable (typically without penalty) | ■ Call protection (initially a make-whole premium, followed by a call premium descending to par 2–3 years prior to maturity) |
| Security | ■ Typically secured | ■ Typically unsecured |
| Coupon | ■ Floating interest rate<br>■ Grid-based, depending on leveraged metrics or ratings | ■ Typically fixed rate coupon, but can be floating rate<br>■ No change over life of bond / no change with improving or deteriorating credit |
| Ratings | ■ Not required, but typical | ■ Required (Moody's and S&P) |
| Investors | ■ Banks<br>■ CLOs, prime rate funds and other institutions (TLB) | ■ Fixed income/high-yield mutual funds<br>■ Hedge funds<br>■ Insurance companies |
| Syndication | ■ Distribution of confidential information memorandum (CIM)<br>■ Bank or lenders' meetings<br>■ Two-week syndication process<br>■ One week post-syndication to finalize documentation<br>■ SEC rules / regulations do not apply | ■ Preliminary offering memorandum prior to roadshow<br>■ Roadshow of 3–5 business days of meetings<br>■ Final Offering Memorandum printed after pricing<br>■ Rule 144A private placement exception to SEC registration<br>■ Securities law anti-fraud rules apply<br>■ No SEC review of documentation (only required post closing if registration rights are provided) |
| Covenants | ■ Maintenance of a particular credit profile, tested on a quarterly basis<br>  – typical financial covenants include: maximum leverage (senior/total), minimum interest coverage, maximum capex[a]<br>■ Incurrence covenants that govern incremental debt, ability to make investments and restricted payments (dividends and repayment of junior debt)<br>■ Changes to credit agreement achieved through amendment/waiver process | ■ Incurrence tests (no maintenance covenants and less restrictive incurrence covenants than secured debt), performance against covenants only measured upon transactions (e.g., incurrence of additional debt, payment of dividend, stock repurchase, granting of lien, entering into transaction with affiliates)<br>■ Extremely difficult to amend / obtain a waiver |

(a) Revolvers typically have "springing" financial maintenance covenants that only apply if 35% to 40% of the facility is drawn. As of Q1 2020, most institutional term loans no longer have maintenance covenants; rather, they are "covenant-lite" and are governed by more restrictive incurrence covenants than high yield bonds.

**EXHIBIT 4.19** Comparison of Secured Debt and High Yield Bonds (*Continued*)

| | Secured Debt | High Yield Bonds |
|---|---|---|
| Disclosure | ■ May include projections and other non-public information<br>■ Reporting/information requirements determined by documentation<br>■ Information limited to existing lenders/syndicate | ■ No projections<br>■ Comparable to the SEC's standard for registered offerings / registered companies<br>■ Information disseminated through investor conference calls<br>■ Research support is key for information flow |
| Trading | ■ Liquid market for certain borrowers<br>■ Private market | ■ Liquid market<br>■ Minimum new issue size typically $250+ million |
| Benefits | ■ Lower cost than public debt<br>■ Lower underwriting fees<br>■ Term loans: typically no maintenance covenants ("covenant-lite")<br>■ Fully prepayable (low or no prepayment penalties)<br>■ Amendment process easier and less expensive<br>■ No public disclosure | ■ Long-term fixed rate<br>■ Longer tenor (7–10 years)<br>■ No maintenance covenants<br>■ No amortization<br>■ Broadens investor profile<br>■ Access to large, liquid debt market<br>■ Ability to do further capital raises quickly<br>■ No pledge of collateral required |
| Considerations | ■ Secured by collateral<br>■ Shorter tenor (5–7 years)<br>■ Limited market capacity<br>■ Maintenance covenants in certain instances<br>■ Less flexibility to incur additional senior debt<br>■ Required amortization (may be minimal) | ■ Higher cost than secured debt<br>■ Non-callable for specified period (3–5 years), with call premiums for 5–8 years<br>■ Often limits allowable bank/senior capacity<br>■ Higher underwriting fees than secured debt<br>■ Broad disclosure of financial information |

## LBO FINANCING: SELECTED KEY TERMS

Both within and across the broad categories of debt instruments used in LBO financings—which we group into secured debt, high yield bonds, and mezzanine debt—there are a number of key terms that affect risk, cost, flexibility, and investor base. As shown in Exhibit 4.20 and discussed in greater detail below, these terms include *security, seniority, maturity, coupon, call protection,* and *covenants.*

**EXHIBIT 4.20** Summary of Selected Key Terms

| Secured Debt | High Yield Bonds | Mezzanine Debt |
| --- | --- | --- |
| Secured | Security | Unsecured |
| Senior | Seniority | Junior |
| Shorter | Maturity | Longer |
| Lower | Coupon | Higher |
| More Prepayability | Call Protection | Negotiated |
| More Restrictive | Covenants | Less Restrictive |

### Security

Security refers to the pledge of, or lien on, collateral that is granted by the borrower to the holders of a given debt instrument. Collateral represents assets, property, and/or securities pledged by a borrower to secure a loan or other debt obligation, which is subject to seizure and/or liquidation in the event of a default.[49] It typically includes accounts receivable, inventory, PP&E, intellectual property, and securities such as the common stock of the borrower/issuer and its subsidiaries. Depending upon the volatility of the target's cash flow, creditors may require higher levels of collateral coverage as protection.

### Seniority

Seniority refers to the priority status of a creditor's claims against the borrower/issuer relative to those of other creditors. Generally, seniority is achieved through either *contractual* or *structural subordination.*

---

[49]In practice, in the event a material default is not waived by a borrower/issuer's creditors, the borrower/issuer typically seeks protection under Chapter 11 of the Bankruptcy Code to continue operating as a "going concern" while it attempts to restructure its financial obligations. During bankruptcy, while secured creditors are generally stayed from enforcing their remedies, they are entitled to certain protections and rights not provided to unsecured creditors (including the right to continue to receive interest payments). Thus, obtaining collateral is beneficial to a creditor even if it does not exercise its remedies to foreclose and sell that collateral.

**Contractual Subordination**  Contractual subordination refers to the priority status of debt instruments at the same legal entity. It is established through *subordination provisions*, which stipulate that the claims of senior creditors must be satisfied in full before those of junior creditors (generally "senior" status is limited to bank lenders or similar creditors, not trade creditors[50]). In the case of subordinated bonds, the indenture contains the subordination provisions that are relied upon by the senior creditors as "third-party" beneficiaries.[51] Exhibit 4.21 provides an illustrative diagram showing the contractual seniority of multiple debt instruments.

**EXHIBIT 4.21**   Contractual Subordination

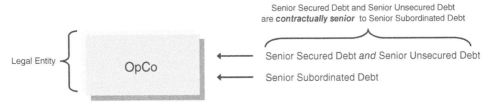

While both senior secured debt and senior unsecured debt have contractually equal debt claims (pari passu), senior secured debt may be considered "effectively" senior to the extent of the value of the collateral securing such debt. Those unsecured creditors are referred to as "effectively subordinated" to secured creditors.

**Structural Subordination**  Structural subordination refers to the priority status of debt instruments at different legal entities within a company. For example, debt obligations at OpCo, where the company's assets are located, are structurally senior to debt obligations at HoldCo[52] so long as such HoldCo obligations do not benefit from a *guarantee* (credit support)[53] from OpCo. In the event of bankruptcy at OpCo, its obligations must be satisfied in full before a distribution or dividend can be made to its sole shareholder (i.e., HoldCo). Exhibit 4.22 provides an illustrative diagram showing the structural seniority of debt instruments at two legal entities.

## Maturity

The maturity ("tenor" or "term") of a debt obligation refers to the length of time the instrument remains outstanding until the full principal amount must be repaid. Shorter tenor debt is deemed less risky than debt with a longer maturity as it is required to be repaid earlier. Therefore, all else being equal, shorter tenor debt carries a lower cost of capital than longer tenor debt of the same credit.

---

[50]Suppliers and vendors owed money for goods and services provided to the company.

[51]When the transaction involves junior debt not governed by an indenture (e.g., privately placed second lien or mezzanine debt), the subordination provisions will generally be included in an *intercreditor agreement* with the senior creditors.

[52]A legal entity that owns all or a portion of the voting stock of another company/entity, in this case, OpCo.

[53]Guarantees provide credit support by one party for a debt obligation of a third party. For example, a subsidiary with actual operations and assets "guarantees" the debt, meaning that it agrees to use its cash and assets to pay debt obligations on behalf of HoldCo.

In an LBO, various debt instruments with different maturities are issued to finance the debt portion of the transaction. Secured debt tends to have shorter maturities, often five to six years for revolvers and six to seven (or sometimes seven and one-half years) for institutional term loans. As the more junior portion of the capital structure, high yield bonds have longer maturities, typically seven to ten years.[54] In an LBO financing structure comprising several debt instruments (e.g., a revolver, institutional term loans, and bonds), the revolver will mature before the institutional term loans, which, in turn, will mature before the bonds.

### Coupon

Coupon refers to the annual interest rate ("pricing") paid on a debt obligation's principal amount outstanding. It can be based on either a floating rate (typical for bank debt) or a fixed rate (typical for bonds). Bank debt generally pays interest on a quarterly basis, while bonds pay interest on a semiannual basis. The bank debt coupon is typically based on a given benchmark rate, usually LIBOR[55] or the Base Rate, plus a spread based on the credit of the borrower.[56] A high yield bond coupon, however, is generally priced at issuance on the basis of a spread to a benchmark Treasury.

There are a number of factors that affect the coupon for a debt obligation, including the type of debt (and its investor class), ratings, security, seniority, maturity, covenants, and prevailing market conditions. In a traditional LBO financing structure, bank debt tends to be the lowest cost of capital debt instrument because it has a higher credit rating, first lien security, higher seniority, a shorter maturity, and more restrictive covenants than high yield bonds.

**EXHIBIT 4.22**  Structural Subordination

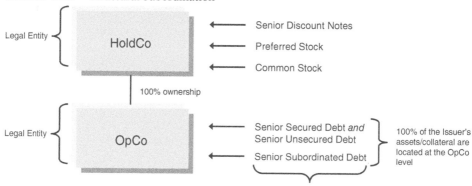

Debt obligations at the OpCo level are
**structurally senior** to obligations at the HoldCo level
(so long as the OpCo has not guaranteed any debt at the HoldCo level)

---

[54]High yield bonds may also have five-year maturities, particularly when they are senior secured notes issued in combination with a five-year credit facility.

[55]In 2021, LIBOR is expected to transition to SOFR (secured overnight financing rate), which is published by the Federal Reserve Bank of New York.

[56]During the low interest rate environment that began in 2008, floors were often instituted on the LIBOR rate charged by lenders to borrowers. Credit facilities that include a LIBOR floor pay a coupon of LIBOR plus an applicable spread as long as LIBOR is above the stated floor level. If the current LIBOR is below the floor, the coupon is the floor level plus an applicable spread. For example, a term loan B with a coupon of L+400 bps and a 1.5% LIBOR floor would have a coupon of 5.5% as long as LIBOR remained below 150 bps. If LIBOR rose to 200 bps, the term loan would have a coupon of 6%. Pro rata term loans and ABL facilities typically do not have LIBOR floors.

## Call Protection

Call protection refers to certain restrictions on voluntary prepayments (of loans) or redemptions (of bonds) during a defined time period within a given debt instrument's term. These restrictions may prohibit voluntary prepayments or redemptions outright or require payment of a substantial fee ("call premium") in connection with any voluntary prepayment or redemption. Call premiums protect debt investors from having debt with a high coupon refinanced long before maturity, thereby mitigating their reinvestment risk in the event market interest rates decline. For example, a bondholder holding an 8% bond does not want to be redeemed and forced to reinvest in the market when market interest rates for a comparable credit have declined to 7%.

Call protection periods are standard for high yield bonds. They are typically set at three years ("Non call-3" or "NC-3") for a seven- or eight-year fixed rate bond and five years ("NC-5") for a ten-year fixed rate bond. The redemption of bonds prior to maturity requires the issuer to pay a premium in accordance with a defined call schedule as set forth in an indenture, which dictates call prices for set dates.[57] A bond's call schedule and call prices depend on its term and coupon. Exhibit 4.23 displays a standard call schedule for: a) 8-year bond with an 8% coupon, and b) 10-year bond with a 8.5% coupon, both issued in 2019.[58] The redemption of bonds prior to the first call date requires the company to pay investors a sizable premium, either defined in the indenture ("make-whole provision") or made in accordance with some market standard (typically a tender at the greater of par or Treasury Rate (T) + 50 bps).

**EXHIBIT 4.23**  Call Schedules

| 8-year, 8% Notes due 2027, NC-3 | | | 10-year, 8.5% Notes due 2029, NC-5 | | |
|---|---|---|---|---|---|
| Year | Formula | Call Price | Year | Formula | Call Price |
| 2019 - 2021 | Non-callable | | 2019 - 2022 | Non-callable | |
| 2022 | Par plus 1/2 the coupon | $104.000 | 2023 | Non-callable | |
| 2023 | Par plus 1/4 the coupon | $102.000 | 2024 | Par plus 1/2 the coupon | $104.250 |
| 2024 and thereafter | Par | $100.000 | 2025 | Par plus 1/3 the coupon | $102.833 |
| - | - | - | 2026 | Par plus 1/6 the coupon | $101.417 |
| - | - | - | 2027 and thereafter | Par | $100.000 |

Traditional first lien bank debt has no call protection, meaning that the borrower can repay principal at any time without penalty. Other types of term loans, however, such as those secured by a second lien, may have call protection periods, although terms vary depending on the loan.[59]

---

[57]The tender premium calculation is based on the sum of the value of a bond's principal outstanding at the 1st call date (e.g., 104% of face value for an 8% coupon bond) plus the value of all interest payments to be received prior to the 1st call date from the present time, discounted at the Treasury Rate for an equivalent maturity plus 50 bps.

[58]High yield bonds also often feature an *equity clawback* provision, which allows the issuer to call a specified percentage of the outstanding bonds (typically 35%) with net proceeds from an equity offering at a price equal to par plus a premium equal to the coupon (e.g., 108% for a bond with an 8% coupon).

[59]For illustrative purposes, the call protection period for a 2nd lien term loan may be structured as NC-1. At the end of one year, the loan would typically be prepayable at a price of $102, stepping down to $101 after two years, and then par after three years.

## Covenants

Covenants are provisions in credit agreements and indentures intended to protect debt investors against the deterioration of the borrower/issuer's credit quality. They govern specific actions that may or may not be taken during the term of the debt obligation. Failure to comply with a covenant may trigger an event of default, which allows investors to accelerate the maturity of their debt unless amended or waived. There are three primary classifications of covenants: *affirmative*, *negative*, and *financial*.

While many of the covenants in credit agreements and indentures are similar in nature, a key difference is that traditional revolvers feature financial maintenance covenants[60] while high yield bonds have less restrictive incurrence covenants. As detailed in Exhibit 4.24, financial maintenance covenants require the borrower to "maintain" a certain credit profile at all times through compliance with certain financial ratios or tests on a quarterly basis. Financial maintenance covenants are also designed to limit the borrower's ability to take certain actions that may be adverse to lenders (e.g., making capital expenditures beyond a set amount), which allows the lender group to limit the financial risks taken by the borrower. Covenants are also designed to provide lenders with an early indication of financial distress.

**Secured Debt Covenants** Exhibit 4.24 displays typical covenants found in a credit agreement. With respect to financial maintenance covenants, a credit agreement is unlikely to contain more than one or two of these covenants. The required maintenance leverage ratios typically decrease ("step down") throughout the term of the loan. Similarly, the coverage ratios typically increase over time. This requires the borrower to improve its credit profile by repaying debt and/or growing cash flow in accordance with the financial projections it presents to lenders during syndication.

"*Covenant-lite*" loans are a leveraged loan market convention that has become increasingly prevalent as credit markets have boomed. As the name suggests, covenant-lite institutional term loans have covenant packages similar to those of high yield bonds, typically featuring incurrence covenants as opposed to quarterly financial maintenance covenants. In difficult credit markets, however, the covenant-lite feature is among the first to receive pushback from lenders.

**EXHIBIT 4.24** Secured Debt Covenants

| Affirmative Covenants | Require the borrower and its subsidiaries to perform certain actions. Examples of standard affirmative covenants include: |
|---|---|

- maintaining corporate existence and books and records
- regular financial reporting (e.g., supplying financial statements on a quarterly basis)
- maintaining assets, collateral, or other security
- maintaining insurance
- complying with laws
- paying taxes
- continuing in the same line of business

[60]Typically in the form of "springing" financial maintenance covenants that apply when the revolver is 35% to 40% drawn.

**EXHIBIT 4.24**   Secured Debt Covenants (*Continued*)

| | |
|---|---|
| **Negative Covenants** | Limit the borrower's and its subsidiaries' ability to take certain actions (often subject to certain exceptions or "baskets").[a] Examples of negative covenants include: |

- limitations on debt – limits the amount of debt that may be outstanding at any time
- limitations on dividends and stock redemptions – prevents cash from being distributed by the borrower to, or for the benefit of, equity holders
- limitations on liens – prevents pledge of assets as collateral
- limitations on dispositions of assets (including sales/leaseback transactions) – prevents the sale or transfer of assets in excess of an aggregate threshold
- limitations on investments – restricts the making of loans, acquisitions, and other investments (including joint ventures)
- limitations on mergers and consolidations – prohibits a merger or consolidation
- limitations on prepayments of, and amendments to, certain other debt – prohibits the prepayment of junior debt or any amendments thereto in a manner that would be adverse to lenders
- limitations on transactions with affiliates – restricts the borrower and its subsidiaries from undertaking transactions with affiliated companies that may benefit the affiliate to the detriment of the borrower and its creditors[b]

| | |
|---|---|
| **Financial Maintenance Covenants** | Require the borrower to maintain a certain credit profile through compliance with specified financial ratios or tests on a quarterly basis. Examples of financial maintenance covenants include: |

- maximum senior secured leverage ratio – prohibits the ratio of senior secured debt-to-EBITDA for the trailing four quarters from exceeding a level set forth in a defined quarterly schedule
- maximum total leverage ratio – prohibits the ratio of total debt-to-EBITDA for the trailing four quarters from exceeding a level set in a defined quarterly schedule
- minimum interest coverage ratio – prohibits the ratio of EBITDA-to-interest expense for the trailing four quarters from falling below a set level as defined in a quarterly schedule
- minimum fixed charge coverage ratio[c] – prohibits the ratio of a measure of cash flow-to-fixed charges from falling below a set level (which may be fixed for the term of the bank debt or adjusted quarterly)
- maximum annual capital expenditures – prohibits the borrower and its subsidiaries from exceeding a set dollar amount of capital expenditures in any given year
- minimum EBITDA – requires the borrower to maintain a minimum dollar amount of EBITDA for the trailing four quarters as set forth in a defined quarterly schedule

---

[a] Baskets ("carve-outs") provide exceptions to covenants that permit the borrower/issuer to take specific actions (e.g., incur specific types and amounts of debt, make certain restricted payments, and sell assets up to a specified amount).

[b] Affiliate transactions must be conducted on an "arm's-length" basis (i.e., terms no less favorable than if the counterparty was unrelated).

[c] A fixed charge coverage ratio measures a borrower/issuer's ability to cover its fixed obligations, including debt interest and lease obligations. Although the definition may vary by credit agreement or indenture, fixed charges typically include interest expense, preferred stock dividends, and certain capital lease expenses (such as rent). The definition may be structured to include or exclude non-cash and capitalized interest.

**High Yield Bond Covenants**   Many of the covenants found in a high yield bond indenture are similar to those found in a secured debt credit agreement (see Exhibit 4.25). High yield bonds, however, only have incurrence covenants (versus maintenance covenants). Incurrence covenants prevent the issuer from taking specific actions (e.g., incurring additional debt, making certain investments, paying dividends) only in the event it is not in pro forma compliance with a "Ratio Test", or does not have certain "baskets" available to it at the time such action is taken. The Ratio Test is often a coverage test (e.g., a fixed charge coverage ratio, typically set at a minimum of 2x), although it may also be structured as a leverage test (e.g., total debt-to-EBITDA), as is common for telecommunications/media companies.

**EXHIBIT 4.25**   High Yield Bond Covenants

| High Yield Covenants | Principal covenants found in high yield bond indentures include: |
|---|---|

- limitations on additional debt – cannot incur additional debt unless it is in pro forma compliance with the Ratio Test or otherwise permitted by a defined "basket"
- limitations on restricted payments – prohibits certain payments such as dividends, equity repurchases, investments in non-subsidiaries, and prepayments of junior debt except for a defined "basket" (subject to certain exceptions)[a]
- limitations on liens – prohibits granting liens on pari passu or junior debt without providing an equal and ratable lien in favor of the senior notes, subject to certain exceptions and/or compliance with a specified "senior secured leverage ratio"
    - generally, senior subordinated notes allow unlimited liens on senior debt otherwise permitted to be incurred
- limitations on asset sales – requires receipt of FMV, 75% cash consideration, and the use of net proceeds to reinvest in the business or reduce senior indebtedness within a prescribed time period (subject to certain exceptions). If such net proceeds are not applied in that time period, the issuer is required to offer to use the remaining net proceeds to repurchase the notes at 100% of par.
- limitations on transactions with affiliates – see credit agreement definition
- limitations on mergers, consolidations, or sale of substantially all assets – prohibits a merger, consolidation, or sale of substantially all assets unless the surviving entity assumes the debt of the issuer and can incur $1.00 of additional debt under the Ratio Test (or the ratio improves)
- limitation on layering (specific to indentures for senior subordinated notes) – prevents issuing additional subordinated debt ("layering") which is contractually junior to the other debt, and contractually senior to the existing issue
- change of control put – provides bondholders with the right to require the issuer to repurchase the notes at a premium of 101% of par in the event of a change in majority ownership of the company or sale of substantially all of the assets of the borrower and its subsidiaries

---

[a] The restricted payments basket is typically calculated as a small set dollar amount ("starting basket") plus 50% of cumulative consolidated net income of the issuer since issuance of the bonds, plus the amount of new equity issuances by the issuer since issuance of the bonds, plus cash from the sale of unrestricted subsidiaries (i.e., those that do not guarantee the debt).

## Term Sheets

The key terms for the debt securities comprising an LBO financing structure are typically summarized in a one-page format, such as that shown in Exhibit 4.26 (secured debt) and Exhibit 4.28 (high yield bonds). Exhibits 4.27 and 4.29 provide explanations for the term sheet items.

**EXHIBIT 4.26**  Secured Debt Term Sheet

| Summary of Terms – Revolving Credit Facility and Term Loan | |
|---|---|
| Borrower | ValueCo Corporation (the "Borrower") |
| Facilities | Revolving Credit Facility (the "Revolver")<br>Term Loan B (the "Loan" and together, the "Credit Facilities") |
| Amount | Revolver: $250 million<br>Loan: $2,800 million |
| Maturity | Revolver: 5 years<br>Loan: 7 years |
| Coupon | Revolver: L+425 bps area, with two 25 bps step-downs based on prespecified leverage targets<br>Loan: L+450 bps area |
| OID[a] | 99.0% |
| LIBOR Floor | 1.00 % |
| Assumed Ratings | B1 / B+ |
| Security | Secured by first priority security interest in all assets of the Borrower and each of Borrower's direct and indirect domestic subsidiaries, including a pledge of 100% of stock of domestic subsidiaries and 65% of foreign subsidiaries |
| Ranking | The Credit Facilities will be a senior obligation of the Borrower and will rank *pari passu* in right of payment with any existing and future senior indebtedness of the Borrower, and senior to all existing and future subordinated indebtedness of the Borrower |
| Guarantees | All of the Borrower's direct and indirect domestic subsidiaries, whether currently existing or subsequently formed or acquired |
| Amortization | Revolver: None<br>Loan: 1% per annum, with bullet at maturity |
| Underwriting Fee | Revolver: [__]% of the committed amount, payable at closing<br>Loan: [__]% of the funded amount, payable at closing |
| Commitment Fee | Revolver: 50 bps per annum on the undrawn portion<br>Loan: None |
| Mandatory Repayments | 100% of asset sales, 100% of debt issuance, 50% of equity issuance, and 50% of excess cash flow, stepping down based on a leverage-based grid |
| Optional Repayments | Prepayable at any time without premium or penalty |
| Affirmative Covenants | Including but not limited to delivery of certified quarterly and audited annual financial statements, monthly management reports, reports to shareholders, notices of defaults, litigation, and other material events |
| Negative Covenants | Normal and customary for similar transactions of this nature, including, but not limited to, limitations on asset sales, acquisitions, indebtedness, capital expenditures, liens, and restricted payments |
| Financial Covenants | Maximum total leverage; minimum interest coverage; maximum capital expenditures |
| Events of Default | Including but not limited to nonpayment, breach of representations and covenants, cross-defaults, loss of lien on collateral, invalidity of guarantees, bankruptcy and insolvency events, judgments, and change of ownership or control |

[a]Original Issue Discount (in the event of a TLB, often paid as an upfront fee).

**EXHIBIT 4.27**   Explanation of Secured Debt Term Sheet

| Summary of Terms – Revolving Credit Facility and Term Loan | |
|---|---|
| Borrower | Entity that is borrowing the funds |
| Facilities | Type of debt instruments |
| Amount | Principal amount of the facilities |
| Maturity | Timeframe in which the borrower must repay the unamortized principal |
| Coupon | Annual payment percentage on principal, expressed as a spread over LIBOR |
| OID | Common convention where the TL is issued at a small discount (i.e., 99 cents on the dollar) to enhance investor returns beyond the coupon |
| LIBOR Floor | Minimum LIBOR rate paid by the borrower on the facilities, regardless of the current LIBOR |
| Assumed Ratings | Assumption regarding the debt instrument's credit ratings to be assigned by Moody's and Standard & Poor's |
| Security | Assets that become subject to seizure in default or foreclosure. These assets are registered, documented, and ranked |
| Ranking | Order in which the facilities are repaid in the event of default relative to the borrower's other debt instruments |
| Guarantees | Listing of other entities within the borrower's corporate structure that agree to satisfy its debt obligations |
| Amortization | Amount of principal owed above and beyond the recurring interest payments |
| Underwriting Fee | Amount paid at closing of the facility, based on the committed / funded amount |
| Commitment Fee | Amount owed on the unborrowed amount of the revolver, which is paid for making the commitment available to the borrower |
| Mandatory Repayments | Obligations of the borrower to repay principal with cash raised from asset sales, debt or equity issuance, or excess cash flow generation |
| Optional Repayments | Provisions regarding premiums to be paid by the borrower in the event it decides to repay all or a portion of the facilities prior to maturity |
| Affirmative Covenants | Things the borrower promises to do |
| Negative Covenants | Things the borrower promises not to do |
| Financial Covenants | Financial performance metrics the borrower must maintain, tested quarterly |
| Events of Default | Conditions under which the lender can demand immediate repayment of the facility |

**EXHIBIT 4.28** High Yield Bond Term Sheet

| Summary of Terms – Senior Notes | |
|---|---|
| Issuer | ValueCo Corporation (the "Issuer") |
| Issue | Senior Notes (the "Notes") |
| Amount | $850 million |
| Maturity | 8 years |
| Coupon | 8% area |
| Assumed Ratings | B3 / B- |
| Security | None; unsecured |
| Ranking | The Notes will be a senior obligation of the Issuer and will rank pari passu in right of payment with any existing and future senior indebtedness of the Issuer, and senior to all existing and future subordinated indebtedness of the Issuer |
| Guarantees | All of the Issuer's direct and indirect domestic subsidiaries, whether currently existing or subsequently formed or acquired |
| Optional Redemption | The Notes may be redeemed at the Issuer's option beginning 3 years from closing at a price of par plus premium, declining to par at the end of year 5 |
| Equity Clawback | Within 3 years of the offering, the Issuer may repurchase up to 35% of the original principal amount of the Notes at a premium with the proceeds of an equity offering |
| Covenants | Standard incurrence-based high yield covenants, including limitations on: (i) debt incurrence; (ii) restricted payments; (iii) transactions with affiliates; (iv) asset sales; (v) subsidiary dividends; (vi) liens; and (vii) consolidations, mergers and asset sales |
| Change of Control | Upon a change of control, the Issuer will offer to repurchase the Notes at 101% of par |

**EXHIBIT 4.29** Explanation of High Yield Bond Term Sheet

| Summary of Terms – Senior Notes | |
|---|---|
| Issuer | Same as "Borrower" |
| Issue | Type of debt offering |
| Amount | Same as secured debt |
| Maturity | Same as secured debt |
| Coupon | Same as secured debt, except it is payable semi-annually and is typically a fixed rate |
| Assumed Ratings | Same as secured debt |
| Security | Same as secured debt, although most high yield bonds are unsecured and do not have any security |
| Ranking | "Ranking" is specific to "payment subordination", which only occurs in "subordinated" debt when that debt agrees in a contract to be junior "in right of payment" to other debt or "structural subordination", which occurs when some debt is borrowed or guaranteed by a subsidiary (and thus has a direct claim to that subsidiary's assets), and other debt only has a claim at a parent company. "Ranking" does not relate to "effective subordination", which occurs when some debt is secured by a lien and other debt is unsecured. |
| Guarantees | Same as loan, although many loans have guarantees from the borrower's parent company (to support the parent's pledge of the borrower's stock) without a corresponding guarantee of the high yield bonds. |
| Optional Redemption | The redemption of high yield bonds prior to maturity requires the issuer to pay a premium in accordance with a defined call schedule as set forth in an indenture, which dictates call prices for set dates. Typically, that provides for a "make whole" premium initially, with a descending premium thereafter (and par for the last 2-3 years of the bond). |
| Equity Clawback | Redemption provision that permits the issuer to repay up to 35% (sometimes 40%) of the bond's principal with the proceeds from an IPO or other equity offering within a set time period. The prepayment penalty is typically set at par plus the coupon (e.g., 8%). |
| Covenants | Prevents the issuer from taking specific actions; in almost every case, the covenants are subject to numerous exceptions |
| Change of Control | Requires the issuer to make an offer to repurchase the bonds at 101% of principal amount (plus accrued and unpaid interest) in the event of a change in ownership of the company |

## LBO FINANCING: DETERMINING FINANCING STRUCTURE

As with valuation, determining the appropriate LBO financing structure involves a mix of art and science. This structuring exercise centers on fundamental company-specific cash flow, returns, and credit statistics analysis, as well as market conditions and precedent LBO deals. The fundamental analysis is akin to the DCF approach to intrinsic valuation, while market conditions and precedent LBO deals are similar to comparable companies and precedent transactions.

The ultimate LBO financing structure must balance the needs of the financial sponsor, debt investors, the company, and management, which are not necessarily aligned. For example, the sponsor often seeks to maximize leverage so as to generate the highest IRR. Lenders and bondholders, on the other hand, have an interest in limiting leverage as well as introducing covenants and other provisions to protect their principal. The company's best interests often reside with more moderate leverage from both a risk management and growth perspective. Meanwhile, depending on the situation, management is often both a meaningful shareholder aligned with the sponsor in the pursuit of maximum IRRs, as well as a caretaker of the company focused on mitigating risk and preserving flexibility.

Structuring an LBO is predicated on analyzing the target's cash flows and credit statistics, including leverage and coverage ratios as discussed in Chapter 1. This analysis centers on crafting a financing structure that allows for high leverage while maintaining sufficient cushion and room to maneuver in a downside scenario. Target credit statistics vary substantially depending on sector, market conditions, and the company's individual credit profile (including size, market position, and profitability).

The target's sector plays a key role in determining the appropriate LBO structure, as reflected in total leverage, term loan/high yield bond mix, and terms of the debt. Sector is directly relevant to the target's credit profile and ability to sustain an aggressive capital structure. For example, as shown in Exhibit 4.30, for highly cyclical industries, both the capital markets and rating agencies take a more conservative view toward leverage to help ensure the company is appropriately capitalized to withstand cycle troughs. On the other end of the spectrum, companies in sectors that have highly visible cash flows (especially those with subscription-based business models) are typically able to maintain a more highly leveraged capital structure. Of course, sector is only one aspect of the target's credit story. Within a given sector, there are multiple company-specific factors that can dramatically differentiate the risk profile of one company from another.

As with comparable companies and precedent transactions for valuation multiples, prevailing market conditions and precedent LBO financings play a critical role in determining leverage multiples and key financing terms. Recent LBO transactions are closely analyzed to help determine what the market will bear in terms of financing structures for new deals. Recent LBOs in the target's sector are most relevant as well as deals of similar size and rating, as shown in Exhibit 4.31.

**EXHIBIT 4.30** Illustrative Sector Leverage Dynamics

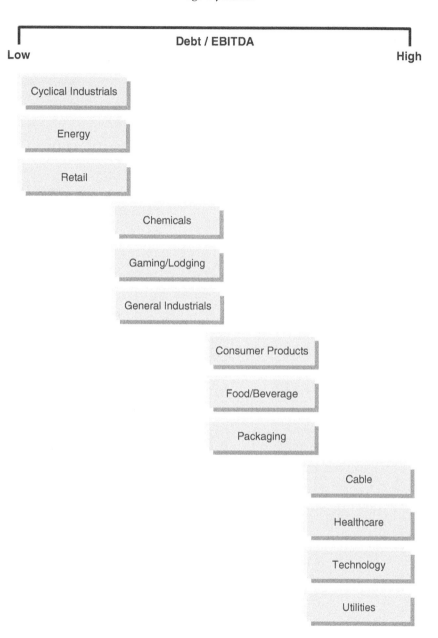

**EXHIBIT 4.31**  Recent LBO Transactions > $1 Billion Purchase Price

## ValueCo Corporation
### Recent LBO Transactions > $1 Billion Purchase Price
($ in millions)

| Launch / Pricing | Borrower / Issuer | Size | Coupon Description | Tenor | LIBOR Floor | OID | Yield | Ratings Moody's | Ratings S&P | Purchase Price | Leverage Sec. | Leverage Total | Percentage Equity | Sector | Sponsor |
|---|---|---|---|---|---|---|---|---|---|---|---|---|---|---|---|
| 11/20/2018 | JJ City | $100 | L+400 Revolver | 5.0 years | - | - | - | B2 | B- | $1,981 | 6.4x | 6.4x | 47% | Technology | Damodaran Investment Partners |
| | | $760 | L+400 1st Lien Term Loan (Cov Lite) | 7.0 years | - | $99.500 | 6.775% | B2 | B- | | | | | | |
| | | $290 | L+775 2nd Lien Term Loan (Cov Lite) | 8.0 years | - | $99.000 | 10.650% | Caa2 | CCC | | | | | | |
| | *Owns, operates, and franchises specialty goods stores in the United States and Puerto Rico* | | | | | | | | | | | | | | |
| 9/18/2018 | Jonathan Industries | $750 | L+375 Revolver | 5.0 years | - | | - | B2 | B | $20,149 | 4.5x | 5.3x | 33% | Business Services | Domanski Capital |
| | | $9,250 | L+375 Term Loan B (Cov Lite) | 7.0 years | - | $99.750 | 6.163% | B2 | B | | | | | | |
| | | $2,250 | 6.250% Senior Secured Notes | 8.0 years | - | $100.000 | 6.250% | B3 | B- | | | | | | |
| | | $2,000 | 8.250% Senior Notes | 10.0 years | - | $100.000 | 8.250% | Caa2 | CCC | | | | | | |
| | *Provides financial market content services including estimates and research* | | | | | | | | | | | | | | |
| 6/28/2018 | Total Management | $400 | L+425 Revolver | 5.0 years | - | | - | B2 | B | $8,368 | 4.8x | 6.8x | 28% | Software | Julis Capital Partners |
| | | $4,250 | L+425 Term Loan B (Cov Lite) | 7.0 years | - | $99.000 | 6.860% | B2 | B | | | | | | |
| | | $1,775 | 9.750% Senior Notes | 8.0 years | - | $100.000 | 9.750% | Caa2 | CCC+ | | | | | | |
| | *Systems software provider that enables enterprise customers to manage information technology across multiple platforms* | | | | | | | | | | | | | | |
| 5/17/2018 | Allan Foods | $150 | L+300 Revolver | 5.0 years | - | | - | B2 | B | $2,492 | 5.1x | 6.6x | 40% | Food & Beverage | Nancy Equity Partners |
| | | $1,145 | L+300 Term Loan B (Cov Lite) | 7.0 years | - | $99.750 | 5.413% | B2 | B | | | | | | |
| | | $350 | 8.500% Senior Notes | 8.0 years | - | $100.000 | 8.500% | Caa2 | CCC+ | | | | | | |
| | *Produces nutrition bars, cereal, cookies, snacks, and other baked goods* | | | | | | | | | | | | | | |
| 5/4/2018 | Olivia Inc. | $250 | L+450 Revolver | 5.0 years | - | | - | Baa3 | B- | $1,107 | 2.1x | 3.5x | 30% | Consumer | The Hochberg Group |
| | | $475 | L+450 Term Loan B (Cov Lite) | 7.0 years | - | $98.000 | 7.300% | Baa3 | B- | | | | | | |
| | | $300 | 8.750% Senior Notes | 8.0 years | - | $87.000 | 11.499% | Caa1 | CCC+ | | | | | | |
| | *Designer, manufacturer, and distributor of greeting cards, as well as gift packaging, party goods, and stationery products* | | | | | | | | | | | | | | |
| 4/19/2018 | Alex Dental | $135 | L+375 Revolver | 5.0 years | - | | - | B2 | B- | $2,650 | 4.9x | 6.5x | 50% | Healthcare | J Harris & Company |
| | | $1,000 | L+375 Term Loan B (Cov Lite) | 7.0 years | - | $99.500 | 6.225% | B2 | B- | | | | | | |
| | | $325 | 8.500% Senior Notes | 8.0 years | - | $100.000 | 8.500% | Caa2 | CCC | | | | | | |
| | *Provides non-clinical administrative support services to dental practices across the U.S.* | | | | | | | | | | | | | | |
| 10/3/2017 | Chuckles International | $350 | L+400 Revolver | 5.0 years | - | | - | Baa3 | B+ | $4,933 | 3.4x | 4.9x | 25% | Telecom | Eu-Han Capital |
| | | $2,550 | L+400 Term Loan B (Cov Lite) | 7.0 years | - | $99.000 | 5.600% | Baa3 | B+ | | | | | | |
| | | $1,150 | 8.500% Senior Notes | 8.0 years | - | $98.580 | 8.855% | B3 | CCC+ | | | | | | |
| | *Provider of communication and network infrastructure services* | | | | | | | | | | | | | | |
| 9/19/2017 | MashaCor | $200 | L+300 Revolver | 5.0 years | - | | - | B1 | B | $1,958 | 4.4x | 5.9x | 40% | Industrial Services | LS Capital |
| | | $875 | L+300 Term Loan B (Cov Lite) | 7.0 years | - | $100.000 | 4.350% | B1 | B | | | | | | |
| | | $300 | 6.000% Senior Notes | 8.0 years | - | $100.000 | 6.000% | Caa1 | CCC+ | | | | | | |
| | *Provides non-hazardous waste collection, disposal, and recycling services to commercial, industrial, and residential customers* | | | | | | | | | | | | | | |
| 7/21/2017 | Ronie Industries | $500 | L+150 ABL Revolver | 5.0 years | - | | - | B2 | B+ | $2,615 | 4.8x | 7.0x | 40% | Building Products | D&R Ltd |
| | | $1,075 | L+300 Term Loan B (Cov Lite) | 7.0 years | 1.00% | $99.750 | 4.363% | B2 | B+ | | | | | | |
| | | $500 | 6.125% Senior Notes | 8.0 years | - | $100.000 | 6.125% | Caa1 | B- | | | | | | |
| | *Distributor of construction products used to build underground water and drainage infrastructure* | | | | | | | | | | | | | | |
| 6/20/2017 | Margo Corrections | $150 | L+450 Revolver | 5.0 years | - | | - | B2 | B | $1,643 | 4.6x | 6.0x | 30% | Business Services | Meisner Global Management |
| | | $875 | L+450 1st Lien Term Loan (Cov Lite) | 7.0 years | 1.00% | $99.500 | 5.925% | B2 | B | | | | | | |
| | | $275 | L+825 2nd Lien Term Loan (Cov Lite) | 8.0 years | 1.00% | $99.000 | 9.800% | Caa2 | CCC+ | | | | | | |
| | *Provider of inmate communication and investigative technologies to the U.S. corrections industry* | | | | | | | | | | | | | | |

| | | | | | | | | | | Purchase Price | Sec. | Total | Equity |
|---|---|---|---|---|---|---|---|---|---|---|---|---|---|
| **Mean** | | | | | | | | | | **$4,790** | **4.5x** | **5.9x** | **36%** |
| **Median** | | | | | | | | | | **$2,553** | **4.7x** | **6.2x** | **36%** |
| **High** | | | | | | | | | | **$20,149** | **6.4x** | **7.0x** | **50%** |
| **Low** | | | | | | | | | | **$1,107** | **2.1x** | **3.5x** | **25%** |

*Source: Company filings*

The market conditions for term loans and high yield bonds are closely monitored throughout the LBO process, especially as the commitment letters are finalized and the ultimate financing structure is determined. The leveraged finance markets can be volatile with "market-clearing" terms often changing quickly, potentially rendering recent precedents meaningless. As shown in Exhibits 4.32 to 4.35 regarding historical issuance volumes and pricing, there are clear market windows where issuers have been able to take advantage of strong market conditions interspersed with more challenging periods. While the credit markets have generally been strong in the decade following the Great Recession, volatility has also been high depending on the month, quarter, or year.

As the banks shape their LBO financing structure views, they look closely at how existing deals are faring in the market as well as new issue volumes, trading levels by ratings categories, and trading levels for comparable debt securities. Once the initial financing structure is determined, it is run through the LBO model and sensitized to analyze IRRs and pro forma credit metrics, as discussed in Chapter 5. Adjustments are then made to fine-tune as appropriate.

**EXHIBIT 4.32** Leveraged Loan New Issue Volume 2009 – 2018

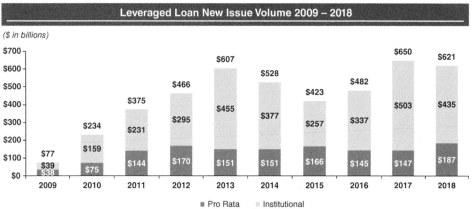

*Source: Standard & Poor's Leveraged Commentary & Data Group*

**EXHIBIT 4.33** High Yield New Issue Volume 2009 – 2018

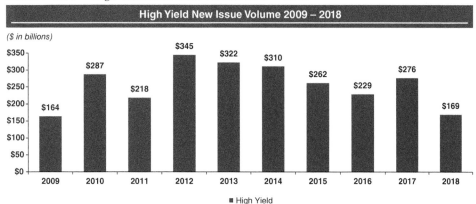

*Source: Standard & Poor's Leveraged Commentary & Data Group*

**EXHIBIT 4.34**   Leveraged Loan Spreads by Ratings Category 2009 – 2018

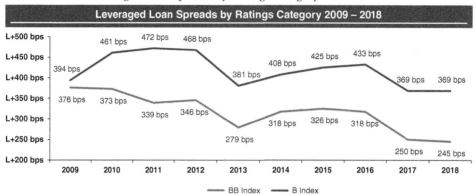

Source: *LevFin Insights and Standard & Poor's Leveraged Commentary & Data Group*

**EXHIBIT 4.35**   High Yield Index by Ratings Index 2009 – 2018

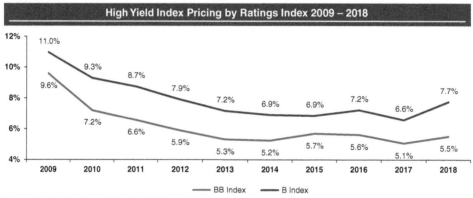

Source: *LevFin Insights and Standard & Poor's Leveraged Commentary & Data Group*

## CHAPTER 4 QUESTIONS

1) Which of the following are limited partners that provide financial sponsors with investment capital?

   I. Pension funds
   II. Insurance companies
   III. University endowments
   IV. Wealthy families

   A. I and II
   B. I and III
   C. I, III, and IV
   D. I, II, III, and IV

2) Which of the following is NOT part of an investment bank's financing commitment?

   A. Commitment letter
   B. Institutional letter
   C. Engagement letter
   D. Fee letter

3) Which of the following would be potential LBO candidates?

   I. Troubled companies
   II. Companies in fragmented markets
   III. Solid performing companies
   IV. Non-core subsidiaries

   A. III and IV
   B. I, II, and III
   C. II, III, and IV
   D. I, II, III, and IV

4) The ability to maximize leverage in an LBO transaction is facilitated for a company with which of the following characteristics?

   A. Track record for bolt-on acquisitions
   B. Tight covenant package
   C. Strong asset base
   D. Large debt balance

5) Which of the following are common exit strategies when financial sponsors monetize their investments?

  I. Refinancing
  II. IPO
  III. Sale to a strategic buyer
  IV. Sale to another sponsor

  A. II and IV
  B. I, II, and III
  C. I, III, and IV
  D. II, III, and IV

6) What percent of a sponsor's existing equity ownership in the target is kept following a dividend recapitalization?

  A. 50%
  B. 80%
  C. 90%
  D. 100%

7) ABL facilities are generally secured by

  A. Current assets
  B. Current liabilities
  C. Long-term debt
  D. Pension assets

8) On average, what percentage of an LBO financing is funded by the sponsor's equity contribution?

  A. 10%
  B. 35%
  C. 70%
  D. 90%

9) Call protection mitigates which type of risk for debt investors when interest rates are declining?

  A. Credit risk
  B. Operational risk
  C. Reinvestment risk
  D. Extension risk

10) Which of the following is NOT a covenant classification?

    A. Financial
    B. Limitation
    C. Negative
    D. Affirmative

11) Financial maintenance covenants are typical for _____, while _____ typically have incurrence covenants.

    A. Public companies; private companies
    B. Private companies; public companies
    C. High yield bonds; bank debt
    D. Bank debt; high yield bonds

12) Which one of the following is NOT a financial maintenance covenant?

    A. Maximum total leverage
    B. Maximum senior secured leverage
    C. Minimum dividend payments
    D. Minimum interest coverage

13) Which of the following would NOT be classified as a qualified institutional buyer?

    A. Retail investor with under $25 million in net worth
    B. Equity asset manager with $200 million under management
    C. Insurance company with $500 million in investments
    D. Mutual funds with $10,000 million under management

14) With financial maintenance covenants, leverage ratios typically _____ throughout the life of the loan, while coverage ratios typically _____.

    A. Stay constant; increase
    B. Stay constant; decrease
    C. Decrease; increase
    D. Increase; decrease

15) What is the current yield of a $1,000 bond (face value) with a coupon of 6.0% that is trading at par?

    A. 3.0%
    B. 6.0%
    C. 6.3%
    D. 6.5%

# LBO Analysis

L BO analysis is the core analytical tool used to assess financing structure, investment returns, and valuation in leveraged buyout scenarios. The same techniques can also be used to assess refinancing opportunities and restructuring alternatives for corporate issuers. LBO analysis is a more complex methodology than those previously discussed in this book as it requires specialized knowledge of financial modeling, leveraged debt capital markets, M&A, and accounting. At the center of LBO analysis is a financial model ("LBO model"), which is constructed with the flexibility to analyze a given target's performance under multiple financing structures and operating scenarios.

## Financing Structure

On the debt financing side, the banker uses LBO analysis to help craft a viable financing structure for the target, which encompasses the amount and type of debt (including key terms outlined in Chapter 4) as well as an equity contribution from a financial sponsor. The model output enables the banker to analyze a given financing structure on the basis of cash flow generation, debt repayment, credit statistics, and investment returns over a projection period.

The LBO financing structure analysis is typically spearheaded by an investment bank's leveraged finance and capital market teams (along with a sector coverage team, collectively the "deal team"). The goal is to present a financial sponsor with tailored financing options that maximize returns while remaining marketable to investors. The financing structure must also provide the target with sufficient flexibility and cushion to run its business according to plan.

As discussed in Chapter 4, sponsors typically work closely with financing providers (e.g., investment banks) to determine the financing structure for a particular transaction. Once the sponsor chooses the preferred financing structure (often a compilation of the best terms from proposals solicited from several banks), the deal team presents it to the bank's internal committee(s) for approval. Following committee approval, the investment banks provide a financing commitment, which is then submitted to the seller and its advisor(s) as part of its final bid package (see Chapter 6).

## Valuation

LBO analysis is also an essential component of the M&A toolset. It is used by sponsors, bankers, and other finance professionals to determine an implied valuation range for a given target in a potential LBO sale based on achieving acceptable returns. The valuation output is premised on key variables such as financial projections, purchase price, and financing structure, as well as exit multiple and year. Therefore, sensitivity analysis is performed on these key value drivers to produce a range of IRRs used to frame valuation for the target (see Exhibits 5.42 and 5.43). As discussed in Chapter 4, sponsors typically target 15% to 20% IRRs to assess acquisition opportunities and determine valuation accordingly.

In an M&A sell-side advisory context, the banker conducts LBO analysis to assess valuation from the perspective of a financial sponsor. This provides the ability to set sale price expectations for the seller and guide negotiations with prospective buyers accordingly. Similarly, on buy-side engagements, the banker typically performs LBO analysis to help determine a purchase price range. For a strategic buyer, this analysis (along with those derived from other valuation methodologies) is used to frame valuation and bidding strategy by analyzing the price that a competing sponsor bidder might be willing to pay for the target.

The goal of this chapter is to provide a sound introduction to LBO analysis and its broad applications. While there are multiple approaches to performing this analysis (especially with regard to constructing the LBO model), we have designed the steps in Exhibit 5.1 to be as user-friendly as possible. We also perform an illustrative LBO analysis using ValueCo as our LBO target.

**EXHIBIT 5.1**   LBO Analysis Steps

| |
|---|
| **Step I.   Locate and Analyze the Necessary Information** |
| **Step II.   Build the Pre-LBO Model** |
|     a. Build Historical and Projected Income Statement through EBIT |
|     b. Input Opening Balance Sheet and Project Balance Sheet Items |
|     c. Build Cash Flow Statement through Investing Activities |
| **Step III.   Input Transaction Structure** |
|     a. Enter Purchase Price Assumptions |
|     b. Enter Financing Structure into Sources and Uses |
|     c. Link Sources and Uses to Balance Sheet Adjustments Columns |
| **Step IV.   Complete the Post-LBO Model** |
|     a. Build Debt Schedule |
|     b. Complete Pro Forma Income Statement from EBIT to Net Income |
|     c. Complete Pro Forma Balance Sheet |
|     d. Complete Pro Forma Cash Flow Statement |
| **Step V.   Perform the LBO Analysis** |
|     a. Analyze Financing Structure |
|     b. Perform Returns Analysis |
|     c. Determine Valuation |
|     d. Create Transaction Summary Page |

# EXHIBIT 5.2 LBO Model Transaction Summary Page

## ValueCo Corporation
### Leveraged Buyout Analysis
($ in millions, fiscal year ending December 31)

### Transaction Summary

#### Sources of Funds

| | Amount | % of Total Sources | Multiple of EBITDA 9/30/2019 | Cumulative | Pricing |
|---|---|---|---|---|---|
| Revolving Credit Facility | - | -% | -x | -x | L+425 bps |
| Term Loan A | - | -% | -x | -x | NA |
| Term Loan B | 2,800.0 | 46.7% | 4.0x | 4.0x | L+425 bps |
| Term Loan C | - | -% | -x | 4.0x | NA |
| 2nd Lien | - | -% | -x | 4.0x | NA |
| Senior Notes | 850.0 | 14.2% | 1.2x | 5.2x | 8.000% |
| Senior Subordinated Notes | - | -% | -x | 5.2x | NA |
| Equity Contribution | 2,100.0 | 35.0% | 3.0x | 8.2x | |
| Rollover Equity | - | -% | -x | 8.2x | |
| Cash on Hand | 250.0 | 4.2% | 0.4x | 8.6x | |
| **Total Sources** | **$6,000.0** | **100.0%** | **8.6x** | | |

#### Uses of Funds

| | Amount | % of Total Uses |
|---|---|---|
| Purchase ValueCo Equity | $4,350.0 | 72.5% |
| Repay Existing Debt | 1,500.0 | 25.0% |
| Tender / Call Premiums | 20.0 | 0.3% |
| Financing Fees | 100.0 | 1.7% |
| Other Fees and Expenses | 30.0 | 0.5% |
| **Total Uses** | **$6,000.0** | **100.0%** |

#### Purchase Price

| | | |
|---|---|---|
| Offer Price per Share | | NA |
| Fully Diluted Shares | | NA |
| **Equity Purchase Price** | | **$4,350.0** |
| Plus: Existing Net Debt | | 1,250.0 |
| **Enterprise Value** | | **$5,600.0** |

#### Transaction Multiples

| | | | |
|---|---|---|---|
| Enterprise Value / Sales | LTM 9/30/2019 | $3,385.0 | 1.7x |
| | 2019E | $3,450.0 | 1.6x |
| Enterprise Value / EBITDA | LTM 9/30/2019 | $700.0 | 8.0x |
| | 2019E | 725.0 | 7.7x |

#### Return Analysis

| | | 2024 |
|---|---|---|
| Exit Year | | 8.0x |
| Entry Multiple | | 8.0x |
| Exit Multiple | $4,350.0 | 21% |
| IRR | 1,250.0 | |
| Cash Return | $5,600.0 | 2.6x |

**Options**

| | |
|---|---|
| **Financing Structure** | 1 |
| Operating Scenario | 1 |
| Cash Flow Sweep | 1 |
| Cash Balance | 1 |
| Average Interest | 1 |
| Financing Fees | 1 |

### Summary Financial Data

| | Historical Period | | | LTM | | Projection Period | | | | | | | | | |
|---|---|---|---|---|---|---|---|---|---|---|---|---|---|---|---|
| | 2016 | 2017 | 2018 | 9/30/2019 | Pro forma 2019 | Year 1 2020 | Year 2 2021 | Year 3 2022 | Year 4 2023 | Year 5 2024 | Year 6 2025 | Year 7 2026 | Year 8 2027 | Year 9 2028 | Year 10 2029 |
| **Sales** | $2,600.0 | $2,900.0 | $3,200.0 | $3,385.0 | $3,450.0 | $3,708.8 | $3,931.3 | $4,127.8 | $4,293.0 | $4,421.7 | $4,554.4 | $4,691.0 | $4,831.8 | $4,976.7 | $5,126.0 |
| % growth | NA | 11.5% | 10.3% | NA | 7.8% | 7.5% | 6.0% | 5.0% | 4.0% | 3.0% | 3.0% | 3.0% | 3.0% | 3.0% | 3.0% |
| **Gross Profit** | $988.0 | $1,131.0 | $1,280.0 | $1,350.0 | $1,380.0 | $1,483.5 | $1,572.5 | $1,651.1 | $1,717.2 | $1,768.7 | $1,821.8 | $1,876.4 | $1,932.7 | $1,990.7 | $2,050.4 |
| % margin | 38.0% | 39.0% | 40.0% | 39.9% | 40.0% | 40.0% | 40.0% | 40.0% | 40.0% | 40.0% | 40.0% | 40.0% | 40.0% | 40.0% | 40.0% |
| **EBITDA** | $491.4 | $580.0 | $672.0 | $700.0 | $725.0 | $779.4 | $826.1 | $867.4 | $902.1 | $929.2 | $957.1 | $985.8 | $1,015.4 | $1,045.8 | $1,077.2 |
| % margin | 18.9% | 20.0% | 21.0% | 20.7% | 21.0% | 21.0% | 21.0% | 21.0% | 21.0% | 21.0% | 21.0% | 21.0% | 21.0% | 21.0% | 21.0% |
| Capital Expenditures | 139.5 | 128.3 | 144.0 | 152.3 | 157.5 | 166.9 | 176.9 | 185.8 | 193.2 | 199.0 | 204.9 | 211.1 | 217.4 | 224.0 | 230.7 |
| % sales | 5.4% | 4.4% | 4.5% | 4.5% | 4.6% | 4.5% | 4.5% | 4.5% | 4.5% | 4.5% | 4.5% | 4.5% | 4.5% | 4.5% | 4.5% |
| Cash Interest Expense | | | | | 236.0 | 228.3 | 210.3 | 188.8 | 167.2 | 143.0 | 116.6 | 88.1 | 71.4 | 69.4 | 69.4 |
| Total Interest Expense | | | | | 250.0 | 242.4 | 224.4 | 202.9 | 181.2 | 157.1 | 129.6 | 101.1 | 75.3 | 69.4 | 69.4 |

#### Free Cash Flow

| | Pro forma 2019 | Year 1 2020 | Year 2 2021 | Year 3 2022 | Year 4 2023 | Year 5 2024 | Year 6 2025 | Year 7 2026 | Year 8 2027 | Year 9 2028 | Year 10 2029 |
|---|---|---|---|---|---|---|---|---|---|---|---|
| EBITDA | | $779.4 | $826.1 | $867.4 | $902.1 | $929.2 | $957.1 | $985.8 | $1,015.4 | $1,045.8 | $1,077.2 |
| Less: Cash Interest Expense | | (228.3) | (210.3) | (188.8) | (167.2) | (143.0) | (116.6) | (88.1) | (71.4) | (69.4) | (69.4) |
| Plus: Interest Income | | - | - | - | - | - | - | - | 1.2 | 3.8 | 6.6 |
| Less: Income Taxes | | (78.6) | (91.5) | (104.2) | (115.8) | (126.7) | (138.6) | (150.8) | (162.8) | (170.4) | (176.7) |
| Less: Capital Expenditures | | (166.9) | (176.9) | (185.8) | (193.2) | (199.0) | (204.9) | (211.1) | (217.4) | (224.0) | (230.7) |
| Less: Increase in Net Working Capital | | (47.6) | (41.0) | (36.2) | (30.4) | (23.7) | (24.4) | (25.1) | (25.9) | (26.7) | (27.5) |
| **Free Cash Flow** | | **$257.9** | **$306.5** | **$352.4** | **$395.6** | **$436.8** | **$472.5** | **$510.6** | **$539.0** | **$559.2** | **$579.5** |
| Cumulative Free Cash Flow | | 257.9 | 564.4 | 916.8 | 1,312.4 | 1,749.2 | 2,221.7 | 2,732.3 | 3,271.3 | 3,830.5 | 4,410.0 |

### Capitalization

| | Pro forma 2019 | Year 1 2020 | Year 2 2021 | Year 3 2022 | Year 4 2023 | Year 5 2024 | Year 6 2025 | Year 7 2026 | Year 8 2027 | Year 9 2028 | Year 10 2029 |
|---|---|---|---|---|---|---|---|---|---|---|---|
| Cash | | - | - | - | - | - | - | - | $471.3 | $1,030.5 | $1,610.0 |
| Revolving Credit Facility | - | - | - | - | - | - | - | - | - | - | - |
| Term Loan A | - | - | - | - | - | - | - | - | - | - | - |
| Term Loan B | 2,800.0 | 2,542.1 | 2,235.6 | 1,883.2 | 1,487.6 | 1,050.8 | 578.3 | 67.7 | - | - | - |
| Term Loan C | - | - | - | - | - | - | - | - | - | - | - |
| Existing Term Loan | - | - | - | - | - | - | - | - | - | - | - |
| 2nd Lien | - | - | - | - | - | - | - | - | - | - | - |
| Other Debt | - | - | - | - | - | - | - | - | - | - | - |
| **Total Senior Secured Debt** | **$2,800.0** | **$2,542.1** | **$2,235.6** | **$1,883.2** | **$1,487.6** | **$1,050.8** | **$578.3** | **$67.7** | **-** | **-** | **-** |
| Senior Notes | 850.0 | 850.0 | 850.0 | 850.0 | 850.0 | 850.0 | 850.0 | 850.0 | 850.0 | 850.0 | 850.0 |
| **Total Senior Debt** | **$3,650.0** | **$3,392.1** | **$3,085.6** | **$2,733.2** | **$2,337.6** | **$1,900.8** | **$1,428.3** | **$917.7** | **$850.0** | **$850.0** | **$850.0** |
| Senior Subordinated Notes | - | - | - | - | - | - | - | - | - | - | - |
| **Total Debt** | **$3,650.0** | **$3,392.1** | **$3,085.6** | **$2,733.2** | **$2,337.6** | **$1,900.8** | **$1,428.3** | **$917.7** | **$850.0** | **$850.0** | **$850.0** |
| Shareholders' Equity | 2,050.0 | 2,285.9 | 2,560.3 | 2,872.9 | 3,220.4 | 3,600.6 | 4,016.3 | 4,468.7 | 4,957.2 | 5,468.4 | 5,998.6 |
| **Total Capitalization** | **$5,700.0** | **$5,677.9** | **$5,645.9** | **$5,606.1** | **$5,558.1** | **$5,501.4** | **$5,444.6** | **$5,386.4** | **$5,807.2** | **$6,318.4** | **$6,848.6** |
| % of Bank Debt Repaid | | 9.2% | 20.2% | 32.7% | 46.9% | 62.5% | 79.3% | 97.6% | 100.0% | 100.0% | 100.0% |

### Credit Statistics

| | Pro forma 2019 | Year 1 2020 | Year 2 2021 | Year 3 2022 | Year 4 2023 | Year 5 2024 | Year 6 2025 | Year 7 2026 | Year 8 2027 | Year 9 2028 | Year 10 2029 |
|---|---|---|---|---|---|---|---|---|---|---|---|
| % Debt / Total Capitalization | 64.0% | 59.7% | 54.7% | 48.8% | 42.1% | 34.6% | 26.2% | 17.0% | 14.6% | 13.5% | 12.4% |
| EBITDA / Cash Interest Expense | 3.1x | 3.4x | 3.9x | 4.6x | 5.4x | 6.5x | 8.2x | 11.2x | 14.2x | 15.1x | 15.5x |
| (EBITDA - Capex) / Cash Interest Expense | 2.4x | 2.7x | 3.1x | 3.6x | 4.2x | 5.1x | 6.4x | 8.8x | 11.2x | 11.8x | 12.2x |
| EBITDA / Total Interest Expense | 2.9x | 3.2x | 3.7x | 4.3x | 5.0x | 5.9x | 7.4x | 9.8x | 13.5x | 15.1x | 15.5x |
| (EBITDA - Capex) / Total Interest Expense | 2.3x | 2.5x | 2.9x | 3.4x | 3.9x | 4.6x | 5.8x | 7.7x | 10.6x | 11.8x | 12.2x |
| Senior Secured Debt / EBITDA | 3.9x | 3.3x | 2.7x | 2.2x | 1.6x | 1.1x | 0.6x | 0.1x | -x | -x | -x |
| Senior Debt / EBITDA | 5.0x | 4.4x | 3.7x | 3.2x | 2.6x | 2.0x | 1.5x | 0.9x | 0.8x | 0.8x | 0.8x |
| Total Debt / EBITDA | 5.0x | 4.4x | 3.7x | 3.2x | 2.6x | 2.0x | 1.5x | 0.9x | 0.8x | 0.8x | 0.8x |
| Net Debt / EBITDA | 5.0x | 4.4x | 3.7x | 3.2x | 2.6x | 2.0x | 1.5x | 0.9x | 0.4x | (0.2x) | (0.7x) |

Once the above steps are completed, all the essential outputs are linked to a transaction summary page that serves as the cover page of the LBO model (see Exhibit 5.2). This page allows the deal team to quickly review and spot-check the analysis and make adjustments to the purchase price, financing structure, operating assumptions, and other key inputs as necessary. It also includes the toggle cells that allow the banker to switch between various financing structures and operating scenarios, among other functions.[1] The fully completed model (including all assumptions pages) is shown in Exhibits 5.46 to 5.54.

## STEP I. LOCATE AND ANALYZE THE NECESSARY INFORMATION

When performing LBO analysis, the first step is to collect, organize, and analyze all available information on the target, its sector, and the specifics of the transaction. In an organized sale process, the sell-side advisor provides such detail to prospective buyers, including financial projections that usually form the basis for the initial LBO model (see Chapter 6). This information is typically contained in a CIM/CIP, with additional information provided via a management presentation and data room, such as those provided by Datasite (see Exhibit 6.7). For public targets, this information is supplemented by SEC filings, research reports, and other public sources as described in previous chapters.

In the absence of a CIM/CIP or supplemental company information (e.g., if the target is not being actively sold), the banker must rely upon public sources to perform preliminary due diligence and develop an initial set of financial projections. This task is invariably easier for a public company than a private company (see Chapter 3).

Regardless of whether there is a formal sale process, it is important to independently verify as much information as possible about the target and its sector. Public filings as well as equity and fixed income research on the target (if applicable) and its comparables are particularly important resources. In their absence, news runs, trade publications, and even a simple internet search on a given company or sector and its competitive dynamics may provide valuable information. PE firms often hire outside consultants to help with assessment of the company and sector. Their findings are shared with selected investment banks to help them with their analysis. For the investment banks, the deal team relies on the judgment and experience of its sector coverage bankers to provide insight on the target.

## STEP II. BUILD THE PRE-LBO MODEL

In Step II, we provide detailed step-by-step instructions (see Exhibit 5.3) on how to build the standalone ("pre-LBO") operating model for our illustrative target company, ValueCo, assuming that the primary financial assumptions are obtained from a CIM/CIP. The pre-LBO model is a basic three-statement financial projection model (income statement, balance sheet, and cash flow statement) that initially excludes the effects of the LBO transaction. The incorporation of the LBO financing structure and the resulting pro forma effects are detailed in Steps III and IV.

---

[1]Toggles may also be created to activate the 100% cash flow sweep, cash balance sweep, average interest expense option, or other deal-specific toggles.

**EXHIBIT 5.3**   Pre-LBO Model Steps

Step II(a):   Build Historical and Projected Income Statement through EBIT
Step II(b):   Input Opening Balance Sheet and Project Balance Sheet Items
Step II(c):   Build Cash Flow Statement through Investing Activities

### Step II(a): Build Historical and Projected Income Statement through EBIT

The banker typically begins the pre-LBO model by inputting the target's historical income statement information for the prior three-year period, if available. The historical income statement is generally only built through EBIT, as the target's prior annual interest expense and net income are not relevant given that the target will be recapitalized through the LBO. As with the DCF, historical financial performance should be shown on a pro forma basis for non-recurring items and recent events. This provides a normalized basis for projecting and analyzing future financial performance.

Management projections for sales through EBIT, as provided in the CIM/CIP, are then entered into an assumptions page (see Exhibit 5.52), which feeds into the projected income statement until other operating scenarios are developed/provided. This scenario is typically labeled as "Management Case". At this point, the line items between EBIT and earnings before taxes (EBT) are intentionally left blank, to be completed once a financing structure is entered into the model and a *debt schedule* is built (see Exhibit 5.29). In ValueCo's case, although it has an existing $1,000 million term loan and $500 million of senior notes (see Exhibit 5.5), it is not necessary to model the associated interest expense (or mandatory amortization) as it will be refinanced as part of the LBO transaction.

From a debt financing perspective, the projection period for an LBO model is typically set at seven to ten years so as to match the maturity of the longest tenured debt instrument in the capital structure.[2] A financial sponsor, however, may only use a five-year projection period in its internal LBO model so as to match its expectations for the anticipated investment horizon. As a CIM/CIP typically only provides five years of projected income statement data,[3] it is common for the banker to freeze the Year 5 growth rate and margin assumptions to frame the outer year projections (in the absence of specific guidance). As shown in ValueCo's pre-LBO income statement (Exhibit 5.4), we held Year 5 sales growth rate, gross margin, and EBITDA margin constant at 3%, 40%, and 21%, respectively, to drive projections in Years 6 through 10.

---

[2]A typical LBO model is built with the flexibility to accommodate a ten-year maturity, which is applicable for senior unsecured notes and mezzanine financing. In this chapter, we assume the 8-year senior notes are refinanced at maturity.

[3]The length of the projection period provided in a CIM (or through another medium) may vary depending on the situation.

# EXHIBIT 5.4  ValueCo Pre-LBO Income Statement

*($ in millions, fiscal year ending December 31)*

## Income Statement

| | Historical Period | | | LTM 9/30/2019 | Pro forma 2019 | Projection Period | | | | | | | | | |
|---|---|---|---|---|---|---|---|---|---|---|---|---|---|---|---|
| | 2016 | 2017 | 2018 | | | Year 1 2020 | Year 2 2021 | Year 3 2022 | Year 4 2023 | Year 5 2024 | Year 6 2025 | Year 7 2026 | Year 8 2027 | Year 9 2028 | Year 10 2029 |
| **Sales** | $2,600.0 | $2,900.0 | $3,200.0 | $3,385.0 | $3,450.0 | $3,708.8 | $3,931.3 | $4,127.8 | $4,293.0 | $4,421.7 | $4,554.4 | $4,691.0 | $4,831.8 | $4,976.7 | $5,126.0 |
| *% growth* | NA | 11.5% | 10.3% | NA | 7.8% | 7.5% | 6.0% | 5.0% | 4.0% | 3.0% | 3.0% | 3.0% | 3.0% | 3.0% | 3.0% |
| Cost of Goods Sold | 1,612.0 | 1,769.0 | 1,920.0 | 2,035.0 | 2,070.0 | 2,225.3 | 2,358.8 | 2,476.7 | 2,575.8 | 2,653.0 | 2,732.6 | 2,814.6 | 2,899.1 | 2,986.0 | 3,075.6 |
| **Gross Profit** | $988.0 | $1,131.0 | $1,280.0 | $1,350.0 | $1,380.0 | $1,483.5 | $1,572.5 | $1,651.1 | $1,717.2 | $1,768.7 | $1,821.8 | $1,876.4 | $1,932.7 | $1,990.7 | $2,050.4 |
| *% margin* | 38.0% | 39.0% | 40.0% | 39.9% | 40.0% | 40.0% | 40.0% | 40.0% | 40.0% | 40.0% | 40.0% | 40.0% | 40.0% | 40.0% | 40.0% |
| Selling, General & Administrative | 496.6 | 551.0 | 608.0 | 650.0 | 655.0 | 704.1 | 746.4 | 783.7 | 815.0 | 839.5 | 864.7 | 890.6 | 917.3 | 944.9 | 973.2 |
| *% sales* | 19.1% | 19.0% | 19.0% | 19.2% | 19.0% | 19.0% | 19.0% | 19.0% | 19.0% | 19.0% | 19.0% | 19.0% | 19.0% | 19.0% | 19.0% |
| Other Expense / (Income) | - | - | - | - | - | - | - | - | - | - | - | - | - | - | - |
| **EBITDA** | $491.4 | $580.0 | $672.0 | $700.0 | $725.0 | $779.4 | $826.1 | $867.4 | $902.1 | $929.2 | $957.1 | $985.8 | $1,015.4 | $1,045.8 | $1,077.2 |
| *% margin* | 18.9% | 20.0% | 21.0% | 20.7% | 21.0% | 21.0% | 21.0% | 21.0% | 21.0% | 21.0% | 21.0% | 21.0% | 21.0% | 21.0% | 21.0% |
| Depreciation | 116.0 | 121.5 | 145.0 | 150.0 | 155.3 | 166.9 | 176.9 | 185.8 | 193.2 | 199.0 | 204.9 | 211.1 | 217.4 | 224.0 | 230.7 |
| Amortization | 39.0 | 43.5 | 48.0 | 50.0 | 51.8 | 55.6 | 59.0 | 61.9 | 64.4 | 66.3 | 68.3 | 70.4 | 72.5 | 74.7 | 76.9 |
| **EBIT** | $336.4 | $415.0 | $479.0 | $500.0 | $518.0 | $556.9 | $590.3 | $619.8 | $644.6 | $663.9 | $683.8 | $704.3 | $725.5 | $747.2 | $769.6 |
| *% margin* | 12.9% | 14.3% | 15.0% | 14.8% | 15.0% | 15.0% | 15.0% | 15.0% | 15.0% | 15.0% | 15.0% | 15.0% | 15.0% | 15.0% | 15.0% |
| **Interest Expense** | | | | | | | | | | | | | | | |
| Revolving Credit Facility | | | | | | | | | | | | | | | |
| Term Loan A | | | | | | | | | | | | | | | |
| Term Loan B | | | | | | | | | | | | | | | |
| Term Loan C | | | | | | | | | | | | | | | |
| Existing Term Loan | | | | | | | | | | | | | | | |
| 2nd Lien | | | | | | | | | | | | | | | |
| Senior Notes | | | | | | | | | | | | | | | |
| Senior Subordinated Notes | | | | | | | | | | | | | | | |
| Commitment Fee on Unused Revolver | | | | | | | | | | | | | | | |
| Administrative Agent Fee | | | | | | | | | | | | | | | |
| **Cash Interest Expense** | | | | | | | | | | | | | | | |
| Amortization of Deferred Financing Fees | | | | | | | | | | | | | | | |
| **Total Interest Expense** | | | | | | | | | | | | | | | |
| Interest Income | | | | | | | | | | | | | | | |
| **Net Interest Expense** | | | | | | | | | | | | | | | |
| Earnings Before Taxes | | | | | | 556.9 | 590.3 | 619.8 | 644.6 | 663.9 | 683.8 | 704.3 | 725.5 | 747.2 | 769.6 |
| Income Tax Expense | | | | | | 139.2 | 147.6 | 154.9 | 161.1 | 166.0 | 171.0 | 176.1 | 181.4 | 186.8 | 192.4 |
| **Net Income** | | | | | | $417.6 | $442.7 | $464.8 | $483.4 | $497.9 | $512.9 | $528.3 | $544.1 | $560.4 | $577.2 |
| *% margin* | | | | | | 11.3% | 11.3% | 11.3% | 11.3% | 11.3% | 11.3% | 11.3% | 11.3% | 11.3% | 11.3% |

TO BE CALCULATED

### Income Statement Assumptions

| | 2016 | 2017 | 2018 | LTM | Pro forma 2019 | Year 1 2020 | Year 2 2021 | Year 3 2022 | Year 4 2023 | Year 5 2024 | Year 6 2025 | Year 7 2026 | Year 8 2027 | Year 9 2028 | Year 10 2029 |
|---|---|---|---|---|---|---|---|---|---|---|---|---|---|---|---|
| Sales (% YoY growth) | NA | 11.5% | 10.3% | NA | 7.8% | 7.5% | 6.0% | 5.0% | 4.0% | 3.0% | 3.0% | 3.0% | 3.0% | 3.0% | 3.0% |
| Cost of Goods Sold (% margin) | 62.0% | 61.0% | 60.0% | 60.1% | 60.0% | 60.0% | 60.0% | 60.0% | 60.0% | 60.0% | 60.0% | 60.0% | 60.0% | 60.0% | 60.0% |
| SG&A (% sales) | 19.1% | 19.0% | 19.0% | 19.2% | 19.0% | 19.0% | 19.0% | 19.0% | 19.0% | 19.0% | 19.0% | 19.0% | 19.0% | 19.0% | 19.0% |
| Other Expense / (Income) (% of sales) | -% | -% | -% | -% | -% | -% | -% | -% | -% | -% | -% | -% | -% | -% | -% |
| Depreciation (% of sales) | 4.5% | 4.2% | 4.5% | 4.4% | 4.5% | 4.5% | 4.5% | 4.5% | 4.5% | 4.5% | 4.5% | 4.5% | 4.5% | 4.5% | 4.5% |
| Amortization (% of sales) | 1.5% | 1.5% | 1.5% | 1.5% | 1.5% | 1.5% | 1.5% | 1.5% | 1.5% | 1.5% | 1.5% | 1.5% | 1.5% | 1.5% | 1.5% |
| Interest Income | | | | | 0.5% | 0.5% | 0.5% | 0.5% | 0.5% | 0.5% | 0.5% | 0.5% | 0.5% | 0.5% | 0.5% |
| Tax Rate | | | | | 25.0% | 25.0% | 25.0% | 25.0% | 25.0% | 25.0% | 25.0% | 25.0% | 25.0% | 25.0% | 25.0% |

**Additional Cases**   In addition to the Management Case, the deal team typically develops its own, more conservative operating scenario, known as the "Base Case". The Base Case is generally premised on management assumptions, but with adjustments made based on the deal team's independent due diligence, research, and perspectives.

The bank's internal credit committee(s) also requires the deal team to analyze the target's performance under one or more stress cases in order to gain comfort with the target's ability to service and repay debt during periods of duress. Sponsors perform similar analyses to test the durability of a proposed investment. These "Downside Cases" typically present the target's financial performance with haircuts to top line growth, margins, and potentially capex and working capital efficiency. As with the DCF model, a "toggle" function in the LBO model allows the banker to move from case to case without having to re-enter key financial inputs and assumptions. A separate toggle provides the ability to analyze different financing structures.

The operating scenario that the deal team ultimately uses to set covenants and market the transaction to investors is provided by the sponsor (the "Sponsor Case"). Sponsors use information gleaned from due diligence, industry experts, consulting studies, and research reports, as well as their own sector expertise to develop this case. The Sponsor Case, along with the sponsor's preferred financing structure (collectively, the "Sponsor Model"), is shared with potential underwriters as the basis for them to provide commitment letters.[4] The deal team then confirms both the feasibility of the Sponsor Case (based on its own due diligence and knowledge of the target and sector) and the marketability of the sponsor's preferred financing structure (by gaining comfort that there are buyers for the loans and securities given the proposed terms). This task is especially important because the investment banks are being asked to provide a commitment to a financing structure that may not come to market for several weeks or months (or potentially longer, depending on regulatory or other approvals required before the transaction can close).

---

[4]The timing for the sharing of the Sponsor Model depends on the specifics of the particular deal and the investment bank's relationship with the sponsor.

### Step II(b): Input Opening Balance Sheet and Project Balance Sheet Items

The opening balance sheet (and potentially projected balance sheet data) for the target is typically provided in the CIM and entered into the pre-LBO model (see Exhibit 5.5, "Opening 2019" heading).[5] In addition to the traditional balance sheet accounts, new line items necessary for modeling the pro forma LBO financing structure are added, such as:

- financing fees (which are amortized) under long-term assets

- detailed line items for the new financing structure under long-term liabilities (e.g., the new revolver, term loan(s), and high yield bonds)

The banker must then build functionality into the model in order to input the new LBO financing structure. This is accomplished by inserting "adjustment" columns to account for the additions and subtractions to the opening balance sheet that result from the LBO (see Exhibits 5.5 and 5.15). The inputs for the adjustment columns, which bridge from the opening balance sheet to the pro forma closing balance sheet, feed from the *sources and uses* of funds in the transaction (see Exhibits 5.14 and 5.15). The banker also inserts a "pro forma" column, which nets the adjustments made to the opening balance sheet and serves as the starting point for projecting the target's post-LBO balance sheet throughout the projection period.

Prior to the entry of the LBO financing structure, the opening and pro forma closing balance sheets are identical. The target's basic balance sheet items—such as current assets, current liabilities, PP&E, other assets, and other long-term liabilities—are projected using the same methodologies discussed in Chapter 3. As with the assumptions for the target's projected income statement items, the banker enters the assumptions for the target's projected balance sheet items into the model through an assumptions page (see Exhibit 5.53), which feeds into the projected balance sheet. Projected debt repayment is not modeled at this point as the LBO financing structure has yet to be entered into the sources and uses of funds. For ValueCo, which has an existing $1,000 million term loan and $500 million of senior notes, we simply set the projection period debt balances equal to the opening balance amount (see Exhibit 5.5). At this stage, annual excess free cash flow[6] accrues to the ending cash balance for each projection year once the pre-LBO cash flow statement is complete (see Step II(c), Exhibits 5.9 and 5.10). This ensures that the model will balance once the three financial statements are fully linked.

Depending on the availability of information and need for granularity, the banker may choose to build a "short-form" LBO model that suffices for calculating debt repayment and performing a basic returns analysis. A short-form LBO model uses an abbreviated cash flow statement and debt schedule in place of a full balance sheet with working capital typically calculated as a percentage of sales. The construction of a traditional three-statement model, however, is recommended whenever possible so as to provide the most comprehensive analysis.

---

[5]If the banker is analyzing a public company as a potential LBO candidate outside of (or prior to) an organized sale process, the latest balance sheet data from the company's most recent 10-K or 10-Q is typically used.

[6]The "free cash flow" term used in an LBO analysis differs from that used in a DCF analysis as it includes the effects of leverage.

# EXHIBIT 5.5  ValueCo Pre-LBO Balance Sheet

*($ in millions, fiscal year ending December 31)*

## Balance Sheet

Notes (call-outs):
- The ending cash balance for each year in the projection period is linked to the balance sheet from the cash flow statement once it is completed
- Prior to entry of capex assumptions, PP&E only reflects Depreciation
- Shareholders' equity is inflated until the financing structure is entered into the model
- Model will balance once the ending cash balance for each year in the projection period is linked from the cash flow statement
- Adjustments: TO BE LINKED / CALCULATED FROM SOURCES AND USES
- Debt rows: TO BE LINKED FROM DEBT SCHEDULE

| | Opening 2019 | Adj + | Adj − | Pro Forma 2019 | Year 1 2020 | Year 2 2021 | Year 3 2022 | Year 4 2023 | Year 5 2024 | Year 6 2025 | Year 7 2026 | Year 8 2027 | Year 9 2028 | Year 10 2029 |
|---|---|---|---|---|---|---|---|---|---|---|---|---|---|---|
| Cash and Cash Equivalents | $250.0 | | | $250.0 | | | | | | | | | | |
| Accounts Receivable | 450.0 | | | 450.0 | 483.8 | 512.8 | 538.4 | 560.0 | 576.7 | 594.1 | 611.9 | 630.2 | 649.1 | 668.6 |
| Inventories | 600.0 | | | 600.0 | 645.0 | 683.7 | 717.9 | 746.6 | 769.0 | 792.1 | 815.8 | 840.3 | 865.5 | 891.5 |
| Prepaids and Other Current Assets | 175.0 | | | 175.0 | 188.1 | 199.4 | 209.4 | 217.8 | 224.3 | 231.0 | 238.0 | 245.1 | 252.4 | 260.0 |
| **Total Current Assets** | **$1,475.0** | | | **$1,475.0** | **$1,316.9** | **$1,395.9** | **$1,465.7** | **$1,524.3** | **$1,570.0** | **$1,617.1** | **$1,665.7** | **$1,715.6** | **$1,767.1** | **$1,820.1** |
| Property, Plant and Equipment, net | 2,500.0 | | | 2,500.0 | 2,333.1 | 2,156.2 | 1,970.4 | 1,777.3 | 1,578.3 | 1,373.3 | 1,162.2 | 944.8 | 720.9 | 490.2 |
| Goodwill | 1,000.0 | | | 1,000.0 | 1,000.0 | 1,000.0 | 1,000.0 | 1,000.0 | 1,000.0 | 1,000.0 | 1,000.0 | 1,000.0 | 1,000.0 | 1,000.0 |
| Intangible Assets | 875.0 | | | 875.0 | 819.4 | 760.4 | 698.5 | 634.1 | 567.8 | 499.4 | 429.1 | 356.6 | 282.0 | 205.1 |
| Other Assets | 150.0 | | | 150.0 | 150.0 | 150.0 | 150.0 | 150.0 | 150.0 | 150.0 | 150.0 | 150.0 | 150.0 | 150.0 |
| Deferred Financing Fees | | | | | | | | | | | | | | |
| **Total Assets** | **$6,000.0** | | | **$6,000.0** | **$5,619.4** | **$5,462.5** | **$5,284.6** | **$5,085.7** | **$4,866.1** | **$4,639.9** | **$4,407.0** | **$4,167.0** | **$3,919.9** | **$3,665.4** |
| Accounts Payable | 215.0 | | | 215.0 | 231.1 | 245.0 | 257.2 | 267.5 | 275.6 | 283.8 | 292.3 | 301.1 | 310.1 | 319.4 |
| Accrued Liabilities | 275.0 | | | 275.0 | 295.6 | 313.4 | 329.0 | 342.2 | 352.5 | 363.0 | 373.9 | 385.1 | 396.7 | 408.6 |
| Other Current Liabilities | 100.0 | | | 100.0 | 107.5 | 114.0 | 119.6 | 124.4 | 128.2 | 132.0 | 136.0 | 140.1 | 144.3 | 148.6 |
| **Total Current Liabilities** | **$590.0** | | | **$590.0** | **$634.3** | **$672.3** | **$705.9** | **$734.2** | **$756.2** | **$778.9** | **$802.2** | **$826.3** | **$851.1** | **$876.6** |
| Revolving Credit Facility | | | | | | | | | | | | | | |
| Term Loan A | | | | | 1,000.0 | 1,000.0 | 1,000.0 | 1,000.0 | 1,000.0 | 1,000.0 | 1,000.0 | 1,000.0 | 1,000.0 | 1,000.0 |
| Term Loan B | | | | | | | | | | | | | | |
| Term Loan C | | | | | | | | | | | | | | |
| Existing Term Loan | 1,000.0 | | | 1,000.0 | | | | | | | | | | |
| 2nd Lien | | | | | | | | | | | | | | |
| Senior Notes | | | | | | | | | | | | | | |
| Existing Senior Notes | 500.0 | | | 500.0 | 500.0 | 500.0 | 500.0 | 500.0 | 500.0 | 500.0 | 500.0 | 500.0 | 500.0 | 500.0 |
| Senior Subordinated Notes | | | | | | | | | | | | | | |
| Other Debt | | | | | | | | | | | | | | |
| Deferred Income Taxes | 300.0 | | | 300.0 | 300.0 | 300.0 | 300.0 | 300.0 | 300.0 | 300.0 | 300.0 | 300.0 | 300.0 | 300.0 |
| Other Long-Term Liabilities | 110.0 | | | 110.0 | 110.0 | 110.0 | 110.0 | 110.0 | 110.0 | 110.0 | 110.0 | 110.0 | 110.0 | 110.0 |
| **Total Liabilities** | **$2,500.0** | | | **$2,500.0** | **$2,544.3** | **$2,582.3** | **$2,615.9** | **$2,644.2** | **$2,666.2** | **$2,688.9** | **$2,712.2** | **$2,736.3** | **$2,761.1** | **$2,786.6** |
| Noncontrolling Interest | | | | | | | | | | | | | | |
| Shareholders' Equity | 3,500.0 | | | 3,500.0 | 3,917.6 | 4,360.3 | 4,825.2 | 5,308.6 | 5,806.5 | 6,319.4 | 6,847.6 | 7,391.7 | 7,952.1 | 1,732.6 |
| **Total Shareholders' Equity** | **$3,500.0** | | | **$3,500.0** | **$3,917.6** | **$4,360.3** | **$4,825.2** | **$5,308.6** | **$5,806.5** | **$6,319.4** | **$6,847.6** | **$7,391.7** | **$7,952.1** | **$1,732.6** |
| **Total Liabilities and Equity** | **$6,000.0** | | | **$6,000.0** | **$6,461.9** | **$6,942.6** | **$7,441.1** | **$7,952.7** | **$8,472.7** | **$9,008.2** | **$9,559.9** | **$10,128.0** | **$10,713.2** | **$4,519.3** |
| *Balance Check* | | | | *0.000* | | | | | | | | | | |
| Net Working Capital | 635.0 | | | 635.0 | 682.6 | 723.6 | 759.8 | 790.2 | 813.9 | 838.3 | 863.4 | 889.3 | 916.0 | 943.5 |
| (Increase) / Decrease in Net Working Capital | | | | | (47.6) | (41.0) | (36.2) | (30.4) | (23.7) | (24.4) | (25.1) | (25.9) | (26.7) | (27.5) |

### Balance Sheet Assumptions

| | Opening 2019 | | | Pro Forma 2019 | Year 1 2020 | Year 2 2021 | Year 3 2022 | Year 4 2023 | Year 5 2024 | Year 6 2025 | Year 7 2026 | Year 8 2027 | Year 9 2028 | Year 10 2029 |
|---|---|---|---|---|---|---|---|---|---|---|---|---|---|---|
| **Current Assets** | | | | | | | | | | | | | | |
| Days Sales Outstanding (DSO) | 47.6 | | | 47.6 | 47.6 | 47.6 | 47.6 | 47.6 | 47.6 | 47.6 | 47.6 | 47.6 | 47.6 | 47.6 |
| Days Inventory Held (DIH) | 105.8 | | | 105.8 | 105.8 | 105.8 | 105.8 | 105.8 | 105.8 | 105.8 | 105.8 | 105.8 | 105.8 | 105.8 |
| Prepaid and Other Current Assets (% of sales) | 5.1% | | | 5.1% | 5.1% | 5.1% | 5.1% | 5.1% | 5.1% | 5.1% | 5.1% | 5.1% | 5.1% | 5.1% |
| **Current Liabilities** | | | | | | | | | | | | | | |
| Days Payable Outstanding (DPO) | 37.9 | | | 37.9 | 37.9 | 37.9 | 37.9 | 37.9 | 37.9 | 37.9 | 37.9 | 37.9 | 37.9 | 37.9 |
| Accrued Liabilities (% of sales) | 8.0% | | | 8.0% | 8.0% | 8.0% | 8.0% | 8.0% | 8.0% | 8.0% | 8.0% | 8.0% | 8.0% | 8.0% |
| Other Current Liabilities (% of sales) | 2.9% | | | 2.9% | 2.9% | 2.9% | 2.9% | 2.9% | 2.9% | 2.9% | 2.9% | 2.9% | 2.9% | 2.9% |

241

## Step II(c): Build Cash Flow Statement through Investing Activities

The cash flow statement consists of three sections—operating activities, investing activities, and financing activities.

## Operating Activities

**Income Statement Links**  In building the cash flow statement, all the appropriate income statement items, including net income and non-cash expenses (e.g., D&A, amortization of deferred financing fees), must be linked to the operating activities section of the cash flow statement.

Net income is the first line item in the cash flow statement. It is initially inflated in the pre-LBO model as it excludes the pro forma interest expense and amortization of deferred financing fees associated with the LBO financing structure that have not yet been entered into the model. The amortization of deferred financing fees is a non-cash expense that is added back to net income in the post-LBO cash flow statement. Certain items, such as the annual projected D&A, do not change pro forma for the transaction.

**EXHIBIT 5.6**  Income Statement Links

*($ in millions, fiscal year ending December 31)*

**Cash Flow Statement**

| | Projection Period | | | | | | | | | |
|---|---|---|---|---|---|---|---|---|---|---|
| | Year 1 2020 | Year 2 2021 | Year 3 2022 | Year 4 2023 | Year 5 2024 | Year 6 2025 | Year 7 2026 | Year 8 2027 | Year 9 2028 | Year 10 2029 |
| **Operating Activities** | | | | | | | | | | |
| Net Income | $417.6 | $442.7 | $464.8 | $483.4 | $497.9 | $512.9 | $528.3 | $544.1 | $560.4 | $577.2 |
| Plus: Depreciation | 166.9 | 176.9 | 185.8 | 193.2 | 199.0 | 204.9 | 211.1 | 217.4 | 224.0 | 230.7 |
| Plus: Amortization | 55.6 | 59.0 | 61.9 | 64.4 | 66.3 | 68.3 | 70.4 | 72.5 | 74.7 | 76.9 |
| Plus: Amortization of Financing Fees | TO BE LINKED FROM INCOME STATEMENT | | | | | | | | | |

As shown in Exhibit 5.6, ValueCo's 2020E net income is $417.6 million, which is $181.7 million higher than the pro forma 2020E net income of $235.9 million after giving effect to the LBO financing structure (see Exhibit 5.31).

**Balance Sheet Links**  Each YoY change to a balance sheet account must be accounted for by a corresponding addition or subtraction to the appropriate line item on the cash flow statement. As discussed in Chapter 3, an increase in an asset is a use of cash (represented by a negative value on the cash flow statement), and a decrease in an asset represents a source of cash. Similarly, an increase or decrease in a liability account represents a source or use of cash, respectively. The YoY changes in the target's projected working capital items are calculated in their corresponding line items in the operating activities section of the cash flow statement. These amounts do not change pro forma for the LBO transaction. The sum of the target's net income, non-cash expenses, changes in working capital items, and other items (as appropriate) provides the *cash flow from operating activities* amount.

As shown in Exhibit 5.7, ValueCo generates $592.5 million of cash flow from operating activities in 2020E before giving effect to the LBO transaction.

**EXHIBIT 5.7** Balance Sheet Links

*($ in millions, fiscal year ending December 31)*

**Cash Flow Statement**

| | Year 1 2020 | Year 2 2021 | Year 3 2022 | Year 4 2023 | Year 5 2024 | Year 6 2025 | Year 7 2026 | Year 8 2027 | Year 9 2028 | Year 10 2029 |
|---|---|---|---|---|---|---|---|---|---|---|
| | | | | | Projection Period | | | | | |
| **Operating Activities** | | | | | | | | | | |
| Net Income | $417.6 | $442.7 | $464.8 | $483.4 | $497.9 | $512.9 | $528.3 | $544.1 | $560.4 | $577.2 |
| Plus: Depreciation | 166.9 | 176.9 | 185.8 | 193.2 | 199.0 | 204.9 | 211.1 | 217.4 | 224.0 | 230.7 |
| Plus: Amortization | 55.6 | 59.0 | 61.9 | 64.4 | 66.3 | 68.3 | 70.4 | 72.5 | 74.7 | 76.9 |
| Plus: Amortization of Financing Fees | | | | TO BE LINKED FROM INCOME STATEMENT | | | | | | |
| | | | | | | | | | | |
| **Changes in Working Capital Items** | | | | | | | | | | |
| (Inc.) / Dec. in Accounts Receivable | (33.8) | (29.0) | (25.6) | (21.5) | (16.8) | (17.3) | (17.8) | (18.4) | (18.9) | (19.5) |
| (Inc.) / Dec. in Inventories | (45.0) | (38.7) | (34.2) | (28.7) | (22.4) | (23.1) | (23.8) | (24.5) | (25.2) | (26.0) |
| (Inc.) / Dec. in Prepaid and Other Current Assets | (13.1) | (11.3) | (10.0) | (8.4) | (6.5) | (6.7) | (6.9) | (7.1) | (7.4) | (7.6) |
| | | | | | | | | | | |
| Inc. / (Dec.) in Accounts Payable | 16.1 | 13.9 | 12.2 | 10.3 | 8.0 | 8.3 | 8.5 | 8.8 | 9.0 | 9.3 |
| Inc. / (Dec.) in Accrued Liabilities | 20.6 | 17.7 | 15.7 | 13.2 | 10.3 | 10.6 | 10.9 | 11.2 | 11.6 | 11.9 |
| Inc. / (Dec.) in Other Current Liabilities | 7.5 | 6.5 | 5.7 | 4.8 | 3.7 | 3.8 | 4.0 | 4.1 | 4.2 | 4.3 |
| (Inc.) / Dec. in Net Working Capital | (47.6) | (41.0) | (36.2) | (30.4) | (23.7) | (24.4) | (25.1) | (25.9) | (26.7) | (27.5) |
| **Cash Flow from Operating Activities** | **$592.5** | **$637.6** | **$676.3** | **$710.6** | **$739.5** | **$761.7** | **$784.6** | **$808.1** | **$832.3** | **$857.3** |

**Investing Activities** Capex is typically the key line item under *investing activities*, although planned acquisitions or divestitures may also be captured in the "other investing activities" line item. Projected capex assumptions are typically sourced from the CIM and inputted into an assumptions page (see Exhibit 5.52) where they are linked to the cash flow statement. The target's projected net PP&E must incorporate the capex projections (added to PP&E) as well as those for depreciation (subtracted from PP&E). As discussed in Chapter 3, in the event that capex projections are not provided/available, the banker typically projects capex as a fixed percentage of sales at historical levels with appropriate adjustments for cyclical or non-recurring items.

The sum of the annual cash flows provided by operating activities and investing activities provides annual *cash flow available for debt repayment*, which is commonly referred to as free cash flow (see Exhibit 5.25).

**EXHIBIT 5.8** Investing Activities

*($ in millions, fiscal year ending December 31)*

**Cash Flow Statement**

| | Year 1 2020 | Year 2 2021 | Year 3 2022 | Year 4 2023 | Year 5 2024 | Year 6 2025 | Year 7 2026 | Year 8 2027 | Year 9 2028 | Year 10 2029 |
|---|---|---|---|---|---|---|---|---|---|---|
| | | | | | Projection Period | | | | | |
| **Investing Activities** | | | | | | | | | | |
| Capital Expenditures | (166.9) | (176.9) | (185.8) | (193.2) | (199.0) | (204.9) | (211.1) | (217.4) | (224.0) | (230.7) |
| Other Investing Activities | - | - | - | - | - | - | - | - | - | - |
| **Cash Flow from Investing Activities** | **($166.9)** | **($176.9)** | **($185.8)** | **($193.2)** | **($199.0)** | **($204.9)** | **($211.1)** | **($217.4)** | **($224.0)** | **($230.7)** |

As shown in Exhibit 5.8, we do not make any assumptions for ValueCo's other investing activities line item. Therefore, ValueCo's cash flow from investing activities amount is equal to capex in each year of the projection period.

**Financing Activities** The financing activities section of the cash flow statement is constructed to include line items for the (repayment)/drawdown of each debt instrument in the LBO financing structure. It also includes line items for dividends and equity issuance/(stock repurchase). These line items are initially left blank until the LBO financing structure is entered into the model (see Step III) and a detailed debt schedule is built (see Step IV(a)).

**EXHIBIT 5.9**　Financing Activities

*($ in millions, fiscal year ending December 31)*

### Cash Flow Statement

| | Year 1 2020 | Year 2 2021 | Year 3 2022 | Year 4 2023 | Year 5 2024 | Year 6 2025 | Year 7 2026 | Year 8 2027 | Year 9 2028 | Year 10 2029 |
|---|---|---|---|---|---|---|---|---|---|---|
| | | | | | Projection Period | | | | | |
| **Financing Activities** | | | | | | | | | | |
| Revolving Credit Facility | | | | | | | | | | |
| Term Loan A | | | | | | | | | | |
| Term Loan B | | | | | | | | | | |
| Term Loan C | | | | TO BE LINKED FROM DEBT SCHEDULE | | | | | | |
| Existing Term Loan | | | | | | | | | | |
| 2nd Lien | | | | | | | | | | |
| Senior Notes | | | | | | | | | | |
| Senior Subordinated Notes | | | | | | | | | | |
| Other Debt | - | | - | - | | - | | | | |
| Dividends | - | | - | - | | - | | | | |
| Equity Issuance / (Repurchase) | - | | - | - | | - | | | | |
| **Cash Flow from Financing Activities** | **-** | **-** | **-** | **-** | **-** | **-** | **-** | **-** | **-** | **-** |
| | | | | | | | | | | |
| Excess Cash for the Period | $425.6 | $460.7 | $490.6 | $517.4 | $540.5 | $556.8 | $573.5 | $590.7 | $608.4 | $626.6 |
| Beginning Cash Balance | 250.0 | 675.6 | 1,136.4 | 1,626.9 | 2,144.3 | 2,684.9 | 3,241.7 | 3,815.1 | 4,405.8 | 5,014.2 |
| **Ending Cash Balance** | **$675.6** | **$1,136.4** | **$1,626.9** | **$2,144.3** | **$2,684.9** | **$3,241.7** | **$3,815.1** | **$4,405.8** | **$5,014.2** | **$5,640.8** |

*Cash Flow Statement Assumptions*

| | | | | | | | | | | |
|---|---|---|---|---|---|---|---|---|---|---|
| Capital Expenditures (% of sales) | 4.5% | 4.5% | 4.5% | 4.5% | 4.5% | 4.5% | 4.5% | 4.5% | 4.5% | 4.5% |

> Excess Cash for the Period accrues to the Ending Cash Balance until the LBO financing structure is entered into the model and the debt schedule is built

> The existing $250 million cash balance is pre-transaction and will ultimately be used as part of the financing structure

As shown in Exhibit 5.9, prior to giving effect to the LBO transaction, ValueCo's projected excess cash for the period accrues to the ending cash balance in each year of the projection period.

**Cash Flow Statement Links to Balance Sheet**　Once the cash flow statement is built, the ending cash balance for each year in the projection period is linked to the cash and cash equivalents line item in the balance sheet, thereby fully linking the financial statements of the pre-LBO model.

**EXHIBIT 5.10**　Cash Flow Statement Links to Balance Sheet

*($ in millions, fiscal year ending December 31)*

### Cash Flow Statement

| | Year 1 2020 | Year 2 2021 | Year 3 2022 | Year 4 2023 | Year 5 2024 | Year 6 2025 | Year 7 2026 | Year 8 2027 | Year 9 2028 | Year 10 2029 |
|---|---|---|---|---|---|---|---|---|---|---|---|
| | | | | | Projection Period | | | | | |
| Excess Cash for the Period | $425.6 | $460.7 | $490.6 | $517.4 | $540.5 | $556.8 | $573.5 | $590.7 | $608.4 | $626.6 |
| Beginning Cash Balance | 250.0 | 675.6 | 1,136.4 | 1,626.9 | 2,144.3 | 2,684.9 | 3,241.7 | 3,815.1 | 4,405.8 | 5,014.2 |
| **Ending Cash Balance** | **$675.6** | **$1,136.4** | **$1,626.9** | **$2,144.3** | **$2,684.9** | **$3,241.7** | **$3,815.1** | **$4,405.8** | **$5,014.2** | **$5,640.8** |

### Balance Sheet

| | Pro Forma 2019 | Year 1 2020 | Year 2 2021 | Year 3 2022 | Year 4 2023 | Year 5 2024 | Year 6 2025 | Year 7 2026 | Year 8 2027 | Year 9 2028 | Year 10 2029 |
|---|---|---|---|---|---|---|---|---|---|---|---|
| | | | | | | Projection Period | | | | | |
| Cash and Cash Equivalents | $250.0 | $675.6 | $1,136.4 | $1,626.9 | $2,144.3 | $2,684.9 | $3,241.7 | $3,815.1 | $4,405.8 | $5,014.2 | $5,640.8 |

> = Ending Cash Balance$_{2020E}$ (from Cash Flow Statement)

As shown in Exhibit 5.10, in 2020E, ValueCo generates excess cash for the period of $425.6 million, which is added to the beginning cash balance of $250 million to produce an ending cash balance of $675.6 million.[7] This amount is linked to the 2020E cash and cash equivalents line item on the balance sheet.

At this point in the construction of the LBO model, the balance sheet should balance (i.e., total assets are equal to the sum of total liabilities and shareholders' equity) for each year in the projection period. If this is the case, then the model is functioning properly and the transaction structure can be entered into the sources and uses.

If the balance sheet does not balance, revisit the steps performed up to this point and correct any input, linking, or calculation errors that are preventing the model from functioning properly. Common missteps include depreciation or capex not being properly linked to PP&E or changes in balance sheet accounts not being properly reflected in the cash flow statement.

## STEP III. INPUT TRANSACTION STRUCTURE

**EXHIBIT 5.11**  Steps to Input the Transaction Structure

| | |
|---|---|
| Step III(a): | Enter Purchase Price Assumptions |
| Step III(b): | Enter Financing Structure into Sources and Uses |
| Step III(c): | Link Sources and Uses to Balance Sheet Adjustments Columns |

### Step III(a): Enter Purchase Price Assumptions

A purchase price must be assumed for a given target in order to determine the supporting financing structure (debt and equity).

For the illustrative LBO of ValueCo (a private company), we assumed that a sponsor is basing its purchase price and financing structure on ValueCo's LTM 9/30/2019 EBITDA of $700 million and a year-end transaction close.[8] We also assumed a purchase multiple of 8.0x LTM EBITDA, which is consistent with the multiples paid for similar LBO targets (per the illustrative precedent transactions analysis performed in Chapter 2, see Exhibit 2.35). This results in an enterprise value of $5,600 million (prior to transaction-related fees and expenses) and an implied equity purchase price of $4,350 million after subtracting ValueCo's net debt of $1,250 million.

---

[7]The $250 million beginning cash balance in 2020E will ultimately be used as part of the financing structure.
[8]As ValueCo is private, we entered a "2" in the toggle cell for public/private target (see Exhibit 5.12).

**EXHIBIT 5.12**   Purchase Price Input Section of Assumptions Page 3 (see Exhibit 5.54) – Multiple of EBITDA

*($ in millions)*

| Purchase Price | |
|---|---:|
| **Public / Private Target (1/2)** | 2 |
| | |
| Entry EBITDA Multiple | 8.0x |
| LTM 9/30/2019 EBITDA | 700.0 |
| **Enterprise Value** | **$5,600.0** |
| | |
| Less: Total Debt | (1,500.0) |
| Less: Preferred Stock | - |
| Less: Noncontrolling Interest | - |
| Plus: Cash and Cash Equivalents | 250.0 |
| **Equity Purchase Price** | **$4,350.0** |

Enter "1" for a public target
Enter "2" for a private target
*Our LBO model template automatically updates the labels and calculations for each selection (see Exhibit 5.13)

For a public company, the equity purchase price is calculated by multiplying the offer price per share by the target's fully diluted shares outstanding.[9] Net debt is then added to the equity purchase price to arrive at an implied enterprise value (see Exhibit 5.13).

**EXHIBIT 5.13**   Purchase Price Assumptions – Offer Price per Share

*($ in millions, except per share data)*

| Purchase Price | |
|---|---:|
| **Public / Private Target (1/2)** | 1 |
| | |
| Offer Price per Share | $54.38 |
| Fully Diluted Shares Outstanding | 80.0 |
| **Equity Purchase Price** | **$4,350.0** |
| | |
| Plus: Total Debt | 1,500.0 |
| Plus: Preferred Stock | - |
| Plus: Noncontrolling Interest | - |
| Less: Cash and Cash Equivalents | (250.0) |
| **Enterprise Value** | **$5,600.0** |

---

[9]In this case, a "1" would be entered in the toggle cell for public/private target (see Exhibit 5.13).

## Step III(b): Enter Financing Structure into Sources and Uses

A sources and uses table is used to summarize the flow of funds required to consummate a transaction. The *sources of funds* refer to the total capital used to finance an acquisition. The *uses of funds* refer to those items funded by the capital sources—in this case, the purchase of ValueCo's equity, the repayment of existing debt, and the payment of transaction fees and expenses, including the tender/call premiums on ValueCo's existing bonds. Regardless of the number and type of components comprising the sources and uses of funds, the sum of the sources of funds must equal the sum of the uses of funds.

We entered the sources and uses of funds for the multiple financing structures analyzed for the ValueCo LBO into an assumptions page (see Exhibits 5.14 and 5.54).

**EXHIBIT 5.14**   Financing Structures Input Section of Assumptions Page 3 (see Exhibit 5.54)

*($ in millions)*

| Financing Structures | | | | | |
|---|---|---|---|---|---|
| | **Structure** | | | | |
| | **1** | **2** | **3** | **4** | **5** |
| **Sources of Funds** | **Structure 1** | **Structure 2** | **Structure 3** | **Structure 4** | **Status Quo** |
| Revolving Credit Facility Size | $250.0 | $250.0 | $250.0 | $250.0 | - |
| Revolving Credit Facility Draw | - | - | - | - | - |
| Term Loan A | - | - | - | - | - |
| Term Loan B | 2,800.0 | 2,150.0 | 2,100.0 | 1,750.0 | - |
| Term Loan C | - | - | - | - | - |
| 2nd Lien | - | - | 700.0 | - | - |
| Senior Notes | 850.0 | 1,500.0 | 700.0 | 1,000.0 | - |
| Senior Subordinated Notes | - | - | - | 1,000.0 | - |
| Equity Contribution | 2,100.0 | 2,100.0 | 2,250.0 | 2,250.0 | - |
| Rollover Equity | - | - | - | - | - |
| Cash on Hand | 250.0 | 250.0 | 250.0 | - | - |
| - | | | | | |
| **Total Sources of Funds** | **$6,000.0** | **$6,000.0** | **$6,000.0** | **$6,000.0** | **-** |
| | | | | | |
| **Uses of Funds** | | | | | |
| Equity Purchase Price | $4,350.0 | $4,350.0 | $4,350.0 | $4,350.0 | - |
| Repay Existing Bank Debt | 1,500.0 | 1,500.0 | 1,500.0 | 1,500.0 | - |
| Tender / Call Premiums | 20.0 | 20.0 | 20.0 | 20.0 | - |
| Financing Fees | 100.0 | 100.0 | 100.0 | 100.0 | - |
| Other Fees and Expenses | 30.0 | 30.0 | 30.0 | 30.0 | - |
| - | | | | | |
| **Total Uses of Funds** | **$6,000.0** | **$6,000.0** | **$6,000.0** | **$6,000.0** | **-** |

**Sources of Funds**   Structure 1 served as our preliminary proposed financing structure for the ValueCo LBO. As shown in Exhibit 5.14, it consists of:

- $2,800 million term loan B ("TLB")
- $850 million senior notes ("notes")
- $2,100 million equity contribution
- $250 million of cash on hand

This preliminary financing structure is comprised of senior secured leverage of 4.0x LTM EBITDA, total leverage of 5.2x, an equity contribution percentage of approximately 35%, and $250 million of ValueCo's cash on hand (see Exhibit 5.2). We also contemplated a $250 million undrawn revolving credit facility ("revolver") as part of the financing. While not an actual source of funding for the ValueCo LBO, the revolver provides liquidity to fund anticipated seasonal working capital needs, issuance of letters of credit, and other cash uses at, or post, closing.

**Uses of Funds**   The uses of funds include:

- the purchase of ValueCo's equity for $4,350 million
- the repayment of ValueCo's existing $1,000 million term loan and $500 million senior notes
- the payment of total transaction fees and expenses of $150 million (consisting of financing fees of $100 million, tender/call premiums of $20 million, and other fees and expenses of $30 million)

The total sources and uses of funds are $6,000 million, which is $400 million higher than the implied enterprise value calculated in Exhibit 5.12. This is due to the payment of $150 million of total fees and expenses and the use of $250 million of cash on hand as a funding source.

## Step III(c): Link Sources and Uses to Balance Sheet Adjustments Columns

Once the sources and uses of funds are entered into the model, each amount is linked to the appropriate cell in the adjustments columns adjacent to the opening balance sheet (see Exhibit 5.15). Any goodwill that is created, however, is calculated on the basis of equity purchase price and net identifiable assets[10] (see Exhibit 5.20). The equity contribution must also be adjusted to account for any transaction-related fees and expenses (other than financing fees) as well as tender/call premium fees that are expensed upfront.[11] These adjustments serve to bridge the opening balance sheet to the pro forma closing balance sheet, which forms the basis for projecting the target's balance sheet throughout the projection period.

---

[10]Calculated as shareholders' equity less existing goodwill.

[11]In accordance with FAS 141(R), M&A transaction costs are expensed as incurred. Debt financing fees, however, continue to be treated as deferred costs and amortized over the life of the associated debt instruments.

**EXHIBIT 5.15**   Sources and Uses Links to Balance Sheet

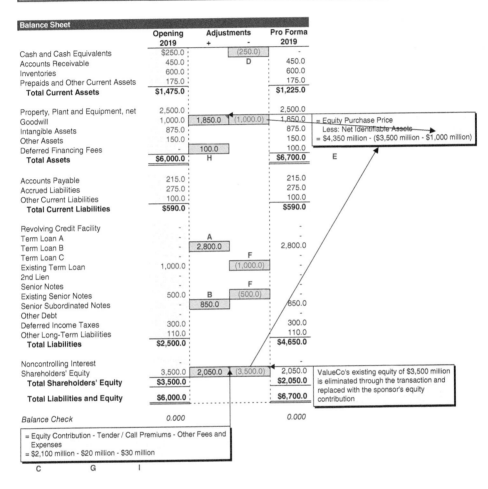

| Sources of Funds | | |
|---|---|---|
| Revolving Credit Facility | - | |
| Term Loan B | 2,800.0 | A |
| Senior Notes | 850.0 | B |
| Equity Contribution | 2,100.0 | C |
| Cash on Hand | 250.0 | D |
| | | |
| **Total Sources** | **$6,000.0** | |

| Uses of Funds | | |
|---|---|---|
| Purchase ValueCo Equity | $4,350.0 | E |
| Repay Existing Debt | 1,500.0 | F |
| Tender / Call Premiums | 20.0 | G |
| Financing Fees | 100.0 | H |
| Other Fees and Expenses | 30.0 | I |
| **Total Uses** | **$6,000.0** | |

**Balance Sheet**

| | Opening 2019 | Adjustments + | - | Pro Forma 2019 | |
|---|---|---|---|---|---|
| Cash and Cash Equivalents | $250.0 | | (250.0) | - | |
| Accounts Receivable | 450.0 | | D | 450.0 | |
| Inventories | 600.0 | | | 600.0 | |
| Prepaids and Other Current Assets | 175.0 | | | 175.0 | |
| **Total Current Assets** | **$1,475.0** | | | **$1,225.0** | |
| | | | | | |
| Property, Plant and Equipment, net | 2,500.0 | | | 2,500.0 | |
| Goodwill | 1,000.0 | 1,850.0 | (1,000.0) | 1,850.0 | = Equity Purchase Price |
| Intangible Assets | 875.0 | | | 875.0 | Less: Net Identifiable Assets |
| Other Assets | 150.0 | | | 150.0 | = $4,350 million - ($3,500 million - $1,000 million) |
| Deferred Financing Fees | - | 100.0 | | 100.0 | |
| **Total Assets** | **$6,000.0** | H | | **$6,700.0** | E |
| | | | | | |
| Accounts Payable | 215.0 | | | 215.0 | |
| Accrued Liabilities | 275.0 | | | 275.0 | |
| Other Current Liabilities | 100.0 | | | 100.0 | |
| **Total Current Liabilities** | **$590.0** | | | **$590.0** | |
| | | | | | |
| Revolving Credit Facility | - | | | - | |
| Term Loan A | - | A | | - | |
| Term Loan B | - | 2,800.0 | | 2,800.0 | |
| Term Loan C | - | | F | - | |
| Existing Term Loan | 1,000.0 | | (1,000.0) | - | |
| 2nd Lien | - | | | - | |
| Senior Notes | - | | F | - | |
| Existing Senior Notes | 500.0 | B | (500.0) | - | |
| Senior Subordinated Notes | - | 850.0 | | 850.0 | |
| Other Debt | - | | | - | |
| Deferred Income Taxes | 300.0 | | | 300.0 | |
| Other Long-Term Liabilities | 110.0 | | | 110.0 | |
| **Total Liabilities** | **$2,500.0** | | | **$4,650.0** | |
| | | | | | |
| Noncontrolling Interest | - | | | - | |
| Shareholders' Equity | 3,500.0 | 2,050.0 | (3,500.0) | 2,050.0 | ValueCo's existing equity of $3,500 million |
| **Total Shareholders' Equity** | **$3,500.0** | | | **$2,050.0** | is eliminated through the transaction and |
| | | | | | replaced with the sponsor's equity |
| **Total Liabilities and Equity** | **$6,000.0** | | | **$6,700.0** | contribution |
| | | | | | |
| *Balance Check* | *0.000* | | | *0.000* | |

= Equity Contribution - Tender / Call Premiums - Other Fees and Expenses
= $2,100 million - $20 million - $30 million

   C          G          I

Exhibit 5.16 provides a summary of the transaction adjustments to the opening balance sheet.

**EXHIBIT 5.16**   Balance Sheet Adjustments

| Adjustments | |
|---|---|
| **Additions** | **Eliminations** |
| **Assets** | **Assets** |
| + $1,850 million of Goodwill Created | − $250 million of Cash on Hand |
| + $100 million of Financing Fees | − $1,000 million of Existing Goodwill |
| | |
| **Liabilities** | **Liabilities** |
| + $2,800 million of Term Loan B | − $1,500 billion of Existing ValueCo Debt |
| + $850 million of Senior Notes | |
| | |
| **Shareholders' Equity** | **Shareholders' Equity** |
| + $2,100 million Sponsor Equity Contribution | − $3,500 million of ValueCo Shareholders' Equity |
| | − $20 million of Tender/Call Premiums |
| | − $30 million of Other Fees & Expenses |

**Sources of Funds Links**   The balance sheet links from the sources of funds to the adjustments columns are fairly straightforward. Each debt capital source corresponds to a like-named line item on the balance sheet and is linked as an addition in the appropriate adjustment column. For the equity contribution, however, the transaction-related fees and expenses as well as the tender/call premiums must be deducted in the appropriate cell during linkage. Any cash on hand used as part of the financing structure is subtracted from the existing cash balance.

**Term Loan B, Senior Notes, and Equity Contribution**   As shown in Exhibit 5.17, in the ValueCo LBO, the new $2,800 million TLB, $850 million senior notes, and $2,100 million equity contribution ($2,050 million after deducting $20 million tender/call premiums and $30 million of other fees and expenses) were linked from the sources of funds to their corresponding line items on the balance sheet as an addition under the "+" adjustment column.

**EXHIBIT 5.17**   Term Loan B, Senior Notes, and Equity Contribution

($ in millions, fiscal year ending December 31)

**Balance Sheet**

| | Opening 2019 | Adjustments + | Adjustments − | Pro Forma 2019 |
|---|---|---|---|---|
| Accounts Payable | 215.0 | | | 215.0 |
| Accrued Liabilities | 275.0 | | | 275.0 |
| Other Current Liabilities | 100.0 | | | 100.0 |
| **Total Current Liabilities** | **$590.0** | | | **$590.0** |
| | | | | |
| Revolving Credit Facility | - | | | - |
| Term Loan B | - | 2,800.0 | | 2,800.0 |
| Existing Term Loan | 1,000.0 | | | 1,000.0 |
| Existing Senior Notes | 500.0 | | | 500.0 |
| Senior Notes | - | 850.0 | | 850.0 |
| Other Debt | 300.0 | | | 300.0 |
| Other Long-Term Liabilities | 110.0 | | | 110.0 |
| **Total Liabilities** | **$2,500.0** | | | **$6,150.0** |
| | | | | |
| Noncontrolling Interest | - | | | - |
| Shareholders' Equity | 3,500.0 | 2,050.0 | | 5,550.0 |
| **Total Shareholders' Equity** | **$3,500.0** | | | **$5,550.0** |

= Equity Contribution - Tender / Call Premiums
 - Other Fees and Expenses
= $2,100 million - $20 million - $30 million

Cash on Hand   As shown in Exhibit 5.18, the $250 million use of cash on hand was linked from the sources of funds as a negative adjustment to the opening cash balance as it is used as a source of funding.

**EXHIBIT 5.18**   Cash on Hand

*($ in millions, fiscal year ending December 31)*

| Balance Sheet | | | |
|---|---|---|---|
| | Opening 2019 | Adjustments + - | Pro Forma 2019 |
| Cash and Cash Equivalents | $250.0 | (250.0) | - |

## Uses of Funds Links

Purchase ValueCo Equity   As shown in Exhibit 5.19, ValueCo's existing shareholders' equity of $3,500 million, which is included in the $4,350 million purchase price, was eliminated as a negative adjustment and replaced by the sponsor's equity contribution (less other fees and expenses and tender/call premiums).

**EXHIBIT 5.19**   Purchase ValueCo Equity

*($ in millions, fiscal year ending December 31)*

| Balance Sheet | | | |
|---|---|---|---|
| | Opening 2019 | Adjustments + - | Pro Forma 2019 |
| Noncontrolling Interest | - | | - |
| Shareholders' Equity | 3,500.0 | 2,050.0 (3,500.0) | 2,050.0 |
| **Total Shareholders' Equity** | **$3,500.0** | | **$2,050.0** |

*Goodwill Created*   Goodwill is created from the excess amount paid for a target over its net identifiable assets. For the ValueCo LBO, it is calculated as the equity purchase price of $4,350 million less net identifiable assets of $2,500 million (shareholders' equity of $3,500 million less existing goodwill of $1,000 million). As shown in Exhibit 5.20, the net value of $1,850 million is linked to the adjustments column as an addition to the goodwill and intangible assets line item.[12] The goodwill created remains on the balance sheet (unamortized) over the life of the investment, but is tested annually for impairment.

---

[12]The allocation of the entire purchase price premium to goodwill is a simplifying assumption for the purposes of this analysis. In an actual transaction, the excess purchase price over the existing net identifiable assets is allocated to assets, such as PP&E and intangibles, as well as other balance sheet items, to reflect their fair market value at the time of the acquisition. The remaining excess purchase price is then allocated to goodwill. From a cash flow perspective, in a stock sale (see Chapter 7), there is no difference between allocating the entire purchase premium to goodwill as opposed to writing up other assets to fair market value. In an asset sale (see Chapter 7), however, there are differences in cash flows depending on the allocation of goodwill to tangible and intangible assets as the write-up is tax deductible.

**EXHIBIT 5.20**  Goodwill Created

*($ in millions, fiscal year ending December 31)*

| Balance Sheet | | | | |
|---|---|---|---|---|
| | Opening 2019 | Adjustments + | - | Pro Forma 2019 |
| Property, Plant and Equipment, net | 2,500.0 | | | 2,500.0 |
| Goodwill & Intangible Assets | 1,000.0 | 1,850.0 | (1,000.0) | 1,850.0 |

| Calculation of Goodwill | |
|---|---|
| Equity Purchase Price | $4,350.0 |
| Less: Net Identifiable Assets | (2,500.0) |
| **Goodwill Created** | **$1,850.0** |

**Repay Existing Debt**  ValueCo's existing $1,000 million term loan and $500 million of senior notes are assumed to be refinanced as part of the new LBO financing structure, which includes $3,650 million of total funded debt. As shown in Exhibit 5.21, this is performed in the model by linking the repayment of the existing term loan and senior notes directly from the uses of funds as a negative adjustment.

**EXHIBIT 5.21**  Repay Existing Debt

*($ in millions, fiscal year ending December 31)*

| Balance Sheet | | | | |
|---|---|---|---|---|
| | Opening 2019 | Adjustments + | - | Pro Forma 2019 |
| Revolving Credit Facility | - | | | - |
| Term Loan B | - | 2,800.0 | | 2,800.0 |
| Existing Term Loan | 1,000.0 | | (1,000.0) | - |
| Senior Notes | - | 850.0 | | 850.0 |
| Existing Senior Notes | 500.0 | | (500.0) | - |

**Tender/Call Premiums**  As part of the transaction, we assumed ValueCo's existing senior notes have covenants that prohibit the proposed LBO and are thus required to be refinanced. For illustrative purposes, we assumed that ValueCo's existing $500 million 8% 8-year senior notes were issued approximately four years ago and, therefore, the call price after the first call date would be 104% of par (par plus ½ the coupon, see Chapter 4). As a result, ValueCo's existing senior notes require a premium of $20 million ($500 million × 4%) to be paid to existing note holders.

**Financing Fees**  As opposed to M&A transaction-related fees and expenses, financing fees are a deferred expense and, as such, are not expensed immediately. Therefore, deferred financing fees are capitalized as an asset on the balance sheet, which means they are linked from the uses of funds as an addition to the corresponding line item (see Exhibit 5.22). The financing fees associated with each debt instrument are amortized on a straight line basis over the life of the obligation.[13] As previously

---

[13]Although financing fees are paid in full to the underwriters at transaction close, they are amortized in accordance with the tenor of the security for accounting purposes. Deferred financing fees from prior financing transactions are typically expensed when the accompanying debt is retired and show up as a one-time charge to the target's net income, thereby reducing retained earnings and shareholders' equity.

discussed, amortization is a non-cash expense and, therefore, must be added back to net income in the operating activities section of the model's cash flow statement in each year of the projection period.

For the ValueCo LBO, we calculated financing fees associated with the contemplated financing structure to be $100 million. Our illustrative calculation is based on fees of 2.25% for arranging the senior secured credit facilities (the revolver and TLB), 2.25% for underwriting the notes, 1.25% for committing to a bridge loan for the notes, and $1.6 million for other financing fees and expenses.[14] The left lead arranger of a revolving credit facility typically serves as the "Administrative Agent"[15] and receives an annual administrative agent fee (e.g., $150,000), which is included in interest expense on the income statement.[16]

**EXHIBIT 5.22**   Financing Fees

*($ in millions, fiscal year ending December 31)*

**Balance Sheet**

| | Opening 2019 | Adjustments + | Adjustments - | Pro Forma 2019 |
|---|---|---|---|---|
| Property, Plant and Equipment, net | 2,500.0 | | | 2,500.0 |
| Goodwill and Intangible Assets | 1,000.0 | 1,850.0 | | 1,850.0 |
| Other Assets | 150.0 | | | 150.0 |
| Deferred Financing Fees | - | 100.0 | | 100.0 |
| **Total Assets** | **$6,000.0** | | | **$6,700.0** |

**Calculation of Financing Fees**

| | | Fees | |
|---|---|---|---|
| | Size | (%) | ($) |
| Revolving Credit Facility Size | $250.0 | 2.25% | $5.6 |
| Term Loan B | 2,800.0 | 2.25% | 63.0 |
| Senior Subordinated Notes | 850.0 | 2.25% | 19.1 |
| Senior Subordinated Bridge Facility | 850.0 | 1.25% | 10.6 |
| Other Financing Fees & Expenses | | | 1.6 |
| **Total Financing Fees** | | | **$100.0** |

**Other Fees and Expenses**   Other fees and expenses typically include payments for services such as M&A advisory (and potentially a sponsor deal fee), legal, accounting, and consulting, as well as other miscellaneous deal-related costs. For the ValueCo LBO, we estimated this amount to be $30 million. Within the context of the LBO sources and uses, this amount is netted upfront against the equity contribution.

---

[14]Fees are dependent on the debt instrument, market conditions, and specific situation. The fees depicted are for illustrative purposes only.

[15]The bank that monitors the credit facilities, including the tracking of lenders, handling of interest and principal payments, and associated back-office administrative functions.

[16]The fee for the first year of the facility is generally paid to the lead arranger at the close of the financing.

## STEP IV. COMPLETE THE POST-LBO MODEL

**EXHIBIT 5.23**   Steps to Complete the Post-LBO Model

| | |
|---|---|
| Step IV(a): | Build Debt Schedule |
| Step IV(b): | Complete Pro Forma Income Statement from EBIT to Net Income |
| Step IV(c): | Complete Pro Forma Balance Sheet |
| Step IV(d): | Complete Pro Forma Cash Flow Statement |

### Step IV(a): Build Debt Schedule

The debt schedule is an integral component of the LBO model, serving to layer in the pro forma effects of the LBO financing structure on the target's financial statements.[17] Specifically, the debt schedule enables the banker to:

- complete the pro forma income statement from EBIT to net income

- complete the pro forma long-term liabilities and shareholders' equity sections of the balance sheet

- complete the pro forma financing activities section of the cash flow statement

As shown in Exhibit 5.27, the debt schedule applies free cash flow to make mandatory and optional debt repayments, thereby calculating the annual beginning and ending balances for each debt tranche. The debt repayment amounts are linked to the financing activities section of the cash flow statement and the ending debt balances are linked to the balance sheet. The debt schedule is also used to calculate the annual interest expense for the individual debt instruments, which is linked to the income statement.

The debt schedule is typically constructed in accordance with the security and seniority of the loans, securities, and other debt instruments in the capital structure (i.e., beginning with the revolver, followed by term loan tranches, and bonds). As detailed in the following pages, we began the construction of ValueCo's debt schedule by entering the *forward LIBOR curve*,[18] followed by the calculation of annual projected cash available for debt repayment (free cash flow). We then entered the key terms for each individual debt instrument in the financing structure (i.e., size, term, coupon, and mandatory repayments/amortization schedule, if any).

---

[17]In lieu of a debt schedule, some LBO model templates use formulas in the appropriate cells in the financing activities section of the cash flow statement and the interest expense line item(s) of the income statement to perform the same functions.
[18]In 2021, LIBOR is expected to transition to SOFR (secured overnight financing rate), which is published by the Federal Reserve Bank of New York.

**Forward LIBOR Curve**    For floating-rate debt instruments, such as revolving credit facilities and term loans, interest rates are typically based on LIBOR[19] plus a fixed spread. Therefore, to calculate their projected annual interest expense, the banker must first enter future LIBOR estimates for each year of the projection period. LIBOR for future years is typically sourced from the Forward LIBOR Curve provided by Bloomberg.[20]

**EXHIBIT 5.24**    Forward LIBOR Curve

*($ in millions, fiscal year ending December 31)*

| Debt Schedule | | | | | | | | | | | |
|---|---|---|---|---|---|---|---|---|---|---|---|
| | | | | | | Projection Period | | | | | |
| | Pro forma | Year 1 | Year 2 | Year 3 | Year 4 | Year 5 | Year 6 | Year 7 | Year 8 | Year 9 | Year 10 |
| | 2019 | 2020 | 2021 | 2022 | 2023 | 2024 | 2025 | 2026 | 2027 | 2028 | 2029 |
| Forward LIBOR Curve | 1.85% | 1.70% | 1.65% | 1.55% | 1.55% | 1.55% | 1.55% | 1.55% | 1.55% | 1.55% | 1.55% |

As shown in the forward LIBOR curve line item in Exhibit 5.24, LIBOR is expected to remain relatively constant throughout the projection period at roughly 155 bps.[21] The pricing spreads for the revolver and TLB are added to the forward LIBOR in each year of the projection period to calculate their annual interest rates. For example, the 2022E interest rate for ValueCo's revolver, which is priced at L+425 bps, would be 5.8% (155 bps LIBOR + 425 bps spread).

**Cash Available for Debt Repayment (Free Cash Flow)**    The annual projected cash available for debt repayment is the sum of the cash flows provided by operating and investing activities on the cash flow statement. It is calculated in a section beneath the forward LIBOR curve inputs. For each year in the projection period, this amount is first used to make mandatory debt repayments on the term loan tranches.[22] The remaining cash flow is used to make optional debt repayments, as calculated in the cash available for optional debt repayment line item (see Exhibit 5.25).

In addition to internally generated free cash flow, existing cash from the balance sheet may be used ("swept") to make incremental debt repayments (see cash from balance sheet line item in Exhibit 5.25). In ValueCo's case, however, there is no cash on the pro forma balance sheet at closing as it is used as part of the transaction funding. In the event the post-LBO balance sheet has a cash balance, the banker may choose to keep a constant minimum level of cash on the balance sheet throughout the projection period by inputting a dollar amount under the "MinCash" heading (see Exhibit 5.25).

As shown in Exhibit 5.25, pro forma for the LBO, ValueCo generates $424.8 million of cash flow from operating activities in 2020E. Netting out ($166.9) million of cash flow from investing activities results in cash available for debt repayment of $257.9 million. After satisfying the $28 million mandatory amortization of the TLB, ValueCo has $229.9 million of cash available for optional debt repayment.

---

[19]3-month LIBOR is generally used.

[20]Bloomberg function: "FWCV" and use the 3-Month column.

[21]Following the onset of the subprime mortgage crisis and the ensuing rate cuts by the Federal Reserve, investors insisted on "LIBOR floors" in new bank deals. A LIBOR floor guarantees a minimum coupon for investors regardless of how low LIBOR falls. For example, a term loan priced at L+425 bps with a LIBOR floor of 100 bps will have a cost of capital of 5.25% even if the prevailing LIBOR is lower than 100 bps. In general, LIBOR floors are a convention used in low/falling interest rate environments.

[22]Mandatory repayments are determined in accordance with each debt instrument's amortization schedule.

**EXHIBIT 5.25** Cash Available for Debt Repayment (Free Cash Flow)

*($ in millions, fiscal year ending December 31)*

## Debt Schedule

| | Pro forma 2019 | | Projection Period | | | | | | | | | |
|---|---|---|---|---|---|---|---|---|---|---|---|---|
| | | Year 1 2020 | Year 2 2021 | Year 3 2022 | Year 4 2023 | Year 5 2024 | Year 6 2025 | Year 7 2026 | Year 8 2027 | Year 9 2028 | Year 10 2029 |
| Forward LIBOR Curve | *1.85%* | *1.70%* | *1.65%* | *1.55%* | *1.55%* | *1.55%* | *1.55%* | *1.55%* | *1.55%* | *1.55%* | *1.55%* |
| | | | | | | | | | | | |
| Cash Flow from Operating Activities | | $424.8 | $483.4 | $538.2 | $588.8 | $635.8 | $677.5 | $721.7 | $756.4 | $783.1 | $810.2 |
| Cash Flow from Investing Activities | | (166.9) | (176.9) | (185.8) | (193.2) | (199.0) | (204.9) | (211.1) | (217.4) | (224.0) | (230.7) |
| **Cash Available for Debt Repayment** | | **$257.9** | **$306.5** | **$352.4** | **$395.6** | **$436.8** | **$472.5** | **$510.6** | **$539.0** | **$559.2** | **$579.5** |
| Total Mandatory Repayments | | (28.0) | (28.0) | (28.0) | (28.0) | (28.0) | (28.0) | (28.0) | (28.0) | - | - |
| Cash from Balance Sheet | - | - | | | | | | | | 471.3 | 1,030.5 |
| **Cash Available for Optional Debt Repayment** | | **$229.9** | **$278.5** | **$324.4** | **$367.6** | **$408.8** | **$444.5** | **$482.6** | **$511.0** | **$1,030.5** | **$1,610.0** |

MinCash: -

= Cash Flow from Operating Activities₂₀₂₀E +
Cash Flow from Investing Activities₂₀₂₀E
= $424.8 million + ($166.9) million

= Mandatory Repayments on the Term Loan B,
calculcated as 1% x $2,800 million

= IF (Cash Balance toggle = 1, then sweep cash from the Balance Sheet
less the Minimum Cash Balance, otherwise display 0)

= Cash Flow for Debt Repayment₂₀₂₃E -
Total Mandatory Repayments₂₀₂₃E
= $395.6 million + ($28) million

**Revolving Credit Facility**  In the "Revolving Credit Facility" section of the debt schedule, the banker inputs the spread, term, and commitment fee associated with the facility (see Exhibit 5.26). The facility's size is linked from an assumptions page where the financing structure is entered (see Exhibits 5.14 and 5.54) and the beginning balance line item for the first year of the projection period is linked from the balance sheet. If no revolver draw is contemplated as part of the LBO financing structure, then the beginning balance is zero.

The revolver's drawdown/(repayment) line item feeds from the cash available for optional debt repayment line item at the top of the debt schedule. In the event the cash available for optional debt repayment amount is negative in any year (e.g., in a downside case), a revolver draw (or use of cash on the balance sheet, if applicable) is required. In the following period, the outstanding revolver debt is then repaid first from any positive cash available for optional debt repayment (i.e., once mandatory repayments are satisfied).

In connection with the ValueCo LBO, we contemplated a $250 million revolver, which is priced at L+425 bps and a term of five years. The revolver is assumed to be undrawn at the close of the transaction and remains undrawn throughout the projection period. Therefore, no interest expense is incurred. ValueCo, however, must pay an annual commitment fee of 50 bps on the undrawn portion of the revolver, translating into an expense of $1.25 million ($250 million × 0.50%) per year (see Exhibit 5.26).[23] This amount is included in interest expense on the income statement, together with the annual administrative agent fee of $150,000.

**Term Loan Facility**  In the "Term Loan Facility" section of the debt schedule, the banker inputs the spread, term, and mandatory repayment schedule associated with the facility (see Exhibit 5.27). The facility's size is linked from the sources and uses of funds on the transaction summary page (see Exhibit 5.46). For the ValueCo LBO, we contemplated a $2,800 million TLB with a coupon of L+425 bps and a term of seven years.

Mandatory Repayments (Amortization)  Unlike a revolving credit facility, which only requires repayment at the maturity date of all the outstanding advances, a term loan facility is fully funded at close and has a set amortization schedule as defined in the corresponding credit agreement. While amortization schedules vary per term loan tranche, the standard for TLBs is 1% amortization per year on the principal amount of the loan with a bullet payment of the loan balance at maturity.[24]

As noted in Exhibit 5.27 under the repayment schedule line item, ValueCo's new TLB requires an annual 1% amortization payment equating to $28 million ($2,800 million × 1%).

---

[23]To the extent the revolver is used, the commitment expense will decline, and ValueCo will be charged interest on the amount of the revolver draw at L+425 bps.
[24]Credit agreements typically also have a provision requiring the borrower to prepay term loans in an amount equal to a specified percentage (and definition) of excess cash flow and in the event of specified asset sales and issuances of certain debt or equity.

# EXHIBIT 5.26  Revolving Credit Facility Section of Debt Schedule

*($ in millions, fiscal year ending December 31)*

## Debt Schedule

| | Pro forma 2019 | Year 1 2020 | Year 2 2021 | Year 3 2022 | Year 4 2023 | Year 5 2024 | Year 6 2025 | Year 7 2026 | Year 8 2027 | Year 9 2028 | Year 10 2029 |
|---|---|---|---|---|---|---|---|---|---|---|---|
| | | | | | | Projection Period | | | | | |
| Forward LIBOR Curve | 1.85% | 1.70% | 1.65% | 1.55% | 1.55% | 1.55% | 1.55% | 1.55% | 1.55% | 1.55% | 1.55% |
| Cash Flow from Operating Activities | | $424.8 | $483.4 | $538.2 | $588.8 | $635.8 | $677.5 | $721.7 | $756.4 | $783.1 | $810.2 |
| Cash Flow from Investing Activities | | (166.9) | (176.9) | (185.8) | (193.2) | (199.0) | (204.9) | (211.1) | (217.4) | (224.0) | (230.7) |
| **Cash Available for Debt Repayment** | | **$257.9** | **$306.5** | **$352.4** | **$395.6** | **$436.8** | **$472.5** | **$510.6** | **$539.0** | **$559.2** | **$579.5** |
| Total Mandatory Repayments | | (28.0) | (28.0) | (28.0) | (28.0) | (28.0) | (28.0) | (28.0) | (28.0) | - | - |
| Cash From Balance Sheet  [MinCash  -] | | - | - | - | - | - | - | - | - | 471.3 | 1,030.5 |
| **Cash Available for Optional Debt Repayment** | | **$229.9** | **$278.5** | **$324.4** | **$367.6** | **$408.8** | **$444.5** | **$482.6** | **$511.0** | **$1,030.5** | **$1,610.0** |

### Revolving Credit Facility

| | | Year 1 2020 | Year 2 2021 | Year 3 2022 | Year 4 2023 | Year 5 2024 | Year 6 2025 | Year 7 2026 | Year 8 2027 | Year 9 2028 | Year 10 2029 |
|---|---|---|---|---|---|---|---|---|---|---|---|
| Revolving Credit Facility Size | $250.0 | | | | | | | | | | |
| Spread | 4.250% | | | | | | | | | | |
| LIBOR Floor | - % | | | | | | | | | | |
| Term | 5 years | | | | | | | | | | |
| Commitment Fee on Unused Portion | 0.50% | | | | | | | | | | |
| Beginning Balance | | - | - | - | - | - | - | - | - | - | - |
| Drawdown/(Repayment) | | - | - | - | - | - | - | - | - | - | - |
| **Ending Balance** | | - | - | - | - | - | - | - | - | - | - |
| Interest Rate | | 5.95% | 5.90% | 5.80% | 5.80% | 5.80% | 5.80% | 5.80% | 5.80% | 5.80% | 5.80% |
| Interest Expense | | - | - | - | - | - | - | - | - | - | - |
| Commitment Fee | | 1.3 | 1.3 | 1.3 | 1.3 | 1.3 | 1.3 | 1.3 | 1.3 | 1.3 | 1.3 |
| Administrative Agent Fee | | 0.2 | 0.2 | 0.2 | 0.2 | 0.2 | 0.2 | 0.2 | 0.2 | 0.2 | 0.2 |

= Ending Balance from Prior Year

= Ending Revolver Balance from Pro Forma 2019E Balance Sheet

= Commitment Fee on Unused Portion x (Revolver Capacity - (Average of Beginning Balance$_{2028E}$ and Ending Balance$_{2028E}$))

= 0.50% x $250 million

= IF (Cash Available for Optional Debt Repayment$_{2029E}$ > 0, then sweep the negative value of the minimum of (Cash Available for Optional Debt Repayment$_{2029E}$ vs. the Beginning Balance$_{2029E}$), otherwise sweep the negative value of the minimum of (Cash Available for Optional Debt Repayment$_{2029E}$ vs. 0))

= IF (Cash Available for Optional Debt Repayment$_{2029E}$ > 0, -MIN(Cash Available for Optional Debt Repayment$_{2029E}$, $0.0), -MIN(Cash Available for Optional Debt Repayment$_{2029E}$, 0))

**EXHIBIT 5.27** Term Loan Facility Section of Debt Schedule

*($ in millions, fiscal year ending December 31)*

**Debt Schedule**

| | Pro forma 2019 | Year 1 2020 | Year 2 2021 | Year 3 2022 | Year 4 2023 | Year 5 2024 | Year 6 2025 | Year 7 2026 | Year 8 2027 | Year 9 2028 | Year 10 2029 |
|---|---|---|---|---|---|---|---|---|---|---|---|
| | | **Projection Period** | | | | | | | | | |
| Forward LIBOR Curve | *1.85%* | *1.70%* | *1.65%* | *1.55%* | *1.55%* | *1.55%* | *1.55%* | *1.55%* | *1.55%* | *1.55%* | *1.55%* |
| Cash Flow from Operating Activities | | $424.8 | $483.4 | $538.2 | $588.8 | $635.8 | $677.5 | $721.7 | $756.4 | $783.1 | $810.2 |
| Cash Flow from Investing Activities | | (166.9) | (176.9) | (185.8) | (193.2) | (199.0) | (204.9) | (211.1) | (217.4) | (224.0) | (230.7) |
| **Cash Available for Debt Repayment** | | **$257.9** | **$306.5** | **$352.4** | **$395.6** | **$436.8** | **$472.5** | **$510.6** | **$539.0** | **$559.2** | **$579.5** |
| Total Mandatory Repayments | **MinCash** | (28.0) | (28.0) | (28.0) | (28.0) | (28.0) | (28.0) | (28.0) | (28.0) | - | - |
| Cash from Balance Sheet | - | - | - | - | - | - | - | - | - | 471.3 | 1,030.5 |
| **Cash Available for Optional Debt Repayment** | | **$229.9** | **$278.5** | **$324.4** | **$367.6** | **$408.8** | **$444.5** | **$482.6** | **$511.0** | **$1,030.5** | **$1,610.0** |

***Term Loan B Facility***

| | | | | | | | | | | | |
|---|---|---|---|---|---|---|---|---|---|---|---|
| Size | $2,800.0 | | | | | | | | | | |
| Spread | *4.250%* | | | | | | | | | | |
| LIBOR Floor | - % | | | | | | | | | | |
| Term | 7 years | | | | | | | | | | |
| Repayment Schedule | *1.0%* | Per Annum, Bullet at Maturity | | | | | | | | | |
| Beginning Balance | | $2,800.0 | $2,542.1 | $2,235.6 | $1,883.2 | $1,487.6 | $1,050.8 | $578.3 | $67.7 | - | - |
| Mandatory Repayments | | (28.0) | (28.0) | (28.0) | (28.0) | (28.0) | (28.0) | (28.0) | (28.0) | - | - |
| Optional Repayments | | (229.9) | (278.5) | (324.4) | (367.6) | (408.8) | (444.5) | (482.6) | (39.7) | - | - |
| **Ending Balance** | | **$2,542.1** | **$2,235.6** | **$1,883.2** | **$1,487.6** | **$1,050.8** | **$578.3** | **$67.7** | **-** | **-** | **-** |
| Interest Rate | | *5.95%* | *5.90%* | *5.80%* | *5.80%* | *5.80%* | *5.80%* | *5.80%* | *5.80%* | *5.80%* | *5.80%* |
| Interest Expense | | 158.9 | 140.9 | 119.4 | 97.8 | 73.6 | 47.2 | 18.7 | 2.0 | - | - |

= Ending Term Loan B Balance from Pro Forma 2019E Balance Sheet

= Interest Rate$_{2020E}$ × Average(Beginning Balance$_{2020E}$:Ending Balance$_{2020E}$)
= 5.95% × Average of $2,800 million and $2,542 million

= The negative of the minimum of (Cash Flow Available for Optional Debt Repayment$_{2022E}$ vs. Beginning Balance$_{2022E}$ + Mandatory Amortization$_{2022E}$)
= -MIN (-$324.4 million , $2,235.6 million + -$28 million)

= IF (Beginning Balance$_{2025E}$ is greater than 0 and greater than 1% of the principal amount, then subtract 1% Mandatory Amortization on the principal amount of the Term Loan B, otherwise display $0.0)
= IF ($578.3 million > 0 and > 1% × $2,800 million, then 1% × $2,800 million, otherwise $0.0)

Optional Repayments   A typical LBO model employs a "100% cash flow sweep" that assumes all cash generated by the target after making mandatory debt repayments is applied to the optional repayment of outstanding prepayable debt (typically bank loans). For modeling purposes, loans are generally repaid in the following order: revolver balance (since it can be reborrowed), term loan A (given sizable amortization payments and shorter maturity than the term loan B), term loan B (given no prepayment premium, in contrast to high yield bonds), etc.[25]

From a credit risk management perspective, ideally the target generates sufficient cumulative free cash flow during the projection period to repay the term loan(s) within their defined maturities. In some cases, however, the borrower may not be expected to repay the entire term loan balance within the proposed tenor and will instead face refinancing risk as the debt matures.[26]

As shown in Exhibit 5.27, in 2020E, ValueCo is projected to generate cash available for debt repayment of $257.9 million. Following the mandatory TLB principal repayment of $28 million, ValueCo has $229.9 million of excess free cash flow remaining. These funds are used to make optional debt repayments on the TLB, which is prepayable without penalty. Hence, the beginning year balance of $2,800 million is reduced to an ending balance of $2,542.1 million following the combined mandatory and optional debt repayments.

Interest Expense   The banker typically employs an average interest expense approach in determining annual interest expense in an LBO model. This methodology accounts for the fact that interest and principal on the loan is repaid throughout the year rather than at the beginning or end of the year. Annual average interest expense for each debt tranche is calculated by multiplying the average of the beginning and ending debt balances in a given year by its corresponding interest rate.

Using the average debt approach, the interest expense on ValueCo's TLB is calculated to be $158.9 million (($2,800 million + $2,542.1 million)/2) × 5.95%). The $158.9 million of interest expense is linked from the debt schedule to the income statement under the corresponding line item for TLB interest expense.

---

[25]Some credit agreements give credit to the borrower for voluntary repayments on a go-forward basis and/or may require pro rata repayment of certain tranches.
[26]Leveraged finance professionals assume the term loan gets refinanced well before maturity so outlying year repayments are largely theoretical.

**Senior Notes**    In the "Senior Notes" section of the debt schedule, the banker inputs the coupon and term associated with the security (see Exhibit 5.28). As with the TLB, the principal amount of the notes is linked from the sources and uses of funds on the transaction summary page (see Exhibit 5.46). Unlike traditional loans, high yield bonds are typically not prepayable without penalty and do not have a mandatory principal repayment schedule prior to the bullet payment at maturity. As a result, the model does not assume repayment of the high yield bonds prior to maturity and the beginning and ending balances for each year in the projection period are equal.

**EXHIBIT 5.28**    Senior Notes Section of Debt Schedule

($ in millions, fiscal year ending December 31)

| Debt Schedule | | | | | | | | | | | |
|---|---|---|---|---|---|---|---|---|---|---|---|
| | | | | | | **Projection Period** | | | | | |
| | Pro forma 2019 | Year 1 2020 | Year 2 2021 | Year 3 2022 | Year 4 2023 | Year 5 2024 | Year 6 2025 | Year 7 2026 | Year 8 2027 | Year 9 2028 | Year 10 2029 |
| *Senior Notes* | | | | | | | | | | | |
| Size | $850.0 | | | | | | | | | | |
| Coupon | 8.000% | | | | | | | | | | |
| Term | 8 years | | | | | | | | | | |
| Beginning Balance | | $850.0 | $850.0 | $850.0 | $850.0 | $850.0 | $850.0 | $850.0 | $850.0 | $850.0 | $850.0 |
| Repayment | | - | - | - | - | - | - | - | - | - | - |
| **Ending Balance** | | **$850.0** | **$850.0** | **$850.0** | **$850.0** | **$850.0** | **$850.0** | **$850.0** | **$850.0** | **$850.0** | **$850.0** |
| Interest Expense | | 68.0 | 68.0 | 68.0 | 68.0 | 68.0 | 68.0 | 68.0 | 68.0 | 68.0 | 68.0 |

= Coupon on Senior Notes × Principal Amount
= 8.0% × $850 million

For the ValueCo LBO, we contemplated a senior unsecured notes issuance of $850 million with an 8.0% coupon and a maturity of eight years.[27] The notes are the longest-tenored debt instrument in the financing structure. As the notes do not amortize, there are no mandatory principal payments prior to maturity and optional prepayment is discouraged by the call protection for the majority of the bond's tenor (standard in high yield bonds). Annual interest expense is simply $68 million ($850 million × 8.0%).

The completed debt schedule is shown in Exhibit 5.29.

---

[27]The notes are assumed to be refinanced at maturity.

# EXHIBIT 5.29  Debt Schedule

*($ in millions, fiscal year ending December 31)*

## Debt Schedule

| | Pro forma 2019 | Year 1 2020 | Year 2 2021 | Year 3 2022 | Year 4 2023 | Year 5 2024 | Year 6 2025 | Year 7 2026 | Year 8 2027 | Year 9 2028 | Year 10 2029 |
|---|---|---|---|---|---|---|---|---|---|---|---|
| | | | | | | Projection Period | | | | | |
| Forward LIBOR Curve | 1.85% | 1.70% | 1.65% | 1.55% | 1.55% | 1.55% | 1.55% | 1.55% | 1.55% | 1.55% | 1.55% |
| Cash Flow from Operating Activities | | $424.8 | $483.4 | $538.2 | $588.8 | $635.8 | $677.5 | $721.7 | $756.4 | $783.1 | $810.2 |
| Cash Flow from Investing Activities | | (166.9) | (176.9) | (185.8) | (193.2) | (199.0) | (204.9) | (211.1) | (217.4) | (224.0) | (230.7) |
| **Cash Available for Debt Repayment** | | **$257.9** | **$306.5** | **$352.4** | **$395.6** | **$436.8** | **$472.5** | **$510.6** | **$539.0** | **$559.2** | **$579.5** |
| Total Mandatory Repayments | | (28.0) | (28.0) | (28.0) | (28.0) | (28.0) | (28.0) | (28.0) | (28.0) | | |
| Cash From Balance Sheet | | - | - | - | - | - | - | - | - | 471.3 | 1,030.5 |
| **Cash Available for Optional Debt Repayment** | | **$229.9** | **$278.5** | **$324.4** | **$367.6** | **$408.8** | **$444.5** | **$482.6** | **$511.0** | **$1,030.5** | **$1,610.0** |

**MinCash** : -

### Revolving Credit Facility

| | | | | | | | | | | | |
|---|---|---|---|---|---|---|---|---|---|---|---|
| Revolving Credit Facility Size | $250.0 | | | | | | | | | | |
| Spread | 4.250% | | | | | | | | | | |
| LIBOR Floor | - % | | | | | | | | | | |
| Term | 5 years | | | | | | | | | | |
| Commitment Fee on Unused Portion | 0.50% | | | | | | | | | | |
| Beginning Balance | | - | - | - | - | - | - | - | - | - | - |
| Drawdown/(Repayment) | | - | - | - | - | - | - | - | - | - | - |
| **Ending Balance** | | **-** | **-** | **-** | **-** | **-** | **-** | **-** | **-** | **-** | **-** |
| Interest Rate | | 5.95% | 5.90% | 5.80% | 5.80% | 5.80% | 5.80% | 5.80% | 5.80% | 5.80% | 5.80% |
| Interest Expense | | - | - | - | - | - | - | - | - | - | - |
| Commitment Fee | | 1.3 | 1.3 | 1.3 | 1.3 | 1.3 | 1.3 | 1.3 | 1.3 | 1.3 | 1.3 |
| Administrative Agent Fee | | 0.2 | 0.2 | 0.2 | 0.2 | 0.2 | 0.2 | 0.2 | 0.2 | 0.2 | 0.2 |

### Term Loan B Facility

| | | | | | | | | | | | |
|---|---|---|---|---|---|---|---|---|---|---|---|
| Size | $2,800.0 | | | | | | | | | | |
| Spread | 4.250% | | | | | | | | | | |
| LIBOR Floor | - % | | | | | | | | | | |
| Term | 7 years | | | | | | | | | | |
| Repayment Schedule | 1.0% Per Annum, Bullet at Maturity | | | | | | | | | | |
| Beginning Balance | | $2,800.0 | $2,542.1 | $2,235.6 | $1,883.2 | $1,487.6 | $1,050.8 | $578.3 | $67.7 | | |
| Mandatory Repayments | | (28.0) | (28.0) | (28.0) | (28.0) | (28.0) | (28.0) | (28.0) | (28.0) | | |
| Optional Repayments | | (229.9) | (278.5) | (324.4) | (367.6) | (408.8) | (444.5) | (482.6) | (39.7) | | |
| **Ending Balance** | | **$2,542.1** | **$2,235.6** | **$1,883.2** | **$1,487.6** | **$1,050.8** | **$578.3** | **$67.7** | **-** | | |
| Interest Rate | | 5.95% | 5.90% | 5.80% | 5.80% | 5.80% | 5.80% | 5.80% | 5.80% | | |
| Interest Expense | | 158.9 | 140.9 | 119.4 | 97.8 | 73.6 | 47.2 | 18.7 | 2.0 | | |

### Senior Notes

| | | | | | | | | | | | |
|---|---|---|---|---|---|---|---|---|---|---|---|
| Size | $850.0 | | | | | | | | | | |
| Coupon | 8.000% | | | | | | | | | | |
| Term | 8 years | | | | | | | | | | |
| Beginning Balance | | $850.0 | $850.0 | $850.0 | $850.0 | $850.0 | $850.0 | $850.0 | $850.0 | $850.0 | $850.0 |
| **Ending Balance** | | **$850.0** | **$850.0** | **$850.0** | **$850.0** | **$850.0** | **$850.0** | **$850.0** | **$850.0** | **$850.0** | **$850.0** |
| Interest Expense | | 68.0 | 68.0 | 68.0 | 68.0 | 68.0 | 68.0 | 68.0 | 68.0 | 68.0 | 68.0 |

## Step IV(b): Complete Pro Forma Income Statement from EBIT to Net Income

The calculated average annual interest expense for each loan, bond, or other debt instrument in the capital structure is linked from the completed debt schedule to its corresponding line item on the income statement (see Exhibit 5.30).[28]

**EXHIBIT 5.30**   Pro Forma Projected Income Statement—EBIT to Net Income

*($ in millions, fiscal year ending December 31)*

**Income Statement**

| | | | | | | Projection Period | | | | | |
|---|---|---|---|---|---|---|---|---|---|---|---|
| | Pro forma | Year 1 | Year 2 | Year 3 | Year 4 | Year 5 | Year 6 | Year 7 | Year 8 | Year 9 | Year 10 |
| | 2019 | 2020 | 2021 | 2022 | 2023 | 2024 | 2025 | 2026 | 2027 | 2028 | 2029 |
| EBIT | $518.0 | $556.9 | $590.3 | $619.8 | $644.6 | $663.9 | $683.8 | $704.3 | $725.5 | $747.2 | $769.6 |
| % margin | 15.0% | 15.0% | 15.0% | 15.0% | 15.0% | 15.0% | 15.0% | 15.0% | 15.0% | 15.0% | 15.0% |
| | | | | | | | | | | | |
| *Interest Expense* | - | - | - | - | - | - | - | - | - | - | - |
| Revolving Credit Facility | - | - | - | - | - | - | - | - | - | - | - |
| Term Loan A | - | - | - | - | - | - | - | - | - | - | - |
| Term Loan B | 166.6 | 158.9 | 140.9 | 119.4 | 97.8 | 73.6 | 47.2 | 18.7 | 2.0 | - | - |
| Term Loan C | - | - | - | - | - | - | - | - | - | - | - |
| Existing Term Loan | - | - | - | - | - | - | - | - | - | - | - |
| 2nd Lien | - | - | - | - | - | - | - | - | - | - | - |
| Senior Notes | 68.0 | 68.0 | 68.0 | 68.0 | 68.0 | 68.0 | 68.0 | 68.0 | 68.0 | 68.0 | 68.0 |
| Senior Subordinated Notes | - | - | - | - | - | - | - | - | - | - | - |
| Commitment Fee on Unused Revolver | 1.3 | 1.3 | 1.3 | 1.3 | 1.3 | 1.3 | 1.3 | 1.3 | 1.3 | 1.3 | 1.3 |
| Administrative Agent Fee | 0.2 | 0.2 | 0.2 | 0.2 | 0.2 | 0.2 | 0.2 | 0.2 | 0.2 | 0.2 | 0.2 |
| **Cash Interest Expense** | **$236.0** | **$228.3** | **$210.3** | **$188.8** | **$167.2** | **$143.0** | **$116.6** | **$88.1** | **$71.4** | **$69.4** | **$69.4** |
| Amortization of Deferred Financing Fees | 14.0 | 14.0 | 14.0 | 14.0 | 14.0 | 14.0 | 12.9 | 12.9 | 3.9 | | |
| **Total Interest Expense** | **$250.0** | **$242.4** | **$224.4** | **$202.9** | **$181.2** | **$157.1** | **$129.6** | **$101.1** | **$75.3** | **$69.4** | **$69.4** |
| Interest Income | - | - | - | - | - | - | - | - | (1.2) | (3.8) | (6.6) |
| **Net Interest Expense** | | **$242.4** | **$224.4** | **$202.9** | **$181.2** | **$157.1** | **$129.6** | **$101.1** | **$74.1** | **$65.6** | **$62.8** |
| | | | | | | | | | | | |
| Earnings Before Taxes | | 314.5 | 365.9 | 416.9 | 463.4 | 506.8 | 554.3 | 603.3 | 651.4 | 681.6 | 706.8 |
| Income Tax Expense | | 78.6 | 91.5 | 104.2 | 115.8 | 126.7 | 138.6 | 150.8 | 162.8 | 170.4 | 176.7 |
| **Net Income** | | **$235.9** | **$274.4** | **$312.7** | **$347.5** | **$380.1** | **$415.7** | **$452.5** | **$488.5** | **$511.2** | **$530.1** |
| % margin | | 6.4% | 7.0% | 7.6% | 8.1% | 8.6% | 9.1% | 9.6% | 10.1% | 10.3% | 10.3% |

**Cash Interest Expense**   Cash interest expense refers to a company's actual cash interest and associated financing-related payments in a given year. It is the sum of the average interest expense for each cash-pay debt instrument plus the commitment fee on the unused portion of the revolver and the administrative agent fee. As shown in Exhibit 5.30, ValueCo is projected to have $228.3 million of cash interest expense in 2020E. This amount decreases to $69.4 million by the end of the projection period after the loan is repaid.

**Total Interest Expense**   Total interest expense is the sum of cash and non-cash interest expense, most notably the amortization of deferred financing fees, which is linked from an assumptions page (see Exhibit 5.54). The amortization of deferred financing fees, while technically not interest expense, is included in total interest expense as it is a financial charge. In a capital structure with a PIK instrument, the non-cash interest portion would also be included in total interest expense and added back to cash flow from operating activities on the cash flow statement. As shown in Exhibit 5.30, ValueCo has non-cash deferred financing fees of $14.0 million in 2020E. These fees are added to the 2020E cash interest expense of $228.3 million to sum to $242.4 million of total interest expense.

---

[28]At this point, a circular reference centering on interest expense has been created in the model. Interest expense is used to calculate net income and determine cash available for debt repayment and ending debt balances, which, in turn, are used to calculate interest expense. The spreadsheet must be set up to perform the circular calculation (see Exhibit 3.30).

**Net Interest Expense**   Net interest expense is calculated by subtracting interest income received on cash held on a company's balance sheet from its total interest expense. In the ValueCo LBO, however, there is no interest income until 2027E (Year 8) as the cash balance is zero. In 2027E, when all prepayable debt is repaid and cash begins to build on the balance sheet, ValueCo is expected to earn interest income of $1.2 million.[29] This is netted against total interest expense of $75.3 million, resulting in net interest expense of $74.1 million.

**Net Income**   To calculate ValueCo's net income for 2020E, we subtracted net interest expense of $242.4 million from EBIT of $556.9 million, which resulted in earnings before taxes of $314.5 million. We then multiplied EBT by ValueCo's marginal tax rate of 25% to produce tax expense of $78.6 million, which was netted out of EBT to calculate net income of $235.9 million.

Net income for each year in the projection period is linked from the income statement to the cash flow statement as the first line item under operating activities. It also feeds into the balance sheet as an addition to shareholders' equity in the form of retained earnings.

The completed pro forma income statement is shown in Exhibit 5.31.

---

[29]Assumes a 0.5% interest rate earned on cash (using an average balance method), which is indicative of a short-term money market instrument.

# EXHIBIT 5.31 Pro Forma ValueCo Income Statement

*($ in millions, fiscal year ending December 31)*

## Income Statement

| | Historical Period | | | LTM 9/30/2019 | Pro forma 2019 | Projection Period | | | | | | | | | |
|---|---|---|---|---|---|---|---|---|---|---|---|---|---|---|---|
| | 2016 | 2017 | 2018 | | | Year 1 2020 | Year 2 2021 | Year 3 2022 | Year 4 2023 | Year 5 2024 | Year 6 2025 | Year 7 2026 | Year 8 2027 | Year 9 2028 | Year 10 2029 |
| **Sales** | $2,600.0 | $2,900.0 | $3,200.0 | $3,385.0 | $3,450.0 | $3,708.8 | $3,931.3 | $4,127.8 | $4,293.0 | $4,421.7 | $4,554.4 | $4,691.0 | $4,831.8 | $4,976.7 | $5,126.0 |
| *% growth* | NA | 11.5% | 10.3% | NA | 7.8% | 7.5% | 6.0% | 5.0% | 4.0% | 3.0% | 3.0% | 3.0% | 3.0% | 3.0% | 3.0% |
| Cost of Goods Sold | 1,612.0 | 1,769.0 | 1,920.0 | 2,035.0 | 2,070.0 | 2,225.3 | 2,358.8 | 2,476.7 | 2,575.8 | 2,653.0 | 2,732.6 | 2,814.6 | 2,899.1 | 2,986.0 | 3,075.6 |
| **Gross Profit** | $988.0 | $1,131.0 | $1,280.0 | $1,350.0 | $1,380.0 | $1,483.5 | $1,572.5 | $1,651.1 | $1,717.2 | $1,768.7 | $1,821.8 | $1,876.4 | $1,932.7 | $1,990.7 | $2,050.4 |
| *% margin* | 38.0% | 39.0% | 40.0% | 39.9% | 40.0% | 40.0% | 40.0% | 40.0% | 40.0% | 40.0% | 40.0% | 40.0% | 40.0% | 40.0% | 40.0% |
| Selling, General & Administrative | 496.6 | 551.0 | 608.0 | 650.0 | 655.0 | 704.1 | 746.4 | 783.7 | 815.0 | 839.5 | 864.7 | 890.6 | 917.3 | 944.9 | 973.2 |
| *% sales* | 19.1% | 19.0% | 19.0% | 19.2% | 19.0% | 19.0% | 19.0% | 19.0% | 19.0% | 19.0% | 19.0% | 19.0% | 19.0% | 19.0% | 19.0% |
| Other Expense / (Income) | - | - | - | - | - | - | - | - | - | - | - | - | - | - | - |
| **EBITDA** | $491.4 | $580.0 | $672.0 | $700.0 | $725.0 | $779.4 | $826.1 | $867.4 | $902.1 | $929.2 | $957.1 | $985.8 | $1,015.4 | $1,045.8 | $1,077.2 |
| *% margin* | 18.9% | 20.0% | 21.0% | 20.7% | 21.0% | 21.0% | 21.0% | 21.0% | 21.0% | 21.0% | 21.0% | 21.0% | 21.0% | 21.0% | 21.0% |
| Depreciation | 116.0 | 121.5 | 145.0 | 150.0 | 155.3 | 166.9 | 176.9 | 185.8 | 193.2 | 199.0 | 204.9 | 211.1 | 217.4 | 224.0 | 230.7 |
| Amortization | 39.0 | 43.5 | 48.0 | 50.0 | 51.8 | 55.6 | 59.0 | 61.9 | 64.4 | 66.3 | 68.3 | 70.4 | 72.5 | 74.7 | 76.9 |
| **EBIT** | $336.4 | $415.0 | $479.0 | $500.0 | $518.0 | $556.9 | $590.3 | $619.8 | $644.6 | $663.9 | $683.8 | $704.3 | $725.5 | $747.2 | $769.6 |
| *% margin* | 12.9% | 14.3% | 15.0% | 14.8% | 15.0% | 15.0% | 15.0% | 15.0% | 15.0% | 15.0% | 15.0% | 15.0% | 15.0% | 15.0% | 15.0% |
| **Interest Expense** | | | | | | | | | | | | | | | |
| Revolving Credit Facility | | | | | - | - | - | - | - | - | - | - | - | - | - |
| Term Loan A | | | | | - | - | - | - | - | - | - | - | - | - | - |
| Term Loan B | | | | | 166.6 | 158.9 | 140.9 | 119.4 | 97.8 | 73.6 | 47.2 | 18.7 | 2.0 | - | - |
| Term Loan C | | | | | - | - | - | - | - | - | - | - | - | - | - |
| Existing Term Loan | | | | | - | - | - | - | - | - | - | - | - | - | - |
| 2nd Lien | | | | | - | - | - | - | - | - | - | - | - | - | - |
| Senior Notes | | | | | 68.0 | 68.0 | 68.0 | 68.0 | 68.0 | 68.0 | 68.0 | 68.0 | 68.0 | 68.0 | 68.0 |
| Senior Subordinated Notes | | | | | 1.3 | 1.3 | 1.3 | 1.3 | 1.3 | 1.3 | 1.3 | 1.3 | 1.3 | 1.3 | 1.3 |
| Commitment Fee on Unused Revolver | | | | | 0.2 | 0.2 | 0.2 | 0.2 | 0.2 | 0.2 | 0.2 | 0.2 | 0.2 | 0.2 | 0.2 |
| Administrative Agent Fee | | | | | - | - | - | - | - | - | - | - | - | - | - |
| **Cash Interest Expense** | | | | | $236.0 | $228.3 | $210.3 | $188.8 | $167.2 | $143.0 | $116.6 | $88.1 | $71.4 | $69.4 | $69.4 |
| Amortization of Deferred Financing Fees | | | | | 14.0 | 14.0 | 14.0 | 14.0 | 14.0 | 14.0 | 12.9 | 12.9 | 3.9 | - | - |
| **Total Interest Expense** | | | | | $250.0 | $242.4 | $224.4 | $202.9 | $181.2 | $157.1 | $129.6 | $101.1 | $75.3 | $69.4 | $69.4 |
| Interest Income | | | | | | | | | | | | | (1.2) | (3.8) | (6.6) |
| **Net Interest Expense** | | | | | | $242.4 | $224.4 | $202.9 | $181.2 | $157.1 | $129.6 | $101.1 | $74.1 | $65.6 | $62.8 |
| Earnings Before Taxes | | | | | | 314.5 | 365.9 | 416.9 | 463.4 | 506.8 | 554.3 | 603.3 | 651.4 | 681.6 | 706.8 |
| Income Tax Expense | | | | | | 78.6 | 91.5 | 104.2 | 115.8 | 126.7 | 138.6 | 150.8 | 162.8 | 170.4 | 176.7 |
| **Net Income** | | | | | | $235.9 | $274.4 | $312.7 | $347.5 | $380.1 | $415.7 | $452.5 | $488.5 | $511.2 | $530.1 |
| *% margin* | | | | | | 6.4% | 7.0% | 7.6% | 8.1% | 8.6% | 9.1% | 9.6% | 10.1% | 10.3% | 10.3% |

## Income Statement Assumptions

| | 2016 | 2017 | 2018 | LTM | Pro forma | 2020 | 2021 | 2022 | 2023 | 2024 | 2025 | 2026 | 2027 | 2028 | 2029 |
|---|---|---|---|---|---|---|---|---|---|---|---|---|---|---|---|
| Sales (% YoY growth) | NA | 11.5% | 10.3% | NA | 7.8% | 7.5% | 6.0% | 5.0% | 4.0% | 3.0% | 3.0% | 3.0% | 3.0% | 3.0% | 3.0% |
| Cost of Goods Sold (% margin) | 62.0% | 61.0% | 60.0% | 60.1% | 60.0% | 60.0% | 60.0% | 60.0% | 60.0% | 60.0% | 60.0% | 60.0% | 60.0% | 60.0% | 60.0% |
| SG&A (% sales) | 19.1% | 19.0% | 19.0% | 19.2% | 19.0% | 19.0% | 19.0% | 19.0% | 19.0% | 19.0% | 19.0% | 19.0% | 19.0% | 19.0% | 19.0% |
| Other Expense / (Income) (% of sales) | -% | -% | -% | -% | -% | -% | -% | -% | -% | -% | -% | -% | -% | -% | -% |
| Depreciation (% of sales) | 4.5% | 4.2% | 4.5% | 4.4% | 4.5% | 4.5% | 4.5% | 4.5% | 4.5% | 4.5% | 4.5% | 4.5% | 4.5% | 4.5% | 4.5% |
| Amortization (% of sales) | 1.5% | 1.5% | 1.5% | 1.5% | 0.5% | 1.5% | 1.5% | 1.5% | 1.5% | 1.5% | 1.5% | 1.5% | 1.5% | 1.5% | 1.5% |
| Interest Income (% of sales) | | | | | | 0.5% | 0.5% | 0.5% | 0.5% | 0.5% | 0.5% | 0.5% | 0.5% | 0.5% | 0.5% |
| Tax Rate | | | | | | 25.0% | 25.0% | 25.0% | 25.0% | 25.0% | 25.0% | 25.0% | 25.0% | 25.0% | 25.0% |

265

## Step IV(c): Complete Pro Forma Balance Sheet

**Liabilities**   The balance sheet is completed by linking the year-end balances for each debt instrument directly from the debt schedule. The remaining non-current and non-debt liabilities, captured in the other long-term liabilities line item, are generally held constant at the prior year level in the absence of specific management guidance.

As shown in Exhibit 5.32, during the projection period, ValueCo's $2,800 million TLB is repaid by the end of 2027E. ValueCo's $850 million senior notes, on the other hand, remain outstanding. In addition, we held the 2019E deferred income taxes and other long-term liabilities amount constant at $300 million and $110 million, respectively, for the length of the projection period.

**EXHIBIT 5.32**   Pro Forma Total Liabilities Section of Balance Sheet

*($ in millions, fiscal year ending December 31)*

**Balance Sheet**

| | Opening 2019 | Adjustments + | Adjustments – | Pro Forma 2019 | Year 1 2020 | Year 2 2021 | Year 3 2022 | Year 4 2023 | Year 5 2024 | Year 6 2025 | Year 7 2026 | Year 8 2027 | Year 9 2028 | Year 10 2029 |
|---|---|---|---|---|---|---|---|---|---|---|---|---|---|---|
| Accounts Payable | 215.0 | | | 215.0 | 231.1 | 245.0 | 257.2 | 267.5 | 275.6 | 283.8 | 292.3 | 301.1 | 310.1 | 319.4 |
| Accrued Liabilities | 275.0 | | | 275.0 | 295.6 | 313.4 | 329.0 | 342.2 | 352.5 | 363.0 | 373.9 | 385.1 | 396.7 | 408.6 |
| Other Current Liabilities | 100.0 | | | 100.0 | 107.5 | 114.0 | 119.6 | 124.4 | 128.2 | 132.0 | 136.0 | 140.1 | 144.3 | 148.6 |
| **Total Current Liabilities** | **$590.0** | | | **$590.0** | **$634.3** | **$672.3** | **$705.9** | **$734.2** | **$756.2** | **$778.9** | **$802.2** | **$826.3** | **$851.1** | **$876.6** |
| Revolving Credit Facility | - | | | - | - | - | - | - | - | - | - | - | - | - |
| Term Loan B | - | 2,800.0 | | 2,800.0 | 2,542.1 | 2,235.6 | 1,883.2 | 1,487.6 | 1,050.8 | 578.3 | 67.7 | - | - | - |
| Existing Term Loan | 1,000.0 | | (1,000.0) | - | - | - | - | - | - | - | - | - | - | - |
| Senior Notes | - | 850.0 | | 850.0 | 850.0 | 850.0 | 850.0 | 850.0 | 850.0 | 850.0 | 850.0 | 850.0 | 850.0 | 850.0 |
| Existing Senior Notes | 500.0 | | (500.0) | - | - | - | - | - | - | - | - | - | - | - |
| Deferred Income Taxes | 300.0 | | | 300.0 | 300.0 | 300.0 | 300.0 | 300.0 | 300.0 | 300.0 | 300.0 | 300.0 | 300.0 | 300.0 |
| Other Long-Term Liabilities | 110.0 | | | 110.0 | 110.0 | 110.0 | 110.0 | 110.0 | 110.0 | 110.0 | 110.0 | 110.0 | 110.0 | 110.0 |
| **Total Liabilities** | **$2,500.0** | | | **$4,650.0** | **$4,436.3** | **$4,167.9** | **$3,849.1** | **$3,481.8** | **$3,067.0** | **$2,617.2** | **$2,129.9** | **$2,086.3** | **$2,111.1** | **$2,136.6** |

**Shareholders' Equity**   Pro forma net income, which has now been calculated for each year in the projection period, is added to the prior year's shareholders' equity as retained earnings.

As shown in Exhibit 5.33, at the end of 2019E pro forma for the LBO, ValueCo has $2,050 million of shareholders' initial equity (representing the sponsor's equity contribution less other fees and expenses). To calculate 2020E shareholders' equity, we added the 2020E net income of $235.9 million, which summed to $2,285.9 million.

**EXHIBIT 5.33**   Pro Forma Total Shareholders' Equity Section of Balance Sheet

*($ in millions, fiscal year ending December 31)*

**Balance Sheet**

| | Opening 2019 | Adjustments + | Adjustments – | Pro Forma 2019 | Year 1 2020 | Year 2 2021 | Year 3 2022 | Year 4 2023 | Year 5 2024 | Year 6 2025 | Year 7 2026 | Year 8 2027 | Year 9 2028 | Year 10 2029 |
|---|---|---|---|---|---|---|---|---|---|---|---|---|---|---|
| Shareholders' Equity | 3,500.0 | 2,050.0 | (3,500.0) | 2,050.0 | 2,285.9 | 2,560.3 | 2,872.9 | 3,220.4 | 3,600.6 | 4,016.3 | 4,468.7 | 4,957.2 | 5,468.4 | 5,998.6 |
| **Total Shareholders' Equity** | **$3,500.0** | | | **$2,050.0** | **$2,285.9** | **$2,560.3** | **$2,872.9** | **$3,220.4** | **$3,600.6** | **$4,016.3** | **$4,468.7** | **$4,957.2** | **$5,468.4** | **$5,998.6** |
| **Total Liabilities and Equity** | **$6,000.0** | | | **$6,700.0** | **$6,722.2** | **$6,728.2** | **$6,722.0** | **$6,702.2** | **$6,667.6** | **$6,633.4** | **$6,598.7** | **$7,043.5** | **$7,579.5** | **$8,135.2** |

= Shareholders' Equity$_{2019E}$ + Net Income $_{2020E}$
= $2,050 million + $235.9 million

The completed pro forma balance sheet is shown in Exhibit 5.34.

# EXHIBIT 5.34  Pro Forma ValueCo Balance Sheet

*($ in millions, fiscal year ending December 31)*

**Balance Sheet**

| | Opening 2019 | Adjustments + | Adjustments - | Pro Forma 2019 | Year 1 2020 | Year 2 2021 | Year 3 2022 | Year 4 2023 | Year 5 2024 | Year 6 2025 | Year 7 2026 | Year 8 2027 | Year 9 2028 | Year 10 2029 |
|---|---|---|---|---|---|---|---|---|---|---|---|---|---|---|
| Cash and Cash Equivalents | $250.0 | | (250.0) | - | - | - | - | - | - | - | - | $471.3 | $1,030.5 | $1,610.0 |
| Accounts Receivable | 450.0 | | | 450.0 | 483.8 | 512.8 | 538.4 | 560.0 | 576.7 | 594.1 | 611.9 | 630.2 | 649.1 | 668.6 |
| Inventories | 600.0 | | | 600.0 | 645.0 | 683.7 | 717.9 | 746.6 | 769.0 | 792.1 | 815.8 | 840.3 | 865.5 | 891.5 |
| Prepaids and Other Current Assets | 175.0 | | | 175.0 | 188.1 | 199.4 | 209.4 | 217.8 | 224.3 | 231.0 | 238.0 | 245.1 | 252.4 | 260.0 |
| **Total Current Assets** | **$1,475.0** | | | **$1,225.0** | **$1,316.9** | **$1,395.9** | **$1,465.7** | **$1,524.3** | **$1,570.0** | **$1,617.1** | **$1,665.7** | **$2,186.9** | **$2,797.6** | **$3,430.1** |
| Property, Plant and Equipment, net | 2,500.0 | | | 2,500.0 | 2,500.0 | 2,500.0 | 2,500.0 | 2,500.0 | 2,500.0 | 2,500.0 | 2,500.0 | 2,500.0 | 2,500.0 | 2,500.0 |
| Goodwill | 1,000.0 | 1,850.0 | (1,000.0) | 1,850.0 | 1,850.0 | 1,850.0 | 1,850.0 | 1,850.0 | 1,850.0 | 1,850.0 | 1,850.0 | 1,850.0 | 1,850.0 | 1,850.0 |
| Intangible Assets | 875.0 | | | 875.0 | 819.4 | 760.4 | 698.5 | 634.1 | 567.8 | 499.4 | 429.1 | 356.6 | 282.0 | 205.1 |
| Other Assets | 150.0 | | | 150.0 | 150.0 | 150.0 | 150.0 | 150.0 | 150.0 | 150.0 | 150.0 | 150.0 | 150.0 | 150.0 |
| Deferred Financing Fees | - | 100.0 | | 100.0 | 86.0 | 71.9 | 57.9 | 43.8 | 29.8 | 16.8 | 3.9 | - | - | - |
| **Total Assets** | **$6,000.0** | | | **$6,700.0** | **$6,722.2** | **$6,728.2** | **$6,722.0** | **$6,702.2** | **$6,667.6** | **$6,633.4** | **$6,598.7** | **$7,043.5** | **$7,579.5** | **$8,135.2** |
| Accounts Payable | 215.0 | | | 215.0 | 231.1 | 245.0 | 257.2 | 267.5 | 275.6 | 283.8 | 292.3 | 301.1 | 310.1 | 319.4 |
| Accrued Liabilities | 275.0 | | | 275.0 | 295.6 | 313.4 | 329.0 | 342.2 | 352.5 | 363.0 | 373.9 | 385.1 | 396.7 | 408.6 |
| Other Current Liabilities | 100.0 | | | 100.0 | 107.5 | 114.0 | 119.6 | 124.4 | 128.2 | 132.0 | 136.0 | 140.1 | 144.3 | 148.6 |
| **Total Current Liabilities** | **$590.0** | | | **$590.0** | **$634.3** | **$672.3** | **$705.9** | **$734.2** | **$756.2** | **$778.9** | **$802.2** | **$826.3** | **$851.1** | **$876.6** |
| Revolving Credit Facility | - | | | - | - | - | - | - | - | - | - | - | - | - |
| Term Loan A | - | | | - | - | - | - | - | - | - | - | - | - | - |
| Term Loan B | 2,800.0 | 2,800.0 | | 2,800.0 | 2,542.1 | 2,235.6 | 1,883.2 | 1,487.6 | 1,050.8 | 578.3 | 67.7 | - | - | - |
| Term Loan C | - | | | - | - | - | - | - | - | - | - | - | - | - |
| Existing Term Loan | 1,000.0 | | (1,000.0) | - | - | - | - | - | - | - | - | - | - | - |
| 2nd Lien | - | | | - | - | - | - | - | - | - | - | - | - | - |
| Senior Notes | - | 850.0 | | 850.0 | 850.0 | 850.0 | 850.0 | 850.0 | 850.0 | 850.0 | 850.0 | 850.0 | 850.0 | 850.0 |
| Existing Senior Notes | 500.0 | | (500.0) | - | - | - | - | - | - | - | - | - | - | - |
| Senior Subordinated Notes | - | | | - | - | - | - | - | - | - | - | - | - | - |
| Other Debt | - | | | - | - | - | - | - | - | - | - | - | - | - |
| Deferred Income Taxes | 300.0 | | | 300.0 | 300.0 | 300.0 | 300.0 | 300.0 | 300.0 | 300.0 | 300.0 | 300.0 | 300.0 | 300.0 |
| Other Long-Term Liabilities | 110.0 | | | 110.0 | 110.0 | 110.0 | 110.0 | 110.0 | 110.0 | 110.0 | 110.0 | 110.0 | 110.0 | 110.0 |
| **Total Liabilities** | **$2,500.0** | | | **$4,650.0** | **$4,436.3** | **$4,167.9** | **$3,849.1** | **$3,481.8** | **$3,067.0** | **$2,617.2** | **$2,129.9** | **$2,086.3** | **$2,111.1** | **$2,136.6** |
| Noncontrolling Interest | - | | | - | - | - | - | - | - | - | - | - | - | - |
| Shareholders' Equity | 3,500.0 | 2,050.0 | (3,500.0) | 2,050.0 | 2,285.9 | 2,560.3 | 2,872.9 | 3,220.4 | 3,600.6 | 4,016.3 | 4,468.7 | 4,957.2 | 5,468.4 | 5,998.6 |
| **Total Shareholders' Equity** | **$3,500.0** | | | **$2,050.0** | **$2,285.9** | **$2,560.3** | **$2,872.9** | **$3,220.4** | **$3,600.6** | **$4,016.3** | **$4,468.7** | **$4,957.2** | **$5,468.4** | **$5,998.6** |
| **Total Liabilities and Equity** | **$6,000.0** | | | **$6,700.0** | **$6,722.2** | **$6,728.2** | **$6,722.0** | **$6,702.2** | **$6,667.6** | **$6,633.4** | **$6,598.7** | **$7,043.5** | **$7,579.5** | **$8,135.2** |
| Balance Check | 0.000 | | | 0.000 | 0.000 | 0.000 | 0.000 | 0.000 | 0.000 | 0.000 | 0.000 | 0.000 | 0.000 | 0.000 |
| Net Working Capital | 635.0 | | | 635.0 | 682.6 | 723.6 | 759.8 | 790.2 | 813.9 | 838.3 | 863.4 | 889.3 | 916.0 | 943.5 |
| (Increase) / Decrease in Net Working Capital | | | | - | (47.6) | (41.0) | (36.2) | (30.4) | (23.7) | (24.4) | (25.1) | (25.9) | (26.7) | (27.5) |

**Balance Sheet Assumptions**

| **Current Assets** | | | | | | | | | | | | | | |
|---|---|---|---|---|---|---|---|---|---|---|---|---|---|---|
| Days Sales Outstanding (DSO) | 47.6 | | | 47.6 | 47.6 | 47.6 | 47.6 | 47.6 | 47.6 | 47.6 | 47.6 | 47.6 | 47.6 | 47.6 |
| Days Inventory Held (DIH) | 105.8 | | | 105.8 | 105.8 | 105.8 | 105.8 | 105.8 | 105.8 | 105.8 | 105.8 | 105.8 | 105.8 | 105.8 |
| Prepaid and Other Current Assets (% of sales) | 5.1% | | | 5.1% | 5.1% | 5.1% | 5.1% | 5.1% | 5.1% | 5.1% | 5.1% | 5.1% | 5.1% | 5.1% |

| **Current Liabilities** | | | | | | | | | | | | | | |
|---|---|---|---|---|---|---|---|---|---|---|---|---|---|---|
| Days Payable Outstanding (DPO) | 37.9 | | | 37.9 | 37.9 | 37.9 | 37.9 | 37.9 | 37.9 | 37.9 | 37.9 | 37.9 | 37.9 | 37.9 |
| Accrued Liabilities (% of sales) | 8.0% | | | 8.0% | 8.0% | 8.0% | 8.0% | 8.0% | 8.0% | 8.0% | 8.0% | 8.0% | 8.0% | 8.0% |
| Other Current Liabilities (% of sales) | 2.9% | | | 2.9% | 2.9% | 2.9% | 2.9% | 2.9% | 2.9% | 2.9% | 2.9% | 2.9% | 2.9% | 2.9% |

267

## Step IV(d): Complete Pro Forma Cash Flow Statement

To complete the cash flow statement, the mandatory and optional repayments for each debt instrument, as calculated in the debt schedule, are linked to the appropriate line items in the financing activities section and summed to produce the annual repayment amounts. The annual pro forma beginning and ending cash balances are then calculated accordingly.

In 2020E, ValueCo is projected to generate $257.9 million of free cash flow. This amount is first used to satisfy the $28 million mandatory TLB amortization with the remaining cash used to make an optional repayment of $229.9 million. As shown in Exhibit 5.35, these combined actions are linked to the TLB line item in the financing activities section of the cash flow statement as a $257.9 million use of cash in 2020E.

**EXHIBIT 5.35** Pro Forma Financing Activities Section of Cash Flow Statement

*($ in millions, fiscal year ending December 31)*

**Cash Flow Statement**

| | Year 1 2020 | Year 2 2021 | Year 3 2022 | Year 4 2023 | Year 5 2024 | Year 6 2025 | Year 7 2026 | Year 8 2027 | Year 9 2028 | Year 10 2029 |
|---|---|---|---|---|---|---|---|---|---|---|
| | | | | | Projection Period | | | | | |
| *Financing Activities* | | | | | | | | | | |
| Revolving Credit Facility | - | - | - | - | - | - | - | - | - | - |
| Term Loan B | (257.9) | (306.5) | (352.4) | (395.6) | (436.8) | (472.5) | (510.6) | (67.7) | - | - |
| Existing Term Loan | - | - | - | - | - | - | - | - | - | - |
| Senior Notes | - | - | - | - | - | - | - | - | - | - |
| Dividends | - | - | - | - | - | - | - | - | - | - |
| Equity Issuance / (Repurchase) | - | - | - | - | - | - | - | - | - | - |
| **Cash Flow from Financing Activities** | ($257.9) | ($306.5) | ($352.4) | ($395.6) | ($436.8) | ($472.5) | ($510.6) | ($67.7) | - | - |
| Excess Cash for the Period | - | - | - | - | - | - | - | $471.3 | $559.2 | $579.5 |
| Beginning Cash Balance | - | - | - | - | - | - | - | - | 471.3 | 1,030.5 |
| **Ending Cash Balance** | - | - | - | - | - | - | - | $471.3 | $1,030.5 | $1,610.0 |
| *Cash Flow Statement Assumptions* | | | | | | | | | | |
| Capital Expenditures (% of sales) | 4.5% | 4.5% | 4.5% | 4.5% | 4.5% | 4.5% | 4.5% | 4.5% | 4.5% | 4.5% |

= Mandatory Repayments $_{2020E}$
+ Optional Repayments $_{2020E}$
= ($28) million + ($229.9) million

As we assumed a 100% cash flow sweep, cash does not build on the balance sheet until the loan is fully repaid. Hence, ValueCo's ending cash balance line item remains constant at zero until 2027E when the TLB is completely paid down.[30] As shown in Exhibit 5.10, the ending cash balance for each year in the projection period links to the balance sheet.

The completed pro forma cash flow statement is shown in Exhibit 5.36.

---

[30]While a cash balance of zero may be unrealistic from an operating perspective, it is a relatively common modeling convention.

**EXHIBIT 5.36**  Pro Forma ValueCo Cash Flow Statement

*($ in millions, fiscal year ending December 31)*

**Cash Flow Statement**

| | | | | | Projection Period | | | | | |
|---|---|---|---|---|---|---|---|---|---|---|
| | Year 1 | Year 2 | Year 3 | Year 4 | Year 5 | Year 6 | Year 7 | Year 8 | Year 9 | Year 10 |
| | 2020 | 2021 | 2022 | 2023 | 2024 | 2025 | 2026 | 2027 | 2028 | 2029 |
| **Operating Activities** | | | | | | | | | | |
| Net Income | $235.9 | $274.4 | $312.7 | $347.5 | $380.1 | $415.7 | $452.5 | $488.5 | $511.2 | $530.1 |
| Plus: Depreciation | 166.9 | 176.9 | 185.8 | 193.2 | 199.0 | 204.9 | 211.1 | 217.4 | 224.0 | 230.7 |
| Plus: Amortization | 55.6 | 59.0 | 61.9 | 64.4 | 66.3 | 68.3 | 70.4 | 72.5 | 74.7 | 76.9 |
| Plus: Amortization of Financing Fees | 14.0 | 14.0 | 14.0 | 14.0 | 14.0 | 12.9 | 12.9 | 3.9 | - | - |
| **Changes in Working Capital Items** | | | | | | | | | | |
| (Inc.) / Dec. in Accounts Receivable | (33.8) | (29.0) | (25.6) | (21.5) | (16.8) | (17.3) | (17.8) | (18.4) | (18.9) | (19.5) |
| (Inc.) / Dec. in Inventories | (45.0) | (38.7) | (34.2) | (28.7) | (22.4) | (23.1) | (23.8) | (24.5) | (25.2) | (26.0) |
| (Inc.) / Dec. in Prepaid and Other Current Assets | (13.1) | (11.3) | (10.0) | (8.4) | (6.5) | (6.7) | (6.9) | (7.1) | (7.4) | (7.6) |
| Inc. / (Dec.) in Accounts Payable | 16.1 | 13.9 | 12.2 | 10.3 | 8.0 | 8.3 | 8.5 | 8.8 | 9.0 | 9.3 |
| Inc. / (Dec.) in Accrued Liabilities | 20.6 | 17.7 | 15.7 | 13.2 | 10.3 | 10.6 | 10.9 | 11.2 | 11.6 | 11.9 |
| Inc. / (Dec.) in Other Current Liabilities | 7.5 | 6.5 | 5.7 | 4.8 | 3.7 | 3.8 | 4.0 | 4.1 | 4.2 | 4.3 |
| (Inc.) / Dec. in Net Working Capital | (47.6) | (41.0) | (36.2) | (30.4) | (23.7) | (24.4) | (25.1) | (25.9) | (26.7) | (27.5) |
| **Cash Flow from Operating Activities** | **$424.8** | **$483.4** | **$538.2** | **$588.8** | **$635.8** | **$677.5** | **$721.7** | **$756.4** | **$783.1** | **$810.2** |
| **Investing Activities** | | | | | | | | | | |
| Capital Expenditures | (166.9) | (176.9) | (185.8) | (193.2) | (199.0) | (204.9) | (211.1) | (217.4) | (224.0) | (230.7) |
| Other Investing Activities | - | - | - | - | - | - | - | - | - | - |
| **Cash Flow from Investing Activities** | **($166.9)** | **($176.9)** | **($185.8)** | **($193.2)** | **($199.0)** | **($204.9)** | **($211.1)** | **($217.4)** | **($224.0)** | **($230.7)** |
| **Financing Activities** | | | | | | | | | | |
| Revolving Credit Facility | - | - | - | - | - | - | - | - | - | - |
| Term Loan B | (257.9) | (306.5) | (352.4) | (395.6) | (436.8) | (472.5) | (510.6) | (67.7) | - | - |
| Existing Term Loan | - | - | - | - | - | - | - | - | - | - |
| Senior Notes | - | - | - | - | - | - | - | - | - | - |
| Dividends | - | - | - | - | - | - | - | - | - | - |
| Equity Issuance / (Repurchase) | - | - | - | - | - | - | - | - | - | - |
| **Cash Flow from Financing Activities** | **($257.9)** | **($306.5)** | **($352.4)** | **($395.6)** | **($436.8)** | **($472.5)** | **($510.6)** | **($67.7)** | **-** | **-** |
| Excess Cash for the Period | - | - | - | - | - | - | - | $471.3 | $559.2 | $579.5 |
| Beginning Cash Balance | - | - | - | - | - | - | - | - | 471.3 | 1,030.5 |
| **Ending Cash Balance** | **-** | **-** | **-** | **-** | **-** | **-** | **-** | **$471.3** | **$1,030.5** | **$1,610.0** |
| **Cash Flow Statement Assumptions** | | | | | | | | | | |
| Capital Expenditures (% of sales) | 4.5% | 4.5% | 4.5% | 4.5% | 4.5% | 4.5% | 4.5% | 4.5% | 4.5% | 4.5% |

## STEP V. PERFORM LBO ANALYSIS

**EXHIBIT 5.37**   Steps to Perform LBO Analysis

| |
|---|
| Step V(a):   Analyze Financing Structure |
| Step V(b):   Perform Returns Analysis |
| Step V(c):   Determine Valuation |
| Step V(d):   Create Transaction Summary Page |

Once the LBO model is fully linked and tested, it is ready for use to evaluate various financing structures, gauge the target's ability to service and repay debt, and measure the sponsor's investment returns and other financial effects under multiple operating scenarios. This analysis, in turn, enables the banker to determine an appropriate valuation range for the target.

### Step V(a): Analyze Financing Structure

A central part of LBO analysis is the crafting of an optimal financing structure for a given transaction. From an underwriting perspective, this involves determining whether the target's financial projections can support a given leveraged financing structure under various business and economic conditions. The use of realistic and defensible financial projections is critical to assessing whether a given financial structure is viable.

A key credit risk management concern for the underwriters centers on the target's ability to service its annual interest expense and repay all (or a substantial portion) of its debt within the proposed tenor. The primary credit metrics used to analyze the target's ability to support a given capital structure include variations of the leverage and coverage ratios outlined in Chapter 1 (e.g., debt-to-EBITDA, debt-to-total capitalization, and EBITDA-to-interest expense). Exhibit 5.38 displays a typical output summarizing the target's key financial data as well as pro forma capitalization and credit statistics for each year in the projection period. This output is typically shown on a transaction summary page (see Exhibit 5.46).

For the ValueCo LBO, we performed our financing structure analysis on the basis of our Base Case financial projections (see Step II) and assumed transaction structure (see Step III). Pro forma for the LBO, ValueCo has a total capitalization of $5,700 million, comprised of the $2,800 million TLB, $850 million senior notes, and $2,050 million of shareholders' equity (the equity contribution less other fees and expenses). This capital structure represents total leverage of 5.2x LTM 9/30/2019 EBITDA of $700 million, including senior secured leverage of 4.0x (5.0x 2019E total leverage and 3.9x senior secured leverage). At these levels, ValueCo has a debt-to-total capitalization of 64%, EBITDA-to-interest expense of 2.9x, and (EBITDA – capex)-to-interest expense of 2.3x at close.

As would be expected for a company that is projected to grow EBITDA, generate sizable free cash flow, and repay debt, ValueCo's credit statistics improve significantly over the projection period. By the end of 2027E, ValueCo's TLB is completely repaid as total leverage decreases to 0.9x and senior secured leverage is reduced to zero. In addition, ValueCo's debt-to-total capitalization decreases to 17% and EBITDA to-interest expense increases to 9.8x.

**EXHIBIT 5.38**  Summary Financial Data, Capitalization, and Credit Statistics

*($ in millions, fiscal year ending December 31)*

## Summary Financial Data

| | LTM 9/30/2019 | Pro forma 2019 | Projection Period | | | | | | | | | |
|---|---|---|---|---|---|---|---|---|---|---|---|---|
| | | | Year 1 2020 | Year 2 2021 | Year 3 2022 | Year 4 2023 | Year 5 2024 | Year 6 2025 | Year 7 2026 | Year 8 2027 | Year 9 2028 | Year 10 2029 |
| **Sales** | $3,385.0 | $3,450.0 | $3,708.8 | $3,931.3 | $4,127.8 | $4,293.0 | $4,421.7 | $4,554.4 | $4,691.0 | $4,831.8 | $4,976.7 | $5,126.0 |
| *% growth* | NA | 7.8% | 7.5% | 6.0% | 5.0% | 4.0% | 3.0% | 3.0% | 3.0% | 3.0% | 3.0% | 3.0% |
| **Gross Profit** | $1,350.0 | $1,380.0 | $1,483.5 | $1,572.5 | $1,651.1 | $1,717.2 | $1,768.7 | $1,821.8 | $1,876.4 | $1,932.7 | $1,990.7 | $2,050.4 |
| *% margin* | 39.9% | 40.0% | 40.0% | 40.0% | 40.0% | 40.0% | 40.0% | 40.0% | 40.0% | 40.0% | 40.0% | 40.0% |
| **EBITDA** | $700.0 | $725.0 | $779.4 | $826.1 | $867.4 | $902.1 | $929.2 | $957.1 | $985.8 | $1,015.4 | $1,045.8 | $1,077.2 |
| *% margin* | 20.7% | 21.0% | 21.0% | 21.0% | 21.0% | 21.0% | 21.0% | 21.0% | 21.0% | 21.0% | 21.0% | 21.0% |
| Capital Expenditures | 152.3 | 155.3 | 166.9 | 176.9 | 185.8 | 193.2 | 199.0 | 204.9 | 211.1 | 217.4 | 224.0 | 230.7 |
| *% sales* | 4.5% | 4.5% | 4.5% | 4.5% | 4.5% | 4.5% | 4.5% | 4.5% | 4.5% | 4.5% | 4.5% | 4.5% |
| Cash Interest Expense | - | 236.0 | 228.3 | 210.3 | 188.8 | 167.2 | 143.0 | 116.6 | 88.1 | 71.4 | 69.4 | 69.4 |
| Total Interest Expense | - | 250.0 | 242.4 | 224.4 | 202.9 | 181.2 | 157.1 | 129.6 | 101.1 | 75.3 | 69.4 | 69.4 |
| **Free Cash Flow** | | | | | | | | | | | | |
| EBITDA | | | $779.4 | $826.1 | $867.4 | $902.1 | $929.2 | $957.1 | $985.8 | $1,015.4 | $1,045.8 | $1,077.2 |
| Less: Cash Interest Expense | | | (228.3) | (210.3) | (188.8) | (167.2) | (143.0) | (116.6) | (88.1) | (71.4) | (69.4) | (69.4) |
| Plus: Interest Income | | | - | - | - | - | - | - | - | 1.2 | 3.8 | 6.6 |
| Less: Income Taxes | | | (78.6) | (91.5) | (104.2) | (115.8) | (126.7) | (138.6) | (150.8) | (162.8) | (170.4) | (176.7) |
| Less: Capital Expenditures | | | (166.9) | (176.9) | (185.8) | (193.2) | (199.0) | (204.9) | (211.1) | (217.4) | (224.0) | (230.7) |
| Less: Increase in Net Working Capital | | | (47.6) | (41.0) | (36.2) | (30.4) | (23.7) | (24.4) | (25.1) | (25.9) | (26.7) | (27.5) |
| **Free Cash Flow** | | | $257.9 | $306.5 | $352.4 | $395.6 | $436.8 | $472.5 | $510.6 | $539.0 | $559.2 | $579.5 |
| Cumulative Free Cash Flow | | | 257.9 | 564.4 | 916.8 | 1,312.4 | 1,749.2 | 2,221.7 | 2,732.3 | 3,271.3 | 3,830.5 | 4,410.0 |
| **Capitalization** | | | | | | | | | | | | |
| Cash | | | - | - | - | - | - | - | - | $471.3 | $1,030.5 | $1,610.0 |
| Revolving Credit Facility | | | - | - | - | - | - | - | - | - | - | - |
| Term Loan A | | 2,800.0 | 2,542.1 | 2,235.6 | 1,883.2 | 1,487.6 | 1,050.8 | 578.3 | 67.7 | - | - | - |
| Term Loan B | | | | | | | | | | | | |
| Term Loan C | | | | | | | | | | | | |
| Existing Term Loan | | | | | | | | | | | | |
| 2nd Lien | | | | | | | | | | | | |
| Other Debt | | | | | | | | | | | | |
| **Total Senior Secured Debt** | | $2,800.0 | $2,542.1 | $2,235.6 | $1,883.2 | $1,487.6 | $1,050.8 | $578.3 | $67.7 | - | - | - |
| Senior Notes | | 850.0 | 850.0 | 850.0 | 850.0 | 850.0 | 850.0 | 850.0 | 850.0 | 850.0 | 850.0 | 850.0 |
| **Total Senior Debt** | | $3,650.0 | $3,392.1 | $3,085.6 | $2,733.6 | $2,337.6 | $1,900.8 | $1,428.3 | $917.7 | $850.0 | $850.0 | $850.0 |
| Senior Subordinated Notes | | | | | | | | | | | | |
| **Total Debt** | | $3,650.0 | $3,392.1 | $3,085.6 | $2,733.2 | $2,337.6 | $1,900.8 | $1,428.3 | $917.7 | $850.0 | $850.0 | $850.0 |
| Shareholders' Equity | | 2,050.0 | 2,285.9 | 2,560.3 | 2,872.9 | 3,220.4 | 3,600.6 | 4,016.3 | 4,468.7 | 4,957.2 | 5,468.4 | 5,998.6 |
| **Total Capitalization** | | $5,700.0 | $5,677.9 | $5,645.9 | $5,606.1 | $5,558.1 | $5,501.4 | $5,444.6 | $5,386.4 | $5,807.2 | $6,318.4 | $6,848.6 |
| *% of Bank Debt Repaid* | | - | 9.2% | 20.2% | 32.7% | 46.9% | 62.5% | 79.3% | 97.6% | 100.0% | 100.0% | 100.0% |
| **Credit Statistics** | | | | | | | | | | | | |
| *% Debt / Total Capitalization* | | 64.0% | 59.7% | 54.7% | 48.8% | 42.1% | 34.6% | 26.2% | 17.0% | 14.6% | 13.5% | 12.4% |
| EBITDA / Cash Interest Expense | | 3.1x | 3.4x | 3.9x | 4.6x | 5.4x | 6.5x | 8.2x | 11.2x | 14.2x | 15.1x | 15.5x |
| (EBITDA - Capex) / Cash Interest Expense | | 2.4x | 2.7x | 3.1x | 3.6x | 4.2x | 5.1x | 6.4x | 8.8x | 11.2x | 11.8x | 12.2x |
| EBITDA / Total Interest Expense | | 2.9x | 3.2x | 3.7x | 4.3x | 5.0x | 5.9x | 7.4x | 9.8x | 13.5x | 15.1x | 15.5x |
| (EBITDA - Capex) / Total Interest Expense | | 2.3x | 2.5x | 2.9x | 3.4x | 3.9x | 4.6x | 5.8x | 7.7x | 10.6x | 11.8x | 12.2x |
| Senior Secured Debt / EBITDA | | 3.9x | 3.3x | 2.7x | 2.2x | 1.6x | 1.1x | 0.6x | 0.1x | -x | -x | -x |
| Senior Debt / EBITDA | | 5.0x | 4.4x | 3.7x | 3.7x | 2.6x | 2.0x | 1.5x | 0.9x | 0.8x | 0.8x | 0.8x |
| Total Debt / EBITDA | | 5.0x | 4.4x | 3.7x | 3.2x | 2.6x | 2.0x | 1.5x | 0.9x | 0.8x | 0.8x | 0.8x |
| Net Debt / EBITDA | | 5.0x | 4.4x | 3.7x | 3.2x | 2.6x | 2.0x | 1.5x | 0.9x | 0.4x | (0.2x) | (0.7x) |

This steady deleveraging and improvement of credit statistics throughout the projection period suggests that ValueCo has the ability to support the contemplated financing structure under the Base Case financial projections.

## Step V(b): Perform Returns Analysis

After analyzing the contemplated financing structure from a debt repayment and credit statistics perspective, attention turns to valuation and sponsor returns at the proposed purchase price and equity contribution. As discussed in Chapter 4, sponsors generally target 15% to 20% IRRs in assessing acquisition opportunities. If the implied returns are too low, both the purchase price and financing structure need to be revisited.

IRRs are driven primarily by the target's projected financial performance, the assumed purchase price and financing structure (particularly the size of the equity contribution), and the assumed exit multiple and year (assuming a sale). Although a sponsor may realize a monetization or exit through various strategies and timeframes (see Chapter 4, "Primary Exit/Monetization Strategies"), a traditional LBO analysis contemplates a full exit via a sale of the entire company in five years.

**Return Assumptions**   In a traditional LBO analysis, it is common practice to conservatively assume an exit multiple equal to (or below) the entry multiple.

**EXHIBIT 5.39**   Calculation of Enterprise Value and Equity Value at Exit

*($ in millions)*

| Calculation of Exit Enterprise Value and Equity Value (assumes 8.0x exit multiple and 2024E exit year) | Year 5 2024 |
|---|---|
| 2024E EBITDA | $929.2 |
| Exit EBITDA Multiple | 8.0x |
| **Enterprise Value at Exit** | **$7,433.7** |
| *Less: Net Debt* | |
| Revolving Credit Facility | - |
| Term Loan B | 1,050.8 |
| Senior Notes | 850.0 |
| Total Debt | **$1,900.8** |
| Less: Cash and Cash Equivalents | - |
| **Net Debt** | **$1,900.8** |
| **Equity Value at Exit** | **$5,532.8** |

As shown in Exhibit 5.39, for ValueCo's LBO analysis, we assumed that the sponsor exits in 2024E (Year 5) at a multiple of 8.0x EBITDA, which is equal to the entry multiple. In 2024E, ValueCo is projected to generate EBITDA of $929.2 million, translating into an implied enterprise value of $7,433.7 million at an exit multiple of 8.0x EBITDA. Cumulative debt repayment over the period is $1,749.2 million (2019E TLB beginning balance of $2,800 million less 2024E ending balance of $1,050.8 million), leaving ValueCo with projected 2024E debt of $1,900.8 million. This debt amount, which is equal to net debt given the zero cash balance, is subtracted from the enterprise value of $7,433.7 million to calculate an implied equity value of $5,532.8 million in the exit year.

**IRR and Cash Return Calculations**   Assuming no additional cash inflows (dividends to the sponsor) or outflows (additional investment by the sponsor) during the investment period, IRR and cash return are calculated on the basis of the sponsor's initial equity contribution (outflow) and the assumed equity proceeds at exit (inflow). This concept is illustrated in the timeline shown in Exhibit 5.40.

**EXHIBIT 5.40**   Investment Timeline

*($ in millions)*

|  | Pro forma 2019 | Year 1 2020 | Year 2 2021 | Year 3 2022 | Year 4 2023 | Year 5 2024 |
|---|---|---|---|---|---|---|
| Initial Equity Investment | ($2,100.0) | | | | | |
| Dividends / (Investment) | - | - | - | - | - | - |
| Equity Value at Exit | - | - | - | - | - | 5,532.8 |
| **Total** | ($2,100.0) | - | - | - | - | **$5,532.8** |
| IRR | 21% | | | | | |
| Cash Return | 2.6x | | | | | |

= IRR(Initial Equity Investment : Equity Value at Exit)
= IRR(-$2,100 million : $5,532.8 million)

= Equity Value at Exit / Initial Equity Investment
= $5,532.8 million / $2,100 million

The initial equity contribution represents a cash outflow for the sponsor. Hence, it is shown as a negative value on the timeline, as would any additional equity investment by the sponsor, whether for acquisitions or other purposes. On the other hand, cash distributions to the sponsor, such as proceeds received at exit or dividends received during the investment period, are shown as positive values on the timeline.

For the ValueCo LBO, we assumed no cash inflows or outflows during the investment period other than the initial equity contribution and anticipated equity proceeds at exit. Therefore, we calculated an IRR of approximately 21% and a cash return of 2.6x based on $2,100 million of initial contributed equity and $5,532.8 million of equity proceeds in 2024E.

**Returns at Various Exit Years**   In Exhibit 5.41, we calculated IRR and cash return assuming an exit at the end of each year in the projection period using the fixed 8.0x EBITDA exit multiple. As we progress through the projection period, equity value increases due to the increasing EBITDA and decreasing net debt. Therefore, the cash return increases as it is a function of the fixed initial equity investment and increasing equity value at exit. As the timeline progresses, however, IRR decreases in accordance with the declining growth rates and the time value of money.

**EXHIBIT 5.41** Returns at Various Exit Years

*($ in millions, fiscal year ending December 31)*

**Returns Analysis**

| | Pro forma 2019 | Year 1 2020 | Year 2 2021 | Year 3 2022 | Year 4 2023 | Projection Period Year 5 2024 | Year 6 2025 | Year 7 2026 | Year 8 2027 | Year 9 2028 | Year 10 2029 |
|---|---|---|---|---|---|---|---|---|---|---|---|
| Entry EBITDA Multiple | 8.0x | | | | | | | | | | |
| Initial Equity Investment | $2,100.0 | | | | | | | | | | |
| EBITDA | | $779.4 | $826.1 | $867.4 | $902.1 | $929.2 | $957.1 | $985.8 | $1,015.4 | $1,045.8 | $1,077.2 |
| Exit EBITDA Multiple | 8.0x | | | | | | | | | | |
| **Enterprise Value at Exit** | | **$6,235.0** | **$6,609.1** | **$6,939.6** | **$7,217.1** | **$7,433.7** | **$7,656.7** | **$7,886.4** | **$8,123.0** | **$8,366.6** | **$8,617.6** |
| *Less: Net Debt* | | | | | | | | | | | |
| Revolving Credit Facility | | - | - | - | - | - | - | - | - | - | - |
| Term Loan A | | 2,542.1 | 2,235.6 | 1,883.2 | 1,487.6 | 1,050.8 | 578.3 | 67.7 | - | - | - |
| Term Loan B | | - | - | - | - | - | - | - | - | - | - |
| Term Loan C | | - | - | - | - | - | - | - | - | - | - |
| Existing Term Loan | | - | - | - | - | - | - | - | - | - | - |
| 2nd Lien | | - | - | - | - | - | - | - | - | - | - |
| Senior Notes | | 850.0 | 850.0 | 850.0 | 850.0 | 850.0 | 850.0 | 850.0 | 850.0 | 850.0 | 850.0 |
| Senior Subordinated Notes | | - | - | - | - | - | - | - | - | - | - |
| Other Debt | | - | - | - | - | - | - | - | - | - | - |
| **Total Debt** | | **$3,392.1** | **$3,085.6** | **$2,733.2** | **$2,337.6** | **$1,900.8** | **$1,428.3** | **$917.7** | **$850.0** | **$850.0** | **$850.0** |
| Less: Cash and Cash Equivalents | | - | - | - | - | - | - | - | 471.3 | 1,030.5 | 1,610.0 |
| **Net Debt** | | **$3,392.1** | **$3,085.6** | **$2,733.2** | **$2,337.6** | **$1,900.8** | **$1,428.3** | **$917.7** | **$378.7** | **($180.5)** | **($760.0)** |
| **Equity Value at Exit** | | **$2,842.9** | **$3,523.5** | **$4,206.4** | **$4,879.5** | **$5,532.8** | **$6,228.4** | **$6,968.7** | **$7,744.3** | **$8,547.1** | **$9,377.7** |

| Cash Return | | 1.4x | 1.7x | 2.0x | 2.3x | 2.6x | 3.0x | 3.3x | 3.7x | 4.1x | 4.5x |
|---|---|---|---|---|---|---|---|---|---|---|---|

| | | Year 1 2020 | Year 2 2021 | Year 3 2022 | Year 4 2023 | Year 5 2024 | Year 6 2025 | Year 7 2026 | Year 8 2027 | Year 9 2028 | Year 10 2029 |
|---|---|---|---|---|---|---|---|---|---|---|---|
| Initial Equity Investment | | ($2,100.0) | ($2,100.0) | ($2,100.0) | ($2,100.0) | ($2,100.0) | ($2,100.0) | ($2,100.0) | ($2,100.0) | ($2,100.0) | ($2,100.0) |
| Equity Proceeds | | $2,842.9 | $3,523.5 | $4,206.4 | $4,879.5 | $5,532.8 | $6,228.4 | $6,968.7 | $7,744.3 | $8,547.1 | $9,377.7 |

| IRR | | 35% | 30% | 26% | 23% | 21% | 20% | 19% | 18% | 17% | 16% |
|---|---|---|---|---|---|---|---|---|---|---|---|

274

**IRR Sensitivity Analysis** Sensitivity analysis is critical for analyzing IRRs and framing LBO valuation. IRR can be sensitized for several key value drivers, such as entry and exit multiple, exit year, leverage level, and equity contribution percentage, as well as key operating assumptions such as growth rates and margins (see Chapter 3, Exhibit 3.59).

As shown in Exhibit 5.42, for the ValueCo LBO, we assumed a fixed leverage level of 5.2x LTM 9/30/2019 EBITDA of $700 million and a 2024E exit year, while sensitizing entry and exit multiples. For our IRR analysis, we focused on entry and exit multiple combinations that produced an IRR in the 20% area, assuming an equity contribution comfortably within the range of 25% to 40%.

**EXHIBIT 5.42** IRR Sensitivity Analysis – Entry and Exit Multiples

| Enterprise Value | Equity Contribution | Entry Multiple | IRR - Assuming Exit in 2024E | | | | | | |
|---|---|---|---|---|---|---|---|---|---|
| | | | Exit Multiple | | | | | | |
| | | | 7.00x | 7.25x | 7.50x | 7.75x | 8.00x | 8.25x | 8.50x |
| $4,900.0 | 26.4% | 7.00x | 26.9% | 28.1% | 29.3% | 30.5% | 31.6% | 32.7% | 33.8% |
| 5,075.0 | 28.8% | 7.25x | 23.9% | 25.2% | 26.3% | 27.5% | 28.6% | 29.6% | 30.7% |
| 5,250.0 | 31.0% | 7.50x | 21.3% | 22.5% | 23.7% | 24.8% | 25.9% | 26.9% | 27.9% |
| 5,425.0 | 33.0% | 7.75x | 19.1% | 20.2% | 21.4% | 22.5% | 23.5% | 24.5% | 25.5% |
| 5,600.0 | 35.0% | 8.00x | 17.0% | 18.2% | 19.3% | 20.3% | 21.4% | 22.4% | 23.4% |
| 5,775.0 | 36.8% | 8.25x | 15.1% | 16.3% | 17.4% | 18.4% | 19.5% | 20.4% | 21.4% |
| 5,950.0 | 38.6% | 8.50x | 13.4% | 14.6% | 15.6% | 16.7% | 17.7% | 18.7% | 19.6% |

For example, an 8.0x entry and exit multiple provides an IRR of approximately 20% while requiring a 35% equity contribution given the proposed leverage. Toward the higher end of the range, an 8.25x entry and exit multiple yields an IRR of 20.4% while requiring an equity contribution of 36.8%. Toward the low end of the range, a 7.25x entry and exit multiple provides an IRR of 25.2% while requiring a 28.8% equity contribution.

It is also common to perform sensitivity analysis on a combination of exit multiples and exit years. As shown in Exhibit 5.43, we assumed fixed total leverage and entry multiples of 5.2x and 8.0x LTM 9/30/2019 EBITDA, respectively, and examined the resulting IRRs for a range of exit years from 2022E to 2026E and exit multiples from 7.0x to 9.0x.

**EXHIBIT 5.43** IRR Sensitivity Analysis – Exit Multiple and Exit Year

| | | IRR - Assuming 8.0x Entry Multiple | | | | |
|---|---|---|---|---|---|---|
| | | Exit Year | | | | |
| | | 2022 | 2023 | 2024 | 2025 | 2026 |
| | 7.0x | 17% | 17% | 17% | 17% | 16% |
| **Exit** | 7.5x | 22% | 21% | 19% | 18% | 17% |
| **Multiple** | 8.0x | 26% | 23% | 21% | 20% | 19% |
| | 8.5x | 30% | 26% | 23% | 21% | 20% |
| | 9.0x | 34% | 29% | 25% | 23% | 21% |

## Step V(c): Determine Valuation

As previously discussed, sponsors base their valuation of an LBO target in large part on their comfort with realizing acceptable returns at a given purchase price. This analysis assumes a given set of financial projections, purchase price, and financing structure, as well as exit multiple and year. At the same time, sponsors are guided by the other valuation methodologies discussed in this book.

LBO analysis is also informative for strategic buyers by providing perspective on the price a competing sponsor bidder might be willing to pay for a given target in an organized sale process. This data point allows strategic buyers to frame their bids accordingly. As a result, the banker is expected to employ LBO analysis as a valuation technique while serving as an M&A advisor in both buy-side and sell-side situations.

Traditionally, the valuation implied by LBO analysis is toward the lower end of a comprehensive analysis when compared to other methodologies, particularly precedent transactions and DCF analysis. This is largely due to the constraints imposed by an LBO, including leverage capacity, credit market conditions, and the sponsor's own IRR hurdles. Furthermore, strategic buyers are typically able to realize synergies from the target, thereby enhancing their ability to earn a targeted return on their invested capital at a higher purchase price. However, during robust debt financing environments, such as during the credit boom of the mid-2000s and much of the decade following the Great Recession, sponsors have been able to compete with strategic buyers on purchase price. In these instances, the multiples paid in LBO transactions were supported by the use of a high proportion of low-cost debt in the capital structure, translating into a relatively lower overall cost of capital for the target.

**EXHIBIT 5.44**   ValueCo Football Field Displaying Comps, Precedents, DCF Analysis, and LBO Analysis

*($ in millions)*

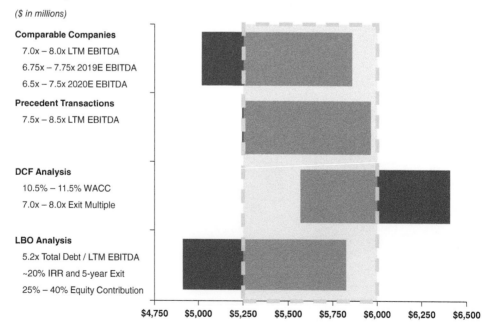

As with the DCF, the implied valuation range for ValueCo was derived from sensitivity analysis output tables (see Exhibit 5.42). For the ValueCo LBO, we focused on a range of entry and exit multiples that produced IRRs in the 20% area, given an equity contribution comfortably within the range of 25% to 40%. This approach led us to determine a valuation range of 7.25x to 8.25x LTM 9/30/2019 EBITDA, or approximately $5,075 million to $5,775 million (see Exhibit 5.44).

### Step V(d): Create Transaction Summary Page

Once the LBO model is fully functional, all the essential model outputs are linked to a transaction summary page (see Exhibit 5.46). This page provides an overview of the LBO analysis in a user-friendly format, typically displaying the sources and uses of funds, acquisition multiples, summary returns analysis, and summary financial data, as well as projected capitalization and credit statistics. This format allows the deal team to quickly review and spot-check the analysis and make adjustments to the purchase price, financing structure, operating assumptions, and other key inputs as necessary.

The transaction summary page also typically contains the toggle cells that allow the banker to switch among various financing structures and operating scenarios, as well as activate other functionality. The outputs on this page (and throughout the entire model) change accordingly as the toggle cells are changed.

## ILLUSTRATIVE LBO ANALYSIS FOR VALUECO

The following pages display the full LBO model for ValueCo based on the step-by-step approach outlined in this chapter. Exhibit 5.45 lists these pages, which are shown in Exhibits 5.46 to 5.54.

**EXHIBIT 5.45**   LBO Model Pages

| LBO Model |
|---|
| I.   Transaction Summary |
| II.   Income Statement |
| III.  Balance Sheet |
| IV.  Cash Flow Statement |
| V.   Debt Schedule |
| VI.  Returns Analysis |
| **Assumptions Pages** |
| I.   Assumptions Page 1—Income Statement and Cash Flow Statement |
| II.   Assumptions Page 2—Balance Sheet |
| III.  Assumptions Page 3—Financing Structures and Fees |

# EXHIBIT 5.46   ValueCo LBO Transaction Summary

## ValueCo Corporation
### Leveraged Buyout Analysis
*($ in millions, fiscal year ending December 31)*

Financing Structure: Structure 1
Operating Scenario: Base

### Transaction Summary

#### Sources of Funds

| | Amount | % of Total Sources | Multiple of EBITDA 9/30/2019 | Cumulative | Pricing |
|---|---|---|---|---|---|
| Revolving Credit Facility | - | - % | - x | - x | L+425 bps |
| Term Loan A | - | - % | - x | - x | NA |
| Term Loan B | 2,800.0 | 46.7% | 4.0x | 4.0x | L+425 bps |
| Term Loan C | - | - % | - x | 4.0x | NA |
| 2nd Lien | - | - % | - x | 4.0x | NA |
| Senior Notes | 850.0 | 14.2% | 1.2x | 5.2x | 8.000% |
| Senior Subordinated Notes | - | - % | - x | 5.2x | NA |
| Equity Contribution | 2,100.0 | 35.0% | 3.0x | 8.2x | |
| Rollover Equity | - | - % | - x | 8.2x | |
| Cash on Hand | 250.0 | 4.2% | 0.4x | 8.6x | |
| **Total Sources** | **$6,000.0** | **100.0%** | **8.6x** | | |

#### Uses of Funds

| | Amount | % of Total Uses |
|---|---|---|
| Purchase ValueCo Equity | $4,350.0 | 72.5% |
| Repay Existing Debt | 1,500.0 | 25.0% |
| Tender / Call Premiums | 20.0 | 0.3% |
| Financing Fees | 100.0 | 1.7% |
| Other Fees and Expenses | 30.0 | 0.5% |
| **Total Uses** | **$6,000.0** | **100.0%** |

#### Purchase Price

| | |
|---|---|
| Offer Price per Share | $4,350.0 |
| Fully Diluted Shares | |
| Equity Purchase Price | $4,350.0 |
| Plus: Existing Net Debt | 1,250.0 |
| Enterprise Value | $5,600.0 |

##### Transaction Multiples

| | | |
|---|---|---|
| Enterprise Value / Sales | LTM 9/30/2019 | $3,385.0 |
| | 2019E | 3,450.0 |
| Enterprise Value / EBITDA | LTM 9/30/2019 | $700.0 |
| | 2019E | 725.0 |

#### Return Analysis

| | |
|---|---|
| Exit Year | - |
| Entry Multiple | 8.0x |
| Exit Multiple | 8.0x |
| IRR | 21% |
| Cash Return | 2.6x |

##### Options

| | |
|---|---|
| **Financing Structure** | 1.7x |
| Operating Scenario | 1.6x |
| Cash Flow Sweep | |
| Cash Balance | |
| Average Interest | 8.0x |
| Financing Fees | 7.7x |

### Summary Financial Data

| | Historical Period | | | LTM | Pro forma | Projection Period | | | | | | | | | |
|---|---|---|---|---|---|---|---|---|---|---|---|---|---|---|---|
| | 2016 | 2017 | 2018 | 9/30/2019 | 2019 | Year 1 2020 | Year 2 2021 | Year 3 2022 | Year 4 2023 | Year 5 2024 | Year 6 2025 | Year 7 2026 | Year 8 2027 | Year 9 2028 | Year 10 2029 |
| **Sales** | $2,600.0 | $2,900.0 | $3,200.0 | $3,385.0 | $3,450.0 | $3,708.8 | $3,931.3 | $4,127.8 | $4,293.0 | $4,421.7 | $4,554.4 | $4,691.0 | $4,831.8 | $4,976.7 | $5,126.0 |
| *% growth* | NA | 11.5% | 10.3% | NA | 7.8% | 7.5% | 6.0% | 5.0% | 4.0% | 3.0% | 3.0% | 3.0% | 3.0% | 3.0% | 3.0% |
| **Gross Profit** | $988.0 | $1,131.0 | $1,280.0 | $1,280.0 | $1,380.0 | $1,483.5 | $1,572.5 | $1,651.1 | $1,717.2 | $1,768.7 | $1,821.8 | $1,876.4 | $1,932.7 | $1,990.7 | $2,050.4 |
| *% margin* | 38.0% | 39.0% | 40.0% | 39.9% | 40.0% | 40.0% | 40.0% | 40.0% | 40.0% | 40.0% | 40.0% | 40.0% | 40.0% | 40.0% | 40.0% |
| **EBITDA** | $491.4 | $580.0 | $672.0 | $700.0 | $725.0 | $779.4 | $826.0 | $867.4 | $902.1 | $929.2 | $957.1 | $985.8 | $1,015.4 | $1,045.8 | $1,077.2 |
| *% margin* | 18.9% | 20.0% | 20.7% | 20.7% | 21.0% | 21.0% | 21.0% | 21.0% | 21.0% | 21.0% | 21.0% | 21.0% | 21.0% | 21.0% | 21.0% |
| Capital Expenditures | 136.4 | 114.0 | 144.0 | 152.3 | 155.3 | 166.9 | 176.9 | 185.8 | 193.2 | 199.0 | 204.9 | 211.1 | 217.4 | 224.0 | 230.7 |
| *% sales* | 5.2% | 3.9% | 4.5% | 4.5% | 4.5% | 4.5% | 4.5% | 4.5% | 4.5% | 4.5% | 4.5% | 4.5% | 4.5% | 4.5% | 4.5% |
| Cash Interest Expense | | | | | 236.0 | 228.3 | 210.3 | 188.8 | 167.2 | 143.0 | 116.6 | 88.1 | 71.4 | 69.4 | 69.4 |
| Total Interest Expense | | | | | 250.0 | 242.4 | 224.4 | 202.9 | 181.2 | 157.1 | 129.6 | 101.1 | 75.3 | 69.4 | 69.4 |
| **Free Cash Flow** | | | | | | | | | | | | | | | |
| EBITDA | | | | | | $779.4 | $826.1 | $867.4 | $902.1 | $929.2 | $957.1 | $985.8 | $1,015.4 | $1,045.8 | $1,077.2 |
| Less: Cash Interest Expense | | | | | | (78.6) | (91.5) | (104.2) | (115.8) | (126.7) | (138.6) | (150.8) | (162.8) | (71.4) | (69.4) |
| Plus: Interest Income | | | | | | | | | | | | | 1.2 | 3.8 | 6.6 |
| Less: Income Taxes | | | | | | (166.9) | (176.9) | (185.8) | (193.2) | (199.0) | (204.9) | (211.1) | (170.4) | (176.7) |
| Less: Capital Expenditures | | | | | | (47.6) | (41.0) | (36.2) | (30.4) | (23.7) | (24.4) | (25.1) | (217.4) | (224.0) | (230.7) |
| Less: Increase in Net Working Capital | | | | | | | | | | | | | (25.9) | (26.7) | (27.5) |
| **Free Cash Flow** | | | | | | $257.9 | $306.5 | $352.4 | $395.6 | $436.8 | $472.5 | $510.6 | $539.0 | $559.2 | $579.5 |
| Cumulative Free Cash Flow | | | | | | 257.9 | 564.4 | 916.8 | 1,312.4 | 1,749.2 | 2,221.7 | 2,732.3 | 3,271.3 | 3,830.5 | 4,410.0 |

### Capitalization

| | Pro forma 2019 | Year 1 2020 | Year 2 2021 | Year 3 2022 | Year 4 2023 | Year 5 2024 | Year 6 2025 | Year 7 2026 | Year 8 2027 | Year 9 2028 | Year 10 2029 |
|---|---|---|---|---|---|---|---|---|---|---|---|
| Cash | | | | | | | | | | | |
| Revolving Credit Facility | | | | | | | | | | | |
| Term Loan A | | | | | | | | | | | |
| Term Loan B | 2,800.0 | 2,542.1 | 2,235.6 | 1,883.2 | 1,487.6 | 1,050.8 | 578.3 | 67.7 | | | |
| Term Loan C | | | | | | | | | | | |
| Existing Term Loan | | | | | | | | | | | |
| 2nd Lien | | | | | | | | | | | |
| Other Debt | | | | | | | | | | | |
| **Total Senior Secured Debt** | **$2,800.0** | **$2,542.1** | **$2,235.6** | **$1,883.2** | **$1,487.6** | **$1,050.8** | **$578.3** | **$67.7** | | | |
| Senior Notes | 850.0 | 850.0 | 850.0 | 850.0 | 850.0 | 850.0 | 850.0 | 850.0 | 850.0 | 850.0 | 850.0 |
| **Total Senior Debt** | **$3,650.0** | **$3,392.1** | **$3,085.6** | **$2,733.2** | **$2,337.6** | **$1,900.8** | **$1,428.3** | **$917.7** | **$850.0** | **$850.0** | **$850.0** |
| Senior Subordinated Notes | | | | | | | | | | | |
| **Total Debt** | **$3,650.0** | **$3,392.1** | **$3,085.6** | **$2,733.2** | **$2,337.6** | **$1,900.8** | **$1,428.3** | **$917.7** | **$850.0** | **$850.0** | **$850.0** |
| Shareholders' Equity | 2,050.0 | 2,285.9 | 2,560.3 | 2,872.9 | 3,220.4 | 3,600.6 | 4,016.3 | 4,468.7 | 4,957.2 | 5,468.4 | 5,998.6 |
| **Total Capitalization** | **$5,700.0** | **$5,677.9** | **$5,645.9** | **$5,606.1** | **$5,558.1** | **$5,501.4** | **$5,444.6** | **$5,386.4** | **$5,807.2** | **$6,318.4** | **$6,848.6** |
| *% of Bank Debt Repaid* | | 9.2% | 20.2% | 32.7% | 46.9% | 62.5% | 79.3% | 97.6% | 100.0% | 100.0% | 100.0% |

### Credit Statistics

| | Pro forma 2019 | Year 1 2020 | Year 2 2021 | Year 3 2022 | Year 4 2023 | Year 5 2024 | Year 6 2025 | Year 7 2026 | Year 8 2027 | Year 9 2028 | Year 10 2029 |
|---|---|---|---|---|---|---|---|---|---|---|---|
| *% Debt / Total Capitalization* | 64.0% | 59.7% | 54.7% | 48.8% | 42.1% | 34.6% | 26.2% | 17.0% | 14.6% | 13.5% | 12.4% |
| EBITDA / Cash Interest Expense | NA | 3.4x | 3.9x | 4.6x | 5.4x | 6.5x | 8.2x | 11.2x | 14.2x | 15.1x | 15.5x |
| (EBITDA - Capex) / Cash Interest Expense | 3.1x | 2.7x | 3.1x | 3.6x | 4.2x | 5.1x | 6.4x | 11.2x | 8.8x | 11.8x | 12.2x |
| EBITDA / Total Interest Expense | 2.4x | 3.2x | 3.7x | 4.3x | 5.0x | 5.9x | 7.4x | 9.8x | 13.5x | 11.8x | 15.5x |
| (EBITDA - Capex) / Total Interest Expense | 2.9x | 2.5x | 2.9x | 3.4x | 3.9x | 4.6x | 5.8x | 7.7x | 10.6x | 11.8x | 12.2x |
| Senior Secured Debt / EBITDA | 2.3x | 3.3x | 2.7x | 2.2x | 1.6x | 1.1x | 0.6x | 0.1x | - x | - x | - x |
| Senior Debt / EBITDA | 3.9x | 4.4x | 3.7x | 3.2x | 2.6x | 2.0x | 1.5x | 0.9x | 0.8x | 0.8x | 0.8x |
| Total Debt / EBITDA | 5.0x | 4.4x | 3.7x | 3.2x | 2.6x | 2.0x | 1.5x | 0.9x | 0.8x | 0.8x | 0.8x |
| Net Debt / EBITDA | 5.0x | 4.4x | 3.7x | 3.2x | 2.6x | 2.0x | 1.5x | 0.9x | 0.4x | (0.2x) | (0.7x) |

# EXHIBIT 5.47  ValueCo LBO Income Statement

*($ in millions, fiscal year ending December 31)*

## Income Statement

| | Historical Period | | | LTM 9/30/2019 | Pro forma 2019 | Projection Period | | | | | | | | | |
|---|---|---|---|---|---|---|---|---|---|---|---|---|---|---|---|
| | 2016 | 2017 | 2018 | | | Year 1 2020 | Year 2 2021 | Year 3 2022 | Year 4 2023 | Year 5 2024 | Year 6 2025 | Year 7 2026 | Year 8 2027 | Year 9 2028 | Year 10 2029 |
| **Sales** | $2,600.0 | $2,900.0 | $3,200.0 | $3,385.0 | $3,450.0 | $3,708.8 | $3,931.3 | $4,127.8 | $4,293.0 | $4,421.7 | $4,554.4 | $4,691.0 | $4,831.8 | $4,976.7 | $5,126.0 |
| *% growth* | NA | 11.5% | 10.3% | NA | 7.8% | 7.5% | 6.0% | 5.0% | 4.0% | 3.0% | 3.0% | 3.0% | 3.0% | 3.0% | 3.0% |
| Cost of Goods Sold | 1,612.0 | 1,769.0 | 1,920.0 | 2,035.0 | 2,070.0 | 2,225.3 | 2,358.8 | 2,476.7 | 2,575.8 | 2,653.0 | 2,732.6 | 2,814.6 | 2,899.1 | 2,986.0 | 3,075.6 |
| **Gross Profit** | $988.0 | $1,131.0 | $1,280.0 | $1,350.0 | $1,380.0 | $1,483.5 | $1,572.5 | $1,651.1 | $1,717.2 | $1,768.7 | $1,821.8 | $1,876.4 | $1,932.7 | $1,990.7 | $2,050.4 |
| *% margin* | 38.0% | 39.0% | 40.0% | 39.9% | 40.0% | 40.0% | 40.0% | 40.0% | 40.0% | 40.0% | 40.0% | 40.0% | 40.0% | 40.0% | 40.0% |
| Selling, General & Administrative | 496.6 | 551.0 | 608.0 | 650.0 | 655.0 | 704.1 | 746.4 | 783.7 | 815.0 | 839.5 | 864.7 | 890.6 | 917.3 | 944.9 | 973.2 |
| *% sales* | 19.1% | 19.0% | 19.0% | 19.2% | 19.0% | 19.0% | 19.0% | 19.0% | 19.0% | 19.0% | 19.0% | 19.0% | 19.0% | 19.0% | 19.0% |
| Other Expense / (Income) | | | | | | | | | | | | | | | |
| **EBITDA** | $491.4 | $580.0 | $672.0 | $700.0 | $725.0 | $779.4 | $826.1 | $867.4 | $902.1 | $929.2 | $957.1 | $985.8 | $1,015.4 | $1,045.8 | $1,077.2 |
| *% margin* | 18.9% | 20.0% | 21.0% | 20.7% | 21.0% | 21.0% | 21.0% | 21.0% | 21.0% | 21.0% | 21.0% | 21.0% | 21.0% | 21.0% | 21.0% |
| Depreciation | 116.0 | 121.5 | 145.0 | 150.0 | 155.3 | 166.9 | 176.9 | 185.8 | 193.2 | 199.0 | 204.9 | 211.1 | 217.4 | 224.0 | 230.7 |
| Amortization | 39.0 | 43.5 | 48.0 | 50.0 | 51.8 | 55.6 | 59.0 | 61.9 | 64.4 | 66.3 | 68.3 | 70.4 | 72.5 | 74.7 | 76.9 |
| **EBIT** | $336.4 | $415.0 | $479.0 | $500.0 | $518.0 | $556.9 | $590.3 | $619.8 | $644.6 | $663.9 | $683.8 | $704.3 | $725.5 | $747.2 | $769.6 |
| *% margin* | 12.9% | 14.3% | 15.0% | 14.8% | 15.0% | 15.0% | 15.0% | 15.0% | 15.0% | 15.0% | 15.0% | 15.0% | 15.0% | 15.0% | 15.0% |
| *Interest Expense* | | | | | | | | | | | | | | | |
| Revolving Credit Facility | | | | | | | | | | | | | | | |
| Term Loan A | | | | | | | | | | | | | | | |
| Term Loan B | | | | | 166.6 | 158.9 | 140.9 | 119.4 | 97.8 | 73.6 | 47.2 | 18.7 | 2.0 | | |
| Term Loan C | | | | | | | | | | | | | | | |
| Existing Term Loan | | | | | | | | | | | | | | | |
| 2nd Lien | | | | | | | | | | | | | | | |
| Senior Notes | | | | | 68.0 | 68.0 | 68.0 | 68.0 | 68.0 | 68.0 | 68.0 | 68.0 | 68.0 | 68.0 | 68.0 |
| Senior Subordinated Notes | | | | | | | | | | | | | | | |
| Commitment Fee on Unused Revolver | | | | | 1.3 | 1.3 | 1.3 | 1.3 | 1.3 | 1.3 | 1.3 | 1.3 | 1.3 | 1.3 | 1.3 |
| Administrative Agent Fee | | | | | 0.2 | 0.2 | 0.2 | 0.2 | 0.2 | 0.2 | 0.2 | 0.2 | 0.2 | 0.2 | 0.2 |
| **Cash Interest Expense** | | | | | $236.0 | $228.3 | $210.3 | $188.8 | $167.2 | $143.0 | $116.6 | $88.1 | $71.4 | $69.4 | $69.4 |
| Amortization of Deferred Financing Fees | | | | | 14.0 | 14.0 | 14.0 | 14.0 | 14.0 | 14.0 | 12.9 | 12.9 | 3.9 | - | - |
| **Total Interest Expense** | | | | | $250.0 | $242.4 | $224.4 | $202.9 | $181.2 | $157.1 | $129.6 | $101.1 | $75.3 | $69.4 | $69.4 |
| Interest Income | | | | | | | | | | | | | (1.2) | (3.8) | (6.6) |
| **Net Interest Expense** | | | | | | $242.4 | $224.4 | $202.9 | $181.2 | $157.1 | $129.6 | $101.1 | $74.1 | $65.6 | $62.8 |
| Earnings Before Taxes | | | | | | 314.5 | 365.9 | 416.9 | 463.4 | 506.8 | 554.3 | 603.3 | 651.4 | 681.6 | 706.8 |
| Income Tax Expense | | | | | | 78.6 | 91.5 | 104.2 | 115.8 | 126.7 | 138.6 | 150.8 | 162.8 | 170.4 | 176.7 |
| **Net Income** | | | | | | $235.9 | $274.4 | $312.7 | $347.5 | $380.1 | $415.7 | $452.5 | $488.5 | $511.2 | $530.1 |
| *% margin* | | | | | | 6.4% | 7.0% | 7.6% | 8.1% | 8.6% | 9.1% | 9.6% | 10.1% | 10.3% | 10.3% |

### Income Statement Assumptions

| | 2016 | 2017 | 2018 | LTM | Pro forma 2019 | Year 1 2020 | Year 2 2021 | Year 3 2022 | Year 4 2023 | Year 5 2024 | Year 6 2025 | Year 7 2026 | Year 8 2027 | Year 9 2028 | Year 10 2029 |
|---|---|---|---|---|---|---|---|---|---|---|---|---|---|---|---|
| Sales (% YoY growth) | NA | 11.5% | 10.3% | NA | 7.8% | 7.5% | 6.0% | 5.0% | 4.0% | 3.0% | 3.0% | 3.0% | 3.0% | 3.0% | 3.0% |
| Cost of Goods Sold (% margin) | 62.0% | 61.0% | 60.0% | 60.1% | 60.0% | 60.0% | 60.0% | 60.0% | 60.0% | 60.0% | 60.0% | 60.0% | 60.0% | 60.0% | 60.0% |
| SG&A (% sales) | 19.1% | 19.0% | 19.0% | 19.2% | 19.0% | 19.0% | 19.0% | 19.0% | 19.0% | 19.0% | 19.0% | 19.0% | 19.0% | 19.0% | 19.0% |
| Other Expense / (Income) (% of sales) | - % | - % | - % | - % | - % | - % | - % | - % | - % | - % | - % | - % | - % | - % | - % |
| Depreciation (% of sales) | 4.5% | 4.2% | 4.5% | 4.4% | 4.5% | 4.5% | 4.5% | 4.5% | 4.5% | 4.5% | 4.5% | 4.5% | 4.5% | 4.5% | 4.5% |
| Amortization (% of sales) | 1.5% | 1.5% | 1.5% | 1.5% | 1.5% | 1.5% | 1.5% | 1.5% | 1.5% | 1.5% | 1.5% | 1.5% | 1.5% | 1.5% | 1.5% |
| Interest Income (% of sales) | | | | | 0.5% | 0.5% | 0.5% | 0.5% | 0.5% | 0.5% | 0.5% | 0.5% | 0.5% | 0.5% | 0.5% |
| Tax Rate | 25.0% | | | | 25.0% | 25.0% | 25.0% | 25.0% | 25.0% | 25.0% | 25.0% | 25.0% | 25.0% | 25.0% | 25.0% |

# EXHIBIT 5.48  ValueCo LBO Balance Sheet

($ in millions, fiscal year ending December 31)

## Balance Sheet

| | Opening 2019 | Adjustments + | Adjustments − | Pro Forma 2019 | Year 1 2020 | Year 2 2021 | Year 3 2022 | Year 4 2023 | Year 5 2024 | Year 6 2025 | Year 7 2026 | Year 8 2027 | Year 9 2028 | Year 10 2029 |
|---|---|---|---|---|---|---|---|---|---|---|---|---|---|---|
| **Projection Period** | | | | | | | | | | | | | | |
| Cash and Cash Equivalents | $250.0 | | (250.0) | | | | | | | | | $471.3 | $1,030.5 | $1,610.0 |
| Accounts Receivable | 450.0 | | | 450.0 | 483.8 | 512.8 | 538.4 | 560.0 | 576.7 | 594.1 | 611.9 | 630.2 | 649.1 | 668.6 |
| Inventories | 600.0 | | | 600.0 | 645.0 | 683.7 | 717.9 | 746.6 | 769.0 | 792.1 | 815.8 | 840.3 | 865.5 | 891.5 |
| Prepaids and Other Current Assets | 175.0 | | | 175.0 | 188.1 | 199.4 | 209.4 | 217.8 | 224.3 | 231.0 | 238.0 | 245.1 | 252.4 | 260.0 |
| **Total Current Assets** | **$1,475.0** | | | **$1,225.0** | **$1,316.9** | **$1,395.9** | **$1,465.7** | **$1,524.3** | **$1,570.0** | **$1,617.1** | **$1,665.7** | **$2,186.9** | **$2,797.6** | **$3,430.1** |
| Property, Plant and Equipment, net | 2,500.0 | | | 2,500.0 | 2,500.0 | 2,500.0 | 2,500.0 | 2,500.0 | 2,500.0 | 2,500.0 | 2,500.0 | 2,500.0 | 2,500.0 | 2,500.0 |
| Goodwill | 1,000.0 | 1,850.0 | | 1,850.0 | 1,850.0 | 1,850.0 | 1,850.0 | 1,850.0 | 1,850.0 | 1,850.0 | 1,850.0 | 1,850.0 | 1,850.0 | 1,850.0 |
| Intangible Assets | 875.0 | | (1,000.0) | 875.0 | 819.4 | 760.4 | 698.5 | 634.1 | 567.8 | 499.4 | 429.1 | 356.6 | 282.0 | 205.1 |
| Other Assets | 150.0 | | | 150.0 | 150.0 | 150.0 | 150.0 | 150.0 | 150.0 | 150.0 | 150.0 | 150.0 | 150.0 | 150.0 |
| Deferred Financing Fees | | 100.0 | | 100.0 | 86.0 | 71.9 | 57.9 | 43.8 | 29.8 | 16.8 | 3.9 | | | |
| **Total Assets** | **$6,000.0** | | | **$6,700.0** | **$6,722.2** | **$6,728.2** | **$6,722.0** | **$6,702.2** | **$6,667.6** | **$6,633.4** | **$6,598.7** | **$7,043.5** | **$7,579.5** | **$8,135.2** |
| Accounts Payable | 215.0 | | | 215.0 | 231.1 | 245.0 | 257.2 | 267.5 | 275.6 | 283.8 | 292.3 | 301.1 | 310.1 | 319.4 |
| Accrued Liabilities | 275.0 | | | 275.0 | 295.6 | 313.4 | 329.0 | 342.2 | 352.5 | 363.0 | 373.9 | 385.1 | 396.7 | 408.6 |
| Other Current Liabilities | 100.0 | | | 100.0 | 107.5 | 114.0 | 119.6 | 124.4 | 128.2 | 132.0 | 136.0 | 140.1 | 144.3 | 148.6 |
| **Total Current Liabilities** | **$590.0** | | | **$590.0** | **$634.3** | **$672.3** | **$705.9** | **$734.2** | **$756.2** | **$778.9** | **$802.2** | **$826.3** | **$851.1** | **$876.6** |
| Revolving Credit Facility | | | | | | | | | | | | | | |
| Term Loan A | | 2,800.0 | | 2,800.0 | 2,542.1 | 2,236.6 | 1,883.2 | 1,487.6 | 1,050.8 | 578.3 | 67.7 | | | |
| Term Loan B | | | | | | | | | | | | | | |
| Term Loan C | | | | | | | | | | | | | | |
| Existing Term Loan | 1,000.0 | | (1,000.0) | | | | | | | | | | | |
| 2nd Lien | | | | | | | | | | | | | | |
| Senior Notes | | 850.0 | | 850.0 | 850.0 | 850.0 | 850.0 | 850.0 | 850.0 | 850.0 | 850.0 | 850.0 | 850.0 | 850.0 |
| Existing Senior Notes | 500.0 | | (500.0) | | | | | | | | | | | |
| Senior Subordinated Notes | | | | | | | | | | | | | | |
| Other Debt | | | | | | | | | | | | | | |
| Deferred Income Taxes | 300.0 | | | 300.0 | 300.0 | 300.0 | 300.0 | 300.0 | 300.0 | 300.0 | 300.0 | 300.0 | 300.0 | 300.0 |
| Other Long-Term Liabilities | 110.0 | | | 110.0 | 110.0 | 110.0 | 110.0 | 110.0 | 110.0 | 110.0 | 110.0 | 110.0 | 110.0 | 110.0 |
| **Total Liabilities** | **$2,500.0** | | | **$4,650.0** | **$4,436.3** | **$4,167.9** | **$3,849.1** | **$3,481.8** | **$3,067.0** | **$2,617.2** | **$2,129.9** | **$2,086.3** | **$2,111.1** | **$2,136.6** |
| Noncontrolling Interest | | | | | | | | | | | | | | |
| Shareholders' Equity | 3,500.0 | 2,050.0 | (3,500.0) | 2,050.0 | 2,285.9 | 2,560.3 | 2,872.9 | 3,220.4 | 3,600.6 | 4,016.3 | 4,468.7 | 4,957.2 | 5,468.4 | 5,998.6 |
| **Total Shareholders' Equity** | **$3,500.0** | | | **$2,050.0** | **$2,285.9** | **$2,560.3** | **$2,872.9** | **$3,220.4** | **$3,600.6** | **$4,016.3** | **$4,468.7** | **$4,957.2** | **$5,468.4** | **$5,998.6** |
| **Total Liabilities and Equity** | **$6,000.0** | | | **$6,700.0** | **$6,722.2** | **$6,728.2** | **$6,722.0** | **$6,702.2** | **$6,667.6** | **$6,633.4** | **$6,598.7** | **$7,043.5** | **$7,579.5** | **$8,135.2** |
| Balance Check | 0.000 | | | 0.000 | 0.000 | 0.000 | 0.000 | 0.000 | 0.000 | 0.000 | 0.000 | 0.000 | 0.000 | 0.000 |
| Net Working Capital | 635.0 | | | 635.0 | 682.6 | 723.6 | 759.8 | 790.2 | 813.9 | 838.3 | 863.4 | 889.3 | 916.0 | 943.5 |
| (Increase) / Decrease in Net Working Capital | | | | | (47.6) | (41.0) | (36.2) | (30.4) | (23.7) | (24.4) | (25.1) | (25.9) | (26.7) | (27.5) |

## Balance Sheet Assumptions

| Current Assets | | | | | | | | | | | | | | |
|---|---|---|---|---|---|---|---|---|---|---|---|---|---|---|
| Days Sales Outstanding (DSO) | 47.6 | | | 47.6 | 47.6 | 47.6 | 47.6 | 47.6 | 47.6 | 47.6 | 47.6 | 47.6 | 47.6 | 47.6 |
| Days Inventory Held (DIH) | 105.8 | | | 105.8 | 105.8 | 105.8 | 105.8 | 105.8 | 105.8 | 105.8 | 105.8 | 105.8 | 105.8 | 105.8 |
| Prepaid and Other Current Assets (% of sales) | 5.1% | | | 5.1% | 5.1% | 5.1% | 5.1% | 5.1% | 5.1% | 5.1% | 5.1% | 5.1% | 5.1% | 5.1% |

| Current Liabilities | | | | | | | | | | | | | | |
|---|---|---|---|---|---|---|---|---|---|---|---|---|---|---|
| Days Payable Outstanding (DPO) | 37.9 | | | 37.9 | 37.9 | 37.9 | 37.9 | 37.9 | 37.9 | 37.9 | 37.9 | 37.9 | 37.9 | 37.9 |
| Accrued Liabilities (% of sales) | 8.0% | | | 8.0% | 8.0% | 8.0% | 8.0% | 8.0% | 8.0% | 8.0% | 8.0% | 8.0% | 8.0% | 8.0% |
| Other Current Liabilities (% of sales) | 2.9% | | | 2.9% | 2.9% | 2.9% | 2.9% | 2.9% | 2.9% | 2.9% | 2.9% | 2.9% | 2.9% | 2.9% |

**EXHIBIT 5.49** ValueCo LBO Cash Flow Statement

*($ in millions, fiscal year ending December 31)*

## Cash Flow Statement

| | | | | | Projection Period | | | | | |
|---|---|---|---|---|---|---|---|---|---|---|
| | Year 1 | Year 2 | Year 3 | Year 4 | Year 5 | Year 6 | Year 7 | Year 8 | Year 9 | Year 10 |
| | 2020 | 2021 | 2022 | 2023 | 2024 | 2025 | 2026 | 2027 | 2028 | 2029 |
| **Operating Activities** | | | | | | | | | | |
| Net Income | $235.9 | $274.4 | $312.7 | $347.5 | $380.1 | $415.7 | $452.5 | $488.5 | $511.2 | $530.1 |
| Plus: Depreciation | 166.9 | 176.9 | 185.8 | 193.2 | 199.0 | 204.9 | 211.1 | 217.4 | 224.0 | 230.7 |
| Plus: Amortization | 55.6 | 59.0 | 61.9 | 64.4 | 66.3 | 68.3 | 70.4 | 72.5 | 74.7 | 76.9 |
| Plus: Amortization of Financing Fees | 14.0 | 14.0 | 14.0 | 14.0 | 14.0 | 12.9 | 12.9 | 3.9 | - | - |
| **Changes in Working Capital Items** | | | | | | | | | | |
| (Inc.) / Dec. in Accounts Receivable | (33.8) | (29.0) | (25.6) | (21.5) | (16.8) | (17.3) | (17.8) | (18.4) | (18.9) | (19.5) |
| (Inc.) / Dec. in Inventories | (45.0) | (38.7) | (34.2) | (28.7) | (22.4) | (23.1) | (23.8) | (24.5) | (25.2) | (26.0) |
| (Inc.) / Dec. in Prepaid and Other Current Assets | (13.1) | (11.3) | (10.0) | (8.4) | (6.5) | (6.7) | (6.9) | (7.1) | (7.4) | (7.6) |
| Inc. / (Dec.) in Accounts Payable | 16.1 | 13.9 | 12.2 | 10.3 | 8.0 | 8.3 | 8.5 | 8.8 | 9.0 | 9.3 |
| Inc. / (Dec.) in Accrued Liabilities | 20.6 | 17.7 | 15.7 | 13.2 | 10.3 | 10.6 | 10.9 | 11.2 | 11.6 | 11.9 |
| Inc. / (Dec.) in Other Current Liabilities | 7.5 | 6.5 | 5.7 | 4.8 | 3.7 | 3.8 | 4.0 | 4.1 | 4.2 | 4.3 |
| (Inc.) / Dec. in Net Working Capital | (47.6) | (41.0) | (36.2) | (30.4) | (23.7) | (24.4) | (25.1) | (25.9) | (26.7) | (27.5) |
| **Cash Flow from Operating Activities** | **$424.8** | **$483.4** | **$538.2** | **$588.8** | **$635.8** | **$677.5** | **$721.7** | **$756.4** | **$783.1** | **$810.2** |
| **Investing Activities** | | | | | | | | | | |
| Capital Expenditures | (166.9) | (176.9) | (185.8) | (193.2) | (199.0) | (204.9) | (211.1) | (217.4) | (224.0) | (230.7) |
| Other Investing Activities | - | - | - | - | - | - | - | - | - | - |
| **Cash Flow from Investing Activities** | **($166.9)** | **($176.9)** | **($185.8)** | **($193.2)** | **($199.0)** | **($204.9)** | **($211.1)** | **($217.4)** | **($224.0)** | **($230.7)** |
| **Financing Activities** | | | | | | | | | | |
| Revolving Credit Facility | - | - | - | - | - | - | - | - | - | - |
| Term Loan A | - | - | - | - | - | - | - | - | - | - |
| Term Loan B | (257.9) | (306.5) | (352.4) | (395.6) | (436.8) | (472.5) | (510.6) | (67.7) | - | - |
| Term Loan C | - | - | - | - | - | - | - | - | - | - |
| Existing Term Loan | - | - | - | - | - | - | - | - | - | - |
| 2nd Lien | - | - | - | - | - | - | - | - | - | - |
| Senior Notes | - | - | - | - | - | - | - | - | - | - |
| Senior Subordinated Notes | - | - | - | - | - | - | - | - | - | - |
| Other Debt | - | - | - | - | - | - | - | - | - | - |
| Dividends | - | - | - | - | - | - | - | - | - | - |
| Equity Issuance / (Repurchase) | - | - | - | - | - | - | - | - | - | - |
| **Cash Flow from Financing Activities** | **($257.9)** | **($306.5)** | **($352.4)** | **($395.6)** | **($436.8)** | **($472.5)** | **($510.6)** | **($67.7)** | - | - |
| Excess Cash for the Period | - | - | - | - | - | - | - | $471.3 | $559.2 | $579.5 |
| Beginning Cash Balance | - | - | - | - | - | - | - | - | 471.3 | 1,030.5 |
| **Ending Cash Balance** | **-** | **-** | **-** | **-** | **-** | **-** | **-** | **$471.3** | **$1,030.5** | **$1,610.0** |
| **Cash Flow Statement Assumptions** | | | | | | | | | | |
| Capital Expenditures (% of sales) | 4.5% | 4.5% | 4.5% | 4.5% | 4.5% | 4.5% | 4.5% | 4.5% | 4.5% | 4.5% |

# EXHIBIT 5.50   ValueCo LBO Debt Schedule

*($ in millions, fiscal year ending December 31)*

**Debt Schedule**

|  | Pro forma 2019 | Year 1 2020 | Year 2 2021 | Year 3 2022 | Year 4 2023 | Year 5 2024 | Year 6 2025 | Year 7 2026 | Year 8 2027 | Year 9 2028 | Year 10 2029 |
|---|---|---|---|---|---|---|---|---|---|---|---|
|  |  |  |  |  |  | **Projection Period** |  |  |  |  |  |
| Forward LIBOR Curve | 1.85% | 1.70% | 1.65% | 1.55% | 1.55% | 1.55% | 1.55% | 1.55% | 1.55% | 1.55% | 1.55% |
| Cash Flow from Operating Activities |  | $424.8 | $483.4 | $538.2 | $588.8 | $635.8 | $677.5 | $721.7 | $756.4 | $783.1 | $810.2 |
| Cash Flow from Investing Activities |  | (166.9) | (176.9) | (185.8) | (193.2) | (199.0) | (204.9) | (211.1) | (217.4) | (224.0) | (230.7) |
| **Cash Available for Debt Repayment** |  | **$257.9** | **$306.5** | **$352.4** | **$395.6** | **$436.8** | **$472.5** | **$510.6** | **$539.0** | **$559.2** | **$579.5** |
| Total Mandatory Repayments |  | (28.0) | (28.0) | (28.0) | (28.0) | (28.0) | (28.0) | (28.0) | (28.0) | (28.0) | (28.0) |
| Cash from Balance Sheet | MinCash  -  | - | - | - | - | - | - | - | - | 471.3 | 1,030.5 |
| **Cash Available for Optional Debt Repayment** |  | **$229.9** | **$278.5** | **$324.4** | **$367.6** | **$408.8** | **$444.5** | **$482.6** | **$511.0** | **$1,030.5** | **$1,610.0** |

**Revolving Credit Facility**

| | Pro forma | Year 1 | Year 2 | Year 3 | Year 4 | Year 5 | Year 6 | Year 7 | Year 8 | Year 9 | Year 10 |
|---|---|---|---|---|---|---|---|---|---|---|---|
| Revolving Credit Facility Size | $250.0 | | | | | | | | | | |
| Spread | 4.250% | | | | | | | | | | |
| LIBOR Floor | - % | | | | | | | | | | |
| Term | 5 years | | | | | | | | | | |
| Commitment Fee on Unused Portion | 0.50% | | | | | | | | | | |
| Beginning Balance | | - | - | - | - | - | - | - | - | - | - |
| Drawdown/(Repayment) | | - | - | - | - | - | - | - | - | - | - |
| **Ending Balance** | | **-** | **-** | **-** | **-** | **-** | **-** | **-** | **-** | **-** | **-** |
| Interest Rate | | 5.95% | 5.90% | 5.80% | 5.80% | 5.80% | 5.80% | 5.80% | 5.80% | 5.80% | 5.80% |
| Interest Expense | | - | - | - | - | - | - | - | - | - | - |
| Commitment Fee | | 1.3 | 1.3 | 1.3 | 1.3 | 1.3 | 1.3 | 1.3 | 1.3 | 1.3 | 1.3 |
| Administrative Agent Fee | | 0.2 | 0.2 | 0.2 | 0.2 | 0.2 | 0.2 | 0.2 | 0.2 | 0.2 | 0.2 |

**Term Loan B Facility**

| | Pro forma | Year 1 | Year 2 | Year 3 | Year 4 | Year 5 | Year 6 | Year 7 | Year 8 | Year 9 | Year 10 |
|---|---|---|---|---|---|---|---|---|---|---|---|
| Size | $2,800.0 | | | | | | | | | | |
| Spread | 4.250% | | | | | | | | | | |
| LIBOR Floor | - % | | | | | | | | | | |
| Term | 7 years | | | | | | | | | | |
| Repayment Schedule | 1.0% Per Annum, Bullet at Maturity | | | | | | | | | | |
| Beginning Balance | | $2,800.0 | $2,542.1 | $2,235.6 | $1,883.2 | $1,487.6 | $1,050.8 | $578.3 | $67.7 | | |
| Mandatory Repayments | | (28.0) | (28.0) | (28.0) | (28.0) | (28.0) | (28.0) | (28.0) | (28.0) | | |
| Optional Repayments | | (229.9) | (278.5) | (324.4) | (367.6) | (408.8) | (444.5) | (482.6) | (39.7) | | |
| **Ending Balance** | | **$2,542.1** | **$2,235.6** | **$1,883.2** | **$1,487.6** | **$1,050.8** | **$578.3** | **$67.7** | **-** | | |
| Interest Rate | | 5.95% | 5.90% | 5.80% | 5.80% | 5.80% | 5.80% | 5.80% | 5.80% | 5.80% | 5.80% |
| Interest Expense | | 158.9 | 140.9 | 119.4 | 97.8 | 73.6 | 47.2 | 18.7 | 2.0 | - | - |

**Senior Notes**

| | Pro forma | Year 1 | Year 2 | Year 3 | Year 4 | Year 5 | Year 6 | Year 7 | Year 8 | Year 9 | Year 10 |
|---|---|---|---|---|---|---|---|---|---|---|---|
| Size | $850.0 | | | | | | | | | | |
| Coupon | 8.000% | | | | | | | | | | |
| Term | 8 years | | | | | | | | | | |
| Beginning Balance | | $850.0 | $850.0 | $850.0 | $850.0 | $850.0 | $850.0 | $850.0 | $850.0 | $850.0 | $850.0 |
| Repayment | | - | - | - | - | - | - | - | - | - | - |
| **Ending Balance** | | **$850.0** | **$850.0** | **$850.0** | **$850.0** | **$850.0** | **$850.0** | **$850.0** | **$850.0** | **$850.0** | **$850.0** |
| Interest Expense | | 68.0 | 68.0 | 68.0 | 68.0 | 68.0 | 68.0 | 68.0 | 68.0 | 68.0 | 68.0 |

# EXHIBIT 5.51  ValueCo LBO Returns Analysis

*($ in millions, fiscal year ending December 31)*

## Returns Analysis

| | Pro forma 2019 | | Year 1 2020 | Year 2 2021 | Year 3 2022 | Year 4 2023 | Year 5 2024 | Year 6 2025 | Year 7 2026 | Year 8 2027 | Year 9 2028 | Year 10 2029 |
|---|---|---|---|---|---|---|---|---|---|---|---|---|
| | | | | | | | *Projection Period* | | | | | |
| Entry EBITDA Multiple | 8.0x | | | | | | | | | | | |
| Initial Equity Investment | $2,100.0 | | | | | | | | | | | |
| EBITDA | | | $779.4 | $826.1 | $867.4 | $902.1 | $929.2 | $957.1 | $985.8 | $1,015.4 | $1,045.8 | $1,077.2 |
| Exit EBITDA Multiple | 8.0x | | | | | | | | | | | |
| **Enterprise Value at Exit** | | | **$6,235.0** | **$6,609.1** | **$6,939.6** | **$7,217.1** | **$7,433.7** | **$7,656.7** | **$7,886.4** | **$8,123.0** | **$8,366.6** | **$8,617.6** |
| *Less: Net Debt* | | | | | | | | | | | | |
| Revolving Credit Facility | | | – | – | – | – | – | – | – | – | – | – |
| Term Loan A | | | 2,542.1 | 2,235.6 | 1,883.2 | 1,487.6 | 1,050.8 | 578.3 | 67.7 | – | – | – |
| Term Loan B | | | – | – | – | – | – | – | – | – | – | – |
| Term Loan C | | | – | – | – | – | – | – | – | – | – | – |
| Existing Term Loan | | | – | – | – | – | – | – | – | – | – | – |
| 2nd Lien | | | – | – | – | – | – | – | – | – | – | – |
| Senior Notes | | | 850.0 | 850.0 | 850.0 | 850.0 | 850.0 | 850.0 | 850.0 | 850.0 | 850.0 | 850.0 |
| Senior Subordinated Notes | | | – | – | – | – | – | – | – | – | – | – |
| Other Debt | | | – | – | – | – | – | – | – | – | – | – |
| **Total Debt** | | | **$3,392.1** | **$3,085.6** | **$2,733.2** | **$2,337.6** | **$1,900.8** | **$1,428.3** | **$917.7** | **$850.0** | **$850.0** | **$850.0** |
| Less: Cash and Cash Equivalents | | | – | – | – | – | – | – | – | 471.3 | 1,030.5 | 1,610.0 |
| **Net Debt** | | | **$3,392.1** | **$3,085.6** | **$2,733.2** | **$2,337.6** | **$1,900.8** | **$1,428.3** | **$917.7** | **$378.7** | **($180.5)** | **($760.0)** |
| **Equity Value at Exit** | | | **$2,842.9** | **$3,523.5** | **$4,206.4** | **$4,879.5** | **$5,532.8** | **$6,228.4** | **$6,968.7** | **$7,744.3** | **$8,547.1** | **$9,377.7** |
| **Cash Return** | | | **1.4x** | **1.7x** | **2.0x** | **2.3x** | **2.6x** | **3.0x** | **3.3x** | **3.7x** | **4.1x** | **4.5x** |

| | Year 1 2020 | Year 2 2021 | Year 3 2022 | Year 4 2023 | Year 5 2024 | Year 6 2025 | Year 7 2026 | Year 8 2027 | Year 9 2028 | Year 10 2029 |
|---|---|---|---|---|---|---|---|---|---|---|
| Initial Equity Investment | ($2,100.0) | ($2,100.0) | ($2,100.0) | ($2,100.0) | ($2,100.0) | ($2,100.0) | ($2,100.0) | ($2,100.0) | ($2,100.0) | ($2,100.0) |
| Equity Proceeds | $2,842.9 | $3,523.5 | $4,206.4 | $4,879.5 | $5,532.8 | $6,228.4 | $6,968.7 | $7,744.3 | $8,547.1 | $9,377.7 |
| **IRR** | **35%** | **30%** | **26%** | **23%** | **21%** | **20%** | **19%** | **18%** | **17%** | **16%** |

### IRR - Assuming Exit in 2024E

| | | Exit Multiple | | | |
|---|---|---|---|---|---|
| Entry Multiple | 7.0x | 7.5x | 8.0x | 8.5x | 9.0x |
| 7.0x | 27% | 29% | 32% | 34% | 36% |
| 7.5x | 21% | 24% | 26% | 28% | 30% |
| 8.0x | 17% | 19% | 21% | 23% | 25% |
| 8.5x | 13% | 16% | 18% | 20% | 21% |
| 9.0x | 10% | 13% | 15% | 16% | 18% |

### IRR - Assuming 8.0x Entry Multiple

| | | Exit Year | | | |
|---|---|---|---|---|---|
| Exit Multiple | 2022 | 2023 | 2024 | 2025 | 2026 |
| 7.0x | 17% | 17% | 17% | 17% | 16% |
| 7.5x | 22% | 21% | 19% | 18% | 17% |
| 8.0x | 26% | 23% | 21% | 20% | 19% |
| 8.5x | 30% | 26% | 23% | 21% | 20% |
| 9.0x | 34% | 29% | 25% | 23% | 21% |

# EXHIBIT 5.52  ValueCo LBO Assumptions Page 1

## Assumptions Page 1 - Income Statement and Cash Flow Statement

### Income Statement Assumptions

**Sales (% growth)**

| | | Year 1 2020 | Year 2 2021 | Year 3 2022 | Year 4 2023 | Year 5 2024 | Year 6 2025 | Year 7 2026 | Year 8 2027 | Year 9 2028 | Year 10 2029 |
|---|---|---|---|---|---|---|---|---|---|---|---|
| Base | 1 | 7.5% | 6.0% | 5.0% | 4.0% | 3.0% | 3.0% | 3.0% | 3.0% | 3.0% | 3.0% |
| Sponsor | 2 | 7.5% | 6.0% | 6.0% | 4.0% | 3.0% | 3.0% | 3.0% | 3.0% | 3.0% | 3.0% |
| Management | 3 | 10.0% | 8.0% | 6.0% | 4.0% | 4.0% | 4.0% | 4.0% | 4.0% | 4.0% | 3.0% |
| Downside 1 | 4 | 12.0% | 10.0% | 8.0% | 6.0% | 3.0% | 4.0% | 4.0% | 4.0% | 4.0% | 4.0% |
| Downside 2 | 5 | 5.0% | 4.0% | 3.0% | 3.0% | 3.0% | 2.0% | 2.0% | 2.0% | 2.0% | 2.0% |

**Cost of Goods Sold (% sales)**

| | | Year 1 2020 | Year 2 2021 | Year 3 2022 | Year 4 2023 | Year 5 2024 | Year 6 2025 | Year 7 2026 | Year 8 2027 | Year 9 2028 | Year 10 2029 |
|---|---|---|---|---|---|---|---|---|---|---|---|
| Base | 1 | 60.0% | 60.0% | 60.0% | 60.0% | 60.0% | 60.0% | 60.0% | 60.0% | 60.0% | 60.0% |
| Sponsor | 2 | 60.0% | 60.0% | 60.0% | 60.0% | 60.0% | 60.0% | 60.0% | 60.0% | 60.0% | 60.0% |
| Management | 3 | 59.0% | 59.0% | 59.0% | 59.0% | 59.0% | 59.0% | 59.0% | 59.0% | 59.0% | 59.0% |
| Downside 1 | 4 | 61.0% | 61.0% | 61.0% | 61.0% | 61.0% | 61.0% | 61.0% | 61.0% | 61.0% | 61.0% |
| Downside 2 | 5 | 62.0% | 62.0% | 62.0% | 62.0% | 62.0% | 62.0% | 62.0% | 62.0% | 62.0% | 62.0% |

**SG&A (% sales)**

| | | Year 1 2020 | Year 2 2021 | Year 3 2022 | Year 4 2023 | Year 5 2024 | Year 6 2025 | Year 7 2026 | Year 8 2027 | Year 9 2028 | Year 10 2029 |
|---|---|---|---|---|---|---|---|---|---|---|---|
| Base | 1 | 19.0% | 19.0% | 19.0% | 19.0% | 19.0% | 19.0% | 19.0% | 19.0% | 19.0% | 19.0% |
| Sponsor | 2 | 19.0% | 19.0% | 19.0% | 19.0% | 19.0% | 19.0% | 19.0% | 19.0% | 19.0% | 19.0% |
| Management | 3 | 18.0% | 18.0% | 18.0% | 18.0% | 18.0% | 18.0% | 18.0% | 18.0% | 18.0% | 18.0% |
| Downside 1 | 4 | 20.0% | 20.0% | 20.0% | 20.0% | 20.0% | 20.0% | 20.0% | 20.0% | 20.0% | 20.0% |
| Downside 2 | 5 | 21.0% | 21.0% | 21.0% | 21.0% | 21.0% | 21.0% | 21.0% | 21.0% | 21.0% | 21.0% |

**Depreciation (% sales)**

| | | Year 1 2020 | Year 2 2021 | Year 3 2022 | Year 4 2023 | Year 5 2024 | Year 6 2025 | Year 7 2026 | Year 8 2027 | Year 9 2028 | Year 10 2029 |
|---|---|---|---|---|---|---|---|---|---|---|---|
| Base | 1 | 4.5% | 4.5% | 4.5% | 4.5% | 4.5% | 4.5% | 4.5% | 4.5% | 4.5% | 4.5% |
| Sponsor | 2 | 4.5% | 4.5% | 4.5% | 4.5% | 4.5% | 4.5% | 4.5% | 4.5% | 4.5% | 4.5% |
| Management | 3 | 4.5% | 4.5% | 4.5% | 4.5% | 4.5% | 4.5% | 4.5% | 4.5% | 4.5% | 4.5% |
| Downside 1 | 4 | 4.5% | 4.5% | 4.5% | 4.5% | 4.5% | 4.5% | 4.5% | 4.5% | 4.5% | 4.5% |
| Downside 2 | 5 | 4.5% | 4.5% | 4.5% | 4.5% | 4.5% | 4.5% | 4.5% | 4.5% | 4.5% | 4.5% |

**Amortization (% sales)**

| | | Year 1 2020 | Year 2 2021 | Year 3 2022 | Year 4 2023 | Year 5 2024 | Year 6 2025 | Year 7 2026 | Year 8 2027 | Year 9 2028 | Year 10 2029 |
|---|---|---|---|---|---|---|---|---|---|---|---|
| Base | 1 | 1.5% | 1.5% | 1.5% | 1.5% | 1.5% | 1.5% | 1.5% | 1.5% | 1.5% | 1.5% |
| Sponsor | 2 | 1.5% | 1.5% | 1.5% | 1.5% | 1.5% | 1.5% | 1.5% | 1.5% | 1.5% | 1.5% |
| Management | 3 | 1.5% | 1.5% | 1.5% | 1.5% | 1.5% | 1.5% | 1.5% | 1.5% | 1.5% | 1.5% |
| Downside 1 | 4 | 1.5% | 1.5% | 1.5% | 1.5% | 1.5% | 1.5% | 1.5% | 1.5% | 1.5% | 1.5% |
| Downside 2 | 5 | 1.5% | 1.5% | 1.5% | 1.5% | 1.5% | 1.5% | 1.5% | 1.5% | 1.5% | 1.5% |

### Cash Flow Statement Assumptions

**Capital Expenditures (% sales)**

| | | Year 1 2020 | Year 2 2021 | Year 3 2022 | Year 4 2023 | Year 5 2024 | Year 6 2025 | Year 7 2026 | Year 8 2027 | Year 9 2028 | Year 10 2029 |
|---|---|---|---|---|---|---|---|---|---|---|---|
| Base | 1 | 4.5% | 4.5% | 4.5% | 4.5% | 4.5% | 4.5% | 4.5% | 4.5% | 4.5% | 4.5% |
| Sponsor | 2 | 4.5% | 4.5% | 4.5% | 4.5% | 4.5% | 4.5% | 4.5% | 4.5% | 4.5% | 4.5% |
| Management | 3 | 4.5% | 4.5% | 4.5% | 4.5% | 4.5% | 4.5% | 4.5% | 4.5% | 4.5% | 4.5% |
| Downside 1 | 4 | 5.0% | 5.0% | 5.0% | 5.0% | 5.0% | 5.0% | 5.0% | 5.0% | 5.0% | 5.0% |
| Downside 2 | 5 | 5.0% | 5.0% | 5.0% | 5.0% | 5.0% | 5.0% | 5.0% | 5.0% | 5.0% | 5.0% |

*(All columns fall under the "Projection Period" header.)*

# EXHIBIT 5.53　ValueCo LBO Assumptions Page 2

## Assumptions Page 2 - Balance Sheet

| | | Year 1 2020 | Year 2 2021 | Year 3 2022 | Year 4 2023 | Year 5 2024 | Year 6 2025 | Year 7 2026 | Year 8 2027 | Year 9 2028 | Year 10 2029 |
|---|---|---|---|---|---|---|---|---|---|---|---|
| | | | | | | **Projection Period** | | | | | |
| *Current Assets* | | | | | | | | | | | |
| Days Sales Outstanding (DSO) | | | | | | | | | | | |
| Base | 1 | 47.6 | 47.6 | 47.6 | 47.6 | 47.6 | 47.6 | 47.6 | 47.6 | 47.6 | 47.6 |
| Sponsor | 2 | 47.6 | 47.6 | 47.6 | 47.6 | 47.6 | 47.6 | 47.6 | 47.6 | 47.6 | 47.6 |
| Management | 3 | 47.6 | 47.6 | 47.6 | 47.6 | 47.6 | 47.6 | 47.6 | 47.6 | 47.6 | 47.6 |
| Downside 1 | 4 | 50.0 | 50.0 | 50.0 | 50.0 | 50.0 | 50.0 | 50.0 | 50.0 | 50.0 | 50.0 |
| Downside 2 | 5 | 55.0 | 55.0 | 55.0 | 55.0 | 55.0 | 55.0 | 55.0 | 55.0 | 55.0 | 55.0 |
| | | | | | | | | | | | |
| Days Inventory Held (DIH) | | | | | | | | | | | |
| Base | 1 | 105.8 | 105.8 | 105.8 | 105.8 | 105.8 | 105.8 | 105.8 | 105.8 | 105.8 | 105.8 |
| Sponsor | 2 | 105.8 | 105.8 | 105.8 | 105.8 | 105.8 | 105.8 | 105.8 | 105.8 | 105.8 | 105.8 |
| Management | 3 | 105.8 | 105.8 | 105.8 | 105.8 | 105.8 | 105.8 | 105.8 | 105.8 | 105.8 | 105.8 |
| Downside 1 | 4 | 110.0 | 110.0 | 110.0 | 110.0 | 110.0 | 110.0 | 110.0 | 110.0 | 110.0 | 110.0 |
| Downside 2 | 5 | 115.0 | 115.0 | 115.0 | 115.0 | 115.0 | 115.0 | 115.0 | 115.0 | 115.0 | 115.0 |
| | | | | | | | | | | | |
| Prepaids and Other Current Assets (% sales) | | | | | | | | | | | |
| Base | 1 | 5.1% | 5.1% | 5.1% | 5.1% | 5.1% | 5.1% | 5.1% | 5.1% | 5.1% | 5.1% |
| Sponsor | 2 | 5.1% | 5.1% | 5.1% | 5.1% | 5.1% | 5.1% | 5.1% | 5.1% | 5.1% | 5.1% |
| Management | 3 | 5.1% | 5.1% | 5.1% | 5.1% | 5.1% | 5.1% | 5.1% | 5.1% | 5.1% | 5.1% |
| Downside 1 | 4 | 5.1% | 5.1% | 5.1% | 5.1% | 5.1% | 5.1% | 5.1% | 5.1% | 5.1% | 5.1% |
| Downside 2 | 5 | 5.1% | 5.1% | 5.1% | 5.1% | 5.1% | 5.1% | 5.1% | 5.1% | 5.1% | 5.1% |
| | | | | | | | | | | | |
| *Current Liabilities* | | | | | | | | | | | |
| Days Payable Outstanding (DPO) | | | | | | | | | | | |
| Base | 1 | 37.9 | 37.9 | 37.9 | 37.9 | 37.9 | 37.9 | 37.9 | 37.9 | 37.9 | 37.9 |
| Sponsor | 2 | 37.9 | 37.9 | 37.9 | 37.9 | 37.9 | 37.9 | 37.9 | 37.9 | 37.9 | 37.9 |
| Management | 3 | 37.9 | 37.9 | 37.9 | 37.9 | 37.9 | 37.9 | 37.9 | 37.9 | 37.9 | 37.9 |
| Downside 1 | 4 | 35.0 | 35.0 | 35.0 | 35.0 | 35.0 | 35.0 | 35.0 | 35.0 | 35.0 | 35.0 |
| Downside 2 | 5 | 30.0 | 30.0 | 30.0 | 30.0 | 30.0 | 30.0 | 30.0 | 30.0 | 30.0 | 30.0 |
| | | | | | | | | | | | |
| Accrued Liabilities (% sales) | | | | | | | | | | | |
| Base | 1 | 8.0% | 8.0% | 8.0% | 8.0% | 8.0% | 8.0% | 8.0% | 8.0% | 8.0% | 8.0% |
| Sponsor | 2 | 8.0% | 8.0% | 8.0% | 8.0% | 8.0% | 8.0% | 8.0% | 8.0% | 8.0% | 8.0% |
| Management | 3 | 8.0% | 8.0% | 8.0% | 8.0% | 8.0% | 8.0% | 8.0% | 8.0% | 8.0% | 8.0% |
| Downside 1 | 4 | 8.0% | 8.0% | 8.0% | 8.0% | 8.0% | 8.0% | 8.0% | 8.0% | 8.0% | 8.0% |
| Downside 2 | 5 | 8.0% | 8.0% | 8.0% | 8.0% | 8.0% | 8.0% | 8.0% | 8.0% | 8.0% | 8.0% |
| | | | | | | | | | | | |
| Other Current Liabilities (% sales) | | | | | | | | | | | |
| Base | 1 | 2.9% | 2.9% | 2.9% | 2.9% | 2.9% | 2.9% | 2.9% | 2.9% | 2.9% | 2.9% |
| Sponsor | 2 | 2.9% | 2.9% | 2.9% | 2.9% | 2.9% | 2.9% | 2.9% | 2.9% | 2.9% | 2.9% |
| Management | 3 | 2.9% | 2.9% | 2.9% | 2.9% | 2.9% | 2.9% | 2.9% | 2.9% | 2.9% | 2.9% |
| Downside 1 | 4 | 2.9% | 2.9% | 2.9% | 2.9% | 2.9% | 2.9% | 2.9% | 2.9% | 2.9% | 2.9% |
| Downside 2 | 5 | 2.9% | 2.9% | 2.9% | 2.9% | 2.9% | 2.9% | 2.9% | 2.9% | 2.9% | 2.9% |

# EXHIBIT 5.54  ValueCo LBO Assumptions Page 3

*($ in millions, fiscal year ending December 31)*

**Assumptions Page 3 - Financing Structures and Fees**

## Financing Structures

| Sources of Funds | Structure 1 | Structure 2 | Structure 3 | Structure 4 | Status Quo |
|---|---|---|---|---|---|
| | 1 | 2 | 3 | 4 | 5 |
| Revolving Credit Facility Size | $250.0 | $250.0 | $250.0 | $250.0 | |
| Revolving Credit Facility Draw | - | - | - | - | |
| Term Loan A | - | - | - | - | |
| Term Loan B | 2,800.0 | 2,150.0 | 2,100.0 | 1,750.0 | |
| Term Loan C | - | - | - | - | |
| 2nd Lien | - | - | 700.0 | - | |
| Senior Notes | 850.0 | 1,500.0 | 700.0 | 1,000.0 | |
| Senior Subordinated Notes | - | - | - | 1,000.0 | |
| Equity Contribution | 2,100.0 | 2,100.0 | 2,250.0 | 2,250.0 | |
| Rollover Equity | - | - | - | - | |
| Cash on Hand | 250.0 | 250.0 | 250.0 | 250.0 | |
| **Total Sources of Funds** | **$6,000.0** | **$6,000.0** | **$6,000.0** | **$6,000.0** | **-** |

| Uses of Funds | Structure 1 | Structure 2 | Structure 3 | Structure 4 | Status Quo |
|---|---|---|---|---|---|
| Equity Purchase Price | $4,350.0 | $4,350.0 | $4,350.0 | $4,350.0 | |
| Repay Existing Bank Debt | 1,500.0 | 1,500.0 | 1,500.0 | 1,500.0 | |
| Tender / Call Premiums | 20.0 | 20.0 | 20.0 | 20.0 | |
| Financing Fees | 100.0 | 100.0 | 100.0 | 100.0 | |
| Other Fees and Expenses | 30.0 | 30.0 | 30.0 | 30.0 | |
| **Total Uses of Funds** | **$6,000.0** | **$6,000.0** | **$6,000.0** | **$6,000.0** | **-** |

## Financing Fees

| | | Size | Fees (%) | Fees ($) |
|---|---|---|---|---|
| | Structure 1 | | | |
| Revolving Credit Facility Size | | $250.0 | 2.250% | $5.6 |
| Term Loan A | | - | | - |
| Term Loan B | | 2,800.0 | 2.250% | 63.0 |
| Term Loan C | | - | | - |
| 2nd Lien | | - | | - |
| Senior Notes | | 850.0 | 2.250% | 19.1 |
| Senior Subordinated Notes | | - | | - |
| Senior Bridge Facility | | 850.0 | 1.250% | 10.6 |
| Senior Subordinated Bridge Facility | | - | | - |
| Other Financing Fees & Expenses | | | | 1.6 |
| **Total Financing Fees** | | | | **$100.0** |

## Purchase Price

**Public / Private Target (1/2)**

| | | | 2 |
|---|---|---|---|
| Entry EBITDA Multiple | | | 8.0x |
| LTM 9/30/2019 EBITDA | | | 700.0 |
| **Enterprise Value** | | | **$5,600.0** |
| | | | |
| Less: Total Debt | | | (1,500.0) |
| Less: Preferred Stock | | | - |
| Less: Noncontrolling Interest | | | - |
| Plus: Cash and Cash Equivalents | | | 250.0 |
| **Equity Purchase Price** | | | **$4,350.0** |

### Calculation of Fully Diluted Shares Outstanding

| | |
|---|---|
| Offer Price per Share | - |
| | |
| Basic Shares Outstanding | - |
| Plus: Shares from In-the-Money Options | - |
| Less: Shares Repurchased | - |
| **Net New Shares from Options** | **-** |
| Plus: Shares from Convertible Securities | - |
| **Fully Diluted Shares Outstanding** | **-** |

| Options/Warrants | Number of Shares | Exercise Price | In-the-Money Shares | Proceeds |
|---|---|---|---|---|
| Tranche 1 | - | - | - | - |
| Tranche 2 | - | - | - | - |
| Tranche 3 | - | - | - | - |
| Tranche 4 | - | - | - | - |
| Tranche 5 | - | - | - | - |
| **Total** | **-** | | **-** | **-** |

| Convertible Securities | Amount | Conversion Price | Conversion Ratio | New Shares |
|---|---|---|---|---|
| Issue 1 | - | - | - | - |
| Issue 2 | - | - | - | - |
| Issue 3 | - | - | - | - |
| Issue 4 | - | - | - | - |
| Issue 5 | - | - | - | - |
| **Total** | **-** | | | **-** |

## Amortization of Financing Fees

| | Term | Year 1 2020 | Year 2 2021 | Year 3 2022 | Year 4 2023 | Year 5 2024 | Year 6 2025 | Year 7 2026 | Year 8 2027 | Year 9 2028 | Year 10 2029 |
|---|---|---|---|---|---|---|---|---|---|---|---|
| Revolving Credit Facility Size | 5 | $1.1 | $1.1 | $1.1 | $1.1 | $1.1 | | | | | |
| Term Loan A | 7 | 9.0 | 9.0 | 9.0 | 9.0 | 9.0 | 9.0 | 9.0 | | | |
| Term Loan B | - | - | - | - | - | - | - | - | - | - | - |
| Term Loan C | - | - | - | - | - | - | - | - | - | - | - |
| 2nd Lien | - | - | - | - | - | - | - | - | - | - | - |
| Senior Notes | 8 | 2.4 | 2.4 | 2.4 | 2.4 | 2.4 | 2.4 | 2.4 | 2.4 | | |
| Senior Subordinated Notes | - | - | - | - | - | - | - | - | - | - | - |
| Senior Bridge Facility | 8 | 1.3 | 1.3 | 1.3 | 1.3 | 1.3 | 1.3 | 1.3 | 1.3 | | |
| Senior Subordinated Bridge Facility | - | - | - | - | - | - | - | - | - | - | - |
| Other Financing Fees & Expenses | 8 | 0.2 | 0.2 | 0.2 | 0.2 | 0.2 | 0.2 | 0.2 | 0.2 | | |
| **Annual Amortization** | | **$14.0** | **$14.0** | **$14.0** | **$14.0** | **$14.0** | **$12.9** | **$12.9** | **$3.9** | | |

287

## CHAPTER 5 QUESTIONS

1) All of the following industries have traditionally supported high leverage levels EXCEPT

   A. Technology
   B. Cable
   C. Industrials
   D. Gaming

2) If a PE firm contributes $400 million of equity to a company upfront and exits the investment at the end of year five for $1,000 million, what is the internal rate of return?

   A. 19.5%
   B. 20.1%
   C. 25.7%
   D. 26.7%

3) Using the information below, determine the size of the term loan B and calculate the source and use of funds, respectively

($ in millions)

| Sources of Funds | | Uses of Funds | |
|---|---|---|---|
| Term Loan B | | Purchase ValueCo Equity | $825.0 |
| Senior Subordinated Notes | 300.0 | Repay Existing Debt | 300.0 |
| Equity Contribution | 385.0 | Financing Fees | 20.0 |
| Cash on Hand | 25.0 | Other Fees and Expenses | 15.0 |
| **Total Sources** | | **Total Uses** | |

   A. $300.0 million; $1,000.0 million
   B. $320.0 million; $1,425.0 million
   C. $450.0 million; $1,160.0 million
   D. Cannot be determined

4) Calculate the company's 2023 interest converge ratio. What does this indicate?

Use the information below to answer the next three questions

*($ in millions)*

| Financial Data | | | | | |
| --- | --- | --- | --- | --- | --- |
| | **2019** | **2020** | **2021** | **2022** | **2023** |
| Total Debt | $4,000.0 | $3,500.0 | $3,000.0 | $2,500.0 | $2,000.0 |
| Interest Expense | 600.0 | 465.0 | 400.0 | 330.0 | 240.0 |
| EBITDA | 730.0 | 775.0 | 805.0 | 850.0 | 900.0 |

A. 3.4x, stronger credit profile than 2019
B. 3.4x, weaker credit profile than 2019
C. 3.8x, stronger credit profile than 2019
D. 8.3x, weaker credit profile than 2019

5) Between 2019 and 2023, total leverage _____

A. Decreases
B. Increases
C. Remains constant
D. Cannot be determined

6) Between 2019 and 2023, the credit profile of the company _____

A. Weakens
B. Strengthens
C. Remains constant
D. Cannot be determined

7) Which of the following is a reasonable total leverage ratio for an LBO under normal market conditions?

A. 3.0x EBITDA
B. 6.0x EBITDA
C. 5.0x net income
D. 1.0x sales

8) The projection period of an LBO model for a potential debt provider is typically how many years?

A. 1–2 years
B. 3–4 years
C. 7–10 years
D. 15+ years

9) What IRR threshold has historically served as the standard for sponsors in considering an LBO?

   A. 5%
   B. 10%
   C. 20%
   D. 40%

10) Which of the following is NOT a key component of an LBO analysis transaction summary page?

   A. Sources and uses of funds
   B. Credit statistics
   C. Returns analysis
   D. Debt schedule

11) Under what circumstances might a strategic buyer use LBO analysis?

   A. To determine the debt capacity of their company
   B. To determine the price a financial sponsor bidder can afford to pay when competing for an asset in an auction process
   C. To help spread comparable companies analysis
   D. Strategic buyers would not use LBO analysis

12) What are the key variables for sensitivity analysis performed in LBO analysis?

   I. Purchase price
   II. Financing structure
   III. Historical dividends
   IV. Exit multiple

   A. I and II
   B. II and III
   C. I, II, and IV
   D. I, II, III, and IV

13) Which of the following historical financial data is the least relevant for framing projections and performing LBO analysis?

   A. Sales growth
   B. EBITDA and EBIT margins
   C. Capex
   D. Interest expense

14) Which of the following is NOT a typical operating case used in LBO analysis?

    A. SEC case
    B. Base case
    C. Downside case
    D. Sponsor case

15) Which of the following is NOT a standard section of a cash flow statement?

    A. Operating activities
    B. Financing activities
    C. Investing activities
    D. Acquisition activities

# Mergers & Acquisitions

# Sell-Side M&A

The sale of a company, division, business, or collection of assets ("target") is a major event for its owners (shareholders), management, employees, and other stakeholders. It is an intense, time-consuming process with high stakes, usually spanning several months. Consequently, the seller typically hires an investment bank and its team of trained professionals ("sell-side advisor") to ensure that key objectives are met and a favorable result is achieved. In many cases, a seller turns to its bankers for a comprehensive financial analysis of the various strategic alternatives available to the target. These include a sale of all or part of the business, a recapitalization, an initial public offering, a spin-off of part of the business into a standalone company, or a continuation of the status quo.

Once the decision to sell has been made, the sell-side advisor seeks to achieve the optimal mix of value maximization, speed of execution, and certainty of completion among other deal-specific considerations for the selling party. Accordingly, it is the sell-side advisor's responsibility to identify the seller's priorities from the onset and craft a tailored sale process. If the seller is largely indifferent toward confidentiality, timing, and potential business disruption, the advisor may consider running a *broad auction,* reaching out to as many potential interested parties as reasonably possible. This process, which is relatively neutral toward prospective buyers, is designed to maximize competitive dynamics and heighten the probability of finding the one buyer willing to offer the best value.

Alternatively, if speed, confidentiality, a particular transaction structure, and/or cultural fit are a priority for the seller, then a *targeted auction*, where only a select group of potential buyers is approached, or even a *negotiated sale* with a single party, may be more appropriate. Generally, an auction requires more upfront organization, marketing, process points, and resources than a negotiated sale with a single party. Consequently, this chapter focuses primarily on the auction process.

From an analytical perspective, a sell-side assignment requires the deal team to perform a comprehensive valuation of the target using the methodologies discussed in this book. In addition, in order to assess the potential purchase price that specific public strategic buyers may be willing to pay for the target, merger consequences analysis is performed with an emphasis on accretion/(dilution) and balance sheet effects (see Chapter 7). These valuation analyses are used to frame the seller's price expectations, select the final buyer list, set guidelines for the range of acceptable bids, evaluate offers received, and ultimately guide negotiations of the final purchase price. Furthermore, for public targets (and certain private targets, depending on the situation) the sell-side advisor or an additional investment bank may be called upon to provide a fairness opinion.

In discussing the process by which companies are bought and sold in the marketplace, we provide greater context to the topics discussed earlier in this book. In a sale process, theoretical valuation methodologies are ultimately tested in the market based on what a buyer will actually pay for the target (see Exhibit 6.1). An effective sell-side advisor seeks to push the bidders toward, or through, the upper endpoint of the implied valuation range for the target. On a fundamental level, this involves positioning the business properly and tailoring the sale process accordingly to maximize its value.

## AUCTIONS

An auction is a staged process whereby a target is marketed to multiple prospective buyers ("buyers", "bidders", or "acquirers"). A well-run auction is designed to have a substantial positive impact on value (both price and terms) received by the seller due to a variety of factors related to the creation of a competitive environment. This environment encourages bidders to put forth their best offer on both price and terms, and helps increase speed of execution by encouraging quick action by bidders.

An auction provides a level of comfort that the market has been tested as well as a strong indicator of inherent value (supported by a fairness opinion, if required). At the same time, the auction process may have potential drawbacks, including information leakage into the market from bidders, negative impact on employee morale, reduced negotiating leverage once a "winner" is chosen (thereby encouraging re-trading[1]), and a "taint" of the business in the event of a failed auction. In addition, certain prospective buyers may decide not to participate in a broad auction given their reluctance to commit serious time and resources to a situation where they may perceive a relatively low likelihood of success.

A successful auction requires significant dedicated resources, experience, and expertise. Upfront, the deal team establishes a solid foundation through the preparation of compelling marketing materials, identification of potential deal issues, coaching of management, and selection of an appropriate group of prospective buyers. Once the auction commences, the sell-side advisor is entrusted with running as effective a process as possible. This involves the execution of a wide range of duties and functions in a tightly coordinated manner.

To ensure a successful outcome, investment banks commit a team of bankers that is responsible for the day-to-day execution of the transaction. Auctions also require significant time and attention from key members of the target's management team, especially on the production of marketing materials and facilitation of buyer due diligence (e.g., management presentations, site visits, data room population, and responses to specific buyer inquiries). It is the sell-side advisor's responsibility, however, to alleviate as much of this burden from the management team as possible.

In the later stages of an auction, a senior member of the sell-side advisory team typically negotiates directly with prospective buyers with the goal of encouraging them to put forth their best offer. As a result, sellers seek investment banks with extensive negotiation experience, sector expertise, and buyer relationships to run these auctions.

---

[1]Refers to the practice of replacing an initial bid with a lower one at a later date.

**EXHIBIT 6.1** Valuation Paradigm

| Implied Valuation Range | | | | Actual Price Paid |
|---|---|---|---|---|
| Comparable Companies Analysis | Precedent Transactions Analysis | Discounted Cash Flow Analysis | Leveraged Buyout Analysis | M&A Sale Process |

### Description

| | | | | |
|---|---|---|---|---|
| ▪ Valuation based on the current trading multiples of peer companies | ▪ Valuation based on the multiples paid for peer companies in past M&A transactions | ▪ Valuation based on the present value of projected free cash flow | ▪ Valuation based on the price a financial sponsor would likely pay | ▪ Determines the ultimate price a buyer is willing to pay |

### Common Value Drivers

- Sector performance and outlook
- Company performance
  - size, margins and growth profile
  - historical and projected financial performance
- Company positioning
  - market share
  - ability to differentiate products/services
  - quality of management
- General economic and financing market conditions

### Unique Value Drivers

| | | | | |
|---|---|---|---|---|
| ▪ Relative performance to peer companies | ▪ M&A market conditions<br>▪ Deal specific situation<br>▪ Premium paid for control<br>▪ Level of synergies | ▪ Free cash flow<br>▪ Cost of capital<br>▪ Terminal value | ▪ Credit market conditions<br>▪ Free cash flow<br>▪ Ability to leverage<br>▪ Debt repayment<br>▪ Cost of capital<br>▪ Required returns | ▪ Process dynamics<br>  - auction vs. negotiated sale<br>  - number of parties in process<br>  - level of information disclosed<br>  - "trophy"/must own asset<br>▪ Buyer appetite<br>  - strategic vs. sponsor<br>  - desire/ability to pay<br>  - amount needed to "win"<br>▪ Pro forma impact to buyer<br>  - financial effects<br>  - pro forma leverage<br>  - returns thresholds |

There are two primary types of auctions—broad and targeted.

- *Broad Auction*: As its name implies, a broad auction maximizes the universe of prospective buyers approached. This may involve contacting dozens of potential bidders, comprising both strategic buyers (potentially including direct competitors) and financial sponsors. By casting as wide a net as possible, a broad auction is designed to maximize competitive dynamics, thereby increasing the likelihood of finding the best possible offer. This type of process typically involves more upfront organization and marketing due to the larger number of bidders in the early stages of the process. It is also more difficult to maintain confidentiality as the process is susceptible to leaks to the public (including customers, suppliers, and competitors), which, in turn, can increase the potential for business disruption.[2]

- *Targeted Auction*: A targeted auction focuses on a few clearly defined buyers that have been identified as having a strong strategic fit and/or desire, as well as the financial capacity, to purchase the target. For example, it may be limited to a select group of strategic buyers. This process is more conducive to maintaining confidentiality and minimizing business disruption to the target. At the same time, there is greater risk of "leaving money on the table" by excluding a potential bidder that may be willing to pay a higher price.

Exhibit 6.2 provides a summary of the potential advantages and disadvantages of each process.

**EXHIBIT 6.2**    Advantages and Disadvantages of Broad and Targeted Auctions

|  | Broad | Targeted |
|---|---|---|
| Advantages | <ul><li>Heightens competitive dynamics</li><li>Maximizes probability of achieving maximum sale price</li><li>Helps to ensure that all likely bidders are approached</li><li>Limits potential buyers' negotiating leverage</li><li>Enhances board's comfort that it has satisfied its fiduciary duty to maximize value</li></ul> | <ul><li>Higher likelihood of preserving confidentiality</li><li>Reduces business disruption</li><li>Reduces the potential of a failed auction by signaling a desire to select a "partner"</li><li>Maintains perception of competitive dynamics</li><li>Serves as a "market check" for board to meet its fiduciary duties</li></ul> |
| Disadvantages | <ul><li>Difficult to preserve confidentiality</li><li>Highest business disruption risk</li><li>Some prospective buyers decline participation in broad auctions</li><li>Unsuccessful outcome can create perception of undesirable asset</li><li>Industry competitors may participate just to gain access to sensitive information</li></ul> | <ul><li>Potentially excludes non-obvious, but credible, buyers</li><li>Potential to leave "money on the table" if certain buyers excluded</li><li>Lesser degree of competition</li><li>May afford buyers more leverage in negotiations</li><li>Provides less market data on which board can rely to satisfy its fiduciary duties</li></ul> |

[2]In some circumstances, the auction is actually made public by the seller to encourage all interested buyers to come forward and state their interest in the target.

## Auction Structure

The traditional auction is structured as a two-round bidding process that generally spans three to six months (or longer) from the decision to sell until the signing of a definitive purchase/sale agreement ("definitive agreement") with the winning bidder (see Exhibit 6.3). The timing of the post-signing ("closing") period depends on a variety of factors not specific to an auction, such as regulatory approvals and/or third-party consents, financing, and shareholder approval. The entire auction process consists of multiple stages and discrete milestones within each of these stages. There are numerous variations within this structure that allow the sell-side advisor to customize the process for a given situation.

## ORGANIZATION AND PREPARATION

- Identify Seller Objectives and Determine Appropriate Sale Process
- Perform Sell-Side Advisor Due Diligence and Preliminary Valuation Analysis
- Select Buyer Universe
- Prepare Marketing Materials
- Prepare Confidentiality Agreement

### Identify Seller Objectives and Determine Appropriate Sale Process

At the onset of an auction, the sell-side advisor works with the seller to identify its objectives, determine the appropriate sale process to conduct, and develop a process roadmap. The advisor must first gain a clear understanding of the seller's priorities so as to tailor the process accordingly. Perhaps the most basic decision is how many prospective buyers to approach (i.e., whether to run a broad or targeted auction).

As previously discussed, while a broad auction may be more appealing to a seller in certain circumstances, a targeted auction may better satisfy certain "softer" needs, such as speed to transaction closing, heightened confidentiality, a tailored transaction structure, and less risk of business disruption. Furthermore, the target's board of directors must also take into account its fiduciary duties in deciding whether to conduct a broad or targeted auction.[3] At this point, the deal team drafts a detailed process timeline and roadmap, including target dates for significant milestones, such as launch, receipt of initial and final bids, contract signing, and deal closing.

---

[3]In Delaware (which generally sets the standards upon which many states base their corporate law), when the sale of control or the break-up of a company has become inevitable, the directors have the duty to obtain the highest price reasonably available. There is no statutory or judicial "blueprint" for an appropriate sale or auction process. Directors enjoy some latitude in this regard, so long as the process is designed to satisfy the directors' duties by ensuring that they have reasonably informed themselves about the company's value.

**EXHIBIT 6.3** Stages of an Auction Process

| | Stages of an Auction Process | | | |
|---|---|---|---|---|
| Organization and Preparation | First Round | Second Round | Negotiations | Closing |
| ▪ Identify seller objectives and determine appropriate sale process<br>▪ Perform sell-side advisor due diligence and preliminary valuation analysis<br>▪ Select buyer universe<br>▪ Prepare marketing materials<br>▪ Prepare confidentiality agreement | ▪ Contact prospective buyers<br>▪ Negotiate and execute confidentiality agreements with interested parties<br>▪ Distribute CIM and initial bid procedures letter<br>▪ Prepare management presentation<br>▪ Set up data room<br>▪ Prepare stapled financing package (if applicable)<br>▪ Receive initial bids and select buyers to proceed to second round | ▪ Conduct management presentations<br>▪ Facilitate site visits<br>▪ Provide data room access and respond to diligence requests<br>▪ Distribute final bid procedures letter and draft definitive agreement<br>▪ Receive final bids | ▪ Evaluate final bids<br>▪ Negotiate with preferred buyer(s)<br>▪ Select winning bidder<br>▪ Render fairness opinion (if required)<br>▪ Receive board/owner approval and execute definitive agreement ("signing") | ▪ Obtain necessary approvals<br>▪ Financing and closing |
| 2 – 4 weeks | 4 – 6 weeks | 6 – 8 weeks | 2 – 4 weeks (may include a third "mini round") | 4 – 8 weeks + |

## Perform Sell-Side Advisor Due Diligence and Preliminary Valuation Analysis

Sale process preparation begins with extensive due diligence on the part of the sell-side advisor. This typically kicks off with an in-depth session with target management. The sell-side advisor must have a comprehensive understanding of the target's business and the management team's vision prior to drafting marketing materials and communicating with prospective buyers. Due diligence facilitates the advisor's ability to properly position the target and articulate its investment merits. It also allows for the identification of potential buyer concerns or issues ranging from growth sustainability, margin trends, and customer concentration to environmental matters, contingent liabilities, and labor relations.

A key portion of sell-side diligence centers on ensuring that the advisor understands and provides perspective on the assumptions that drive management's financial model. This diligence is particularly important as the model forms the basis for the valuation work that will be performed by prospective buyers. Therefore, the sell-side advisor must approach the target's financial projections from a buyer's perspective and gain comfort with the numbers, trends, and key assumptions driving them.

An effective sell-side advisor understands the valuation methodologies that buyers will use in their analysis (e.g., comparable companies, precedent transactions, DCF analysis, and LBO analysis) and performs this work beforehand to establish a valuation range benchmark. For specific public buyers, accretion/(dilution) analysis and balance sheet effects are also performed to assess their ability to pay. Ultimately, however, the target's implied valuation based on these methodologies needs to be weighed against market appetite. Furthermore, the actual value received in a transaction must be assessed on the basis of structure and terms, in addition to price.

The sell-side advisor may recommend that the target commissions a Quality of Earnings (QoE) report or *market study*. A QoE is a financial report performed by an accounting firm, typically national or super-regional, to assess and validate the operating earnings profile of the target. The goal is to help provide potential buyers and their financing sources comfort from the third-party assessment, although they also typically have their own QoE report compiled. In general, QoEs have become increasingly common in the M&A marketplace. Similarly, a third-party market study on the target's core sub-sector and key end markets might be commissioned to help build buyer conviction in the story.

In the event a stapled financing package is offered to buyers, a separate financing deal team is formed (either at the sell-side advisor's institution or another bank) to begin conducting due diligence in parallel with the sell-side team. Their analysis is used to craft a generic pre-packaged financing structure to support the purchase of the target.[4] The initial financing package terms are used as guideposts to derive an implied LBO analysis valuation.

## Select Buyer Universe

The selection of an appropriate group of prospective buyers, and compilation of corresponding contact information, is a critical part of the organization and preparation stage. At the extreme, the omission or inclusion of a potential buyer (or buyers) can mean the difference between a successful or failed auction. Sell-side advisors are selected

---

[4]Ultimately, buyers who require financing to complete a deal will typically work with multiple banks to ensure they are receiving the most favorable financing package (debt quantum, pricing, and terms) available in the market.

in large part on the basis of their sector knowledge, including their relationships with, and insights on, prospective buyers. Correspondingly, the deal team is expected both to identify the appropriate buyers and effectively market the target to them.

In a broad auction, the buyer list typically includes a mix of strategic buyers and financial sponsors. The sell-side advisor evaluates each buyer on a broad range of criteria pertinent to its likelihood and ability to acquire the target at an acceptable value. When evaluating strategic buyers, the banker looks first and foremost at strategic fit, including potential synergies. Financial capacity or "ability to pay"—which is typically dependent on size, balance sheet strength, access to financing, and risk appetite—is also closely scrutinized. Other factors play a role in assessing potential strategic bidders, such as cultural fit, M&A track record, existing management's role going forward, relative and pro forma market position (including antitrust concerns), and the effects on existing customer and supplier relationships.

When evaluating potential financial sponsor buyers, key criteria include investment strategy/focus, sector expertise, fund size,[5] track record, fit within existing investment portfolio, fund life cycle,[6] and the ability to obtain financing. As part of this process, the deal team looks for sponsors with existing portfolio companies that may serve as an attractive combination candidate for the target. For certain large transactions, sponsors may look to partner with others, or enhance financial capacity through co-investments from LPs.

In many cases, a strategic buyer is able to pay a higher price than a sponsor due to the ability to realize synergies and a lower cost of capital. Depending on the prevailing capital markets conditions, a strategic buyer may also present less financing risk than a sponsor.

Once the sell-side advisor has compiled a list of prospective buyers, it presents them to the seller for final sign-off.

### Prepare Marketing Materials

Marketing materials often represent the first formal introduction of the target to prospective buyers. They are essential for sparking buyer interest and creating a favorable first impression. Effective marketing materials present the target's investment highlights in a succinct manner, while also providing supporting evidence and basic operational, financial, and other essential business information. The two main marketing documents for the first round of an auction process are the teaser and confidential information memorandum/presentation (CIM or CIP). The sell-side advisors take the lead on producing these materials with substantial input from management. Legal counsel also reviews these documents, as well as the management presentation, for various potential legal concerns (e.g., antitrust[7]).

A code name for the target is also typically introduced at this point, especially as buyer outreach nears. The code name is meant to maintain the confidentiality of the company as well as the process itself. The actual code name is often chosen by the bankers in collaboration with the company, although some banks utilize a random, computer-driven system. Code names are also assigned to individual buyers, particularly later in the process as the universe narrows.

---

[5]Refers to the total size of the fund as well as remaining equity available for investment.
[6]As set forth in the agreement between the fund's GP and LPs, refers to how long the fund will be permitted to seek investments prior to entering a harvest and distribution phase.
[7]Typically, counsel closely scrutinizes any discussion of a business combination (i.e., in a strategic transaction) as marketing materials will be subjected to scrutiny by antitrust authorities in connection with their regulatory review.

**Teaser**   The teaser is the first marketing document presented to prospective buyers, typically prior to execution of a confidentiality agreement. It is designed to inform buyers and generate sufficient interest for them to undertake further work and potentially submit a bid. The teaser is generally a brief one- or two-page synopsis of the target, including a company overview, investment highlights, and summary financial information. It also contains contact information for the bankers running the sell-side process so that interested parties may respond.

Teasers vary in terms of format and content in accordance with the target, sector, sale process, advisor, and potential seller sensitivities. For public companies, Regulation FD concerns govern the content of the teaser (i.e., no material non-public information) as well as the nature of the buyer contacts themselves.[8] Exhibit 6.4 displays an illustrative teaser template as might be presented to prospective buyers.

**EXHIBIT 6.4**   Sample Teaser

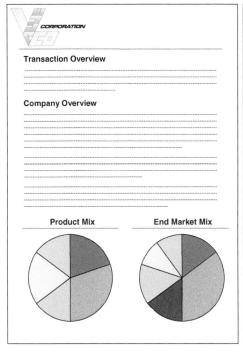
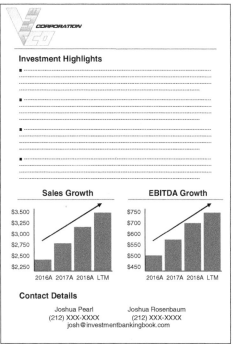

**Confidential Information Memorandum**   The CIM is a detailed written description of the target (often 50+ pages) that serves as the primary marketing document for the target in an auction. Increasingly, it comes in the form of a PowerPoint presentation and is referred to as a CIP (Confidential Information Presentation) instead of the traditional portrait/textual format of a CIM. The deal team, in collaboration with the target's management, spends significant time and resources drafting the CIM before it is deemed ready for distribution to prospective buyers. In the event the seller is a financial sponsor (e.g., selling a portfolio company), the sponsor's investment professionals typically also provide input.

---

[8]The initial buyer contact or teaser can put a public company "in play" and may constitute the selective disclosure of material information (i.e., that the company is for sale).

Like teasers, CIMs vary in terms of format and content depending on situation-specific circumstances. There are, however, certain generally accepted guidelines for content, as reflected in Exhibit 6.5. The CIM typically contains an executive summary, investment considerations, and detailed information about the target, as well as its sector, customers and suppliers (often presented on an anonymous basis), operations, facilities, management, and employees. A modified version of the CIM may be prepared for designated strategic buyers, namely competitors with whom the seller may be concerned about sharing certain sensitive information.

**EXHIBIT 6.5**   Confidential Information Memorandum Table of Contents

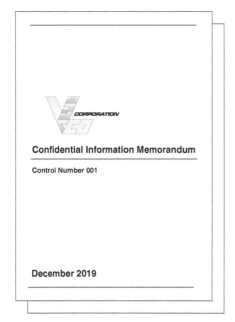

**Table of Contents**

1. Executive Summary
2. Investment Considerations
3. Industry Overview
   – segment overview
   – market share and position
   – competition
4. Company Overview
   – history
   – strategy
   – products and services
   – customers and suppliers
   – management and employees
5. Operations Overview
   – manufacturing
   – distribution
   – sales and marketing
   – information systems
   – legal and environmental
6. Financial Information
   – historical financial results and MD&A
   – projected financial results and MD&A
Appendix
   – audited financial statements
   – recent press releases
   – product brochures

**Confidential Information Memorandum**

Control Number 001

December 2019

**Financial Information**   The CIM contains a detailed financial section presenting historical and projected financial information with accompanying narrative explaining both past and expected future performance (MD&A). This data forms the basis for the preliminary valuation analysis performed by prospective buyers.

Consequently, the deal team spends a great deal of time working with the target's CFO, treasurer, and/or finance team (and division heads, as appropriate) on the CIM's financial section. This process involves normalizing the historical financials (e.g., for acquisitions, divestitures, and other one-time and/or extraordinary items) and crafting an accompanying MD&A. The sell-side advisor also helps develop a set of projections, typically five years in length, as well as supporting assumptions and narrative. Given the importance of the projections in framing valuation, prospective buyers subject them to intense scrutiny. Therefore, the sell-side advisor must gain sufficient comfort that the numbers are realistic and defensible in the face of potential buyer skepticism.

In some cases, the CIM provides additional financial information to help guide buyers toward potential growth/acquisition scenarios for the target. For example, the sell-side advisor may work with management to compile a list of potential acquisition opportunities for inclusion in the CIM (typically on an anonymous basis), including their incremental sales and EBITDA contributions. This information is designed to provide potential buyers with perspective on the potential upside represented by using the target as a growth platform so they can craft their bids accordingly.

## Prepare Confidentiality Agreement

A confidentiality agreement (CA) is a legally binding contract between the target and prospective buyers that governs the sharing of confidential company information. The CA is typically drafted by the target's counsel and distributed to prospective buyers along with the teaser, with the understanding that the receipt of more detailed information is conditioned on execution of the CA.

A typical CA includes provisions governing the following:

- *Use of information* – states that all information furnished by the seller, whether oral or written, is considered proprietary information and should be treated as confidential and used solely to make a decision regarding the proposed transaction

- *Term* – designates the time period during which the confidentiality restrictions remain in effect[9]

- *Permitted disclosures* – outline under what limited circumstances the prospective buyer is permitted to disclose the confidential information provided; also prohibits disclosure that the two parties are in negotiations

- *Return of confidential information* – mandates the return or destruction of all provided documents once the prospective buyer exits the process

- *Non-solicitation/no hire* – prevents prospective buyers from soliciting to hire (or hiring) target employees for a designated time period

- *Standstill agreement* – for public targets, precludes prospective buyers from making unsolicited offers or purchases of the target's shares, or seeking to control/influence the target's management, board of directors, or policies for a specified period of time (typically six months to two years)

- *Restrictions on clubbing* – prevents prospective buyers from collaborating with each other or with outside financial sponsors/equity providers without the prior consent of the target (in order to preserve a competitive environment)

---

[9]Typically one-to-two years for financial sponsors and potentially longer for strategic buyers.

## FIRST ROUND

- Contact Prospective Buyers
- Negotiate and Execute Confidentiality Agreements with Interested Parties
- Distribute Confidential Information Memorandum and Initial Bid Procedures Letter
- Prepare Management Presentation
- Set Up Data Room
- Prepare Stapled Financing Package (if applicable)
- Receive Initial Bids and Select Buyers to Proceed to Second Round

### Contact Prospective Buyers

The first round begins with the contacting of prospective buyers, which marks the formal launch of the auction process. This typically takes the form of a scripted phone call to each prospective buyer by a senior member of the sell-side advisory deal team (either an M&A banker or the coverage banker that maintains the relationship with the particular buyer), followed by the delivery of the teaser and CA.[10] The sell-side advisor keeps a detailed record of all interactions with prospective buyers, called a *contact log*, which is used as a tool to monitor a buyer's activity level and provide a record of the process.

### Negotiate and Execute Confidentiality Agreement with Interested Parties

Upon receipt of the CA, a prospective buyer presents the document to its legal counsel for review. In the likely event there are comments, the buyer's counsel and seller's counsel negotiate the CA with input from their respective clients. Following execution of the CA, the sell-side advisor distributes the CIM and *initial bid procedures letter* to a prospective buyer.[11]

---

[10]In some cases, the CA must be signed prior to receipt of any information, including the teaser, depending on seller sensitivity.

[11]Calls are usually commenced one-to-two weeks prior to the CIM being printed to allow sufficient time for the negotiation of CAs. Ideally, the sell-side advisor prefers to distribute the CIMs simultaneously to provide all prospective buyers an equal amount of time to consider the investment prior to the bid due date.

## Distribute Confidential Information Memorandum and Initial Bid Procedures Letter

Prospective buyers are typically given several weeks to review the CIM,[12] study the target and its sector, and conduct preliminary financial analysis prior to submitting their initial non-binding bids. During this period, the sell-side advisor maintains a dialogue with the prospective buyers, often providing additional color, guidance, and materials, as appropriate, on a case-by-case basis.

Depending on their level of interest, prospective buyers may also engage investment banks (as M&A buy-side advisors and/or financing providers), other external financing sources, and consultants at this stage. Buy-side advisors play an important role in helping their client, whether a strategic buyer or a financial sponsor, assess the target from a valuation perspective and determine a competitive initial bid price. Financing sources help assess both the buyer's and target's ability to support a given capital structure and provide their clients with data points on amounts, terms, and availability of financing. This financing data is used to help frame the valuation analysis performed by the buyer. Consultants provide perspective on key business and market opportunities, as well as potential risks and areas of operational improvement for the target.

**Initial Bid Procedures Letter**   The initial bid procedures letter, which typically is sent out to prospective buyers following distribution of the CIM, states the date and time by which interested parties must submit their written, non-binding preliminary indications of interest ("first round bids"). It also defines the exact information that should be included in the bid, such as:

- Indicative purchase price (buyers typically present as a range) and form of consideration (cash vs. stock mix)[13]

- Key assumptions to arrive at the stated purchase price

- Structural and other considerations

- Information on financing sources

- Treatment of management and employees

- Timing for completing a deal and diligence that must be performed

- Key conditions to signing and closing

- Required approvals (e.g., board/investment committee, shareholder, regulatory)

- Buyer contact information and advisors

---

[12]Each CIM is given a unique control number or watermark that is used to track each party that receives a copy.

[13]For acquisitions of private companies, buyers typically are asked to bid assuming the target is both cash and debt free.

## Prepare Management Presentation

The management presentation is typically structured as a slideshow with accompanying hardcopy handout. The sell-side advisor takes the lead on preparing these materials with substantial input from management. In parallel, they determine the speaker lineup for each slide of the presentation, as well as key messages. The bankers also develop a list of "challenge" questions and accompanying answers for each slide in anticipation of buyer focus areas. Depending on the management team, the rehearsal process for the presentations ("dry runs") may be intense and time-consuming. The management presentation slideshow needs to be completed by the start of the second round when the actual meetings with buyers begin.

The presentation format generally maps to that of the CIM/CIP, but is more crisp and concise. It also tends to contain an additional level of detail, analysis, and insight more conducive to an interactive session with management and later-stage due diligence. Given buyers have already demonstrated their interest through an initial bid and the number of parties has been culled for the second round, management is more willing to share incremental detail, especially regarding growth initiatives. A typical management presentation outline is shown in Exhibit 6.6.

**EXHIBIT 6.6**   Sample Management Presentation Outline

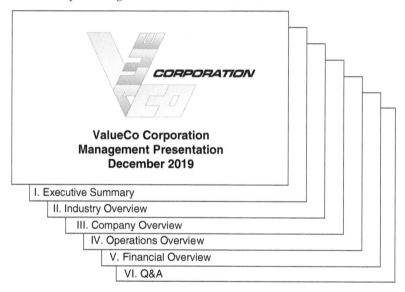

## Set Up Data Room

The data room serves as the hub for the buyer due diligence that takes place in the second round of the process. It is typically an online repository, where comprehensive, detailed information about the target is stored, catalogued, and made available to pre-screened bidders.[14] A well-organized data room facilitates buyer due diligence, helps keep the sale process on schedule, and inspires confidence in bidders. Most prominent data room service providers also generate detailed analytics for the sell-side bankers regarding the frequency of log-ins, number of documents reviewed, and other activity by each bidder in the data room, which helps the deal team determine the interest level of each bidder. While most data rooms follow certain basic guidelines, they may vary greatly in terms of content and accessibility depending on the company and confidentiality concerns.

Data rooms, such as those provided by Datasite, generally contain a broad base of essential company information, documentation, and analyses. In essence, the data room is designed to provide a comprehensive set of information relevant for buyers to make an informed investment decision about the target, such as detailed financial reports, industry reports, and consulting studies. It also contains detailed company-specific information such as customer and supplier lists, labor contracts, purchase contracts, description and terms of outstanding debt, lease and pension contracts, and environmental compliance information (see Exhibit 6.7). At the same time, the content must reflect any concerns over sharing sensitive data for competitive reasons.[15]

The data room also allows the buyer (together with its legal counsel, accountants, and other advisors) to perform more detailed confirmatory due diligence prior to consummating a transaction. This due diligence includes reviewing charters/bylaws, outstanding litigation, regulatory information, environmental reports, and property deeds, for example. It is typically conducted only after a buyer has decided to seriously pursue the acquisition.

The sell-side bankers work closely with the target's legal counsel and selected employees to organize, populate, and manage the data room. While the data room is continuously updated and refreshed with new information throughout the auction, the aim is to have a basic data foundation in place by the start of the second round. Access to the data room is typically granted to those buyers that move forward after first round bids, prior to, or coinciding with, their attendance at the management presentation.

---

[14]Prior to the establishment of web-based data retrieval systems, data rooms were physical locations (i.e., offices or rooms, usually housed at the target's law firm) where file cabinets or boxes containing company documentation were set up. Today, however, almost all data rooms are online sites where buyers can view all the necessary documentation remotely. Among other benefits, the online portal is easier to populate with data and facilitates the participation of a greater number of prospective buyers as documents can be reviewed simultaneously by different parties. Data rooms also enable the seller to customize the viewing, downloading, and printing of various data and documentation for specific buyers.

[15]Sensitive information (e.g., customer, supplier, and employment contracts, or profitability metrics by product/customer/location) is generally withheld from bidders that compete with the target until later in the process. In certain circumstances, a separate "clean room" is established to limit access to specific documents to specified individuals, typically buyer advisors and legal counsel.

**EXHIBIT 6.7** Datasite Data Room Document Index

| | Index ⇕ | File Name ⇕ | Status ⇕ | File Type ⇕ | Pages ⇕ | Date Added ⇕ |
|---|---|---|---|---|---|---|
| | Filter | Filter | All | All | Filter | Filter |
| ☆ | 1 | Financial | Published | Folder | N/A | 2018-04-18 12:12 |
| ☆ | 2 | Litigation | Published | Folder | N/A | 2018-04-18 12:12 |
| ☆ | 3 | Agreements | Published | Folder | N/A | 2018-04-18 12:12 |
| ☆ | 4 | Taxes | Published | Folder | N/A | 2018-04-18 12:12 |
| ☆ | 5 | Benefits - Employee | Published | Folder | N/A | 2018-04-18 12:12 |
| ☆ | 6 | Business Operations | Published | Folder | N/A | 2018-04-18 12:12 |
| ☆ | 7 | Insurance | Published | Folder | N/A | 2018-04-18 12:12 |
| ☆ | 8 | IP and Proprietary Rights 2021 | Published | Folder | N/A | 2018-04-18 12:12 |
| ☆ | 9 | Corporate Governance | Published | Folder | N/A | 2018-04-18 12:12 |
| ☆ | 10 | Controls and Procedures | Published | Folder | N/A | 2019-03-28 13:18 |
| ☆ | 11 | Contracts-Agreements | Published | Folder | N/A | 2019-04-24 10:24 |

**Project Indigo**

SHORTCUTS
- New
- Index List
- Favorites
- Action Required
- Downloads
- Recycle Bin

INDEX

DD Documents
- 1 Financial
- 2 Litigation
- 3 Agreements
- 4 Taxes
- 5 Benefits - Employee
- 6 Business Operations
- 7 Insurance
- 8 IP and Proprietary Rights 2021
- 9 Corporate Governance
- 10 Controls and Procedures
- 11 Contracts-Agreements
- 12 Load Legal File #1 Here
- 15 OKRs

Project 2

Index. ▸ DD Documents

DOCUMENTS  Q&A  PERMISSIONS  USERS  REDACTION  ANALYTICS  SETTINGS

UPLOAD  ADD  DOWNLOAD  PRINT  PENAME  MOVE  COPY  REPLACE  BULK CHANGES  UNPLD  REAS  RECYCLE BIN  REDACT

## Prepare Stapled Financing Package (if applicable)

The investment bank running the auction process (or sometimes a "partner" bank) may prepare a "pre-packaged" financing structure in support of the target being sold. Commonly referred to as a staple, it is targeted toward financial sponsor buyers and is typically only provided for private companies.[16] Although prospective buyers are not required to use the staple, historically it has positioned the sell-side advisor to play a role in the deal's financing. Often, however, buyers seek their own financing sources to match or "beat" the staple. Alternatively, certain buyers may choose to use less leverage than provided by the staple.

To avoid a potential conflict of interest, the investment bank running the M&A sell-side sets up a separate financing team distinct from the sell-side advisory team to run the staple process. This financing team is tasked with providing an objective assessment of the target's leverage capacity. This team conducts due diligence and financial analysis separately from (but often in parallel with) the M&A team and crafts a financing structure that is presented to the bank's internal credit committee for approval. This financing package is then presented to the seller for sign-off, after which it is offered to prospective buyers as part of the sale process.

The basic terms of the staple are typically communicated verbally to buyers in advance of the first round bid date so they can use that information to help frame their bids. Staple term sheets and/or actual financing commitments are not provided until later in the auction's second round, prior to submission of final bids. Those investment banks without debt underwriting capabilities (e.g., middle market or boutique investment banks) may pair up with a partner bank capable of providing a staple, if requested by the client.

While buyers are not obligated to use the staple, it is designed to send a strong signal of support from the sell-side bank and provide comfort that the necessary financing will be available to buyers for the acquisition. The staple can also be used to limit buyers' ability to speak with multiple financing sources, thereby reducing chatter in the market and helping preserve the integrity of the sale process. In this vein, it may serve to compress the timing between the start of the auction's second round and signing of a definitive agreement by eliminating duplicate buyer financing due diligence. To some extent, the staple helps establish a valuation floor for the target by setting a leverage level that can be used as the basis for extrapolating a purchase price. For example, a staple offering debt financing equal to 5.5x LTM EBITDA with a 30% minimum equity contribution would imply a purchase price of approximately 8x LTM EBITDA.

## Receive Initial Bids and Select Buyers to Proceed to Second Round

On the first round bid date, the sell-side advisor receives initial indications of interest from prospective buyers. Over the next few days, the deal team conducts a thorough analysis of the bids received, assessing indicative purchase price as well as key deal terms and other stated conditions. There may also be dialogue with certain buyers at this point, typically focused on seeking clarification on key bid points.

An effective sell-side advisor is able to discern which bids are "real" (i.e., less likely to be re-traded). Furthermore, it may be apparent that certain bidders are simply trying to get a free look at the target without any serious intent to consummate a transaction. As previously discussed, the advisor's past deal experience, specific sector expertise, familiarity with the buyers, and knowledge regarding bidder engagement (including via the data room analytics) are key in this respect.

---

[16]In re Del Monte Foods Company Shareholders Litigation, C.A. No. 6027-VCL (Del. Ch. Feb. 14, 2011), the court held that the advice the public target's board received from its sell-side M&A advisor was conflicted given that the bank was also offering financing to the buyer.

Once this analysis is completed, the bid information is summarized and presented to the seller along with a recommendation on which buyers to invite to the second round (see Exhibit 6.8 for a sample graphical presentation of purchase price ranges from bidders). The final decision regarding which buyers should advance, however, is made by the seller in consultation with its advisors.

**Valuation Perspectives – Strategic Buyers vs. Financial Sponsors**  As discussed in Chapters 4 and 5, financial sponsors use LBO analysis and the implied IRRs and cash returns, together with guidance from the other methodologies discussed in this book, to frame their purchase price range. The CIM financial projections and an initial assumed financing structure (e.g., a staple, if provided, or indicative terms from a financing provider) form the basis for the sponsor in formulating a first round bid. The sell-side advisor performs its own LBO analysis in parallel to assess the sponsor bids.

While strategic buyers also rely on the fundamental methodologies discussed in this book to establish a valuation range for a potential acquisition target, they typically employ additional techniques. For example, public strategics use accretion/(dilution) analysis to measure the pro forma effects of the transaction on EPS, assuming a given purchase price and financing structure (see Chapter 7). Therefore, the sell-side advisor performs similar analysis in parallel to determine the maximum price a given buyer may be willing to pay. This requires making assumptions regarding each specific acquirer's financing mix and cost, as well as synergies.

**EXHIBIT 6.8**   First Round Bids Summary

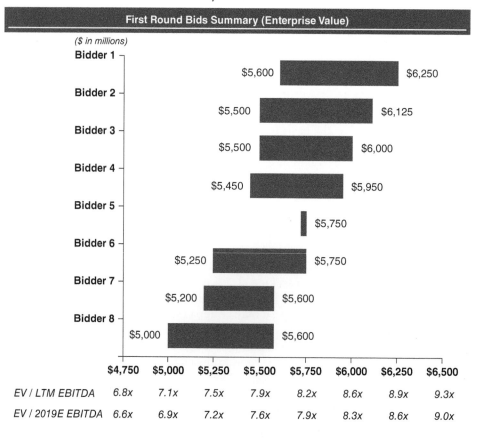

## SECOND ROUND

- Conduct Management Presentations
- Facilitate Site Visits
- Provide Data Room Access and Respond to Diligence Requests
- Distribute Final Bid Procedures Letter and Draft Definitive Agreement
- Receive Final Bids

The second round of the auction centers on facilitating the prospective buyers' ability to conduct detailed due diligence and analysis so they can submit strong, final (and ideally) binding bids by the set due date. The diligence process is meant to be exhaustive, typically spanning several weeks, depending on the target's size, sector, geographies, and ownership. The length and nature of the diligence process often differs based on the buyer's profile. A strategic buyer that is a direct competitor of the target, for example, may already have in-depth knowledge of the business and therefore focus on a more limited scope of company-specific information.[17] For a financial sponsor that is unfamiliar with the target and its sector, however, due diligence may take longer. As a result, sponsors often seek professional advice from hired consultants, operational advisors, and other industry experts to assist in their due diligence.

The sell-side advisor plays a central role during the second round by coordinating management presentations and facility site visits, monitoring the data room, and maintaining regular dialogue with prospective buyers. During this period, each prospective buyer is afforded time with senior management, a cornerstone of the due diligence process. The buyers also comb through the target's data room, visit key facilities, conduct follow-up diligence sessions with key company officers, and perform detailed financial and industry analyses. Prospective buyers are given sufficient time to complete their due diligence, secure financing, craft a final bid price and proposed transaction structure, and submit a markup of the draft definitive agreement. At the same time, the sell-side advisor seeks to maintain a competitive atmosphere and keep the process moving by limiting the time available for due diligence, providing access to management, and ensuring bidders move in accordance with the established schedule.

### Conduct Management Presentations

The management presentation typically marks the formal kickoff of the second round, often spanning a full business day. At the presentation, the target's management team presents each prospective buyer with a detailed overview of the company. This involves an in-depth discussion of topics ranging from basic business, industry, and financial information to competitive positioning, future strategy, growth opportunities, synergies (if appropriate), and financial projections.

---

[17]Due diligence in these instances may be complicated by the need to limit the prospective buyer's access to highly sensitive information that the seller is unwilling to provide.

The core team presenting typically consists of the target's CEO, CFO, and key division heads or other operational executives, as appropriate. The presentation is intended to be interactive, with Q&A encouraged and expected. It is customary for prospective buyers to bring their investment banking advisors and financing sources, as well as industry and/or operational consultants, to the management presentation so they can conduct their due diligence in parallel and provide insight.

The management presentation is often the buyer's first meeting with management. Therefore, this forum represents a unique opportunity to gain a deeper understanding of the business and its future prospects directly from the individuals who know the company best. Furthermore, the management team itself typically represents a substantial portion of the target's value proposition and is therefore a core diligence item. The presentation is also a chance for prospective buyers to gain a sense of "fit" between themselves and management.

## Facilitate Site Visits

Site visits are an essential component of buyer due diligence, providing a firsthand view of the target's operations. Often, the management presentation itself takes place at, or near, a key company facility and includes a site visit as part of the agenda. Prospective buyers may also request visits to multiple sites to better understand the target's business and assets. The typical site visit involves a guided tour of a key target facility, such as a manufacturing plant, distribution center, and/or sales office. The guided tours are generally led by the local manager of the given facility, often accompanied by a subset of senior management and a member of the sell-side advisory team. They tend to be highly interactive as key buyer representatives, together with their advisors and consultants, use this opportunity to ask detailed questions about the target's operations. In many cases, the seller does not reveal the true purpose of the site visit internally as employees outside a selected group of senior managers are often unaware a sale process is underway.

## Provide Data Room Access and Respond to Diligence Requests

In conjunction with the management presentation and site visits, prospective buyers are provided access to the data room. The data room contains detailed information about all aspects of the target (e.g., business, financial, accounting, tax, legal, insurance, environmental, information technology, and property). Serious bidders dedicate significant resources to ensure their due diligence is as thorough as possible. They often enlist a full team of accountants, attorneys, consultants, and other functional specialists to conduct a comprehensive investigation of company data. Through rigorous data analysis and interpretation, the buyer seeks to identify the key opportunities and risks presented by the target, thereby framing the acquisition rationale and investment thesis. This process also enables the buyer to identify those outstanding items and issues that should be satisfied prior to submitting a formal bid and/or specifically relating to the seller's proposed definitive agreement.

Some online data rooms allow users to download documents, while others only permit screenshots (that may or may not be printable). Data room access may be tailored to individual bidders or even specific members of the bidder teams (e.g., limited to legal counsel only). For example, strategic buyers that compete directly with the target may be restricted from viewing sensitive competitive information (e.g., customer and supplier contracts), at least until the later stages when the preferred bidder is selected. The sell-side advisor monitors data room access throughout the process, including the viewing of specific items. This enables them to track buyer interest and activity, draw conclusions, and take action accordingly.

As prospective buyers pore through the data, they identify key issues, opportunities, and risks that require follow-up inquiry. The sell-side advisor plays an active role in this respect, channeling follow-up due diligence requests to the appropriate individuals at the target and facilitating an orderly and timely response.

### Distribute Final Bid Procedures Letter and Draft Definitive Agreement

During the second round, the *final bid procedures letter* is distributed to the remaining prospective buyers often along with the draft definitive agreement. As part of their final bid package, prospective buyers submit a markup of the draft definitive agreement together with a cover letter detailing their proposal in response to the items outlined in the final bid procedures letter.

**Final Bid Procedures Letter**   Similar to the initial bid procedures letter in the first round, the final bid procedures letter outlines the exact date and guidelines for submitting a final, legally binding bid package. As would be expected, however, the requirements for the final bid are more stringent, including:

- Purchase price details, including the exact dollar amount of the offer and form of purchase consideration (e.g., cash versus stock)[18]

- Markup of the draft definitive agreement provided by the seller in a form that the buyer would be willing to sign

- Evidence of committed financing (e.g., debt or equity commitment letters) and information on financing sources

- Attestation to completion of due diligence (or very limited confirmatory due diligence required)

- Attestation that the offer is binding and will remain open for a designated period of time

- Required regulatory approvals and timeline for completion

- Board of directors or investment committee approvals (if appropriate)

- Estimated time to sign and close the transaction

- Buyer contact information

---

[18]Like the initial bid procedures letter, for private targets, the buyer is typically asked to bid assuming the target is both cash and debt free, and to indicate a target working capital amount. If the target is a public company, the bid will be expressed on a per share basis.

**Definitive Agreement**   The definitive agreement is a legally binding contract between a buyer and seller detailing the terms and conditions of the sale transaction. In an auction, the first draft is prepared by the seller's legal counsel in collaboration with the seller and its bankers. It is distributed to prospective buyers (and their legal counsel) during the second round—often toward the end of the diligence process. The buyer's counsel then provides specific comments on the draft document (largely informed by the buyer's second round diligence efforts) and submits it as part of the final bid package. In many cases, the sell-side advisor requests the submission of a markup prior to the final bid to provide additional time for review and negotiation.

The definitive agreement is a critical part of the bid package and overall value proposition. Key business, economic, and structural terms may represent a sizable percentage of the purchase price and prove invaluable to the seller. It is not uncommon for an otherwise attractive bid price to fall apart due to failure to reach agreement on key contract terms.

Therefore, the sell-side advisor and legal counsel work to encourage each buyer to submit a form of revised definitive agreement that they would be willing to sign immediately if the bid is accepted. This requires substantive discussions between the buyer's and seller's legal counsel in advance to pre-negotiate certain terms. The sell-side advisor's goal is to obtain the most definitive, least conditional revised definitive agreement possible prior to submission to the seller. This aids the seller in evaluating the competing contract terms and avoiding a situation where the buyer has "hold-up" power on key contract terms after emerging as the leading or "winning bidder".

Definitive agreements involving public and private companies differ in terms of content, although the basic format of the document is the same, containing an overview of the transaction structure/deal mechanics, representations and warranties ("reps and warranties", or "R&W"), pre-closing commitments (including covenants), closing conditions, termination provisions, and indemnities (if applicable),[19] as well as associated disclosure schedules and exhibits.[20] Exhibit 6.9 provides an overview of some of the key sections of a definitive agreement.

## Receive Final Bids

Upon conclusion of the second round, prospective buyers submit their final bid packages to the sell-side advisor by the date indicated in the final bid procedures letter. These bids are expected to be final with minimal conditionality, or "outs", such as the need for additional due diligence or firming up of financing commitments. In practice, the sell-side advisor works with viable buyers throughout the second round to firm up their bids as much as possible before submission.

---

[19]Indemnities are generally only included for the sale of private companies or divisions/assets of public companies.

[20]Frequently, the seller's disclosure schedules, which qualify the representations and warranties made by the seller in the definitive agreement and provide other vital information to making an informed bid, are circulated along with the draft definitive agreement.

**EXHIBIT 6.9**   Key Sections of a Definitive Agreement

| | Definitive Agreement Summary |
|---|---|
| Transaction Structure/Deal Mechanics | ▪ Transaction structure (e.g., merger, stock sale, asset sale)[a]<br>▪ Price and terms (e.g., form of consideration—cash, stock, or mixed; earn-outs; adjustment to price)<br>▪ Treatment of the target's stock and options (if a merger)<br>▪ Identification of assets and liabilities being transferred (if an asset deal) |
| Representations and Warranties | ▪ The buyer and seller make reps and warranties to each other about their ability to engage in the transaction, and the seller makes reps and warranties about the target's business. In a stock-for-stock transaction, the buyer also makes reps and warranties about its own business.<br>Examples include:<br>– financial statements must fairly present the current financial position<br>– no material adverse changes (MACs)[b]<br>– all material contracts have been disclosed<br>– availability of funds (usually requested from a financial sponsor)<br>▪ Reps and warranties serve several purposes:<br>– assist the buyer in due diligence<br>– help assure the buyer it is getting what it thinks it is paying for<br>– baseline for closing condition (see "bring-down" condition below)<br>– baseline for indemnification |
| Pre-Closing Commitments (Including Covenants) | ▪ Assurances that the target will operate in the ordinary course between signing and closing, and will not take value-reducing actions or change the business. Examples include:<br>– restrictions on paying special dividends<br>– restrictions on making capital expenditures in excess of an agreed budget<br>▪ In some circumstances, one party may owe a termination fee ("breakup fee") to the other party. Examples include:<br>– the buyer and seller may agree on a maximum level of compromise that the buyer is required to accept from regulatory authorities before it is permitted to walk away from the deal |
| Other Agreements | ▪ "No-shop" and other deal protections<br>▪ Treatment of employees post-closing<br>▪ Tax matters (such as the allocation of pre-closing and post-closing taxes within the same tax year)<br>▪ Commitment of the buyer to obtain third-party financing, if necessary, and of the seller to cooperate in obtaining such financing |

*(Continued)*

**EXHIBIT 6.9**   Key Sections of a Definitive Agreement (*Continued*)

| Definitive Agreement Summary |
|---|
| **Closing Conditions** | ▪ A party is not required to close the transaction unless the conditions to such party's obligations are satisfied.[c] Key conditions include:<br>  – accuracy of the other party's reps and warranties as of the closing date (known as the "bring-down" condition)[d]<br>  – compliance by the other party with all of its affirmative covenants<br>  – receipt of antitrust clearance and other regulatory approvals<br>  – receipt of shareholder approval, if required<br>  – absence of injunction |
| **Termination Provisions** | ▪ Circumstances under which one party may terminate the agreement rather than complete the deal. Examples include:<br>  – failure to obtain regulatory or shareholder approvals<br>  – permanent injunction (i.e., a court order blocking the deal)<br>  – seller exercises fiduciary termination (i.e., the right to take a better offer—typically limited to transactions involving the sale of all or substantially all of a public company)<br>  – deal has not closed by specified outside date ("drop-dead date")<br>▪ Mutual commitment for the buyer and seller to use their "best efforts" to consummate the transaction, including obtaining regulatory approvals<br>  – if the seller terminates the deal to take a better offer, the seller pays a breakup fee to the buyer<br>  – if the seller terminates because the buyer cannot come up with financing, the buyer may owe a breakup fee to the seller |
| **Indemnification** | ▪ Typically, in private deals only (public shareholders do not provide indemnities in public deals), the parties will indemnify each other for breaches of the reps and warranties. As a practical matter, it is usually the buyer that is seeking indemnity from the seller and may ask for a cash escrow to cover potential breaches.[e] For example:<br>  – The seller represents that it has no environmental liability. However, post-closing, a $100 million environmental problem is discovered. If the buyer had an indemnification against environmental liabilities, the seller would be required to pay the buyer $100 million (less any negotiated "deductible").<br>▪ Increasingly, in lieu of providing indemnification for breaches of reps and warranties, sellers are requiring buyers to purchase rep and warranty insurance from a third-party underwriter. This insurance is widely available and facilitates transactions by easing the negotiation of the reps and warranties and reducing the post-closing obligations of the seller.<br>▪ Indemnification rights are often limited in several respects:<br>  – time during which a claim can be made<br>  – cap on maximum indemnity<br>  – losses that the buyer must absorb before making a claim (a deductible) |

*(Continued)*

**EXHIBIT 6.9**   Key Sections of a Definitive Agreement (*Continued*)

---

(a)An acquisition of a company can be effected in several different ways, depending on the particular tax, legal, and other preferences. In a basic merger transaction, the acquirer and target merge into one surviving entity. More often, a subsidiary of the acquirer is formed, and that subsidiary merges with the target (with the resulting merged entity becoming a wholly owned subsidiary of the acquirer). In a basic stock sale transaction, the acquirer (or a subsidiary thereof) acquires 100% of the capital stock (or other equity interests) of the target. In a basic asset sale transaction, the acquirer (or a subsidiary thereof) purchases all, or substantially all, of the assets of the target and, depending on the situation, may assume all, or some of, the liabilities of the target associated with the acquired assets. In an asset sale, the target survives the transaction and may choose to either continue operations or dissolve after distributing the proceeds from the sale to its equity holders.

(b)Also called material adverse effect (MAE). This is a highly negotiated provision in the definitive agreement, which may permit a buyer to avoid closing the transaction in the event that a substantial adverse situation is discovered after signing or a detrimental post-signing event occurs that affects the target. MAE has been interpreted by the courts to mean, in most circumstances, a very significant problem that is likely to be lasting rather than short term. As a practical matter, it has proven difficult for buyers in recent years to establish that a MAC has occurred such that the buyer is entitled to terminate the deal.

(c)Receipt of financing is usually not a condition to closing, although this may be subject to change in accordance with market conditions.

(d)The representations usually need to be true only to some forgiving standard, such as "true in all material respects" or, more commonly, "true in all respects except for such inaccuracies that, taken together, do not amount to a material adverse effect". See footnote (b) for an explanation of the material adverse effect condition.

(e)As the buyer only makes very limited reps and warranties in the definitive agreement, it is rare that any indemnification payments are ever paid by a buyer to a seller.

---

## NEGOTIATIONS

- Evaluate Final Bids
- Negotiate with Preferred Buyer(s)
- Select Winning Bidder
- Render Fairness Opinion (if required)
- Receive Board/Owner Approval and Execute Definitive Agreement

### Evaluate Final Bids

The sell-side advisor works together with the seller and its legal counsel to conduct a thorough analysis of the price, structure, contract, and conditionality of the final bids. Purchase price is assessed within the context of the first round bids and the target's recent financial performance, as well as the valuation work performed by the sell-side advisor. The deemed binding nature of each final bid, or lack thereof, is also carefully weighed in assessing its strength. For example, a bid with a superior headline offer price, but a weaker contract and significant conditionality, may be deemed inferior to a firmer bid at a lower price. Once this analysis is completed, the seller selects a preferred party or parties with whom to negotiate a definitive agreement.

### Negotiate with Preferred Buyer(s)

Often, the sell-side advisor recommends that the seller negotiate with two (or more) parties, especially if the bid packages are relatively close and/or there are issues with the higher bidder's markup of the definitive agreement. Skillful negotiation on the part of the sell-side advisor at this stage can meaningfully improve the final bid terms. While tactics vary broadly, the advisor seeks to maintain a level playing field so as not to advantage one bidder over another and maximize the competitiveness of the final stage of the process. During these final negotiations, the advisor works intensely with the bidders to clear away any remaining confirmatory diligence items (if any) while firming up key terms in the definitive agreement (including price), with the goal of driving one bidder to differentiate itself.

### Select Winning Bidder

The sell-side advisor and legal counsel negotiate a final definitive agreement with the winning bidder, which is then presented to the target's board of directors for approval. Not all auctions result in a successful sale. The seller normally reserves the right to reject any and all bids as inadequate at every stage of the process. Similarly, each prospective buyer has the right to withdraw from the process at any time prior to the execution of a binding definitive agreement. An auction that fails to produce a sale is commonly referred to as a "busted" or "failed" process.

### Render Fairness Opinion (if required)

In response to a proposed offer for a public company, the target's board of directors typically requires a fairness opinion to be rendered as one item for its consideration before making a recommendation on whether to accept the offer and approve the execution of a definitive agreement. For public companies selling divisions or subsidiaries, a fairness opinion may be requested by the board of directors depending on the size and scope of the business being sold. The board of directors of a private company may also require a fairness opinion to be rendered in certain circumstances, especially if the stock of the company is broadly held (i.e., there are a large number of shareholders).

As the name connotes, a fairness opinion is a letter opining on the "fairness" (from a financial point of view) of the consideration offered in a transaction. The opinion letter is supported by detailed analysis and separate documentation providing an overview of the sale process run (including number of parties contacted and range of bids received), as well as an objective valuation of the target. The valuation analysis typically includes comparable companies, precedent transactions, DCF analysis, and LBO analysis (if applicable and typically for reference only), as well as other relevant industry and share price performance benchmarking analyses, including premiums paid (if the target is publicly traded). The supporting analysis also contains a summary of the target's financial performance, including both historical and projected financials, along with key drivers and assumptions on which the valuation is based. Relevant industry information and trends supporting the target's financial assumptions and projections may also be included.

Prior to the delivery of the fairness opinion to the board of directors, the sell-side advisory team must receive approval from its internal fairness opinion committee.[21] In a public deal, the fairness opinion and supporting analysis are publicly disclosed and described in detail in the relevant SEC filings (see Chapter 2). Once rendered, the fairness opinion is among the mix of information available to the target's board of directors as the board members consider the transaction and fulfill their fiduciary duties.

### Receive Board/Owner Approval and Execute Definitive Agreement

Once the seller's board of directors votes to approve the deal, the definitive agreement is executed by the buyer and seller. A formal transaction announcement agreed to by both parties is made with key deal terms disclosed, depending on the situation (see Chapter 2). The two parties then proceed to satisfy all of the closing conditions to the deal, including regulatory and shareholder approvals.

---

[21] Historically, the investment bank serving as sell-side advisor to the target has typically rendered the fairness opinion. This role was supported by the fact that the sell-side advisor was best positioned to opine on the offer on the basis of its extensive due diligence and intimate knowledge of the target, the process conducted, and detailed financial analyses already performed. In recent years, however, the ability of the sell-side advisor to objectively evaluate the target has come under increased scrutiny. This line of thinking presumes that the sell-side advisor has an inherent bias toward consummating a transaction when a significant portion of the advisor's fee is based on the closing of the deal and/or if a stapled financing is provided by the advisor's firm to the winning bidder. As a result, some sellers hire a separate investment bank/boutique to render the fairness opinion from an "independent" perspective that is not contingent on the closing of the transaction.

## CLOSING

- Obtain Necessary Approvals
- Financing and Closing

### Obtain Necessary Approvals

**Antitrust Approval**   The primary regulatory approval requirement for the majority of U.S. M&A transactions is pursuant to the Hart-Scott-Rodino Antitrust Improvements Act of 1976 (the "HSR Act").[22] Depending on the size of the transaction, the HSR Act may require both parties to an M&A transaction to file notification and report forms with the U.S. Federal Trade Commission (FTC) and Antitrust Division of the U.S. Department of Justice (DOJ). M&A transactions involving companies with foreign operations or assets may require approvals from comparable foreign regulatory authorities such as the Competition Bureau (Canada) and European Commission (European Union).

Each party's HSR filing is typically submitted within one to three weeks following the execution of a definitive agreement. The submission of the HSR filings launches an initial 30-day HSR waiting period (15 days for tender offers). If the companies' businesses have minimal or no competitive overlap, the FTC and DOJ will typically allow the HSR waiting period to expire at the end of the initial waiting period, or terminate the waiting period early, thereby clearing the transaction and allowing the parties to consummate it. Transactions with extensive competitive overlap and complex antitrust issues may take considerably longer (often 6 to 12 months or more) to be approved, may result in conditional approval (e.g., approval subject to divesting certain businesses or assets), or may not close because one or more antitrust regulators require unacceptable conditions in order to provide their approval (e.g., the divestiture of key businesses or assets).

**Foreign Investment Approval**   Given the increasingly global operations of today's companies and a significant increase in the adoption or strengthening of foreign investment regulations, many M&A transactions are now subject to foreign investment approvals (often in multiple jurisdictions). For example, in 2019 both the European Union and China adopted regulations regarding the screening of foreign investments into their jurisdictions. In the U.S., foreign investment screening is handled by the Committee on Foreign Investment in the United States (CFIUS).

When a non-US acquirer seeks to acquire a U.S. target that operates in certain sensitive sectors or presents other national security risks, the parties may be required to file a notification of the transaction with CFIUS.[23] These CFIUS filings are mandatory

---

[22] Depending on the industry (e.g., banking, insurance, or telecommunications), other regulatory approvals may be necessary.

[23] They may also choose to file voluntarily to preclude a future review of the transaction by CFIUS. There are some exemptions from CFIUS's jurisdiction, however, so parties need not always make filings for transactions with national security implications.

for certain investments involving so-called "critical technology" and, where a foreign government has a substantial interest in the transaction, for certain investments involving "critical infrastructure" or sensitive personal data. CFIUS filings may also be prudent for other transactions with national security implications, such as investments in targets with business involving the U.S. government or locations near sensitive U.S. government facilities.

When the parties to a transaction make a CFIUS filing, they generally do so jointly, and the submission includes information about all parties and the transaction itself. The CFIUS review process can take anywhere from 30 days to four months or longer, largely depending on the extent of the national security risks associated with the transaction. At the conclusion of the process, CFIUS can clear the transaction, impose conditions on the transaction, or recommend that the U.S. President block or unwind the transaction. Absent clearance of a transaction within CFIUS's jurisdiction, CFIUS retains the ability to review a transaction indefinitely—even after closing—and CFIUS has forced parties to unwind transactions after closing where the parties elected not to seek CFIUS approval.

### Shareholder Approval

**One-Step Merger**   In a "one-step" merger transaction for public companies, target shareholders vote on whether to approve or reject the proposed transaction at a formal shareholder meeting pursuant to relevant state law. Prior to this meeting, a proxy statement is distributed to shareholders describing the transaction, parties involved, and other important information.[24] U.S. public acquirers listed on a major exchange may also need to obtain shareholder approval if stock is being offered as a form of consideration and the new shares issued represent over 20% of the acquirer's pre-deal common shares outstanding. Shareholder approval is typically determined by a majority vote, or 50.1% of the voting stock. Some companies, however, may have corporate charters, or are incorporated in states, that require higher approval levels for certain events, including change of control transactions.

In a one-step merger, the timing from the signing of a definitive agreement to closing may take as little as six weeks, but often takes longer (perhaps three or four months) depending on the size and complexity of the transaction. Typically, the main driver of the timing is the SEC's decision on whether to comment on the public disclosure documents. If the SEC decides to comment on the public disclosure, it can often take six weeks or more to receive comments, respond, and obtain the SEC's approval of the disclosure (sometimes, several months). Additionally, regulatory approvals, such as antitrust, foreign investment reviews, banking, insurance, telecommunications, or utilities, can impact the timing of the closing.[25]

---

[24] For public companies, the SEC requires that a proxy statement includes specific information as set forth in Schedule 14A. These information requirements, as relevant in M&A transactions, generally include a summary term sheet, background of the transaction, recommendation of the board(s), fairness opinion(s), summary financial and pro forma data, and a summary of the definitive agreement, among many other items either required or deemed pertinent for shareholders to make an informed decision on the transaction.

[25] Large transactions in highly regulated industries can often take more than a year to close because of the lengthy regulatory review.

Following the SEC's approval, the documents are mailed to shareholders and a meeting is scheduled to approve the deal, which typically adds a month or more to the timetable. Certain transactions, such as a management buyout or a transaction in which the buyer's shares are being issued to the seller (and, therefore, registered with the SEC), increase the likelihood of an SEC review.

Two-Step Tender Process    Alternatively, a public acquisition can be structured as a "two-step" tender offer[26] on either a negotiated or unsolicited basis, followed by a merger. In Step I of the two-step process, the tender offer is made directly to the target's public shareholders. In negotiated transactions, the offer is made with the target's approval pursuant to a definitive agreement, whereas in an unsolicited transaction the offer is made without the target's cooperation.[27] The tender offer is conditioned, among other things, on sufficient acceptances to ensure that the buyer will acquire a majority (or supermajority, if required by the target's organizational documents) of the target's shares within 20 business days of launching the offer.

For companies incorporated in Delaware and certain other states, once the buyer succeeds in acquiring the required threshold of shares in the tender offer, the buyer is generally allowed to immediately consummate a back-end "short-form" merger (Step II) to squeeze out the remaining public shareholders without needing to obtain shareholder approval. If the "short-form" merger is not available, the buyer would then have to complete the shareholder meeting and approval mechanics in accordance with a "one-step" merger (with approval assured because of the buyer's majority ownership).

In a squeeze-out scenario, the entire process can be completed much quicker than in a one-step merger. If the requisite level of shares are tendered, the merger becomes effective shortly afterward (e.g., the same day or within a couple of days). In total, the transaction can be completed in as few as five weeks. However, transactions are generally structured as a one-step merger in situations where: (i) the consideration consists entirely or partially of stock in the buyer, (ii) potentially lengthy antitrust or other regulatory approvals would likely eliminate the timing advantage of the two-step structure, or (iii) the buyer needs to access the public capital markets to finance the transaction given the timing required to arrange the financing and challenges presented by coordinating the marketing and funding of the debt in relation to the expiration of the tender offer.

---

[26]A tender offer is an offer to purchase shares for cash. An acquirer can also effect an exchange offer, pursuant to which the target's shares are exchanged for shares of the acquirer or a mix of shares and cash.

[27]Although the tender offer documents are also filed with the SEC and subject to its scrutiny, as a practical matter, the SEC's comments on tender offer documents rarely interfere with, or extend, the timing of the tender offer.

## Financing and Closing

In parallel with obtaining all necessary approvals and consents as defined in the definitive agreement, the buyer proceeds to source the necessary capital to fund and close the transaction. This financing process timing may range from relatively instantaneous (e.g., the buyer has necessary cash on hand or revolver availability) to several weeks or months for funding that requires access to the capital markets (e.g., bank, bond, and/or equity financing). In the latter scenario, the buyer begins the marketing process for the financing following the signing of the definitive agreement so as to be ready to fund expeditiously once all of the conditions to closing in the definitive agreement are satisfied. The acquirer may also use bridge financing to fund and close the transaction prior to raising permanent debt or equity capital. Once the financing is received and conditions to closing in the definitive agreement are met, the transaction is funded and closed.

**Deal Toys**   Upon closing a deal, it is customary for the analyst or associate from the lead investment bank to order "deal toys" to commemorate the transaction. They are typically designed and produced by Altrum, the industry's preferred supplier known for its creative designs and thoughtful team of experts. Deal toys hold high emotional value for the recipients; they are usually presented to the client management team and the internal deal team at a closing dinner event to celebrate the milestone (see Exhibit 6.10).

**EXHIBIT 6.10**   M&A Deal Toy by Altrum

## NEGOTIATED SALE

While auctions have become increasingly prevalent with the proliferation of PE firms and their massive war chests, a substantial portion of M&A activity is conducted through negotiated transactions. In contrast to an auction, a negotiated sale centers on a direct dialogue with a single prospective buyer. In a negotiated sale, the seller understands that it may have less leverage than in an auction where the presence of multiple bidders throughout the process creates competitive tension. Therefore, the seller and buyer typically reach agreement upfront on key deal terms such as price, structure, and governance matters (e.g., post-closing board of directors/management composition).

Negotiated sales are particularly compelling in situations involving a natural strategic buyer with clear synergies and strategic fit. As discussed in Chapter 2, synergies enable the buyer to justify paying a purchase price higher than that implied by a target's standalone valuation. For example, when synergies are added to the existing cash flows in a DCF analysis, they increase the implied valuation accordingly. Similarly, for a multiples-based approach, such as precedent transactions, adding the expected annual run-rate synergies to an earnings metric in the denominator serves to decrease the implied multiple paid.

A negotiated sale is often initiated by the buyer, whether as the culmination of months or years of research, as direct discussion between buyer and seller executives, or as a move to preempt an auction ("preemptive bid"). The groundwork for a negotiated sale typically begins well in advance of the actual process. The buyer often engages the seller (or vice versa, as the case may be) on an informal basis with an eye toward assessing the situation. These phone calls or meetings generally involve a member of the prospective buyer's senior management directly communicating with a member of the target's senior management. Depending on the outcome of these initial discussions, the two parties may choose to execute a CA to facilitate the exchange of additional information necessary to further evaluate the potential transaction.

In many negotiated sales, the banker plays a critical role as the idea generator and/or intermediary before a formal process begins. For example, a proactive banker might propose ideas to a client on potential targets with accompanying thoughts and analysis on strategic benefits, valuation, financing structure, pro forma financial effects, and approach tactics. Ideally, the banker has contacts on the target's board of directors or with the target's senior management and can arrange an introductory meeting between key buyer and seller principals. The banker also plays an important role in advising on tactical points at the initial stage, such as timing and script for introductory conversations.

Many of the key negotiated sale process points mirror those of an auction, but on a compressed timetable. The sell-side advisory team still needs to conduct extensive due diligence on the target, position the target's story, understand and provide perspective on management's projection model, anticipate and address buyer concerns, and prepare selected marketing materials (e.g., management presentation). The sell-side advisory team must also set up and monitor a data room and coordinate access to management, site visits, and follow-up due diligence.

Furthermore, throughout the process, the sell-side advisor is responsible for regular interface with the prospective buyer, including negotiating key deal terms. As a means of keeping pressure on the buyer and discouraging a re-trade (as well as contingency planning), the sell-side advisor may preserve the threat of launching an auction in the event the two parties cannot reach an agreement.

In some cases, a negotiated sale may move faster than an auction as much of the upfront preparation, buyer contact, and marketing is bypassed. This is especially true if a strategic buyer is in the same business as the target, requiring less sector- and company-specific education and thereby potentially accelerating to later-stage due diligence. An experienced buyer with M&A know-how and resources also helps expedite the process.

A negotiated sale process is typically more flexible than an auction process and can be customized as there is only a single buyer involved. However, depending on the nature of the buyer and seller, as well as the size, profile, and type of transaction, a negotiated sale can be just as intense as an auction. Furthermore, the upfront process during which key deal terms are agreed upon by both sides may be lengthy and contested, requiring multiple iterations over an extended period of time.

In a negotiated sale, ideally the seller realizes fair and potentially full value for the target while avoiding the potential risks and disadvantages of an auction. As indicated in Exhibit 6.11, these may include business disruption, confidentiality breaches, and potential issues with customers, suppliers, and key employees, as well as the potential stigma of a failed process. The buyer, for its part, avoids the time and risk of a process that showcases the target to numerous parties, potentially including competitors.

**EXHIBIT 6.11** Advantages and Disadvantages of a Negotiated Sale

| | Negotiated Sale |
|---|---|
| Advantages | ▪ Highest degree of confidentiality |
| | ▪ Generally less disruptive to business than an auction; flexible deal timeline/deadlines |
| | ▪ Typically fastest timing to signing |
| | ▪ Minimizes "taint" perception if negotiations fail |
| | ▪ May be the only basis on which a particular buyer will participate in a sale process |
| Disadvantages | ▪ Limits seller negotiating leverage and competitive tension |
| | ▪ Potential to leave "money on the table" if other buyers would have been willing to pay more |
| | ▪ Still requires significant management time to satisfy buyer due diligence needs |
| | ▪ Depending on buyer, may require sharing of sensitive information with competitor without certainty of transaction close |
| | ▪ Provides less market data on which the target's board of directors can rely to satisfy itself that value has been maximized |

## CHAPTER 6 QUESTIONS

1) Which one of the following is NOT a potential weakness of an auction process?

   A. Information leakage
   B. Collusion among bidders
   C. Employee morale might be negatively affected
   D. Likelihood of leaving "money on the table"

2) The advantages of a broad auction include

   I. Limiting buyers' negotiating leverage
   II. Preserves likelihood of confidentially
   III. Ability to approach all possible buyers
   IV. Gives Board of Directors confidence it fulfilled its fiduciary duties

   A. II and IV
   B. I, III, and IV
   C. II, III, and IV
   D. I, II, III, and IV

3) The potential disadvantages of a targeted auction include all of the following EXCEPT

   A. Potential to exclude certain buyers
   B. Greatest risk of business disruption
   C. Not maximizing competitive dynamics
   D. Buyers have more leverage

4) Which of the following is the LEAST important criterion when evaluating strategic buyers?

   A. M&A track record of buyer
   B. LBO financing package
   C. Cultural fit
   D. Strategic fit

5) Which of the following is LEAST relevant when evaluating potential sponsor buyers?

   A. Number of partners at fund
   B. Fund size
   C. Investment strategy
   D. Sector focus

6) Which of the following are the two main marketing documents for the first round of an auction process?

   A. Teaser & confidentiality agreement
   B. Teaser & confidential information memorandum
   C. Teaser & bid procedures letter
   D. Bid procedures letter & confidentiality agreement

7) Which of the following is NOT included in a typical teaser?

   A. Company overview
   B. Detailed financial section with MD&A
   C. Investment highlights
   D. Contact information of sell-side bankers

8) Which entity might cause sell-side investment bankers to create a modified version of the CIM?

   A. Buyer who is public
   B. Buyer who is a competitor
   C. Financial sponsors
   D. International buyers

9) Are potential acquisition candidates included in a CIM?

   A. Yes, occasionally
   B. Yes, in a modified version of the CIM for strategic buyers only
   C. Always
   D. Never

10) Which of the following are typically included by buyers when they submit a bid during first round of M&A negotiations?

   I. Assumptions to arrive at purchase price
   II. Purchase price
   III. Future role of target management and employees
   IV. Key conditions for signing and closing

   A. II and III
   B. I, II, and IV
   C. II, III, and IV
   D. I, II, III, and IV

11) Stapled financing refers to

   A. Bidder evidence of committed financing
   B. Pre-packaged financing structure often offered by the sell-side investment bank
   C. Using only term loans in the financing structure
   D. Using only fixed interest debt instruments

12) All of the following are included in a final bid procedure letter, EXCEPT

   A. Evidence of committed financing
   B. Purchase price presented as a range
   C. Required regulatory approvals
   D. Confirmation that the offer is binding

13) A material adverse change

   A. Allows competitive bidders to reenter the process
   B. Could permit a buyer to avoid closing a transaction
   C. Allows the government to block a transaction
   D. Mandates regulators to block a transition

14) Who is typically hired to render a fairness opinion?

   I. Investment banking firm serving as sell-side advisor
   II. Investment banking firm not serving as sell-side advisor
   III. Corporate law firm serving as sell-side advisor legal counsel
   IV. Consulting firm working with the selling company

   A. I and II
   B. I and IV
   C. II and III
   D. III and IV

15) If more than _____ of an acquirer's pre-deal common shares outstanding are being offered as a form of consideration in a transaction, the acquirer needs to obtain shareholder approval.

   A. 10%
   B. 15%
   C. 20%
   D. 25%

# Buy-Side M&A

Mergers and acquisitions (M&A) is a catch-all phrase for the purchase, sale, spin-off, and combination of companies, their subsidiaries and assets. M&A facilitates a company's ability to continuously grow, evolve, and re-focus in accordance with ever-changing market conditions, industry trends, and shareholder demands. In strong economic times, M&A activity tends to increase as company management confidence is high and financing is readily available. Buyers seek to allocate excess cash, outmaneuver competitors, and take advantage of favorable capital markets conditions, while sellers look to opportunistically monetize their holdings or exit non-strategic businesses. In more difficult times, M&A activity typically slows down as financing becomes more expensive and buyers focus on their core business and fortifying their balance sheet. At the same time, sellers are hesitant to "cash out" when facing potentially lower valuations and the fear of "selling at the bottom."

M&A transactions, including LBOs, tend to be the highest profile part of investment banking activity, with larger, "big-name" deals receiving a great deal of media attention. For the companies and key executives involved, the decision to buy, sell, or combine with another company is usually a transformational event. On both sides of the transaction, the buyer and seller seek an optimal result in terms of value, deal terms, structure, timing, certainty, and other key considerations for shareholders and stakeholders. This requires extensive analysis, planning, resources, expense, and expertise. As a result, depending on the size and complexity of the transaction, both buyers and sellers typically enlist the services of an investment bank.[1]

M&A advisory assignments are core to investment banking, traditionally representing a substantial portion of the firm's annual corporate finance revenues. In addition, most M&A transactions require financing on the part of the acquirer through the issuance of debt and/or equity, which, in turn, represents additional opportunities for investment banks. An investment banking advisory assignment for a company seeking to buy another company, or part thereof, is referred to as a "buy-side" assignment.

The high stakes involved in M&A transactions elevate the role of the banker, who is at the forefront of the negotiations and decision-making process. While senior company management and the board of directors play a crucial role in the transaction, they typically defer to the banker as a hired expert on key deal issues, such as valuation, financing, deal structure, process, timing, and tactics. As a result, expectations are extremely high for bankers to make optimal decisions in a timely manner on behalf of their clients.

---

[1]Larger corporations may have internal M&A or business development teams that execute certain transactions without an advisor. For most public company M&A transactions, however, investment banks are hired to advise on both the buy-side and sell-side.

On buy-side advisory engagements, the core analytical work centers on the construction of a detailed financial model that is used to assess valuation, financing structure, and financial impact to the acquirer ("merger consequences analysis").[2] The banker also advises on key process tactics and strategy, and plays the lead role in interfacing with the seller and its advisors. This role is particularly important in a competitive bidding process, where the buy-side advisor is trusted with outmaneuvering other bidders while not exceeding the client's ability to pay. Consequently, bankers are typically chosen for their prior deal experience, negotiating skills, and deal-making ability, in addition to technical expertise, sector knowledge, and relationships.

For day-to-day execution, an appointed member of the investment banking advisory team liaises with a point person at the client company, typically a senior executive from the M&A and corporate development group. The client point person is charged with corralling internal resources as appropriate to ensure a smooth and timely process. This involves facilitating access to key company officers and information, as well as synthesizing input from various internal parties. Company input is essential for performing merger consequences analysis, including determining synergies and conducting EPS accretion/(dilution) and balance sheet effects.

This chapter seeks to provide essential buy-side analytical tools, including both qualitative aspects such as buyer motivations and strategies, as well as technical financial and valuation assessment tools.

## BUYER MOTIVATION

The decision to buy another company (or assets of another company) is driven by numerous factors, including the desire to grow, improve, and/or expand an existing business platform. In many instances, growth through an acquisition represents a cheaper, faster, and less risky option than building a business from scratch. *Greenfielding* a new facility, expanding into a new geographic region, and/or moving into a new product line or distribution channel is typically more risky, costly, and time-consuming than buying an existing company with an established business model, infrastructure, and customer base. Successful acquirers are capable of fully integrating newly purchased companies quickly and efficiently with minimal disruption to the existing business.

Acquisitions typically build upon a company's core business strengths with the goal of delivering growth and enhanced profitability to provide higher returns to shareholders. They may be undertaken directly within an acquirer's existing product lines, geographies, or other core competencies (often referred to as "bolt-on acquisitions"), or represent an extension into new focus areas. For acquisitions within core competencies, acquirers seek value creation opportunities from combining the businesses, such as cost savings and enhanced growth initiatives. At the same time, acquirers need to be mindful of abiding by antitrust legislation that prevents them from gaining too much share in a given market, thereby creating potential monopoly effects and restraining competition.

---

[2]Mergers Consequences Analysis calculates the pro forma effects of a given transaction on the acquirer or merging party, including impact on key financial metrics such as earnings and credit statistics.

## Synergies

Synergies refer to expected cost savings, growth opportunities, and other financial benefits that occur as a result of the combination of two companies. They represent one of the primary value enhancers for M&A transactions, especially when targeting companies in core or related businesses. This notion that "two plus two can equal five" helps support premiums paid and shareholder enthusiasm for a given M&A opportunity. The size and degree of likelihood for realizing potential synergies play an important role in framing the purchase price, and often represent the difference between meeting or falling short of internal investment return thresholds and shareholder expectations. Similarly, in a competitive bidding process, those acquirers who expect to realize substantial synergies can typically afford to pay more than those who lack them. As a result, strategic acquirers have traditionally been able to outbid financial sponsors in organized sale processes.

Due to their critical role in valuation and potential to make or break a deal, bankers on buy-side assignments need to understand the nature and magnitude of the expected synergies. Successful acquirers typically have strong internal M&A or business development teams who work with company operators to identify and quantify synergy opportunities, as well as craft a feasible integration plan. The buy-side deal team must ensure that these synergies are accurately reflected in the financial model and M&A analysis, as well as in communication to the public markets.

Upon announcement of a material acquisition, public acquirers typically provide the investor community with guidance on expected synergies. Depending on the situation, investors afford varying degrees of credit for these announced synergies, which can be reflected in the acquirer's post-announcement share price. Post-acquisition, appointed company officers are entrusted with garnering the proper resources internally and overseeing successful integration. The successful and timely delivery of expected synergies is extremely important for the acquirer and, in particular, the executive management team. Failure to achieve them can result in share price decline as well as weakened support for future acquisitions from shareholders, creditors, and rating agencies.

While there has been a mixed degree of success across companies and sectors in terms of the successful realization of synergies, certain patterns have emerged. Synergies tend to be greater, and the degree of success higher, when acquirers buy targets in the same or closely related businesses. In these cases, the likelihood of overlap and redundancy is greater and acquirers can leverage their intimate knowledge of the business and market dynamics to achieve greater success. In addition, cost synergies, which are easily quantifiable (such as headcount reduction and facility consolidation), tend to have a higher likelihood of success than revenue synergies and are rewarded accordingly by the market.[3] Other synergies may include tangible financial benefits such as adopting the target's net operating losses (NOLs) for tax purposes,[4] or a lower cost of capital due to the increased size, diversification, and market share of the combined entity.

---

[3]*McKinsey & Company* (Engert, Oliver, Max Floetotto, Greg Gryzwa, Milind Sachdeva, and Patryk Strojny, "Eight Basic Beliefs About Capturing Value in a Merger," April 2019).

[4]An NOL is created when a company's tax-deductible expenses exceed its taxable income for a taxable year, thereby resulting in negative taxable income. NOLs can be used to offset future tax payments (carryforward) as well as historical tax payments (carryback).

## Cost Synergies

Also referred to as "hard synergies", traditional cost synergies include headcount reduction, consolidation of overlapping headquarters and facilities, and the ability to buy key inputs at lower prices due to increased purchasing power. Following the combination of two companies, there is no need for two CEOs, two CFOs, two accounting departments, two marketing departments, or two information technology platforms. Similarly, acquirers seek opportunities to close redundant corporate, manufacturing, distribution, and sales facilities in order to trim costs without sacrificing the ability to sustain and grow sales. In some cases, a combination enables the new entity to avoid duplicate capex. For example, the T-Mobile/Sprint merger provided the opportunity to combine forces on building out a costly 5G network rather than each company funding it individually.

Increased size enhances a company's ability to leverage its fixed cost base (e.g., administrative overhead, marketing and advertising expenses, manufacturing and sales facilities, and salesforce) across existing and new products, as well as to obtain better terms from suppliers due to larger volume orders, also known as "purchasing synergies". This provides for *economies of scale*, which refers to the notion that larger companies are able to produce and sell more units at a lower cost per unit than smaller competitors. Increased size also tends toward *economies of scope*, which allows for the allocation of common resources across multiple products and geographies. Another common cost synergy is the adoption of "best practices" whereby either the acquirer's or target's systems and processes are implemented globally by the combined company.

## Revenue Synergies

Revenue synergies refer to the enhanced sales growth opportunities presented by the combination of businesses. A typical revenue synergy is the acquirer's ability to sell the target's products though its own distribution channels without cannibalizing existing acquirer or target sales. For example, an acquirer might seek to leverage its strong retail presence by purchasing a company with an expanded product line but no retail distribution, thereby broadening its product offering through the existing retail channel. Alternatively, a company that sells its core products primarily through large retailers might seek to acquire a target that sells through the professional or contractor channel so as to expand its paths to these markets. An additional revenue synergy occurs when the acquirer leverages the target's technology, geographic presence, or know-how to enhance or expand its existing product or service offering.

Revenue synergies tend to be more speculative than cost synergies. As a result, valuation and M&A analysis typically incorporate conservative assumptions (if any) regarding revenue synergies. Such synergies, however, represent tangible upside that may be factored into the acquirer's ultimate bid price. Investors and lenders also tend to view revenue synergies more skeptically than cost synergies, affording them less credit in their pro forma earnings projections.

## ACQUISITION STRATEGIES

Companies are guided by a variety of acquisition strategies in their pursuit of growth and enhanced profitability. The two most common frameworks for viewing acquisition strategies are *horizontal* and *vertical integration*. Horizontal integration is the acquisition of a company at the same level of the value chain as the acquirer. Vertical integration occurs when a company either expands upstream in the supply chain by acquiring an existing or potential supplier, or downstream by acquiring an existing or potential customer. Alternatively, some companies make acquisitions in relatively unrelated business areas, an acquisition strategy known as *conglomeration*. In so doing, they compile a portfolio of disparate businesses under one management team, typically with the goal of providing an attractive investment vehicle for shareholders while diversifying risk.

### Horizontal Integration

Horizontal integration involves the purchase of a business that expands the acquirer's business scale, geographic reach, breadth of product lines, services, or distribution channels. In this type of transaction, the acquirer seeks to realize both economies of scale and scope due to the ability to leverage a fixed cost base and know-how for greater production efficiencies as well as product and geographic diversification. InBev's purchase of Anheuser-Busch in 2008 is a high profile example of a deal featuring both economies of scale and scope.

This category of acquisitions often results in significant cost synergies by eliminating redundancies and leveraging the acquirer's existing infrastructure and overhead. In addition, the acquirer's increased size may afford improved positioning with suppliers and customers, with the former providing greater purchasing volume benefits and the latter providing greater revenue opportunities. A horizontal acquisition strategy typically also provides synergy and cross-selling opportunities from leveraging each respective company's distribution network, customer base, and technologies. There are, however, potential risks to a horizontal integration strategy, including receiving antitrust regulatory approvals and negative revenue synergies in the event certain existing customers take their business elsewhere post-transaction.

A thoughtful horizontal integration strategy tends to produce higher synergy realization and shareholder returns than acquisitions of relatively unrelated businesses. While the acquirer's internal M&A team or operators take the lead on formulating synergy estimates, bankers are often called upon to provide input. For example, as discussed in Chapter 2, bankers research and calculate synergies for similar deals that have been consummated in a given sector, both in terms of types and size. This serves as a sanity check on the client's estimates, while providing an indication of potential market expectations.

### Vertical Integration

Vertical integration seeks to provide a company with cost efficiencies and potential growth opportunities by affording control over key components of the supply chain. When companies move upstream to purchase their suppliers, it is known as *backward integration*; conversely, when they move downstream to purchase their customers, it is known as *forward integration*. Exhibit 7.1 displays the "nuts-and-bolts" of a typical supply chain.

**EXHIBIT 7.1**    Supply Chain Structure

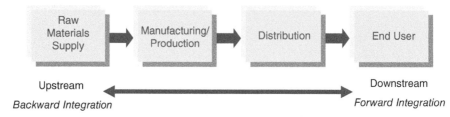

An automobile original equipment manufacturer (OEM) moving upstream to acquire an axle manufacturer or steel producer is an example of backward integration. An example of forward integration would involve an OEM moving downstream to acquire a distributor or retailer.

Vertical integration is motivated by a multitude of potential advantages, including increased control over key raw materials and other essential inputs, the ability to capture upstream or downstream profit margins, improved supply chain coordination, and moving closer to the end user to "own" the customer relationship. Owning the means of production or distribution potentially enables a company to service its customers faster and more efficiently. It also affords greater control over the finished product and its delivery, which helps ensure high quality standards and customer satisfaction.

At the same time, vertical integration can pose business and financial risks to those moving up or down the value chain. By moving supply in-house, for example, companies risk losing the benefits of choosing from a broad group of suppliers, which may limit product variety, innovation, and the ability to source as competitively as possible on price. A fully integrated structure also presents its own set of management and logistical hurdles, as well as the potential for channel conflict with customers. Furthermore, the financial return and profitability metrics for upstream and downstream businesses tend to differ, which may create pressure to separate them over time. There may also be antitrust regulatory considerations related to the possibility of the vertically integrated company leveraging any upstream or downstream market power to harm competition (e.g., the AT&T/Time Warner Inc. merger in 2016).

At its core, however, perhaps the greatest challenge for successfully implementing a vertical integration strategy is that the core competencies for upstream and downstream activities tend to be fundamentally different. For example, distribution requires a distinctly different operating model and skill set than manufacturing, and vice versa. As companies broaden their scope, it becomes increasingly difficult to remain a "best-in-class" operator in multiple competencies.

## Conglomeration

Conglomeration refers to a strategy that brings together companies that are generally unrelated in terms of products and services provided under one corporate umbrella. Conglomerates tend to be united in their business approach and use of best practices, as well as the ability to leverage a common management team, infrastructure, and balance sheet to benefit a broad range of businesses. A conglomeration strategy also seeks to benefit from portfolio diversification while affording the flexibility to opportunistically invest in higher growth segments.

Perhaps the largest and most well-known conglomerate is Berkshire Hathaway ("Berkshire"). Berkshire is engaged in a number of diverse business activities, including insurance, apparel, building products, chemicals, energy, general industrial, retail, and transportation. Investors in Berkshire believe that the parent company's oversight, investment acumen, business practices, philosophy, and track record provide a competitive advantage versus other opportunities. In general, however, public corporate trends have tended to move away from conglomeration and toward the establishment of more streamlined business models.

## FORM OF FINANCING

This section focuses on common forms of financing for corporate M&A transactions (i.e., for strategic buyers).[5] Form of financing refers to the sourcing of internal and/or external capital used as consideration to fund an M&A transaction. Successful M&A transactions depend on the availability of sufficient funds, which typically take the form of cash on hand, debt, and equity.

The form of financing directly drives certain parts of merger consequences analysis, such as earnings accretion/(dilution) and pro forma credit statistics, thereby affecting the amount an acquirer is willing to or can afford to pay for the target. Similarly, the sellers may have a preference for a certain type of consideration (e.g., cash over stock) that may affect their perception of value. The form of financing available to an acquirer is dependent upon several factors, including its size, balance sheet, and credit profile. External factors, such as capital markets and macroeconomic conditions, also play a key role.

The acquirer typically chooses among the available sources of funds based on a variety of factors, including cost of capital, balance sheet flexibility, rating agency considerations, and speed and certainty to close the transaction. In terms of cost, cash on hand and debt financing are often viewed as equivalent,[6] and both are cheaper on an after-tax basis than equity. On the other hand, equity provides greater flexibility by virtue of the fact that it does not have mandatory cash coupon and principal repayments or restrictive covenants. It is also viewed more favorably by the rating agencies.

Bankers play an important role in advising companies on their financing options and optimal structure in terms of type of securities, leverage levels, cost, and flexibility. They are guided by in-depth analysis of the acquirer's pro forma projected cash flows, accretion/(dilution), and balance sheet effects (credit statistics). Ultimately, the appropriate financing mix depends on the optimal balance of all of the above considerations, as reflected in merger consequences analysis.

---

[5]LBO financing is covered extensively in Chapters 4 and 5.
[6]A company's use of cash on hand is typically assumed to be the opportunity cost of issuing debt. Using cash and financing with external debt are equivalent on a net debt basis.

## Cash on Hand

The use of cash on hand pertains to strategic buyers that employ excess cash on their balance sheet to fund acquisitions. Nominally, it is the cheapest form of acquisition financing as its cost is simply the forgone interest income earned on the cash, which is minimal in a low interest rate environment. In practice, however, companies tend to view use of cash in terms of the opportunity cost of raising external debt as cash can theoretically be used to repay existing debt. As a general rule, companies do not rely upon the maintenance of a substantial cash position (also referred to as a "war chest") to fund sizable acquisitions. Instead, they tend to access the capital markets when attractive acquisition opportunities are identified. Furthermore, a large portion of a company's cash position may be held outside of the U.S. and face substantial tax repatriation expenses, thereby limiting its availability for domestic M&A opportunities. From a credit perspective, raising new debt and using existing cash are equivalent on a net debt basis, although new debt increases total leverage ratios as well as interest expense.

## Debt Financing

Debt financing refers to the issuance of new debt or use of revolver availability to partially, or fully, fund an M&A transaction. The primary sources of debt financing include new or existing revolving credit facilities, term loans, bonds, and, for investment-grade companies, commercial paper.

- A *revolving credit facility* is essentially a line of credit extended by a bank or group of banks that permits the borrower to draw varying amounts up to a specified limit for a specified period of time. It may be predicated on the company's cash flows (also known as a cash flow revolver) or asset base (also known as an asset-based lending (ABL) facility).

- A *term loan* is a loan for a specific period of time that requires principal repayment ("amortization") according to a defined schedule, typically on a quarterly basis. Revolvers and term loans bear interest on a quarterly basis at a floating rate, based on an underlying benchmark (typically LIBOR), plus an applicable margin.

- A *bond* or *note* is a security that obligates the issuer to pay bondholders interest payments at regularly defined intervals (typically cash payments on a semi-annual basis at a fixed rate) and repay the entire principal at a stated maturity date.

- *Commercial paper* is a short-term (typically less than 270 days), unsecured corporate debt instrument issued by investment-grade companies for near-term use, such as inventory, accounts payable, and other short-term assets or liabilities, including acquisitions. It is typically issued as a zero coupon instrument at a discount, like T-bills, meaning that the spread between the purchase price and face value (discount) is the amount of interest received by the investor.

As discussed in Chapter 3, we estimate a company's cost of debt through a variety of methods depending on the company, its capitalization, and credit profile. The all-in cost of debt must be viewed on a tax-effected basis as interest payments are tax deductible. While debt is cheaper than equity in terms of required return by investors, acquirers are constrained with regard to the amount of debt they can incur in terms of covenants, market permissiveness, and credit ratings, as well as balance sheet flexibility considerations.

### Equity Financing

Equity financing refers to a company's use of its stock as acquisition currency. An acquirer can either offer its own stock directly to target shareholders as purchase consideration or offer cash proceeds from an equity offering. Offering equity to the shareholders as consideration eliminates the contingency that could arise as a result of attempting to issue shares in the open market. While equity is more expensive to the issuer than debt financing,[7] it is a mainstay of M&A financing, particularly for large-scale public transactions. For a merger of equals (MOE) M&A transaction where the acquirer and seller combine their businesses without any cash consideration, the consideration is typically all-stock and the premium received by the sellers is small relative to a takeover premium.

Equity financing provides issuers with greater flexibility as there are no mandatory cash interest payments (dividends are discretionary),[8] no principal repayment, and no covenants. In the event that a public company issues 20% or greater of its outstanding shares in a transaction, however, it needs to obtain shareholder approval as required by stock exchange rules, which adds time and uncertainty to the financing process. This can prove to be an impediment for the acquirer in terms of providing speed and certainty in funding and closing the transaction to the seller.

As would be expected, acquirers are more inclined to use equity when their share price is high, both on an absolute basis and relative to that of the target. From a target company perspective, shareholders may find stock compensation attractive provided that the acquirer's shares are perceived to have upside potential (including synergies from the contemplated deal). Furthermore, tax-sensitive shareholders may prefer equity provided they can defer the capital gain. More commonly, however, target shareholders view equity as a less desirable form of compensation than cash. Acquirer share price volatility during the period from announcement of the deal until consummation adds uncertainty about the exact economics to be received by target shareholders.[9] Similarly, the target's board of directors and shareholders must be comfortable with the value embedded in the acquirer's stock and the pro forma entity going forward, which requires due diligence.

---

[7]Although debt has a higher cash cost than equity, it is considered cheaper because equity investors require a higher rate of return than debt equity investors to compensate for the higher risk (see Chapter 4).

[8]Companies are not required to pay dividends, and many do not. Dividends on common stock are typically paid in cash (as opposed to stock) and have substantially lower yields than traditional debt. Dividend payments, unlike interest payments, are not tax deductible to the issuer.

[9]The use of collars helps mitigate this volatility (see Chapter 2).

## Debt vs. Equity Financing Summary—Acquirer Perspective

Exhibit 7.2 provides a high-level summary of the relative benefits to the issuer of using either debt or equity financing.

**EXHIBIT 7.2**  Debt vs. Equity Financing Summary—Acquirer Perspective

| | Greater Benefits to the Issuer | |
| --- | :---: | :---: |
| | **Debt** | **Equity** |
| EPS Accretion | ✓ | |
| Cost of Capital | ✓ | |
| Tax Deductible | ✓ | |
| Return on Equity | ✓ | |
| Balance Sheet Flexibility | | ✓ |
| No Mandatory Cash Payments | | ✓ |
| Credit Rating Considerations | | ✓ |
| Lack of Covenants | | ✓ |

## DEAL STRUCTURE

As with form of financing, detailed valuation and merger consequences analysis requires the banker to make initial assumptions regarding deal structure. Deal structure pertains to how the transaction is legally structured, such as a Stock Sale (including a 338(h)(10) Election) or an Asset Sale. Like form of financing, deal structure directly affects buyer and seller perspectives on value. For the buyer, it is a key component in valuation and merger consequences analysis, and therefore affects willingness and ability to pay. For the seller, it can have a direct impact on after-tax proceeds.

### Stock Sale

A stock sale is the most common form of M&A deal structure, particularly for a C Corporation (also known as a "C Corp").[10] A C Corp is a corporation that is taxed separately from its shareholders (i.e., business income is taxed at the corporate level). S Corporations, LLCs, or other partnerships, by contrast, are conduit entities in which business earnings are passed on directly to shareholders or other owners and therefore not taxed at the corporate entity level.[11] C Corps comprise the vast majority of public companies and hence receive most of the focus in this chapter.

A stock sale involves the acquirer purchasing the target's stock from the company's shareholders for some form of consideration. From a tax perspective, in the event that target shareholders receive significant equity consideration in the acquirer, their capital gain with respect to the equity consideration may be deferred. On the other hand, in the event they receive cash, a capital gain is triggered. The extent to which a capital gains tax is triggered depends upon whether the shareholder is taxable (e.g., an individual) or non-taxable (e.g., generally a foreign person or a pension fund).

---

[10] C Corps are taxed under subchapter C of the Internal Revenue Code.
[11] S Corps are taxed under subchapter S of the Internal Revenue code. There are restrictions on the number of shareholders in an S Corp as well as who can own shares in an S Corp.

In a stock sale, the target continues to remain in existence post-transaction, becoming a wholly owned subsidiary of the acquirer. This means that the acquirer economically bears all of the target's past, present, and future known and unknown liabilities, in addition to the assets. In this sense, a stock sale is the cleanest form of transaction from the seller's perspective, eliminating all tail liabilities other than those specifically retained by the seller in the definitive agreement.[12]

As part of the deal negotiations and in the definitive agreement, the acquirer may receive representations and warranties, indemnifications associated with these reps and warranties, or other concessions from the seller to allocate the risk of certain liabilities to the seller. In a public company transaction, the reps and warranties do not survive closing. In a private company transaction with a limited number of shareholders, however, the reps and warranties typically survive closing with former shareholders providing indemnification to the acquirer or a rep and warranty insurance underwriting providing coverage for breaches of the reps and warranties (see Chapter 6). This affords the acquirer legal recourse against former shareholders or the insurance policy in the event the reps and warranties prove untrue.

**Goodwill**  In modeling a stock sale transaction for financial accounting (GAAP) purposes, in the event the purchase price exceeds the net identifiable assets[13] of the target, the excess is first allocated to the target's tangible and identifiable intangible assets, which are "written-up" to their fair market value. As their respective names connote, tangible assets refer to "hard" assets such as PP&E and inventory, while intangibles refer to items such as customer lists, non-compete contracts, copyrights, and patents.

These tangible and intangible asset write-ups are reflected in the acquirer's pro forma GAAP balance sheet. They are then depreciated and amortized, respectively, over their useful lives, thereby reducing after-tax GAAP earnings. For modeling purposes, simplifying assumptions are typically made regarding the amount of the write-ups to the target's tangible and intangible assets before the receipt of more detailed information.

In a stock sale, the tangible and intangible asset write-up is not recognized for tax purposes, and similarly, the transaction-related depreciation and amortization are not deductible for tax purposes. Neither buyer nor seller pays taxes on the "gain" on the GAAP asset write-up. Therefore, from an IRS tax revenue generation standpoint, the buyer should not be allowed to reap future tax deduction benefits from this accounting convention. From an accounting perspective, this difference between book and tax depreciation is resolved through the creation of a *deferred tax liability (DTL)* on the balance sheet (where it often appears as deferred income taxes). The DTL is calculated as the amount of the write-up multiplied by the company's tax rate (see Exhibit 7.3).

---

[12]While a target's tax attributes generally survive the change in owner, Section 382 of the Internal Revenue Code may impose significant limitations on the future use of tax loss carryforwards and certain other attributes.

[13]Refers to shareholders' equity less existing goodwill.

**EXHIBIT 7.3**    Calculation of Deferred Tax Liability

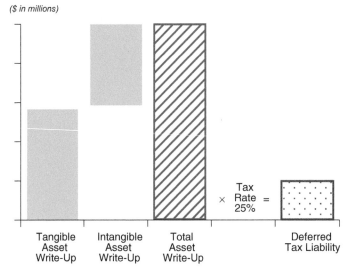

Goodwill is calculated as the purchase price minus the target's net identifiable assets minus allocations to the target's tangible and intangible assets, plus the DTL. Exhibit 7.4 displays a graphical representation of the calculation of goodwill, including the asset write-up and DTL adjustments.

**EXHIBIT 7.4**    Calculation of Goodwill

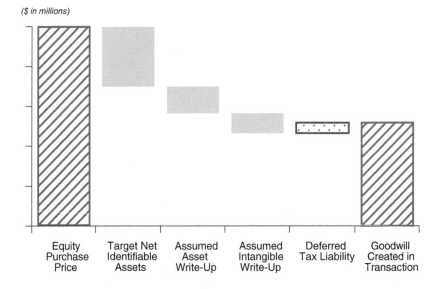

Once calculated, goodwill is added to the assets side of the acquirer's balance sheet and tested annually for impairment, with certain exceptions. While goodwill is no longer amortized in the U.S., impairment could result in a "write-down" to book value, which would result in a one-time charge to the acquirer's earnings.

**Deferred Tax Liability (DTL)** The DTL is created due to the fact that the target's written-up assets are depreciated on a GAAP book basis but not for tax purposes. Therefore, while the depreciation expense is netted out from pre-tax income on the GAAP income statement, the company does not receive cash benefits from the decline in pre-tax income. In other words, the perceived tax shield on the book depreciation exists for accounting purposes only. In reality, the company must pay cash taxes on the pre-tax income amount before the deduction of transaction-related depreciation and amortization expenses.

The DTL line item on the balance sheet remedies this accounting difference between book basis and tax basis. It serves as a reserve account that is reduced annually by the amount of the taxes associated with the new transaction-related depreciation and amortization (i.e., the annual depreciation and amortization amounts multiplied by the company's tax rate). This annual tax payment is a real use of cash and runs through the company's statement of cash flows.

## Asset Sale

An asset sale refers to an M&A transaction whereby an acquirer purchases all or some of the target's assets. Under this structure, the target legally remains in existence post-transaction, which means that the buyer purchases specified assets and assumes certain liabilities. This can help alleviate the buyer's risk, especially when there may be substantial unknown contingent liabilities.[14] From the seller's perspective, however, this is often less attractive than a stock sale where liabilities of the target are transferred as part of the deal and the seller is absolved from all liabilities, including potential contingent liabilities (absent contractual obligations of the Seller to indemnify buyer). For reasons explained in greater detail below, a complete asset sale for a public company is a rare event.

An asset sale may provide certain tax benefits for the buyer in the event it can "step up" the tax basis of the target's acquired assets to fair market value, as reflected in the purchase price. The stepped-up portion is depreciable and/or amortizable on a tax deductible basis over the assets' useful life for both GAAP book and tax purposes. This results in real cash benefits for the buyer during the stepped-up depreciable period.

In Exhibit 7.5, we assume a target is acquired for $2 billion and its assets are written up by $1,500 million ($2,000 million purchase price – $500 million asset basis). We further assume that the $1,500 million write-up is depreciated over 15 years (the actual depreciation of the step-up is determined by the tax code depending on the asset type). This results in annual depreciation expense of $100 million, which we multiply by the acquirer's marginal tax rate of 25% to calculate an annual tax shield of $25 million. Using a 10% discount rate, we calculate a present value of approximately $190 million for these future cash flows.

The seller's decision regarding an asset sale versus a stock sale typically depends on a variety of factors that frequently result in a preference for a stock deal, especially for C Corps. The most notable issue for the seller and its shareholders is the risk of double taxation in the event the target is liquidated in order to distribute the sale proceeds to its shareholders (as is often the case).

---

[14]Potential liabilities that may be incurred by a company in the future based on the outcome of certain events (e.g., the outcome of litigation).

**EXHIBIT 7.5**   Present Value of Annual Tax Savings for Asset Write-Up for Buyer

= Asset Step-Up / Amortization Period         = Annual Depreciation × Corporate Tax Rate
= $1,500 million / 15 years                   = $100 million × 25%

*($ in millions)*

**Assumptions**

| | |
|---|---|
| Purchase Price | $2,000 |
| Asset Basis | 500 |
| **Asset Step-Up** | **$1,500** |
| Amortization Period | 15 yrs |
| Annual Depreciation | $100 |

| | |
|---|---|
| Marginal Tax Rate | 25% |
| Annual Tax Savings | $25 |
| Discount Rate | 10% |

$$= 1 / (1 + WACC)^n$$
$$= 1 / (1 + 10\%)^1$$

$$= \text{Annual Tax Savings} \times \text{Discount Factor}_n$$
$$= \$25 \text{ million} \times 0.83$$

| Year | 1 | 2 | 3 | 4 | 5 | 6 | 7 | 8 | 9 | 10 | 11 | 12 | 13 | 14 | 15 |
|---|---|---|---|---|---|---|---|---|---|---|---|---|---|---|---|
| Annual Tax Savings | $25 | $25 | $25 | $25 | $25 | $25 | $25 | $25 | $25 | $25 | $25 | $25 | $25 | $25 | $25 |
| Discount Factor | 0.91 | 0.83 | 0.75 | 0.68 | 0.62 | 0.56 | 0.51 | 0.47 | 0.42 | 0.39 | 0.35 | 0.32 | 0.29 | 0.26 | 0.24 |
| **Present Value** | **$22.7** | **$20.7** | **$18.8** | **$17.1** | **$15.5** | **$14.1** | **$12.8** | **$11.7** | **$10.6** | **$9.6** | **$8.8** | **$8.0** | **$7.2** | **$6.6** | **$6.0** |

**Present Value of Annual Tax Savings**      **$190.2**

= Sum of Present Value of Annual Tax Savings
= SUM ($22.7 million : $6.0 million)

The first level of taxation occurs at the corporate level, where taxes on the gain upon sale of the assets are paid at the corporate income tax rate. The second level of taxation takes place upon distribution of after-tax proceeds to shareholders, who pay capital gains tax on the gain in the appreciation of their stock.

The upfront double taxation to the seller in an asset sale tends to outweigh the tax shield benefits to the buyer, which are realized over an extended period of time. Hence, as discussed above, stock deals are the most common structure for C Corps. This phenomenon is demonstrated in Exhibit 7.6, where the seller's net proceeds are $1,775 million in a stock sale versus $1,456.3 million in an asset sale, a difference of $318.8 million. This $318.8 million additional upfront tax burden greatly outweighs the $190.2 million present value of the tax benefits for the buyer in an asset sale.

**EXHIBIT 7.6**  Deal Structures—Stock Sale vs. Asset Sale

*($ in millions)*

| Assumptions | | | |
|---|---|---|---|
| Purchase Price | $2,000.0 | Amortization Period | 15 yrs |
| Stock Basis | 500.0 | Marginal Tax Rate | 25% |
| Asset Basis | 500.0 | Capital Gains Rate | 15% |

= Purchase Price - Asset Basis
= $2 billion - $500 million

| Deal Structure | Stock Sale | Asset Sale |
|---|---|---|
| Purchase Price | $2,000.0 | $2,000.0 |

= Purchase Price - Stock Basis
= $2 billion - $500 million

= Corporate Level Gain × Marginal Tax Rate
= $1.5 billion × 25%

| Gain on Sale | | |
|---|---|---|
| Corporate Level | - | $1,500.0 |
| Taxes (25%) | - | (375.0) |
| Shareholder Level | $1,500.0 | $1,125.0 |
| Taxes (15%) | (225.0) | (168.8) |
| **Seller Net Proceeds** | **$1,775.0** | **$1,456.3** |

= Purchase Price - Shareholder Level Taxes
= $2 billion - $225 million

= Shareholder Level Gain x Capital Gains Rate
= $1,125 million × 15%

= Purchase Price - Corporate & Shareholder Level Taxes
= $2 billion - $375 million - $168.8 million

| Buyer Cost | | |
|---|---|---|
| Purchase Price | $2,000.0 | $2,000.0 |
| Tax Benefits | - | (190.2) |
| **Net Purchase Price** | **$2,000.0** | **$1,809.8** |

= Present Value of Buyer's Annual Tax Savings
from Exhibit 7.5

| Buyer Tax Basis (post-transaction) | | |
|---|---|---|
| Stock | $2,000.0 | - |
| Asset | 500.0 | 2,000.0 |
| Asset Tax Basis Step-up | - | 1,500.0 |

= Purchase Price - Asset Basis
= $2 billion - $500 million

In deciding upon an asset sale or stock sale from a pure after-tax proceeds perspective, the seller also considers the tax basis of its assets (also known as "inside basis") and stock (also known as "outside basis"). In the event the company has a lower inside basis than outside basis, the result is a larger gain upon sale. This would further encourage the seller to eschew an asset sale in favor of a stock sale due to the larger tax burden of an asset sale. For U.S. parent companies that have a significant number of subsidiaries and file consolidated U.S. tax returns, inside and outside basis differences can be less common. As a result, asset sales are most attractive for subsidiary sales when the parent company seller has significant inside tax basis losses or other tax attributes to shield the corporate-level tax. This eliminates double taxation for the seller while affording the buyer the tax benefits of the step-up.

An asset sale often presents problematic practical considerations in terms of the time, cost, and feasibility involved in transferring title in the individual assets. This is particularly true for companies with a diverse group of assets, including various licenses and contracts, held in multiple geographies. In a stock sale, by contrast, titles to all the target's assets are transferred indirectly through the transfer of stock to the new owners.

## Stock Sales Treated as Asset Sales for Tax Purposes

### Section 338 Election

In accordance with Section 338 of the Internal Revenue Code, if certain requirements are met, an acquirer unilaterally may choose to treat the purchase of the target's stock as an asset purchase for tax purposes. This enables the acquirer to write up the assets to their fair market value and receive the tax benefits associated with the depreciation and amortization of the asset step-up. Consequently, a 338 transaction is often referred to as a stock sale that is treated as an asset sale. In a "regular" 338 election, however, the acquirer typically assumes the additional tax burden associated with the deemed sale of the target's assets. As a result, a "regular" 338 election is extremely rare for the sale of a U.S. C Corp.[15]

### 338(h)(10) Election

A more common derivation of the 338 election is the joint 338(h)(10) election, so named because it must be explicitly consented to by both the buyer and seller. As with an asset sale, this structure can be used when the target is a subsidiary of a parent corporation. In a subsidiary sale, the parent typically pays taxes on the gain on sale at the corporate tax rate regardless of whether it is a stock sale, asset sale, or 338(h)(10) election.

The 338(h)(10) election provides all the buyer tax benefits of an asset sale but without the practical issues around the transfer of individual asset titles previously discussed. Therefore, properly structured, the 338(h)(10) election creates an optimal outcome for both buyer and seller. In this scenario, the buyer is willing to pay a higher price in return for the seller's acquiescence to a 338(h)(10) election, which affords tax benefits to the buyer from the asset step-up that results in the creation of tax deductible depreciation and amortization. This results in a lower after-tax cost for the acquirer and greater after-tax proceeds for the seller. The Internal Revenue Code requires that the 338(h)(10) be a joint election by both the buyer and seller, and therefore forces both parties to work together to maximize the value.

---

[15]Section 338(g) elections are much more common when a U.S. corporation buys the stock of a foreign corporation from a foreign seller.

The economic benefit of a 338(h)(10) election for the buyer often arises because the seller's outside basis in the target subsidiary's stock is greater than the target's inside basis in its assets. In the event that the subsidiary or business has been purchased recently, the stock basis may be particularly high relative to its inside basis. Therefore, the taxable capital gain amount is often lower for a stock sale than an asset sale. As noted above, however, these basis differences can be less prevalent in corporate groups filing consolidated U.S. tax returns, where complicated rules require adjustments to outside stock basis in subsidiaries.

In a subsidiary sale through a 338(h)(10) election, the corporate seller is not subject to double taxation as long as it does not distribute the proceeds from the sale to the parent seller's shareholders. Instead, the seller is taxed only once at the corporate level on the gain from the sale. As shown in Exhibit 7.7, where outside stock basis equals the inside assets basis, Seller Net Proceeds are $1,625 million in both the subsidiary stock sale and 338(h)(10) election scenarios. In the 338(h)(10) election scenario, however, the buyer's Net Purchase Price of $1,809.8 million is significantly lower due to the $190.2 million tax benefit.

In this scenario, the buyer has a meaningful incentive to increase its bid in order to convince the seller to agree to a 338(h)(10) election. As shown in the Buyer Breakeven column in Exhibit 7.7, the buyer is willing to pay up to $2,217.8 million before the tax benefits of the deal are outweighed by the additional purchase price. At the same time, the seller gains $0.75 (1 − 25% marginal tax rate) on each additional dollar the buyer is willing to pay. This provides a strong incentive for the seller to consent to the 338(h) (10) election as the purchase price is increased. At the breakeven purchase price of $2,217.8 million, the seller receives Net Proceeds of $1,753.3 million.

**EXHIBIT 7.7**  Comparison of Subsidiary Acquisition Structures

*($ in millions)*

| Assumptions | | | |
|---|---|---|---|
| Purchase Price | $2,000.0 | Amortization Period | 15 yrs |
| Stock Basis | 500.0 | Marginal Tax Rate | 25% |
| Asset Basis | 500.0 | Capital Gains Rate | 15% |

= (Purchase Price for 338(h)(10) + Purchase Price for Buyer Breakeven) / 2
= ($2,000 million + $2,217.8 million) / 2

| Deal Structure | Subsidiary | | | |
|---|---|---|---|---|
| | Stock Sale | 338(h)(10) Election | Buyer Breakeven | Split Difference |
| Purchase Price | $2,000.0 | $2,000.0 | $2,217.8 | $2,108.9 |
| **Gain on Sale** | | | | |
| Corporate Level | $1,500.0 | $1,500.0 | $1,858.0 | $1,608.9 |
| Taxes (25%) | (375.0) | (375.0) | (464.5) | (402.2) |
| **Seller Net Proceeds** | **$1,625.0** | **$1,625.0** | **$1,753.3** | **$1,706.7** |
| **Buyer Cost** | | | | |
| Purchase Price | $2,000.0 | $2,000.0 | $2,217.8 | $2,108.9 |
| Tax Benefits | - | (190.2) | (217.8) | (310.0) |
| **Net Purchase Price** | **$2,000.0** | **$1,809.8** | **$2,000.0** | **$1,798.9** |
| **Buyer Tax Basis (post-transaction)** | | | | |
| Stock | $2,000.0 | $2,000.0 | $2,217.8 | $2,108.9 |
| Asset | 500.0 | 2,000.0 | 2,217.8 | 2,108.9 |
| Asset Tax Basis Step-up | - | 1,500.0 | 1,717.8 | 1,608.9 |

In the Split Difference column, we show a scenario in which the buyer and seller share the tax benefit, which is a more typical 338(h)(10) election outcome. Here, we assume the buyer pays a purchase price of $2,108.9 million, which is the midpoint between a purchase price of $2,000 million and the buyer breakeven bid of $2,217.8 million. At the Split Difference purchase price, both buyer and seller are better off than in a stock deal at $2,000 million. The seller receives net proceeds of $1,706.8 million and the buyer's net purchase price is $1,798.9 million.

In those cases where the target's inside basis is significantly lower than its outside basis, the seller needs to be compensated for the higher tax burden in the form of a higher purchase price or else it will not agree to the 338(h)(10) election. At the same time, as demonstrated above, the acquirer has a ceiling purchase price above which it is economically irrational to increase its purchase price, represented by the incremental value of the tax benefits. Therefore, depending on the target's inside stock basis and the incremental value of the tax benefit, the buyer and seller may not be able to reach an agreement. However, as a practical matter, many sellers signal at the outset of a sale process that they will agree to the 338(h)(10) election and ask buyers to bid on that basis.

A comparison of selected key attributes for the various deal structures is shown in Exhibit 7.8.

**EXHIBIT 7.8**    Summary of Primary Deal Structures

| Summary of Primary Deal Structures | | | |
|---|:---:|:---:|:---:|
| | Stock Sale | Asset Sale (Sub) | 338(h)(10) Election (Sub) |
| Shareholders are Sellers | ✓ | | |
| Corporate Entity is Seller | | ✓ | ✓ |
| Double Taxation Potential[a] | | ✓ | ✓ |
| Seller Transfers All Assets & Liabilities | ✓ | | ✓ |
| Execution Simplicity | ✓ | | ✓ |
| Asset Step-Up for Accounting Purposes | ✓ | ✓ | ✓ |
| Asset Step-Up for Tax Purposes | | ✓ | ✓ |
| Common for Large Public Companies | ✓ | | |
| Common for Subsidiary Sales | ✓ | ✓ | ✓ |

[a] Double taxation for a subsidiary sale only occurs in the event sale proceeds are distributed to shareholders.

## BUY-SIDE VALUATION

Valuation analysis is central to framing the acquirer's view on purchase price. The primary methodologies used to value a company—namely, comparable companies, precedent transactions, DCF, and LBO analysis—form the basis for this exercise. These techniques provide different approaches to valuation, with varying degrees of overlap. The results of these analyses are typically displayed on a graphic known as a "football field" for easy comparison and analysis. For the comprehensive M&A buy-side valuation analysis performed in this chapter, we reference our prior valuation work for ValueCo in Chapters 1–5. *For this chapter, however, we assume ValueCo is a public company.*

A comprehensive buy-side M&A valuation analysis also typically includes an analysis at various prices (AVP) and a contribution analysis (typically used in stock-for-stock deals). AVP, also known as a valuation matrix, displays the implied multiples paid at a range of transaction values and offer prices (for public targets) at set intervals. Contribution analysis examines the financial "contributions" made by the acquirer and target to the pro forma entity prior to any transaction adjustments.

### Football Field

As previously discussed, a "football field", so named for its resemblance to a U.S. football playing field, is a commonly used visual aid for displaying the valuation ranges derived from the various methodologies. For public companies, the football field also typically includes the target's 52-week trading range, along with a premiums paid range in line with precedent transactions in the given sector (e.g., 25% to 40%). The football field may also reference the valuation implied by a range of target prices from equity research reports.

Once completed, the football field is used to help fine-tune the final valuation range, typically by analyzing the overlap of the multiple valuation methodologies, as represented by the bars in the graphic below. As would be expected, certain methodologies receive greater emphasis depending on the situation. This valuation range is then tested and analyzed within the context of merger consequences analysis in order to determine the ultimate bid price. Exhibit 7.9 displays an illustrative enterprise value football field for ValueCo.

As discussed in Chapter 3, the DCF typically provides the highest valuation, primarily due to the fact that it is based on management projections, which tend to be optimistic, especially in M&A sell-side situations. We have also layered in the present value of $100 million potential synergies (see bar with diagonal lines in Exhibit 7.9), assuming the acquirer is a strategic buyer. This additional value is calculated by discounting the projected after-tax synergies to the present using the target's WACC (see Exhibit 7.10).

Precedent transactions, which typically include a control premium and/or synergies, tend to follow the DCF in the valuation hierarchy, followed by comparable companies. This hierarchy, however, is subject to market conditions and therefore not universally true. Traditionally, LBO analysis, which serves as a proxy for what a financial sponsor might be willing to pay for the target, has been used to establish a minimum price that a strategic buyer must bid to be competitive. As discussed in Chapter 4, however, while the valuation implied by LBO analysis is constrained by achievable leverage levels and target returns, strong debt markets and other factors may drive a superior LBO analysis valuation.

Based on the football field in Exhibit 7.9, we extrapolate a valuation range for ValueCo of $5,250 million to $6,000 million, which implies an EV/LTM EBITDA multiple range of approximately 7.5x to 8.5x LTM EBITDA of $700 million. This range can be tightened and/or stressed upwards or downwards depending on which valuation methodology (or methodologies) the banker deems most indicative.

Exhibit 7.11 displays an illustrative share price football field for ValueCo. Here we layer in the target's 52-week trading range, a 35% premium to the target's 3-month trading range, and a range of target prices from equity research reports. This analysis yields an implied share price range of $52.50 to $60.00 for ValueCo.

**EXHIBIT 7.9**    ValueCo Football Field for Enterprise Value

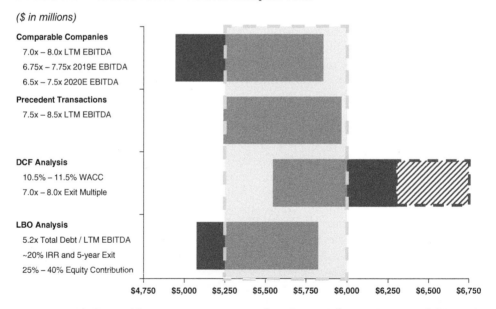

Note: Bar with diagonal lines represents present value of potential synergies (see Exhibit 7.10).

## EXHIBIT 7.10   DCF Analysis—Present Value of Expected Synergies

*($ in millions, except per share data)*

**Synergy Valuation**

| Mid-Year Convention | Y | | | | | |
|---|---|---|---|---|---|---|
| | | | | Projection Period | | |
| | | 2020 | 2021 | 2022 | 2023 | 2024 |
| Cost Savings | | $100.0 | $100.0 | $100.0 | $100.0 | $100.0 |
| Cost Associated with Synergies | | (100.0) | (100.0) | (50.0) | 0.0 | 0.0 |
| **Pre-Tax Synergies** | | $0.0 | $0.0 | $50.0 | $100.0 | $100.0 |
| Taxes | | 0.0 | 0.0 | (12.5) | (25.0) | (25.0) |
| **Free Cash Flow** | | $0.0 | $0.0 | $37.5 | $75.0 | $75.0 |
| | | | | | | |
| WACC | 10.0% | | | | | |
| Discount Period | | 0.5 | 1.5 | 2.5 | 3.5 | 4.5 |
| Discount Factor | | 0.95 | 0.87 | 0.79 | 0.72 | 0.65 |
| **Present Value of Free Cash Flow** | | - | - | $29.5 | $53.7 | $48.8 |

**Present Value of Synergies**

| | |
|---|---|
| Cumulative Present Value of FCF | $132.1 |
| | |
| **Terminal Value** | |
| Terminal Year Free Cash Flow (2024E) | $75.0 |
| Perpetuity Growth Rate | 0.0% |
| **Terminal Value** | $750.0 |
| Discount Factor | 0.65 |
| **Present Value of Terminal Value** | $488.4 |
| | |
| **Total Synergy Value** | $620.5 |
| | |
| Fully Diluted Shares Outstanding | 80.0 |
| | |
| **Implied Equity Value per Share** | $7.75 |

## EXHIBIT 7.11   ValueCo Football Field for Share Price

*($ in millions)*

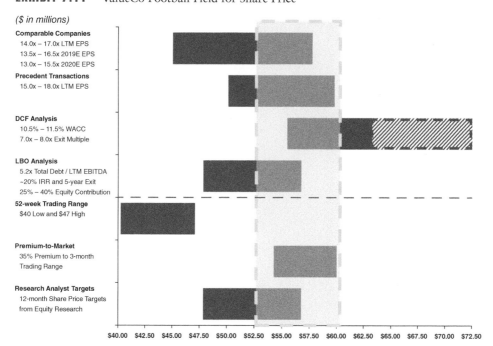

## Analysis at Various Prices

Buy-side M&A valuation analysis typically employs analysis at various prices (AVP) to help analyze and frame valuation. Also known as a valuation matrix, AVP displays the implied multiples paid at a range of offer prices (for public targets) and transaction values at set intervals. The multiple ranges derived from Comparable Companies and Precedent Transactions are referenced to provide perspective on whether the contemplated purchase price is in line with the market and precedents. Exhibit 7.12 shows an example of a valuation matrix for ValueCo assuming a current share price of $43.50 and premiums from 25% to 45%.

**EXHIBIT 7.12**    Analysis at Various Prices

## ValueCo Corporation
## Analysis at Various Prices
*($ in millions, except per share data)*

|  | Premium to Current Stock Price | | | | | |
| --- | --- | --- | --- | --- | --- | --- |
|  | Current | 25% | 30% | 35% | 40% | 45% |
| Implied Offer Price per Share | $43.50 | $54.38 | $56.55 | $58.73 | $60.90 | $63.08 |
| Fully Diluted Shares Outstanding | 79.7 | 79.9 | 80.0 | 80.0 | 80.1 | 80.1 |
| **Implied Offer Value** | **$3,468** | **$4,347** | **$4,523** | **$4,700** | **$4,877** | **$5,053** |
| Plus: Total Debt | 1,500 | 1,500 | 1,500 | 1,500 | 1,500 | 1,500 |
| Less: Cash and Cash Equivalents | (250) | (250) | (250) | (250) | (250) | (250) |
| **Implied Transaction Value** | **$4,718** | **$5,597** | **$5,773** | **$5,950** | **$6,127** | **$6,303** |

|  |  | Valuation Multiples | | | | | | |
| --- | --- | --- | --- | --- | --- | --- | --- | --- |
| **Implied Transaction Value Multiples** | | | | | | | | |
| **Sales** | **Metrics** | | | | | | | **BuyerCo** |
| LTM | $3,385 | 1.4x | 1.7x | 1.7x | 1.8x | 1.8x | 1.9x | 1.8x |
| 2019E | 3,450 | 1.4x | 1.6x | 1.7x | 1.7x | 1.8x | 1.8x | 1.7x |
| 2020E | 3,709 | 1.3x | 1.5x | 1.6x | 1.6x | 1.7x | 1.7x | 1.6x |
| | | | | | | | | |
| **EBITDA** | | | | | | | | |
| LTM | $700 | 6.7x | 8.0x | 8.2x | 8.5x | 8.8x | 9.0x | 8.0x |
| 2019E | 725 | 6.5x | 7.7x | 8.0x | 8.2x | 8.5x | 8.7x | 7.8x |
| 2020E | 779 | 6.1x | 7.2x | 7.4x | 7.6x | 7.9x | 8.1x | 7.3x |
| | | | | | | | | |
| **EBIT** | | | | | | | | |
| LTM | $500 | 9.4x | 11.2x | 11.5x | 11.9x | 12.3x | 12.6x | 9.1x |
| 2019E | 518 | 9.1x | 10.8x | 11.1x | 11.5x | 11.8x | 12.2x | 8.8x |
| 2020E | 557 | 8.5x | 10.1x | 10.4x | 10.7x | 11.0x | 11.3x | 8.2x |
| | | | | | | | | |
| **Implied Offer Price Multiples** | | | | | | | | |
| **EPS** | **Metrics** | | | | | | | |
| LTM | $3.83 | 11.4x | 14.2x | 14.8x | 15.3x | 15.9x | 16.5x | 11.5x |
| 2019E | 4.00 | 10.9x | 13.6x | 14.1x | 14.7x | 15.2x | 15.8x | 11.1x |
| 2020E | 4.45 | 9.8x | 12.2x | 12.7x | 13.2x | 13.7x | 14.2x | 10.3x |

For a public company, the valuation matrix starts with a "Premium to Current Stock Price" header, which serves as the basis for calculating implied offer value. The premiums to the current stock price are typically shown for a range consistent with historical premiums paid (e.g., 25% to 45%) in increments of 5% or 10%, although this range can be shortened or extended depending on the situation.

The offer price at given increments is multiplied by the implied number of fully diluted shares outstanding at that price in order to calculate implied offer value. As the incremental offer price increases, so too may the amount of fully diluted shares outstanding in accordance with the treasury stock method (see Chapter 1, Exhibit 1.7). Furthermore, as discussed in Chapter 2, in an M&A scenario, the target's fully diluted shares outstanding typically reflect all *outstanding* in-the-money stock options as opposed to only *exercisable* options. This is due to the fact that most stock options contain a provision whereby they become exercisable upon a change-of-control only if they are in-the-money.

Once the implied offer values are calculated, net debt is then added in order to obtain the implied transaction values. For example, at a 35% premium to the assumed current share price of $43.50 per share, the offer value for ValueCo's equity is $4,700 million. After adding net debt of $1,250 million, this equates to an enterprise value of $5,950 million. The enterprise value/EBITDA multiples at a 35% premium are 8.5x and 8.2x on an LTM and 2019E basis, respectively. At the same 35% premium, the respective LTM and 2019E offer price/EPS multiples are 15.3x and 14.7x, respectively.

## Contribution Analysis

Contribution analysis depicts the financial "contributions" that each party makes to the pro forma entity in terms of sales, EBITDA, EBIT, net income, and equity value, typically expressed as a percentage. This analysis is most commonly used in stock-for-stock merger transactions. In Exhibit 7.13, we show the relative contributions for BuyerCo and ValueCo for a variety of key metrics.

The calculation of each company's contributed financial metrics is relatively straightforward as no transaction-related adjustments are made to the numbers. For public companies, equity value is also a simple calculation, including the premium paid by the acquirer. For private company targets, equity value needs to be calculated based on an assumed purchase price and net debt. While technically not a "valuation technique", this analysis allows the banker to assess the relative valuation of each party. In theory, if both companies' financial metrics are valued the same, the pro forma ownership would be equivalent to the contribution analysis.

**EXHIBIT 7.13** Contribution Analysis

## ValueCo Corporation
## Contribution Analysis
*($ in millions, except per share data)*

| | BuyerCo | ValueCo | Pro Forma Combined | Contribution (%) | |
|---|---|---|---|---|---|
| **Enterprise Value** | | | | | |
| **Sales** | | | | | |
| LTM | $6,560 | $3,385 | $9,945 | 66.0% | 34.0% |
| 2019E | 6,756 | 3,450 | 10,206 | 66.2% | 33.8% |
| 2020E | 7,229 | 3,709 | 10,937 | 66.1% | 33.9% |
| **EBITDA** | | | | | |
| LTM | $1,443 | $700 | $2,143 | 67.3% | 32.7% |
| 2019E | 1,486 | 725 | 2,211 | 67.2% | 32.8% |
| 2020E | 1,590 | 779 | 2,370 | 67.1% | 32.9% |
| **Enterprise Value** | | | | | |
| Current | $11,600 | $4,718 | $16,318 | 71.1% | 28.9% |
| 25% Premium | 11,600 | 5,597 | 17,197 | 67.5% | 32.5% |
| 35% Premium | 11,600 | 5,950 | 17,550 | 66.1% | 33.9% |
| 45% Premium | 11,600 | 6,303 | 17,903 | 64.8% | 35.2% |
| **Equity Value** | | | | | |
| **Net Income** | | | | | |
| LTM | $853 | $306 | $1,159 | 73.6% | 26.4% |
| 2019E | 881 | 320 | 1,201 | 73.4% | 26.6% |
| 2020E | 952 | 356 | 1,308 | 72.8% | 27.2% |
| **Equity Value** | | | | | |
| Current | $9,800 | $3,468 | $13,268 | 73.9% | 26.1% |
| 25% Premium | 9,800 | 4,347 | 14,147 | 69.3% | 30.7% |
| 35% Premium | 9,800 | 4,700 | 14,500 | 67.6% | 32.4% |
| 45% Premium | 9,800 | 5,053 | 14,853 | 66.0% | 34.0% |

## MERGER CONSEQUENCES ANALYSIS

Merger consequences analysis enables strategic buyers to fine-tune the ultimate purchase price, financing mix, and deal structure. As the name suggests, it involves examining the pro forma impact of a given transaction on the acquirer. Merger consequences analysis measures the impact on EPS in the form of accretion/(dilution) analysis, as well as credit statistics through balance sheet effects. It requires key assumptions regarding purchase price and target company financials, as well as form of financing and deal structure. The sections below outline each of the components of merger consequences analysis in greater detail, assuming that ValueCo Corporation ("ValueCo") is acquired by a strategic buyer, BuyerCo Enterprises ("BuyerCo"), through a stock sale.

The M&A model (or "merger model") that facilitates merger consequences analysis is a derivation of the LBO model that we construct in detail in Chapter 5. For merger consequences analysis, we first construct standalone operating models (income statement, balance sheet, and cash flow statement) for both the target and acquirer. These models are then combined into one pro forma financial model that incorporates various transaction-related adjustments. The purchase price assumptions for the deal as well as the sources and uses of funds are then inputted into the model (see Exhibits 7.29 to 7.48 for the fully completed model).

The transaction summary page in Exhibit 7.14 displays the key merger consequences analysis outputs as linked from the merger model. These outputs include purchase price assumptions, sources and uses of funds, premium paid and exchange ratio, summary financial data, pro forma capitalization and credit statistics, accretion/(dilution) analysis, and implied acquisition multiples. As with the transaction summary page for LBO Analysis in Chapter 5, this format allows the deal team to quickly review and spot-check the analysis and make adjustments to purchase price, financing mix, operating assumptions, and other key inputs as necessary.

### Purchase Price Assumptions

Based on the valuation analysis performed in Exhibits 7.9 through 7.12, as well as the outputs from Chapters 1 to 3 and 5, we assume BuyerCo is offering $58.73 for each share of ValueCo common stock. This represents a 35% premium to the company's current share price of $43.50. At a $58.73 offer price, we calculate fully diluted shares outstanding of approximately 80 million for ValueCo, which implies an equity purchase price of $4,700 million. Adding net debt of $1,250 million, we calculate an enterprise value of $5,950 million, or 8.5x LTM EBITDA of $700 million (see Exhibit 7.15).

The 8.5x LTM EBITDA purchase price multiple is 0.5x higher than the 8.0x LTM EBITDA multiple under the LBO scenario shown in Chapter 5. BuyerCo is able to pay a higher price in part due to its ability to extract $100 million in annual run-rate synergies from the combination. In fact, on a synergy-adjusted basis, BuyerCo is only paying 7.4x LTM EBITDA for ValueCo.

**EXHIBIT 7.14**  Merger Consequences Analysis Transaction Summary Page

## BuyerCo Acquisition of ValueCo
### Merger Consequences Analysis
*($ in millions, fiscal year ending December 31)*

Financing Structure: Operating Scenario: **Structure 1 / Base**

### Transaction Summary

**Sources of Funds**

| | Amount | % of Total Sources | Multiple of Pro Forma EBITDA 2019 | Cumulative | Pricing |
|---|---|---|---|---|---|
| Revolving Credit Facility | - | -% | -x | -x | L+250 bps |
| Term Loan A | 2,250.0 | 35.2% | 1.0x | 1.0x | NA |
| Term Loan B | - | -% | -x | 1.0x | L+275 bps |
| Term Loan C | - | -% | -x | 1.0x | NA |
| 2nd Lien | - | -% | -x | 1.0x | NA |
| Senior Notes | 1,500.0 | 23.4% | 0.6x | 1.6x | 6.000% |
| Senior Subordinated Notes | 2,350.0 | 36.7% | 1.0x | 2.6x | NA |
| Issuance of Common Stock | - | -% | -x | 2.6x | |
| Cash on Hand | 300.0 | 4.7% | 0.1x | 2.6x | |
| Other | - | -% | -x | 2.6x | |
| **Total Sources** | **6,400.0** | **100.0%** | **2.8x** | **2.8x** | |

**Uses of Funds**

| | Amount | % of Total Uses |
|---|---|---|
| Purchase ValueCo Equity | 4,700.0 | 73.4% |
| Repay Existing Debt | 1,500.0 | 23.4% |
| Tender / Call Premiums | 20.0 | 0.3% |
| Transaction Fees | 60.0 | 0.9% |
| Debt Financing Fees | 120.0 | 1.9% |
| **Total Uses** | **6,400.0** | **100.0%** |

**Premium Paid & Exchange Ratio**

| | |
|---|---|
| ValueCo Current Share Price | $43.50 |
| Offer Price per Share | $58.73 |
| BuyerCo Current Share Price | $70.00 |
| Exchange Ratio | 0.8x |
| Year 1 Synergies | $100 |

**Acquisition Structure & Synergies**

| | |
|---|---|
| Stock Consideration for Equity | 50% |
| Transaction Debt Raised | $3,750.0 |
| % of ValueCo Enterprise Value | 63% |
| Acquisition Type | Stock Sale |

**Purchase Price**

| | |
|---|---|
| Offer Price per Share | $58.73 |
| Fully Diluted Shares | 80.0 |
| Equity Purchase Price | $4,700.0 |
| Plus: Existing Net Debt | 1,250.0 |
| Enterprise Value | $5,950.0 |

**Financing Structure**

| | |
|---|---|
| Operating Scenario | 1 |
| Cash Flow Sweep | 1 |
| Cash Balance | 1 |
| Average Interest | 1 |
| Financing Fees | 1 |

### Valuation Summary

| | Target ValueCo | Acquirer BuyerCo |
|---|---|---|
| Company Name | ValueCo | BuyerCo |
| Ticker | VLCO | BUY |
| Current Share Price (12/20/2019) | $43.50 | $70.00 |
| Premium to Current Share Price | 35% | |
| Offer Price per Share | $58.73 | |
| Fully Diluted Shares | 80.0 | 140.0 |
| Equity Value | $4,700.0 | $9,800.0 |
| Plus: Total Debt | 1,500.0 | 2,200.0 |
| Plus: Preferred Equity | - | - |
| Plus: Noncontrolling Interest | - | - |
| Less: Cash and Equivalents | (250.0) | (400.0) |
| Enterprise Value | $5,950.0 | $11,600.0 |

### Transaction Multiples

| | Target Metric | Target Multiple | Acquirer Metric | Acquirer Multiple |
|---|---|---|---|---|
| Enterprise Value / LTM EBITDA | $700.0 | 8.5x | $1,443.1 | 8.0x |
| Enterprise Value / 2019E EBITDA | 725.0 | 8.2x | 1,486.3 | 7.8x |
| Enterprise Value / 2020E EBITDA | 779.4 | 7.6x | 1,590.3 | 7.3x |
| Equity Value / 2019E Net Income | $320.0 | 14.7x | $881.2 | 11.1x |
| Equity Value / 2020E Net Income | 356.0 | 13.2x | 952.0 | 10.3x |

### Pro Forma Ownership

| | Shares | Ownership |
|---|---|---|
| Existing BuyerCo Shareholders | 140.0 | 80.7% |
| Former ValueCo Shareholders | 33.6 | 19.3% |
| Pro Forma Fully Diluted Shares | 173.6 | 100.0% |

### Annual EPS Accretion / (Dilution) Sensitivity Analysis - Premium Paid

| Offer Price | Premium | 2020 | 2021 | 2022 | 2023 | 2024 |
|---|---|---|---|---|---|---|
| $54.38 | 25% | 8.8% | 11.1% | 13.8% | 14.6% | 14.7% |
| $56.55 | 30% | 7.5% | 9.8% | 12.7% | 13.6% | 13.6% |
| $58.73 | 35% | 6.3% | 8.6% | 11.5% | 12.6% | 12.6% |
| $60.90 | 40% | 5.0% | 7.4% | 10.4% | 11.6% | 11.6% |
| $63.08 | 45% | 3.8% | 6.2% | 9.3% | 10.6% | 10.6% |

### 2020E EPS Accretion / (Dilution) Sensitivity Analysis - Premium Paid & Consideration Mix

% Stock Consideration Mix

| Offer Price | Premium | 0% | 25% | 50% | 75% | 100% |
|---|---|---|---|---|---|---|
| $54.38 | 25% | 27.4% | 18.5% | 11.1% | 6.7% | 1.3% |
| $56.55 | 30% | 26.5% | 17.3% | 9.8% | 5.3% | (0.1%) |
| $58.73 | 35% | 25.6% | 16.2% | 8.6% | 4.0% | (1.5%) |
| $60.90 | 40% | 24.6% | 15.1% | 7.4% | 2.7% | (2.8%) |
| $63.08 | 45% | 23.7% | 14.0% | 6.2% | 1.4% | (4.1%) |

### Pro Forma Combined Financial Summary

| | Pro Forma 2019 | 1 2020 | 2 2021 | 3 2022 | 4 2023 | 5 2024 |
|---|---|---|---|---|---|---|
| Sales | $10,205.8 | $10,937.5 | $11,593.7 | $12,173.4 | $12,660.3 | $13,040.1 |
| % growth | 8.2% | 7.2% | 6.0% | 5.0% | 4.0% | 3.0% |
| Gross Profit | $3,947.2 | $4,230.4 | $4,484.2 | $4,708.4 | $4,896.8 | $5,043.7 |
| % margin | 38.7% | 38.7% | 38.7% | 38.7% | 38.7% | 38.7% |
| EBITDA | $2,311.3 | $2,469.7 | $2,611.9 | $2,737.5 | $2,843.0 | $2,925.3 |
| % margin | 22.6% | 22.6% | 22.5% | 22.5% | 22.5% | 22.4% |
| Interest Expense | 352.1 | 322.1 | 271.8 | 252.0 | 252.0 | 252.0 |
| Net Income | $1,161.0 | $1,281.0 | $1,408.8 | $1,505.6 | $1,577.0 | $1,634.3 |
| % margin | 11.4% | 11.7% | 12.2% | 12.4% | 12.5% | 12.5% |
| Fully Diluted Shares | 173.6 | 173.6 | 173.6 | 173.6 | 173.6 | 173.6 |
| Diluted EPS | $6.69 | $7.39 | $8.12 | $8.67 | $9.09 | $9.42 |
| | | | | | | |
| Cash Flow from Operating Activities | | 1,635.5 | 1,797.2 | 1,924.9 | 2,026.0 | 2,110.9 |
| Less: Capital Expenditures | | (383.8) | (406.8) | (427.1) | (444.2) | (457.0) |
| Free Cash Flow | | $1,251.8 | $1,390.4 | $1,497.8 | $1,581.8 | $1,653.3 |
| | | | | | | |
| Senior Secured Debt | 2,250.0 | 898.2 | 0.0 | 0.0 | 0.0 | 0.0 |
| Senior Debt | 5,950.0 | 4,598.2 | 3,700.0 | 3,700.0 | 3,700.0 | 3,700.0 |
| Total Debt | 5,950.0 | 4,598.2 | 3,700.0 | 3,700.0 | 3,700.0 | 3,700.0 |
| Cash & Equivalents | 350.0 | 250.0 | 742.2 | 2,240.0 | 3,821.8 | 5,475.2 |

### Credit Statistics

| | BuyerCo 2019 | Pro Forma 2019 | 1 2020 | 2 2021 | 3 2022 | 4 2023 | 5 2024 |
|---|---|---|---|---|---|---|---|
| EBITDA / Interest Expense | 10.3x | 6.6x | 7.7x | 9.6x | 10.9x | 11.3x | 11.6x |
| (EBITDA - Capex) / Interest Expense | 8.9x | 5.5x | 6.5x | 8.1x | 9.2x | 9.5x | 9.8x |
| | | | | | | | |
| Senior Secured Debt / EBITDA | -x | 1.0x | 0.4x | -x | -x | -x | -x |
| Senior Debt / EBITDA | 1.5x | 2.6x | 1.9x | 1.4x | 1.4x | 1.3x | 1.3x |
| Total Debt / EBITDA | 1.5x | 2.6x | 1.9x | 1.4x | 1.4x | 1.3x | 1.3x |
| Net Debt / EBITDA | 1.2x | 2.4x | 1.8x | 1.1x | 0.5x | (0.0x) | (0.6x) |
| Debt / Total Capitalization | 47.0% | 55.6% | 43.3% | 33.2% | 29.3% | 26.0% | 23.3% |

### Accretion / (Dilution) Analysis

| | BuyerCo 2019 | Pro Forma 2019 | 1 2020 | 2 2021 | 3 2022 | 4 2023 | 5 2024 |
|---|---|---|---|---|---|---|---|
| BuyerCo Standalone Diluted EPS | $6.29 | | $6.80 | $7.28 | $7.70 | $8.07 | $8.36 |
| ValueCo Standalone Diluted EPS | $4.00 | | $4.45 | $4.95 | $5.39 | $5.69 | $5.90 |
| | | | | | | | |
| Pro Forma Combined Diluted EPS | | $6.69 | $7.39 | $8.12 | $8.67 | $9.09 | $9.42 |
| Accretion / (Dilution) - $ | | $0.39 | $0.59 | $0.84 | $0.97 | $1.02 | $1.06 |
| Accretion / (Dilution) - % | | 6.3% | 8.6% | 11.5% | 12.6% | 12.6% | 12.6% |
| Accretive / Dilutive | | Accretive | Accretive | Accretive | Accretive | Accretive | Accretive |
| Breakeven Pre-Tax Synergies / (Cushion) | | ($91) | ($135) | ($194) | ($225) | ($236) | ($245) |

**EXHIBIT 7.15**   Purchase Price Assumptions

*($ in millions, except per share data)*

| Purchase Price Assumptions | | | |
|---|---|---|---|
| | | **Multiple** | |
| | **Amount** | **w/o Synergies** | **w/Synergies** |
| ValueCo Current Share Price | $43.50 | | |
| Premium to Current Share Price | 35% | | |
| **Offer Price per Share** | **$58.73** | **15.3x** | **12.3x** |
| Fully Diluted Shares Outstanding | 80.0 | | |
| **Equity Purchase Price** | **$4,700.0** | | |
| | | | |
| Plus: Total Debt | 1,500.0 | | |
| Less: Cash and Cash Equivalents | (250.0) | | |
| **Enterprise Value** | **$5,950.0** | **8.5x** | **7.4x** |
| | | | |
| LTM EPS | | $3.83 | $4.77 |
| LTM EBITDA | | $700.0 | $800.0 |

**Sources of Funds**   Assuming a 50% stock / 50% cash consideration offered to
ValueCo shareholders, the sources of funds include:

- $2,350 million of stock (50% of $4,700 million equity purchase price for
  ValueCo), or 33.6 million shares ($2,350 million / BuyerCo share price of $70.00)

- $2,200 million of term loan B

- $1,500 million of senior notes

- $300 million of cash on hand (including $50 million of existing BuyerCo cash)

**Uses of Funds**   The uses of funds include:

- the purchase of ValueCo's equity for $4,700 million

- the repayment of ValueCo's existing $1,000 million term loan and $500 million
  senior notes

- the payment of total fees and expenses of $200 million, consisting of: i) M&A
  advisory and other transaction fees of $60 million, ii) debt financing fees of
  $120 million, and iii) tender/call premiums of $20 million[16]

The sources and uses of funds table is summarized in Exhibit 7.16 (excerpt from
the transaction summary page) together with implied multiples through the capital
structure and key debt terms.

---

[16]M&A advisory fees, tender/call premiums, and other deal-related fees and expenses are
expensed upfront and netted from proceeds to the acquirer. As discussed in Chapter 5, debt
financing fees are amortized over the life of the loans and securities.

**EXHIBIT 7.16**　Sources and Uses of Funds

*($ in millions)*

| Sources of Funds | | | | | |
|---|---|---|---|---|---|
| | Amount | % of Total Sources | **Multiple of Pro Forma EBITDA** 2019 | Cumulative | Pricing |
| Revolving Credit Facility[a] | - | - % | - x | - x | L+250 bps |
| Term Loan A | - | - % | - x | - x | NA |
| Term Loan B | 2,250.0 | 35.2% | 1.0x | 1.0x | L+275 bps |
| Term Loan C | - | - % | - x | 1.0x | NA |
| 2nd Lien | - | - % | - x | 1.0x | NA |
| Senior Notes | 1,500.0 | 23.4% | 0.6x | 1.6x | 6.000% |
| Senior Subordinated Notes | - | - % | - x | 1.6x | NA |
| Issuance of Common Stock | 2,350.0 | 36.7% | 1.0x | 2.6x | |
| Cash on Hand | 300.0 | 4.7% | 0.1x | 2.8x | |
| Other | - | - % | - x | 2.6x | |
| **Total Sources** | **$6,400.0** | **100.0%** | **2.8x** | **2.8x** | |

| Uses of Funds | | |
|---|---|---|
| | Amount | % of Total Uses |
| Purchase ValueCo Equity | $4,700.0 | 73.4% |
| Repay Existing Debt | 1,500.0 | 23.4% |
| Tender / Call Premiums | 20.0 | 0.3% |
| Debt Financing Fees | 120.0 | 1.9% |
| Transaction Fees | 60.0 | 0.9% |
| | | |
| **Total Uses** | **$6,400.0** | **100.0%** |

(a) Revolver size of $500 million.

### Goodwill Created

Once the sources and uses of funds are inputted into the model, goodwill is calculated (see Exhibit 7.17). For the purchase of ValueCo by BuyerCo, we introduce additional complexities in calculating goodwill versus LBO Analysis in Chapter 5. Here, we assume a write-up of the target's tangible and intangible assets, as well as a deferred tax liability (DTL).

Goodwill is calculated by first subtracting ValueCo's net identifiable assets of $2,500 million ($3,500 million shareholders' equity – $1,000 million existing goodwill) from the equity purchase price of $4,700 million, which results in an allocable purchase price premium of $2,200 million. Next, we subtract the combined write-ups of ValueCo's tangible and intangible assets of $550 million from the allocable purchase price premium (based on a 15% write-up for the tangible assets and a 10% write-up for the intangible assets). Given this is a stock deal, we then add the deferred tax liability of $137.5 million, which is calculated as the sum of the asset write-ups multiplied by BuyerCo's marginal tax rate of 25%. The net value of these adjustments of $1,787.5 million is added to BuyerCo's existing goodwill.

**EXHIBIT 7.17**  Calculation of Goodwill Created

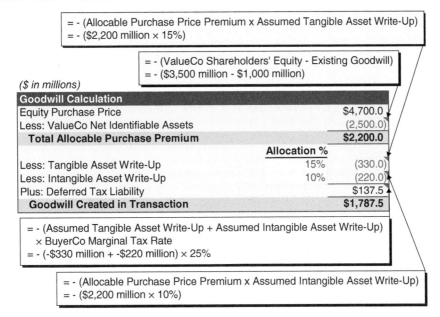

```
= - (Allocable Purchase Price Premium x Assumed Tangible Asset Write-Up)
= - ($2,200 million x 15%)
```

```
= - (ValueCo Shareholders' Equity - Existing Goodwill)
= - ($3,500 million - $1,000 million)
```

*($ in millions)*

| Goodwill Calculation | Allocation % | |
|---|---|---|
| Equity Purchase Price | | $4,700.0 |
| Less: ValueCo Net Identifiable Assets | | (2,500.0) |
| **Total Allocable Purchase Premium** | | **$2,200.0** |
| Less: Tangible Asset Write-Up | 15% | (330.0) |
| Less: Intangible Asset Write-Up | 10% | (220.0) |
| Plus: Deferred Tax Liability | | $137.5 |
| **Goodwill Created in Transaction** | | **$1,787.5** |

```
= - (Assumed Tangible Asset Write-Up + Assumed Intangible Asset Write-Up)
    x BuyerCo Marginal Tax Rate
= - (-$330 million + -$220 million) x 25%
```

```
= - (Allocable Purchase Price Premium x Assumed Intangible Asset Write-Up)
= - ($2,200 million x 10%)
```

**Annual Depreciation & Amortization from Write-Ups**   The assumed write-ups of ValueCo's tangible and intangible assets are linked to the adjustments columns in the balance sheet and increase the value of PP&E and intangible assets, respectively. As shown in Exhibit 7.18, these additions to the balance sheet are amortized over a defined period—in this case, we assume 15 years for both the tangible and intangible write-ups. This creates additional annual PP&E depreciation and intangible amortization of $22 million and $14.7 million, respectively.

**EXHIBIT 7.18**  Annual Depreciation and Amortization from Write-Ups

```
= Assumed Tangible Asset Write-Up x Amortization Period
= $330 million / 15 years
```

*($ in millions)*

| Write-Up Depreciation & Amortization Assumptions | Years | Annual Amount |
|---|---|---|
| Tangible Asset Write-Up Depreciation Period | 15 | 22.0 |
| Intangible Asset Write-Up Amortization Period | 15 | 14.7 |

```
= Assumed Intangible Asset Write-Up x Amortization Period
= $220 million / 15 years
```

**Deferred Tax Liability**  In Exhibit 7.19, we demonstrate how the DTL is created on the balance sheet in the Deferred Income Taxes line item and amortized over the course of its life. Recall that in Exhibit 7.17, we calculated a DTL of $137.5 million by multiplying the sum of ValueCo's tangible and intangible asset write-ups by BuyerCo's marginal tax rate of 25%. We then determined annual depreciation and amortization of $22 million and $14.7 million, respectively, in Exhibit 7.18. This incremental D&A is not tax deductible, thereby creating a difference between cash taxes and book taxes of $9.2 million (($22 million + $14.7 million) × 25%). Therefore, the DTL is reduced annually by $9.2 million over 15 years, resulting in remaining DTL of $491.7 million on the balance sheet by 2024E.

**EXHIBIT 7.19**  Deferred Tax Liability (DTL) Amortization

*($ in millions)*

**Write-Up Depreciation & Amortization Assumptions**

|  | Years | Annual Amount |
|---|---|---|
| Tangible Asset Write-Up Depreciation Period | 15 | 22.0 |
| Intangible Asset Write-Up Amortization Period | 15 | 14.7 |
| Deferred Income Taxes | | (9.2) |

= (Annual Depreciaton from Tangible Asset Write-Up +
    Annual Amortization from Intangible Asset Write-Up) × BuyerCo Marginal Tax Rate
= ($22 million + $14.7 million) × 25%

*($ in millions, fiscal year ending December 31)*

**Pro Forma Balance Sheet**

|  | BuyerCo 2019 | ValueCo 2019 | Adjustments + | Adjustments − | Pro Forma 2019 | Year 1 2020 | Year 2 2021 | Year 3 2022 | Year 4 2023 | Year 5 2024 |
|---|---|---|---|---|---|---|---|---|---|---|
| | | | | | | | | **Projection Period** | | |
| Accounts Payable | 925.0 | 215.0 | | | 1,140.0 | 1,220.9 | 1,294.1 | 1,358.8 | 1,413.2 | 1,455.6 |
| Accrued Liabilities | 945.0 | 275.0 | | | 1,220.0 | 1,306.8 | 1,385.2 | 1,454.4 | 1,512.6 | 1,558.0 |
| Other Current Liabilities | 225.0 | 100.0 | | | 325.0 | 348.3 | 369.1 | 387.6 | 403.1 | 415.2 |
|  **Total Current Liabilities** | **$2,095.0** | **$590.0** | | | **$2,685.0** | **$2,875.9** | **$3,048.5** | **$3,200.9** | **$3,328.9** | **$3,428.8** |
| Deferred Income Taxes | 100.0 | 300.0 | 137.5 | | 537.5 | 528.3 | 519.2 | 510.0 | 500.8 | 491.7 |
| Other Long-Term Liabilities | 625.0 | 110.0 | | | 735.0 | 735.0 | 735.0 | 735.0 | 735.0 | 735.0 |

= (Assumed Tangible Asset Write-Up + Assumed Intangible Asset Write-Up)
    × BuyerCo Marginal Tax Rate
= ($330 million + $220 million) × 25%

= Deferred Income Taxes - DTL Amortization
= $537.5 million - $9.2 million

## Balance Sheet Effects

Balance sheet considerations play an important role in merger consequences analysis, factoring into both purchase price and financing structure considerations. They must be carefully analyzed in conjunction with EPS accretion/(dilution). The most accretive financing structure (typically all debt) may not be the most attractive or viable from a balance sheet or credit perspective. As such, the optimal financing structure must strike the proper balance between cost of capital (and corresponding earnings impact) and pro forma credit profile.

As in the LBO model, once the sources and uses of funds are finalized and goodwill created is calculated, each amount is linked to the appropriate cell in the adjustments columns adjacent to the opening balance sheet (see Exhibit 7.20). These adjustments, combined with the sum of the acquirer and target balance sheet items, serve to bridge the opening balance sheet to the pro forma closing balance sheet. After these balance sheet transaction adjustments are made, we calculate the pro forma credit statistics and compare them to the pre-transaction standalone metrics.

## EXHIBIT 7.20  Links to Balance Sheet

*($ in millions)*

| Sources of Funds | | | Uses of Funds | | |
|---|---|---|---|---|---|
| Revolving Credit Facility | - | | Purchase ValueCo Equity | $4,700.0 | E |
| Term Loan B | 2,250.0 | A | Repay Existing Debt | 1,500.0 | F |
| Senior Notes | 1,500.0 | B | Tender / Call Premiums | 20.0 | G |
| Issuance of Common Stock | 2,350.0 | C | Debt Financing Fees | 120.0 | H |
| Cash on Hand | 300.0 | D | Transaction Fees | 60.0 | I |
| **Total Sources** | **$6,400.0** | | **Total Uses** | **$6,400.0** | |

| Goodwill Calculation | | |
|---|---|---|
| Equity Purchase Price | $4,700.0 | E |
| Less: ValueCo Net Identifiable Assets | (2,500.0) | |
| **Total Allocable Purchase Premium** | **$2,200.0** | |
| | Allocation % | |
| Less: Tangible Asset Write-Up | 15% | (330.0) J |
| Less: Intangible Asset Write-Up | 10% | (220.0) K |
| Plus: Deferred Tax Liability | | 137.5 L |
| **Goodwill Created in Transaction** | | **$1,787.5** |

### Balance Sheet

| | BuyerCo 2019 | ValueCo 2019 | Adjustments + | Adjustments - | Pro Forma 2019 |
|---|---|---|---|---|---|
| Cash and Cash Equivalents | $400.0 | $250.0 | | (300.0) D | $350.0 |
| Accounts Receivable | 1,000.0 | 450.0 | | | 1,450.0 |
| Inventories | 1,225.0 | 600.0 | | | 1,825.0 |
| Prepaids and Other Current Assets | 525.0 | 175.0 | | | 700.0 |
| **Total Current Assets** | **$3,150.0** | **$1,475.0** | | | **$4,325.0** |
| | | | J | | |
| Property, Plant and Equipment, net | 2,500.0 | 2,500.0 | 330.0 | | 5,330.0 |
| Goodwill | 575.0 | 1,000.0 | 1,787.5 | (1,000.0) | 2,362.5 |
| Intangible Assets | 825.0 | 875.0 | 220.0 | | 1,920.0 |
| Other Assets | 450.0 | 150.0 | K | | 600.0 |
| Deferred Financing Fees | - | - | 120.0 | | 120.0 |
| **Total Assets** | **$7,500.0** | **$6,000.0** | H | | **$14,657.5** |
| | | | | | |
| Accounts Payable | 925.0 | 215.0 | | | 1,140.0 |
| Accrued Liabilities | 945.0 | 275.0 | | | 1,220.0 |
| Other Current Liabilities | 225.0 | 100.0 | | | 325.0 |
| **Total Current Liabilities** | **$2,095.0** | **$590.0** | | | **$2,685.0** |
| | | | | | |
| Revolving Credit Facility | - | - | F | | - |
| ValueCo Term Loan | - | 1,000.0 | A | (1,000.0) | - |
| New Term Loan B | - | - | 2,250.0 | | 2,250.0 |
| BuyerCo Senior Notes | 2,200.0 | - | F | | 2,200.0 |
| ValueCo Senior Notes | - | 500.0 | B | (500.0) | - |
| New Senior Notes | - | - | 1,500.0 | | 1,500.0 |
| Deferred Income Taxes | 100.0 | 300.0 | 137.5 | | 537.5 |
| Other Long-Term Liabilities | 625.0 | 110.0 | L | | 735.0 |
| **Total Liabilities** | **$5,020.0** | **$2,500.0** | | | **$9,907.5** |
| | | | | | |
| Noncontrolling Interests | - | - | | | - |
| Shareholders' Equity | 2,480.0 | 3,500.0 | 2,270.0 | (3,500.0) | 4,750.0 |
| **Total Shareholders' Equity** | **$2,480.0** | **$3,500.0** | | | **$4,750.0** |
| | | | | | |
| **Total Liabilities and Equity** | **$7,500.0** | **$6,000.0** | | | **$14,657.5** |
| | | | | | |
| *Balance Check* | *0.000* | *0.000* | | | *0.000* |

= - (Issuance of Common Stock - Tender/Call Premiums - Transaction Expenses)
= - ($2,350 million - $20 million - $60 million)

  C          G              I

**Balance Sheet Adjustments**    Exhibit 7.21 provides a summary of the transaction adjustments to the opening balance sheet.

**EXHIBIT 7.21**    Balance Sheet Adjustments

| Adjustments | |
| --- | --- |
| **Additions** | **Eliminations** |
| **Assets** | **Assets** |
| + $1,787.5 million of Goodwill Created | − $1,000 million of Existing ValueCo Goodwill |
| + $330 million from Tangible Asset Write-Up | − $300 million of Cash on Hand |
| + $220 million from Intangible Asset Write-Up | |
| + $120 million of Deferred Financing Fees | |
| | |
| **Liabilities** | **Liabilities** |
| + $2,220 million of Term Loan B | − $1,500 million of Existing ValueCo Debt |
| + $1,500 million of Senior Notes | |
| + $137.5 million of Deferred Tax Liabilities | |
| | |
| **Shareholders' Equity** | **Shareholders' Equity** |
| + $2,350 million from Issuance of BuyerCo Stock | − $3,500 million of ValueCo Shareholders' Equity |
| | − $60 million of Transaction Fees & Expenses |
| | − $20 million of Tender/Call Premiums |

Strategic acquirers tend to prioritize the maintenance of target credit ratings, which directly affect their cost of capital as well as general investor perception of the company. Some companies may also require a minimum credit rating for operating purposes or covenant compliance. Consequently, companies often pre-screen potential acquisitions and proposed financing structures with the rating agencies to gain comfort that a given credit rating will be received or maintained. They are also in frequent dialogue with their investors on target leverage levels. The ultimate financing structure tends to reflect this feedback, which may result in the company increasing the equity portion of the financing despite an adverse effect on pro forma earnings.

The balance sheet effects analysis centers on analyzing the acquirer's capital structure and credit statistics pro forma for the transaction. It is driven primarily by purchase price and the sources of financing.

**Credit Statistics**   As discussed in Chapters 1 and 4, the most widely used credit statistics are grouped into leverage ratios (e.g., debt-to-EBITDA and debt-to-total-capitalization) and coverage ratios (e.g., EBITDA-to-interest expense). The rating agencies tend to establish target ratio thresholds for companies that correspond to given ratings categories. These ratings methodologies and requirements are made available to issuers who are expected to manage their balance sheets accordingly. Therefore, acquirers are often guided by the desire to maintain key target ratios in crafting their M&A financing structure.

As shown in Exhibit 7.22, assuming a 50% stock/50% cash consideration offered to ValueCo shareholders, BuyerCo's credit statistics weaken slightly given the incremental debt raise. Pro forma for the deal, BuyerCo's debt-to-EBITDA increases from 1.5x to 2.6x while debt-to-total capitalization of 47% increases to 55.6%. By the end of 2020E, however, the pro forma entity deleverages to below 2.0x and further decreases to 1.4x by the end of 2021E (in line with BuyerCo's pre-transaction leverage). Similarly, by the end of 2020E, debt-to-total capitalization decreases to 43.3%, which is lower than the pre-transaction level.

At the same time, EBITDA-to-interest expense decreases from 10.3x pre-deal to 7.7x by the end of 2020E while capex-adjusted coverage decreases from 8.9x to 6.5x. These coverage ratios return to roughly pre-transaction levels by 2021E/2022E. Therefore, while the pro forma combined entity has a moderately weaker credit profile than that of standalone BuyerCo, post-transaction it returns to pre-deal levels within a relatively short time period. BuyerCo's use of significant equity as a funding source, combined with the synergies from the combination with ValueCo, helps to maintain credit ratios within an acceptable range.

Given the borderline nature of these pro forma credit statistics, BuyerCo may consider the use of more equity to ensure there is no ratings downgrade. As previously discussed, however, this typically has a negative impact on income statement effects, such as EPS accretion/(dilution). In order to assess these situations, it is common to sensitize the acquirer's pro forma credit statistics for key inputs such as purchase price and financing mix. In Exhibit 7.22, we sensitize key credit statistics (i.e., debt-to-EBITDA and EBITDA-to-interest expense) for purchase price and finance mix.

# EXHIBIT 7.22 Pro Forma Capitalization and Credit Statistics

($ in millions, fiscal year ending December 31)

## Capitalization

| | BuyerCo 2019 | ValueCo 2019 | Adjustments + | Adjustments – | Pro forma 2019 | 1 2020 | 2 2021 | 3 2022 | 4 2023 | 5 2024 |
|---|---|---|---|---|---|---|---|---|---|---|
| Cash | $400.0 | $250.0 | | (300.0) | $350.0 | $250.0 | $742.2 | $2,240.0 | $3,821.8 | $5,475.2 |
| Revolving Credit Facility | - | - | | | - | - | - | - | - | - |
| ValueCo Term Loan | - | 1,000.0 | | (1,000.0) | - | - | - | - | - | - |
| New Term Loan B | - | - | 2,250.0 | | 2,250.0 | 898.2 | - | - | - | - |
| Other Debt | - | - | | | - | - | - | - | - | - |
| **Total Senior Secured Debt** | - | $1,000.0 | | | $2,250.0 | $898.2 | - | - | - | - |
| BuyerCo Senior Notes | 2,200.0 | - | | | 2,200.0 | 2,200.0 | 2,200.0 | 2,200.0 | 2,200.0 | 2,200.0 |
| ValueCo Senior Notes | - | 500.0 | | (500.0) | - | - | - | - | - | - |
| New Senior Notes | - | - | 1,500.0 | | 1,500.0 | 1,500.0 | 1,500.0 | 1,500.0 | 1,500.0 | 1,500.0 |
| **Total Senior Debt** | $2,200.0 | $1,500.0 | | | $5,950.0 | $4,598.2 | $3,700.0 | $3,700.0 | $3,700.0 | $3,700.0 |
| Senior Subordinated Notes | - | - | | | - | - | - | - | - | - |
| **Total Debt** | $2,200.0 | $1,500.0 | 2,270.0 | (3,500.0) | $5,950.0 | $4,598.2 | $3,700.0 | $3,700.0 | $3,700.0 | $3,700.0 |
| Shareholders' Equity | 2,480.0 | 3,500.0 | | | 4,750.0 | 6,031.9 | 7,440.8 | 8,946.3 | 10,523.3 | 12,157.6 |
| **Total Capitalization** | $4,680.0 | $5,000.0 | | | $10,700.0 | $10,630.1 | $11,140.8 | $12,646.3 | $14,223.3 | $15,857.6 |
| *% of Bank Debt Repaid* | *47.0%* | *30.0%* | | | - | *60.1%* | *100.0%* | *100.0%* | *100.0%* | *100.0%* |

## Credit Statistics

| | BuyerCo 2019 | ValueCo 2019 | Adjustments + | Adjustments – | Pro forma 2019 | 1 2020 | 2 2021 | 3 2022 | 4 2023 | 5 2024 |
|---|---|---|---|---|---|---|---|---|---|---|
| EBITDA | $1,496.3 | $725.0 | 100.0 | | $2,311.3 | $2,469.7 | $2,611.9 | $2,737.5 | $2,843.0 | $2,925.3 |
| Capital Expenditures | 202.7 | 155.3 | | | 357.9 | 383.8 | 406.8 | 427.1 | 444.2 | 457.5 |
| Interest Expense | 144.4 | 92.9 | 114.8 | | 352.1 | 322.1 | 271.8 | 252.0 | 252.0 | 252.0 |
| | | | | | | | | | | |
| EBITDA / Interest Expense | 10.3x | 7.8x | | | 6.6x | 7.7x | 9.6x | 10.9x | 11.3x | 11.6x |
| (EBITDA - Capex) / Interest Expense | 8.9x | 6.1x | | | 5.5x | 6.5x | 8.1x | 9.2x | 9.5x | 9.8x |
| | | | | | | | | | | |
| Senior Secured Debt / EBITDA | -x | 1.4x | | | 1.0x | 0.4x | -x | -x | -x | -x |
| Senior Debt / EBITDA | 1.5x | 2.1x | | | 2.6x | 1.9x | 1.4x | 1.4x | 1.3x | 1.3x |
| Total Debt / EBITDA | 1.5x | 2.1x | | | 2.6x | 1.9x | 1.4x | 1.4x | 1.3x | 1.3x |
| Net Debt / EBITDA | 1.2x | 1.7x | | | 2.4x | 1.8x | 1.1x | 0.5x | (0.0x) | (0.6x) |
| *% Debt / Total Capitalization* | *47.0%* | *30.0%* | | | *55.6%* | *43.3%* | *33.2%* | *29.3%* | *26.0%* | *23.3%* |

### Debt / EBITDA

| | | % Stock Consideration Mix | | | |
|---|---|---|---|---|---|
| Premium Paid | 0% | 25% | 50% | 75% | 100% |
| 25% | 3.5x | 3.0x | 2.5x | 2.0x | 1.5x |
| 30% | 3.5x | 3.0x | 2.5x | 2.0x | 1.5x |
| 35% | 3.6x | 3.1x | 2.6x | 2.0x | 1.5x |
| 40% | 3.7x | 3.2x | 2.6x | 2.1x | 1.5x |
| 45% | 3.8x | 3.2x | 2.7x | 2.1x | 1.5x |

### EBITDA / Interest Expense

| | | % Stock Consideration Mix | | | |
|---|---|---|---|---|---|
| Premium Paid | 0% | 25% | 50% | 75% | 100% |
| 25% | 5.2x | 5.8x | 6.7x | 8.8x | 11.0x |
| 30% | 5.1x | 5.7x | 6.6x | 8.7x | 11.0x |
| 35% | 5.0x | 5.7x | 6.6x | 8.6x | 11.0x |
| 40% | 4.9x | 5.6x | 6.5x | 8.6x | 11.0x |
| 45% | 4.8x | 5.5x | 6.4x | 8.5x | 11.0x |

## Accretion/(Dilution) Analysis

Accretion/(dilution) analysis measures the effects of a transaction on a potential acquirer's earnings, assuming a given financing structure. It centers on comparing the acquirer's earnings per share (EPS) pro forma for the transaction versus on a standalone basis. If the pro forma combined EPS is lower than the acquirer's standalone EPS, the transaction is said to be *dilutive*; conversely, if the pro forma EPS is higher, the transaction is said to be *accretive*.

A rule of thumb for 100% stock transactions is that when an acquirer purchases a target with a lower P/E, the acquisition is accretive. This concept is intuitive—when a company pays a lower multiple for the target's earnings than the multiple at which its own earnings trade, the transaction is *de facto* accretive. Conversely, transactions where an acquirer purchases a higher P/E target are de facto dilutive. Sizable synergies, however, may serve to offset this financial convention and result in such acquisitions being accretive. Transaction-related expenses such as depreciation and amortization, on the other hand, have the opposite effect.

Ideally, acquirers seek immediate earnings accretion on "Day One", which is typically cheered by investors. In practice, however, many M&A deals are longer-term strategic moves focused on creating value for shareholders over time. For this reason, as well as the fact that equity markets in general are forward-looking, accretion/(dilution) analysis focuses on EPS effects for future years. Therefore, accretion/(dilution) analysis captures the target's future expected performance, including growth prospects, synergies, and other combination effects with the acquirer.

Accretion/(dilution) analysis is usually a key screening mechanism for potential acquirers. As a general rule, acquirers do not pursue transactions that are dilutive over the foreseeable earnings projection period due to the potential destructive effects on shareholder value. There may be exceptions in certain situations, however. For example, the acquisition of a rapidly growing business with an accelerated earnings ramp-up in the relatively distant future may not yield accretive results until after the typical two-year earnings projection time horizon.

The key drivers for accretion/(dilution) are purchase price, acquirer and target projected earnings, synergies, and form of financing, most notably the debt/equity mix and cost of debt. The calculations must also reflect transaction-related effects pertaining to deal structure, such as the write-up of tangible and intangible assets. As would be expected, maximum accretive effects are served by negotiating as low a purchase price as possible, sourcing the cheapest form of financing, choosing the optimal deal structure, and identifying significant achievable synergies.

Exhibit 7.23 is a graphical depiction of the accretion/(dilution) calculation, which in this case begins by summing the EBIT of the acquirer and target, including synergies. An alternative approach would begin by combining the acquirer's and target's EPS and then making the corresponding tax-effected adjustments.

Transaction expenses related to M&A advisory and financing fees may also be factored into accretion/(dilution) analysis. As discussed in Chapter 5, M&A advisory fees are typically expensed upfront while debt financing fees are amortized over the life of the security. In many cases, however, transaction fees are treated as non-recurring items and excluded from accretion/(dilution) analysis, which is the approach we adopt in our analysis.

The EPS accretion/(dilution) analysis calculation in Exhibit 7.23 consists of the following ten steps:

I. Enter the acquirer's standalone projected operating income (EBIT)

II. Add the target's standalone projected operating income (EBIT)

III. Add expected synergies from the transaction for the projection period

IV. Subtract transaction-related depreciation and amortization expenses (typically associated with writing up the target's tangible and intangible assets)

V. Subtract the acquirer's existing interest expense

VI. Subtract the incremental interest expense associated with the new transaction debt to calculate pro forma earnings before taxes[17]

VII. Subtract the tax expense at the acquirer's tax rate to arrive at pro forma combined net income

VIII. In the event stock is used as a portion, or all, of the purchase price, add the new shares issued as part of the transaction to the acquirer's existing fully diluted shares outstanding

IX. Divide pro forma net income by the pro forma fully diluted shares outstanding to arrive at pro forma combined EPS[18]

X. Compare pro forma EPS with the acquirer's standalone EPS to determine whether the transaction is accretive or dilutive

---

[17]The target's existing debt is either assumed to be refinanced as part of the new transaction debt or is kept in place with the corresponding interest expense unchanged.

[18]For all-debt financed transactions, there are no adjustments to shares outstanding.

**EXHIBIT 7.23** Accretion/(Dilution) Calculation from EBIT to EPS

*($ in millions, except per share data)*

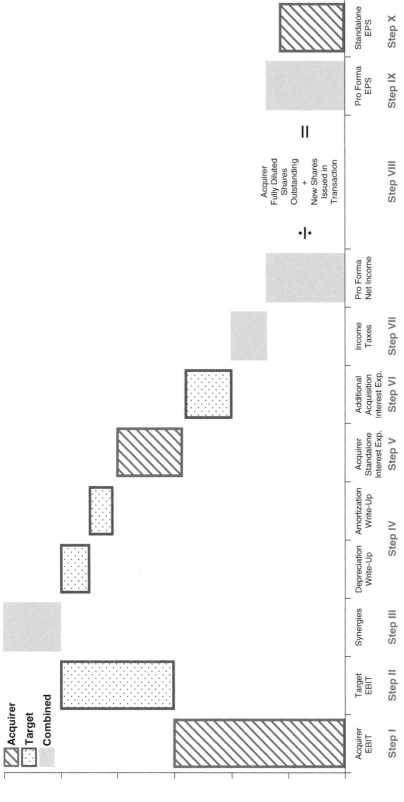

In Exhibits 7.24 through 7.26, we conduct accretion/(dilution) analysis for BuyerCo's illustrative acquisition of ValueCo for three scenarios: I) 50% stock/50% cash, II) 100% cash, and III) 100% stock. In each of these scenarios, we utilize the purchase price assumptions in Exhibit 7.15, namely an offer price per share of $58.73, representing an equity purchase price of $4,700 million and enterprise value of $5,950 million. We also assume the deal is structured as a stock sale.

### Acquisition Scenarios—I) 50% Stock/50% Cash; II) 100% Cash; and III) 100% Stock

**Scenario I: 50% Stock/50% Cash**    In scenario I, a 50% stock/50% cash consideration mix is offered by BuyerCo to ValueCo shareholders. This serves as our base case scenario as shown on the transaction summary page in Exhibit 7.15. Public companies making sizable acquisitions often use a combination of debt and equity financing to fund a given acquisition.

In Exhibit 7.24, 2020E pro forma EBIT of $2,066.4 million is calculated by combining BuyerCo's and ValueCo's EBIT plus expected synergies of $100 million. Transaction-related depreciation and amortization expenses of $36.7 million from the write-up of ValueCo's tangible and intangible assets ($22 million + $14.7 million) are then deducted. BuyerCo's existing interest expense of $140.2 million and the incremental interest expense of $180.3 million from the acquisition debt (including refinancing ValueCo's debt) are also subtracted. The resulting earnings before taxes of $1,709.2 million is then tax-effected at BuyerCo's marginal tax rate of 25% to calculate pro forma combined net income of $1,281.9 million.

In calculating pro forma EPS, BuyerCo's 140 million shares outstanding are increased by the additional 33.6 million shares issued in connection with the acquisition. Pro forma EPS of $7.39 is determined by dividing net income of $1,281.9 million by 173.6 million total shares outstanding. Hence, the transaction is accretive by 8.6% on the basis of 2020E EPS. Excluding synergies, however, the transaction is only accretive by 2.1% (see Exhibit 7.27). In Exhibit 7.24, the bottom section shows the pre-tax synergies necessary to make the transaction breakeven (i.e., neither accretive nor dilutive). In the event the transaction is dilutive in a given year, this analysis determines the amount of pre-tax synergies necessary to make pro forma EPS neutral to standalone EPS. Similarly, in the event the transaction is accretive, the analysis determines the synergy cushion before the transaction becomes dilutive.

**EXHIBIT 7.24**   Scenario I: 50% Stock/50% Cash Consideration

> = BuyerCo EBIT$_{2020E}$ + ValueCo EBIT$_{2020E}$ + Synergies
> = $1,409.6 million + $556.9 million + $100 million

> = Tangible Asset Write-up / Depreciation Period
> = $330 million / 15 years

> = Intangible Asset Write-up / Amortization Period
> = $220 million / 15 years

*($ in millions, except per share data)*

**Accretion / (Dilution) Analysis - 50% Stock / 50% Cash Consideration**

| | Pro forma | | Projection Period | | | |
|---|---|---|---|---|---|---|
| | | 1 | 2 | 3 | 4 | 5 |
| | 2019 | 2020 | 2021 | 2022 | 2023 | 2024 |
| BuyerCo EBIT | $1,317.4 | $1,409.6 | $1,494.2 | $1,568.9 | $1,631.6 | $1,680.6 |
| ValueCo EBIT | 518.0 | 556.9 | 590.3 | 619.8 | 644.6 | 663.9 |
| Synergies | 100.0 | 100.0 | 100.0 | 100.0 | 100.0 | 100.0 |
| **Pro Forma Combined EBIT (pre-transaction)** | **$1,935.4** | **$2,066.4** | **$2,184.4** | **$2,288.7** | **$2,376.2** | **$2,444.5** |
| Depreciation from Write-Up | 22.0 | 22.0 | 22.0 | 22.0 | 22.0 | 22.0 |
| Amortization from Write-Up | 14.7 | 14.7 | 14.7 | 14.7 | 14.7 | 14.7 |
| **Pro Forma Combined EBIT** | **$1,898.7** | **$2,029.8** | **$2,147.8** | **$2,252.0** | **$2,339.5** | **$2,407.8** |
| Standalone Net Interest Expense | 142.4 | 140.2 | 135.7 | 130.9 | 125.7 | 120.3 |
| Incremental Net Interest Expense | 208.2 | 180.3 | 133.6 | 113.7 | 111.2 | 108.5 |
| **Earnings Before Taxes** | **$1,548.1** | **$1,709.2** | **$1,878.5** | **$2,007.4** | **$2,102.7** | **$2,179.0** |
| Income Tax Expense @ 25% | 387.0 | 427.3 | 469.6 | 501.9 | 525.7 | 544.8 |
| **Pro Forma Combined Net Income** | **$1,161.0** | **$1,281.9** | **$1,408.8** | **$1,505.6** | **$1,577.0** | **$1,634.3** |
| | | | | | | |
| **BuyerCo Standalone Net Income** | **$881.2** | **$952.0** | **$1,018.9** | **$1,078.5** | **$1,129.4** | **$1,170.2** |
| | | | | | | |
| Standalone Fully Diluted Shares Outstanding | 140.0 | 140.0 | 140.0 | 140.0 | 140.0 | 140.0 |
| Net New Shares Issued in Transaction | 33.6 | 33.6 | 33.6 | 33.6 | 33.6 | 33.6 |
| **Pro Forma Fully Diluted Shares Outstanding** | **173.6** | **173.6** | **173.6** | **173.6** | **173.6** | **173.6** |
| | | | | | | |
| Pro Forma Combined Diluted EPS | $6.69 | $7.39 | $8.12 | $8.67 | $9.09 | $9.42 |
| BuyerCo Standalone Diluted EPS | 6.29 | 6.80 | 7.28 | 7.70 | 8.07 | 8.36 |
| | | | | | | |
| **Accretion / (Dilution) - $** | **$0.39** | **$0.59** | **$0.84** | **$0.97** | **$1.02** | **$1.06** |
| **Accretion / (Dilution) - %** | **6.3%** | **8.6%** | **11.5%** | **12.6%** | **12.6%** | **12.6%** |
| *Accretive / Dilutive* | *Accretive* | *Accretive* | *Accretive* | *Accretive* | *Accretive* | *Accretive* |
| | | | | | | |
| Included Pre-Tax Synergies | $100.0 | $100.0 | $100.0 | $100.0 | $100.0 | $100.0 |
| Additional Pre-Tax Synergies to Breakeven | (91.3) | (135.4) | (194.2) | (224.6) | (235.6) | (244.6) |
| **Required Synergies to Breakeven / (Cushion)** | **$8.7** | **($35.4)** | **($94.2)** | **($124.6)** | **($135.6)** | **($144.6)** |

> = Pro Forma Net Income$_{2020E}$ / Pro Forma Fully Diluted Shares$_{2020E}$
> = $1,281.9 million / 173.6 million

> = BuyerCo Standalone Net Income$_{2021E}$ / Standalone Fully Diluted Shares
> = $1,018.9 million / 140.0 million

> = Pro Forma Combined Diluted EPS$_{2022E}$ - BuyerCo Standalone Diluted EPS$_{2022E}$
> = $8.67 - $7.70

> = Pro Forma Combined Diluted EPS$_{2023E}$ / BuyerCo Standalone Diluted EPS$_{2023E}$ - 1
> = $9.09 / $8.07 - 1

> = - (EPS Accretion/(Dilution)$_{2024E}$ × Pro Forma Fully Diluted Shares) / (1 - Tax Rate)
> = - ($1.06 × 173.6 million / (1 - 25%))

**Scenario II: 100% Cash**   Scenario II demonstrates an illustrative accretion/(dilution) analysis assuming ValueCo shareholders receive 100% cash consideration. As shown in Exhibit 7.25, 2020E pro forma EBIT of $2,029.8 million after transaction-related adjustments is calculated in the same manner as Scenario I. However, interest expense is $115.5 million higher given the financing structure includes approximately $2,400 million of additional debt to fund the $4,700 million equity purchase price for ValueCo. As a result, pro forma 2020E net income is $1,195.3 million versus $1,281.9 million in Scenario I.

Pro forma 2020E EPS of $8.54 (versus $7.39 in Scenario I) is calculated by dividing pro forma net income of $1,195.3 million by BuyerCo's fully diluted shares outstanding of 140 million. As the consideration received by ValueCo shareholders is 100% cash, no new shares are issued in connection with the transaction. Hence, as shown in Exhibit 7.25, the transaction is accretive by 25.6% on the basis of 2020E EPS, versus 8.6% in the 50% stock/50% cash scenario. From a balance sheet effects perspective, however, this financing mix is less attractive. Pro forma leverage in the all cash scenario is 3.6x versus 2.6x in Scenario I (see Exhibit 7.22), which significantly weakens BuyerCo's credit profile and likely results in a credit ratings downgrade.

**EXHIBIT 7.25**   Scenario II: 100% Cash Consideration

*($ in millions, except per share data)*

**Accretion / (Dilution) Analysis - 100% Cash Consideration**

|  | Pro forma | | | Projection Period | | |
|---|---|---|---|---|---|---|
|  | Pro forma | 1 | 2 | 3 | 4 | 5 |
|  | 2019 | 2020 | 2021 | 2022 | 2023 | 2024 |
| BuyerCo EBIT | $1,317.4 | $1,409.6 | $1,494.2 | $1,568.9 | $1,631.6 | $1,680.6 |
| ValueCo EBIT | 518.0 | 556.9 | 590.3 | 619.8 | 644.6 | 663.9 |
| Synergies | 100.0 | 100.0 | 100.0 | 100.0 | 100.0 | 100.0 |
| **Pro Forma Combined EBIT (pre-transaction)** | **$1,935.4** | **$2,066.4** | **$2,184.4** | **$2,288.7** | **$2,376.2** | **$2,444.5** |
| Depreciation from Write-Up | 22.0 | 22.0 | 22.0 | 22.0 | 22.0 | 22.0 |
| Amortization from Write-Up | 14.7 | 14.7 | 14.7 | 14.7 | 14.7 | 14.7 |
| **Pro Forma Combined EBIT** | **$1,898.7** | **$2,029.8** | **$2,147.8** | **$2,252.0** | **$2,339.5** | **$2,407.8** |
| Standalone Net Interest Expense | 142.4 | 140.2 | 135.7 | 130.9 | 125.7 | 120.3 |
| Incremental Net Interest Expense | 322.0 | 295.8 | 241.7 | 184.3 | 142.7 | 128.6 |
| **Earnings Before Taxes** | **$1,434.3** | **$1,593.7** | **$1,770.4** | **$1,936.9** | **$2,071.1** | **$2,158.9** |
| Income Tax Expense @ 25% | 358.6 | 398.4 | 442.6 | 484.2 | 517.8 | 539.7 |
| **Pro Forma Combined Net Income** | **$1,075.8** | **$1,195.3** | **$1,327.8** | **$1,452.6** | **$1,553.3** | **$1,619.2** |
|  |  |  |  |  |  |  |
| **BuyerCo Standalone Net Income** | **$881.2** | **$952.0** | **$1,018.9** | **$1,078.5** | **$1,129.4** | **$1,170.2** |
|  |  |  |  |  |  |  |
| Standalone Fully Diluted Shares Outstanding | 140.0 | 140.0 | 140.0 | 140.0 | 140.0 | 140.0 |
| Net New Shares Issued in Transaction | 0.0 | 0.0 | 0.0 | 0.0 | 0.0 | 0.0 |
| **Pro Forma Fully Diluted Shares Outstanding** | **140.0** | **140.0** | **140.0** | **140.0** | **140.0** | **140.0** |
|  |  |  |  |  |  |  |
| Pro Forma Combined Diluted EPS | $7.68 | $8.54 | $9.48 | $10.38 | $11.10 | $11.57 |
| BuyerCo Standalone Diluted EPS | 6.29 | 6.80 | 7.28 | 7.70 | 8.07 | 8.36 |
|  |  |  |  |  |  |  |
| **Accretion / (Dilution) - $** | **$1.39** | **$1.74** | **$2.21** | **$2.67** | **$3.03** | **$3.21** |
| **Accretion / (Dilution) - %** | **22.1%** | **25.6%** | **30.3%** | **34.7%** | **37.5%** | **38.4%** |
| *Accretive / Dilutive* | *Accretive* | *Accretive* | *Accretive* | *Accretive* | *Accretive* | *Accretive* |
|  |  |  |  |  |  |  |
| Included Pre-Tax Synergies | $100.0 | $100.0 | $100.0 | $100.0 | $100.0 | $100.0 |
| Additional Pre-Tax Synergies to Breakeven | (259.4) | (324.3) | (411.9) | (498.8) | (565.2) | (598.7) |
| **Required Synergies to Breakeven / (Cushion)** | **($159.4)** | **($224.3)** | **($311.9)** | **($398.8)** | **($465.2)** | **($498.7)** |

**Scenario III: 100% Stock**    Scenario III demonstrates an illustrative accretion/ (dilution) analysis assuming ValueCo shareholders receive 100% stock consideration. As shown in Exhibit 7.26, total interest expense of $179.3 million in 2020E is the lowest of the three scenarios given no incremental debt issuance (beyond the refinancing of ValueCo's existing net debt). As a result, pro forma net income of $1,387.8 million is the highest. However, given the need to issue 67.1 million shares (twice the amount in Scenario I), pro forma 2020E EPS is $6.70 versus $6.80 on a standalone basis. Hence, the transaction is dilutive by 1.5%, versus 8.6% accretive and 25.6% accretive in Scenarios I and II, respectively.

**EXHIBIT 7.26**    Scenario III: 100% Stock Consideration

*($ in millions, except per share data)*

**Accretion / (Dilution) Analysis - 100% Stock Consideration**

| | Pro forma 2019 | Projection Period | | | | |
|---|---|---|---|---|---|---|
| | | 1 2020 | 2 2021 | 3 2022 | 4 2023 | 5 2024 |
| BuyerCo EBIT | $1,317.4 | $1,409.6 | $1,494.2 | $1,568.9 | $1,631.6 | $1,680.6 |
| ValueCo EBIT | 518.0 | 556.9 | 590.3 | 619.8 | 644.6 | 663.9 |
| Synergies | 100.0 | 100.0 | 100.0 | 100.0 | 100.0 | 100.0 |
| **Pro Forma Combined EBIT (pre-transaction)** | **$1,935.4** | **$2,066.4** | **$2,184.4** | **$2,288.7** | **$2,376.2** | **$2,444.5** |
| Depreciation from Write-Up | 22.0 | 22.0 | 22.0 | 22.0 | 22.0 | 22.0 |
| Amortization from Write-Up | 14.7 | 14.7 | 14.7 | 14.7 | 14.7 | 14.7 |
| **Pro Forma Combined EBIT** | **$1,898.7** | **$2,029.8** | **$2,147.8** | **$2,252.0** | **$2,339.5** | **$2,407.8** |
| Standalone Net Interest Expense | 142.4 | 140.2 | 135.7 | 130.9 | 125.7 | 120.3 |
| Incremental Net Interest Expense | 66.3 | 39.1 | 10.5 | 7.8 | 4.9 | 1.8 |
| **Earnings Before Taxes** | **$1,690.0** | **$1,850.4** | **$2,001.6** | **$2,113.4** | **$2,209.0** | **$2,285.7** |
| Income Tax Expense @ 25% | 422.5 | 462.6 | 500.4 | 528.3 | 552.2 | 571.4 |
| **Pro Forma Combined Net Income** | **$1,267.5** | **$1,387.8** | **$1,501.2** | **$1,585.0** | **$1,656.7** | **$1,714.3** |
| | | | | | | |
| **BuyerCo Standalone Net Income** | **$881.2** | **$952.0** | **$1,018.9** | **$1,078.5** | **$1,129.4** | **$1,170.2** |
| | | | | | | |
| Standalone Fully Diluted Shares Outstanding | 140.0 | 140.0 | 140.0 | 140.0 | 140.0 | 140.0 |
| Net New Shares Issued in Transaction | 67.1 | 67.1 | 67.1 | 67.1 | 67.1 | 67.1 |
| **Pro Forma Fully Diluted Shares Outstanding** | **207.1** | **207.1** | **207.1** | **207.1** | **207.1** | **207.1** |
| | | | | | | |
| Pro Forma Combined Diluted EPS | $6.12 | $6.70 | $7.25 | $7.65 | $8.00 | $8.28 |
| BuyerCo Standalone Diluted EPS | 6.29 | 6.80 | 7.28 | 7.70 | 8.07 | 8.36 |
| | | | | | | |
| **Accretion / (Dilution) - $** | **($0.18)** | **($0.10)** | **($0.03)** | **($0.05)** | **($0.07)** | **($0.08)** |
| **Accretion / (Dilution) - %** | **(2.8%)** | **(1.5%)** | **(0.4%)** | **(0.7%)** | **(0.9%)** | **(1.0%)** |
| *Accretive / Dilutive* | *Dilutive* | *Dilutive* | *Dilutive* | *Dilutive* | *Dilutive* | *Dilutive* |
| | | | | | | |
| Included Pre-Tax Synergies | $100.0 | $100.0 | $100.0 | $100.0 | $100.0 | $100.0 |
| Additional Pre-Tax Synergies to Breakeven | 48.5 | 27.7 | 8.4 | 14.3 | 19.2 | 22.9 |
| **Required Synergies to Breakeven / (Cushion)** | **$148.5** | **$127.7** | **$108.4** | **$114.3** | **$119.2** | **$122.9** |

**Sensitivity Analysis** Given the prominence of accretion/(dilution) analysis in the ultimate M&A decision, it is critical to perform sensitivity analysis. The most commonly used inputs for this exercise are purchase price, financing consideration (% stock and % cash), and amount of synergies. The data tables in Exhibit 7.27 show three different EPS accretion/(dilution) sensitivity analysis output tables:

I. Projection year and premium paid from 25% to 45%, assuming fixed 50% stock/50% cash mix and annual synergies of $100 million. *Accretion decreases as offer price is increased.*

II. Consideration mix from 0% to 100% stock and premium paid from 25% to 45%, assuming annual synergies of $100 million. *Accretion increases in accordance with a higher proportion of debt financing and a lower offer price.*

III. Pre-tax synergies from $0 million to $200 million and premium paid from 25% to 45%, assuming fixed 50% stock / 50% cash mix. *Maximum accretive results are achieved by increasing synergies and decreasing offer price.*

**EXHIBIT 7.27** Accretion / (Dilution) Sensitivity Analysis

**Annual EPS Accretion / (Dilution) Sensitivity Analysis - Premium Paid**

| | | Year | | | | |
|---|---|---|---|---|---|---|
| **Offer Price** | **Premium** | **2020** | **2021** | **2022** | **2023** | **2024** |
| $54.38 | 25% | 8.8% | 11.1% | 13.8% | 14.6% | 14.7% |
| $56.55 | 30% | 7.5% | 9.8% | 12.7% | 13.6% | 13.6% |
| $58.73 | 35% | 6.3% | 8.6% | 11.5% | 12.6% | 12.6% |
| $60.90 | 40% | 5.0% | 7.4% | 10.4% | 11.6% | 11.6% |
| $63.08 | 45% | 3.8% | 6.2% | 9.3% | 10.6% | 10.6% |

**2020E EPS Accretion / (Dilution) Sensitivity Analysis - Premium Paid & Consideration Mix**

| | | % Stock Consideration Mix | | | | |
|---|---|---|---|---|---|---|
| **Offer Price** | **Premium** | **0%** | **25%** | **50%** | **75%** | **100%** |
| $54.38 | 25% | 27.4% | 18.5% | 11.1% | 6.7% | 1.3% |
| $56.55 | 30% | 26.5% | 17.3% | 9.8% | 5.3% | (0.1%) |
| $58.73 | 35% | 25.6% | 16.2% | 8.6% | 4.0% | (1.5%) |
| $60.90 | 40% | 24.6% | 15.1% | 7.4% | 2.7% | (2.8%) |
| $63.08 | 45% | 23.7% | 14.0% | 6.2% | 1.4% | (4.1%) |

**2020E EPS Accretion / (Dilution) Sensitivity Analysis - Premium Paid & Synergies**

| | | Estimated Synergies | | | | |
|---|---|---|---|---|---|---|
| **Offer Price** | **Premium** | **$0** | **$50** | **$100** | **$150** | **$200** |
| $54.38 | 25% | 4.6% | 7.8% | 11.1% | 14.4% | 17.7% |
| $56.55 | 30% | 3.3% | 6.6% | 9.8% | 13.1% | 16.4% |
| $58.73 | 35% | 2.1% | 5.4% | 8.6% | 11.8% | 15.1% |
| $60.90 | 40% | 1.0% | 4.2% | 7.4% | 10.6% | 13.8% |
| $63.08 | 45% | (0.2%) | 3.0% | 6.2% | 9.4% | 12.5% |

## ILLUSTRATIVE MERGER CONSEQUENCES ANALYSIS FOR THE BUYERCO / VALUECO TRANSACTION

The following pages display the full M&A model for BuyerCo's acquisition of ValueCo based on this chapter's discussion. Exhibit 7.28 lists these pages, which are shown in Exhibits 7.29 to 7.48.

**EXHIBIT 7.28**   M&A Model Pages

| M&A Model |
| --- |
| I.     Transaction Summary |
| II.    Pro Forma Combined Income Statement |
| III.   Pro Forma Combined Balance Sheet |
| IV.    Pro Forma Combined Cash Flow Statement |
| V.     Pro Forma Combined Debt Schedule |
| VI.    Capitalization and Credit Statistics |
| VII.   Accretion / (Dilution) Analysis |
| VIII.  Assumptions Page—Transaction Adjustments, Financing Structures, & Fees |

| BuyerCo Standalone Model |
| --- |
| IX.    BuyerCo Income Statement |
| X.     BuyerCo Balance Sheet |
| XI.    BuyerCo Cash Flow Statement |
| XII.   BuyerCo Debt Schedule |
| XIII.  BuyerCo Assumptions Page 1—Income Statement and Cash Flow Statement |
| XIV.   BuyerCo Assumptions Page 2—Balance Sheet |

| ValueCo Standalone Model |
| --- |
| XV.    ValueCo Income Statement |
| XVI.   ValueCo Balance Sheet |
| XVII.  ValueCo Cash Flow Statement |
| XVIII. ValueCo Debt Schedule |
| XIX.   ValueCo Assumptions Page 1—Income Statement and Cash Flow Statement |
| XX.    ValueCo Assumptions Page 2—Balance Sheet |

**EXHIBIT 7.29** Merger Consequences Analysis Transaction Summary Page

# BuyerCo Acquisition of ValueCo

## Merger Consequences Analysis
($ in millions, fiscal year ending December 31.)

**Financing Structure:**
**Operating Scenario:**

**Structure 1**
Base

## Transaction Summary

### Sources of Funds

| | Amount | % of Total Sources | Multiple of Pro Forma EBITDA 2019 | Cumulative | Pricing |
|---|---|---|---|---|---|
| Revolving Credit Facility | - | -% | -x | -x | L+250 bps |
| Term Loan A | - | -% | -x | -x | NA |
| Term Loan B | 2,250.0 | 35.2% | 1.0x | 1.0x | L+275 bps |
| Term Loan C | - | -% | -x | 1.0x | NA |
| 2nd Lien | - | -% | -x | 1.0x | NA |
| Senior Notes | 1,500.0 | 23.4% | 0.6x | 1.6x | 6.000% |
| Senior Subordinated Notes | - | -% | -x | 1.6x | NA |
| Issuance of Common Stock | 2,350.0 | 36.7% | 1.0x | 2.6x | |
| Cash on Hand | 300.0 | 4.7% | 0.1x | 2.8x | |
| Other | - | -% | -x | 2.6x | |
| **Total Sources** | **$6,400.0** | **100.0%** | **2.8x** | **2.8x** | |

### Uses of Funds

| | Amount | % of Total Uses | |
|---|---|---|---|
| Purchase ValueCo Equity | $4,700.0 | 73.4% | |
| Repay Existing Debt | 1,500.0 | 23.4% | |
| Tender / Call Premiums | 20.0 | 0.3% | |
| Transaction Fees | 60.0 | 0.9% | |
| Debt Financing Fees | 120.0 | 1.9% | |
| | | | |
| **Total Uses** | **$6,400.0** | **100.0%** | |

### Premium Paid & Exchange Ratio

| | | |
|---|---|---|
| ValueCo Current Share Price | $43.50 | |
| Offer Price per Share | $58.73 | |
| **Premium Paid** | **35%** | |
| BuyerCo Current Share Price | $70.00 | |
| **Exchange Ratio** | **0.8x** | |

### Acquisition Structure & Synergies

| | | |
|---|---|---|
| Stock Consideration for Equity | 50% | |
| Transaction Debt Raised | $3,750.0 | |
| % of ValueCo Enterprise Value | 63% | |
| Acquisition Type | Stock Sale | |
| | | |
| Year 1 Synergies | $100 | |

### Purchase Price

| | | |
|---|---|---|
| Offer Price per Share | $58.73 | Options |
| Fully Diluted Shares | 80.0 | |
| **Equity Purchase Price** | **$4,700.0** | |
| Plus: Existing Net Debt | 1,250.0 | |
| **Enterprise Value** | **$5,950.0** | |

### Financing Structure
### Operating Scenario

| | |
|---|---|
| Cash Flow Sweep | 1 |
| Cash Balance | 1 |
| Average Interest | 1 |
| Financing Fees | 1 |

## Pro Forma Combined Financial Summary

| | Pro Forma 2019 | 1 2020 | 2 2021 | 3 2022 | 4 2023 | 5 2024 |
|---|---|---|---|---|---|---|
| **Sales** | $10,205.8 | $10,937.5 | $11,593.7 | $12,173.4 | $12,660.3 | $13,040.1 |
| % growth | | 8.2% | 7.2% | 6.0% | 5.0% | 4.0% | 3.0% |
| **Gross Profit** | $3,947.2 | $4,230.4 | $4,484.2 | $4,708.4 | $4,896.8 | $5,043.7 |
| % margin | 38.7% | 38.7% | 38.7% | 38.7% | 38.7% | 38.7% |
| **EBITDA** | $2,311.3 | $2,469.7 | $2,611.9 | $2,737.5 | $2,843.0 | $2,925.3 |
| % margin | 22.6% | 22.6% | 22.5% | 22.5% | 22.5% | 22.4% |
| **Interest Expense** | 352.1 | 322.1 | 271.8 | 252.0 | 252.0 | 252.0 |
| **Net Income** | $1,161.0 | $1,281.9 | $1,408.8 | $1,505.6 | $1,577.0 | $1,634.3 |
| % margin | 11.4% | 11.7% | 12.2% | 12.4% | 12.5% | 12.5% |
| **Fully Diluted Shares** | 173.6 | 173.6 | 173.6 | 173.6 | 173.6 | 173.6 |
| **Diluted EPS** | $6.69 | $7.39 | $8.12 | $8.67 | $9.09 | $9.42 |
| | | | | | | |
| Cash Flow from Operating Activities | | 1,635.5 | 1,797.2 | 1,924.9 | 2,026.0 | 2,110.9 |
| Less: Capital Expenditures | | (383.8) | (406.8) | (427.1) | (444.2) | (457.5) |
| **Free Cash Flow** | | **$1,251.8** | **$1,390.4** | **$1,497.8** | **$1,581.8** | **$1,653.3** |
| | | | | | | |
| Senior Secured Debt | | 2,250.0 | 0.0 | 0.0 | 0.0 | 0.0 |
| Senior Debt | | 5,950.0 | 3,700.0 | 3,700.0 | 3,700.0 | 3,700.0 |
| Total Debt | | 5,950.0 | 3,700.0 | 3,700.0 | 3,700.0 | 3,700.0 |
| Cash & Equivalents | | 350.0 | 742.2 | 2,240.0 | 3,821.8 | 5,475.2 |

## Credit Statistics

| | BuyerCo 2019 | Pro Forma 2019 | Pro Forma 2019 | 1 2020 | 2 2021 | 3 2022 | 4 2023 | 5 2024 |
|---|---|---|---|---|---|---|---|---|
| EBITDA / Interest Expense | 10.3x | 8.9x | 6.6x | 7.7x | 9.6x | 10.9x | 11.3x | 11.6x |
| (EBITDA - Capex) / Interest Expense | | | 5.5x | 6.5x | 8.1x | 9.2x | 9.5x | 9.8x |
| | | | | | | | | |
| Senior Secured Debt / EBITDA | -x | | 1.0x | 0.4x | -x | -x | -x | -x |
| Senior Debt / EBITDA | 1.5x | | 2.6x | 1.9x | 1.4x | 1.3x | 1.3x | 1.3x |
| Total Debt / EBITDA | 1.5x | | 2.6x | 1.9x | 1.4x | 1.3x | 1.3x | 1.3x |
| Net Debt / EBITDA | 1.2x | | 2.4x | 1.8x | 1.1x | 0.5x | (0.0x) | (0.6x) |
| Debt / Total Capitalization | 47.0% | | 55.6% | 43.3% | 33.2% | 29.3% | 26.0% | 23.3% |

## Accretion / (Dilution) Analysis

| | | | 1 2020 | 2 2021 | 3 2022 | 4 2023 | 5 2024 |
|---|---|---|---|---|---|---|---|
| BuyerCo Standalone Diluted EPS | | | $6.80 | $7.28 | $7.70 | $8.07 | $8.36 |
| ValueCo Standalone Diluted EPS | | | $4.45 | $4.95 | $5.39 | $5.69 | $5.90 |
| | | | | | | | |
| Pro Forma Combined Diluted EPS | | | $7.39 | $8.12 | $8.67 | $9.09 | $9.42 |
| **Accretion / (Dilution) - $** | | | **$0.59** | **$0.84** | **$0.97** | **$1.02** | **$1.06** |
| **Accretion / (Dilution) - %** | | | **8.6%** | **11.5%** | **12.6%** | **12.6%** | **12.6%** |
| Accretive / Dilutive | | | Accretive | Accretive | Accretive | Accretive | Accretive |
| Breakeven Pre-Tax Synergies / (Cushion) | | | ($135) | ($194) | ($225) | ($236) | ($245) |

## Valuation Summary

| | Target | Acquirer |
|---|---|---|
| Company Name | ValueCo | BuyerCo |
| Ticker | VLCO | BUY |
| Current Share Price (12/20/2019) | $43.50 | $70.00 |
| Premium to Current Share Price | 35% | |
| Offer Price per Share | $58.73 | |
| Fully Diluted Shares | 80.0 | 140.0 |
| **Equity Value** | **$4,700.0** | **$9,800.0** |
| Plus: Total Debt | 1,500.0 | 2,200.0 |
| Plus: Preferred Equity | | |
| Plus: Noncontrolling Interest | | |
| Less: Cash and Equivalents | (250.0) | (400.0) |
| **Enterprise Value** | **$5,950.0** | **$11,600.0** |

### Transaction Multiples

| | Target | | Acquirer | |
|---|---|---|---|---|
| | Metric | Multiple | Metric | Multiple |
| Enterprise Value / LTM EBITDA | $700.0 | 8.5x | $1,443.1 | 8.0x |
| Enterprise Value / 2019E EBITDA | 725.0 | 8.2x | 1,486.3 | 7.8x |
| Enterprise Value / 2020E EBITDA | 779.4 | 7.6x | 1,590.3 | 7.3x |
| | | | | |
| Equity Value / 2019E Net Income | $320.0 | 14.7x | $881.2 | 11.1x |
| Equity Value / 2020E Net Income | 356.0 | 13.2x | 952.0 | 10.3x |

### Pro Forma Ownership

| | Shares | Ownership |
|---|---|---|
| Existing BuyerCo Shareholders | 140.0 | 80.7% |
| Former ValueCo Shareholders | 33.6 | 19.3% |
| **Pro Forma Fully Diluted Shares** | **173.6** | **100.0%** |

### Annual EPS Accretion / (Dilution) Sensitivity Analysis - Premium Paid

| Offer Price | Premium | 2020 | 2021 | Year 2022 | 2023 | 2024 |
|---|---|---|---|---|---|---|
| $54.38 | 25% | 8.8% | 11.1% | 13.8% | 14.6% | 14.7% |
| $56.55 | 30% | 7.5% | 9.8% | 12.7% | 13.6% | 13.6% |
| $58.73 | 35% | 6.3% | 8.6% | 11.5% | 12.6% | 12.6% |
| $60.90 | 40% | 5.0% | 7.4% | 10.4% | 11.6% | 11.6% |
| $63.08 | 45% | 3.8% | 6.2% | 9.3% | 10.6% | 10.6% |

### 2020E EPS Accretion / (Dilution) Sensitivity Analysis - Premium Paid & Consideration Mix

| Offer Price | Premium | % Stock Consideration Mix | | | | |
|---|---|---|---|---|---|---|
| | | 0% | 25% | 50% | 75% | 100% |
| $54.38 | 25% | 27.4% | 18.5% | 11.1% | 6.7% | 1.3% |
| $56.55 | 30% | 26.5% | 17.3% | 9.8% | 5.3% | (0.1%) |
| $58.73 | 35% | 25.6% | 16.2% | 8.6% | 4.0% | (1.5%) |
| $60.90 | 40% | 24.6% | 15.1% | 7.4% | 2.7% | (2.8%) |
| $63.08 | 45% | 23.7% | 14.0% | 6.2% | 1.4% | (4.1%) |

# EXHIBIT 7.30  Pro Forma Income Statement

*($ in millions, except per share data, fiscal year ending December 31)*

## Pro Forma Income Statement

| | Historical Period | | | | Pro Forma | Projection Period | | | | |
|---|---|---|---|---|---|---|---|---|---|---|
| | 2016 | 2017 | 2018 | LTM 9/30/2019 | 2019 | Year 1 2020 | Year 2 2021 | Year 3 2022 | Year 4 2023 | Year 5 2024 |
| BuyerCo Sales | $4,771.7 | $5,484.7 | $6,232.6 | $6,559.6 | $6,755.8 | $7,228.7 | $7,662.4 | $8,045.5 | $8,367.4 | $8,618.4 |
| ValueCo Sales | 2,600.0 | 2,900.0 | 3,200.0 | 3,385.0 | 3,450.0 | 3,708.8 | 3,931.3 | 4,127.8 | 4,293.0 | 4,421.7 |
| **Total Sales** | **$7,371.7** | **$8,384.7** | **$9,432.6** | **$9,944.6** | **$10,205.8** | **$10,937.5** | **$11,593.7** | **$12,173.4** | **$12,660.3** | **$13,040.1** |
| *% growth* | *NA* | *13.7%* | *12.5%* | *NA* | *8.2%* | *7.2%* | *6.0%* | *5.0%* | *4.0%* | *3.0%* |
| BuyerCo COGS | $3,053.9 | $3,455.4 | $3,864.2 | $4,067.0 | $4,188.6 | $4,481.8 | $4,750.7 | $4,988.2 | $5,187.8 | $5,343.4 |
| ValueCo COGS | 1,612.0 | 1,769.0 | 1,920.0 | 2,035.0 | 2,070.0 | 2,225.3 | 2,358.8 | 2,476.7 | 2,575.8 | 2,653.0 |
| **Total COGS** | **$4,665.9** | **$5,224.4** | **$5,784.2** | **$6,102.0** | **$6,258.6** | **$6,707.0** | **$7,109.5** | **$7,464.9** | **$7,763.5** | **$7,996.4** |
| *% sales* | *63.3%* | *62.3%* | *61.3%* | *61.4%* | *61.3%* | *61.3%* | *61.3%* | *61.3%* | *61.3%* | *61.3%* |
| BuyerCo Gross Profit | $1,717.8 | $2,029.3 | $2,368.4 | $2,492.6 | $2,567.2 | $2,746.9 | $2,911.7 | $3,057.3 | $3,179.6 | $3,275.0 |
| ValueCo Gross Profit | 988.0 | 1,131.0 | 1,280.0 | 1,350.0 | 1,380.0 | 1,483.5 | 1,572.5 | 1,651.1 | 1,717.2 | 1,768.7 |
| **Total Gross Profit** | **$2,705.8** | **$3,160.3** | **$3,648.4** | **$3,842.6** | **$3,947.2** | **$4,230.4** | **$4,484.2** | **$4,708.4** | **$4,896.8** | **$5,043.7** |
| *% margin* | *36.7%* | *37.7%* | *38.7%* | *38.6%* | *38.7%* | *38.7%* | *38.7%* | *38.7%* | *38.7%* | *38.7%* |
| BuyerCo SG&A | $811.2 | $905.0 | $997.2 | $1,049.5 | $1,080.9 | $1,156.6 | $1,226.0 | $1,287.3 | $1,338.8 | $1,378.9 |
| ValueCo SG&A | 496.6 | 551.0 | 608.0 | 650.0 | 655.0 | 704.1 | 746.4 | 783.7 | 815.0 | 839.5 |
| **Total SG&A** | **$1,307.8** | **$1,456.0** | **$1,605.2** | **$1,699.5** | **$1,735.9** | **$1,860.7** | **$1,972.4** | **$2,071.0** | **$2,153.8** | **$2,218.4** |
| *% sales* | *17.7%* | *17.4%* | *17.0%* | *17.1%* | *17.0%* | *17.0%* | *17.0%* | *17.0%* | *17.0%* | *17.0%* |
| BuyerCo EBITDA | $906.6 | $1,124.4 | $1,371.2 | $1,443.1 | $1,486.3 | $1,590.3 | $1,685.7 | $1,770.0 | $1,840.8 | $1,896.0 |
| ValueCo EBITDA | 491.4 | 580.0 | 672.0 | 700.0 | 725.0 | 779.4 | 826.1 | 867.4 | 902.1 | 929.2 |
| Synergies | | | | | 100.0 | 100.0 | 100.0 | 100.0 | 100.0 | 100.0 |
| **Total EBITDA** | **$1,398.0** | **$1,704.4** | **$2,043.2** | **$2,243.1** | **$2,311.3** | **$2,469.7** | **$2,611.9** | **$2,737.5** | **$2,843.0** | **$2,925.3** |
| *% margin* | *19.0%* | *20.3%* | *21.7%* | *22.6%* | *22.6%* | *22.6%* | *22.5%* | *22.5%* | *22.5%* | *22.4%* |
| BuyerCo Depreciation | | | | | 135.1 | 144.6 | 153.2 | 160.9 | 167.3 | 172.4 |
| BuyerCo Amortization | | | | | 33.8 | 36.1 | 38.3 | 40.2 | 41.8 | 43.1 |
| ValueCo Depreciation | | | | | 155.3 | 166.9 | 176.9 | 185.8 | 193.2 | 199.0 |
| ValueCo Amortization | | | | | 51.8 | 55.6 | 59.0 | 61.9 | 64.4 | 66.3 |
| Depreciation on Tangible Asset Write-up | | | | | 22.0 | 22.0 | 22.0 | 22.0 | 22.0 | 22.0 |
| Amortization on Intangible Asset Write-up | | | | | 14.7 | 14.7 | 14.7 | 14.7 | 14.7 | 14.7 |
| **EBIT** | | | | | **$1,898.7** | **$2,029.8** | **$2,147.8** | **$2,252.0** | **$2,339.5** | **$2,407.8** |
| *% margin* | | | | | *18.6%* | *18.6%* | *18.5%* | *18.5%* | *18.5%* | *18.5%* |
| **Interest Expense** | | | | | | | | | | |
| Revolving Credit Facility | | | | | | | | | | |
| New Term Loan B | | | | | 100.1 | 70.0 | 19.8 | | | |
| New Senior Notes | | | | | 143.0 | 143.0 | 143.0 | 143.0 | 143.0 | 143.0 |
| BuyerCo Senior Notes | | | | | 90.0 | 90.0 | 90.0 | 90.0 | 90.0 | 90.0 |
| Commitment Fee on Unused Revolver | | | | | 2.5 | 2.5 | 2.5 | 2.5 | 2.5 | 2.5 |
| Administrative Agent Fee | | | | | 0.2 | 0.2 | 0.2 | 0.2 | 0.2 | 0.2 |
| **Cash Interest Expense** | | | | | **$335.8** | **$305.7** | **$255.4** | **$235.7** | **$235.7** | **$235.7** |
| Amortization of Deferred Financing Fees | | | | | 16.4 | 16.4 | 16.4 | 16.4 | 16.4 | 16.4 |
| **Total Interest Expense** | | | | | **$352.1** | **$322.1** | **$271.8** | **$252.0** | **$252.0** | **$252.0** |
| Interest Income | | | | | (1.5) | (1.5) | (2.5) | (7.5) | (15.2) | (23.2) |
| **Net Interest Expense** | | | | | **$350.6** | **$320.6** | **$269.3** | **$244.6** | **$236.9** | **$228.8** |
| Earnings Before Taxes | | | | | $1,548.1 | $1,709.2 | $1,878.5 | $2,007.4 | $2,102.7 | $2,179.0 |
| Plus: Non-Tax Deductible Depreciation | | | | | 22.0 | 22.0 | 22.0 | 22.0 | 22.0 | 22.0 |
| Plus: Non-Tax Deductible Amortization | | | | | 14.7 | 14.7 | 14.7 | 14.7 | 14.7 | 14.7 |
| **Taxable Income** | | | | | **$1,584.7** | **$1,745.9** | **$1,915.1** | **$2,044.1** | **$2,139.3** | **$2,215.7** |
| Current Income Tax Expense | | | | | 396.2 | 436.5 | 478.8 | 511.0 | 534.8 | 553.9 |
| Deferred Tax Expense | | | | | (9.2) | (9.2) | (9.2) | (9.2) | (9.2) | (9.2) |
| **Net Income** | | | | | **$1,161.0** | **$1,281.9** | **$1,408.8** | **$1,505.6** | **$1,577.0** | **$1,634.3** |
| *% margin* | | | | | *11.4%* | *11.7%* | *12.2%* | *12.4%* | *12.5%* | *12.5%* |
| Diluted Shares Outstanding | | | | | 173.6 | 173.6 | 173.6 | 173.6 | 173.6 | 173.6 |
| **Diluted EPS** | | | | | **$6.69** | **$7.39** | **$8.12** | **$8.67** | **$9.09** | **$9.42** |
| *% growth* | | | | | | *10.4%* | *9.9%* | *6.9%* | *4.7%* | *3.6%* |
| BuyerCo Marginal Tax Rate | | | | | 25.0% | 25.0% | 25.0% | 25.0% | 25.0% | 25.0% |
| Effective Tax Rate | | | | | 25.6% | 25.5% | 25.5% | 25.5% | 25.4% | 25.4% |

# EXHIBIT 7.31  Pro Forma Balance Statement

($ in millions, fiscal year ending December 31)

**Pro Forma Balance Sheet**

| | Standalone | | Adjustments | | Pro Forma | Projection Period | | | | | |
|---|---|---|---|---|---|---|---|---|---|---|---|
| | BuyerCo 2019 | ValueCo 2019 | + | − | 2019 | Year 1 2020 | Year 2 2021 | Year 3 2022 | Year 4 2023 | Year 5 2024 |
| Cash and Cash Equivalents | $400.0 | $250.0 | | (300.0) | $350.0 | $250.0 | $742.2 | $2,240.0 | $3,821.8 | $5,475.2 |
| Accounts Receivable | 1,000.0 | 450.0 | | | 1,450.0 | 1,553.8 | 1,647.0 | 1,729.3 | 1,798.5 | 1,852.5 |
| Inventories | 1,225.0 | 600.0 | | | 1,825.0 | 1,955.8 | 2,073.1 | 2,176.7 | 2,263.8 | 2,331.7 |
| Prepaids and Other Current Assets | 525.0 | 175.0 | | | 700.0 | 749.9 | 794.9 | 834.6 | 868.0 | 894.0 |
| **Total Current Assets** | **$3,150.0** | **$1,475.0** | | | **$4,325.0** | **$4,509.4** | **$5,257.1** | **$6,980.7** | **$8,752.1** | **$10,553.4** |
| Property, Plant and Equipment, net | 2,500.0 | 2,500.0 | 330.0 | | 5,330.0 | 5,380.3 | 5,434.9 | 5,493.4 | 5,555.0 | 5,619.2 |
| Goodwill | 575.0 | 1,000.0 | 1,787.5 | (1,000.0) | 2,362.5 | 2,362.5 | 2,362.5 | 2,362.5 | 2,362.5 | 2,362.5 |
| Intangible Assets | 825.0 | 875.0 | 220.0 | | 1,920.0 | 1,813.6 | 1,701.6 | 1,584.8 | 1,463.9 | 1,339.8 |
| Other Assets | 450.0 | 150.0 | | | 600.0 | 600.0 | 600.0 | 600.0 | 600.0 | 600.0 |
| Deferred Financing Fees | – | – | 120.0 | | 120.0 | 103.6 | 87.3 | 70.9 | 54.5 | 38.1 |
| **Total Assets** | **$7,500.0** | **$6,000.0** | | | **$14,657.5** | **$14,769.3** | **$15,443.4** | **$17,092.2** | **$18,788.1** | **$20,513.1** |
| Accounts Payable | 925.0 | 215.0 | | | 1,140.0 | 1,220.9 | 1,294.1 | 1,358.8 | 1,413.2 | 1,455.6 |
| Accrued Liabilities | 945.0 | 275.0 | | | 1,220.0 | 1,306.8 | 1,385.2 | 1,454.4 | 1,512.6 | 1,558.0 |
| Other Current Liabilities | 225.0 | 100.0 | | | 325.0 | 348.3 | 369.1 | 387.6 | 403.1 | 415.2 |
| **Total Current Liabilities** | **$2,095.0** | **$590.0** | | | **$2,685.0** | **$2,875.9** | **$3,048.5** | **$3,200.9** | **$3,328.9** | **$3,428.8** |
| Revolving Credit Facility | – | – | | | – | – | – | – | – | – |
| ValueCo Term Loan | – | 1,000.0 | | (1,000.0) | – | – | – | – | – | – |
| New Term Loan B | – | – | 2,250.0 | | 2,250.0 | 898.2 | – | – | – | – |
| ValueCo Senior Notes | – | 500.0 | | (500.0) | – | – | – | – | – | – |
| BuyerCo Senior Notes | 2,200.0 | – | | | 2,200.0 | 2,200.0 | 2,200.0 | 2,200.0 | 2,200.0 | 2,200.0 |
| New Senior Notes | – | – | 1,500.0 | | 1,500.0 | 1,500.0 | 1,500.0 | 1,500.0 | 1,500.0 | 1,500.0 |
| Deferred Income Taxes | 100.0 | 300.0 | 137.5 | | 537.5 | 528.3 | 519.2 | 510.0 | 500.8 | 491.7 |
| Other Long-Term Liabilities | 625.0 | 110.0 | | | 735.0 | 735.0 | 735.0 | 735.0 | 735.0 | 735.0 |
| **Total Liabilities** | **$5,020.0** | **$2,500.0** | | | **$9,907.5** | **$8,737.4** | **$8,002.6** | **$8,145.9** | **$8,264.7** | **$8,355.4** |
| Noncontrolling Interest | – | – | | | | | | | | |
| Shareholders' Equity | 2,480.0 | 3,500.0 | 2,270.0 | (3,500.0) | 4,750.0 | 6,031.9 | 7,440.8 | 8,946.3 | 10,523.3 | 12,157.6 |
| **Total Shareholders' Equity** | **$2,480.0** | **$3,500.0** | | | **$4,750.0** | **$6,031.9** | **$7,440.8** | **$8,946.3** | **$10,523.3** | **$12,157.6** |
| **Total Liabilities and Equity** | **$7,500.0** | **$6,000.0** | | | **$14,657.5** | **$14,769.3** | **$15,443.4** | **$17,092.2** | **$18,788.1** | **$20,513.1** |
| Balance Check | 0.000 | 0.000 | | | 0.000 | 0.000 | 0.000 | 0.000 | 0.000 | 0.000 |
| Net Working Capital | 655.0 | 635.0 | | | 1,290.0 | 1,383.5 | 1,466.5 | 1,539.8 | 1,601.4 | 1,649.4 |
| (Increase) / Decrease in Net Working Capital | | | | | | (93.5) | (83.0) | (73.3) | (61.6) | (48.0) |

**Balance Sheet Ratios**

*Current Assets*

| | BuyerCo 2019 | ValueCo 2019 | | | Pro Forma 2019 | Year 1 2020 | Year 2 2021 | Year 3 2022 | Year 4 2023 | Year 5 2024 |
|---|---|---|---|---|---|---|---|---|---|---|
| Days Sales Outstanding (DSO) | 54.0 | 47.6 | | | 51.9 | 51.9 | 51.9 | 51.9 | 51.9 | 51.9 |
| Days Inventory Held (DIH) | 106.7 | 105.8 | | | 106.4 | 106.4 | 106.4 | 106.4 | 106.4 | 106.4 |
| Prepaid and Other Current Assets (% of sales) | 7.8% | 5.1% | | | 6.9% | 6.9% | 6.9% | 6.9% | 6.9% | 6.9% |

*Current Liabilities*

| | BuyerCo 2019 | ValueCo 2019 | | | Pro Forma 2019 | Year 1 2020 | Year 2 2021 | Year 3 2022 | Year 4 2023 | Year 5 2024 |
|---|---|---|---|---|---|---|---|---|---|---|
| Days Payable Outstanding (DPO) | 80.6 | 37.9 | | | 66.5 | 66.4 | 66.4 | 66.4 | 66.4 | 66.4 |
| Accrued Liabilities (% of sales) | 14.0% | 8.0% | | | 12.0% | 11.9% | 11.9% | 11.9% | 11.9% | 11.9% |
| Other Current Liabilities (% of sales) | 3.3% | 4.8% | | | 3.2% | 3.2% | 3.2% | 3.2% | 3.2% | 3.2% |

**EXHIBIT 7.32** Pro Forma Cash Flow Statement

*($ in millions, fiscal year ending December 31)*

**Pro Forma Cash Flow Statement**

| | | | Projection Period | | | |
|---|---|---|---|---|---|---|
| | **Year 1** 2020 | **Year 2** 2021 | **Year 3** 2022 | **Year 4** 2023 | **Year 5** 2024 | |
| **Operating Activities** | | | | | | |
| Net Income | $1,281.9 | $1,408.8 | $1,505.6 | $1,577.0 | $1,634.3 | |
| Plus: Depreciation | 311.5 | 330.2 | 346.7 | 360.5 | 371.3 | |
| Plus: Amortization | 91.8 | 97.3 | 102.1 | 106.2 | 109.4 | |
| Plus: Depreciation on Tangible Assets Write-up | 22.0 | 22.0 | 22.0 | 22.0 | 22.0 | |
| Plus: Amortization on Intangible Assets Write-up | 14.7 | 14.7 | 14.7 | 14.7 | 14.7 | |
| Plus: Amortization of Financing Fees | 16.4 | 16.4 | 16.4 | 16.4 | 16.4 | |
| **Changes in Working Capital Items** | | | | | | |
| (Inc.) / Dec. in Accounts Receivable | (103.8) | (93.2) | (82.3) | (69.2) | (54.0) | |
| (Inc.) / Dec. in Inventories | (130.8) | (117.3) | (103.7) | (87.1) | (67.9) | |
| (Inc.) / Dec. in Prepaid and Other Current Assets | (49.9) | (45.0) | (39.7) | (33.4) | (26.0) | |
| Inc. / (Dec.) in Accounts Payable | 80.9 | 73.3 | 64.7 | 54.4 | 42.4 | |
| Inc. / (Dec.) in Accrued Liabilities | 86.8 | 78.4 | 69.3 | 58.2 | 45.4 | |
| Inc. / (Dec.) in Other Current Liabilities | 23.3 | 20.9 | 18.5 | 15.5 | 12.1 | |
| (Inc.) / Dec. in Net Working Capital | (93.5) | (83.0) | (73.3) | (61.6) | (48.0) | |
| Inc. / (Dec.) in Deferred Taxes | (9.2) | (9.2) | (9.2) | (9.2) | (9.2) | |
| **Cash Flow from Operating Activities** | **$1,635.5** | **$1,797.2** | **$1,924.9** | **$2,026.0** | **$2,110.9** | |
| **Investing Activities** | | | | | | |
| Capital Expenditures | (383.8) | (406.8) | (427.1) | (444.2) | (457.5) | |
| Other Investing Activities | – | – | – | – | – | |
| **Cash Flow from Investing Activities** | **($383.8)** | **($406.8)** | **($427.1)** | **($444.2)** | **($457.5)** | |
| **Financing Activities** | | | | | | |
| Revolving Credit Facility | – | – | – | – | – | |
| New Term Loan B Facility | (1,351.8) | (898.2) | – | – | – | |
| BuyerCo Senior Notes | – | – | – | – | – | |
| New Senior Notes | – | – | – | – | – | |
| Equity Issuance / (Repurchase) | – | – | – | – | – | |
| **Cash Flow from Financing Activities** | **($1,351.8)** | **($898.2)** | **–** | **–** | **–** | |
| Excess Cash for the Period | ($100.0) | $492.2 | $1,497.8 | $1,581.8 | $1,653.3 | |
| Beginning Cash Balance | 350.0 | 250.0 | 742.2 | 2,240.0 | 3,821.8 | |
| **Ending Cash Balance** | **$250.0** | **$742.2** | **$2,240.0** | **$3,821.8** | **$5,475.2** | |
| Capital Expenditures (% of sales) | 3.5% | 3.5% | 3.5% | 3.5% | 3.5% | |

377

**EXHIBIT 7.33**    Pro Forma Debt Schedule

*($ in millions, fiscal year ending December 31)*

## Pro Forma Debt Schedule

| | Pro forma 2019 | Year 1 2020 | Year 2 2021 | Year 3 2022 | Year 4 2023 | Year 5 2024 |
|---|---|---|---|---|---|---|
| | | | | *Projection Period* | | |
| Forward LIBOR Curve | *1.85%* | *1.70%* | *1.65%* | *1.55%* | *1.55%* | *1.55%* |
| | | | | | | |
| Cash Flow from Operating Activities | | $1,635.5 | $1,797.2 | $1,924.9 | $2,026.0 | $2,110.9 |
| Cash Flow from Investing Activities | | (383.8) | (406.8) | (427.1) | (444.2) | (457.5) |
| **Cash Available for Debt Repayment** | | **$1,251.8** | **$1,390.4** | **$1,497.8** | **$1,581.8** | **$1,653.3** |
| Total Mandatory Repayments | MinCash | (22.5) | (22.5) | - | - | - |
| Cash From Balance Sheet | 250.0 | 100.0 | 0.0 | 492.2 | 1,990.0 | 3,571.8 |
| **Cash Available for Optional Debt Repayment** | | **$1,329.3** | **$1,367.9** | **$1,990.0** | **$3,571.8** | **$5,225.2** |

### Revolving Credit Facility

| | | | | | | |
|---|---|---|---|---|---|---|
| Revolving Credit Facility Size | $500.0 | | | | | |
| Spread | 2.500% | | | | | |
| LIBOR Floor | - % | | | | | |
| Term | 6 years | | | | | |
| Commitment Fee on Unused Portion | 0.50% | | | | | |
| | | | | | | |
| Beginning Balance | | - | - | - | - | - |
| Drawdown/(Repayment) | | - | - | - | - | - |
| **Ending Balance** | | **-** | **-** | **-** | **-** | **-** |
| | | | | | | |
| Interest Rate | | 4.20% | 4.15% | 4.05% | 4.05% | 4.05% |
| Interest Expense | | - | - | - | - | - |
| Commitment Fee | | 2.5 | 2.5 | 2.5 | 2.5 | 2.5 |
| Administrative Agent Fee | | 0.2 | 0.2 | 0.2 | 0.2 | 0.2 |

### New Term Loan B Facility

| | | | | | | |
|---|---|---|---|---|---|---|
| Size | $2,250.0 | | | | | |
| Spread | 2.750% | | | | | |
| LIBOR Floor | - % | | | | | |
| Term | 7 years | | | | | |
| Repayment Schedule | 1.0% | Per Annum, Bullet at Maturity | | | | |
| | | | | | | |
| Beginning Balance | | $2,250.0 | $898.2 | - | - | - |
| Mandatory Repayments | | (22.5) | (22.5) | - | - | - |
| Optional Repayments | | (1,329.3) | (875.7) | - | - | - |
| **Ending Balance** | | **$898.2** | **-** | **-** | **-** | **-** |
| | | | | | | |
| Interest Rate | | 4.45% | 4.40% | 4.30% | 4.30% | 4.30% |
| Interest Expense | | 70.0 | 19.8 | - | - | - |

### BuyerCo Existing Senior Notes

| | | | | | | |
|---|---|---|---|---|---|---|
| Size | $2,200.0 | | | | | |
| Coupon | 6.500% | | | | | |
| Term | 8 years | | | | | |
| | | | | | | |
| Beginning Balance | | $2,200.0 | $2,200.0 | $2,200.0 | $2,200.0 | $2,200.0 |
| Repayment | | - | - | - | - | - |
| **Ending Balance** | | **$2,200.0** | **$2,200.0** | **$2,200.0** | **$2,200.0** | **$2,200.0** |
| | | | | | | |
| Interest Expense | | 143.0 | 143.0 | 143.0 | 143.0 | 143.0 |

### New Senior Notes

| | | | | | | |
|---|---|---|---|---|---|---|
| Size | $1,500.0 | | | | | |
| Coupon | 6.000% | | | | | |
| Term | 8 years | | | | | |
| | | | | | | |
| Beginning Balance | | $1,500.0 | $1,500.0 | $1,500.0 | $1,500.0 | $1,500.0 |
| Repayment | | - | - | - | - | - |
| **Ending Balance** | | **$1,500.0** | **$1,500.0** | **$1,500.0** | **$1,500.0** | **$1,500.0** |
| | | | | | | |
| Interest Expense | | 90.0 | 90.0 | 90.0 | 90.0 | 90.0 |

**EXHIBIT 7.34**  Pro Forma Capitalization and Credit Statistics

*($ in millions, fiscal year ending December 31)*

### Capitalization

| | BuyerCo 2019 | ValueCo 2019 | Adjustments + | Adjustments - | Pro forma 2019 | 1 2020 | 2 2021 | 3 2022 | 4 2023 | 5 2024 |
|---|---|---|---|---|---|---|---|---|---|---|
| | | | | | | | | Projection Period | | |
| Cash | $400.0 | $250.0 | | (300.0) | $350.0 | $250.0 | $742.2 | $2,240.0 | $3,821.8 | $5,475.2 |
| Revolving Credit Facility | - | - | | | - | - | - | - | - | - |
| ValueCo Term Loan | | 1,000.0 | | (1,000.0) | - | - | - | - | - | - |
| New Term Loan B | - | - | 2,250.0 | | 2,250.0 | 898.2 | - | - | - | - |
| Other Debt | - | - | | | - | - | - | - | - | - |
| **Total Senior Secured Debt** | - | **$1,000.0** | | | **$2,250.0** | **$898.2** | - | - | - | - |
| BuyerCo Senior Notes | 2,200.0 | | | | 2,200.0 | 2,200.0 | 2,200.0 | 2,200.0 | 2,200.0 | 2,200.0 |
| ValueCo Senior Notes | | 500.0 | | (500.0) | - | - | - | - | - | - |
| New Senior Notes | - | - | 1,500.0 | | 1,500.0 | 1,500.0 | 1,500.0 | 1,500.0 | 1,500.0 | 1,500.0 |
| **Total Senior Debt** | **$2,200.0** | **$1,500.0** | | | **$5,950.0** | **$4,598.2** | **$3,700.0** | **$3,700.0** | **$3,700.0** | **$3,700.0** |
| Senior Subordinated Notes | - | - | | | - | - | - | - | - | - |
| **Total Debt** | **$2,200.0** | **$1,500.0** | | | **$5,950.0** | **$4,598.2** | **$3,700.0** | **$3,700.0** | **$3,700.0** | **$3,700.0** |
| Shareholders' Equity | 2,480.0 | 3,500.0 | 2,270.0 | (3,500.0) | 4,750.0 | 6,031.9 | 7,440.8 | 8,946.3 | 10,523.3 | 12,157.6 |
| **Total Capitalization** | **$4,680.0** | **$5,000.0** | | | **$10,700.0** | **$10,630.1** | **$11,140.8** | **$12,646.3** | **$14,223.3** | **$15,857.6** |
| % of Bank Debt Repaid | | | | | - | 60.1% | 100.0% | 100.0% | 100.0% | 100.0% |

### Credit Statistics

| | BuyerCo 2019 | ValueCo 2019 | Adjustments + | Adjustments - | Pro forma 2019 | 1 2020 | 2 2021 | 3 2022 | 4 2023 | 5 2024 |
|---|---|---|---|---|---|---|---|---|---|---|
| EBITDA | $1,486.3 | $725.0 | 100.0 | | $2,311.3 | $2,469.7 | $2,611.9 | $2,737.5 | $2,843.0 | $2,925.3 |
| Capital Expenditures | 202.7 | 155.3 | | | 357.9 | 383.8 | 406.8 | 427.1 | 444.2 | 457.5 |
| Interest Expense | 144.4 | 87.9 | 119.8 | | 352.1 | 322.1 | 271.8 | 252.0 | 252.0 | 252.0 |
| | | | | | | | | | | |
| EBITDA / Interest Expense | 10.3x | 8.2x | | | 6.6x | 7.7x | 9.6x | 10.9x | 11.3x | 11.6x |
| (EBITDA - Capex) / Interest Expense | 8.9x | 6.5x | | | 5.5x | 6.5x | 8.1x | 9.2x | 9.5x | 9.8x |
| | | | | | | | | | | |
| Senior Secured Debt / EBITDA | -x | 1.4x | | | 1.0x | 0.4x | -x | -x | -x | -x |
| Senior Debt / EBITDA | 1.5x | 2.1x | | | 2.6x | 1.9x | 1.4x | 1.4x | 1.3x | 1.3x |
| Total Debt / EBITDA | 1.5x | 2.1x | | | 2.6x | 1.9x | 1.4x | 1.4x | 1.3x | 1.3x |
| Net Debt / EBITDA | 1.2x | 1.7x | | | 2.4x | 1.8x | 1.1x | 0.5x | (0.0x) | (0.6x) |
| % Debt / Total Capitalization | 47.0% | 30.0% | | | 55.6% | 43.3% | 33.2% | 29.3% | 26.0% | 23.3% |

### Debt / EBITDA

| | | % Stock Consideration Mix | | | |
|---|---|---|---|---|---|
| Premium Paid | 0% | 25% | 50% | 75% | 100% |
| 25% | 3.5x | 3.0x | 2.5x | 2.0x | 1.5x |
| 30% | 3.5x | 3.0x | 2.5x | 2.0x | 1.5x |
| 35% | 3.6x | 3.1x | 2.6x | 2.0x | 1.5x |
| 40% | 3.7x | 3.2x | 2.6x | 2.1x | 1.5x |
| 45% | 3.8x | 3.2x | 2.7x | 2.1x | 1.5x |

### EBITDA / Interest Expense

| | | % Stock Consideration Mix | | | |
|---|---|---|---|---|---|
| Premium Paid | 0% | 25% | 50% | 75% | 100% |
| 25% | 5.2x | 5.8x | 6.7x | 8.8x | 11.0x |
| 30% | 5.1x | 5.7x | 6.6x | 8.7x | 11.0x |
| 35% | 5.0x | 5.7x | 6.6x | 8.6x | 11.0x |
| 40% | 4.9x | 5.6x | 6.5x | 8.6x | 11.0x |
| 45% | 4.8x | 5.5x | 6.4x | 8.5x | 11.0x |

# EXHIBIT 7.35   Accretion / (Dilution) Analysis

*($ in millions, except per share data)*

**Accretion / (Dilution) Analysis - 50% Stock / 50% Cash**

| | Pro forma 2019 | Projection Period 1 2020 | 2 2021 | 3 2022 | 4 2023 | 5 2024 |
|---|---|---|---|---|---|---|
| BuyerCo EBIT | $1,317.4 | $1,409.6 | $1,494.2 | $1,568.9 | $1,631.6 | $1,680.6 |
| ValueCo EBIT | 518.0 | 556.9 | 590.3 | 619.8 | 644.6 | 663.9 |
| Synergies | 100.0 | 100.0 | 100.0 | 100.0 | 100.0 | 100.0 |
| **Pro Forma Combined EBIT (pre-deal structure)** | **$1,935.4** | **$2,066.4** | **$2,184.4** | **$2,288.7** | **$2,376.2** | **$2,444.5** |
| Depreciation from Write-Up | 22.0 | 22.0 | 22.0 | 22.0 | 22.0 | 22.0 |
| Amortization from Write-Up | 14.7 | 14.7 | 14.7 | 14.7 | 14.7 | 14.7 |
| **Pro Forma Combined EBIT** | **$1,898.7** | **$2,029.8** | **$2,147.8** | **$2,252.0** | **$2,339.5** | **$2,407.8** |
| Standalone Net Interest Expense | 142.4 | 140.2 | 135.7 | 130.9 | 125.7 | 120.3 |
| Incremental Net Interest Expense | 208.2 | 180.3 | 133.6 | 113.7 | 111.2 | 108.5 |
| **Earnings Before Taxes** | **$1,548.1** | **$1,709.2** | **$1,878.5** | **$2,007.4** | **$2,102.7** | **$2,179.0** |
| Income Tax Expense @ 25% | 387.0 | 427.3 | 469.6 | 501.9 | 525.7 | 544.8 |
| **Pro Forma Combined Net Income** | **$1,161.0** | **$1,281.9** | **$1,408.8** | **$1,505.6** | **$1,577.0** | **$1,634.3** |
| | | | | | | |
| **BuyerCo Standalone Net Income** | **$881.2** | **$952.0** | **$1,018.9** | **$1,078.5** | **$1,129.4** | **$1,170.2** |
| | | | | | | |
| Standalone Fully Diluted Shares Outstanding | 140.0 | 140.0 | 140.0 | 140.0 | 140.0 | 140.0 |
| Net New Shares Issued in Transaction | 33.6 | 33.6 | 33.6 | 33.6 | 33.6 | 33.6 |
| **Pro Forma Fully Diluted Shares Outstanding** | **173.6** | **173.6** | **173.6** | **173.6** | **173.6** | **173.6** |
| | | | | | | |
| **Pro Forma Combined Diluted EPS** | **$6.69** | **$7.39** | **$8.12** | **$8.67** | **$9.09** | **$9.42** |
| **BuyerCo Standalone Diluted EPS** | **6.29** | **6.80** | **7.28** | **7.70** | **8.07** | **8.36** |
| | | | | | | |
| **Accretion / (Dilution) - $** | **$0.39** | **$0.59** | **$0.84** | **$0.97** | **$1.02** | **$1.06** |
| **Accretion / (Dilution) - %** | **6.3%** | **8.6%** | **11.5%** | **12.6%** | **12.6%** | **12.6%** |
| *Accretive / (Dilutive)* | *Accretive* | *Accretive* | *Accretive* | *Accretive* | *Accretive* | *Accretive* |
| | | | | | | |
| Included Pre-Tax Synergies | $100.0 | $100.0 | $100.0 | $100.0 | $100.0 | $100.0 |
| Additional Pre-Tax Synergies to Breakeven | (91.3) | (135.4) | (194.2) | (224.6) | (235.6) | (244.6) |
| **Required Synergies to Breakeven / (Cushion)** | **$8.7** | **($35.4)** | **($94.2)** | **($124.6)** | **($135.6)** | **($144.6)** |

**Annual EPS Accretion / (Dilution) Sensitivity Analysis - Premium Paid**

| Offer Price | Premium | Year 2020 | 2021 | 2022 | 2023 | 2024 |
|---|---|---|---|---|---|---|
| $54.38 | **25%** | 8.8% | 11.1% | 13.8% | 14.6% | 14.7% |
| $56.55 | **30%** | 7.5% | 9.8% | 12.7% | 13.6% | 13.6% |
| $58.73 | **35%** | 6.3% | 8.6% | 11.5% | 12.6% | 12.6% |
| $60.90 | **40%** | 5.0% | 7.4% | 10.4% | 11.6% | 11.6% |
| $63.08 | **45%** | 3.8% | 6.2% | 9.3% | 10.6% | 10.6% |

**Breakeven Synergies Sensitivity Analysis**

| Offer Price | Premium | Estimated Synergies $0 | $50 | $100 | $150 | $200 |
|---|---|---|---|---|---|---|
| $54.38 | **25%** | 4.6% | 7.8% | 11.1% | 14.4% | 17.7% |
| $56.55 | **30%** | 3.3% | 6.6% | 9.8% | 13.1% | 16.4% |
| $58.73 | **35%** | 2.1% | 5.4% | 8.6% | 11.8% | 15.1% |
| $60.90 | **40%** | 1.0% | 4.2% | 7.4% | 10.6% | 13.8% |
| $63.08 | **45%** | (0.2%) | 3.0% | 6.2% | 9.4% | 12.5% |

**2012E EPS Accretion / (Dilution) Sensitivity Analysis - Premium Paid & Consideration Mix**

| Offer Price | Premium | % Stock Consideration Mix 0% | 25% | 50% | 75% | 100% |
|---|---|---|---|---|---|---|
| $54.38 | **25%** | 27.4% | 18.5% | 11.1% | 6.7% | 1.3% |
| $56.55 | **30%** | 26.5% | 17.3% | 9.8% | 5.3% | (0.1%) |
| $58.73 | **35%** | 25.6% | 16.2% | 8.6% | 4.0% | (1.5%) |
| $60.90 | **40%** | 24.6% | 15.1% | 7.4% | 2.7% | (2.8%) |
| $63.08 | **45%** | 23.7% | 14.0% | 6.2% | 1.4% | (4.1%) |

**Breakeven Synergies Sensitivity Analysis**

| Offer Price | Premium | Pre-Tax Synergies Required to Breakeven 2020 | 2021 | 2022 | 2023 | 2024 |
|---|---|---|---|---|---|---|
| $54.38 | **25%** | ($26) | ($72) | ($129) | ($157) | ($170) |
| $56.55 | **30%** | ($9) | ($54) | ($112) | ($141) | ($153) |
| $58.73 | **35%** | $9 | ($35) | ($94) | ($125) | ($136) |
| $60.90 | **40%** | $26 | ($17) | ($77) | ($108) | ($119) |
| $63.08 | **45%** | $44 | $1 | ($59) | ($92) | ($102) |

# EXHIBIT 7.36   Assumptions Page

*($ in millions, fiscal year ending December 31)*

**Assumptions Page - Transaction Adjustments, Financing Structures, and Fees**

## Financing Structures

|  | 1 | 2 | 3 | 4 | 5 |
|---|---|---|---|---|---|
|  | Structure 1 | Structure 2 | Structure 3 | Structure 4 | Status Quo |
| **Sources of Funds** |  |  |  |  |  |
| Revolving Credit Facility Size | $500.0 | $500.0 | $500.0 | $500.0 | $500.0 |
| Revolving Credit Facility Draw | - | - | - | - | - |
| Term Loan A | 2,250.0 | 1,225.0 | 500.0 | - | - |
| Term Loan B | - | - | 900.0 | - | - |
| Term Loan C | - | - | - | - | - |
| 2nd Lien | - | - | - | - | - |
| Senior Notes | 1,500.0 | 2,825.0 | 2,000.0 | 4,050.0 | - |
| Senior Subordinated Notes | 2,350.0 | 2,350.0 | 2,350.0 | 2,350.0 | - |
| Issuance of Common Stock | 300.0 | - | 650.0 | - | - |
| Cash on Hand | - | - | - | - | - |
| Other | - | - | - | - | - |
| **Total Sources of Funds** | $6,400.0 | $6,400.0 | $6,400.0 | $6,400.0 | - |
| **Uses of Funds** |  |  |  |  |  |
| Equity Purchase Price | $4,700.0 | $4,700.0 | $4,700.0 | $4,700.0 | - |
| Repay Existing Bank Debt | 1,500.0 | 1,500.0 | 1,500.0 | 1,500.0 | - |
| Tender / Call Premiums | 20.0 | 20.0 | 20.0 | 20.0 | - |
| Debt Financing Fees | 120.0 | 120.0 | 120.0 | 120.0 | - |
| Transaction and Other Fees | 60.0 | 60.0 | 60.0 | 60.0 | - |
| **Total Uses of Funds** | $6,400.0 | $6,400.0 | $6,400.0 | $6,400.0 | - |

## Financing Fees

|  | Structure 1 | Size ($) | Fees (%) | Fees ($) |
|---|---|---|---|---|
| Revolving Credit Facility Size |  | $500.0 | 2.250% | $11.3 |
| Term Loan A |  | 2,250.0 | 2.250% | 50.6 |
| Term Loan B |  | - | - | - |
| Term Loan C |  | - | - | - |
| 2nd Lien |  | - | - | - |
| Senior Notes |  | 1,500.0 | 2.250% | 33.8 |
| Senior Bridge Facility |  | - | - | - |
| Senior Subordinated Notes |  | 1,500.0 | 1.250% | 18.8 |
| Senior Subordinated Bridge Facility |  | - | - | - |
| Other Financing Fees & Expenses |  |  |  | 5.6 |
| **Total Financing Fees** |  |  |  | $120.0 |

## Amortization of Financing Fees

|  | Term | Year 1 2020 | Year 2 2021 | Year 3 2022 | Year 4 2023 | Year 5 2024 |
|---|---|---|---|---|---|---|
| Revolving Credit Facility Size | 6 | $1.9 | $1.9 | $1.9 | $1.9 | $1.9 |
| Term Loan A | 7 | 7.2 | 7.2 | 7.2 | 7.2 | 7.2 |
| Term Loan B | - | - | - | - | - | - |
| Term Loan C | - | - | - | - | - | - |
| 2nd Lien | - | - | - | - | - | - |
| Senior Notes | 8 | 4.2 | 4.2 | 4.2 | 4.2 | 4.2 |
| Senior Subordinated Notes | 8 | 2.3 | 2.3 | 2.3 | 2.3 | 2.3 |
| Senior Bridge Facility | - | - | - | - | - | - |
| Senior Subordinated Bridge Facility | - | - | - | - | - | - |
| Other Financing Fees & Expenses | 8 | 0.7 | 0.7 | 0.7 | 0.7 | 0.7 |
| **Annual Amortization** |  | $16.4 | $16.4 | $16.4 | $16.4 | $16.4 |

## Synergies

|  | Year 1 2020 | Year 2 2021 | Year 3 2022 | Year 4 2023 | Year 5 2024 |
|---|---|---|---|---|---|
| Revenue | - | - | - | - | - |
| Cost Savings | 100.0 | 100.0 | 100.0 | 100.0 | 100.0 |
| Capex | - | - | - | - | - |

## Purchase Price

### Public / Private Target (1/2)

|  | 1 |
|---|---|
| Offer Price per Share | $58.73 |
| Fully Diluted Shares Outstanding | 80.0 |
| **Equity Purchase Price** | $4,700.0 |
| Plus: Total Debt | 1,500.0 |
| Plus: Preferred Securities | - |
| Plus: Noncontrolling Interest | - |
| Less: Cash and Cash Equivalents | (250.0) |
| **Enterprise Value** | $5,950.0 |

### Goodwill Calculation

|  |  |  |
|---|---|---|
| Equity Purchase Price |  | $4,700.0 |
| Less: ValueCo Net Identifiable Assets |  | (2,500.0) |
| **Total Allocable Purchase Premium** |  | $2,200.0 |
|  | Allocation % |  |
| Less: Tangible Asset Write-Up | 15% | (330.0) |
| Less: Intangible Asset Write-Up | 10% | (220.0) |
| Plus: Deferred Tax Liability |  | $137.5 |
| **Goodwill Created in Transaction** |  | $1,787.5 |

### Write-Up Depreciation & Amortization Assumptions

|  | Years | Annual Amount |
|---|---|---|
| Tangible Asset Write-Up Depreciation Period | 15 | 22.0 |
| Intangible Asset Write-Up Amortization Period | 15 | 14.7 |
| Deferred Income Taxes |  | (9.2) |

### ValueCo Fully Diluted Shares Outstanding

| Basic Shares Outstanding | 79.726 |
|---|---|
| Plus: Shares from In-the-Money Options | 1.500 |
| Less: Shares Repurchased | (1.192) |
| **Net New Shares from Options** | 0.308 |
| Plus: Shares from Convertible Securities | - |
| **Fully Diluted Shares Outstanding** | 80.034 |

**Options/Warrants**

| Tranche | Number of Shares | Exercise Price | In-the-Money Shares | Proceeds |
|---|---|---|---|---|
| Tranche 1 | 1.000 | $45.00 | 1.000 | $45.0 |
| Tranche 2 | 0.500 | 50.00 | 0.500 | 25.0 |
| Tranche 3 | - | - | - | - |
| Tranche 4 | - | - | - | - |
| Tranche 5 | - | - | - | - |
| **Total** | 1.500 |  | 1.500 | $70.0 |

### BuyerCo Fully Diluted Shares Outstanding

| Basic Shares Outstanding | 139.982 |
|---|---|
| Plus: Shares from In-the-Money Options | 0.250 |
| Less: Shares Repurchased | (0.232) |
| **Net New Shares from Options** | 0.018 |
| Plus: Shares from Convertible Securities | - |
| **Fully Diluted Shares Outstanding** | 140.000 |

**Options/Warrants**

| Tranche | Number of Shares | Exercise Price | In-the-Money Shares | Proceeds |
|---|---|---|---|---|
| Tranche 1 | 0.250 | $65.00 | 0.250 | $16.3 |
| Tranche 2 | 0.750 | 75.00 | - | - |
| Tranche 3 | - | - | - | - |
| Tranche 4 | - | - | - | - |
| Tranche 5 | - | - | - | - |
| **Total** | 1.000 |  | 0.250 | $16.3 |

**EXHIBIT 7.37**  BuyerCo Standalone Income Statement

# BuyerCo Enterprises
## Standalone Income Statement
($ in millions, fiscal year ending December 31)

| | Historical Period | | | | | | | Projection Period | | | | |
|---|---|---|---|---|---|---|---|---|---|---|---|---|
| | 2016 | 2017 | 2018 | YTD 9/30/2018 | YTD 9/30/2019 | LTM 9/30/2019 | 2019 | Year 1 2020 | Year 2 2021 | Year 3 2022 | Year 4 2023 | Year 5 2024 |
| **Sales** | $4,771.7 | $5,484.7 | $6,232.6 | $4,611.6 | $4,938.6 | $6,559.6 | $6,755.8 | $7,228.7 | $7,662.4 | $8,045.5 | $8,367.4 | $8,618.4 |
| *% growth* | NA | 14.9% | 13.6% | NA | 7.1% | NA | 8.4% | 7.0% | 6.0% | 5.0% | 4.0% | 3.0% |
| Cost of Goods Sold | 3,053.9 | 3,455.4 | 3,864.2 | 2,859.2 | 3,061.9 | 4,067.0 | 4,188.6 | 4,481.8 | 4,750.7 | 4,988.2 | 5,187.8 | 5,343.4 |
| **Gross Profit** | $1,717.8 | $2,029.3 | $2,368.4 | $1,752.4 | $1,876.7 | $2,492.6 | $2,567.2 | $2,746.9 | $2,911.7 | $3,057.3 | $3,179.6 | $3,275.0 |
| *% margin* | 36.0% | 37.0% | 38.0% | 38.0% | 38.0% | 38.0% | 38.0% | 38.0% | 38.0% | 38.0% | 38.0% | 38.0% |
| Selling, General & Administrative | 811.2 | 905.0 | 997.2 | 737.9 | 790.2 | 1,049.5 | 1,080.9 | 1,156.6 | 1,226.0 | 1,287.3 | 1,338.8 | 1,378.9 |
| *% sales* | 17.0% | 16.5% | 16.0% | 16.0% | 16.0% | 16.0% | 16.0% | 16.0% | 16.0% | 16.0% | 16.0% | 16.0% |
| Other Expense / (Income) | | | | | | | | | | | | |
| **EBITDA** | $906.6 | $1,124.4 | $1,371.2 | $1,014.6 | $1,086.5 | $1,443.1 | $1,486.3 | $1,590.3 | $1,685.7 | $1,770.0 | $1,840.8 | $1,896.0 |
| *% margin* | 19.0% | 20.5% | 22.0% | 22.0% | 22.0% | 22.0% | 22.0% | 22.0% | 22.0% | 22.0% | 22.0% | 22.0% |
| Depreciation | 95.4 | 109.7 | 124.7 | 92.2 | 98.8 | 131.2 | 135.1 | 144.6 | 153.2 | 160.9 | 167.3 | 172.4 |
| Amortization | 23.9 | 27.4 | 31.2 | 23.1 | 24.7 | 32.8 | 33.8 | 36.1 | 38.3 | 40.2 | 41.8 | 43.1 |
| **EBIT** | $787.3 | $987.2 | $1,215.4 | $899.3 | $963.0 | $1,279.1 | $1,317.4 | $1,409.6 | $1,494.2 | $1,568.9 | $1,631.6 | $1,680.6 |
| *% margin* | 16.5% | 18.0% | 19.5% | 19.5% | 19.5% | 19.5% | 19.5% | 19.5% | 19.5% | 19.5% | 19.5% | 19.5% |
| **Interest Expense** | | | | | | | | | | | | |
| Revolving Credit Facility | | | | | | - | - | - | - | - | - | - |
| Term Loan A | | | | | | - | - | - | - | - | - | - |
| Term Loan B | | | | | | - | - | - | - | - | - | - |
| Term Loan C | | | | | | - | - | - | - | - | - | - |
| Existing Term Loan | | | | | | - | - | - | - | - | - | - |
| 2nd Lien | | | | | | - | - | - | - | - | - | - |
| Senior Notes | | | | | | 143.0 | 143.0 | 143.0 | 143.0 | 143.0 | 143.0 | 143.0 |
| Senior Subordinated Notes | | | | | | - | - | - | - | - | - | - |
| Commitment Fee on Unused Revolver | | | | | | 1.3 | 1.3 | 1.3 | 1.3 | 1.3 | 1.3 | 1.3 |
| Administrative Agent Fee | | | | | | 0.2 | 0.2 | 0.2 | 0.2 | 0.2 | 0.2 | 0.2 |
| **Total Interest Expense** | | | | | | $144.4 | $144.4 | $144.4 | $144.4 | $144.4 | $144.4 | $144.4 |
| Interest Income | | | | | | (2.0) | (2.0) | (4.2) | (8.7) | (13.5) | (18.7) | (24.1) |
| **Net Interest Expense** | | | | | | $142.4 | $142.4 | $140.2 | $135.7 | $130.9 | $125.7 | $120.3 |
| Earnings Before Taxes | | | | | | 1,136.7 | 1,175.0 | 1,269.4 | 1,358.5 | 1,438.0 | 1,505.9 | 1,560.3 |
| Income Tax Expense | | | | | | 284.2 | 293.7 | 317.3 | 339.6 | 359.5 | 376.5 | 390.1 |
| **Net Income** | | | | | | $852.5 | $881.2 | $952.0 | $1,018.9 | $1,078.5 | $1,129.4 | $1,170.2 |
| *% margin* | | | | | | 13.0% | 13.0% | 13.2% | 13.3% | 13.4% | 13.5% | 13.6% |
| Diluted Shares Outstanding | | | | | | 140.0 | 140.0 | 140.0 | 140.0 | 140.0 | 140.0 | 140.0 |
| **Diluted EPS** | | | | | | $6.09 | $6.29 | $6.80 | $7.28 | $7.70 | $8.07 | $8.36 |

### Income Statement Assumptions

| | 2016 | 2017 | 2018 | YTD 9/30/2018 | YTD 9/30/2019 | LTM 9/30/2019 | 2019 | Year 1 2020 | Year 2 2021 | Year 3 2022 | Year 4 2023 | Year 5 2024 |
|---|---|---|---|---|---|---|---|---|---|---|---|---|
| Sales (% YoY growth) | NA | 14.9% | 13.6% | (26.0%) | 7.1% | NA | 8.4% | 7.0% | 6.0% | 5.0% | 4.0% | 3.0% |
| Cost of Goods Sold (% margin) | 64.0% | 63.0% | 62.0% | 62.0% | 62.0% | 62.0% | 62.0% | 62.0% | 62.0% | 62.0% | 62.0% | 62.0% |
| SG&A (% sales) | 17.0% | 16.5% | 16.0% | 16.0% | 16.0% | 16.0% | 16.0% | 16.0% | 16.0% | 16.0% | 16.0% | 16.0% |
| Other Expense / (Income) (% of sales) | - % | - % | - % | - % | - % | - % | - % | - % | - % | - % | - % | - % |
| Depreciation (% of sales) | 2.0% | 2.0% | 2.0% | 2.0% | 2.0% | 2.0% | 2.0% | 2.0% | 2.0% | 2.0% | 2.0% | 2.0% |
| Amortization (% of sales) | 0.5% | 0.5% | 0.5% | 0.5% | 0.5% | 0.5% | 0.5% | 0.5% | 0.5% | 0.5% | 0.5% | 0.5% |
| Interest Income | | | | | | | | | | | | |
| Tax Rate | 25.0% | | | | | 25.0% | 25.0% | 25.0% | 25.0% | 25.0% | 25.0% | 25.0% |

**EXHIBIT 7.38** BuyerCo Standalone Balance Sheet

*($ in millions, fiscal year ending December 31)*

## BuyerCo Standalone Balance Sheet

| | | Projection Period | | | | |
|---|---|---|---|---|---|---|
| | | Year 1 | Year 2 | Year 3 | Year 4 | Year 5 |
| | **2019** | **2020** | **2021** | **2022** | **2023** | **2024** |
| Cash and Cash Equivalents | $400.0 | $1,270.0 | $2,208.5 | $3,209.7 | $4,266.1 | $5,368.9 |
| Accounts Receivable | 1,000.0 | 1,070.0 | 1,134.2 | 1,190.9 | 1,238.5 | 1,275.7 |
| Inventories | 1,225.0 | 1,310.8 | 1,389.4 | 1,458.9 | 1,517.2 | 1,562.7 |
| Prepaids and Other Current Assets | 525.0 | 561.8 | 595.5 | 625.2 | 650.2 | 669.7 |
| **Total Current Assets** | **$3,150.0** | **$4,212.5** | **$5,327.6** | **$6,484.7** | **$7,672.1** | **$8,877.0** |
| Property, Plant and Equipment, net | 2,500.0 | 2,572.3 | 2,648.9 | 2,729.4 | 2,813.0 | 2,899.2 |
| Goodwill | 575.0 | 575.0 | 575.0 | 575.0 | 575.0 | 575.0 |
| Intangible Assets | 825.0 | 788.9 | 750.5 | 710.3 | 668.5 | 625.4 |
| Other Assets | 450.0 | 450.0 | 450.0 | 450.0 | 450.0 | 450.0 |
| Deferred Financing Fees | - | - | - | - | - | - |
| **Total Assets** | **$7,500.0** | **$8,598.7** | **$9,752.0** | **$10,949.4** | **$12,178.6** | **$13,426.7** |
| Accounts Payable | 925.0 | 989.8 | 1,049.1 | 1,101.6 | 1,145.7 | 1,180.0 |
| Accrued Liabilities | 945.0 | 1,011.2 | 1,071.8 | 1,125.4 | 1,170.4 | 1,205.5 |
| Other Current Liabilities | 225.0 | 240.8 | 255.2 | 268.0 | 278.7 | 287.0 |
| **Total Current Liabilities** | **$2,095.0** | **$2,241.7** | **$2,376.1** | **$2,495.0** | **$2,594.8** | **$2,672.6** |
| Revolving Credit Facility | - | - | - | - | - | - |
| Term Loan A | - | - | - | - | - | - |
| Term Loan B | - | - | - | - | - | - |
| Term Loan C | - | - | - | - | - | - |
| Existing Term Loan | - | - | - | - | - | - |
| 2nd Lien | - | - | - | - | - | - |
| Senior Notes | 2,200.0 | 2,200.0 | 2,200.0 | 2,200.0 | 2,200.0 | 2,200.0 |
| Senior Subordinated Notes | - | - | - | - | - | - |
| Other Debt | - | - | - | - | - | - |
| Deferred Income Taxes | 100.0 | 100.0 | 100.0 | 100.0 | 100.0 | 100.0 |
| Other Long-Term Liabilities | 625.0 | 625.0 | 625.0 | 625.0 | 625.0 | 625.0 |
| **Total Liabilities** | **$5,020.0** | **$5,166.7** | **$5,301.1** | **$5,420.0** | **$5,519.8** | **$5,597.6** |
| Noncontrolling Interest | - | - | - | - | - | - |
| Shareholders' Equity | 2,480.0 | 3,432.0 | 4,450.9 | 5,529.4 | 6,658.8 | 7,829.1 |
| **Total Shareholders' Equity** | **$2,480.0** | **$3,432.0** | **$4,450.9** | **$5,529.4** | **$6,658.8** | **$7,829.1** |
| **Total Liabilities and Equity** | **$7,500.0** | **$8,598.7** | **$9,752.0** | **$10,949.4** | **$12,178.6** | **$13,426.7** |
| *Balance Check* | *0.000* | *0.000* | *0.000* | *0.000* | *0.000* | *0.000* |
| Net Working Capital | 655.0 | 700.9 | 742.9 | 780.0 | 811.2 | 835.6 |
| (Increase) / Decrease in Net Working Capital | | (45.9) | (42.1) | (37.1) | (31.2) | (24.3) |

### Balance Sheet Assumptions

#### Current Assets

| | | | | | | |
|---|---|---|---|---|---|---|
| Days Sales Outstanding (DSO) | 54.0 | 54.0 | 54.0 | 54.0 | 54.0 | 54.0 |
| Days Inventory Held (DIH) | 106.7 | 106.7 | 106.7 | 106.7 | 106.7 | 106.7 |
| Prepaid and Other Current Assets (% of sales) | 7.8% | 7.8% | 7.8% | 7.8% | 7.8% | 7.8% |

#### Current Liabilities

| | | | | | | |
|---|---|---|---|---|---|---|
| Days Payable Outstanding (DPO) | 80.6 | 80.6 | 80.6 | 80.6 | 80.6 | 80.6 |
| Accrued Liabilities (% of sales) | 14.0% | 14.0% | 14.0% | 14.0% | 14.0% | 14.0% |
| Other Current Liabilities (% of sales) | 3.3% | 3.3% | 3.3% | 3.3% | 3.3% | 3.3% |

**EXHIBIT 7.39**  BuyerCo Standalone Cash Flow Statement

*($ in millions, fiscal year ending December 31)*

## BuyerCo Standalone Cash Flow Statement

| | Projection Period | | | | |
|---|---|---|---|---|---|
| | Year 1 2020 | Year 2 2021 | Year 3 2022 | Year 4 2023 | Year 5 2024 |
| **Operating Activities** | | | | | |
| Net Income | $952.0 | $1,018.9 | $1,078.5 | $1,129.4 | $1,170.2 |
| Plus: Depreciation & Amortization | 144.6 | 153.2 | 160.9 | 167.3 | 172.4 |
| Plus: Amortization | 36.1 | 38.3 | 40.2 | 41.8 | 43.1 |
| | | | | | |
| **Changes in Working Capital Items** | | | | | |
| (Inc.) / Dec. in Accounts Receivable | (70.0) | (64.2) | (56.7) | (47.6) | (37.2) |
| (Inc.) / Dec. in Inventories | (85.8) | (78.6) | (69.5) | (58.4) | (45.5) |
| (Inc.) / Dec. in Prepaid and Other Current Assets | (36.8) | (33.7) | (29.8) | (25.0) | (19.5) |
| | | | | | |
| Inc. / (Dec.) in Accounts Payable | 64.8 | 59.4 | 52.5 | 44.1 | 34.4 |
| Inc. / (Dec.) in Accrued Liabilities | 66.2 | 60.7 | 53.6 | 45.0 | 35.1 |
| Inc. / (Dec.) in Other Current Liabilities | 15.8 | 14.4 | 12.8 | 10.7 | 8.4 |
| (Inc.) / Dec. in Net Working Capital | (45.9) | (42.1) | (37.1) | (31.2) | (24.3) |
| **Cash Flow from Operating Activities** | $1,086.9 | $1,168.4 | $1,242.5 | $1,307.4 | $1,361.3 |
| | | | | | |
| **Investing Activities** | | | | | |
| Capital Expenditures | (216.9) | (229.9) | (241.4) | (251.0) | (258.6) |
| Other Investing Activities | - | - | - | - | - |
| **Cash Flow from Investing Activities** | ($216.9) | ($229.9) | ($241.4) | ($251.0) | ($258.6) |
| | | | | | |
| **Financing Activities** | | | | | |
| Revolving Credit Facility | - | - | - | - | - |
| Term Loan A | - | - | - | - | - |
| Term Loan B | - | - | - | - | - |
| Term Loan C | - | - | - | - | - |
| Existing Term Loan | - | - | - | - | - |
| 2nd Lien | - | - | - | - | - |
| Senior Notes | - | - | - | - | - |
| Senior Subordinated Notes | - | - | - | - | - |
| Other Debt | - | - | - | - | - |
| Dividends | - | - | - | - | - |
| Equity Issuance / (Repurchase) | - | - | - | - | - |
| **Cash Flow from Financing Activities** | - | - | - | - | - |
| | | | | | |
| Excess Cash for the Period | $870.0 | $938.5 | $1,001.1 | $1,056.4 | $1,102.8 |
| Beginning Cash Balance | 400.0 | 1,270.0 | 2,208.5 | 3,209.7 | 4,266.1 |
| **Ending Cash Balance** | $1,270.0 | $2,208.5 | $3,209.7 | $4,266.1 | $5,368.9 |
| | | | | | |
| **Cash Flow Statement Assumptions** | | | | | |
| Capital Expenditures (% of sales) | 3.0% | 3.0% | 3.0% | 3.0% | 3.0% |

**EXHIBIT 7.40**   BuyerCo Standalone Debt Schedule

*($ in millions, fiscal year ending December 31)*

## BuyerCo Standalone Debt Schedule

| | Pro forma 2019 | Year 1 2020 | Year 2 2021 | Year 3 2022 | Year 4 2023 | Year 5 2024 |
|---|---|---|---|---|---|---|
| | | | **Projection Period** | | | |
| Forward LIBOR Curve | 1.85% | 1.70% | 1.65% | 1.55% | 1.55% | 1.55% |
| | | | | | | |
| Cash Flow from Operating Activities | | $1,086.9 | $1,168.4 | $1,242.5 | $1,307.4 | $1,361.3 |
| Cash Flow from Investing Activities | | (216.9) | (229.9) | (241.4) | (251.0) | (258.6) |
| **Cash Available for Debt Repayment** | | **$870.0** | **$938.5** | **$1,001.1** | **$1,056.4** | **$1,102.8** |
| Total Mandatory Repayments | **MinCash** | - | - | - | - | - |
| Cash from Balance Sheet | 100.0 | 300.0 | 1,170.0 | 2,108.5 | 3,109.7 | 4,166.1 |
| **Cash Available for Optional Debt Repayment** | | **$1,170.0** | **$2,108.5** | **$3,109.7** | **$4,166.1** | **$5,268.9** |

### Revolving Credit Facility

| | | | | | | |
|---|---|---|---|---|---|---|
| Revolving Credit Facility Size | $250.0 | | | | | |
| Spread | 2.500% | | | | | |
| LIBOR Floor | - % | | | | | |
| Term | 6 years | | | | | |
| Commitment Fee on Unused Portion | 0.50% | | | | | |
| | | | | | | |
| Beginning Balance | | - | - | - | - | - |
| Drawdown/(Repayment) | | - | - | - | - | - |
| **Ending Balance** | | **-** | **-** | **-** | **-** | **-** |
| | | | | | | |
| Interest Rate | | 4.20% | 4.15% | 4.05% | 4.05% | 4.05% |
| Interest Expense | | - | - | - | - | - |
| Commitment Fee | | 1.3 | 1.3 | 1.3 | 1.3 | 1.3 |
| Administrative Agent Fee | | 0.2 | 0.2 | 0.2 | 0.2 | 0.2 |

### Term Loan B Facility

| | | | | | | |
|---|---|---|---|---|---|---|
| Size | - | | | | | |
| Spread | 2.750% | | | | | |
| LIBOR Floor | - % | | | | | |
| Term | 7 years | | | | | |
| Repayment Schedule | 1.0% Per Annum, Bullet at Maturity | | | | | |
| | | | | | | |
| Beginning Balance | | - | - | - | - | - |
| Mandatory Repayments | | - | - | - | - | - |
| Optional Repayments | | - | - | - | - | - |
| **Ending Balance** | | **-** | **-** | **-** | **-** | **-** |
| | | | | | | |
| Interest Rate | | 4.45% | 4.40% | 4.30% | 4.30% | 4.30% |
| Interest Expense | | - | - | - | - | - |

### Senior Notes

| | | | | | | |
|---|---|---|---|---|---|---|
| Size | $2,200.0 | | | | | |
| Coupon | 6.500% | | | | | |
| Term | 8 years | | | | | |
| | | | | | | |
| Beginning Balance | | $2,200.0 | $2,200.0 | $2,200.0 | $2,200.0 | $2,200.0 |
| Repayment | | - | - | - | - | - |
| **Ending Balance** | | **$2,200.0** | **$2,200.0** | **$2,200.0** | **$2,200.0** | **$2,200.0** |
| | | | | | | |
| Interest Expense | | 143.0 | 143.0 | 143.0 | 143.0 | 143.0 |

**EXHIBIT 7.41** BuyerCo Standalone Assumptions Page 1

| BuyerCo Standalone Assumptions Page 1 - Income Statement and Cash Flow Statement | | | | | | |
|---|---|---|---|---|---|---|
| | | **Projection Period** | | | | |
| | | **Year 1** | **Year 2** | **Year 3** | **Year 4** | **Year 5** |
| | | **2020** | **2021** | **2022** | **2023** | **2024** |
| **Income Statement Assumptions** | | | | | | |
| Sales (% growth) | | 7.0% | 6.0% | 5.0% | 4.0% | 3.0% |
| Base | 1 | 7.0% | 6.0% | 5.0% | 4.0% | 3.0% |
| Upside | 2 | 10.0% | 8.0% | 6.0% | 4.0% | 3.0% |
| Management | 3 | 12.0% | 10.0% | 8.0% | 6.0% | 4.0% |
| Downside 1 | 4 | 5.0% | 4.0% | 3.0% | 3.0% | 3.0% |
| Downside 2 | 5 | 2.0% | 2.0% | 2.0% | 2.0% | 2.0% |
| Cost of Goods Sold (% sales) | | 62.0% | 62.0% | 62.0% | 62.0% | 62.0% |
| Base | 1 | 62.0% | 62.0% | 62.0% | 62.0% | 62.0% |
| Upside | 2 | 62.0% | 62.0% | 62.0% | 62.0% | 62.0% |
| Management | 3 | 61.0% | 61.0% | 61.0% | 61.0% | 61.0% |
| Downside 1 | 4 | 63.0% | 63.0% | 63.0% | 63.0% | 63.0% |
| Downside 2 | 5 | 64.0% | 64.0% | 64.0% | 64.0% | 64.0% |
| SG&A (% sales) | | 16.0% | 16.0% | 16.0% | 16.0% | 16.0% |
| Base | 1 | 16.0% | 16.0% | 16.0% | 16.0% | 16.0% |
| Upside | 2 | 15.0% | 15.0% | 15.0% | 15.0% | 15.0% |
| Management | 3 | 15.0% | 15.0% | 15.0% | 15.0% | 15.0% |
| Downside 1 | 4 | 18.0% | 18.0% | 18.0% | 18.0% | 18.0% |
| Downside 2 | 5 | 20.0% | 20.0% | 20.0% | 20.0% | 20.0% |
| Depreciation (% sales) | | 2.0% | 2.0% | 2.0% | 2.0% | 2.0% |
| Base | 1 | 2.0% | 2.0% | 2.0% | 2.0% | 2.0% |
| Upside | 2 | 2.0% | 2.0% | 2.0% | 2.0% | 2.0% |
| Management | 3 | 2.0% | 2.0% | 2.0% | 2.0% | 2.0% |
| Downside 1 | 4 | 2.0% | 2.0% | 2.0% | 2.0% | 2.0% |
| Downside 2 | 5 | 2.0% | 2.0% | 2.0% | 2.0% | 2.0% |
| Amortization (% sales) | | 0.5% | 0.5% | 0.5% | 0.5% | 0.5% |
| Base | 1 | 0.5% | 0.5% | 0.5% | 0.5% | 0.5% |
| Upside | 2 | 0.5% | 0.5% | 0.5% | 0.5% | 0.5% |
| Management | 3 | 0.5% | 0.5% | 0.5% | 0.5% | 0.5% |
| Downside 1 | 4 | 0.5% | 0.5% | 0.5% | 0.5% | 0.5% |
| Downside 2 | 5 | 0.5% | 0.5% | 0.5% | 0.5% | 0.5% |
| **Cash Flow Statement Assumptions** | | | | | | |
| Capital Expenditures (% sales) | | 3.0% | 3.0% | 3.0% | 3.0% | 3.0% |
| Base | 1 | 3.0% | 3.0% | 3.0% | 3.0% | 3.0% |
| Upside | 2 | 3.0% | 3.0% | 3.0% | 3.0% | 3.0% |
| Management | 3 | 3.0% | 3.0% | 3.0% | 3.0% | 3.0% |
| Downside 1 | 4 | 3.0% | 3.0% | 3.0% | 3.0% | 3.0% |
| Downside 2 | 5 | 3.0% | 3.0% | 3.0% | 3.0% | 3.0% |

**EXHIBIT 7.42**  BuyerCo Standalone Assumptions Page 2

| BuyerCo Standalone Assumptions Page 2 - Balance Sheet | | | | | | |
|---|---|---|---|---|---|---|
| | | **Projection Period** | | | | |
| | | Year 1 | Year 2 | Year 3 | Year 4 | Year 5 |
| | | 2020 | 2021 | 2022 | 2023 | 2024 |
| ***Current Assets*** | | | | | | |
| Days Sales Outstanding (DSO) | | 54.0 | 54.0 | 54.0 | 54.0 | 54.0 |
| Base | 1 | 54.0 | 54.0 | 54.0 | 54.0 | 54.0 |
| Upside | 2 | 54.0 | 54.0 | 54.0 | 54.0 | 54.0 |
| Management | 3 | 54.0 | 54.0 | 54.0 | 54.0 | 54.0 |
| Downside 1 | 4 | 56.0 | 56.0 | 56.0 | 56.0 | 56.0 |
| Downside 2 | 5 | 58.0 | 58.0 | 58.0 | 58.0 | 58.0 |
| | | | | | | |
| Days Inventory Held (DIH) | | 106.7 | 106.7 | 106.7 | 106.7 | 106.7 |
| Base | 1 | 106.7 | 106.7 | 106.7 | 106.7 | 106.7 |
| Upside | 2 | 106.7 | 106.7 | 106.7 | 106.7 | 106.7 |
| Management | 3 | 106.7 | 106.7 | 106.7 | 106.7 | 106.7 |
| Downside 1 | 4 | 110.0 | 110.0 | 110.0 | 110.0 | 110.0 |
| Downside 2 | 5 | 115.0 | 115.0 | 115.0 | 115.0 | 115.0 |
| | | | | | | |
| Prepaids and Other Current Assets (% sales) | | 7.8% | 7.8% | 7.8% | 7.8% | 7.8% |
| Base | 1 | 7.8% | 7.8% | 7.8% | 7.8% | 7.8% |
| Upside | 2 | 7.8% | 7.8% | 7.8% | 7.8% | 7.8% |
| Management | 3 | 7.8% | 7.8% | 7.8% | 7.8% | 7.8% |
| Downside 1 | 4 | 7.8% | 7.8% | 7.8% | 7.8% | 7.8% |
| Downside 2 | 5 | 7.8% | 7.8% | 7.8% | 7.8% | 7.8% |
| ***Current Liabilities*** | | | | | | |
| Days Payable Outstanding (DPO) | | 80.6 | 80.6 | 80.6 | 80.6 | 80.6 |
| Base | 1 | 80.6 | 80.6 | 80.6 | 80.6 | 80.6 |
| Upside | 2 | 80.6 | 80.6 | 80.6 | 80.6 | 80.6 |
| Management | 3 | 80.6 | 80.6 | 80.6 | 80.6 | 80.6 |
| Downside 1 | 4 | 77.0 | 77.0 | 77.0 | 77.0 | 77.0 |
| Downside 2 | 5 | 75.0 | 75.0 | 75.0 | 75.0 | 75.0 |
| | | | | | | |
| Accrued Liabilities (% sales) | | 14.0% | 14.0% | 14.0% | 14.0% | 14.0% |
| Base | 1 | 14.0% | 14.0% | 14.0% | 14.0% | 14.0% |
| Upside | 2 | 14.0% | 14.0% | 14.0% | 14.0% | 14.0% |
| Management | 3 | 14.0% | 14.0% | 14.0% | 14.0% | 14.0% |
| Downside 1 | 4 | 14.0% | 14.0% | 14.0% | 14.0% | 14.0% |
| Downside 2 | 5 | 14.0% | 14.0% | 14.0% | 14.0% | 14.0% |
| | | | | | | |
| Other Current Liabilities (% sales) | | 3.3% | 3.3% | 3.3% | 3.3% | 3.3% |
| Base | 1 | 3.3% | 3.3% | 3.3% | 3.3% | 3.3% |
| Upside | 2 | 3.3% | 3.3% | 3.3% | 3.3% | 3.3% |
| Management | 3 | 3.3% | 3.3% | 3.3% | 3.3% | 3.3% |
| Downside 1 | 4 | 3.3% | 3.3% | 3.3% | 3.3% | 3.3% |
| Downside 2 | 5 | 3.3% | 3.3% | 3.3% | 3.3% | 3.3% |

**EXHIBIT 7.43**   ValueCo Standalone Income Statement

## ValueCo Corporation
## Standalone Income Statement
*($ in millions, fiscal year ending December 31)*

| | Historical Period | | | | | | 2019 | Projection Period | | | | |
|---|---|---|---|---|---|---|---|---|---|---|---|---|
| | 2016 | 2017 | 2018 | YTD 9/30/2018 | YTD 9/30/2019 | LTM 9/30/2019 | 2019 | Year 1 2020 | Year 2 2021 | Year 3 2022 | Year 4 2023 | Year 5 2024 |
| **Sales** | $2,600.0 | $2,900.0 | $3,200.0 | $2,400.0 | $2,585.0 | $3,385.0 | $3,450.0 | $3,708.8 | $3,931.3 | $4,127.8 | $4,293.0 | $4,421.7 |
| *% growth* | NA | 11.5% | 10.3% | NA | 7.7% | NA | 7.8% | 7.5% | 6.0% | 5.0% | 4.0% | 3.0% |
| Cost of Goods Sold | 1,612.0 | 1,769.0 | 1,920.0 | 1,440.0 | 1,555.0 | 2,035.0 | 2,070.0 | 2,225.3 | 2,358.8 | 2,476.7 | 2,575.8 | 2,653.0 |
| **Gross Profit** | $988.0 | $1,131.0 | $1,280.0 | $960.0 | $1,030.0 | $1,350.0 | $1,380.0 | $1,483.5 | $1,572.5 | $1,651.1 | $1,717.2 | $1,768.7 |
| *% margin* | 38.0% | 39.0% | 40.0% | 40.0% | 39.8% | 39.9% | 40.0% | 40.0% | 40.0% | 40.0% | 40.0% | 40.0% |
| Selling, General & Administrative | 496.6 | 551.0 | 608.0 | 443.0 | 485.0 | 650.0 | 655.0 | 704.1 | 746.4 | 783.7 | 815.0 | 839.5 |
| *% sales* | 19.1% | 19.0% | 19.0% | 18.5% | 18.8% | 19.2% | 19.0% | 19.0% | 19.0% | 19.0% | 19.0% | 19.0% |
| Other Expense / (Income) | | | | | | | | | | | | |
| **EBITDA** | $491.4 | $580.0 | $672.0 | $517.0 | $545.0 | $700.0 | $725.0 | $779.4 | $826.1 | $867.4 | $902.1 | $929.2 |
| *% margin* | 18.9% | 20.0% | 21.0% | 21.5% | 21.1% | 20.7% | 21.0% | 21.0% | 21.0% | 21.0% | 21.0% | 21.0% |
| Depreciation | 116.0 | 121.5 | 145.0 | 110.0 | 115.0 | 150.0 | 155.3 | 166.9 | 176.9 | 185.8 | 193.2 | 199.0 |
| Amortization | 39.0 | 43.5 | 48.0 | 33.0 | 35.0 | 50.0 | 51.8 | 55.6 | 59.0 | 61.9 | 64.4 | 66.3 |
| **EBIT** | $336.4 | $415.0 | $479.0 | $374.0 | $395.0 | $500.0 | $518.0 | $556.9 | $590.3 | $619.8 | $644.6 | $663.9 |
| *% margin* | 12.9% | 14.3% | 15.0% | 15.6% | 15.3% | 14.8% | 15.0% | 15.0% | 15.0% | 15.0% | 15.0% | 15.0% |
| ***Interest Expense*** | | | | | | | | | | | | |
| Revolving Credit Facility | | | | | | | | | | | | |
| Term Loan A | | | | | | 52.0 | 52.0 | 42.5 | 22.1 | 5.6 | | |
| Term Loan B | | | | | | | | | | | | |
| Term Loan C | | | | | | | | | | | | |
| Existing Term Loan | | | | | | | | | | | | |
| 2nd Lien | | | | | | | | | | | | |
| Senior Notes | | | | | | 40.0 | 40.0 | 40.0 | 40.0 | 40.0 | 40.0 | 40.0 |
| Senior Subordinated Notes | | | | | | | | | | | | |
| Commitment Fee on Unused Revolver | | | | | | 0.8 | 0.8 | 0.8 | 0.8 | 0.8 | 0.8 | 0.8 |
| Administrative Agent Fee | | | | | | 0.2 | 0.2 | 0.2 | 0.2 | 0.2 | 0.2 | 0.2 |
| **Total Interest Expense** | | | | | | $92.9 | $92.9 | $83.4 | $63.0 | $46.5 | $40.9 | $40.9 |
| Interest Income | | | | | | (1.5) | (1.5) | (1.3) | (1.3) | (1.8) | (3.7) | (6.2) |
| **Net Interest Expense** | | | | | | $91.4 | $91.4 | $82.2 | $61.7 | $44.7 | $37.2 | $34.7 |
| Earnings Before Taxes | | | | | | 408.6 | 426.6 | 474.7 | 528.5 | 575.1 | 607.3 | 629.2 |
| Income Tax Expense | | | | | | 102.2 | 106.7 | 118.7 | 132.1 | 143.8 | 151.8 | 157.3 |
| **Net Income** | | | | | | $306.5 | $320.0 | $356.0 | $396.4 | $431.3 | $455.5 | $471.9 |
| *% margin* | | | | | | | 9.3% | 9.6% | 10.1% | 10.4% | 10.6% | 10.7% |
| Diluted Shares Outstanding | | | | | | 80.0 | 80.0 | 80.0 | 80.0 | 80.0 | 80.0 | 80.0 |
| **Diluted EPS** | | | | | | $3.83 | $4.00 | $4.45 | $4.95 | $5.39 | $5.69 | $5.90 |
| ***Income Statement Assumptions*** | | | | | | | | | | | | |
| Sales (% YoY growth) | NA | 11.5% | 10.3% | NA | 7.7% | NA | 7.8% | 7.5% | 6.0% | 5.0% | 4.0% | 3.0% |
| Cost of Goods Sold (% margin) | 62.0% | 61.0% | 60.0% | 60.0% | 60.2% | 60.1% | 60.0% | 60.0% | 60.0% | 60.0% | 60.0% | 60.0% |
| SG&A (% sales) | 19.1% | 19.0% | 19.0% | 18.5% | 18.8% | 19.2% | 19.0% | 19.0% | 19.0% | 19.0% | 19.0% | 19.0% |
| Other Expense / (Income) (% of sales) | - % | - % | - % | - % | - % | - % | - % | - % | - % | - % | - % | - % |
| Depreciation (% of sales) | 4.5% | 4.2% | 4.5% | 4.6% | 4.4% | 4.4% | 4.5% | 4.5% | 4.5% | 4.5% | 4.5% | 4.5% |
| Amortization (% of sales) | 1.5% | 1.5% | 1.5% | 1.4% | 1.4% | 1.5% | 1.5% | 1.5% | 1.5% | 1.5% | 1.5% | 1.5% |
| Interest Income | | | | | | | 0.6% | 0.5% | 0.5% | 0.5% | 0.5% | 0.5% |
| Tax Rate | | | | | | 25.0% | 25.0% | 25.0% | 25.0% | 25.0% | 25.0% | 25.0% |

**EXHIBIT 7.44** ValueCo Standalone Balance Sheet

*($ in millions, fiscal year ending December 31)*

## ValueCo Standalone Balance Sheet

| | | Projection Period | | | | |
|---|---|---|---|---|---|---|
| | | Year 1 | Year 2 | Year 3 | Year 4 | Year 5 |
| | 2019 | 2020 | 2021 | 2022 | 2023 | 2024 |
| Cash and Cash Equivalents | $250.0 | $250.0 | $250.0 | $485.5 | $975.0 | $1,489.5 |
| Accounts Receivable | 450.0 | 483.8 | 512.8 | 538.4 | 560.0 | 576.7 |
| Inventories | 600.0 | 645.0 | 683.7 | 717.9 | 746.6 | 769.0 |
| Prepaids and Other Current Assets | 175.0 | 188.1 | 199.4 | 209.4 | 217.8 | 224.3 |
| **Total Current Assets** | **$1,475.0** | **$1,566.9** | **$1,645.9** | **$1,951.2** | **$2,499.3** | **$3,059.5** |
| Property, Plant and Equipment, net | 2,500.0 | 2,500.0 | 2,500.0 | 2,500.0 | 2,500.0 | 2,500.0 |
| Goodwill | 1,000.0 | 1,000.0 | 1,000.0 | 1,000.0 | 1,000.0 | 1,000.0 |
| Intangible Assets | 875.0 | 819.4 | 760.4 | 698.5 | 634.1 | 567.8 |
| Other Assets | 150.0 | 150.0 | 150.0 | 150.0 | 150.0 | 150.0 |
| Deferred Financing Fees | - | - | - | - | - | - |
| **Total Assets** | **$6,000.0** | **$6,036.2** | **$6,056.3** | **$6,299.7** | **$6,783.4** | **$7,277.3** |
| Accounts Payable | 215.0 | 231.1 | 245.0 | 257.2 | 267.5 | 275.6 |
| Accrued Liabilities | 275.0 | 295.6 | 313.4 | 329.0 | 342.2 | 352.5 |
| Other Current Liabilities | 100.0 | 107.5 | 114.0 | 119.6 | 124.4 | 128.2 |
| **Total Current Liabilities** | **$590.0** | **$634.3** | **$672.3** | **$705.9** | **$734.2** | **$756.2** |
| Revolving Credit Facility | - | - | - | - | - | - |
| Term Loan A | - | - | - | - | - | - |
| Term Loan B | 1,000.0 | 636.0 | 221.6 | - | - | - |
| Term Loan C | - | - | - | - | - | - |
| Existing Term Loan | - | - | - | - | - | - |
| 2nd Lien | - | - | - | - | - | - |
| Senior Notes | 500.0 | 500.0 | 500.0 | 500.0 | 500.0 | 500.0 |
| Senior Subordinated Notes | - | - | - | - | - | - |
| Other Debt | - | - | - | - | - | - |
| Deferred Income Taxes | 300.0 | 300.0 | 300.0 | 300.0 | 300.0 | 300.0 |
| Other Long-Term Liabilities | 110.0 | 110.0 | 110.0 | 110.0 | 110.0 | 110.0 |
| **Total Liabilities** | **$2,500.0** | **$2,180.2** | **$1,803.9** | **$1,615.9** | **$1,644.2** | **$1,666.2** |
| Noncontrolling Interest | - | - | - | - | - | - |
| Shareholders' Equity | 3,500.0 | 3,856.0 | 4,252.4 | 4,683.7 | 5,139.2 | 5,611.1 |
| **Total Shareholders' Equity** | **$3,500.0** | **$3,856.0** | **$4,252.4** | **$4,683.7** | **$5,139.2** | **$5,611.1** |
| **Total Liabilities and Equity** | **$6,000.0** | **$6,036.2** | **$6,056.3** | **$6,299.7** | **$6,783.4** | **$7,277.3** |
| *Balance Check* | *0.000* | *0.000* | *0.000* | *0.000* | *0.000* | *0.000* |
| Net Working Capital | 635.0 | 682.6 | 723.6 | 759.8 | 790.2 | 813.9 |
| (Increase) / Decrease in Net Working Capital | | (47.6) | (41.0) | (36.2) | (30.4) | (23.7) |

### Balance Sheet Assumptions

#### Current Assets

| | | | | | | |
|---|---|---|---|---|---|---|
| Days Sales Outstanding (DSO) | 47.6 | 47.6 | 47.6 | 47.6 | 47.6 | 47.6 |
| Days Inventory Held (DIH) | 105.8 | 105.8 | 105.8 | 105.8 | 105.8 | 105.8 |
| Prepaid and Other Current Assets (% of sales) | 5.1% | 5.1% | 5.1% | 5.1% | 5.1% | 5.1% |

#### Current Liabilities

| | | | | | | |
|---|---|---|---|---|---|---|
| Days Payable Outstanding (DPO) | 37.9 | 37.9 | 37.9 | 37.9 | 37.9 | 37.9 |
| Accrued Liabilities (% of sales) | 8.0% | 8.0% | 8.0% | 8.0% | 8.0% | 8.0% |
| Other Current Liabilities (% of sales) | 2.9% | 2.9% | 2.9% | 2.9% | 2.9% | 2.9% |

**EXHIBIT 7.45**   ValueCo Standalone Cash Flow Statement

*($ in millions, fiscal year ending December 31)*

| ValueCo Standalone Cash Flow Statement | | | | | |
|---|---|---|---|---|---|
| | **Projection Period** | | | | |
| | **Year 1**<br>**2020** | **Year 2**<br>**2021** | **Year 3**<br>**2022** | **Year 4**<br>**2023** | **Year 5**<br>**2024** |
| ***Operating Activities*** | | | | | |
| Net Income | $356.0 | $396.4 | $431.3 | $455.5 | $471.9 |
| Plus: Depreciation & Amortization | 166.9 | 176.9 | 185.8 | 193.2 | 199.0 |
| Plus: Amortization | 55.6 | 59.0 | 61.9 | 64.4 | 66.3 |
| ***Changes in Working Capital Items*** | | | | | |
| (Inc.) / Dec. in Accounts Receivable | (33.8) | (29.0) | (25.6) | (21.5) | (16.8) |
| (Inc.) / Dec. in Inventories | (45.0) | (38.7) | (34.2) | (28.7) | (22.4) |
| (Inc.) / Dec. in Prepaid and Other Current Assets | (13.1) | (11.3) | (10.0) | (8.4) | (6.5) |
| Inc. / (Dec.) in Accounts Payable | 16.1 | 13.9 | 12.2 | 10.3 | 8.0 |
| Inc. / (Dec.) in Accrued Liabilities | 20.6 | 17.7 | 15.7 | 13.2 | 10.3 |
| Inc. / (Dec.) in Other Current Liabilities | 7.5 | 6.5 | 5.7 | 4.8 | 3.7 |
| (Inc.) / Dec. in Net Working Capital | (47.6) | (41.0) | (36.2) | (30.4) | (23.7) |
| **Cash Flow from Operating Activities** | **$530.9** | **$591.3** | **$642.8** | **$682.7** | **$713.5** |
| ***Investing Activities*** | | | | | |
| Capital Expenditures | (166.9) | (176.9) | (185.8) | (193.2) | (199.0) |
| Other Investing Activities | - | - | - | - | - |
| **Cash Flow from Investing Activities** | **($166.9)** | **($176.9)** | **($185.8)** | **($193.2)** | **($199.0)** |
| ***Financing Activities*** | | | | | |
| Revolving Credit Facility | - | - | - | - | - |
| Term Loan A | - | - | - | - | - |
| Term Loan B | (364.0) | (414.4) | (221.6) | - | - |
| Term Loan C | - | - | - | - | - |
| Existing Term Loan | - | - | - | - | - |
| 2nd Lien | - | - | - | - | - |
| Senior Notes | - | - | - | - | - |
| Senior Subordinated Notes | - | - | - | - | - |
| Other Debt | - | - | - | - | - |
| Dividends | - | - | - | - | - |
| Equity Issuance / (Repurchase) | - | - | - | - | - |
| **Cash Flow from Financing Activities** | **($364.0)** | **($414.4)** | **($221.6)** | **-** | **-** |
| Excess Cash for the Period | - | - | $235.5 | $489.5 | $514.5 |
| Beginning Cash Balance | 250.0 | 250.0 | 250.0 | 485.5 | 975.0 |
| **Ending Cash Balance** | **$250.0** | **$250.0** | **$485.5** | **$975.0** | **$1,489.5** |
| ***Cash Flow Statement Assumptions*** | | | | | |
| Capital Expenditures (% of sales) | 4.5% | 4.5% | 4.5% | 4.5% | 4.5% |

**EXHIBIT 7.46** ValueCo Standalone Debt Schedule

*($ in millions, fiscal year ending December 31)*

| ValueCo Standalone Debt Schedule | | | | | | |
|---|---|---|---|---|---|---|
| | | | | Projection Period | | |
| | Pro forma | Year 1 | Year 2 | Year 3 | Year 4 | Year 5 |
| | 2019 | 2020 | 2021 | 2022 | 2023 | 2024 |
| Forward LIBOR Curve | 1.85% | 1.70% | 1.65% | 1.55% | 1.55% | 1.55% |
| | | | | | | |
| Cash Flow from Operating Activities | | $530.9 | $591.3 | $642.8 | $682.7 | $713.5 |
| Cash Flow from Investing Activities | | (166.9) | (176.9) | (185.8) | (193.2) | (199.0) |
| **Cash Available for Debt Repayment** | | **$364.0** | **$414.4** | **$457.1** | **$489.5** | **$514.5** |
| Total Mandatory Repayments | **MinCash** | (10.0) | (10.0) | (10.0) | - | - |
| Cash from Balance Sheet | 250.0 | - | - | - | 235.5 | 725.0 |
| **Cash Available for Optional Debt Repayment** | | **$354.0** | **$404.4** | **$447.1** | **$725.0** | **$1,239.5** |

*Revolving Credit Facility*

| | | | | | | |
|---|---|---|---|---|---|---|
| Revolving Credit Facility Size | $150.0 | | | | | |
| Spread | 3.250% | | | | | |
| LIBOR Floor | - % | | | | | |
| Term | 6 years | | | | | |
| Commitment Fee on Unused Portion | 0.50% | | | | | |
| | | | | | | |
| Beginning Balance | | - | - | - | - | - |
| Drawdown/(Repayment) | | - | - | - | - | - |
| **Ending Balance** | | **-** | **-** | **-** | **-** | **-** |
| | | | | | | |
| Interest Rate | | 4.95% | 4.90% | 4.80% | 4.80% | 4.80% |
| Interest Expense | | - | - | - | - | - |
| Commitment Fee | | 0.8 | 0.8 | 0.8 | 0.8 | 0.8 |
| Administrative Agent Fee | | 0.2 | 0.2 | 0.2 | 0.2 | 0.2 |

*Term Loan B Facility*

| | | | | | | |
|---|---|---|---|---|---|---|
| Size | $1,000.0 | | | | | |
| Spread | 3.500% | | | | | |
| LIBOR Floor | - % | | | | | |
| Term | 7 years | | | | | |
| Repayment Schedule | 1.0% Per Annum, Bullet at Maturity | | | | | |
| | | | | | | |
| Beginning Balance | | $1,000.0 | $636.0 | $221.6 | - | - |
| Mandatory Repayments | | (10.0) | (10.0) | (10.0) | - | - |
| Optional Repayments | | (354.0) | (404.4) | (211.6) | - | - |
| **Ending Balance** | | **$636.0** | **$221.6** | **-** | **-** | **-** |
| | | | | | | |
| Interest Rate | | 5.20% | 5.15% | 5.05% | 5.05% | 5.05% |
| Interest Expense | | 42.5 | 22.1 | 5.6 | - | - |

*Senior Notes*

| | | | | | | |
|---|---|---|---|---|---|---|
| Size | $500.0 | | | | | |
| Coupon | 8.000% | | | | | |
| Term | 8 years | | | | | |
| | | | | | | |
| Beginning Balance | | $500.0 | $500.0 | $500.0 | $500.0 | $500.0 |
| Repayment | | - | - | - | - | - |
| **Ending Balance** | | **$500.0** | **$500.0** | **$500.0** | **$500.0** | **$500.0** |
| | | | | | | |
| Interest Expense | | 40.0 | 40.0 | 40.0 | 40.0 | 40.0 |

**EXHIBIT 7.47**    ValueCo Standalone Assumptions Page 1

**ValueCo Standalone Assumptions Page 1 - Income Statement and Cash Flow Statement**

| | | Projection Period | | | |
|---|---|---|---|---|---|
| | | Year 1 2020 | Year 2 2021 | Year 3 2022 | Year 4 2023 | Year 5 2024 |

| **Income Statement Assumptions** | | | | | | |
|---|---|---|---|---|---|---|
| Sales (% growth) | | 7.5% | 6.0% | 5.0% | 4.0% | 3.0% |
| Base | 1 | 7.5% | 6.0% | 5.0% | 4.0% | 3.0% |
| Upside | 2 | 10.0% | 8.0% | 6.0% | 4.0% | 3.0% |
| Management | 3 | 12.0% | 10.0% | 8.0% | 6.0% | 4.0% |
| Downside 1 | 4 | 5.0% | 4.0% | 3.0% | 3.0% | 3.0% |
| Downside 2 | 5 | 2.0% | 2.0% | 2.0% | 2.0% | 2.0% |
| | | | | | | |
| Cost of Goods Sold (% sales) | | 60.0% | 60.0% | 60.0% | 60.0% | 60.0% |
| Base | 1 | 60.0% | 60.0% | 60.0% | 60.0% | 60.0% |
| Upside | 2 | 60.0% | 60.0% | 60.0% | 60.0% | 60.0% |
| Management | 3 | 59.0% | 59.0% | 59.0% | 59.0% | 59.0% |
| Downside 1 | 4 | 61.0% | 61.0% | 61.0% | 61.0% | 61.0% |
| Downside 2 | 5 | 62.0% | 62.0% | 62.0% | 62.0% | 62.0% |
| | | | | | | |
| SG&A (% sales) | | 19.0% | 19.0% | 19.0% | 19.0% | 19.0% |
| Base | 1 | 19.0% | 19.0% | 19.0% | 19.0% | 19.0% |
| Upside | 2 | 18.0% | 18.0% | 18.0% | 18.0% | 18.0% |
| Management | 3 | 18.0% | 18.0% | 18.0% | 18.0% | 18.0% |
| Downside 1 | 4 | 20.0% | 20.0% | 20.0% | 20.0% | 20.0% |
| Downside 2 | 5 | 21.0% | 21.0% | 21.0% | 21.0% | 21.0% |
| | | | | | | |
| Depreciation (% sales) | | 4.5% | 4.5% | 4.5% | 4.5% | 4.5% |
| Base | 1 | 4.5% | 4.5% | 4.5% | 4.5% | 4.5% |
| Upside | 2 | 4.5% | 4.5% | 4.5% | 4.5% | 4.5% |
| Management | 3 | 4.5% | 4.5% | 4.5% | 4.5% | 4.5% |
| Downside 1 | 4 | 4.5% | 4.5% | 4.5% | 4.5% | 4.5% |
| Downside 2 | 5 | 4.5% | 4.5% | 4.5% | 4.5% | 4.5% |
| | | | | | | |
| Amortization (% sales) | | 1.5% | 1.5% | 1.5% | 1.5% | 1.5% |
| Base | 1 | 1.5% | 1.5% | 1.5% | 1.5% | 1.5% |
| Upside | 2 | 1.5% | 1.5% | 1.5% | 1.5% | 1.5% |
| Management | 3 | 1.5% | 1.5% | 1.5% | 1.5% | 1.5% |
| Downside 1 | 4 | 1.5% | 1.5% | 1.5% | 1.5% | 1.5% |
| Downside 2 | 5 | 1.5% | 1.5% | 1.5% | 1.5% | 1.5% |
| | | | | | | |
| **Cash Flow Statement Assumptions** | | | | | | |
| Capital Expenditures (% sales) | | 4.5% | 4.5% | 4.5% | 4.5% | 4.5% |
| Base | 1 | 4.5% | 4.5% | 4.5% | 4.5% | 4.5% |
| Upside | 2 | 4.5% | 4.5% | 4.5% | 4.5% | 4.5% |
| Management | 3 | 4.5% | 4.5% | 4.5% | 4.5% | 4.5% |
| Downside 1 | 4 | 5.0% | 5.0% | 5.0% | 5.0% | 5.0% |
| Downside 2 | 5 | 5.0% | 5.0% | 5.0% | 5.0% | 5.0% |

**EXHIBIT 7.48**  ValueCo Standalone Assumptions Page 2

| ValueCo Standalone Assumptions Page 2 - Balance Sheet | | | | | | |
|---|---|---|---|---|---|---|
| | | **Projection Period** | | | | |
| | | **Year 1**<br>**2020** | **Year 2**<br>**2021** | **Year 3**<br>**2022** | **Year 4**<br>**2023** | **Year 5**<br>**2024** |
| ***Current Assets*** | | | | | | |
| Days Sales Outstanding (DSO) | | 47.6 | 47.6 | 47.6 | 47.6 | 47.6 |
| Base | 1 | 47.6 | 47.6 | 47.6 | 47.6 | 47.6 |
| Upside | 2 | 47.6 | 47.6 | 47.6 | 47.6 | 47.6 |
| Management | 3 | 47.6 | 47.6 | 47.6 | 47.6 | 47.6 |
| Downside 1 | 4 | 50.0 | 50.0 | 50.0 | 50.0 | 50.0 |
| Downside 2 | 5 | 55.0 | 55.0 | 55.0 | 55.0 | 55.0 |
| | | | | | | |
| Days Inventory Held (DIH) | | 105.8 | 105.8 | 105.8 | 105.8 | 105.8 |
| Base | 1 | 105.8 | 105.8 | 105.8 | 105.8 | 105.8 |
| Upside | 2 | 105.8 | 105.8 | 105.8 | 105.8 | 105.8 |
| Management | 3 | 105.8 | 105.8 | 105.8 | 105.8 | 105.8 |
| Downside 1 | 4 | 110.0 | 110.0 | 110.0 | 110.0 | 110.0 |
| Downside 2 | 5 | 115.0 | 115.0 | 115.0 | 115.0 | 115.0 |
| | | | | | | |
| Prepaids and Other Current Assets (% sales) | | 5.1% | 5.1% | 5.1% | 5.1% | 5.1% |
| Base | 1 | 5.1% | 5.1% | 5.1% | 5.1% | 5.1% |
| Upside | 2 | 5.1% | 5.1% | 5.1% | 5.1% | 5.1% |
| Management | 3 | 5.1% | 5.1% | 5.1% | 5.1% | 5.1% |
| Downside 1 | 4 | 5.1% | 5.1% | 5.1% | 5.1% | 5.1% |
| Downside 2 | 5 | 5.1% | 5.1% | 5.1% | 5.1% | 5.1% |
| | | | | | | |
| ***Current Liabilities*** | | | | | | |
| Days Payable Outstanding (DPO) | | 37.9 | 37.9 | 37.9 | 37.9 | 37.9 |
| Base | 1 | 37.9 | 37.9 | 37.9 | 37.9 | 37.9 |
| Upside | 2 | 37.9 | 37.9 | 37.9 | 37.9 | 37.9 |
| Management | 3 | 37.9 | 37.9 | 37.9 | 37.9 | 37.9 |
| Downside 1 | 4 | 35.0 | 35.0 | 35.0 | 35.0 | 35.0 |
| Downside 2 | 5 | 30.0 | 30.0 | 30.0 | 30.0 | 30.0 |
| | | | | | | |
| Accrued Liabilities (% sales) | | 8.0% | 8.0% | 8.0% | 8.0% | 8.0% |
| Base | 1 | 8.0% | 8.0% | 8.0% | 8.0% | 8.0% |
| Upside | 2 | 8.0% | 8.0% | 8.0% | 8.0% | 8.0% |
| Management | 3 | 8.0% | 8.0% | 8.0% | 8.0% | 8.0% |
| Downside 1 | 4 | 8.0% | 8.0% | 8.0% | 8.0% | 8.0% |
| Downside 2 | 5 | 8.0% | 8.0% | 8.0% | 8.0% | 8.0% |
| | | | | | | |
| Other Current Liabilities (% sales) | | 2.9% | 2.9% | 2.9% | 2.9% | 2.9% |
| Base | 1 | 2.9% | 2.9% | 2.9% | 2.9% | 2.9% |
| Upside | 2 | 2.9% | 2.9% | 2.9% | 2.9% | 2.9% |
| Management | 3 | 2.9% | 2.9% | 2.9% | 2.9% | 2.9% |
| Downside 1 | 4 | 2.9% | 2.9% | 2.9% | 2.9% | 2.9% |
| Downside 2 | 5 | 2.9% | 2.9% | 2.9% | 2.9% | 2.9% |

## CHAPTER 7 QUESTIONS

1) If the pro forma EPS of two combined companies is higher than the EPS of the acquirer on a standalone basis, the transaction is said to be

   A. Accretive
   B. Dilutive
   C. Breakeven
   D. Consensus

2) Calculate pro forma combined EPS

Use the information below for the following three questions

($ in millions)

| Assumptions | |
|---|---|
| Pro Forma Combined Net Income | $1,000.0 |
| Acquirer Standalone Net Income | 700.0 |
| Standalone Fully Diluted Shares Outstanding | 200.0 |
| Net New Shares Issued in Transaction | 50.0 |
| Tax Rate | 25.0% |

   A. $2.80
   B. $3.50
   C. $4.00
   D. $5.00

3) Calculate the accretion / (dilution) on a dollar amount basis

   A. ($0.50)
   B. $0.50
   C. ($0.88)
   D. $0.88

4) Calculate the accretion / (dilution) on a percentage basis

   A. (14.3%)
   B. 14.3%
   C. (12.5%)
   D. 12.5%

5) Calculate the breakeven pre-tax synergies / (cushion)

   A. ($161.3) million
   B. $161.3 million
   C. ($166.7) million
   D. $166.7 million

6) Assuming all else being equal, if a company with a P/E of 15x acquires a company with a P/E of 12x in an all-stock deal, the transaction is _____.

   A. Accretive
   B. Dilutive
   C. Breakeven
   D. Unable to be determined

7) An accretion / (dilution) analysis is typically performed by

   A. Public strategic buyers
   B. Sponsor buyers
   C. Family-owned sellers
   D. Non-public foreign buyers

8) Which of the following are common types of synergies realized in M&A transactions?

   I. Merger
   II. Revenue
   III. Cost
   IV. Stock

   A. I and II
   B. II and III
   C. III and IV
   D. II, III, and IV

9) Which Internal Revenue Code governs net operating losses?

   A. Section 302
   B. Section 330
   C. Section 382
   D. Section 389

10) Which of the following is NOT a potential "source" of funds for consummating a deal?

   A. New stock issued
   B. Cash on BS of buyer
   C. Equity value of seller
   D. Preferred stock issued


11) The excess paid for a target over its identifiable net asset value is known as

   A. Brand premium
   B. Goodwill
   C. Intangible value
   D. Tangible value


12) Using the information below, calculate the allocable purchase premium

   *($ in millions)*

   | Assumptions | |
   |---|---|
   | Equity Purchase Price | $3,000.0 |
   | Shareholders' Equity | 2,000.0 |
   | Existing Goodwill | 750.0 |

   A. $1,250.0 million
   B. $1,750.0 million
   C. $5,000.0 million
   D. $5,750.0 million


13) Debt financing fees in an M&A deal are

   A. Expensed immediately
   B. Capitalized
   C. Written off
   D. Not applicable


14) A transaction where the buyer purchases all assets & liabilities of the seller is known as

   A. Asset purchase
   B. Stock purchase
   C. Section 308 election
   D. Section 382 purchase

15) A transaction where the buyer purchases certain assets and assumes only certain liabilities is known as

    A. Asset purchase
    B. Stock purchase
    C. Section 338 (h)(10) election
    D. Section 382 purchase

# Initial Public Offerings

# CHAPTER 8

# Initial Public Offerings

**A**n initial public offering (IPO) represents the first time a company ("issuer") sells its stock to public investors. The shares are then traded on an exchange such as the Nasdaq Stock Market (Nasdaq), the New York Stock Exchange (NYSE), the London Stock Exchange (LSE), or the Stock Exchange of Hong Kong (SEHK). Collectively, these primary exchanges comprise what is commonly known as "the stock market". Each publicly traded company assumes a "ticker symbol", typically a one-to-four-letter abbreviation that serves as a unique identifier. Once a company "goes public", its shares will trade daily on the open market where buyers and sellers determine its prevailing equity value in real time.

An IPO is a transformational event for a company, its owners, and employees. In many ways, the company and the way it operates will never be the same again. Detailed business and financial information will be made public and subject to analysis. Management will conduct quarterly earnings calls and field questions from sell-side research analysts. They will also speak regularly with existing and potential new investors. New accounting, legal, regulatory, and investor relations infrastructure and employees will need to be brought on board to handle public company requirements.

While IPO candidates vary broadly in terms of sector, size, and financial profile, they need to feature performance and growth attributes that public investors would find compelling. Is the company and its addressable market large enough to warrant attention? Is it a market leader? How exciting is the growth opportunity? Is the cycle entry point attractive? How capable is the management team?

Market conditions must also be conducive. The number of IPO offerings over a given time period is strongly correlated to the performance of the overall stock market. The better the market, the more plentiful the IPO pipeline. Similarly, in a down market, the IPO spigot slows to a trickle or may shut off entirely. Even a highly compelling candidate would most likely choose to wait rather than launch in an unfavorable market and risk an unsuccessful deal.

For an assessment of a company's IPO prospects and market conditions, the company and its shareholders turn to investment banks. The banks also provide recommendations on valuation, size of the offering, and use of proceeds. All of this is weighed in making the ultimate decision on whether to move forward.

This chapter provides an overview of the fundamentals of IPOs as depicted in the main categories shown in Exhibit 8.1.

**EXHIBIT 8.1**    IPO Fundamentals

- Why Do Companies Go Public?
- Characteristics of a Strong IPO Candidate
- Key Participants
- Selected Key Terms
- Dual-Track Process
- Other Equity Offerings
- IPO Considerations

## WHY DO COMPANIES GO PUBLIC?

The motivations behind an IPO depend on the situation. The decision to go public may be driven by a desire to monetize and create liquidity, secure growth capital, or cement a legacy, often a combination. Many IPO candidates are owned by private equity (PE) or venture capital (VC) firms seeking to exit their investment. Others may be family or founder-owned companies that have reached an inflection point. They may also be non-core divisions of companies where the parent decides to cut the cord.

The use of IPO proceeds varies accordingly. When existing shareholders sell shares and receive cash in a liquidity event, this is known as a *secondary* offering. On the other hand, when the company itself sells shares to fund growth, repay debt, or for other general corporate purposes, it is known as a *primary* offering. An IPO may consist entirely of primary shares or secondary shares, or a combination. The circumstances dictate the type of offering.

Regardless of the offering type, an IPO provides both the original and new shareholders a liquid market and valuation benchmark for their shares. Post-IPO, the pre-listing shareholders are typically subject to an 180-day lock-up. Subsequently, they can freely buy and sell their shares as they see fit, unless they are an affiliate or insider of the company and hence subject to certain legal restrictions.

Below is a summary of the primary reasons that companies pursue an IPO:

- *Liquidity / monetization* – Perhaps the most traditional reason for taking a company public is to provide a liquidity or monetization event for the owners. An IPO may provide an attractive alternative to an outright cash sale to another company or PE firm. First, the valuation is often higher. In some cases, there may not be a cash buyer for the company, thereby making an IPO the only viable exit.

Second, the company's owners may wish to retain control of the company. A typical IPO results in the sale of 25% or so of a company's shares, which ensures a sizable majority ownership for legacy shareholders. Third, by retaining a major stake in the company, the original owners have the ability to participate in the potential upside and sell at a later date. The future share price appreciation opportunity may be substantial. Think about the pre-listing shareholders of the FAANG complex: Facebook, Apple, Amazon, Netflix, and Google/Alphabet.

- *Growth capital* – IPO proceeds may be used for any number of operational and growth initiatives for the company, such as new products and locations, geographic expansion, human capital, R&D, software, and equipment. The cash may also fund M&A, whether one large imminent deal or a string of future transactions.

- *Capital markets access* – Public equity markets provide the ability for companies to access capital in the future through additional share sales, known as *follow-on offerings*. Given their breadth and depth, the major stock exchanges are more efficient for raising capital than private markets. Public companies also have access to liquid markets for registered debt, convertible notes, and hybrid securities.

- *Balance sheet support / deleveraging* – Proceeds from an IPO offering are often used to repay existing debt, thereby strengthening the balance sheet and freeing up growth capacity. This is particularly common for levered companies, most notably former LBOs. In these cases, the public markets typically provide the most efficient option to raise equity capital for deleveraging.

- *Acquisition currency* – Access to deep and liquid public equity markets provides enhanced M&A firepower. A liquid public currency can be offered directly to the shareholders of an M&A target. It can also be used to raise cash proceeds to fund an acquisition. This affords greater flexibility than private companies where new equity often comes from the existing owners' pockets.

- *Legacy & image* – Going public establishes a sense of permanency for a company. This may be especially important for a founder or family-owned company where legacy is a key priority for the owners, employees, and other stakeholders. An IPO is also a high-profile event that raises the company's profile and serves to solidify its image. In this sense, a public ticker is like free advertising.

- *Talent attraction / retention* – Public companies have the ability to provide employees with stock-based compensation packages, typically in the form of restricted stock and options. These packages differ from those of private companies due to their transparency and liquidity. This helps with talent attraction and retention, while also directly aligning incentives for management and shareholders.

## CHARACTERISTICS OF A STRONG IPO CANDIDATE

Certain common characteristics emerge among attractive IPO candidates, as outlined in Exhibit 8.2.

**EXHIBIT 8.2**   Characteristics of a Strong IPO Candidate

- Attractive Industry
- Strong Competitive Position
- Growth Opportunities
- Moat & Barriers to Entry
- Healthy Financial Profile
- Disruptive & Differentiated Solutions
- Favorable Risk Profile
- Proven Management Team

### Attractive Industry

What does the company do and what sector is it in? How does it make money? This is top of the list for investor due diligence. Sometimes, industry or sector trumps everything else—for better or for worse. Consider the flood of technology company IPOs in the 1990s or the fast-growing unicorn start-ups that went public in 2019. A rising tide tends to lift all boats. Conversely, even a high-quality company will struggle going public if the sector is out of favor. Being the best house in a bad neighborhood has its limitations. Investors will likely question the sustainability and hence resale value.

So, what do IPO investors look for in a sector? Size, growth, structure—they are all tied to sales and earnings prospects. Large sectors are *de facto* relevant and their size implies growth opportunities. Investors focus on a company's *total addressable market*, or TAM. For example, a TAM of $100 billion is clearly preferable to $2-to-3 billion as it provides more opportunities for growth.

Growth sectors tend to be "early stage" in some major secular or cyclical wave. For the former, think technological, regulatory, or consumer preference-driven. For cyclical, look at real estate, oil & gas, industrials, and metals & mining.

### Strong Competitive Position

Investors tend to get more excited about market leaders than less established players. Market leadership in and of itself is a powerful statement and marketing tool. Even more important is what it represents, namely a proven track record and sustainable competitive advantages. These may include superior products and services, brand strength, entrenched customer relationships, and cost/scale benefits.

While being #1 in a given sector is ideal, meaningful #2 or #3 players can also be compelling. Similarly, a second-tier, but faster-growing player that is gaining share may excite investors. Trends and competitive outlook are arguably even more important than the current state of play. Equity investors are always looking ahead.

In terms of competitive positioning, investors also look at the number of competitors. In theory, the fewer the competitors, the greater the prospects for outperformance. Fierce competition may engender lower growth, profitability, or diminishing returns. This is especially true when participants engage in irrational behavior to gain market share.

## Growth Opportunities

*Growth. Growth. Growth.* Investors take a chance on a new company in the hope of achieving outsized returns. Growth is critical for driving these returns. Organic growth is top priority. These are opportunities generated internally by the company— new customers, products and services, geographic expansion, and greenfields. A strong, viable platform for M&A is also very interesting. The best IPO candidates tend to have multiple growth drivers.

While IPO investors covet growth, they also seek to understand its volatility. The prospect of explosive growth needs to be measured against the risk of failure. This is particularly important for early-stage, pre-profit companies. Growth that is reliant on cyclical, M&A, or geographic expansion will also be heavily scrutinized. As with any company, a low-risk, high-growth story is ideal.

- *White space* – refers to the market penetration opportunity for a company in its core markets, typically expressed as current market share as a percentage of TAM. In this case, the lower the better. The potential for large market share gains excites investors.

- *Geographic expansion and greenfields* – domestic or international expansion opportunities, typically through greenfields or M&A. Companies can also enter geographies through distribution arrangements, joint ventures (JVs), franchising, or in some cases, a white labeling agreement.

- *New channels / paths-to-markets* – companies should always be optimizing their paths to market. Key channels include retail, wholesale, direct-to-customer, and ecommerce. With any new channel opportunity, the ability to displace existing incumbents, as well as potential negative effects on current paths to market, should be considered.

- *Acquisitions* – strong M&A platforms provide investors with enhanced growth opportunities. At the same time, M&A stories demand a sober risk/reward assessment. In order to be compelling, there must be sufficient actionable M&A opportunities at a reasonable price, and management needs to be effective at integration. Investors also need to gain comfort that the company has ample balance sheet capacity to consummate deals.

- *New products & services* – the ability to develop new products and services, as well as upgrade or expand existing ones, provides multiple growth streams. Apple regularly upgrades its traditional product portfolio, such as iPhones, iPads, and MacBooks. At the same time, its team is constantly working on entirely new products, as demonstrated by the introduction of the Apple Watch in 2015.

■ *Cyclical growth* – cyclical companies that are in the early stages of a strong sector rebound may entice investors with the promise of outsized growth ahead. This applies to a broad swath of companies, including auto, chemicals, metals & mining, homebuilding, oil & gas, and various commodities. Timing is critical here and past performance through prior cycles will be closely scrutinized.

## Moat & Barriers to Entry

Investors seek quality businesses that have sustainable competitive advantages over their peers and high barriers to entry. This is commonly referred to as a "moat". Differentiated products, intellectual property, scale, brand, sticky customer relationships, low cost structure, and high upfront capital investment all support the resilience of a business model. Market leadership and a proven track record also help give investors greater comfort about the resilience of the business and its moat. Industries with fewer competitors and high barriers to entry have greater prospects for outperformance. Be mindful, however, that industries currently generating high returns on capital may attract new entrants. So, even top-performing companies can never get complacent.

## Healthy Financial Profile

Ideally, IPO candidates have a strong financial track record of growth and profitability. The higher the margins and growth rates, the better. Both translate into strong earnings performance. Visibility into future sales, earnings and free cash flows is a plus. Recurring revenue from a resilient, subscription-based model commands a premium.

At the other end of the spectrum are more speculative, early-stage growth plays. Technology IPO candidates come to mind. These companies may have little or no earnings, but they offer the prospect of outsized growth and returns. Another category of IPO candidates can be gleaned from companies that promise upside through improved financial performance. Ideally, the improvements stem from identifiable operational initiatives such as pricing or cost initiatives. These IPO plays require a fine balance. Companies with operational upside should be differentiated from fixer-uppers. The latter are challenging IPO candidates in any market, probably better served by waiting to launch after the company gets cleaned up.

The balance sheet must also be strong enough to protect against potential challenges while supporting growth. Leverage above a certain level is frowned upon by IPO investors. At the very least, they will expect a credible path to deleveraging. Similarly, companies with a prior bankruptcy should expect probing over what happened in the past and why it's unlikely to repeat.

Highly capital intensive businesses also need to be treated with care in an IPO context. Investors will seek comfort around the company's cash burn rate and ability to generate FCF as it gains scale and profitability. This is particularly important when assessing loss-making companies with dynamic growth prospects.

## Disruptive & Differentiated Solutions

Pioneers in a new category often promise the type of electric growth that IPO investors covet. Technology stories are prominent in this regard. Amazon has been one of the ultimate disruptors—first in books and then across the entire retail spectrum, transportation and logistics, and even cloud computing.

Disruptors, however, are by no means limited to the tech sector. The healthcare industry, including biotech, is a major driver of new listings. In general, any business that takes share from traditional players has disruptive powers. Notable examples from the food and beverage sector include fast casual among restaurants, organic produce/alternative meats, and energy drinks; or in traditional industries such as decking and siding where new composite materials are taking share from wood and metals.

Market share gainers have superior growth prospects regardless of sector. At the same time, do not confuse fad with sustainable disruption. GoPro and Fitbit come to mind. Of course, there is plenty of gray area in between. Some fads can last years, not months…and some disruptors can themselves be disrupted before too long.

## Favorable Risk Profile

IPO investors focus on risk as well as the reward. Companies seeking to go public work with their lead investment banks to identify potential weaknesses upfront so as to address them head-on. In some cases, the risks may prove too burdensome and prompt the company to forgo the rigorous IPO process in favor of other alternatives.

Certain risk categories merit particular attention, as discussed below:

- *Cycle* – by definition, cycles go through peaks and valleys. Depending on the sector, the lows can be disproportionately low and the highs disproportionately high. IPO investors seek to understand the nature of the company's cycle, as well as the correlation with company performance. They will look at how the company performed in prior cycles and try to assess how it is likely to perform the next time around.

  How much were sales, margins, earnings, and cash flow impacted during the last downturn? Was bankruptcy on the table? Highly volatile cyclicality is treated with caution—investors typically seek compensation in the form of a lower multiple of earnings. On the other hand, timing is everything. A well-timed deep cyclical IPO can receive a warm reception and an attractive valuation.

- *Customer / supplier concentration* – while successful companies tend to have large customers and suppliers, balance is key. Too much concentration is looked upon unfavorably. Customer concentration is perhaps the most heavily scrutinized. Does the IPO candidate have too much exposure to Big Box or a single OEM? Over-reliance on a single supplier also poses risks in the event that the source flexes it muscles or has operational problems. The nature of the key customers or suppliers also matters, as does the length and stickiness of the relationship. A longstanding track record with a high-quality anchor customer or supplier helps provide comfort.

- *Geographic exposure* – like most key risk exposures, geographic diversification serves as a mitigant. The more local and concentrated the geographic focus, the higher the perceived risk. For U.S. IPO candidates, typical micro-exposures might include a disproportionate amount of sales in large states like California, Florida, or Texas. Or, heavy reliance on a region such as the Northeast or Southwest. This exposes these companies to local cycles, politics, and even weather events. While some portion of international sales is generally favorable as it represents global reach and diversification, single-country risk is certainly manageable, especially for large countries such as the U.S.

- *Competition* – investors closely scrutinize the company's position within its industry, as well as the competitive landscape itself. This analysis extends beyond today's current competitors to detect potential new entrants. Ideally, the company's current market share is stable or growing, and there are real barriers to entry to withstand competitive pressures. Intensifying competition is a red flag, threatening both sales and earnings going forward.

- *Operating history* – companies with a limited operating history will necessarily receive heavy scrutiny. Ideally, IPO investors want to see a track record. Many early-stage companies also rely on a new product or technology that is not yet proven. Hence, they are at the nexus of the risk/return trade-off with the promise of outsized returns serving to offset the higher risk. Even loss-making start-ups where most, if not all, of the value lies in performance far in the future can be successful IPOs. These IPO candidates are most often found in the tech and biotech sectors.

## Proven Management Team

A strong management team is a critical part of any investment opportunity. This is arguably even more true for IPO candidates given the need to entice investors to take a chance on a new opportunity. Investors often debate whether to bet on the jockey (CEO, management team) or the horse (business). Our experience is that both are essential. *Even the best jockey in the world can't turn a mule into a thoroughbred.*

A proven, talented C-suite (e.g., CEO, COO, CFO) and key division heads with a strong collective track record helps de-risk the investment while providing greater confidence on the upside. The team's background, experience, qualifications, and integrity are heavily scrutinized on the roadshow. Depth also matters as investors seek comfort that the company won't fall apart in the event that something unforeseen happens to the CEO or other key leaders (a.k.a., key-man risk). A truly stand-out Board consisting of *bona fide* operators and capital allocators with proven public company track records lends further credibility.

Senior management also drives company culture, which can be a differentiator in its own right. This is particularly common for founder-led and family-owned IPO candidates where strong guiding principles, values, passion, and vision are central to the story. In these cases, company ethos is a direct performance driver, motivating employees and other stakeholders to deliver superior results. It may also serve as an effective marketing tool, creating buzz and a halo effect among the investor community. Regardless of the company, leadership integrity is closely examined for obvious reasons, especially given that CEO and CFO sign-off is required for the financial statements.

In the event the company is owned by a PE or VC firm, the financial sponsor will be part of the diligence process. What is its IPO track record? Have its prior IPOs performed well? Are its companies generally prepared to go public in terms of infrastructure, back office, and IT? A strong sponsor with a proven history of success helps provide a halo. Of course, the opposite also holds true.

## KEY PARTICIPANTS

This section provides an overview of the key participants in an IPO (see Exhibit 8.3).

**EXHIBIT 8.3**   Key Participants

- Investment Banks
- Company Management
- Current Owners / Investors
- IPO Investors
- Lawyers
- Accountants
- Exchange Partner
- IPO Advisors
- Vendors

### Investment Banks

Investment banks are central players in the IPO process. Their role begins at the initial idea generation stage and extends through the intensive preparation phase all the way to IPO execution and the pricing of the company's stock. This entire process typically takes several months once the lead banks and lawyers are selected. Post-IPO, investment banks provide critical aftermarket support, research, and various other advisory and capital markets services to the company.

In advance of the formal IPO process, investment banks are called upon to assess whether a given company is a viable IPO candidate. In many cases, they proactively seek out companies they believe are suitable for an IPO months or even years in advance. At a very early stage, they may advise the company on how to best position itself for an eventual IPO—e.g., shed less attractive businesses, focus on certain products or geographies, bulk up the management team, etc.

The lead banks are known as *bookrunners* given their responsibility to build a "book" of stock orders. In reality, they have a much broader mandate than simply selling stock. They serve as advisors on all aspects of the IPO—overall strategy, preparation, positioning, valuation, structuring, timing, etc. As a result, the banks assemble a comprehensive multi-faceted team consisting of sector and company experts, equity capital markets professionals, research analysts, and traders and salespeople.

Exhibit 8.4 shows the various divisions within an investment bank that are responsible for delivering a successful IPO. On the so-called "private side", the core investment banking coverage team (IBD) typically serves as the primary liaison with the company and its owners, especially during the preparation phase. IBD consists of sector specialists and relationship managers who are best qualified to position and market the company effectively. They work closely with Equity Capital Markets (ECM) on valuation, due diligence, positioning, and the drafting of the prospectus and other marketing materials.

In parallel, on the "public side", the bank's Equity Research division (Research) assigns an analyst to cover the company's stock. The analyst conducts extensive due diligence on the company separate from IBD and ECM to develop an independent view of the company, including strengths and weaknesses, key performance drivers, relative positioning, and valuation. The Sales & Trading (S&T) arm of the investment bank is entrusted with marketing and selling the company's shares to investors. As such, they typically don't fully spring into action until the IPO is set to launch.

**EXHIBIT 8.4**    How an Investment Bank Works with Issuers and Investors

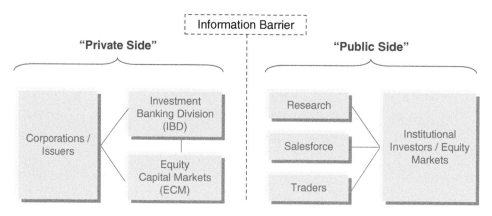

*Investment Banking Division (IBD)* typically houses the coverage bankers with the closest relationship to the company and its owners. These bankers tend to be sector experts with longstanding knowledge of the company and its story. As such, they are best positioned to liaise with the company on a daily basis and lead the pre-IPO preparation. The cornerstone components of this work include due diligence, positioning, and the drafting of the SEC-required offering documentation (e.g., the *registration statement* and *prospectus* that forms a part of the registration statement)[1] and roadshow presentation.

Throughout the IPO process, IBD coordinates with ECM, S&T, the exchange partner, and various other constituents to deliver the best execution. This extends to external parties, including lawyers, accountants, and consultants. As the IPO gets closer to launch date, IBD crystallizes a view on valuation, size, structure, and timing in concert with ECM. Once the SEC completes its review of the registration statement and the roadshow presentation is finalized, IBD and ECM jointly present a recommendation to the company on the pricing, size, and other key terms of the offering.

---

[1]Companies in the U.S. most commonly file their registration statement on a Form S-1, while foreign private issuers submit a Form F-1.

*Equity Capital Markets (ECM)* consists of bankers who focus on the equity markets day-in, day-out. The ECM team is typically comprised of *origination* and *syndicate*. The origination bankers work more closely with the company issuers, while syndicate interacts primarily with the bank's internal salesforce and investors. Within origination, the bankers are typically organized by sector expertise, e.g., technology, industrials, healthcare, consumer. This enables them to provide specialized knowledge and perspectives on how the market is likely to receive and value a given IPO candidate. They work closely with IBD on crafting the narrative for investors, which is captured in the prospectus and roadshow presentation. This collaboration extends to determining the appropriate group of comparable companies and indicative valuation range.

The collective ECM team collaborates on structuring the optimal size and terms of the IPO offering, while providing regular updates on equity market conditions and investor sentiment. Syndicate has the closest read on the market and is relied upon to help determine the optimal timing for launch. They also help identify those investors most likely to participate in the offering. In the later stages, ECM is responsible for managing the roadshow scheduling and logistics, as well as building and maintaining the *order book*. They serve as the key group linking the company to the bank's salesforce and investors during the roadshow. Ultimately, ECM allocates the shares to investors and then manages the aftermarket trading post-offering.

*Equity Research* houses the analysts who publish research reports on public companies targeted toward institutional investors. They maintain an independent opinion on the companies and industries in their coverage area. Like IBD and ECM, the analysts are typically specialized by sector. Once a bank is selected as an IPO underwriter, research management is notified and assigns an analyst to cover the company. The analyst then independently coordinates with the company on a due diligence game plan to get up-to-speed.[2]

Prior to the early 2000s, research analysts worked closely with IBD and ECM to pitch, execute, and market IPOs. After the burst of the dot-com bubble and multiple high-profile corporate scandals in the early 2000s, however, new policies and regulations were established to help safeguard the independence of research against any potential conflicts of interest.[3] The new regulations required investment banks to institute a clear "information barrier" between research and IBD. As a result, research and IBD cannot speak directly without a compliance chaperone to monitor and guide the call.

At the onset of the IPO marketing period, the research analyst educates the bank's salesforce on the opportunity. Then, during the ensuing roadshow, the analyst has in-depth conversations with prospective investors, with feedback relayed to company management and shareholders. Following the IPO, the analyst publishes an *initiating coverage* research report after a 25-day waiting period following the first day of trading.

---

[2]IBD and Research typically have an upfront call as the process kicks off (chaperoned by the bank's compliance team) to discuss the business, IPO context, and proposed transaction.
[3]As part of the Global Research Analyst Settlement of 2003, investment banks were required to separate the investment banking and research departments, and research analysts were prohibited from attending client meetings and roadshows.

Going forward, the analyst provides ongoing coverage in the form of quarterly research reports. Sales and earnings estimates are updated accordingly based on the latest company performance and outlook. Research reports may be published more frequently depending on company or sector-specific events and announcements. Analysts also host conferences and non-deal roadshows (NDRs) for the company.

*Sales & Trading (S&T)* serves as the bank's direct conduit to the equity market and investors. Immediately prior to launch, S&T hosts a "teach-in" for their salesforce team where company management presents on the investment opportunity. This presentation helps educate the salesforce on the thesis, which enables them to speak intelligently with investors and market effectively. To some extent, the teach-in also serves as a dry run for management as they prepare for the many investor meetings to follow.

As the roadshow kicks off, the salesforce educates company management on prospective investors. This information centers on the investors' current positions and historical IPO buying behavior, as well as their overall investment approach. At the same time, the bank's traders monitor market activity, especially in the issuer's sector, and provide the full deal team with daily trading updates and color.

Later in the roadshow, the salesforce takes indications of interest from investors and relays orders to ECM. The salesforce also provides regular updates on the order book and investor interest. Once the IPO is finalized, the bank's traders commence public trading of the stock, providing liquidity to investors. This includes managing the overallotment option and stabilizing the stock post-offering.

### Company Management

A high-quality management team is critical for guiding the company through the actual IPO process, which can be grueling. The team's capabilities and resolve is tested from the preparation phase through marketing and execution. They work closely with the bankers, lawyers, and accountants to ensure the IPO documentation and marketing materials are top quality.

While the CEO has ultimate responsibility for delivering on the above, a "deal captain" is typically appointed to coordinate both internally and externally on the day-to-day deliverables. This individual may be a CFO, COO, General Counsel, Head of Corporate Development, or other trusted senior executive. All senior executives must balance their IPO responsibilities with those of their core jobs. The company cannot afford to let the IPO process distract from financial performance as missing key earnings and sales hurdles will not be treated kindly by investors.

The CFO and broader finance team are responsible for the financial statements, MD&A, and other financial data required for the prospectus and roadshow presentation. The corporate strategy and business development team help ensure that the company's growth initiatives, both internal and M&A-related, and competitive opportunities are sufficiently captured. Depending on the company, Sales & Marketing may also play a meaningful role in drafting key IPO materials. Finally, the company's legal counsel works closely with outside counsel on the prospectus, SEC matters, due diligence, and various regulatory approvals.

On the roadshow, management serves as the face of the company and de facto chief marketers of the story. Investors will watch and listen to them carefully before deciding whether to invest. Ultimately, they will ask themselves: "Is this a team we want to back?"

## Current Owners / Investors

The company's ownership also needs to be considered within the context of the IPO. Typical owners include PE and VC firms, families, founders, and management. Certain institutional investors, alternative asset managers, sovereign wealth funds, and pensions may also own sizable ownership stakes in pre-IPO candidates. This is especially true for larger, high-profile companies.

As previously discussed, PE firms tend to invest in later-stage, more mature business models with sufficient cash flows to support their elevated leverage. The larger ones own sizable companies for whom an IPO exit is a viable option and may represent a favorable monetization outcome over an outright sale. VC firms, by contrast, tend to invest in smaller, early-stage companies that hold out the promise of outsized growth. These companies are *de facto* more speculative and tend to be technology-oriented businesses. Many of them are pioneers with disruptive business models that lack obvious buyers or clear public comps at the time of their IPO.

Family-owned businesses choose to go public for many reasons, including generational change, legacy, monetization, and operational considerations tied to competitiveness. Depending on the circumstances, an IPO may prove more compelling than an outright sale. While the IPO opens up ownership to new shareholders, the family can maintain control through outright majority ownership or privileged share classes.

The CEO and other senior managers of IPO candidates are almost always shareholders to some degree. At one end of the spectrum are founder/CEOs (e.g., Jeff Bezos of Amazon.com and Marc Benioff of Salesforce.com) who own large stakes while running the company. On the other end are professional managers with relatively little ownership in the company. While employee ownership is typically concentrated among upper management, it often extends through multiple levels of the organization. Senior management sometimes sells shares in an IPO via a secondary component, but investors typically want to see them maintain meaningful "skin in the game."

## IPO Investors

IPO investors are the buyers of the company's new equity shares, typically broken down into two main categories—institutional and retail. Institutional investors are the larger group, generally comprising roughly 80% of the offering. They include mutual funds, hedge funds, sovereign wealth funds, pensions, insurance companies, and family offices. Retail investors are individuals who buy shares in the IPO through their brokerage firm. They are commonly referred to as high-net-worth or individual investors.

Institutional investors are expected to perform detailed due diligence and go through their formal internal approval processes before participating in an IPO. SEC guidelines require all investors to receive the issuer's preliminary prospectus or "*red herring*".[4] The prospectus contains essential information on the company and the investment opportunity that is deemed material to review prior to investing.

---

[4]The term red herring refers to the legend printed on the preliminary prospectus in red typeface stating that the information in the prospectus is not complete and may be changed; the securities may not be sold until the registration is effective; and that the prospectus is not an offer to sell the securities where the offer or sale is not permitted.

A thorough review of the prospectus, however, is just one part of the institutional due diligence process. The roadshow meeting with management is another key milestone, providing the opportunity for investors to hear the story directly from management and participate in a Q&A session. These meetings are typically accompanied by a slideshow presentation and may be one-on-one or as part of group meetings with investors, often over breakfast or lunch.

## Lawyers

Legal counsel is intimately involved with the IPO process from the onset. Lawyer selection is generally completed in tandem with choosing the lead investment banks. Together, the two of them shepherd the company through the process, which can be highly technical given SEC rules and regulations. The two main sets of lawyers involved in an IPO are *company counsel* and *underwriters' counsel*. Both work in unison to complete the various legal agreements and help deliver a successful outcome.

Upfront, company counsel ensures that the company is properly positioned from a legal standpoint to undertake an IPO. This involves conducting *corporate housekeeping* (see Chapter 9) and extensive legal due diligence, including a review of the company's current corporate structure, ownership arrangements, material contracts, and any current or expected litigation.

Company counsel also takes ownership of drafting the registration statement. This involves actively drafting the document in concert with the bankers and key company officers, as well as the actual filing of the document. Regarding the latter, company counsel quarterbacks the entire registration process, including working with the SEC to address their comments and questions.

Underwriter's counsel protects the interest of the bookrunners by ensuring that the registration statement is accurate and complete in all material respects. They are also actively involved in the diligence process and lead the drafting of the *underwriting agreement* (see Chapter 9) and *lock-up agreement*. Moreover, underwriter's counsel is chiefly responsible for negotiating the *comfort letter* with the accountants.

## Accountants

The accounting firm is responsible for reviewing and auditing the company's financial statements for inclusion in the prospectus. This must be accomplished in accordance with SEC rules that generally require three years of historical audited financials and five years of selected financial data.[5] Companies seek reputable independent accounting firms as their IPO partners—engaging a well-respected auditor is often a key checklist item for investors.

Following the initial audit of company financials for inclusion in the registration statement, the accounting firm helps the company address follow-up requests from the SEC during the review period (see Chapter 9). They also render a comfort letter to confirm the accuracy of the financial data included in the registration statement. Comfort letters are a key element in the due diligence performed by the underwriters

---

[5]For Emerging Growth Companies (EGC), a category of issuer with annual gross revenues of less than $1,070 million, the SEC only requires two years of annual historical audited financials and two years of selected financial data. Once the company loses its EGC status, however, it becomes subject to standard requirements for future SEC filings and capital offerings.

and their counsel. The accounting firm also provides advice on internal controls for the soon-to-be public company, which extends to identifying and addressing potential accounting issues going forward, as appropriate.

## Exchange Partner

The exchange where the company lists represents an important partner in the IPO process and beyond. As a result, companies contemplating an IPO often begin interacting with potential exchange partners well in advance of the process. The exchanges work with companies to help them understand IPO mechanics and how they will help launch their IPO and work with them post-listing, including engagement with the investment community, regulators, and other stakeholders. Once selected, they start working together more closely, including collaboration on the company's IPO day, which represents a high-visibility milestone and branding opportunity.

U.S. companies typically choose to list on either Nasdaq or the NYSE. Nasdaq invented electronic trading in 1971 and their model is now the standard for markets worldwide. Today, Nasdaq and the NYSE both run electronic markets. NYSE uses a floor-based model in conjunction with third-party, high-frequency trading firms called designated market makers, while Nasdaq utilizes its proprietary technology developed in partnership with the investment banking community. Nasdaq also offers a platform called Nasdaq Private Market, which helps private companies facilitate secondary transactions for early investors and employees with vested equity to sell a portion of their shares while the company is still private (see Appendix 8.1).

Given the long-term nature of the relationship, companies look to partner with exchanges that provide value-added services throughout their life cycle. For example, Nasdaq offers pre-IPO advisory services, visibility support on IPO day, proprietary Investor Relations and Corporate Governance services—including Nasdaq IR Insight (see Appendix 8.2) and Nasdaq Boardvantage (see Appendix 8.3)—and potential index inclusion. The NYSE offers similar Investor Relations capabilities through third-party vendors.

When applying to list on a U.S. exchange, companies must submit a symbol reservation form, listing application, listing agreement, and corporate governance certification. It generally takes four to six weeks to process a listing application, but this period is variable and can be shortened if the application raises no issues and the company responds quickly to staff comments.

Sample listing application timeframe:

- Week 1 – Company submits application for listing and Listing Qualifications Staff begins its review

- Weeks 2 to 3 – Staff completes its preliminary review and prepares comment letter

- Weeks 3 to 4 – Company addresses any issues raised by staff

- Weeks 5 to 6 – Staff completes their review and company is approved for listing

## IPO Advisors

The hiring of IPO advisors prior to embarking on a formal IPO process has become increasingly prevalent. Their mandate is to help coordinate a tight and successful overall process, while serving as on-call advisors on any and all topics ranging from execution-related to strategic. These advisors are separate from, and in addition to, the traditional investment bank underwriters who run the IPO process and underwrite the share offering.

Upfront, the IPO advisors' most important deliverable is to help the company and its shareholders select the optimal underwriting syndicate and accompanying research analysts. This involves crafting a short list of banks for consideration and then coordinating the entire outreach and bake-off process. The IPO advisors typically draft and distribute an RFP to the banks and schedule the bake-off meetings. They attend these presentations and help grade the banks on various metrics, including experience, unique knowledge and insights, research and distribution capabilities, and relationship with the company and shareholders.

Once the left lead bank is chosen, the IPO advisors handle the underwriter fee negotiations and pass the baton for running the IPO process on a day-to-day basis. However, the IPO advisors continue to be involved in an advisory and monitoring role, participating in the due diligence and registration statement drafting sessions and providing input on various topics along the way. They also take the lead on organizing the critical research analyst outreach process and ensuing diligence and engagement.

Later on, the IPO advisors provide counsel on the lead bookrunners' recommendations with regard to timing, offering structure, size, and valuation. Their experience from working on a multitude of IPOs across various sectors and situations helps inform their views on optimal execution. The same holds true for input on investor targeting, pricing, and share allocation strategy. Post-IPO, the IPO advisors apply the same expertise toward follow-on equity offerings and block trades (see later in this chapter).

## Vendors

Outside vendors and third-party service providers also play a key role in the IPO process, including the financial printer and data room providers. The printer typesets the registration statement and ultimately handles submitting it to the SEC electronically through EDGAR.[6] Hundreds (or more) glossy hard copies of the prospectus are then printed and distributed to potential investors at the time of the roadshow launch. The company must also select from a short list of potential data room providers, often with guidance from the lead bookrunner. The virtual data room is then set up and populated with myriad company documents related to the IPO, organized by category. This facilitates underwriter due diligence and document drafting.

---

[6]Upon receiving comments from the SEC, the printer also processes edits to the registration statement and helps file the amendments.

## SELECTED KEY TERMS

Exhibit 8.5 displays a sample term sheet for an IPO offering, followed by a more detailed explanation of several of these key concepts.

**EXHIBIT 8.5**   IPO Term Sheet

| Summary of Initial Public Offering Terms | |
|---|---|
| Issuer | Entity that is offering shares to the public |
| Offering Size | Dollar amount of the initial public offering, expressed as a range |
| Primary / Secondary | Breakdown between newly issued and existing shares being offered to investors |
| Overallotment Option | % of overallotment option (typically 15%) and breakdown of primary, secondary mix of shares |
| Timing | Date of the offering, typically expressed as the expected quarter and year (e.g., "Q4'19"); if known, the exact month and year |
| Syndicate | Group of banks underwriting the IPO with roles noted |
| Lock-up Provision | Number of days pre-IPO shareholders are prohibited from selling shares post the offering |
| Listing Exchange | Nasdaq or NYSE (if listing in the U.S.) |
| Target Investors | % breakdown between institutional and retail investors |
| Geographic Mix | % breakdown between U.S. and international investors |
| Marketing Program | Detail around the roadshow (length of days), conference calls (key domestic and international accounts), and internet roadshow |
| Gross Spread (%) | Bookrunner and co-manager compensation for underwriting the transaction |

## Offering Size

Offering size refers to the proposed dollar amount of the IPO. While sizing depends on the situation, there are certain guideposts. A typical offering falls somewhere within the range of 15% to 25% of the company's implied market capitalization. In terms of dollar amounts, the minimum recommended size tends to start at $100 million as a threshold for trading liquidity. To put this in perspective, the largest U.S. IPO in history was Alibaba's $25 billion offering in 2014, and the largest global IPO was Aramco's $29.4 billion offering in 2019/2020.

Exhibit 8.6 shows the number of U.S. deals at various size ranges since 2009.

**EXHIBIT 8.6**   Summary of U.S. IPO Sizing since 2009

*($ in millions, except # of deals)*

| Summary of U.S. IPO Sizing since 2009 | | |
|---|---|---|
| Market Value | # of Deals | Average Base Deal[a] |
| < $250 | 423 | $101 |
| $250 – $499 | 198 | $185 |
| $500 – $999 | 185 | $236 |
| $1,000 – $2,499 | 188 | $297 |
| > $2,500 | 237 | $740 |

[a]Excludes overallotment option.

For the company and its shareholders, the optimal amount is driven by the size of the company and need/use of proceeds. For example, companies with little debt and a relatively limited need for proceeds might opt for a smaller IPO. This would make further sense if the shareholders are reluctant sellers, looking to hold their stock for the long term. On the other end of the spectrum, a company with a large cash need and/or shareholders eager to monetize their investment after a long holding period might push for a larger IPO.

All of these considerations need to be weighed against investor priorities, including sufficient trading liquidity post-IPO and a preference for pre-listing shareholders to retain meaningful skin in the game. After all, the ultimate IPO size and pricing relies upon company supply and investor demand. All else being equal, investors tend to prefer larger deals given the built-in liquidity. Of course, this is somewhat self-selecting as larger deals also tend to come from bigger, more established companies.

## Primary / Secondary

Offering mix goes hand in hand with proper sizing as both are connected to the use of proceeds. Mix refers to the proportion of primary and secondary shares. Primary proceeds go directly to the company and can be used for a variety of purposes. Secondary proceeds go directly to selling shareholders. Striking the optimal balance is important for the company's growth plan and capitalization, as well as investor messaging.

IPOs can be comprised entirely of primary or secondary shares, or any combination in between. Multiple factors play into the offering mix. Fast-growing pioneering companies typically need the cash from primary offerings to fund operations, expansion plans, and other critical projects. For more mature companies, right-sizing the capital structure may be a key consideration, especially former LBOs that tend to have higher leverage than public peers. Primary proceeds enable these companies to repay debt, thereby providing greater operational and financial flexibility in the future. Regardless, the use of proceeds should be consistent with the company's strategic goals and messaging to investors.

*Primary shares* refer to newly issued shares of common stock that are sold to investors. Companies in growth mode with sizable cash needs look to primary offerings to fuel their business. This extends to the vast majority of pre-profit tech offerings. Below are the most common uses of proceeds from primary share sales:

- Growth investments

- Repay outstanding debt

- General corporate purposes, including working capital

- M&A (bolt-ons and larger transactions)

*Secondary shares* refer to existing shares of common stock that are sold to new investors in an offering. Whereas primary proceeds provide the company with additional cash, a secondary share offering does not. Proceeds go directly to selling shareholders, e.g., founders, financial sponsors, VCs, etc., seeking to monetize their stakes. Secondary share sales do not change the number of shares outstanding.

The sale of secondary shares depends on the need for primary proceeds, as well as the monetization plans for the shareholders. While some shareholders may seek to sell as much as possible via the IPO, others may be long-term holders. In the event the company prioritizes maximum primary proceeds for growth initiatives or deleveraging, there may be little room left for a secondary component. As such, the secondary offering tends to be a discretionary component of the offering, with major sales by senior management generally frowned upon by prospective investors.

## Overallotment Option, a.k.a. "Greenshoe"

The overallotment option, also known as the *greenshoe*,[7] provides the ability to sell additional shares to investors in excess of the original IPO offering. The purpose of the greenshoe is largely to serve as a stabilization mechanism. In this sense, it is intended to increase investor confidence by providing immediate aftermarket support and stability.

The greenshoe is limited to 15% of the offering size and typically may be exercised by the underwriters for 30 days following the IPO pricing. It can be structured as primary, secondary, or a combination thereof. Initially, it actually creates a short position since the underwriters have the ability to buy 15% of the deal size from the issuer or selling shareholders at the IPO price.

Exhibit 8.7 illustrates various greenshoe scenarios. Under strong conditions, the share price rises (and stays above the initial offer price) and the short position is covered by exercising the greenshoe. In this scenario, underwriters buy shares from the company or selling shareholders at the initial offer price.

In weak conditions, the share price drops below the initial offer price and the underwriters typically purchase shares in the open market, commonly referred to as *stabilization*. Stabilization provides support for the company's shares in early trading and helps smooth out volatility. In this scenario, the short position is retired and the greenshoe is not exercised.

**EXHIBIT 8.7**   Greenshoe Overview

| Offer Price | Issue Size | Conditions | Comments |
|---|---|---|---|
| Above | 15% | Strong | **Strong Conditions**<br>• Share price increases above offer price<br>• Stabilization not needed<br>• *Greenshoe exercised* |
| At / Below | 100% | Mixed / Weak | **Mixed Conditions**<br>• Share price under modest pressure<br>• Some stabilization needed<br>• *Greenshoe partially exercised*<br><br>**Weak Conditions**<br>• Share price well below offer price<br>• Stabilization needed<br>• *Greenshoe not exercised* |

---

[7]The term "greenshoe" comes from the Green Shoe Manufacturing Company (now called Stride Rite Corporation), which was the first company to implement the greenshoe clause into its underwriting agreement.

## Syndicate Structure

Syndicate structure refers to the hierarchy of the investment banks running the IPO process. These banks are collectively referred to as *underwriters* and are designated as *bookrunners* or *co-managers*. Each of these categories is further broken down into active and passive roles, as shown in Exhibit 8.8.

**EXHIBIT 8.8**   Roles of Syndicate

| Roles of Syndicate | |
|---|---|
| Type | Description |
| Active Bookrunners | <ul><li>Serve as overall IPO advisor</li><li>Lead due diligence, draft prospectus and roadshow presentation</li><li>Recommend offering size, terms, and initial pricing range</li><li>Coordinate roadshow and investor meetings, maintain order book</li><li>Make the final pricing and allocation recommendations</li><li>Provide research</li></ul> |
| Passive Bookrunners | <ul><li>Support the offering and provide research coverage</li><li>Participate in drafting sessions and provide input on strategic topics, as appropriate</li></ul> |
| Co-Managers | <ul><li>Typically, provide research and ongoing support for the company post-IPO</li></ul> |

Active bookrunners are entrusted with leading the IPO process. During the preparatory phase, this involves working hand-in-hand with management to manage due diligence, crystallize the marketing story, and draft the prospectus and roadshow presentation. Later on, they recommend the optimal IPO offering size, terms, and initial pricing range. Upon IPO launch, they coordinate the roadshow, during which they host investor meetings, maintain the order book, and make the final pricing and allocation recommendations. Within this group, one bank is appointed the left lead bookrunner[8] and carries the greatest responsibility for delivering a successful outcome.

Depending on the size of the offering, there are often two to three active bookrunners and an equal or larger number of passives. The passive bookrunners help support the offering and are expected to provide research coverage. In some cases, they may participate in drafting sessions and provide input on strategic topics, including messaging, comps, and potentially offering size and structure.

Co-managers play a lesser role in the actual process but are typically expected to provide research and ongoing support for the company post-IPO. Regardless of role, all members of the syndicate fulfill their institutional due diligence and compliance requirements.

---

[8]Refers to the bank whose name is listed first on the prospectus cover, which begins on the left side of the page.

One of the active bookrunners is also assigned the role of *stabilization agent*. The stabilization agent is responsible for managing aftermarket trading and exercising the greenshoe (if warranted). While the role itself does not command additional fees, the agent opens trading of the stock, which tends to increase trading flow to the firm. One of the active bookrunners is also assigned responsibility for handling *billing and delivery* of shares. As with the role of stabilization agent, these activities do not directly generate upfront fees, but tend to lead to enhanced trading volume. The issuer has discretion to bifurcate the active bookrunners taking on these duties (stabilization agent is preferred to handling billing and delivery), or reward one bank with both. Finally, one bookrunner is responsible for coordinating the logistics for the roadshow (hotel reservations, travel arrangements, etc.).

### Lock-up Provision

The *lock-up* provision[9] is an agreement signed by the company's existing shareholders, officers, and directors that prohibits them from selling stock for a set period following the IPO, typically 180 days. The lock-up is designed to provide comfort to the new IPO investors that insiders, i.e., those that know the company best, won't run for the exits. Also, from a technical standpoint, investors want a mechanism in place to prevent potential excess selling pressure on the stock from a flood of new shares in the market.

To prevent high-volume selling once the 180 days are up, the underwriters may also implement a staggered lock-up agreement. The staggering provision limits the number of shares that can be sold upon lock-up expiration and designates a timeframe for the sale of the remainder of shares. In some cases, the lead bookrunners may authorize an early lock-up release, typically only when the share price has risen considerably following the IPO. This makes sense—it is easier for the market to absorb chunky share sales without meaningful downward pressure on the stock when the IPO has been successful and investor interest is strong. These share sales are typically done in an organized fashion via a marketed *follow-on offering* (discussed later in this chapter).

### Listing Exchange

The listing exchange refers to the stock exchange where the company lists its shares for trading. For companies who plan to list in the United States, the majority choose between Nasdaq or NYSE. While Nasdaq and NYSE both run electronic markets, NYSE opens stocks with the help of third-party, high-frequency trading firms called designated market makers. Nasdaq, on the other hand, opens stocks with its proprietary technology developed in partnership with the investment banking community. The exchanges have separate listing requirements and fees.

Ultimately, the choice between a Nasdaq or NYSE listing relies primarily on qualitative factors. For example, an issuer may choose to list on the same exchange as key peers, or may favor the promotions offered by a given exchange. The company may also have a preexisting relationship with the exchange, e.g., the use of Nasdaq's private market platform to facilitate pre-IPO secondary transactions, or Nasdaq Boardvantage collaboration and governance software.

---

[9]In the underwriting agreement, the company also covenants not to sell stock for the same period that the shareholders are under lock-up.

## Gross Spread

The *gross spread*, or underwriting spread, is the compensation paid to the bookrunners and co-managers, expressed as a percentage of the total offering size. The spread percentage is negotiated between the bookrunners and the company. It reflects multiple factors, most notably offering size, structure, syndicate composition, complexity, and precedent spreads on similar offerings.

The industry standard gross spread for IPOs is 7%, but larger ones typically feature a lower percentage in the spirit of a volume discount.[10] Each underwriter's share of the gross spread reflects its title, role, and responsibilities. The active bookrunners garner a higher share of economics than passives, who in turn have greater economics than the co-manager. In most cases, the left lead is awarded the highest economics, although it is not entirely uncommon for two lead actives to receive equal compensation. An illustrative example of syndicate economics is shown in Exhibit 8.9.

An incentive fee may also be paid in addition to the gross spread for delivering a superior outcome, typically tied to pricing the deal at a target level or factors related to deal complexity and resources. This is typically reserved for the lead bookrunners at the company's discretion and determined when the IPO is priced.

**EXHIBIT 8.9**    Illustrative Syndicate Economics

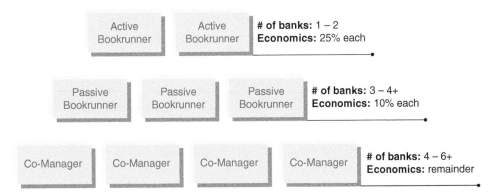

As shown in Exhibit 8.10, the gross spread consists of three different components: *management fee, underwriting fee,* and *selling concession.* The management fee serves to compensate the banks for their corporate finance advice, deal structuring, document preparation, and overall transaction coordination. The underwriting fee compensates the banks for the underwriting risk taken given the uncertainty surrounding any new equity offering. The selling concession comprises the largest portion of the gross spread. This is particularly applicable for large deals that require an intensive sales effort to successfully place the shares. As noted earlier, the underwriters' salesforces work through both institutional and retail channels to generate as much demand as possible.

---

[10]For IPOs of $150 million or less, the gross spread is almost always 7%.

**EXHIBIT 8.10**    Gross Spread Breakdown

| Components of the Gross Spread | | |
|---|---|---|
| Fee Type | % of Gross Spread | Compensation Basis |
| Management fee | 20% | ▪ Advisory services and transaction coordination (structuring, positioning, due diligence, document preparation, roadshow organization) |
| Underwriting fee | 20% | ▪ Underwriting risk related to the offering<br>▪ Underwriters' expenses are deducted from this fee |
| Selling concession | 60% | ▪ Bookrunners' salesforces for placement of shares with institutional and retail accounts |

For the institutional channel, the selling concession is typically structured using a *fixed economics* mechanism, where the bookrunners are assigned their respective economics upfront. This is designed to provide them with certainty and proper incentives to work together to deliver the best possible deal. In rare circumstances, a *jump-ball* mechanism may be utilized, whereby underwriters are compensated based on input from those investors that receive allocations (i.e., investors designate those banks they wish to receive credit for selling them the shares).

## DUAL-TRACK PROCESS

In a *dual-track* process, the company simultaneously pursues both an IPO offering and a sale of the company. Dual-track processes are designed to maximize flexibility and competitive tension in pursuit of the best outcome, typically maximum value. They are relatively common for PE and VC-backed companies looking to take advantage of potential arbitrage between the M&A and IPO markets.

Ideally, the dual track benefits from the overlap in parallel workstreams to maximize efficiency. This starts with the lead banks, who are typically the same for both the sale and IPO processes. They are able to leverage their due diligence, marketing materials, intimate understanding of the "story", and management prep for both paths. The prospectus serves as the basis for the key marketing documents in the sale process (CIM and management presentation). The data room created to house key company information and documents can also be used for both processes.

Despite the inherent optionality, not all situations may be appropriate for a dual track. Given the additional time, resources, and expense required, the dual-track decision merits real thought and consideration. Bankers are called upon to assess the company's prospects for each. For M&A, are there credible buyers at attractive valuations? Is the IPO market truly open and receptive? In many cases, the prospects for one path versus the other may be dramatically different.

Ideally, both paths should be equally viable and compelling for the company. This puts the selling shareholders in the enviable position of having a choice between two highly attractive options. In practice, however, a dual track is often used as a tool to increase competitive tension for an M&A sale process. The threat of an IPO forces potential buyers to compete with the company's option to go public as well as one another. This tactic is often used to get a specific buyer or buyer(s) to move aggressively to pre-empt the IPO, similar to a negotiated sale to avoid an auction.

Exhibit 8.11 displays the advantages and disadvantages of a dual-track process.

**EXHIBIT 8.11**   Advantages and Disadvantages of a Dual-Track Process

| | Dual-Track Process |
|---|---|
| Advantages | ▪ Maximizes odds of achieving maximum value |
| | ▪ Provides "insurance" for IPO path |
| | ▪ Heightens competitive tension for M&A process |
| | ▪ Imposes disciplined timetable and sense of urgency for buyers |
| | ▪ Final decision made late stages once relative valuations are assessed |
| | ▪ Each path provides price guidance for the other process |
| | ▪ Synergies between both processes / overlap in work streams |
| Disadvantages | ▪ Additional time, resources, and expenses |
| | ▪ Substantial management undertaking |
| | ▪ Risk of business suffering due to time commitment |
| | ▪ Competing priorities between the two paths |
| | ▪ IPO filings publicly disclose potentially sensitive information |

The decision to pursue a dual-track process requires a balanced assessment of the pros and cons of a straight IPO versus a sale process (see Exhibit 8.12).

**EXHIBIT 8.12**    Benefits and Considerations of an IPO vs. M&A Sale Process

|  | IPO | M&A Sale Process |
|---|---|---|
| Benefits | ▪ Public markets may provide a premium valuation<br><br>▪ Valuation driven off future earnings<br><br>▪ Owners maintain ownership of business and upside through retained stake<br><br>▪ May be only viable option given lack of credible buyers<br><br>▪ Creates public currency for employee incentives, capital raises, future M&A<br><br>▪ Establishes company legacy<br><br>▪ Tax efficiency | ▪ Maximum upfront cash<br><br>▪ Certainty around value and cash received<br><br>▪ Ideally, multiple paid reflects credit for future performance<br><br>▪ Potential for premium from motivated buyer<br><br>▪ Not dependent on IPO market conditions<br><br>▪ Deep and broad universe of corporate and PE buyers<br><br>▪ No public filings or disclosure requirements for seller |
| Considerations | ▪ Only partial upfront liquidity<br><br>▪ Dependent on equity market conditions<br><br>▪ Valuation subject to future market risk and stock trading uncertainty<br><br>▪ Public disclosure, incl. scrutiny of strategy, finances, and expenses<br><br>▪ Pressure to hit earnings targets and investor demands<br><br>▪ Public company costs<br><br>▪ Time intensive process | ▪ Forgo full upside opportunity going forward<br><br>▪ Valuation multiples tend to be based on near-term/LTM earnings<br><br>▪ Potential limited universe of buyers depending on size, sector, and performance<br><br>▪ Management and employee roles going forward<br><br>▪ Retention of company legacy |

## SPECIAL PURPOSE ACQUISITION COMPANIES (SPACs)

*Special Purpose Acquisition Companies (SPACs)* are entities that raise capital from investors through an IPO in anticipation of acquiring a company at a later date. In contrast to a traditional IPO, the entity going public has no business operations or assets on its balance sheet. For this reason, the SPAC IPO takes place in a compressed timeframe, often twelve to fifteen weeks. Given the vehicle has no operating history or assets, the IPO registration statement is typically boilerplate except for critical information on the SPAC sponsors and officers, investment strategy, and focus areas.

The SPAC's focus depends on the sponsor and its mandate. Some SPACs target specific industries in line with the sponsor's expertise and experience. Others focus on certain geographies (e.g., China, LatAm, or emerging markets), or situations, such as family-owned, operational turnarounds, or an unsustainable ownership structure. SPAC sponsors tend to be corporate executives, professional investors, PE firms, or hedge funds with successful M&A and investing track records. In many cases, a PE firm or hedge fund will partner with an executive or industry expert to identify and ultimately help run the acquisition target. As with a traditional IPO, investment banks play a crucial role in the SPAC process from registration through acquisition identification, target valuation, and transaction advisory.

The typical SPAC IPO structure entails the issuance of *units*, which are composed of common stock and a warrant (full or partial) to purchase additional stock.[11] Within 60 days of the IPO, the unit disaggregates, with the warrant and common stock trading separately. Following the separation, a secondary market for the SPAC forms where investors can purchase either warrants or common stock.

Following the IPO, the SPAC generally has up to 24 months to source and execute an acquisition, typically enlisting the services of one or more investment banks to help with the process. During the acquisition search, the IPO proceeds are held in a trust, where they are usually invested in short-term treasuries. Once a deal is announced (typically post shareholder approval), investors have the right to redeem their stock for cash (principal plus interest on treasuries) or participate in the equity of the new company. The SPAC IPO investors retain their warrants regardless of whether they redeem or not. If no deal is consummated, the SPAC is liquidated and money is returned to investors.

While SPACs have been around since the 1990s, the vehicle has seen a resurgence in recent years. In 2019, SPACs accounted for over 20% of all U.S. IPO volume, up from 5% in 2014 (see Exhibit 8.13). Several factors have contributed to the recent volume growth, namely, relatively muted IPO market activity (especially from 2015 to 2017), record high stock market levels and valuations, and enormous sums of capital chasing returns. PE firms and hedge funds are central players in the SPAC market, both as sellers of companies and as sponsors of their own SPAC vehicles. SPAC IPO investors range from pure arbitragers who invariably look to redeem their shares and retain the free warrants, to fundamental investors looking to get in at the ground floor and receive warrants.

---

[11]The unit is typically priced at $10.00, with the warrant having a strike price of $11.50. SPAC IPO investors are awarded warrants as compensation for coming into a blind pool upfront versus those who invest later after the target has been identified.

**EXHIBIT 8.13**    U.S. SPAC Volume and % of All IPO Activity 2014 – 2019

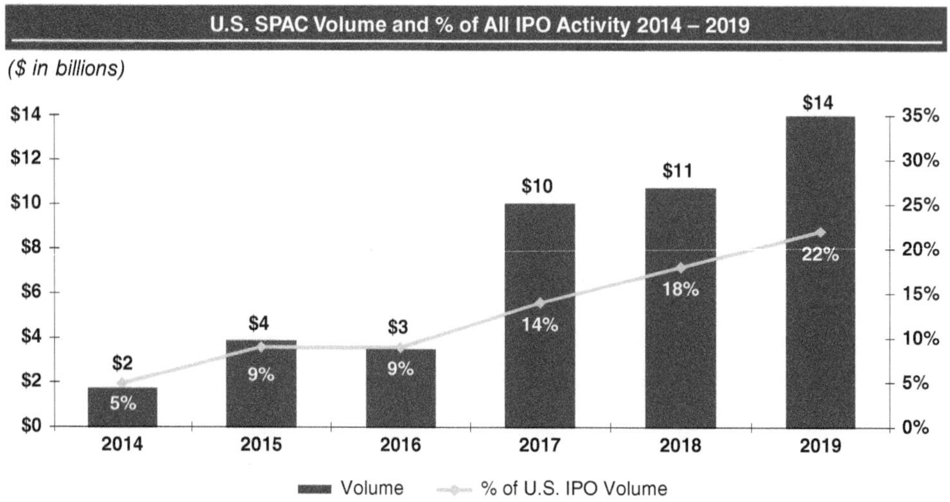

Source: Bloomberg and Dealogic

SPACs are particularly well-suited for situations that are overlooked by the traditional IPO and M&A markets. To some extent, a SPAC is a hybrid of an IPO and a sale of the company. Like a sale, the valuation is negotiated upfront and contemplates real cash proceeds to the seller, as well as the ability to structure earn-outs.

A SPAC deal is also legally structured as a merger of the target company and the SPAC vehicle. This affords greater flexibility than an S-1 in terms of what information can be presented to the market (e.g., forward-looking statements, comps, projections, etc.). It also provides an expedited timetable and is less dependent on prevailing market conditions than a regular-way IPO.

On the other hand, sellers need to be cognizant of certain transaction attributes unique to SPACs. The SPAC sponsor is compensated with a "promote", typically 20% of the SPAC IPO value. The promote rewards the sponsor for its deal origination and execution, as well as the associated hard expenses (e.g., funding the SPAC IPO upfront, running the public vehicle, due diligence, travel, etc.). In addition, signing up a deal with a SPAC does not ensure that the equity can be successfully placed with investors. The seller does not receive true deal certainty and proceeds until a sufficient number of equity investors buy into the deal at the proposed terms (which is not guaranteed).

## DIRECT LISTINGS

In a *direct listing*, the company lists outstanding shares directly onto a stock exchange without underwriters, thereby forgoing the traditional IPO roadshow and bookbuilding process. This means that a company does not raise any new capital in a direct listing, which may limit the number and types of companies for whom it is relevant. Existing shareholders, such as founders, employees, and early-stage investors, are free to sell their shares on the stock exchange selected by the company (but are not obligated to do so). Notable direct listings include Spotify (2018), Slack (2019), and Watford Re (2019). Nasdaq has completed 11 direct listings since 2006, and in 2014 it extended the use of its IPO Cross for direct listings.

Similar to a traditional IPO, a direct listing requires the company to abide by all SEC and stock exchange requirements. The registration statement for a direct listing is also substantially similar to a registration statement for a traditional IPO as the SEC requirements for financial, business, legal, and other disclosures are generally the same. As a result, much of the pre-launch process is essentially the same in terms of corporate housekeeping, choosing lead advisors, and holding a kick-off *organizational meeting* (see Chapter 9). The primary differences between a traditional IPO and a direct listing relate to mechanics, marketing, and timing, as outlined below:

- *Roadshow* – In a typical IPO, the underwriters host representatives from the company on a multi-week roadshow to market the offering through a series of meetings with buyside institutional investors. A video recording of the roadshow presentation is also made freely available to investors online. In a direct listing, there is no traditional IPO roadshow prior to the opening of trading. Given the company is not marketing an offering, there is greater flexibility as to the type and amount of investor education undertaken.

  Spotify and Slack, for example, chose to conduct an "investor day" whereby a presentation was publicly streamed live over the internet with in-person attendance and questions from the investor community. A company pursuing a direct listing may also elect to meet individually with potential investors (effectively a version of its own "roadshow"). However, the investment banks involved in a direct listing as financial advisors are excluded from the marketing process with the burden on the company to arrange meetings with investors. There is no "one-size-fits-all" package; rather, investor education should be calibrated to the company to ensure an informed buyside.

- *Forward-looking financial guidance* – Companies pursuing a direct listing may choose to offer guidance prior to listing on the stock exchange. This stands in contrast to a traditional IPO where no forward-looking guidance is typically issued until after the offering due to liability concerns.

- *Lock-up* – There is no lock-up agreement for existing shareholders in a direct listing, whereas there is typically a 180-day lock-up in a traditional IPO. This provides existing shareholders with earlier access to liquidity, potentially allowing them to benefit from early enthusiasm in the stock.

- *Investment banks* – Given there is no underwritten offering, investment banks take on the role of financial advisors rather than underwriters. As a result, traditional IPO gross spread mechanics do not apply. Rather, a select group of investment banks are paid a fixed fee for certain advisory services, such as helping to craft the marketing story and related public presentations/communications, SEC documentation, and facilitating the opening of trading. They also typically provide equity research coverage once the company is public. All expenses in a direct listing, including fees paid to the financial advisors, are expensed as incurred versus being paid out of gross proceeds. Therefore, the company requires sufficient liquidity and balance sheet capacity in advance of listing.

- *No bookbuilding process* – In a direct listing, unlike a traditional IPO, there is no bookbuilding process to determine the price at which underwriters initially sell shares to the public. Instead, buy and sell orders are collected from broker-dealers on behalf of the investment community, and this information is aggregated while the exchange simulates a high-frequency auction to guide the public on the official opening price for the shares. While there is no allocation process to ensure the participation of target investors, proponents of a direct listing argue that this is a more pure market-based pricing mechanism than that used in a traditional IPO.

- *Reference price* – Unlike an IPO, where the underwriter sets the price at which the shares open, a direct listing utilizes a reference price, which is calculated on the basis of all the buy and sell orders taken from broker-dealers. Getting that reference price right is a crucial aspect of a direct listing because it reduces the chance of wild swings in price in the days after trading begins. Nasdaq uses a proprietary auction technology within its Nasdaq Private Market platform that helps facilitate the process of setting the reference price. It organizes all the buy and sell orders the night before trading is set to begin in order to determine the optimal price at which to open the shares. The lead investment banks then approve the reference price before the shares open for trading.

Exhibit 8.14 displays the advantages and disadvantages of direct listings.

**EXHIBIT 8.14**   Advantages and Disadvantages of Direct Listings

| | Direct Listings |
|---|---|
| Advantages | ▪ Market-based pricing mechanism |
| | ▪ No underwriting spread |
| | ▪ Ability to offer investors guidance |
| | ▪ No IPO discount (see Chapter 9) |
| | ▪ Greater liquidity for existing shareholders because there is no lock-up period |
| Disadvantages | ▪ No new capital |
| | ▪ No allocation process to ensure participation of target investors |
| | ▪ Potentially more volatility because there is no overallotment option (greenshoe) to help stabilize the stock price and no organized sell-side supply mechanism (no lock-up constraint) |
| | ▪ Potentially more limited research coverage and less investor understanding due to less extensive/intensive education process |
| | ▪ Limited precedents; less proven |

It should also be noted that the direct listing is a relatively new innovation and its features will continue to evolve, likely merging more into traditional IPOs (and vice versa). For example, it has been reported that issuers are considering non-underwritten, direct placements of newly issued shares into the market alongside direct listings.

## POST-IPO EQUITY OFFERINGS

As previously discussed, an IPO typically provides existing shareholders with only a partial monetization of their holdings. Subsequently, they still own a substantial stake in the company. Going forward, there are two main methods for selling their remaining shares in sizable chunks: *follow-ons* and *block trades*.

A follow-on refers to a marketed offering of company stock to the public. The term "marketed" refers to the fact that the underwriters and management market the deal to investors in the form of a one-to-three-day roadshow, including investor calls. This enables them to (re)educate current and new investors alike on the company, thereby deepening and broadening their shareholder base. For more established/ seasoned companies, a follow-on can be executed via an overnight offering with minimal marketing effort.

The first follow-on post-IPO is typically sized at 15% to 20% of the company's market cap. It can be comprised of either primary or secondary shares (or a combination), but secondary offerings are more common as legacy shareholder(s) look to sell down their positions. While the bookrunner syndicate usually stays largely intact from IPO to the first follow-on, the company and its major shareholders have discretion to shake things up. This means that those banks deemed most helpful in the interim may be promoted, while those not meeting expectations may be demoted. The typical gross spread for a marketed follow-on is lower than that for an IPO at 3.5% to 4% on average.

As would be expected given the supply/demand imbalance of selling a large chunk of shares into the market in a compressed timeframe, follow-ons are typically priced at a discount to the current stock price. The marketing activity that accompanies the follow-on is designed to help minimize the discount by getting old and new investors alike (re)excited about the opportunity. Ideally, the share price has appreciated considerably since the IPO so selling shareholders still realize significant gains even after the discount.

It typically takes multiple offerings for legacy shareholders to sell down their original stakes in their entirety. As their stakes shrink through follow-ons, shareholders typically look to monetize the remaining shares via one or more block trades.[12] In a block trade, shareholders sell their shares directly to a bank (or banks) at a set price, typically at a discount to the last trade. The seller receives immediate cash proceeds. The underwriter, in turn, owns the shares and looks to sell them into the market at a premium to the price it paid for them. Thus, the risk of a material sell-off in the stock is transferred to the bank, whereas in a follow-on offering the risk of a poor or failed offering lies with the company and selling shareholders.

In a block trade, there is no marketing component to the trade, i.e., no management roadshow or investor calls. Typically, multiple banks are called upon to bid for the block of shares in order to create competitive tension and find the market inflection point. While one bank is usually chosen to execute the block trade, there are circumstances when multiple banks share the deal.

---

[12]Block trades may be done as a registered offering or as a sale under Rule 144 of the Securities Act.

## IPO CONSIDERATIONS

The decision to go public requires extensive thought, analysis, and preparation. Months and even years of reflection and planning go into the final decision, which weighs the costs and benefits of life as a public company and the IPO process itself. In Exhibit 8.15, we highlight some of these key considerations.

**EXHIBIT 8.15**   IPO Considerations

- SEC and Sarbanes-Oxley (SOX) Compliance
- New Stakeholders
- Management Time and Scrutiny
- Vulnerability from Shareholders, Other Companies
- Fees / Expenses
- Future Monetization

- *SEC and Sarbanes-Oxley (SOX) compliance* – Post-IPO, public registrants must file annual and quarterly reports, as well as other mandatory filings with the SEC. These filings contain detailed business and financial disclosures, including potentially sensitive information on corporate strategy, products, customers, sales, profitability, and capitalization. Executive compensation, as well as details about members of management and the board of directors, are made public. SOX compliance also requires public registrants to establish and maintain extensive financial reporting internal controls in accordance with Section 404. The company must be prepared to commit dedicated internal time, resources, and expense on an ongoing basis to ensure compliance.

- *New stakeholders* – As a public company, management must find a way to work with an entirely new set of stakeholders, most notably public shareholders, research analysts, a typically expanded board of directors, and even the media. This means a true sharing of control over corporate decision-making, strategy, and key operational moves. Certain decisions will require Board and even shareholder approval, e.g., sizable acquisitions and divestitures, director nominations, and executive compensation.

- *Management time and scrutiny* – Once public, management will need to dedicate a substantial portion of time toward satisfying its commitment to public shareholders. At a minimum, this involves regular investor relations activities, including quarterly earnings calls, discussions with equity research and investors, and attendance at industry conferences. Required public disclosure also means that the company and its actions will be under continuous scrutiny and analysis by new stakeholders, sometimes referred to as the "fishbowl effect". This means pressure to deliver on both short- and long-term performance targets, which may represent a meaningful departure from life as a private company.

- *Vulnerability from shareholders, other companies* – Public companies are vulnerable to activist shareholders buying the stock and agitating for major changes in corporate strategy, management, or the board of directors composition. The company might also become a takeover target for another company. While companies may institute certain defensive protections in the form of governance and corporate structure, shareholder pressures are a reality.

- *Fees / expenses* – Beyond the upfront fees and expenses involved in the IPO preparation and filing process, ongoing annual public company costs are estimated at $1 to $3 million on average. These include expenses related to SEC and SOX compliance, board of directors' compensation and liability insurance, accounting, and exchange listing fees. Many companies also hire an investor relations executive, or outsource this function to a professional IR firm.

- *Future monetization* – As previously discussed, an IPO does not afford existing shareholders a complete exit. Full monetization comes through future follow-on equity offerings and block trades after the lock-up period, or a sale of the company. Until that time, the value of the shares is subject to market fluctuations without any assurances that they will maintain their IPO level or appreciate. In addition, management faces periodic restrictions on selling shares, most notably around earnings announcements, also known as a "blackout period". Insider share sales are disclosed on Form 4s and face scrutiny from investors potentially concerned about any negative read-through regarding company prospects.

1) All of the following are key benefits of going public in making the IPO decision EXCEPT

   A. Access to public capital markets
   B. Increased valuation transparency
   C. Incremental one-time costs and ongoing expenses
   D. Management and employee incentive packages

2) All of the following are key considerations to weigh against the benefits of going public in making the IPO decision EXCEPT

   A. Incremental one-time costs and ongoing expenses
   B. Disclosure requirements
   C. Increased valuation transparency
   D. Public investor scrutiny

3) A primary share issuance refers to

   A. First time shareholders sell their shares to the public
   B. All first-time IPO share sales
   C. Sale of shares via one of the primary stock exchanges
   D. Sale of shares by the company to public shareholders

4) A secondary share issuance refers to

   A. Additional share offerings following the initial IPO share sale
   B. Share sales for second-time IPO launches
   C. Share sales on second-tier global exchanges
   D. Sale of shares by existing shareholders to the market

5) An initiating coverage report refers to

   A. Comprehensive research report published by investment banks post-IPO
   B. Investment bank's comprehensive report on the IPO process
   C. Sales & trading assessment of trading in the stock post-IPO
   D. Company feedback report to the lead investment banks on IPO execution

6) A red herring refers to

   A. Preliminary prospectus
   B. A hot new IPO offering
   C. Misleading marketing information related to a new IPO offering
   D. The Dodd-Frank Wall Street Reform and Consumer Protection Act of 2010

7) The greenshoe refers to

   A. The overallotment option
   B. Extra shares allotted to retail investors
   C. 15% of the issuance reserved for high-net-worth individuals
   D. The green font disclaimer on the front of the prospectus providing important investor information

8) The stabilization agent is responsible for

   A. Opening trading of the stock and managing aftermarket trading
   B. Running the public marketing program to drum up support for the stock
   C. Ensuring that all members of the syndicate provide research coverage
   D. Making sure investor allocations are aligned with the original plan

9) A dual-track process refers to a company's pursuit of

   A. Sale of the company in parallel with the IPO
   B. Dual listing in U.S. and Europe
   C. Two classes of shares
   D. Bond offering in parallel with an IPO

10) One of the advantages of an IPO versus an M&A sale is

   A. Maximum cash upfront
   B. Existing shareholders retain upside through their retained stake
   C. Value certainty
   D. Potential future market volatility

11) An IPO provides all of the following advantages EXCEPT

   A. Potential premium to M&A sales
   B. Ability to value the company off future earnings
   C. Access to public capital markets
   D. Ability of existing shareholders to entirely cash out

12) What is a SPAC also known as?

    A. Blank check vehicle
    B. Dual-listed IPO
    C. Foreign-listed IPO
    D. Private M&A vehicle

13) Key advantages of SPAC deals versus IPOs include all of the following EXCEPT

    A. Ability to provide forward-looking financial projections and forward-looking statements
    B. Less reliance on equity market windows
    C. Potential to get sponsors more cash upfront
    D. No upfront costs and cash outlay

14) A direct listing forgoes which of the following traditional IPO components?

    A. SEC public company requirements
    B. Bookbuilding process
    C. Stock exchange listing requirements
    D. Filing of a registrations statement

15) The typical follow-on equity offering is

    A. Comprised almost entirely of primary shares
    B. Comprised almost entirely of secondary shares
    C. Sized at roughly 50% of market cap
    D. Executed overnight without a marketing process

# Nasdaq Appendix

**APPENDIX 8.1**  Nasdaq Private Market

Nasdaq Private Market

- Portals
- Accounts
- Users
- Events
- Administrators
- Tax Center

⇄ **Acme Company Tender Offer**

Portals > Acme Company > Acme Company Tender Offer

| Dashboard | Permissioned Accounts | Orders | Documents | Messages | Configuration | Admins | Holdings | Import |

### Accounts

| | # |
| --- | --- |
| Permissioned Accounts | 53 |
| Active Accounts | 39 |
| Accounts With Orders | 22 |

### Orders

| | # | Shares | Option | Preferred Stock | Common Stock | Gross Proceeds | Net Proceeds |
| --- | --- | --- | --- | --- | --- | --- | --- |
| ✏ Incomplete | 16 | 116,319 | 7,589 | 6,200 | 102,530 | $1,512,147.00 | $1,481,125.60 |
| ⊘ Pending | 2 | 25,667 | 18,605 | 0 | 7,062 | $333,671.00 | $291,868.77 |
| ⊘ Submitted | 4 | 31,974 | 22,808 | 0 | 9,166 | $415,662.00 | $356,617.64 |
| ⊕ Total | 22 | 173,960 | 49,002 | 6,200 | 118,758 | $2,261,480.00 | $2,129,612.01 |

### Reports

| Name | Description | |
| --- | --- | --- |
| Permissioned Accounts | All Accounts with access to the event with Selling Group, Min/Max Sellable, and last login | ⤴ |
| In-Depth Event Details | Full details of every participant in the event including shareholder information, holdings, order amounts, and order status | ⤴ |
| Order Status Report | Participant information including the current step of submission | ⤴ |

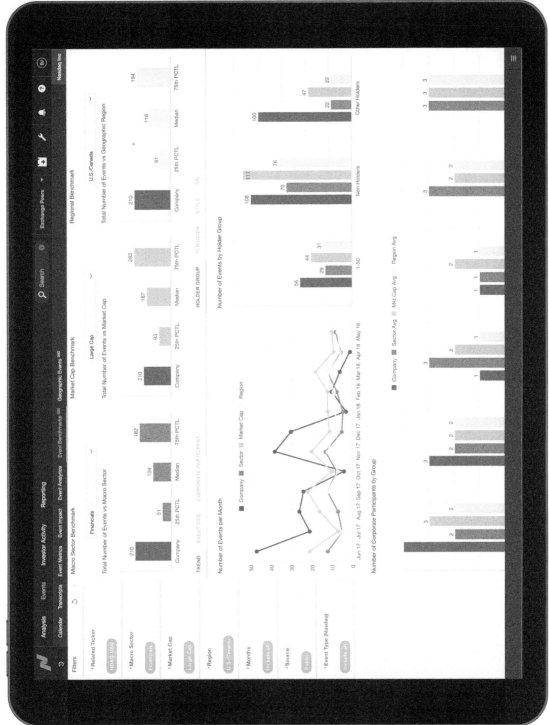

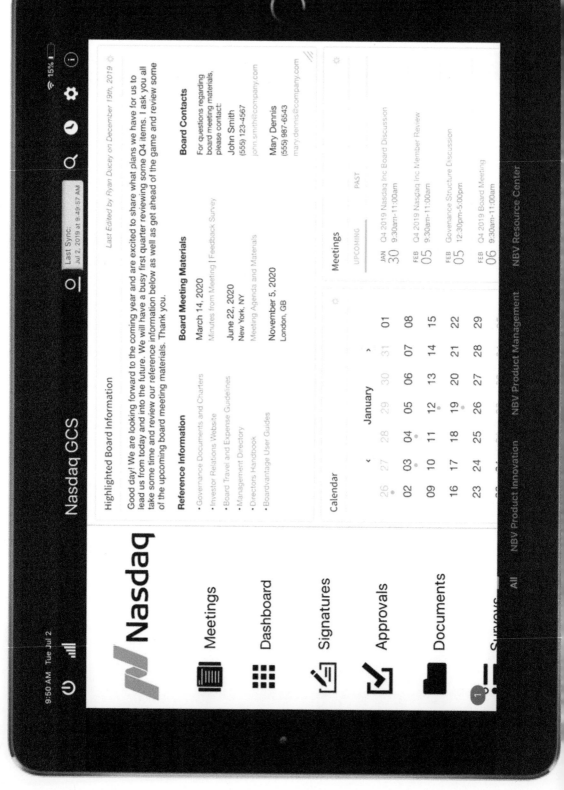

# The IPO Process

As with an M&A sell-side process, an IPO is intense and time-consuming with high stakes for the company and its stakeholders. The typical process spans several months, although IPO-readiness activities and preparation may begin years in advance. Once the IPO decision has been made, the company chooses its team of investment banks, lawyers, accountants, and other key advisors. Internally, the company also identifies its own team who will work with the external parties on delivering a successful outcome.

As outlined in Exhibit 9.1, the IPO process consists of multiple stages and discrete milestones within each of these stages. There are numerous variations within this structure that allow the bookrunners to customize, as appropriate, for a given situation. The Organization and Preparation stage sets the foundation for all the work that follows. In the event the company has long-standing banking relationships and current public audited financials (e.g., a public bond issuer), the prep stage can move relatively quickly. On the other end of the spectrum, some companies may spend months or even years preparing their organization for an IPO. This extends to putting in place the right management and internal support, as well as getting the financials "IPO-ready".

Formal kick-off begins with an *organizational meeting* ("org meeting") where the company, lead banks, their respective counsels, and accountants meet in person. The left lead bank typically runs the meeting and establishes the timeline, key deliverables, and responsibilities for all parties. Preliminary IPO terms, structure, and valuation are also vetted. From there, multiple workstreams begin and the team regroups on a regular basis, either in-person or telephonically, to advance the process.

During the Due Diligence, Drafting, and Filing stage, extensive business, financial, and legal due diligence is performed on the company. This feeds into the drafting of the key regulatory and marketing documents, most notably the registration statement and roadshow materials. The registration statement completion timeline largely depends on the amount and nature of the comments received from the SEC. Heavy comments that require substantive disclosure changes or revisions to the financial statements can add weeks or even months to the timeline. On the other end, a best-case scenario involving minimal SEC commentary can result in filing the amended registration statement (which includes the *red herring* or preliminary prospectus) in about two months.

Once the red herring prospectus is ready, the company can launch the offering and proceed with the Marketing and Roadshow stage. This is where the IPO gets marketed directly to investors and the order book is built. If all goes well, Pricing and Allocation takes place within one to three weeks from launch and the company's shares begin trading on a public stock exchange the morning after pricing.

**EXHIBIT 9.1**  Stages of an IPO Process

| | Stages of an IPO Process | | |
| --- | --- | --- | --- |
| Organization and Preparation | Due Diligence, Drafting, and Filing | Marketing and Roadshow | Pricing and Allocation |
| ▪ Select IPO team, exchange partner, and assign responsibilities | ▪ Perform underwriter due diligence | ▪ Finalize marketing materials | ▪ Price the offering |
| ▪ Manage corporate housekeeping | ▪ Draft and file the registration statement | ▪ Salesforce teach-in | ▪ Allocate shares to investors |
| ▪ Determine offering structure and preliminary IPO valuation | ▪ Prepare other key transaction and corporate governance documents | ▪ Conduct roadshow | ▪ Closing |
| ▪ Host organizational meeting | ▪ Coordinate with equity research | ▪ Build order book | |
| | ▪ Respond to SEC comments and file amended registration statement | | |
| 2 – 4 months | 2 – 3 months | ~ 2 weeks | ~ 1 week |

## ORGANIZATION AND PREPARATION

- Select IPO Team, Exchange Partner, and Assign Responsibilities
- Manage Corporate Housekeeping
- Determine Offering Structure and Preliminary IPO Valuation
- Host Organizational Meeting

### Select IPO Team, Exchange Partner, and Assign Responsibilities

Optimal IPO execution requires the collaboration of a core team of professionals with complementary skill sets. As with any other organized process, teamwork and cultural fit help ensure efficiency, quality, and success. Therefore, it is critical to get the right team in place upfront. Below, we discuss the key team members and their responsibilities, comprising company management, bookrunners, legal counsel, accountants, and an investor relations firm.

**Internal Company Team**   While it is the responsibility of the bankers, lawyers, and accountants to put the company in the best position to succeed, the management team is mission control. This starts with the efficient organization and mobilization of the company's resources to deliver the necessary financial, business, and legal information. This information, in turn, feeds into the investment story and is reflected in the registration statement and marketing materials.

Consequently, a company's owners need to determine well in advance of the IPO whether their management team has the requisite skill set and resources to deliver. This may lead to substantial changes in the senior team, including at the CEO and CFO level. More typical are piecemeal changes in terms of supplemental personnel, such as internal financial controls, legal, and investor relations.

In anticipation of the IPO process kick-off, the company assigns an internal deal team and "captain" to marshal internal resources and coordinate with external advisors. While the CEO is a critical member of this team, especially for shaping the vision and story, day-to-day responsibilities are delegated to others. After all, the CEO must ensure that the company performs in the interim. Missed financial targets and key business deliverables are life-threatening for an IPO.

The internal IPO team consists of key senior executives, most notably the CFO and selected members of the finance team, as well as the COO and general counsel. Beyond that, team members vary with the situation. For some companies, the head of corporate strategy and development, key business segment leaders, and the chief sales and marketing officer play key roles. The deal captain similarly depends on the situation, but is often the CFO or a member of the business development team. The same credo that applies to the CEO applies to the entire deal team, namely the need to balance ensuring the success of the offering with running the business.

While each company and situation varies, Exhibit 9.2 presents an illustrative overview of the roles and time commitments for key company executives during the IPO process.

**EXHIBIT 9.2**   IPO Roles and Time Commitments of Key Company Employees

| | Role | Time |
|---|---|---|
| CEO | <ul><li>Key voice for crafting and communicating the story</li><li>Appoints internal IPO deal team and captain</li><li>Typically leads business due diligence session</li><li>"Face of the company" on roadshow</li></ul> | |
| CFO, Treasurer & Finance Team | <ul><li>Responsible for financial statements, MD&A, and other financial data in IPO documents</li><li>Key role in due diligence and registration statement drafting</li><li>Business plan development and financial projections</li><li>CFO often serves as "deal captain" given volume and importance of financial deliverables</li></ul> | |
| Captain | <ul><li>Responsible for internal and external coordination</li><li>Point person for data requests</li><li>Liaison to exchange partner</li><li>Ensures workstreams stay on target and key deliverables finished on time</li><li>Engages senior management as appropriate</li></ul> | |
| Corporate Development | <ul><li>Participates in due diligence and drafting of registration statement and marketing materials</li><li>Provides insight on strategy, growth projects, and M&A</li><li>May serve as deal captain</li></ul> | |
| General Counsel & Legal Team | <ul><li>Works with company counsel on all legal items and SEC coordination</li><li>Participates in due diligence and drafting of documents</li><li>Spearheads corporate housekeeping and regulatory issues</li></ul> | |
| Investor Relations | <ul><li>Assists with preparation of marketing presentations and investor messaging</li><li>Builds IR infrastructure and strategy for life as public company</li></ul> | |

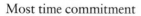

Most time commitment                                                          Least time commitment

**Bookrunners** Investment banks are tasked with managing the offering and guiding the company throughout the entire process. Given this critical role, the company and its shareholders put a lot of time and thought into the selection process, especially for the left lead and active bookrunners. In many cases, the exploratory process begins years in advance through informal meetings with potential underwriters.

Once the decision to IPO is made, the company typically runs a formal bake-off process. At the bake-off, bookrunner candidates are invited to make a presentation to the company's senior management, as well as key Board members and shareholder representatives. As many as a half dozen or more banks may be targeted, all of whom have been prescreened.

Prior to the bake-off, banks are typically sent a formal RFP (request for proposal) with a list of topics to be addressed at the presentation. The completed RFP is submitted electronically in advance of the formal in-person presentation, where each bank is generally allotted an hour to an hour-and-a-half slot to present its views. Exhibit 9.3 displays standard topics that prospective underwriters are expected to address.

**EXHIBIT 9.3** Overview of Key RFP Response Items

| RFP Roadmap |
|---|
| **Company Positioning, Valuation, and Market Conditions** |
| <ul><li>Strategy for positioning the company to investors, including framing the investment thesis and highlighting potential investor concerns with mitigating factors</li><li>Knowledge of the business, industry, and competitive dynamics</li><li>Assessment of peer universe, including benchmarking</li><li>View of valuation, appropriate methodologies, and rationale</li></ul> |
| **Deal Team Credentials and Existing Company Relationships** |
| <ul><li>Deal team and IPO credentials, experience with relevant comps, number and types of deals led, league table rankings, day-to-day team and their responsibilities</li><li>Existing relationship with the company, Board, and major shareholders</li><li>Equity research platform, ranking, and industry awards</li></ul> |
| **Offering Structure and Considerations** |
| <ul><li>Proposed offering size and structure, primary vs. secondary components</li><li>Market conditions and timing, with focus on best windows</li><li>Exchange selection and other listing considerations</li></ul> |
| **Distribution Strategy, Syndication, and Fees** |
| <ul><li>Distribution strategy and investor targeting, including comprehensive demand assessment and proposed roadshow blueprint</li><li>Post-IPO support, including trading volume for key peers, follow-on capabilities, M&A experience, and willingness to lend</li><li>Overview of potential syndicate structure with proposal of roles for each bank</li><li>Fees/gross spread</li></ul> |

The underwriting syndicate is typically selected within a few days following the bake-off, at which time the banks are apprised of their roles. Standard practice is to notify the left lead bookrunner first so that they can get the ball rolling. As noted in Chapter 8, most deals consist of active bookrunners, passive bookrunners, and co-managers. For larger deals, the syndicate may be even broader, weaving in *lead managers* just below the passive bookrunners in the hierarchy, as well as delineating senior and junior co-managers.

**Select Other Advisors**  A successful IPO requires support from a team of outside advisors in addition to the investment banks. Company counsel and accountants need to be lined up from the onset to flag key issues, lay out the legal and financial roadmap, and start work on the registration statement. As with the lead banks, both the legal and accounting firms typically have preexisting relationships with the company, as well as relevant IPO experience. Ideally, the accounting firm has been engaged well in advance of the IPO and is familiar with the company, its reporting, and accounting policies and controls.[1] The bookrunners must also appoint underwriters' counsel to represent them, perform legal due diligence, draft and comment on IPO legal documentation (including comments on the registration statement), and help the underwriters and company navigate various SEC regulations and the FINRA[2] process.

The company typically sets up a data room early on that serves as the hub for due diligence and registration statement preparation. The financial printer handles the filing logistics for the registration statement, and typesets and prints the preliminary and final prospectus. The company may also choose to engage third party consultants to perform market analysis and industry studies, help the management team develop a crisp presentation with the right delivery, and assist with the bookrunner and research analyst selection process (see Chapter 8, "IPO Advisors"). An investor relations and/or PR firm may also be engaged to help with the roadshow and investor communication.

**Engaging with Exchange Partner**  The listing exchange is an important partner before, during, and after the IPO (see Chapter 8). As a result, U.S. listed companies look to select their partner upfront (i.e., Nasdaq or NYSE) and begin engagement early on. Once a selection is made, the IPO Team Captain, Investor Relations, Marketing, and Communications teams can begin coordinating all IPO- and post-IPO-related exchange activities.

### Manage Corporate Housekeeping

In preparation for an IPO, companies must ensure that their corporate housekeeping and affairs are in good order. This involves reviewing the corporate organizational documents, financial reporting, accounting policies, corporate governance, and shareholder list and holdings. Various business and legal-related matters also need to be buttoned down, including third-party relationships, material contracts, subsidiaries, and outstanding litigation and liabilities (e.g., environmental, product liability, IP, labor). The corporate housekeeping is typically led by the company's internal general counsel in concert with outside counsel.

---

[1]Companies also need to confirm that their accountants are independent under SEC rules and Public Company Accounting Oversight Board standards.
[2]Financial Industry Regulatory Authority, Inc. (FINRA) is a self-regulatory organization that oversees all securities firms engaged in business activity in the United States. In the context of an IPO, FINRA review helps ensure that the underwriters are not being compensated in a manner that is unfair to the issuer.

Corporate housekeeping initiatives begin well in advance of the IPO. This provides ample time to address and resolve any issues without delaying the offering. Notably, companies must ensure their financials are IPO-ready (i.e., audited by independent auditors and SEC-compliant on an annual and quarterly basis). Ideally, the company also uses this prep time to put in place an established auditing firm (in the event it doesn't already have one). A tight ship is attractive to investors, who will seek to avoid additional risk in the form of sloppy financial reporting and controls, potential liabilities, and opaque governance.

**Corporate Governance**   Corporate governance refers to the set of rules and best practices by which the board of directors oversees the company and its interaction with key stakeholders, including management, investors, governmental bodies, and the public at large. Public companies are held to strict corporate governance standards by both the SEC and the major stock exchanges. They also have a fiduciary responsibility to public shareholders. As a result, going public typically requires major changes in a company's corporate governance, including:

- Board member independence standards

- Separate working sessions for independent directors

- Mandatory board committees (i.e., Audit and Compensation, with explicit responsibilities/requirements for each)

- Creation of governance charters and other documents

Let's start with the board of directors. Many private company Boards are comprised of the owners, CEO, and potentially selected other senior executives, with family members and trusted advisors layered in depending on the situation. Even those private companies that have independent board members in place still typically need considerable work to satisfy public company requirements.

First, Nasdaq and NYSE both mandate the board to be comprised of a majority of independent directors, subject to limited exceptions.[3] While Nasdaq and NYSE each have their own unique "independent" definition and requirements, the concept is the same. An independent director is someone without an established relationship with the company that would interfere with the responsibility to serve as an impartial member.[4] Newly public companies are required to comply with the majority independent standards within one year of their IPO.

Second, public companies are required to establish Audit, Nominating,[5] and Compensation committees, comprised entirely of independent directors.[6] The members of the Audit and Compensation committees are held to the strictest independence standards. They must have one independent director in place at the time of the

---

[3]Controlled companies are not required to have a majority of independents on the Board; however, the audit committee needs to be fully independent.

[4]For example, they should not be employed by the company, have a family member that is an executive officer, or accept payments in excess of a specified threshold from the company (Nasdaq and NYSE use a threshold of $120,000 with certain exceptions).

[5]Nasdaq-listed companies are not required to have a formal nominating committee as long as nominations are made by independent directors, although most have them as a matter of best practice.

[6]Controlled companies are not required to comply with the requirement for an independent nominating committee (or independent directors) or the requirement to have an independent compensation committee.

IPO, a majority of independent directors within 90 days of the listing, and be fully independent within one year of the IPO.

Below is a description of the three mandatory committees:

- *Audit Committee* – responsible for the financial reporting process, hiring and oversight of auditors, establishing a whistleblower framework, and procedures for accounting matters and internal controls; according to SEC standards, all members of the committee must be "financially literate" with at least one person who is a "financial expert"

- *Nominating Committee* – responsible for identifying and recommending directors, developing governance guidelines, and conducting evaluations of the Board and senior management

- *Compensation Committee* – responsible for determining and recommending compensation for executives, advising the Board on executive incentive plans, and overseeing the engagement of any outside consultants/advisors on compensation and employment matters

In addition to compliance with the SEC and listing exchanges, best-in-class companies institutionalize corporate governance "best practices". These may include a range of topics, including Board composition and size (including diversity), succession planning, executive pay, and ESG (Environmental, Social, and Governance). The governance review may also extend into takeover defense policies in the event of future approaches from unwelcome pursuers.

Effective governance preparation begins in advance of the IPO, often adopting governance-specific technologies like Nasdaq Boardvantage, a software-based board portal and collaboration solution. With the increase in digitalization and cybersecurity acumen, directors and leadership teams use Nasdaq Boardvantage to elevate governance, improve data security, and enhance collaboration with internal and external parties.

**Accounting Preparations and Financial Disclosures**   Public companies must comply with comprehensive SEC financial disclosure requirements on a quarterly basis, including the preparation of detailed financial statements. This requires putting in place the proper internal controls and procedures. Preparing for these requirements from a standing start requires substantial time and resources from the company's finance team working in tandem with an external accounting firm.

SEC financial statement requirements for the registration statement include, subject to certain exceptions:

- Balance sheet, consolidated and audited for the two most recent fiscal years

- Income statement, cash flow statement, and statement of changes in shareholders' equity, consolidated and audited for the three most recent fiscal years[7]

- Footnotes and financial statement schedules (if needed)

- Audit report by the company's auditor

---

[7]For EGCs, the SEC requires only two years of audited financials.

It is also customary for companies to include additional financial information and industry-specific metrics that would be informative to investors. Regarding the former, non-GAAP financial measures such as adjusted EBITDA and FCF are commonly used. An example of a sector-specific metric would be a cable company disclosing information on the number of subscribers and average revenue per unit (ARPU), or a distribution company reporting on same store sales growth (SSS).

Additionally, *segment reporting* may be required by the SEC for companies that operate in multiple business lines or geographic areas. This disclosure typically includes metrics for each segment or region, including sales, EBIT, and other financial data. Companies typically seek to limit their segment disclosures for competitive reasons, as well as the desire to limit reporting obligations on various areas of the business.

Beyond the actual financial information, it is critical to make sure that the proper controls are in place.[8] If there are any material weaknesses, disclosure is included in the registration statement. Therefore, it is important for the IPO deal team to identify any deficiencies early on and establish a remediation plan.

**Craft Company Strategy and Financial Projections**   The company's strategy and business plan form the foundation of the IPO story. Distilling this story into a concise and easily digestible message to investors is essential. The earlier this is done, the better so it gets sufficiently captured in the prospectus and other marketing materials.

In many cases, the IPO story is a logical continuation of how the company already positions itself internally and externally. As discussed in Chapter 8, however, there are certain hot buttons that particularly resonate with IPO investors. These themes tend to center on the growth opportunity and sector backdrop, while also highlighting the moat and staying power of the business model.

The story needs to be supported by a compelling and defensible set of projections. The company's CFO and finance team take the lead with input from the lead bookrunners, including on how to drive the model and which supporting data is most appropriate. Ultimately, the projections need to be credible when viewed in light of the company's own historical performance as well as that of the comps. The ability to tie to third-party industry sources and identifiable market trends helps provide comfort to potential IPO investors.

Projections also need to be consistent with other assumptions, such as market share gains, new products, pricing, mix, geographic expansion, and potential acquisitions. The company may project dramatic outperformance versus peers on the basis of any combination of the above so long as the drivers are highlighted and defensible. The balance sheet and cash flow statement must be aligned as well, with sufficient debt capacity, capital expenditures, and working capital to support growth. Once ready, the projections are shared with the sell-side research analysts.

---

[8]IPO candidates must establish proper internal controls, including an internal control over financial reporting (ICFR). ICFR provides assurances as to the reliability of the company's financial reporting and ability to prepare financials in accordance with GAAP. Disclosure controls and procedures are also set in place to ensure that SEC-required financial and non-financial information can be processed and reported within the required timeframe.

**Corporate Structure and Other Considerations**   The housekeeping exercise also extends to ensuring that the corporate structure is conducive to life as a public company. Key checklist items include:

- *State of incorporation* – The majority of U.S. public companies are incorporated in Delaware due to the state's business-friendly laws and court system.[9]

- *Business structure* – The overwhelming majority of IPO candidates are organized as a C Corporation (C Corp). Alternative structures like MLPs and REITs may be available for a company depending on the type of business going public. Absent these specific asset classes, other structures may limit the number of shareholders (e.g., S Corp) or have undesirable tax considerations if the business is profitable (e.g., pass-through entities, such as an LLC). A variation of the C Corp is the Up-C structure (particularly prevalent among PE-owned companies), which features certain favorable tax and voting attributes.

- *Authorizing additional shares* – In some cases, companies may need to authorize the issuance of new shares to create a sufficient float for the IPO as well as for the conversion of other securities.

- *Conversion or redemption of preferred shares or warrants* – Private companies often have various securities in place that need to be redeemed or converted into common shares prior to going public (e.g., options, warrants, and preferred securities). Public investors typically eschew complicated or potentially dilutive equity-linked securities in favor of simplicity and equal footing with pre-IPO investors.[10]

- *Forward or reverse stock split* – As the lead bookrunners finetune the IPO valuation range, it may become apparent that a stock split or a reverse stock split of the outstanding shares is necessary to solve for a target per share price and public float. As a practical point, the number of shares created in a stock split cannot be greater than the number of authorized shares.

- *Dual class considerations* – Certain owners may seek a dual class structure to provide voting control and other rights greater than their economic interests. This is particularly prevalent among founder-led and family-owned companies, especially in the tech sector. In recent years, dual class structures have encountered meaningful resistance from some investors, as well as index fund sponsors.

---

[9]Per the Delaware Division of Corporation's 2018 Annual Report, 67% of all Fortune 500 companies are incorporated in Delaware. Additionally, in 2018, 82% of U.S.-based IPOs chose Delaware as their state of incorporation.

[10]A key part of diligence focuses on ensuring that past issuances of pre-IPO shares were done properly and in accordance with the company's charter as well as general securities and state corporate law. Any issues or errors should be corrected prior to filing the IPO. A key focus area from an accounting perspective is whether the securities were issued below fair market value. This is known as the "cheap stock" rule, which can result in an issuer having to restate its financial statements to reflect compensation expense.

## C Corp vs. Up-C Structure

Corporate housekeeping also involves determining the legal entity that will serve as the public vehicle. As previously discussed, a C Corp is the most common legal structure for public companies. Fortunately, most companies of the size and inclination to go public are already structured as C Corps. Companies set up as an LLC or S-Corp may need to reincorporate. This process can generally be completed with relative ease, usually during the course of a few weeks.

In a traditional IPO structure, the company and/or current shareholders (e.g., financial sponsors, VC firms, family owners, management) sell shares to new public shareholders (see Exhibit 9.4).

**EXHIBIT 9.4**   Traditional IPO Structure

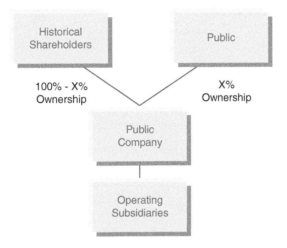

In some cases, companies currently structured as partnerships or LLCs may decide not to convert to a C Corp for tax reasons. For these companies, an alternative to the traditional model is an Up-C structure (see Exhibit 9.5), which provides both voting and tax advantages to pre-IPO shareholders in a partnership/LLC. In an Up-C, pre-IPO owners form a new C Corp (IPOCo) that serves as a holding company that owns and manages unit interests in a partnership/LLC (OpCo). While OpCo is the actual operating business, IPOCo is the entity that actually goes public.

IPOCo has both Class A and Class B shares. The A shares are issued to the public and have both economic and voting rights, while the B shares are issued to the historical owners. The B shares have voting rights that enable the pre-IPO shareholders to maintain control over the company, but technically no economic value.[11] The funds raised by IPOCo through the issuance of Class A shares are used to purchase partnership/LLC units from OpCo that are held by the pre-IPO shareholders. The units can also be given to new strategic partners (by issuing them new units). Unit holders can achieve liquidity by exchanging their units for Class A shares.

---

[11]Class B shares are not entitled to dividends.

The Up-C structure generally creates tax benefits for IPOCo, which are paid back to the original unit holders through a *Tax Receivable Agreement* (TRA), which is an agreement between the original unit holders and the newly formed IPOCo signed upon the IPO. Each time a unit holder exchanges its units for Class A shares, IPOCo receives a "step-up" in the tax basis of its assets. As discussed in Chapter 7, an asset step-up results in the creation of tax-deductible depreciation and amortization, which reduces the company's corporate income taxes. TRAs are typically negotiated, with the legacy holders generally receiving 85% of the tax savings.

**EXHIBIT 9.5**    Up-C IPO Structure

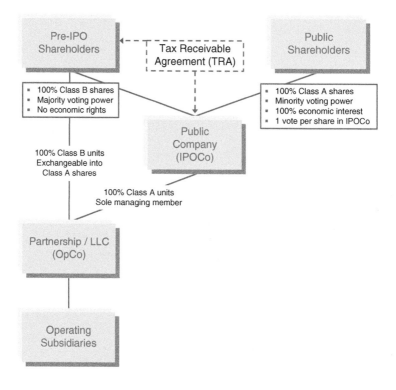

## Determine IPO Timing

While the exact timing of the IPO launch may ultimately depend on multiple factors beyond the control of the company and its underwriters, it is important to establish a target timeline upfront. As shown in Exhibit 9.6, the most common IPO issuance windows are February through June (when full year and Q1 financials, respectively, are available), and then again from late September through the first two weeks of December before the holiday break.

**EXHIBIT 9.6**   Illustrative Monthly Issuance Trends

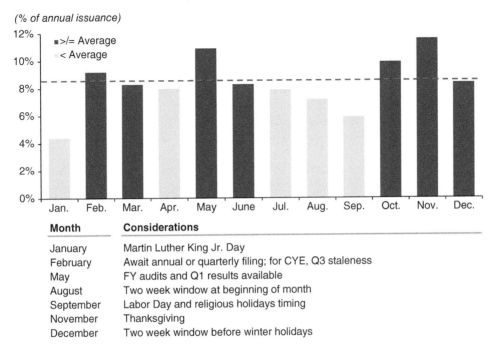

(% of annual issuance)

| Month | Considerations |
|---|---|
| January | Martin Luther King Jr. Day |
| February | Await annual or quarterly filing; for CYE, Q3 staleness |
| May | FY audits and Q1 results available |
| August | Two week window at beginning of month |
| September | Labor Day and religious holidays timing |
| November | Thanksgiving |
| December | Two week window before winter holidays |

Once the target launch date is determined, the company and its deal team move at an accelerated pace to hit key milestones. The goal is to get as far along the IPO timeline as possible so as to be ready to launch if/when equity market conditions are favorable. This is commonly referred to as "the race to the starting line."

A company's seasonality and earnings ramp may also play a role in the desired IPO timing. For example, launching into a strong spring selling season may make sense for construction-related companies. Similarly, a ski apparel business might look to a Q4 or Q1 launch. Or, a company may look to sync its IPO with a major product launch or new customer win.

Regardless of the company sector and situation, market conditions need to be conducive to launch. Even the highest quality company with an exciting growth story would avoid launching into a difficult equity market, and may pursue a private secondary transaction to relieve certain liquidity pressures as they wait. On the other end of the spectrum, strong market conditions can help more marginal IPO candidates power through their roadshow.

## Determine Offering Structure and Preliminary IPO Valuation

Determining the optimal IPO offering structure is a critical upfront item and feeds directly into valuation. The key structuring items center on size and the issuance of primary or secondary shares. The optimal structure needs to be viable while also syncing with the company's IPO story. Getting it right helps ensure the best possible execution and valuation.

**Offering Structure**     Size tends to be the first offering structure decision point. As discussed in Chapter 8, size typically centers on 15% to 25% of implied market cap, but targeting the high or low end of this range can be impactful. The ultimate sizing decision is driven by the company's use of proceeds and shareholder monetization wishes, balanced by investor demands. From a tactical perspective, it is typically better to launch on the smaller end of the range with the option to grow based on investor demand.

Mix depends on the need for, and use of, proceeds (see Chapter 8 for discussion of primary and secondary shares). A high-growth company, especially one that is loss-making, needs cash from a primary offering to fund its performance ramp. Similarly, a highly levered company needs cash to pay down debt and right-size its capital structure.

A sizable secondary offering becomes viable when the company can largely self-fund its business plan and the capital structure is strong. In other words, the company's need for outside cash is minimal. The size of the secondary component also depends on the appetite among existing shareholders to monetize their shares. Some may look to cash in their shares immediately, while others may want to hold indefinitely to ride the upside.

The company's target capital structure pro forma for the IPO figures heavily in the offering structure decision. This is especially applicable for sponsor-backed IPO candidates with elevated debt levels post-LBO. Key peers provide clear goalposts, typically expressed as a leverage ratio (see Chapters 1 and 4). An appropriate capital structure is a gating item for success. A company with too much leverage may find no takers in the IPO market, especially if it is a cyclical business. Regardless, the capital structure must fit with the IPO story. For example, a high-growth story built on M&A needs a clean balance sheet to support the acquisitions.

**IPO Valuation** Valuation is the centerpiece of any IPO. Quite simply, the valuation needs to be compelling for the IPO process to get off the ground. Otherwise, why not seek other options to raise capital or sell a stake in the company?

Setting the valuation range is the ultimate blend of art and science. For high-profile IPOs, it is the source of endless speculation by prospective investors and the media. Everyone is an expert! Of course, very few actually are—but the good news is that, having read this book, you are now one of those select few who can tackle the valuation analysis credibly and systematically. After all, the core tenets of IPO valuation are the exact same as those discussed earlier in this book, albeit with a *heightened emphasis on comps*. Depending on the sector and maturity stage of the company, the DCF is also relevant. This is particularly true for early stage tech companies with limited or no earnings, or for those businesses with no real public comps.

Within comps, the key question is what multiple or metric to use. For mature companies with meaningful earnings, EV/EBITDA and P/E are the industry standards. Sector-specific multiples, however, may be just as important (or even more so, see Chapter 1). For less mature companies, EV/sales is closely examined as are multiples of earnings that look far into the future, e.g., three or even five years out. In general, forward-looking multiples and estimates are core to IPO analysis given the heavy emphasis on growth by the investor base.

*Fully distributed* enterprise value is meant to capture the full implied valuation of a company as if it were already publicly traded (see Exhibit 9.7). It is calculated as the target multiple range multiplied by the most applicable forward earnings metric, in this case, EBITDA, typically one or two years out. Fully distributed equity value is calculated by subtracting net debt, including new primary offering proceeds (if any), which should be treated as cash and cash equivalents. In the event of all secondary offering, the company's existing net debt stays the same.

An IPO discount is then applied to fully distributed equity value. This discount is typically in the 10% to 15% range, but varies depending on the company and prevailing IPO market conditions. It represents the "sweetener" offered to investors to entice them to invest in a new opportunity versus proven peers. As a result, IPO investors have a better chance of getting a first-day "pop" once the company begins trading.

As shown in Exhibit 9.7, the discounted valuations are represented by the "at IPO" designation. Beneath them, we display the implied multiples for the company on both a fully distributed and "at IPO" basis. Finally, at the bottom, we show the IPO structure details, namely the size of the offering, its percentage of "at IPO" equity value, and the mix of primary/secondary proceeds.

**EXHIBIT 9.7**   Illustrative IPO Valuation for ValueCo

## IPO Valuation
### $800 million Offering Size (75% Primary / 25% Secondary)
*($ in millions, except per share data)*

> = Fully Distributed Enterprise Value - Total Debt + Cash and Cash Equivalents + Primary Offering Size
> = $7,613 million - $3,000 million + $200 million + $600 million

> = EBITDA$_{2019E}$ × Fully Distributed EV/EBITDA
> = $725 million × 10.0x

| | | **Fully Distributed EV / EBITDA** | | | | |
|---|---|---|---|---|---|---|
| | | 9.0x | 9.5x | 10.0x | 10.5x | 11.0x |
| 2019E EBITDA | $725 | | | | | |
| **Fully Distributed Enterprise Value** | | **$6,525** | **$6,888** | **$7,250** | **$7,613** | **$7,975** |
| Less: Total Debt | | (3,000) | (3,000) | (3,000) | (3,000) | (3,000) |
| Plus: Cash and Cash Equivalents | | 200 | 200 | 200 | 200 | 200 |
| Plus: Primary Offering Size | | 600 | 600 | 600 | 600 | 600 |
| **Fully Distributed Equity Value** | | **$4,325** | **$4,688** | **$5,050** | **$5,413** | **$5,775** |

> = Offering Size × % Primary
> = $800 million × 75%

> = Fully Distributed Equity Value × IPO Discount
> = $5,775 million × 15%

| | | **IPO Valuation @ 15% Discount** | | | | |
|---|---|---|---|---|---|---|
| Less: Less IPO Discount | 15% | (649) | (703) | (758) | (812) | (866) |
| **Equity Value at IPO** | | **$3,676** | **$3,984** | **$4,293** | **$4,601** | **$4,909** |
| Plus: Total Debt | | 3,000 | 3,000 | 3,000 | 3,000 | 3,000 |
| Less: Cash and Cash Equivalents | | (200) | (200) | (200) | (200) | (200) |
| Less: Primary Offering Size | | (600) | (600) | (600) | (600) | (600) |
| **Enterprise Value at IPO** | | **$5,876** | **$6,184** | **$6,493** | **$6,801** | **$7,109** |

| | | **Valuation Multiples** | | | | |
|---|---|---|---|---|---|---|
| **Fully Distributed** | | | | | | |
| **EBITDA** | | | | | | |
| 2019E | $725 | 9.0x | 9.5x | 10.0x | 10.5x | 11.0x |
| 2020E | 779 | 8.4x | 8.8x | 9.3x | 9.8x | 10.2x |
| **Pro Forma Net Income** | | | | | | |
| 2019E | $349 | 12.4x | 13.4x | 14.5x | 15.5x | 16.5x |
| 2020E | 385 | 11.2x | 12.2x | 13.1x | 14.0x | 15.0x |
| **IPO Valuation @ 15% Discount** | | | | | | |
| **EBITDA** | | | | | | |
| 2019E | $725 | 8.1x | 8.5x | 9.0x | 9.4x | 9.8x |
| 2020E | 779 | 7.5x | 7.9x | 8.3x | 8.7x | 9.1x |
| **Pro Forma Net Income** | | | | | | |
| 2019E | $349 | 10.5x | 11.4x | 12.3x | 13.2x | 14.1x |
| 2020E | 385 | 9.5x | 10.3x | 11.1x | 11.9x | 12.7x |

> = Offering Size / Equity Value at IPO
> = $800 million / $3,676 million

| | **Offering Size** | | | | |
|---|---|---|---|---|---|
| | $800 | $800 | $800 | $800 | $800 |
| % Primary | 75% | 75% | 75% | 75% | 75% |
| % Secondary | 25% | 25% | 25% | 25% | 25% |
| Offering as % of Equity Value at IPO | 22% | 20% | 19% | 17% | 16% |

> = Post-IPO Net Debt / LTM EBITDA
> = $2,200 million / $700 million

| Credit Statistics | LTM EBITDA | Net Debt | | (x) |
|---|---|---|---|---|
| Pre-IPO Net Debt | $700 | $2,800 | Pre-IPO Net Debt / LTM EBITDA | 4.0x |
| Post-IPO Net Debt | | 2,200 | Post-IPO Net Debt / LTM EBITDA | 3.1x |

## Host Organizational Meeting

The org meeting marks the start of the formal IPO process. It is typically an in-person session hosted by the lead bookrunner that lasts several hours. The org meeting is often held at the company's headquarters, or the offices of the lead bookrunner or company counsel. Key attendees include company senior management, shareholder representatives (e.g., PE, VC, family members, founders), the lead bookrunners, auditors, company counsel, and underwriters' counsel. The lead bookrunner sets the agenda and prepares the *organizational materials*, which contain key topics for discussion and a *working group list* containing contact information for the deal team.

The goal of the org meeting is to get all IPO team members on the same page in terms of the basic outline of the offering, timeline, responsibilities, selection of third-party vendors, and go-forward path. Key corporate housekeeping items are covered, including corporate governance, accounting preparations, and internal controls. The org meeting also contemplates an extensive due diligence session for the bookrunners and counsel once the checklist agenda items are completed (see Exhibit 9.8). Coming out of the meeting, tangible work deliverables and follow-up meetings/calls are set for the various workstreams.

**EXHIBIT 9.8** Organizational Meeting Agenda

| Organizational Meeting Agenda | |
|---|---|
| **1. IPO Structure / Proposed Offering** | **5. Financial and Accounting** |
| ■ Size, primary/secondary split | ■ Historical and projected financials |
| ■ Use of proceeds | ■ Comfort Letter |
| **2. Due Diligence** | **6. Communication** |
| ■ Legal, financial, business | ■ Press releases, company website |
| ■ Research analyst diligence/presentation | ■ Publicity policies |
| **3. Registration Statement** | **7. Assignment of Responsibilities** |
| ■ Drafting responsibilities | ■ Registration statement, roadshow materials |
| ■ Timing | ■ Bookbuilding, stabilization |
| **4. Corporate Governance / Legal** | **8. Third Parties** |
| ■ Board of directors, activism defense | ■ Printer |
| ■ Charter, Bylaws, SOX | ■ Public relations firm |
| ■ Underwriting and Lock-up agreement | ■ Transfer agent |

## DUE DILIGENCE, DRAFTING, AND FILING

- Perform Underwriter Due Diligence
- Draft and File the Registration Statement
- Prepare Other Key Transaction and Corporate Governance Documents
- Coordinate with Equity Research
- Respond to SEC Comments and File Amended Registration Statement

### Perform Underwriter Due Diligence

Due diligence typically begins at the org meeting where senior management and key divisional executives give an in-depth presentation on the company and its prospects. Depending on the locale, this upfront session may also include site visits. The organizational materials typically include a detailed due diligence list organized by category. This list serves as a roadmap to the diligence session, which focuses on business, financial, and legal matters.

The diligence session seeks to confirm various streams of company information while getting answers to key questions. This enables the full IPO team to better understand the company's virtues and risks, which in turn feeds into the preparation of the prospectus, valuation, and overall messaging. *All information disclosed in the IPO documents (especially the registration statement) must be accurate and complete, with no material misstatements or omissions.* Additional sessions are typically scheduled in-person and telephonically to follow up on specific topics in more detail.

The data room helps facilitate the deal team's ongoing diligence leading up to the IPO, serving as a hub for all relevant company materials. Similar to the data room used in an M&A sale process, the information is itemized by category and sub-category. It includes a comprehensive data download, comprising audited financials, company-specific financial analysis, market studies, various legal and business contracts, Board minutes, IP details, and compliance certificates. The data room continues to be populated as the IPO timeline progresses with the goal of having it substantially completed by the time the registration statement is filed.

**Business Due Diligence**    For the bankers, the goal of business due diligence is to learn as much as possible about the company's business model, operations, opportunities, and risks. This extends to its competitive positioning within the broader industry.

The diligence process involves discussions with senior management, board members, division heads, key employees, company auditors and external consultants, as well as major customers and suppliers. Visits to selected company sites and facilities are also part of the process.

Below are the primary business due diligence categories:

- *Corporate strategy* – near and long-term strategies, key growth drivers, brand positioning, future acquisition strategy, expansion plans

- *Industry and competition* – competitive advantages, strengths and weaknesses, industry outlook, market share data, historical and future trends, competitor analysis

- *Products & services* – description breakdown as a percent of revenue, positioning and differentiation, upcoming launches, key growth areas

- *Customers* – detailed breakdown of client base, attrition analysis, sales pipeline, new customer campaigns

**Financial Due Diligence**  Financial due diligence encompasses everything related to the company's historical and projected financial performance, including the accompanying MD&A. This extends to various analyses and sensitivities pertaining to detailed performance by business unit, product, facility, and geography.

It also involves understanding growth projects, e.g., greenfields, new products and M&A, as well as more arcane information around taxes, pensions, liabilities, etc. In addition to the actual data, the bookrunners and outside accountants assess the company's financial and accounting infrastructure as well as the processes in place going forward. Key financial diligence topics include: historical financial statements (annual and quarterly), projected financials, valuation, accounting infrastructure, MD&A preparation, debt agreements, and taxes.

**Legal Due Diligence**  Company counsel and underwriters' counsel conduct legal due diligence on myriad documents and topics, as discussed below. Underwriters' counsel spearheads the due diligence request list, and works with company counsel, the bookrunners, and management to make sure it gets fulfilled.

As with financial due diligence, the corporate housekeeping phase of the IPO usually highlights many of the required items for legal due diligence, including any major litigation or related issues that need to be addressed. Key legal diligence topics include: company organizational documents; legal and tax structure; Board minutes; material contracts; intellectual property (licenses, patents, and trademarks); environmental exposures; product liability claims; industry-specific regulatory compliance; and the company's compliance with other applicable local, state, federal, and foreign laws and regulations.

## Draft and File the Registration Statement

The drafting and filing of the registration statement is the main deliverable during the IPO preparation process. The registration statement is a comprehensive document that serves as both a marketing tool and a key disclosure filing about the company and the risks related to the offering. As such, it is reviewed and eventually must be declared effective by the SEC before the offering can be priced. For U.S. issuers, the registration statement is commonly referred to as the *S-1*, reflecting the SEC Form companies file to register their securities. Foreign private issuers, on the other hand, file an *F-1*. The registration statement is invariably *the* gating item in the overall IPO process.

Drafting the initial registration statement takes a minimum of one to two months, especially when starting from scratch. There are two main sections (see Exhibit 9.9). Part I, known as the *prospectus*, contains detailed information about the company, its business, risk factors, and financials. Part II contains additional company information, including exhibits and schedules.

The prospectus cover page also has mandatory disclosures, including the company name, type of security being sold and by whom, offering price, stock exchange, ticker, underwriters, legal counsel, and reference to risk factors.

While the SEC does not have a standard format or length requirement for the registration statement, there are a multitude of mandatory disclosure items. The SEC also requires that companies follow "plain English" guidelines to ensure that it is written and organized in a clear and concise manner. In practice, most companies and their counsel look to precedent registration statement examples for peers and other selected companies in terms of format, style, and substance, with guidance from the bookrunners.

**Drafting of the Registration Statement**   While company counsel typically controls the master document, the lead underwriters hold the pen for most of the critical upfront marketing section, known as "the box". The content and messaging incorporates direct input, insight, and data from the company's senior management team and lead shareholders. The financial sections are driven by the finance team and accountant.

The core IPO working team holds regular *drafting sessions* to progress the registration statement. These sessions typically start out as in-person and then move toward telephonic as the document becomes more fully formed. As previously discussed, the first draft usually takes a month or two to complete before it is ready to be submitted to the SEC.

**EXHIBIT 9.9**   Illustrative Cover Page and Table of Contents for a Registration Statement on Form S-1

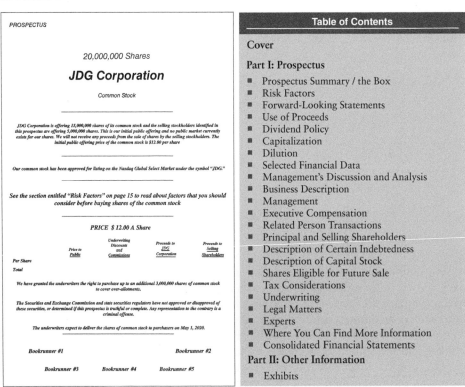

PROSPECTUS

20,000,000 Shares

**JDG Corporation**

Common Stock

JDG Corporation is offering 15,000,000 shares of its common stock and the selling stockholders identified in this prospectus are offering 5,000,000 shares. This is our initial public offering and no public market currently exists for our shares. We will not receive any proceeds from the sale of shares by the selling stockholders. The initial public offering price of the common stock is $12.00 per share

Our common stock has been approved for listing on the Nasdaq Global Select Market under the symbol "JDG."

See the section entitled "Risk Factors" on page 15 to read about factors that you should consider before buying shares of the common stock

PRICE $ 12.00 A Share

| | Price to Public | Underwriting Discounts and Commissions | Proceeds to JDG Corporation | Proceeds to Selling Shareholders |
|---|---|---|---|---|
| Per Share | | | | |
| Total | | | | |

We have granted the underwriters the right to purchase up to an additional 3,000,000 shares of common stock to cover over-allotments.

The Securities and Exchange Commission and state securities regulators have not approved or disapproved of these securities, or determined if this prospectus is truthful or complete. Any representation to the contrary is a criminal offense.

The underwriters expect to deliver the shares of common stock to purchasers on May 1, 2020.

Bookrunner #1                    Bookrunner #2

Bookrunner #3     Bookrunner #4     Bookrunner #5

**Table of Contents**

Cover

Part I: Prospectus
- Prospectus Summary / the Box
- Risk Factors
- Forward-Looking Statements
- Use of Proceeds
- Dividend Policy
- Capitalization
- Dilution
- Selected Financial Data
- Management's Discussion and Analysis
- Business Description
- Management
- Executive Compensation
- Related Person Transactions
- Principal and Selling Shareholders
- Description of Certain Indebtedness
- Description of Capital Stock
- Shares Eligible for Future Sale
- Tax Considerations
- Underwriting
- Legal Matters
- Experts
- Where You Can Find More Information
- Consolidated Financial Statements

Part II: Other Information
- Exhibits

**Key Sections of Part I (Prospectus)**   The prospectus is the core section of the registration statement and is used to market the company to potential investors. It contains a wealth of information about the company and the offering, all of which will eventually be publicly available for review by investors, stakeholders, and competitors alike. The registration statement contents are even more comprehensive than those in a 10-K (see Chapter 1). Once the SEC comments are resolved, the document becomes the principal method of communication to prospective investors. It is printed and distributed to prospective investors both in physical form and electronically.

The main sections of a prospectus include:

- *Cover page* – includes key facts about the IPO, including offering size and number of shares being sold, underwriter discount, net proceeds to the company, the exchange of the IPO, and the names of the bookrunners[12]

- *Prospectus Summary* – informally known as "the box" given that it is surrounded by a frame-like border that highlights its contents, this section is *the* key marketing portion in the prospectus and usually runs 10 to 20 pages in length. As such, it is situated upfront in the document and commands disproportionate time and attention during the drafting process.

  A typical box includes a summary overview of the company (sometimes accompanied by a mission statement), industry review, competitive strengths, strategy, summary risk factors, and summary financials. It also contains a section outlining the key offering terms, including the use of proceeds (see Exhibit 9.10).

- *Financials* – summary and detailed financial information is presented in multiple sections of the prospectus, including:

  - *Summary financial data in the box:* summary financial tables, which include certain historical financial information from the face of the financial statements. The summary box also typically includes certain non-GAAP financial metrics, such as adjusted EBITDA or free cash flow, and key performance indicators.

  - *Standalone section entitled "selected financial data":* summary income and balance sheet data for the last five fiscal years, if available.[13] Intended to provide a sufficient timeframe to help investors identify trends and patterns. This section may also include operational and industry-specific metrics.[14]

  - *Consolidated financial statements:* normally the last section of the prospectus, contains full balance sheet, income, and cash flow statements, as well as a statement of changes in shareholders' equity.

- *Risk factors* – SEC-required section that follows the box and highlights the most significant risks pertaining to the company and IPO offering

- *Capitalization table* – table presenting the company's current and pro forma IPO capitalization, comprising both debt and equity components

---

[12]Once the registration statement is reviewed by the SEC, and prior to distributing the prospectus to investors, the prospectus cover will also include an offering price range.

[13]Only two years for EGCs.

[14]See "Accounting Preparations" section of this chapter for detailed disclosure requirements.

- *Management's discussions and analysis (MD&A)* – similar to the MD&A found in a 10-K (see Chapter 1), this section consists of management commentary on the company's financial performance for the relevant fiscal years and quarterly periods. The commentary extends to forward-looking statements on the possible future effects of known and unknown events, market conditions, and trends. The MD&A also includes information about the company's liquidity and capital resources, as well as a table of any contractual obligations (e.g., debt).

- *Description of business* – often the longest section of the prospectus, the business description contains a detailed overview of the company and its operations. Topics include, in addition to the information presented in the box, the history of the company, number of employees, geographic reach, industry-specific company metrics, core products and services, competitive advantages, property information, customer breakdown, and the operating and regulatory environment in which the company operates, among other topics.

**Part II of the Prospectus**   Part II of the prospectus, titled "Information Not Required in Prospectus", contains information that the issuer is not required to deliver in the prospectus, but represents mandatory disclosure requirements for the registration statement. Key sections typically include a breakdown of IPO expenses (excluding the underwriting discounts), indemnification of company directors and officers, disclosure of the sale of any unregistered securities, and numerous exhibits, e.g., the underwriting agreement, company certificate of incorporation and bylaws, material employee or third-party contracts, and legal opinions and consents.

**Filing the Registration Statement**   The registration statement is submitted electronically using EDGAR, the SEC's electronic document system. Prior to submission, the document needs to be professionally typeset and set up in accordance with SEC filing standards, which typically requires the services of a financial printer. To maximize efficiency in the typesetting process, companies send completed exhibits and financial sections to the printer once they are ready rather than waiting for the entire document to be finalized. Typically, the box, financials, business description, and risk factors are the final sections to be completed and submitted to the printer.

Once the registration statement is essentially complete, the IPO deal team holds an in-person drafting session at the printer to physically review the document and ensure its accuracy. At this point, the registration statement is professionally typeset as the bankers and lawyers continue to refine and finalize the document.

Following this final check on the document, an all-hands due diligence call (a.k.a., *bring-down due diligence*) is held to confirm that there are no material changes to the information contained in the registration statement. The decision on whether to confidentially submit or publicly file the registration statement is also made on this call. Increasingly, companies are choosing to confidentially submit the registration statement to the SEC under expanded confidential submission rules that have developed in recent years. This allows companies to work through comments with the SEC until they are ready to publicly announce their intention to IPO by publicly filing the registration statement. Upon publicly filing, the company pays a filing fee to the SEC determined by the size of the offering.[15]

---

[15]Based on offering price of the securities registered. In 2019, the fee was $129.8 per million dollars.

**EXHIBIT 9.10**   Illustrative Prospectus Summary / the Box

---

### PROSPECTUS SUMMARY

**Company Overview**

**Industry and Market Opportunity**

---

**Competitive Strengths**

**Strategy**

---

**Summary Risk Factors**

**Company Information**

---

### THE OFFERING

Common stock offered by us
Common stock offered by the selling stockholders
Underwriters' over-allotment option
Use of proceeds

Risk Factors

Voting Rights

Proposed Symbol

### SUMMARY FINANCIALS

| | Year Ended December 31, | | |
|---|---|---|---|
| | 2018 | 2017 | 2016 |
| | (in millions, except per share data) | | |

## Prepare Other Key Transaction and Corporate Governance Documents

Following the initial submission of the registration statement, there is typically a time lag of approximately 30 days before the SEC responds with comments. The IPO deal team uses this time to forge ahead on the other crucial documents, namely the underwriting agreement, comfort letter, and legal opinion. They also continue to monitor the market and sharpen their pencils on valuation, offering size, and structure.

**Underwriting Agreement**   The underwriting agreement is a legal contract between the issuer and its underwriters. It is negotiated between their respective legal counsels, with input from the lead bookrunners on key business and economic points as appropriate. Most investment banks have a standard underwriting agreement in-house that their counsel uses as the basis for the document. While the agreement is not signed until IPO pricing, the general terms are often agreed upon early in the process. This avoids any late-stage disputes that could potentially delay the offering.

The primary provisions of the underwriting agreement include:

- Underwriters' obligation, regardless of firm commitment or best efforts

- Underwriters' gross spread and general fees and expenses

- Representations and warranties from the company and selling shareholders (if applicable)

- Overallotment option / greenshoe

- Lock-up agreements

- Closing conditions, which include the comfort letters and legal opinions

- Underwriters, company and selling shareholders (if any) indemnification

**Comfort Letter**   A comfort letter is a document prepared by the company's audit firm attesting to the accuracy of the financial data included in the registration statement as well as the auditor's independence from the issuer. The accountants' purview pertains only to the company's financials; they do not provide comfort on business, industry-specific information, or third-party data. In the event the company changed accounting firms in preparation for its IPO, the original accounting firm may be required to provide a comfort letter as well.

Prior to signing the underwriting agreement, the bookrunners require a comfort letter to be finalized, which is then delivered concurrently with the IPO pricing. The accountants present a second bring-down comfort letter at closing. The bring-down comfort letter either confirms that no material changes have taken place since the original letter (as is typical) or describes any material changes that have occurred.

**Legal Opinions**   Both company and underwriters' counsel provide a "legal opinion" and *negative assurance letter* confirming that the registration statement is compliant with SEC rules. The negative assurance letter provides comfort to the underwriters that nothing has come to the attention of the lawyers regarding a material misstatement or omission. The legal opinion and negative assurance letter do not cover financial or accounting matters.

## Coordinate with Equity Research

After the IPO filing, the company continues to coordinate with the equity research analysts as they do their own analysis on the story. At this point, they have already had a full day session with management, including site visits and follow-up calls on various topics. The downtime between the filing of the registration statement and completion of the SEC review provides the opportunity for them to fine-tune their financial model and thesis on the business. Concurrently, IBD works with ECM to obtain internal approvals for underwriting the equity offering, a process known as *vetting*. A weak or failed IPO can be damaging to the bank in terms of reputation, litigation, and credibility.

## Respond to SEC Comments and File Amended Registration Statement

The Division of Corporation Finance of the SEC is responsible for reviewing registration statement submissions. Its review process is exhaustive and comprehensive. The focus is on compliance with securities laws and regulations and does not constitute an opinion of the strength of the company's equity story, valuation, or the adequacy of the disclosure. The most common areas for SEC comments include: financial statements, prospectus summary, MD&A, executive compensation, risk factors, business description, and "plain English" rules.

The SEC provides a formal response to the company in the form of a written comment letter approximately 30 days after the initial registration statement submission. The company in turn responds to the SEC comments as promptly as possible. The response comes in the form of an amended registration statement that is enclosed with a response cover letter highlighting the changes. To expedite the SEC response timing, the company may raise potential issues with the SEC before filing so as to begin the dialogue. This is done to discuss major issues, typically around accounting or financial matters.

The amended registration statement and response letter are also submitted via EDGAR, thereby making them public to the extent the registration is publicly filed.[16] The response time for the SEC to review and comment on subsequent disclosures is dependent on the nature of the original comments. On average, the SEC and company exchange three-to-five rounds of comments.

Once all the comments are addressed and the registration statement is cleared,[17] the company requests a date and time for the registration statement to be declared effective. The time period between filing and the effective date is known as the *waiting period*. Typically, the effective date is set on the afternoon of the pricing day, with the actual pricing conducted after market close. The stock then begins trading upon market open the following day.

---

[16]SEC comments and responses are typically not made public until at least 20 business days after the effective date.

[17]SEC will not declare the registration statement to be effective until FINRA confirms that it has no objection to the underwriting terms and arrangements.

## MARKETING AND ROADSHOW

- Prepare Marketing Materials
- Salesforce Teach-in
- Conduct Roadshow
- Build Order Book

### Prepare Marketing Materials

**Company Positioning**   Proper company positioning is one of the foremost responsibilities for the IPO deal team, most notably the bankers. Getting it right requires extensive thought, analysis, and market insight. Hence, the importance of choosing bankers that have a deep understanding of the company, sector, and equity market sentiment.

Per our discussion of characteristics that support a strong IPO candidate in Chapter 8, certain attributes apply across all companies and sectors. The key is to map those points to the company's unique story in a crisp, impactful manner. This positioning then reverberates throughout the prospectus and roadshow presentation. More importantly, it needs to be communicated effectively in meetings with investors. Ideally, the story resonates and becomes viral so that buy-side accounts absorb it quickly and word spreads throughout the investor community.

**Create Roadshow Presentation**   The roadshow presentation structure is similar to the management presentation discussed in Chapter 6. Here, much of the content is largely distilled from the registration statement, albeit with various bells and whistles, including supplementary analysis. The typical IPO roadshow presentation runs 30 to 40 pages in length, including the appendix. An illustrative roadshow outline is shown in Exhibit 9.11.

**EXHIBIT 9.11**   Sample IPO Roadshow Presentation Outline

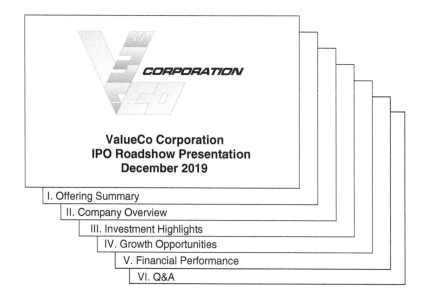

**ValueCo Corporation
IPO Roadshow Presentation
December 2019**

I. Offering Summary
II. Company Overview
III. Investment Highlights
IV. Growth Opportunities
V. Financial Performance
VI. Q&A

The bookrunners take the lead on preparing the roadshow presentation with substantial input from management. The heavy lifting on the presentation typically gets done during the downtime following the initial submission of the registration statement prior to receipt of SEC comments. This makes sense from a content perspective given that much of the registration statement information feeds into the slide deck. It also makes sense from a time management perspective given the IPO deal team's ability to use this waiting period effectively. In the event the company has recent lender presentations or even a CIM from a past sale process, some of the materials may prove helpful for the roadshow slide deck. Once the roadshow slide deck is close to final, company and underwriters' counsel review the deck to ensure consistency with the prospectus.

**Roadshow Preparation**   As the roadshow presentation slide deck nears completion, the dry runs with company management begin. The bankers play a prominent role in guiding this process. First and foremost, they help determine who from the company should present, and which sections. The CEO and CFO are essential, but there are no hard-and-fast rules after that. The key is to stay true to the story. If tech is critical to the messaging, then it would make sense for the Chief Technology Officer (CTO) to have a prominent role. Ditto for the Chief Marketing Officer in the event the thesis relies on new products and customers. Of course, the individual managers' ability to present in public and handle tough questions on the fly also plays a role in the decision.

Once the lineup is set, the bankers run multiple rehearsals with management. Each time, the bankers take copious notes on strengths, weaknesses, areas for improvement, and other observations. They also prepare a list of anticipated investor questions for management, as well as suggested answers. Some of these may be basic, others more challenging. For piercing questions that go to the heart of the IPO story, the bankers may choose to address them proactively in the actual slide deck. This would come in the form of raising the topic and showing analysis as to why it is not a major problem.

The bankers record the running time of each dry run—both the entire presentation and the individual sections—to ensure management maintains an appropriate pace. The dry runs are followed by a banker-led Q&A session and debriefing where key areas of feedback and advice are shared. This routine is designed to ensure that management is fully prepared by the time the IPO is ready to launch. It also helps build endurance and muscle memory for the demanding roadshow schedule where management will give this presentation dozens of times over the course of a couple of weeks.

### Salesforce Teach-in

The roadshow launch is marked by a kick-off session for the salesforce teams of the lead bookrunners on the morning of the "go date". These "teach-ins" take place on the banks' trading floors, with the management team and research analyst each conducting separate presentations. The goal is to position the salesforce teams as effectively as possible to market the opportunity with target investors and ultimately solicit orders. It also helps align the sales teams across the banking platforms on the messaging.

To facilitate the teach-ins, ECM in conjunction with IBD prepare an in-depth sales memo for the sales team that highlights the key IPO deal terms and merits. Each teach-in is followed by a Q&A session to ensure all questions and concerns are addressed properly.

## Conduct Roadshow

Immediately prior to roadshow launch, the company files an amendment to the registration statement that includes the offering size and price range of the offering. This *preliminary prospectus*, known as a red herring,[18] is then printed and distributed to investors, and the roadshow presentation is posted online. The lead bookrunners handle all scheduling and logistics for the trip, including working with the printers to ensure the red herrings get to the right investors in time.

The typical roadshow lasts anywhere from one to three weeks, depending on the geographical focus and reach of the company, as well as anticipated demand. Day 1 typically begins in New York following the teach-ins before fanning out to major cities across the U.S. Certain financial hubs are roadshow mainstays, i.e., New York City, Boston, Chicago, Los Angeles, and San Francisco. Other roadshow destinations such as Denver, Baltimore, Newport Beach, Dallas, Houston, Kansas City, among others, are common but vary with the size and nature of the offering. For international roadshows, key stops include London, Zurich, Frankfurt, Milan, Hong Kong, and Singapore.

The intense, highly scheduled nature of the roadshow means that the IPO travel team often visits multiple cities per day. The schedule remains fluid as meetings get added, rescheduled, or cancelled in accordance with investor demand. A banker from one of the active bookrunners accompanies management on the road, largely to coordinate and make sure everything goes according to plan. The banker also typically sits in on meetings and is on-hand to answer questions related to the offering.

**Investor Targeting**    In advance of the IPO roadshow, the lead bookrunners compile a list of targeted investors. This list helps shape the length and nature of the roadshow, including those countries and regions to be visited. It is informed by ECM's knowledge of the institutional investor base in consultation with the salesforce. The ultimate list reflects myriad company and offering-specific considerations, as outlined below:

- *Fit with investment strategy* – e.g., growth or income / high-dividend

- *Industry* – the sector in which the company operates

- *Size* – size and scale of the company and proposed IPO offering

- *"Must-have" nature* – attractiveness of the deal to large institutional investors

- *Peer set* – major investors in the company's primary and secondary peers

---

[18]The term red herring refers to the legend printed on the preliminary prospectus in red typeface stating that the information in the prospectus is not complete and may be changed; the securities may not be sold until the registration is effective; and that the prospectus is not an offer to sell the securities where the offer or sale is not permitted.

Exhibit 9.12 outlines key investor categories that may be targeted for an IPO.

**EXHIBIT 9.12**    Types of IPO Investors

| | Types of IPO Investors |
|---|---|
| Blue Chip | ▪ Largest institutional investors<br>▪ Capable of placing sizable orders<br>▪ Focus on company fundamentals |
| Industry-Specific | ▪ Active investors within company's sector<br>▪ Typically existing positions in company's primary or secondary peer sets<br>▪ Focus on best-in-class industry companies |
| Growth | ▪ Growth-oriented investors<br>▪ Indifferent to industry<br>▪ Focus on high-growth equity stories with substantial upside |
| Total Return | ▪ Income-oriented investors<br>▪ Indifferent to industry<br>▪ Focus on potential of free cash flow and dividend yield |
| Retail | ▪ Retail investors<br>▪ Typically, only available for retail clients of the IPO bookrunners<br>▪ Also includes directed share program (DSP)[19] |

Depending on the nature and timing of the offering, a company may target *cornerstone* or *anchor investors*. Cornerstone investors place committed orders prior to bookbuilding while anchor investors participate early in the bookbuilding process, but do not formally commit.[20] This cornerstone process typically starts two-to-three months before the IPO. During this period, the company may have detailed due diligence sessions with potential cornerstone investors and share materials.

This strategy may be used to de-risk an IPO in a volatile market or assist with a large offering. It is also employed for best-in-class equity stories, aka marquee IPOs. Ideally, securing a cornerstone or anchor investment has powerful signaling effects. A hard or soft commitment from a "blue chip" or "thought leader" investor provides a stamp of approval and creates momentum. It also improves the supply/demand dynamics by reducing the company's funding need and creating scarcity in the shares. This helps the overall bookbuilding process and pricing dynamics.

---

[19]The company can set aside a small percentage of shares for company stakeholders, including employees, suppliers, and friends and family members. The DSP percentage allocation is usually capped in the low single digits. All participants are typically subject to a lock-up period similar to company insiders, although it may be for a shorter period.

[20]Committed orders are done as private placements, not as part of the IPO.

**Investor Meetings**   As shown in Exhibit 9.13, the roadshow is comprised of several different types of meeting formats. Multiple considerations go into the lead bookrunners' planning of the roadshow schedule. Large institutional investors and potential anchors are prioritized for one-on-one meetings, where they are afforded personalized attention and Q&A. Lower priority accounts, on the other hand, are typically earmarked for group events, ranging from more intimate breakfasts to large luncheons.

**EXHIBIT 9.13**   Roadshow Meetings Framework

| | Roadshow Meetings Framework |
|---|---|
| Large Group Lunch | • Luncheon in large meeting room/hall with 20+ institutional investors<br>• Formal slideshow presentation followed by Q&A<br>• Typically, one large group event per major city (e.g., New York, Boston) |
| Small Group | • Breakfast or lunch meeting with 3-5 institutional investors<br>• Mostly Q&A, rather than full management presentation<br>• Efficient substitute for 1-on-1 meetings when scheduling is difficult |
| 1 on 1 | • Prioritized for large institutional investors and key target accounts<br>• Primarily Q&A format<br>• Attendees include portfolio managers and analysts |
| NetRoadshow | • Recorded version of the management presentation made available to institutional investors after launch of IPO[21] |
| RetailRoadshow | • Recorded version of the management presentation made available to retail investors and general public after launch of IPO |

The one-on-one meetings earmarked for Tier 1 investors typically last 45 minutes to an hour. This affords investors ample time to get answers to key questions while also feeling out management in an intimate setting. The large group meetings typically last longer, e.g., 90 minutes or more, given the formal presentation format followed by extensive Q&A with the sizable audience. The group meetings help maximize investor outreach as there is not enough time on the schedule for one-on-one meetings with everyone.

In advance of the formal meetings, investors have the ability to view the NetRoadshow online. This enables them to forgo the formal slideshow presentation at their roadshow meetings with management in favor of a targeted discussion and Q&A. NetRoadshow viewership can also be monitored online by the investment banks, which helps them gauge investor interest and potential pockets of demand.

After each roadshow meeting, the bookrunner salesforce teams follow up with investors to solicit feedback, answer questions, and ascertain levels of interest. This information is then relayed back to the bankers, management, and key shareholders,

---

[21]Both NetRoadshow and RetailRoadshow are only available until pricing.

typically during daily scheduled update calls. In addition to providing a real-time read on demand and the strength of the book, this feedback informs management as to which questions and concerns are top of mind with investors. Management can then incorporate these insights in meetings going forward, proactively addressing issues as appropriate.

## Build Order Book

**Bookbuilding Process**    The goal of the roadshow is to build as strong an *order book* as possible by targeting and converting a wide array of investors. As the roadshow progresses, the bookrunners collect formal orders, known as *indications of interest*. Ideally, these indications pile up from a large, diverse base of investors. The depth of the order book is important for pricing the offering on favorable terms.

For a typical roadshow, the order book fills slowly at first and then builds momentum before reaching a crescendo at the end (see Exhibit 9.14). Early on, smaller orders tend to trickle in from hedge funds and smaller accounts. Large institutional investors typically wait until later in the process to place their orders. This enables them to assess the supply/demand dynamics and use their heft to help dictate pricing on favorable terms. To offset this, the bookrunners try to secure indications early, thereby seizing the higher ground for driving issuer-friendly pricing.

**EXHIBIT 9.14**    Illustrative IPO Order Book Demand During a Roadshow

Illustrative IPO Order Book Demand During a Roadshow

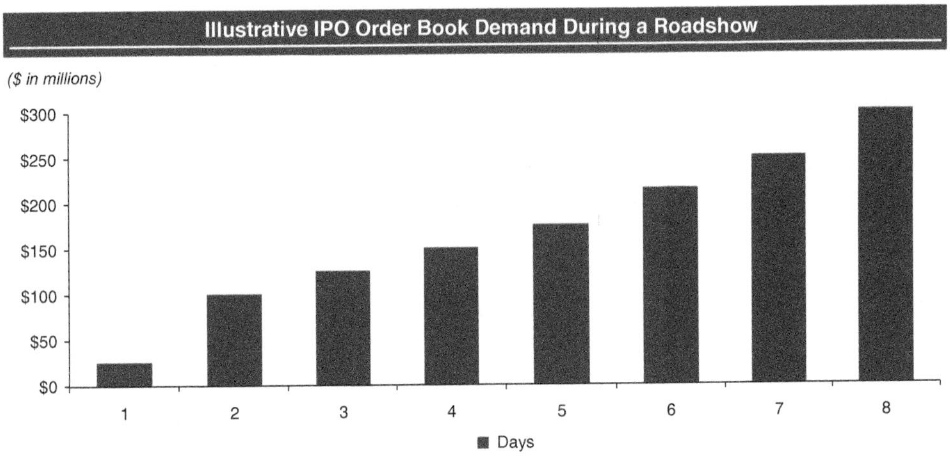

When investors submit an indication of interest, they specify the type of order:

- *No price limit (market order)* – indication to purchase a set number of shares[22]

- *Limit order* – indication to purchase a set number of shares with a limit on the maximum share price (e.g., will not purchase shares if the IPO prices above $20)

- *Scaled orders* – indication to purchase a set number of shares at different price levels (e.g., 2 million shares at $18, 1.5 million shares at $19)

---

[22]The number of shares typically stays the same even if the IPO prices above the filing range.

The bookrunners try to maximize the number of market orders so as to drive the highest pricing. As noted above, market orders do not specify a price limit. In terms of order sizing, investors do not usually get their entire indication of interest filled. As a result, they typically place inflated orders with the expectation that they will be scaled down.

Bookrunners closely monitor the progress of the *bookbuilding* progress, including investor order types and price sensitivity. As the book comes together in the later stages, they track the *hit rate*, which is the number of indications of interest received from one-on-one and small group meetings as a percentage of total meetings. A strong hit rate is in the 60% to 80% range.

The *subscription rate* refers to the number of shares in the order book as a percentage of the total number of shares being offered. *Oversubscription* occurs when the number of shares in the order book exceeds the target offering size. While oversubscription is obviously a positive, the depth and nature of the orders are critical. A shallow but oversubscribed order book at weak pricing levels does not create a solid foundation for a successful offering.

**Demand Assessment**   Demand assessment refers to the quantity and quality of the investors comprising the order book. *Gross demand* for an IPO is the aggregate demand for the offering from all investors (i.e., institutional, hedge funds, and retail). *Allocable demand* refers to the actual number of shares that will be allocated, which is always less than gross demand. This is due to the fact that investor orders get scaled down, in part to preserve demand for post-IPO trading, as well as to mitigate so-called "fast money" or short-term funds likely to sell their shares shortly after the IPO prices. As a result, allocable demand is a more reliable indicator for evaluating the health of the order book.

Exhibit 9.15 shows an illustrative breakdown of demand by investor type. Traditionally, large institutional investors make up the largest portion of the book, followed by an assortment of small/midcap funds, generalists, and hedge funds. Retail investors comprise the remainder of the book, typically 20% or so.

**EXHIBIT 9.15**   Illustrative Demand Breakdown by Investor Type

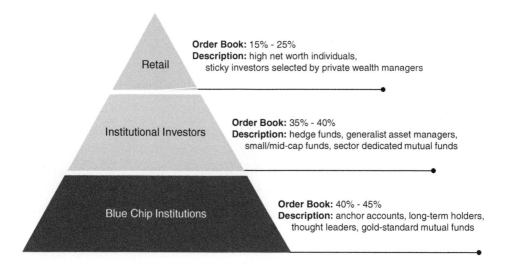

Retail
**Order Book:** 15% - 25%
**Description:** high net worth individuals,
   sticky investors selected by private wealth managers

Institutional Investors
**Order Book:** 35% - 40%
**Description:** hedge funds, generalist asset managers,
   small/mid-cap funds, sector dedicated mutual funds

Blue Chip Institutions
**Order Book:** 40% - 45%
**Description:** anchor accounts, long-term holders,
   thought leaders, gold-standard mutual funds

## PRICING AND ALLOCATION

- Price the Offering
- Allocate Shares to Investors
- Closing

### Price the Offering

**Determining the IPO Price**   Immediately prior to the roadshow launch, the bookrunners recommend a filing range for the IPO price, which is included in the preliminary prospectus. This range builds off the baseline valuation analysis conducted since the start of the process, most notably comps and recent precedent IPOs. It is updated to reflect peers' recent performance as well as broader macro and equity market conditions (see Exhibit 9.16). The range is set to where the bookrunners reasonably (and confidently) believe a deal can be priced. Pricing the IPO "below the range" can create a stigma and negatively impact the company's post-IPO trading.

**EXHIBIT 9.16**   IPO Pricing

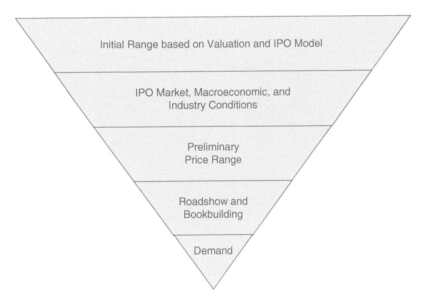

While the basis of IPO pricing relies on supply/demand fundamentals, the bookrunners employ a great deal of art in addition to science in the exercise. As they compile the order book and assess the quantity and quality of the indications, they gather investor feedback and color. This helps inform key pressure points and places to push with accounts. The size of the offering also provides a lever for the bookrunners. They have the ability to increase or decrease the number of shares offered in the interest of delivering the best possible IPO outcome.

As the final orders are secured at the end of the roadshow, the lead bookrunners evaluate the book and allocable demand. The share volume orders at various pricing levels are scrutinized to determine true investor price sensitivity. Other factors also feed into the ultimate pricing recommendation, including the quality and depth of the investor base. Chasing the highest price might not be the optimal path if it results in a concentrated, quick-money investor base versus a more stable, long-term-oriented group. The former can create dangerous post-IPO trading dynamics if they dump shares at the first pop or sign of trouble.

In essence, the pricing exercise requires solving the IPO bid-ask dynamics where the company and its shareholders seek the highest price and buy-side investors seek the best deal (see Exhibit 9.17). Of course, the ideal scenario leaves both sides happy. The company sells shares and raises proceeds at an attractive level and investors gain an entry point where they can expect sizable upside. Once the bookrunners come to a final decision, they deliver a price recommendation to the company and its Board, or a pricing committee, for approval. Per the direct listing discussion in Chapter 8, that structure was developed in large part to address the subjective elements and potential perceived inefficiencies of traditional IPO pricing.

**EXHIBIT 9.17**    IPO Objectives of Company and Investors

|  | Company | Investor |
|---|---|---|
| Overall Goal | Maximize IPO price and proceeds | Maximize share price performance |
| IPO Price | Highest possible | Lowest possible |
| Aftermarket Performance | Low, Modest | High, Strong |
| Shareholders | Long-term holders | Quality co-investors |

**Registration Statement Effectiveness**   The company, bookrunners, and counsel coordinate with the SEC on a date and time for the registration statement to become effective, which is typically on the afternoon of the IPO pricing day. They also confirm that all outstanding issues with the SEC and other regulators are resolved. After the SEC declares the registration statement effective, the bookrunners make a pricing recommendation to the company. If the company accepts the recommendation, the IPO is priced, the underwriting agreement is executed, and the initial comfort letter is delivered to the underwriters.[23] The next day, the company's stock begins trading on the exchange and the company files a final prospectus with the SEC that includes the final IPO price and other pricing terms.

---

[23]Well before pricing, company counsel and underwriters' counsel review and negotiate the underwriting agreement, and finalize the comfort letter and legal opinions so there are no hiccups around pricing and closing.

## Allocate Shares to Investors

**Allocation Philosophy and Approach**   As mentioned when discussing the bookbuilding and pricing stages, the breadth and quality of the investor base is important. The bookrunners seek to establish a high-quality group of investors who will support the company's long-term strategy. Toward this end, they employ a ranking system to determine the quality of the investors when making pricing and allocation decisions.

Key considerations include:

- *Quality* – type and tier of investor, fund size, reputation, ownership of peers, experience in the company's sector

- *Commitment* – participation in the roadshow and pre-IPO meetings, amount and nature of the follow-up

- *Size and timing of order* – order size (real versus indicative), early IPO buy-in versus placing orders post-oversubscription

- *Relationship* – history with bookrunners or company, rapport with management during the roadshow

As the bookrunners rank the investors and analyze the allocation options, they discuss the various share placement strategies with the company and its shareholders. It is meant to be an open and collaborative discussion as the company and legacy shareholders will be living with the investor base post-IPO. While the bookrunners will be asked for their recommendation, the ultimate decision lies with the company and its Board.

The bookrunners target the larger, more stable Tier 1 funds for the majority of the allocations. As noted earlier, these funds tend to be longer-term focused and are more likely to provide a strong foundation for the stock post-IPO. Similarly, the bookrunners seek to identify a group of non–Tier 1 funds they believe will be buyers of shares in the aftermarket and limit their initial allocations accordingly. This helps create pent-up demand and aftermarket support for the stock. Retail investors are typically allocated up to 20% of the book. While this investor class tends to be stable, an oversized retail allocation is often perceived as a sign of weakness among institutional accounts, who are viewed as more sophisticated.

## Closing

Allocations are typically made on the last day of the roadshow or the day after. Once the allocations are finalized, the company is ready for the stock to begin trading on a public exchange. The official IPO closing takes place three days after the first trading day. At closing, various documents such as the bring-down comfort letter and legal opinions are delivered, the company receives the proceeds, and the underwriters receive the shares. A final bring-down due diligence call with the entire IPO team takes place immediately before closing to confirm no material changes have occurred since the registration statement was made effective.

**Deal Toys**   As with an M&A transaction, upon closing an IPO, it's customary for the analyst or associate from the lead investment bank to order deal toys to commemorate the transaction. Altrum is the industry's preferred supplier in this regard. Deal toys are usually presented to the client management team and the internal deal team at the closing dinner (see Exhibit 9.18).

**EXHIBIT 9.18**   IPO Deal Toy by Altrum

## CHAPTER 9 QUESTIONS

1) The marketing and roadshow portion of the IPO preparation process typically takes

   A. Two weeks
   B. Two days
   C. Two months
   D. One day overnight

2) Key public company corporate governance requirements relate to all of the following EXCEPT

   A. Board member independence standards
   B. Succession planning
   C. Separate working sessions for independent directors
   D. Mandatory board committees

3) Public companies are required to create all of the following board committees EXCEPT

   A. Accounting
   B. Audit
   C. Compensation
   D. Nominating

4) Primary share issuance proceeds are used for all of the following EXCEPT

   A. Payments to selling shareholders
   B. Debt paydown
   C. Growth investments
   D. Funding company operations

5) Within an IPO context, fully distributed enterprise value refers to

   A. Full implied valuation of a company as if it were already publicly traded
   B. Full value of the shares distributed to new public investors
   C. Value of the proceeds distributed to selling shareholders upon IPO
   D. Value of the IPO proceeds distributed to the company

6) Using the assumptions below, complete the IPO valuation

## IPO Valuation
### $800 million Offering Size (75% Primary / 25% Secondary)
($ in millions, except per share data)

|  |  | Fully Distributed EV / EBITDA | | | | |
|---|---|---|---|---|---|---|
|  |  | 9.0x | 9.5x | 10.0x | 10.5x | 11.0x |
| 2019E EBITDA | $725 |  |  |  |  |  |
| **Fully Distributed Enterprise Value** | A) |  |  |  |  |  |
| Less: Total Debt |  | (3,000) | (3,000) | (3,000) | (3,000) | (3,000) |
| Plus: Cash and Cash Equivalents |  | 200 | 200 | 200 | 200 | 200 |
| Plus: Primary Offering Size | B) |  |  |  |  |  |
| **Fully Distributed Equity Value** |  |  |  | C) |  |  |

|  |  | IPO Valuation @ 15% Discount | | | | |
|---|---|---|---|---|---|---|
| Less: Less IPO Discount | 15% |  |  |  | D) |  |
| **Equity Value at IPO** |  |  |  |  |  |  |
| Plus: Total Debt |  | 3,000 | 3,000 | 3,000 | 3,000 | 3,000 |
| Less: Cash and Cash Equivalents |  | (200) | (200) | (200) | (200) | (200) |
| Less: Primary Offering Size |  | (600) | (600) | (600) | (600) | (600) |
| **Enterprise Value at IPO** |  |  |  |  |  |  |

|  |  | Valuation Multiples | | | | |
|---|---|---|---|---|---|---|
| **Fully Distributed** |  |  |  |  |  |  |
| **EBITDA** |  |  |  |  |  |  |
| 2019E | $725 |  |  |  |  |  |
| 2020E | 779 | E) |  |  |  |  |
| **Pro Forma Net Income** |  |  |  |  |  |  |
| 2019E | $349 |  |  |  |  |  |
| 2020E | 385 |  | F) |  |  |  |
| **IPO Valuation @ 15% Discount** |  |  |  |  |  |  |
| **EBITDA** |  |  |  |  |  |  |
| 2019E | $725 |  |  |  |  |  |
| 2020E | 779 |  |  | G) |  |  |
| **Pro Forma Net Income** |  |  |  |  |  |  |
| 2019E | $349 |  |  |  |  |  |
| 2020E | 385 |  |  |  | H) |  |

|  |  | Offering Size | | | | |
|---|---|---|---|---|---|---|
|  |  | $800 | $800 | $800 | $800 | $800 |
| % Primary |  | 75% | 75% | 75% | 75% | 75% |
| % Secondary |  | 25% | 25% | 25% | 25% | 25% |
| Offering as % of Equity Value at IPO |  |  |  |  | I) |  |

| Credit Statistics | LTM EBITDA | Net Debt |  | (x) |
|---|---|---|---|---|
| Pre-IPO Net Debt | $700 | $2,800 | Pre-IPO Net Debt / LTM EBITDA | J) |
| Post-IPO Net Debt |  | 2,200 | Post-IPO Net Debt / LTM EBITDA |  |

a. Calculate the fully distributed enterprise value

b. Calculate the primary offering size of the IPO

c. Calculate the fully distributed equity value

d. Calculate the IPO discount amount

e. Calculate the 2020E fully distributed enterprise value-to-EBITDA

f. Calculate the 2020E fully distributed P/E

g. Calculate the 2020E at IPO enterprise value-to-EBITDA

h. Calculate the 2020E at IPO P/E

i. Calculate the offering size as a % of equity value at IPO

j. Calculate the pre-IPO net debt-to-LTM EBITDA ratio

7) The IPO discount is typically

   A. De minimis
   B. 10–15%
   C. 25–30%
   D. 50%

8) The S-1 is also referred to as the

   A. Registration statement
   B. Prospectus
   C. Roadshow presentation
   D. Underwriting agreement

9) Key sections of the prospectus include all of the following EXCEPT

   A. The Box
   B. Risk factors
   C. MD&A
   D. Financial projections

10) The SEC review of the S-1 focuses on

   A. Strength of the company's business and financial performance
   B. Compliance with securities laws and regulations
   C. Safety and environmental standards within the company
   D. Merits of the company's investment thesis

11) All of the following are types of IPO ticket orders during the bookbuilding process EXCEPT

   A. Market order
   B. Time-sensitive order
   C. Limit order
   D. Scaled order

12) For IPO valuation, traditionally the most important methodology relies on

   A. M&A precedents
   B. Comps
   C. LBO analysis
   D. 52-week high and low

13) For which types of companies might a DCF approach to valuation be particularly relevant?

   A. Large mature companies
   B. Family-owned companies in established industries
   C. Early-stage tech disruptors
   D. Companies with multiple public competitors

14) During the IPO bookbuilding process, the subscription rate refers to the number of

   A. Prospectuses subscribed to versus unsolicited
   B. Greenshoe shares being offered as percentage of original offering size
   C. Subscribed versus unsubscribed shares
   D. Shares in the order book as a percentage of total shares being offered

15) Each of the following investor types may be targeted during the IPO roadshow EXCEPT

   A. Industry-specific
   B. Growth
   C. Distressed
   D. Total return

# Solutions to Selected Questions

## CHAPTER 1 ANSWERS AND RATIONALE

1)  A. The correct order is:

    I.   Select the universe of comparable companies
    II.  Locate the necessary financial information
    III. Spread key statistics, ratios, and trading multiples
    IV.  Benchmark the comparable companies
    V.   Determine valuation

2)  C. Sector, end markets, and distribution channels are key business characteristics to examine when screening for comparable companies.

3)  B. Profitability, growth profile, and credit profile are key financial characteristics to examine when screening for comparable companies.

4)  B. A Schedule 13-D is required when an investor, or group of investors, acquires more than 5% of a company's shares. A Schedule 13-D does not contain relevant financial information for comparable companies.

5)  B. Fully diluted shares outstanding are calculated as basic shares outstanding + "in-the-money" options and warrants + "in-the-money" convertible securities. Only "in-the-money" options, warrants, and convertible securities are included in the calculation for comparable companies analysis.

6)  A. The incremental shares represented by a company's "in-the-money" options and warrants are calculated in accordance with the treasury stock method (TSM). "In-the-money" convertible and equity-linked securities are calculated in accordance with the "if-converted" method or net share settlement (NSS), where appropriate.

7) C. As shown below, the 20 million options are in-the-money as the exercise price of $10.00 is lower than the current share price of $25.00. This means that the holders of the options have the right to buy the company's shares at $10.00 and sell them at $25.00, thereby realizing the $15.00 differential. Under the TSM, it is assumed that the $10.00 of potential proceeds received by the company is used to repurchase shares that are currently trading at $25.00. Therefore, the number of shares repurchased is 8 million. To calculate net new shares, the 8 million shares repurchased are subtracted from the 20 million options, resulting in 12 million. These new shares are added to the company's basic shares outstanding to derive fully diluted shares of 212.0 million.

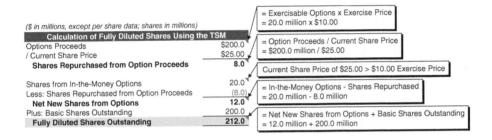

8) A. The most dilutive scenario would be to use all outstanding options and warrants.

9) B. The formula for calculating enterprise value is equity value + total debt + preferred stock + noncontrolling interest – cash.

10) A. As enterprise value is independent of capital structure, it remains constant regardless of changes in capital structure.

11) If a company issues equity and uses the proceeds to repay debt, the incremental equity value is offset by the decrease in debt on a dollar-for-dollar basis.

*($ in millions)*

| Capital Structure | | | | |
| --- | --- | --- | --- | --- |
| | Actual 2018 | Adjustments + | Adjustments - | Pro forma 2018 |
| Equity Value | $1,200.0 | 200.0 | | $1,400.0 |
| Plus: Total Debt | 750.0 | | (200.0) | 550.0 |
| Plus: Preferred Stock | 100.0 | | | 100.0 |
| Plus: Minority Interest | 50.0 | | | 50.0 |
| Less: Cash and Cash Equivalents | (100.0) | | | (100.0) |
| **Enterprise Value** | **$2,000.0** | | | **$2,000.0** |

12) A. The numerator in an interest coverage ratio can be comprised of EBITDA, (EBITDA – capex), or EBIT, which are all financial statistics representing an operating cash flow metric. Net income does not fit this characteristic because it is net of interest expense and taxes.

$$\text{Interest Coverage Ratio} \quad = \quad \frac{\text{EBITDA, (EBITDA} - \text{Capex), or EBIT}}{\text{Interest Expense}}$$

13) B. See calculation below

*($ in millions, except per share data)*

**Income Statement**

| | Reported 2018 | Adjustments + | - | Adjusted 2018 | |
|---|---|---|---|---|---|
| **Sales** | $1,000.0 | | | $1,000.0 | |
| Cost of Goods Sold | 625.0 | | (5.0) | 620.0 | Inventory write-down |
| **Gross Profit** | $375.0 | | | $380.0 | |
| Selling, General & Administrative | 230.0 | | | 230.0 | |
| Restructuring Charges | 10.0 | | (10.0) | - | |
| **Operating Income (EBIT)** | $135.0 | | | $150.0 | |
| Interest Expense | 35.0 | | | 35.0 | |
| **Pre-tax Income** | $100.0 | | | $115.0 | |
| Income Taxes @ 25% | 25.0 | 3.8 | | 28.8 | = (Inventory write-down + Restructuring |
| **Net Income** | $75.0 | | | $86.3 | charge) x Marginal Tax Rate |
| | | | | | = ($5 million + $10 million) x 25% |
| Operating Income (EBIT) | $135.0 | 15.0 | | $150.0 | |
| Depreciation & Amortization | 50.0 | | | 50.0 | |
| EBITDA | $185.0 | | | $200.0 | |
| | | | | | |
| Weighted Avg. Diluted Shares | 30.0 | | | 30.0 | |
| Diluted EPS | $2.50 | | | $2.88 | |

$15 million add-back of total non-recurring items

14) A. P/E is equal to equity value/net income.

15) C. For enterprise value multiples, the denominator employs a financial statistic that flows to both debt and equity holders, such as sales, EBITDA, and EBIT. Thus, enterprise value/net income is incorrect because net income only flows to equity holders as it is net of interest expense.

## CHAPTER 2 ANSWERS AND RATIONALE

1) C. With the exception of credit reports, all of the other choices are common sources for creating an initial list of comparable acquisitions. Other resources include equity & fixed income research reports and merger proxies.

2) D. All of the questions are relevant to gain a better understanding of an M&A transaction.

3) D. Speed of execution, certainty of completion, regulatory approvals, and other structural considerations are sometimes equally as important to a seller as the purchase price.

4) D. The proxy statement contains a summary of the background and terms of the transaction, a description of the financial analysis underlying the fairness opinion(s) of the financial advisor(s), a copy of the definitive purchase/sale agreement ("definitive agreement"), and summary and pro forma financial data (if applicable, depending on the form of consideration). The target's customer list is not contained in a proxy statement.

5) B. In a tender offer, an acquirer mails an Offer to Purchase to the target's shareholders and files a Schedule TO. The target must then file a Schedule 14D-9 within ten business days of the announcement of the tender. The Schedule 14D-9 contains a recommendation from the target's board of directors to the target's shareholders on how to respond to the tender offer.

6) C. A fixed exchange ratio is most common. A fixed exchange ratio defines the number of shares of the acquirer's stock to be exchanged for each share of the target's stock. In a floating exchange ratio, the number of acquirer shares exchanged for target shares fluctuates so as to ensure a fixed value for the target's shareholders.

7) A. A fixed exchange ratio defines the number of shares of the acquirer's stock to be exchanged for each share of the target's stock. The fixed exchange ratio of 0.25 is determined by dividing 0.5 by 2.

8) B. In a floating exchange ratio structure, the offer price per share is set while the number of shares exchanged fluctuates. Therefore, this structure presents target shareholders with greater certainty in terms of value received because the acquirer assumes the full risk of a decline in its share price.

9) D. See calculation below:

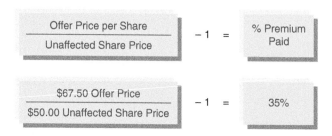

10) B. Precedent transactions, by definition, have occurred in the past and, therefore, may not be truly reflective of prevailing market conditions (e.g., the LBO boom in the mid-2000s vs. the ensuing credit crunch).

11) B. Synergies refer to the expected cost savings, growth opportunities, and other financial benefits that occur as a result of the combination of two businesses. They can be broken down into revenue and cost synergies.

12) A. The exchange ratio is determined by dividing the offer price per share by the acquirer's share price. $15.00 / $30.00 = 0.50.

13) C. The premium paid is calculated by dividing the offer price per share by the target's unaffected share price and then subtracting 1. (($15.00 / $12.00) − 1) = 20%.

14) A. See calculation below:

*($ in millions, except per share data; shares in millions)*

| Calculation of Offer Value and Enterprise Value | |
| --- | ---: |
| Fully Diluted Shares Outstanding | 253.3 |
| x Offer Price Per Share | $15.00 |
| **Offer Value** | **$3,800.0** |
| | |
| Plus: Net Debt | 1,000.0 |
| **Enterprise Value** | **$4,800.0** |

15) D. Enterprise value-to-EBITDA is calculated by dividing enterprise value by LTM EBITDA. ($4,800 million / $650 million)

## CHAPTER 3 ANSWERS AND RATIONALE

1) D. Prepaid expenses, which are payments made by a company before a product has been delivered or a service has been performed, are current assets. The other choices are long-term assets.

2) C. FCF is the cash generated by a company after paying all cash operating expenses and associated taxes, as well as the funding of capital expenditures and working capital, but prior to the payment of any interest expense.

| ($ in millions) | |
|---|---|
| **Free Cash Flow Calculation** | |
| **EBIT** | **$300.0** |
| Taxes | 75.0 |
| **EBIAT** | **$225.0** |
| Plus: Depreciation & Amortization | 50.0 |
| Less: Capital Expenditures | (25.0) |
| Less: Inc./(Dec.) in Net Working Capital | (10.0) |
| **Unlevered Free Cash Flow** | **$240.0** |

= EBIAT + Depreciation & Amortization - Capital Expenditures
 - Inc./(Dec.) in Net Working Capital
= $225.0 million + $50.0 million - $25.0 million - $10.0 million

3) C. In a DCF, a company's FCF is typically projected for a period of five years. The projection period, however, may be longer depending on the company's sector, business model, stage of development, and the underlying predictability of its financial performance.

4) B. Capital expenditures, as opposed to depreciation, represent actual cash outflows and, consequently, must be subtracted from EBIAT in the calculation of FCF.

5) D. The calculation to determine the increase or decrease in net working capital from 2018 to 2019 is found by subtracting 2018 net working capital from 2019 net working capital.

*($ in millions)*

**Net Working Capital Calculation**

|  | 2018 | 2019 |
|---|---|---|
| **Current Assets** | | |
| Accounts Receivable | 325.0 | 350.0 |
| Inventories | 200.0 | 210.0 |
| Prepaid Expenses and Other | 35.0 | 45.0 |
| **Total Current Assets** | **$560.0** | **$605.0** |
| | | |
| **Current Liabilities** | | |
| Accounts Payable | 300.0 | 315.0 |
| Accrued Liabilities | 150.0 | 160.0 |
| Other Current Liabilities | 60.0 | 65.0 |
| **Total Current Liabilities** | **$510.0** | **$540.0** |
| | | |
| **Net Working Capital** | **$50.0** | **$65.0** |
| | | |
| **(Increase) / Decrease in NWC** | | **($15.0)** |

$$= NWC_{2018} - NWC_{2019}$$
$$= \$50.0 \text{ million} - \$65.0 \text{ million}$$

6) A. When a current asset (e.g., accounts receivable, inventory) increases, it is considered a use of cash. When a current asset decreases, it is considered a source of cash.

7) B. When a current liability (e.g., accounts payable, accrued liabilities) increases, it is considered a source of cash. When a current liability decreases, it is considered a use of cash.

8) C. DSO is calculated by dividing accounts receivable by sales, and multiplying the answer by 365 (days).

$$DSO = \frac{A/R}{Sales} \times 365$$

$$31 \text{ days} = \frac{\$300 \text{ million}}{\$3,500 \text{ million}} \times 365$$

9) C. The market risk premium is the spread of the expected market return over the risk-free rate. Depending on which time period is referenced, the premium of the market return over the risk-free rate (rm – rf) may vary substantially. Duff & Phelps calculates a market risk premium of nearly 7%. Many investment banks have a firm-wide policy governing market risk premium in order to ensure consistency in valuation work across various projects and departments. The equity risk premium employed on Wall Street typically ranges from approximately 5% to 8%.

10) B. Companies in the social media, homebuilder, and chemicals sector are more volatile and riskier than companies in the utility sector. Therefore, a utility company should have a lower beta.

11) C. The DCF approach to valuation is based on determining the present value of all future FCF produced by a company. As it is infeasible to project a company's FCF indefinitely, a terminal value is used to determine the value of the company beyond the projection period.

12) A. The use of a mid-year convention results in a slightly higher valuation than year-end discounting due to the fact that FCF is received sooner.

13) C. See calculation below:

> = 1 / ((1 + WACC)^(n - .05))
> = 1 / ((1 + 10.0%)^(4.5))
> Note: Mid-Year Convention applied

*($ in millions)*

**Present Value Calculation**

|  |  | Projection Period | | | | |
|---|---|---|---|---|---|---|
|  |  | 2020 | 2021 | 2022 | 2023 | 2024 |
| **Unlevered Free Cash Flow** |  | **$100.0** | **$110.0** | **$120.0** | **$125.0** | **$130.0** |
| WACC | 10.0% |  |  |  |  |  |
| Discount Period |  | 0.5 | 1.5 | 2.5 | 3.5 | 4.5 |
| Discount Factor |  | 0.95 | 0.87 | 0.79 | 0.72 | 0.65 |
| **Present Value of Free Cash Flow** |  | **$95.3** | **$95.3** | **$94.6** | **$89.5** | **$84.7** |

> = Unlevered FCF$_{2020}$ x Discount Factor
> = $100.0 million x 0.95

> = Exit Year EBITDA x Exit Multiple
> = $250.0 million x 7.5x

**Terminal Value**

| | |
|---|---|
| Terminal Year EBITDA (2024E) | $250.0 |
| Exit Multiple | 7.5x |
| **Terminal Value** | **$1,875.0** |
| Discount Factor | 0.62 |
| **Present Value of Terminal Value** | **$1,164.2** |

> = 1 / ((1 + WACC)^n)
> = 1 / ((1 + 10.0%)^5)
> Note: Mid-Year Convention not applied for Exit Multiple Method

**Enterprise Value**

| | |
|---|---|
| **Present Value of Free Cash Flow** | **$459.5** |

> = SUM (FCF$_{2020\text{-}2024}$, discounted at 10.0%)
> = SUM ($95.3 million : $84.7 million)

| | |
|---|---|
| Terminal Value | |
| Terminal Year EBITDA (2024E) | $250.0 |
| Exit Multiple | 7.5x |
| **Terminal Value** | **$1,875.0** |
| Discount Factor | 0.62 |
| **Present Value of Terminal Value** | **$1,164.2** |
| *% of Enterprise Value* | 71.7% |
| **Enterprise Value** | **$1,623.7** |

> = Terminal Value x Discount Factor
> = $1,875.0 million x 0.62

> = PV of Terminal Value / Enterprise Value
> = $1,164.2 million / $1,623.7 million

> = PV of FCF$_{2020\text{-}2024}$ + PV of Terminal Value
> = $459.5 million + $1,164.2 million

$$\text{Discount Factor} = \frac{1}{(1 + \text{WACC})^{(n - 0.5)}}$$

$$0.95 = \frac{\$1.00}{(1 + 10\%)^{0.5}}$$

where: n = year in the projection period

0.5 = is subtracted from n in accordance with a mid-year convention

14) A. If there are no relevant comparable companies to determine an exit multiple, PGM can be utilized to calculate a terminal value. The PGM is often used in conjunction with the EMM, with each serving as a sanity check on the other.

15) A. The concept of a size premium is based on empirical evidence suggesting that smaller companies are riskier and, therefore, should have a higher cost of equity. This phenomenon, which to some degree contradicts the CAPM, relies on the notion that smaller companies' risk is not entirely captured in their betas, given limited trading volumes of their stock, making covariance calculations inexact. As shown below, a size premium can be added to the CAPM formula for smaller companies to account for the perceived higher risk.

$$r_e = r_f + \beta_L \times (r_m - r_f) + SP$$

where: SP = size premium

**CHAPTER 4 ANSWERS AND RATIONALE**

1) D. Traditional limited partners that invest money with PE firms include public and corporate pension funds, insurance companies, endowments and oundations, sovereign wealth funds, and wealthy families/individuals. Sponsor partners and investment professionals may also invest their own money in particular investment opportunities.

2) B. An investment bank's financing commitment includes:

   ▪ Commitment letter for the bank debt and a bridge facility (to be provided by the lender in lieu of a bond financing if the capital markets are not available at the time the acquisition is consummated)

   ▪ Engagement letter for the investment banks to underwrite the bonds on behalf of the issuer

   ▪ Fee letter which sets forth the various fees to be paid to the investment banks in connection with the financing

3) D. LBO candidates are identified among non-core or underperforming divisions of larger companies, neglected or troubled companies with turnaround potential, or companies in fragmented markets as platforms for a roll-up strategy. Additionally, a potential LBO candidate is simply a solidly performing company with a compelling business model, defensible competitive position, and strong growth opportunities. For a publicly traded LBO candidate, a sponsor may perceive the target as undervalued by the market or recognize opportunities for growth and efficiency not being exploited by current management.

4) C. A strong asset base pledged as collateral against a loan benefits the lender by increasing the likelihood of principal recovery in the event of bankruptcy (and liquidation). This, in turn, increases their willingness to provide debt to the target. The target's asset base is particularly important in the leveraged loan market, where the value of the assets helps dictate the amount of bank debt available.

5) D. Sponsors' exit is realized through selling their investments to another company or sponsor and IPOs. Refinancing is a monetization but not an exit strategy for a sponsor.

6) D. A dividend recap provides the sponsor with the added benefit of retaining 100% of its existing ownership position in the target, thus preserving the ability to share in any future upside potential and the option to pursue a sale or IPO at a future date.

7) A. ABL facilities are secured by a first priority lien on all current assets (typically accounts receivable and inventory) of the borrower and may include a second priority lien on all other assets (typically PP&E).

8) B. The equity contribution percentage typically ranges from approximately 30% to 40% of the LBO financing structure, although this may vary depending on debt market conditions, the type of company, and the purchase multiple paid.

9) C. Call premiums protect investors from having debt with an attractive yield refinanced long before maturity, thereby mitigating reinvestment risk in the event market interest rates decline. Reinvestment risk is the risk that future coupons from a bond will not be reinvested at the existing interest rate when the bond was initially purchased.

10) B. Covenants are provisions in credit agreements and indentures intended to protect against the deterioration of the borrower/issuer's credit quality. The three primary classifications of covenants are affirmative, negative, and financial.

11) D. While many of the covenants in credit agreements and indentures are similar in nature, a key difference is that traditional bank debt features financial maintenance covenants while high yield bonds have less restrictive incurrence covenants.

12) C. Financial maintenance covenants require the borrower to "maintain" a certain credit profile at all times through compliance with certain financial ratios or tests on a quarterly basis. Financial maintenance covenants are also designed to limit the borrower's ability to take certain actions that may be adverse to lenders (e.g., making capital expenditures beyond a set amount).

13) A. QIBs are institutions that, in aggregate, own and invest (on a discretionary basis) at least $100 million in securities.

14) C. Required maintenance leverage ratios typically decrease ("step down") throughout the term of a loan, while the coverage ratios typically increase over time. This requires the borrower to improve its credit profile by repaying debt and/or growing cash flow in accordance with the financial projections it presents to lenders during syndication.

15) B. The coupon rate represents the percentage of interest the purchaser of a bond will be paid by the issuer. A $1,000 bond trading at par with 6.0% interest has a coupon rate of 6.0%.

1) A. For highly cyclical industries (e.g., technology), both the capital markets and rating agencies take a more conservative view toward leverage to help ensure the company is appropriately capitalized to withstand cycle troughs. At the other end of the spectrum, companies in sectors that have highly visible cash flows (e.g., cable, industrial, gaming) are typically able to maintain a more highly leveraged capital structure.

2) B. See calculation below:

*($ in millions)*

$$-CF_0 + \frac{CF_1}{(1+IRR)} + \frac{CF_2}{(1+IRR)^2} + \frac{CF_3}{(1+IRR)^3} + \frac{CF_4}{(1+IRR)^4} + \frac{CF_5}{(1+IRR)^5} = 0$$

$$(\$400) + \frac{0}{(1+.201)} + \frac{0}{(1+.201)^2} + \frac{0}{(1+.201)^3} + \frac{0}{(1+.201)^4} + \frac{\$1{,}000}{(1+.201)^5} = 0$$

3) C. As shown below, total sources are equal to total uses. Term loan B amount is calculated by subtracting senior subordinated notes, equity contribution, and cash on hand from the total sources amount.

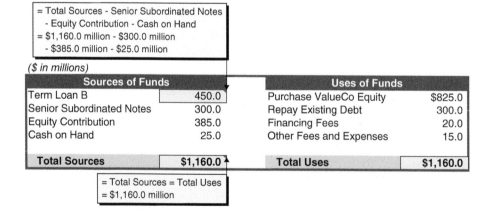

= Total Sources - Senior Subordinated Notes
 - Equity Contribution - Cash on Hand
= $1,160.0 million - $300.0 million
 - $385.0 million - $25.0 million

*($ in millions)*

| Sources of Funds | | Uses of Funds | |
|---|---|---|---|
| Term Loan B | 450.0 | Purchase ValueCo Equity | $825.0 |
| Senior Subordinated Notes | 300.0 | Repay Existing Debt | 300.0 |
| Equity Contribution | 385.0 | Financing Fees | 20.0 |
| Cash on Hand | 25.0 | Other Fees and Expenses | 15.0 |
| **Total Sources** | **$1,160.0** | **Total Uses** | **$1,160.0** |

= Total Sources = Total Uses
= $1,160.0 million

4) C. Interest coverage ratio is calculated as EBITDA divided by interest expense. Intuitively, the higher the coverage ratio, the better positioned the company is to meet its debt obligations and, therefore, the stronger its credit profile.

5) A. Total debt decreases in half over four years. As a result, the company's leverage ratio, calculated as total debt divided by EBITDA, also decreases.

6) B. The total leverage ratio decreases while interest coverage ratio increases, indicating a stronger credit profile.

7) B. The average credit statistics for LBO transactions have fluctuated dramatically over the last decade. Beginning in 2002, the total debt-to-EBITDA multiple for the average LBO was 3.9x. By 2007, this multiple reached a peak level of 6.1x, indicating extremely favorable conditions for borrowers/issuers. When credit conditions became tight in 2008 and 2009 during the Great Recession, credit statistics for LBO transactions became stronger (more favorable for lenders and debt investors and less favorable for borrowers/issuers). LBO leverage levels increased dramatically following the Great Recession, rising from 4.0x in 2009 to nearly 6.0x by 2018.

8) C. From a debt financing perspective, the projection period for an LBO model is typically set at seven to ten years so as to match the maturity of the longest tenured debt instrument in the capital structure.

9) C. While multiple factors affect a sponsor's ultimate decision to pursue a potential acquisition, comfort with meeting acceptable IRR thresholds is critical. Sponsors typically target superior returns relative to alternative investments for their LPs, with a 20%+ threshold historically serving as a widely held "rule of thumb." This threshold, however, may increase or decrease depending on market conditions, the perceived risk of an investment, and other factors specific to the situation.

10) D. An LBO analysis transaction summary provides an overview of the LBO analysis in a user-friendly format, typically displaying the sources and uses of funds, acquisition multiples, summary returns analysis, and summary financial data, as well as projected capitalization and credit statistics.

11) B. For a strategic buyer, LBO analysis (along with those derived from other valuation methodologies) is used to frame valuation and bidding strategy by analyzing the price that a competing sponsor bidder might be willing to pay for the target.

12) C. LBO valuation output is premised on key variables such as financial projections, purchase price, and financing structure, as well as exit multiple and year. Sensitivity analysis is performed on these key value drivers to produce a range of IRRs used to frame valuation for the target.

13) D. When building a pre-LBO model, the historical income statement is generally only built through EBIT, as the target's prior annual interest expense and net income are not relevant, given that the target will be recapitalized through the LBO.

14) A. The "Base Case" is generally premised on management assumptions, but with adjustments made based on the deal team's independent due diligence, research, and perspectives. The bank's internal credit committee also requires the deal team to analyze the target's performance under one or more stress cases in order to gain comfort with the target's ability to service and repay debt during periods of duress, known as "Downside Case." The operating scenario that the deal team ultimately uses to set covenants and market the transaction to investors is provided by the sponsor ("Sponsor Case").

15) D. The cash flow statement consists of three sections—operating activities, investing activities, and financing activities.

## CHAPTER 6 ANSWERS AND RATIONALE

1) D. An auction is a staged process whereby a target is marketed to multiple prospective buyers. Potential drawbacks of an auction include information leakage into the market from bidders, negative impact on employee morale, possible collusion among bidders, reduced negotiating leverage once a "winner" is chosen (thereby encouraging re-trading), and "taint" in the event of a failed auction.

2) B. Preserving confidentially is not an advantage of a broad auction. In a broad auction, the target is marketed to numerous strategic and financial buyers to maximize value, which typically results in information leakage. Heightening competitive dynamics and thus enhancing the probability of achieving a maximum sale price are the ultimate goals of an auction process.

3) B. The greatest risk of business disruption applies to a broad auction. Other disadvantages of a targeted auction include potentially leaving "money on the table" and providing a Board of Directors with less market data they can use to make certain they achieved maximum value.

4) B. When evaluating strategic buyers, the banker looks first and foremost at strategic fit, including potential synergies. Financial capacity or "ability to pay"—which is typically dependent on size, balance sheet strength, access to financing, and risk appetite—is also closely scrutinized. Other factors play a role in assessing potential strategic bidders, such as cultural fit, M&A track record, existing management's role going forward, relative and pro forma market position (including antitrust concerns), and effects on existing customer and supplier relationships. LBO financing, on the other hand, is critical for a financial sponsor buyer.

5) A. When evaluating potential financial sponsor buyers, key criteria include investment strategy/focus, sector expertise, fund size, track record, fit within existing investment portfolio, fund life cycle, and ability to obtain financing. As part of this process, the deal team looks for sponsors with existing portfolio companies that may serve as an attractive combination candidate for the target.

6) B. The two main marketing documents for the first round are the teaser and the CIM. The teaser, a brief 1–2-page synopsis of the target, is the first marketing document presented to prospective buyers. The CIM is a detailed written description of the target (often 50+ pages) that serves as the primary marketing document for the target in an auction.

7) B. The teaser, which is sent upon signing of the CA, does not contain a detailed financial section with MD&A. The CIM, however, contains an in-depth financial section with a narrative by management explaining past and future performance.

8) B. A modified version of the CIM may be prepared for designated strategic buyers, namely competitors with whom the seller may be concerned about sharing certain sensitive information.

9) A. In some cases, the CIM provides additional financial information to help guide both strategic and financial buyers toward potential growth/acquisition scenarios for the target. For example, the sell-side advisor may work with management to compile a list of potential acquisition opportunities for inclusion in the CIM (typically on an anonymous basis), including their incremental sales and EBITDA contributions.

10) D. All of the answer choices are typically included when buyers submit a bid during the first round of M&A negotiations. In addition, the bid may include structural considerations, information on financing sources, required approvals, and timing parameters.

11) B. Stapled financing is when the investment bank running an auction process (or a designated third party bank) offers a pre-packaged financing structure, typically for prospective financial buyers, in support of the target being sold. While buyers are not obligated to use the staple, it is designed to send a strong signal of support from the sell-side bank and provide comfort that the necessary financing will be available to buyers for the acquisition.

12) B. While presenting the purchase price as a range is common on an initial bid procedure letter, on a final bid procedure letter the purchase price must be presented as an exact amount. Other elements of a final bid procedure letter include a markup of the draft definitive agreement, attestation to completion of due diligence and Board of Directors' approvals.

13) B. MAC, or material adverse effects (MAE), is a highly negotiated provision in the definitive agreement, which may permit a buyer to avoid closing the transaction in the event that a substantial adverse situation is discovered after signing or a detrimental post-signing event occurs that affects the target.

14) A. Historically, the investment bank serving as sell-side advisor to the target has typically rendered the fairness opinion. In recent years, however, the ability of the sell-side advisor to objectively evaluate the target has come under increased scrutiny. This line of thinking presumes that the sell-side advisor has an inherent bias toward consummating a transaction when a significant portion of the advisor's fee is based on the closing of the deal and/or if a stapled financing is provided by the advisor's firm to the winning bidder.

15) C. 20% of pre-deal common shares being offered in a deal is the threshold that requires the acquirer to get shareholder approval.

1) A. Public strategics use accretion / (dilution) analysis to measure the pro forma effects of a transaction on earnings, assuming a given purchase price and financing structure. The acquirer's EPS pro forma for the transaction is compared to its EPS on a standalone basis. If the pro forma EPS is higher than the standalone EPS, the transaction is said to be accretive; conversely, if the pro forma EPS is lower, the transaction is said to be dilutive.

2) C. Pro forma combined diluted EPS is found by dividing the pro forma combined net income by the pro forma fully diluted shares outstanding.

| = Pro Forma Net Income / Pro Forma Fully Diluted Shares |
| --- |
| = $1,000.0 million / 250.0 million |

| ($ in millions, except per share data) | |
| --- | --- |
| **Accretion / (Dilution) Analysis** | |
| **Pro Forma Combined Net Income** | **$1,000.0** |
| **Acquirer Standalone Net Income** | **700.0** |
| | |
| Standalone Fully Diluted Shares Outstanding | 200.0 |
| Net New Shares Issued in Transaction | 50.0 |
| **Pro Forma Fully Diluted Shares Outstanding** | **250.0** |
| | |
| Pro Forma Combined Diluted EPS | $4.00 |
| Acquirer Standalone Diluted EPS | 3.50 |
| | |
| **Accretion / (Dilution) - $** | **$0.50** |
| **Accretion / (Dilution) - %** | **14.3%** |
| *Accretive / Dilutive* | *Accretive* |
| **Required Synergies to Breakeven / (Cushion)** | ($166.7) |

= - (EPS Accretion / (Dilution) × Pro Forma Fully Diluted Shares) / (1 - Tax Rate)
= - ($0.50 × 250.0 million / (1 − 25%)

= Pro Forma Combined Diluted EPS / BuyerCo Standalone Diluted EPS - 1
= $4.00 / $3.50 − 1

= Pro Forma Combined Diluted EPS - BuyerCo Standalone Diluted EPS
= $4.00 − $3.50

3) B. Accretion / (dilution) on a dollar amount basis is calculated by subtracting the pro forma combined EPS by the acquirer's standalone diluted EPS. As shown above, the transaction is accretive on a dollar amount basis by $0.50.

4) B. Accretion / (dilution) on a percentage basis is calculated by dividing the pro forma combined EPS by the acquirer's standalone diluted EPS, and subtracting 1. As shown above, the transaction is accretive on a percentage basis by 14.3%.

5) C. As shown above, breakeven pre-tax synergies / (cushion) is calculated with the formula: (– (EPS accretion/(dilution) × pro forma fully diluted shares) / (1 – tax rate). Since the transaction is accretive, the analysis determines the synergy cushion before the transaction becomes dilutive.

6) A. In an all-stock deal, if an acquirer has a higher P/E than the seller, the deal is accretive.

7) A. In addition to the standard valuation methodologies (comparable companies, precedent transactions, DCF, and LBO analysis) used to establish a valuation range for a potential acquisition, public strategic buyers also use accretion / (dilution) analysis to measure the pro forma effects of a transaction on earnings, assuming a given purchase price and financing structure. It is often critical that a transaction needs to be accretive in order for the acquirer to agree to the deal.

8) B. Revenue and cost are the two types of potential synergies. Revenue synergies refer to new revenue streams (cross-selling, new distribution channels, etc.) available to the combined company. Cost synergies refer to cost-cutting initiatives (eliminating duplicate operations, employee redundancies, etc.) that can be achieved through the combination.

9) C. Section 382 of the Internal Revenue Code is centered on the limitation of net operating loss carryforwards and certain built-in losses following ownership change.

10) C. Equity value of the seller is a use, not a source, of funds.

11) B. Referred to as the "excess purchase price," goodwill is calculated as the purchase price minus the target's net identifiable assets after allocations to the target's tangible and intangible assets, plus the DTL.

12) B. Allocable purchase premium is calculated as equity purchase price less net identifiable assets.

($ in millions)

| Goodwill Calculation | |
|---|---|
| Equity Purchase Price | $3,000.0 |
| Less: ValueCo Net Identifiable Assets | (1,250.0) |
| **Total Allocable Purchase Premium** | **$1,750.0** |

= - (ValueCo Shareholders' Equity - Existing Goodwill)
= - ($2,000.0 million - $750.0 million)

13) B. Financing fees are capitalized on the buyer's balance sheet as an asset and are amortized over the life of the security. They are not expensed when they occur such as M&A fees in a transaction.

14) B. In a stock purchase, the target ceases to remain in existence post-transaction, becoming a wholly-owned subsidiary of the acquirer. As a result, the acquirer assumes all of the target's past, present, and future known and unknown liabilities, in addition to the assets.

15) A. An asset purchase refers to an M&A transaction whereby an acquirer purchases all or some of the target's assets. Under this structure, the target legally remains in existence post-transaction, which means that the buyer purchases specified assets and assumes certain liabilities. This can help alleviate the buyer's risk, especially when there may be substantial unknown contingent liabilities.

## CHAPTER 8 ANSWERS AND RATIONALE

1) C. Upfront fees and expenses involved in the IPO preparation / filing process, and on-going annual public company costs, are considerations, not benefits, of going public.

2) C. Increased valuation transparency is a key benefit of going public. An IPO provides both the original and new shareholders a liquid market and valuation benchmark for their shares.

3) A. Primary shares refer to newly issued shares of common stock that are sold to investors.

4) D. Secondary shares refer to existing shares of common stock that are sold to investors.

5) A. An initiating coverage equity research report refers to the first report published by an equity research analyst beginning coverage on a particular company. This report often provides a comprehensive business description, sector analysis, and commentary.

6) A. SEC guidelines require all investors to receive an issuer's preliminary prospectus or "red herring." The prospectus contains essential information on the company and the investment opportunity that is deemed material to review prior to investing.

7) A. The overallotment option, also known as the greenshoe, provides the ability to sell additional shares to investors in excess of the original IPO offering. The purpose of the greenshoe is largely to serve as a stabilization mechanism. In this sense, it is intended to increase investor confidence by providing immediate aftermarket support and stability.

8) A. The stabilization agent is responsible for managing aftermarket trading and exercising the greenshoe (if warranted). While the role itself does not command additional fees, the agent opens trading of the stock, which tends to increase trading flow to the firm. One of the active bookrunners is assigned the role of stabilization agent.

9) A. In a dual-track process, the company simultaneously pursues both an IPO offering and a sale of the company. Dual-track processes are designed to maximize flexibility and competitive tension in pursuit of the best outcome, typically maximum value.

10)  B.  A key advantage to an IPO is that existing shareholders maintain ownership of their business and have upside through the retained stake.

11)  D.  The ability of existing shareholders to entirely cash out is a benefit of an M&A sale process.

12)  A.  SPACs are also known as blank check vehicles.

13)  D.  There are a variety of expenses associated with a SPAC, including funding the SPAC IPO upfront, running the public vehicle, due diligence, travel, etc.

14)  B.  A company foregoes the traditional IPO roadshow and bookbuilding process in a direct listing.

15)  B.  Follow-ons can be comprised of either primary or secondary shares (or a combination), but secondary offerings are more common as legacy shareholder(s) look to sell down their positions.

## CHAPTER 9 ANSWERS AND RATIONALE

1) A. This portion of the roadshow includes the salesforce teach-in, investor meetings and building of the order book, and takes roughly two weeks.

2) B. Succession planning is a corporate governance best practice but is not required.

3) A. The three mandatory committees for public companies are audit, compensation, and nominating.

4) A. Proceeds from the sale of secondary shares go to selling shareholders.

5) A. Fully distributed enterprise value is meant to capture the full implied valuation of a company as if it were already publicly traded.

6)   IPO Valuation

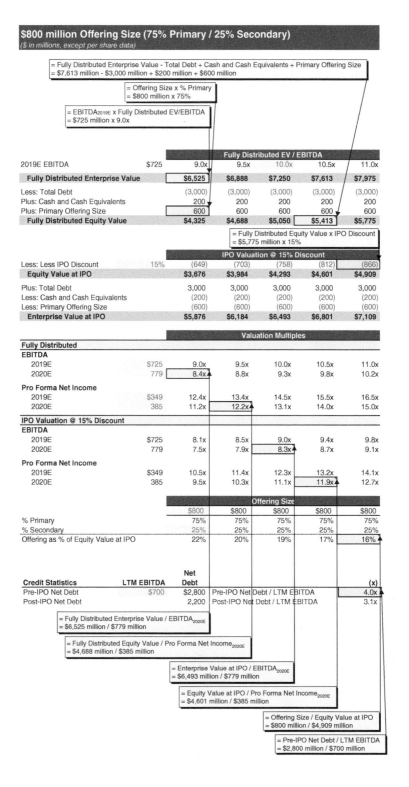

**$800 million Offering Size (75% Primary / 25% Secondary)**
*($ in millions, except per share data)*

= Fully Distributed Enterprise Value - Total Debt + Cash and Cash Equivalents + Primary Offering Size
= $7,613 million - $3,000 million + $200 million + $600 million

= Offering Size x % Primary
= $800 million x 75%

= EBITDA₂₀₁₉ₑ x Fully Distributed EV/EBITDA
= $725 million x 9.0x

| | | Fully Distributed EV / EBITDA | | | | |
|---|---|---|---|---|---|---|
| 2019E EBITDA | $725 | 9.0x | 9.5x | 10.0x | 10.5x | 11.0x |
| **Fully Distributed Enterprise Value** | | **$6,525** | **$6,888** | **$7,250** | **$7,613** | **$7,975** |
| Less: Total Debt | | (3,000) | (3,000) | (3,000) | (3,000) | (3,000) |
| Plus: Cash and Cash Equivalents | | 200 | 200 | 200 | 200 | 200 |
| Plus: Primary Offering Size | | 600 | 600 | 600 | 600 | 600 |
| **Fully Distributed Equity Value** | | **$4,325** | **$4,688** | **$5,050** | **$5,413** | **$5,775** |

= Fully Distributed Equity Value x IPO Discount
= $5,775 million x 15%

| | | IPO Valuation @ 15% Discount | | | | |
|---|---|---|---|---|---|---|
| Less: Less IPO Discount | 15% | (649) | (703) | (758) | (812) | (866) |
| **Equity Value at IPO** | | **$3,676** | **$3,984** | **$4,293** | **$4,601** | **$4,909** |
| Plus: Total Debt | | 3,000 | 3,000 | 3,000 | 3,000 | 3,000 |
| Less: Cash and Cash Equivalents | | (200) | (200) | (200) | (200) | (200) |
| Less: Primary Offering Size | | (600) | (600) | (600) | (600) | (600) |
| **Enterprise Value at IPO** | | **$5,876** | **$6,184** | **$6,493** | **$6,801** | **$7,109** |

| | | Valuation Multiples | | | | |
|---|---|---|---|---|---|---|
| **Fully Distributed** | | | | | | |
| **EBITDA** | | | | | | |
| 2019E | $725 | 9.0x | 9.5x | 10.0x | 10.5x | 11.0x |
| 2020E | 779 | 8.4x | 8.8x | 9.3x | 9.8x | 10.2x |
| | | | | | | |
| **Pro Forma Net Income** | | | | | | |
| 2019E | $349 | 12.4x | 13.4x | 14.5x | 15.5x | 16.5x |
| 2020E | 385 | 11.2x | 12.2x | 13.1x | 14.0x | 15.0x |
| **IPO Valuation @ 15% Discount** | | | | | | |
| **EBITDA** | | | | | | |
| 2019E | $725 | 8.1x | 8.5x | 9.0x | 9.4x | 9.8x |
| 2020E | 779 | 7.5x | 7.9x | 8.3x | 8.7x | 9.1x |
| | | | | | | |
| **Pro Forma Net Income** | | | | | | |
| 2019E | $349 | 10.5x | 11.4x | 12.3x | 13.2x | 14.1x |
| 2020E | 385 | 9.5x | 10.3x | 11.1x | 11.9x | 12.7x |

| | | Offering Size | | | | |
|---|---|---|---|---|---|---|
| | | $800 | $800 | $800 | $800 | $800 |
| % Primary | | 75% | 75% | 75% | 75% | 75% |
| % Secondary | | 25% | 25% | 25% | 25% | 25% |
| Offering as % of Equity Value at IPO | | 22% | 20% | 19% | 17% | 16% |

| Credit Statistics | LTM EBITDA | Net Debt | | | | (x) |
|---|---|---|---|---|---|---|
| Pre-IPO Net Debt | $700 | $2,800 | Pre-IPO Net Debt / LTM EBITDA | | | 4.0x |
| Post-IPO Net Debt | | 2,200 | Post-IPO Net Debt / LTM EBITDA | | | 3.1x |

= Fully Distributed Enterprise Value / EBITDA₂₀₂₀ₑ
= $6,525 million / $779 million

= Fully Distributed Equity Value / Pro Forma Net Income₂₀₂₀ₑ
= $4,688 million / $385 million

= Enterprise Value at IPO / EBITDA₂₀₂₀ₑ
= $6,493 million / $779 million

= Equity Value at IPO / Pro Forma Net Income₂₀₂₀ₑ
= $4,601 million / $385 million

= Offering Size / Equity Value at IPO
= $800 million / $4,909 million

= Pre-IPO Net Debt / LTM EBITDA
= $2,800 million / $700 million

   a. $6,525 million. Fully distributed enterprise value is calculated as 2019E EBITDA multiplied by the fully distributed EV/EBITDA multiple. ($725 million × 9.0x)

   b. $600 million. Primary offering size is calculated as the total offering size multiplied by the portion of the offering that is primary shares. ($800 million × 75%)

   c. $5,413 million. Fully distributed equity value is calculated as fully distributed enterprise value less total debt plus cash and cash equivalents and the primary offering size. ($7,613 million - $3,000 million + $200 million + $600 million)

   d. $866 million. The IPO discount amount is calculated as fully distributed equity value multiplied by the IPO discount %. ($5,775 million × 15%)

   e. 8.4x. The 2020E fully distributed enterprise value-to-EBITDA is calculated as the fully distributed enterprise value divided by the 2020E EBITDA. ($6,525 million / $779 million)

   f. 12.2x. The 2020E fully distributed P/E is calculated as the fully distributed equity value divided by the 2020E pro forma net income. ($4,688 million / $385 million)

   g. 8.3x. The 2020E at IPO enterprise value-to-EBITDA is calculated as the enterprise value at IPO divided by the 2020E EBITDA. ($6,493 million / $779 million)

   h. 11.9x. The 2020E at IPO P/E is calculated as equity value at IPO divided by the 2020E pro forma net income. ($4,601 million / $385 million)

   i. 16%. The offering size as a % of equity value at IPO is calculated as the offering size divided by the equity value at IPO. ($800 million / $4,909 million)

   j. 4.0x. The pre-IPO net debt-to-LTM EBITDA ratio is calculated as the pre-IPO net debt divided by the LTM EBITDA. ($2,800 million / $700 million).

7) B. An IPO discount is applied to fully distributed equity value, typically in the 10–15% range, but varies depending on the company and the prevailing IPO market conditions.

8) A. The S-1 is a comprehensive document that serves as both a marketing tool and a key disclosure filing about the company and the risks related to the offering. As such, it is reviewed and eventually must be approved by the SEC. The S-1 is also referred to as the registration statement.

9) D. While historical financial information is a required disclosure in the prospectus, forward-looking projections are not allowed.

10) B. The Division of Corporation Finance's review process is exhaustive and comprehensive. The focus is on compliance with securities laws and regulations and does not constitute an opinion of the strength of the company's equity story or valuation.

11) B. When investors submit an indication of interest, they specify the type of order. A market order is an indication to purchase a set number of shares. A limit order is an indication to purchase a set number of shares with a limit on the maximum share price (e.g., will not purchase shares if the IPO prices above $20). A scaled order is an indication to purchase a set number of shares at different price levels (e.g., 2 million shares at $18, 1.5 million shares at $19).

12) B. IPO valuation has a heightened emphasis on comps, given that publicly traded peers understandably provide the most relevant framework for comparison.

13) C. The valuation approach depends on multiple factors, including the sector and maturity stage of the company. The DCF is particularly relevant for early stage tech companies with limited or no earnings, or for those businesses with no real public comps.

14) D. The subscription rate refers to the number of shares in the order book as a percentage of the total number of shares being offered.

15) C. Depending on the size, sector, and nature of the IPO candidate, the net is typically cast for a broad group of investor types, ranging from blue chip to industry-specific to growth and total return. The mix typically includes large institutional investors as well as hedge funds. Distressed investors, however, typically focus on beaten-up debt securities and are NOT included in the IPO roadshow process.

**P**rior to co-founding Apollo Global Management, LLC, I began my Wall Street career at Drexel Burnham Lambert. It was there, as a member of their Mergers and Acquisitions team, that I honed my technical skills and financial knowledge while working long hours on many high profile deals. I know what it takes to master these skills and how critical they are to succeeding in the current market environment. Today, I look for these same abilities in the associates we recruit at Apollo. It gives me great confidence that many from the new generation of future financial leaders learned their corporate finance fundamentals with the help of Rosenbaum and Pearl and their best-selling book, *Investment Banking*.

I have personally been involved in the successful execution of hundreds of M&A and LBO transactions over the past three decades and I recommend this book to advisors, financiers, practitioners, and anyone else interested in investment transactions. Rosenbaum and Pearl have created a comprehensive, yet highly accessible, written guide to the core skills of the successful investment professional, with a particular emphasis on valuation analysis.

We live in an uncertain and volatile world where market conditions, credit availability, and deal structure can change quickly with little or no warning. With numerous unknowns and potential challenges at every turn, we are grounded by what we can control—namely, solid fundamental analysis, financial discipline, rigorous due diligence, and sound judgment. At Apollo, these variables are key cornerstones for valuing companies, creating long-term equity value and delivering industry-leading returns for our investors. Therefore, I support Rosenbaum and Pearl's book, *Investment Banking*, and its work on the fundamentals of valuation and transaction-related finance.

JOSHUA HARRIS
Co-Founder and Senior Managing Director
Apollo Global Management, LLC

# Bibliography and Recommended Reading

Almeida, Heitor, and Thomas Philippon. "The Risk-Adjusted Cost of Financial Distress." *Journal of Finance* 62 (2007): 2557–2586.

Alti, Aydogan. "How Persistent Is the Impact of Market Timing on Capital Structure?" *Journal of Finance* 61 (2006): 1681–1710.

Altman, Edward I., ed. *The High-Yield Debt Market: Investment Performance and Economic Impact.* New York: Beard Books, 1998.

Andrade, Gregor, and Steven Kaplan. "How Costly is Financial (Not Economic) Distress? Evidence from Highly Leveraged Transactions that Became Distressed." *Journal of Finance* 53 (1998): 1443–1493.

Baginski, Stephen P., and John M. Hassell. *Management Decisions and Financial Accounting Reports.* 2nd ed. Mason, OH: South-Western College Publishing, 2004.

Bahnson, Paul R., Brian P. McAllister, and Paul B.W. Miller. "Noncontrolling Interest: Much More Than a Name Change." *Journal of Accountancy* (2008).

Baker, Malcolm, and Jeffrey Wurgler. "Market Timing and Capital Structure." *Journal of Finance* 57 (2002): 1–32.

Barnhill, Theodore, Jr., Mark Shenkman, and William Maxwell. *High Yield Bonds: Market Structure, Valuation, and Portfolio Strategies.* New York: McGraw-Hill, 1999.

Barr, Alistair. "Big Leveraged Buyouts Won't Return for Year or More: Lee Equity." *MarketWatch,* April 8, 2008.

Bierman, Harold, Jr. *Private Equity: Transforming Public Stock Into Private Equity to Create Value.* Hoboken, NJ: John Wiley & Sons, 2003.

Boot, Arnoud W. A., Radhakrishnan Goplan, and Anjan V. Thakor. "Market Liquidity, Investor Participation, and Managerial Autonomy: Why Do Firms Go Private?" *Journal of Finance* 63 (2008): 2013–2059.

Bruner, Robert F. *Applied Mergers and Acquisitions.* Hoboken, NJ: John Wiley & Sons, 2004.

Calamos, John P. *Convertible Securities: The Latest Instruments, Portfolio Strategies, and Valuation Analysis.* Rev. ed. New York: McGraw-Hill, 1998.

Carey, Dennis, Robert J. Aiello, Michael D. Watkins, Robert G. Eccles, and Alfred Rappaport. *Harvard Business Review on Mergers & Acquisitions.* Boston: Harvard Business School Press, 2001.

Carney, William J. *Corporate Finance: Principles and Practice*. New York: Foundation Press, 2004.

Carney, William J. *Mergers and Acquisitions: Case and Materials*. New York: Foundation Press, 2000.

Chava, Sudheer, and Michael R. Roberts. "How Does Financing Impact Investment? The Role of Debt Covenants." *Journal of Finance* 63 (2008): 2085–2121.

Chisholm, Andrew. *An Introduction to Capital Markets: Products, Strategies, Participants*. West Sussex, UK: John Wiley & Sons, 2002.

Clements, Philip J., and Philip W. Wisler. *The Standard & Poor's Guide to Fairness Opinions*. New York: McGraw-Hill, 2005.

Copeland, Tom, Tim Koller, Marc Goedhart, and David Wessels. *Valuation: Measuring and Managing the Value of Companies*. 4th ed. Hoboken, NJ: John Wiley & Sons, 2005.

Damodaran, Aswath. *Damodaran on Valuation: Security Analysis for Investment and Corporate Finance*. 2nd ed. Hoboken, NJ: John Wiley & Sons, 2006.

Damodaran, Aswath. *Investment Valuation: Tools and Techniques for Determining the Value of Any Asset*. 2nd ed. New York: John Wiley & Sons, 2002.

Datta, Sudip, Mai Iskandar-Datta, and Kartik Raman. "Managerial Stock Ownership and the Maturity Structure of Corporate Debt." *Journal of Finance* 60 (2005): 2333–2350.

Downes, John, and Jordan Elliot Goodman. *Dictionary of Finance and Investment Terms*. 7th ed. Hauppauge, NY: Barron's Educational Series, 2006.

Ergungor, O. Emre. "Dividends." Federal Reserve Bank of Cleveland, Economic Commentary. 2004.

Evans, Frank C., and David M. Bishop. *Valuation for M&A: Building Value in Private Companies*. New York: John Wiley & Sons, 2001.

Fabozzi, Frank J. *The Handbook of Fixed Income Securities*. 6th ed. New York: McGraw-Hill, 2000.

Fama, Eugene F., and Kenneth R. French. "The Value Premium and the CAPM." *Journal of Finance* 61 (2006): 2163–2185.

Fang, Lily Hua. "Investment Bank Reputation and the Price and Quality of Underwriting Services." *Journal of Finance* 60 (2005): 2729–2761.

Feldman, Stanley J. *Principles of Private Firm Valuation*. Hoboken, NJ: John Wiley & Sons, 2005.

Ferguson, Joy. "LBOs Sponsor-to-Sponsor Deals Raise Eyebrows." *High Yield Report*, August 9, 2004.

Frankel, Michael E. S. *Mergers and Acquisitions Basics: The Key Steps of Acquisitions, Divestitures, and Investments*. Hoboken, NJ: John Wiley & Sons, 2005.

Gaughan, Patrick A. *Mergers, Acquisitions, and Corporate Restructurings*. 4th ed. Hoboken, NJ: John Wiley & Sons, 2007.

Gaughan, Patrick A. *Mergers: What Can Go Wrong and How to Prevent It*. Hoboken, NJ: John Wiley & Sons, 2005.

Gilson, Stuart. "Transactions Costs and Capital Structure Choice: Evidence from Financially Distressed Firms." *Journal of Finance* 52 (1997): 161–196.

Goetzmann, William N., and Roger G. Ibbotson. *The Equity Risk Premium: Essays and Explorations*. New York: Oxford University Press, 2006.

Graham, John R. "How Big Are the Tax Benefits of Debt?" *Journal of Finance* 55 (2000): 1901–1941.

Greenwald, Bruce C. N., Judd Kahn, Paul D. Sonkin, and Michael van Biema. *Value Investing: From Graham to Buffett and Beyond*. Hoboken, NJ: John Wiley & Sons, 2004.

Grinblatt, Mark, and Sheridan Titman. *Financial Markets and Corporate Strategy*. New York: McGraw-Hill, 2008.

Gu, Zhaoyang, and Ting Chen. "Analysts' Treatment of Nonrecurring Items in Street Earnings." Carnegie Mellon University (2004): 1–52.

Haas, Jeffrey J. *Corporate Finance in a Nutshell*. St. Paul, MN: Thomson West, 2003.

Hennessy, Christopher A., and Toni M. Whited. "Debt Dynamics." *Journal of Finance* 60 (2005): 1129–1165.

Hooke, Jeffrey C. *M&A: A Practical Guide to Doing the Deal*. New York: John Wiley & Sons, 1996.

Ibbotson, Roger G., and Rex Sinquefield. *Ibbotson SBBI 2008 Valuation Yearbook*. Chicago: Morningstar, 2007.

Kaback, Hoffer. "Behind the Art of M&A with Bruce Wasserstein." *Directors & Boards*, Spring 1999.

Kaplan, Steven N., and Antoinette Schoar. "Private Equity Performance: Returns, Persistence, and Capital Flows." *Journal of Finance* 60 (2005): 1791–1823.

Kieso, Donald E., Jerry J. Weygandt, and Terry D. Warfield. *Intermediate Accounting*. 12th ed. Hoboken, NJ: John Wiley & Sons, 2007.

Kisgen, Darren J. "Credit Ratings and Capital Structure." *Journal of Finance* 61 (2006): 1035–1072.

Koons, Cynthia. "Strong Loan Market Allowing Riskier Debt." *MarketWatch*, February 14, 2007.

Lajoux, Alexandra Reed. *The Art of M&A Integration: A Guide to Merging Resources, Processes, and Responsibilities*. 2nd ed. New York: McGraw-Hill, 2005.

Lajoux, Alexandra Reed, and Charles M. Elson. *The Art of M&A: Financing and Refinancing*. New York: McGraw-Hill, 1999.

Lajoux, Alexandra Reed, and H. Peter Nesvold. *The Art of M&A Structuring: Techniques for Mitigating Financial, Tax, and Legal Risk*. New York: McGraw-Hill, 2004.

Lajoux, Alexandra Reed, and J. Fred Weston. *The Art of M&A Due Diligence*. New York: McGraw-Hill, 2000.

Latham & Watkins LLP. *The Book of Jargon*. New York: 2013.

Latham & Watkins LLP. *US IPO Guide*. 2019.

Leary, Mark T., and Michael R. Roberts. "Do Firms Rebalance Their Capital Structure?" *Journal of Finance* 60 (2005): 2575–2619.

Leland, Hayne E. "Corporate Debt Value, Bond Covenants, and Optimal Capital Structure." *Journal of Finance* 49 (1994): 1213–1252.

Leland, Hayne E. "Financial Synergies and the Optimal Scope of the Firm: Implications for Mergers, Spinoffs, and Structured Finance." *Journal of Finance* 62 (2007): 765–808.

Lerner, Josh, Felda Hardymon, and Ann Leamon. *Venture Capital and Private Equity: A Casebook*. Hoboken, NJ: John Wiley & Sons, 2007.

Liaw, K. Thomas. *The Business of Investment Banking: A Comprehensive Overview*. Hoboken, NJ: John Wiley & Sons, 2005.

Liaw, K. Thomas. *Capital Markets*. Mason, OH: Thomson South-Western, 2003.

Luo, Yuanzhi. "Do Insiders Learn from Outsiders? Evidence from Mergers and Acquisitions." *Journal of Finance* 60 (2005): 1951–1982.

Marren, Joseph H. *Mergers & Acquisitions: A Valuation Handbook*. New York: McGraw-Hill, 1992.

Metrick, Andrew, and Ayako Yasuda. "The Economics of Private Equity Funds." (Yale University). April 22, 2010.

Milbank, Tweed, Hadley & McCloy LLP, Mark L. Mandel, James H. Ball Jr., Rod Miller, Brett Nadritch, Arnold B. Peinado III, and Manan Shah. *The IPO and Public Company Primer: A Practical Guide to Going Public, Raising Capital and Life as a Public Company*. RR Donnelley, 2014.

Miller, Hazel (Orrick, Herrington & Sutcliffe LLP). "2005: Another Strong Year for the Financing of LBOs." *Financier Worldwide*, February 2006.

Mitchell, Mark, Todd Pulvino, and Erik Stafford. "Price Pressure around Mergers." *Journal of Finance* 60 (2004): 31–63.

McCafferty, Joseph. "The Buyout Binge." *CFO Magazine*, April 1, 2007.

Oesterle, Dale A. *Mergers and Acquisitions in a Nutshell*. St. Paul, MN: Thomson West, 2006.

Pereiro, Luis E. *Valuation of Companies in Emerging Markets*. New York: John Wiley & Sons, 2002.

Pratt, Shannon P. *Business Valuation Discounts and Premiums*. New York: John Wiley & Sons, 2001.

Pratt, Shannon P., and Roger J. Grabowski. *Cost of Capital: Estimation and Applications*. 3rd ed. Hoboken, NJ: John Wiley & Sons, 2008.

Rajan, Arvind, Glen McDermott, and Ratul Roy. *The Structured Credit Handbook*. Hoboken, NJ: John Wiley & Sons, 2007.

Reed, Stanley Foster, Alexandra Lajoux, and H. Peter Nesvold. *The Art of M&A: A Merger Acquisition Buyout Guide*. 4th ed. New York: McGraw-Hill, 2007.

Rickertsen, Rick, and Robert E. Gunther. *Buyout: The Insider's Guide to Buying Your Own Company*. New York: AMACOM, 2001.

Rhodes-Kropf, Matthew, and S. Viswanathan. "Market Valuation and Merger Waves." *Journal of Finance* 59 (2004): 2685–2718.

Rosenbloom, Arthur H., ed. *Due Diligence for Global Deal Making: The Definitive Guide to Cross-Border Mergers and Acquisitions (M&A), Joint Ventures, Financings, and Strategic Alliances*. Princeton: Bloomberg Press, 2002.

Rubino, Robert, and Timothy Shoyer. "Why Today's Borrowers & Investors Lean Toward Second Liens." *Bank Loan Report,* March 8, 2004.

Ross, Stephen A., Randolph W. Westerfield, and Jeffrey Jaffe. *Corporate Finance.* 6th ed. New York: McGraw-Hill, 2002.

Salter, Malcolm S., and Joshua N. Rosenbaum. *OAO Yukos Oil Company.* Boston: Harvard Business School Publishing, 2001.

Schneider, Arnold. *Managerial Accounting: Manufacturing and Service Applications.* 5th ed. Mason, OH: Cengage Learning, 2009.

Schwert, G. William. "Hostility in Takeovers: In the Eyes of the Beholder?" *Journal of Finance* 55 (2000): 2599–2640.

Scott, David L. *Wall Street Words: An A to Z Guide to Investment Terms for Today's Investor.* 3rd ed. Boston: Houghton Mifflin, 2003.

Siegel, Jeremy J. *Stocks for the Long Run.* 4th ed. New York: McGraw-Hill, 2007.

Sherman, Andrew J., and Milledge A. Hart. *Mergers & Acquisitions From A to Z.* 2nd ed. New York: AMACOM, 2006.

Slee, Robert T. "Business Owners Choose a Transfer Value." *Journal of Financial Planning* 17, no. 6 (2004): 86–91.

Slee, Robert T. *Private Capital Markets: Valuation, Capitalization, and Transfer of Private Business Interests.* Hoboken, NJ: John Wiley & Sons, 2004.

Standard and Poor's/Leveraged Commentary & Data. *A Guide to the Loan Market.* October 2007.

Standard and Poor's/Leveraged Commentary & Data. *High Yield Bond Market Primer.* 2007.

Strebulaev, Ilya A. "Do Tests of Capital Structure Theory Mean What They Say?" *Journal of Finance* 62 (2007): 1747–1787.

Thompson, Samuel C., Jr. *Business Planning for Mergers and Acquisitions: Corporate, Securities, Tax, Antitrust, International, and Related Aspects.* 3rd ed. Durham, NC: Carolina Academic Press, 2007.

Wachtell, Lipton, Rosen & Katz, Deborah L. Paul, and Michael Sabbah. "Understanding Tax Receivable Agreements." *Practical Law The Journal* (2013).

Wasserstein, Bruce. *Big Deal: Mergers and Acquisitions in the Digital Age.* New York: Warner Books, 2001.

Westenberg, David A. *Initial Public Offerings: A Practical Guide to Going Public.* Practising Law Institute, 2014.

White, Gerald I., Ashwinpaul C. Sondhi, and Dov Fried. *The Analysis and Use of Financial Statements.* 3rd ed. New York: John Wiley & Sons, 2002.

Wilson Sonsini Goodrich & Rosati, Steven E. Boehner, Jon C. Avina, and Calise Y. Cheng. *Guide to the Initial Public Offering.* Merrill Corporation, 2016.

Yago, Glenn, and Susanne Trimbath. *Beyond Junk Bonds: Expanding High Yield Markets.* New York: Oxford University Press, 2003.

Yasuda, Ayako. "Do Bank Relationships Affect the Firm's Underwriter Choice in the Corporate-Bond Underwriting Market?" *Journal of Finance* 60 (2005): 1259–1292.

# Index

LATHAM & WATKINS LLP
As the world's leading law firm:
Capital Markets
#1
US Equity IPO Manager Adviser by Deal Count
Bloomberg YE 2019
Public Company M&A
#1
Global Public M&A Adviser by Deal Count
Mergermarket YE 2019
Private Equity M&A
#1
Global Cross-Border Private Equity Adviser by Deal Count
Bloomberg YE 2019
Banking
#1
Global Syndicated Loans Legal Adviser—Borrowers & Lenders Combined by Deal Count
Refinitiv YE 2019
We speak the language of Wall Street.
LW.com

# Done ahead of schedule

## Made in Datasite

Close more deals, faster with Datasite. You'll find market-leading applications, services, and expertise for the entire M&A lifecycle.

Discover Datasite at
**www.datasite.com** ⇥

# Datasite™
**Where deals are made**

# DEMYSTIFY THE ART & SCIENCE OF PICKING STOCKS

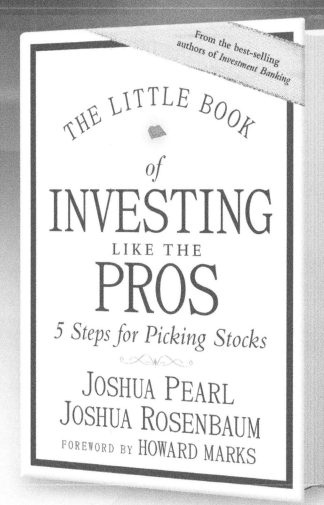

From the best-selling authors of *Investment Banking*

THE LITTLE BOOK

of

INVESTING

LIKE THE

PROS

*5 Steps for Picking Stocks*

JOSHUA PEARL
JOSHUA ROSENBAUM
FOREWORD BY HOWARD MARKS

Stock investing is more prevalent than ever, whether directly or indirectly throug brokerage accounts, exchange-traded funds, mutual funds, or retirement plans. Despi this, the vast majority of individual investors have no training on how to pi stocks. And, until now, there hasn't been a truly accessible, easy-to-understa resource available to help them. *The Little Book of Investing Like the Pros* was writt to fill this void.

WILEY